# The ONE YEAR® *Seasonal* BIBLE

*Winter Devotions*

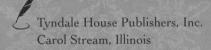

D1449763

Tyndale House Publishers, Inc.
Carol Stream, Illinois

# CONTENTS

# PUBLISHER'S NOTE

*The One Year Bible* has been prepared especially for regular Bible readers who wish to read through the entire Bible in one year. Instead of following a Bible reading chart and experiencing the delay of turning from place to place, you will find the text here in sequence, ready for your quiet reading and meditation. This fulfills our goal at Tyndale to make the Bible as accessible as possible for people no matter what their background or walk of life.

This edition of *The One Year Bible* contains the entire text of the *Holy Bible, New Living Translation,* Second Edition. The New Living Translation was first published in 1996, and it quickly became one of the most popular Bible translations in the English-speaking world. While the NLT's influence was rapidly growing, the Bible Translation Committee determined that an additional investment in scholarly review and text refinement could make it even better. So shortly after its initial publication, the committee began an eight-year process with the purpose of increasing the level of the NLT's precision without sacrificing its easy-to-understand quality. This second-generation text was completed in 2004 and is reflected in this edition of *The One Year Bible.*

The goal of any Bible translation is to convey the meaning and content of the ancient Hebrew, Aramaic, and Greek texts as accurately as possible to contemporary readers. The challenge for our translators was to create a text that would communicate as clearly and powerfully to today's readers as the original texts did to readers and listeners in the ancient biblical world. The resulting translation is easy to read and understand, while also accurately communicating the meaning and content of the original biblical texts. The NLT is a general-purpose text especially good for study, devotional reading, and to be read aloud in public worship.

We believe that the New Living Translation—which combines the latest biblical scholarship with a clear, dynamic writing style—will communicate God's word powerfully to all who read it. We publish it with the prayer that God will use it to speak his timeless truth to the church and the world in a fresh, new way. May this year and every year be enriched as you enjoy daily portions from God's word.

# Introduction to the
# NEW LIVING TRANSLATION

*Translation Philosophy and Methodology.* English Bible translations tend to be governed by one of two general translation theories. The first theory has been called "formal-equivalence," "literal," or "word-for-word" translation. According to this theory, the translator attempts to render each word of the original language into English and seeks to preserve the original syntax and sentence structure as much as possible in translation. The second theory has been called "dynamic-equivalence," "functional-equivalence," or "thought-for-thought" translation. The goal of this translation theory is to produce in English the closest natural equivalent of the message expressed by the original-language text, both in meaning and in style.

Both of these translation theories have their strengths. A formal-equivalence translation preserves aspects of the original text—including ancient idioms, term consistency, and original-language syntax—that are valuable for scholars and professional study. It allows a reader to trace formal elements of the original-language text through the English translation. A dynamic-equivalence translation, on the other hand, focuses on translating the message of the original-language text. It ensures that the meaning of the text is readily apparent to the contemporary reader. This allows the message to come through with immediacy, without requiring the reader to struggle with foreign idioms and awkward syntax. It also facilitates serious study of the text's message and clarity in both devotional and public reading.

The pure application of either of these translation philosophies would create translations at opposite ends of the translation spectrum. But in reality, all translations contain a mixture of these two philosophies. A purely formal-equivalence translation would be unintelligible in English, and a purely dynamic-equivalence translation would risk being unfaithful to the original. That is why translations shaped by dynamic-equivalence theory are usually quite literal when the original text is relatively clear, and the translations shaped by formal-equivalence theory are sometimes quite dynamic when the original text is obscure.

The translators of the New Living Translation set out to render the message of the original texts of Scripture into clear, contemporary English. As they did so, they kept the concerns of both formal-equivalence and dynamic-equivalence in mind. On the one hand, they translated as simply and literally as possible when that approach yielded an accurate, clear, and natural English text. Many words and phrases were rendered literally and consistently into English, preserving essential literary and rhetorical devices, ancient metaphors, and word choices that give structure to the text and provide echoes of meaning from one passage to the next.

On the other hand, the translators rendered the message more dynamically when the literal rendering was hard to understand, was misleading, or yielded archaic or foreign wording. They clarified difficult metaphors and terms to aid in the reader's understanding. The translators first struggled with the meaning of the words and phrases in the ancient context; then they rendered the message into clear, natural English. Their goal was to be both faithful to the ancient texts and eminently readable. The result is a translation that is both exegetically accurate and idiomatically powerful.

*Translation Process and Team.* To produce an accurate translation of the Bible into contemporary English, the translation team needed the skills necessary to enter into the thought patterns of the ancient authors and then to render their ideas, connotations, and effects into clear, contemporary English. To begin this process, qualified biblical scholars were needed to interpret the meaning of the original text and to check it against our base English translation. In order to guard against personal and theological biases, the scholars needed to represent a diverse group of Evangelicals who would employ the best exegetical tools. Then to work alongside the scholars, skilled English stylists were needed to shape the text into clear, contemporary English.

With these concerns in mind, the Bible Translation Committee recruited teams of scholars that represented a broad spectrum of denominations, theological perspectives, and backgrounds within the worldwide Evangelical community. Each book of the Bible was assigned to three different scholars with proven expertise in the book or group of books to be reviewed. Each of these scholars made a thorough review of a base translation and submitted suggested revisions to the appropriate Senior Translator. The Senior Translator then reviewed and summarized these suggestions and proposed a first-draft revision of the base text. This draft served as the basis for several additional phases of exegetical and stylistic committee review. Then the Bible Translation Committee jointly reviewed and approved every verse of the final translation.

Throughout the translation and editing process, the Senior Translators and their scholar teams were given a chance to review the editing done by the team of stylists. This ensured that exegetical errors would not be introduced late in the process and that the entire Bible Translation Committee was happy with the final result. By choosing a team of qualified scholars and skilled stylists and by setting up a process that allowed their interaction throughout the process, the New Living Translation has been refined to preserve the essential formal elements of the original biblical texts, while also creating a clear, understandable English text.

The New Living Translation was first published in 1996. Shortly after its initial publication, the Bible Translation Committee began a process of further committee review and translation refinement. The purpose of this continued revision was to increase the level of precision without sacrificing the text's easy-to-understand quality. This second-edition text was completed in 2004, and this printing of the New Living Translation reflects the updated text.

*Written to Be Read Aloud.* It is evident in Scripture that the biblical documents were written to be read aloud, often in public worship (see Nehemiah 8; Luke 4:16-20; 1 Timothy 4:13; Revelation 1:3). It is still the case today that more people will hear the Bible read aloud in church than are likely to read it for themselves. Therefore, a new translation must communicate with clarity and power when it is read publicly. Clarity was a primary goal for the NLT translators, not only to facilitate private reading and understanding, but also to ensure that it would be excellent for public reading and make an immediate and powerful impact on any listener.

*The Texts behind the New Living Translation.* The Old Testament translators used the Masoretic Text of the Hebrew Bible as represented in *Biblia Hebraica Stuttgartensia* (1977), with its extensive system of textual notes; this is an update of Rudolf Kittel's *Biblia Hebraica* (Stuttgart, 1937). The translators also further compared the Dead Sea Scrolls, the Septuagint and other Greek manuscripts, the Samaritan Pentateuch, the Syriac Peshitta, the Latin Vulgate, and any other versions or manuscripts that shed light on the meaning of difficult passages.

The New Testament translators used the two standard editions of the Greek New Testament: the *Greek New Testament,* published by the United Bible Societies (UBS, fourth revised edition, 1993), and *Novum Testamentum Graece,* edited by Nestle and Aland (NA, twenty-seventh edition, 1993). These two editions, which have the same text but differ in punctuation and textual notes, represent, for the most part, the best in modern textual scholarship. However, in cases where strong textual or other scholarly evidence supported the decision, the translators sometimes chose to differ from the UBS and NA Greek texts and followed variant readings found in other ancient witnesses. Significant textual variants of this sort are always noted in the textual notes of the New Living Translation.

*Translation Issues.* The translators have made a conscious effort to provide a text that can be easily understood by the typical reader of modern English. To this end, we sought to use only vocabulary and language structures in common use today. We avoided using language likely to become quickly dated or that reflects only a narrow sub-dialect of English, with the goal of making the New Living Translation as broadly useful and timeless as possible.

But our concern for readability goes beyond the concerns of vocabulary and sentence structure. We are also concerned about historical and cultural barriers to understanding the Bible, and we have sought to translate terms shrouded in history and culture in ways that can be immediately understood. To this end:

- We have converted ancient weights and measures (for example, "ephah" [a unit of dry volume] or "cubit" [a unit of length]) to modern English (American) equivalents, since the ancient measures are not generally meaningful to today's readers. Then in the textual footnotes we offer the literal Hebrew, Aramaic, or Greek measures, along with modern metric equivalents.

- Instead of translating ancient currency values literally, we have expressed them in common terms that communicate the message. For example, in the Old Testament, "ten shekels of silver" becomes "ten pieces of silver" to convey the intended message. In the New Testament, we have often translated the "denarius" as "the normal daily wage" to facilitate understanding. Then a footnote offers: "Greek *a denarius,* the payment for a full day's wage." In general, we give a clear English rendering and then state the literal Hebrew, Aramaic, or Greek in a textual footnote.

- Since the names of Hebrew months are unknown to most contemporary readers, and since the Hebrew lunar calendar fluctuates from year to year in relation to the solar calendar used today, we have looked for clear ways to communicate the time of year the Hebrew months (such as Abib) refer to. When an expanded or interpretive rendering is given in the text, a textual note gives the literal rendering. Where it is possible to define a specific ancient date in terms of our modern calendar, we use modern dates in the text. A textual footnote then gives the literal Hebrew date and states the rationale for our rendering. For example, Ezra 6:15 pinpoints the date when the post-exilic Temple was completed in Jerusalem: "the third day of the month Adar." This was during the sixth year of King Darius's reign (that is, 515 B.C.). We have translated that date as March 12, with a footnote giving the Hebrew and identifying the year as 515 B.C.

- Since ancient references to the time of day differ from our modern methods of denoting time, we have used renderings that are instantly understandable to the modern reader. Accordingly, we have rendered specific times of day by using approximate equivalents in terms of our common "o'clock" system. On occasion, translations such as "at dawn the next morning" or "as the sun began to set" have been used when the biblical reference is more general.

- When the meaning of a proper name (or a wordplay inherent in a proper name) is relevant to the message of the text, its meaning is often illuminated with a textual footnote. For example, in Exodus 2:10 the text reads: "The princess named him Moses, for she explained, 'I lifted him out of the water.' " The accompanying footnote reads: "*Moses* sounds like a Hebrew term that means 'to lift out.' "
  Sometimes, when the actual meaning of a name is clear, that meaning is included in parentheses within the text itself. For example, the text at Genesis 16:11 reads: "You are to name him Ishmael (*which means 'God hears'*), for the LORD has heard your cry of distress." Since the original hearers and readers would have instantly understood the meaning of the name "Ishmael," we have provided modern readers with the same information so they can experience the text in a similar way.

- Many words and phrases carry a great deal of cultural meaning that was obvious to the original readers but needs explanation in our own culture. For example, the phrase "they beat their breasts" (Luke 23:48) in ancient times meant that people were very upset, often in mourning. In our translation we chose to translate this phrase dynamically for clarity: "They went home *in deep sorrow.*" Then we included a footnote with the literal Greek, which reads: "Greek *went home beating their breasts.*" In other similar cases, however, we have sometimes chosen to illuminate the existing literal expression to make it immediately understandable. For example, here we might have expanded the literal Greek phrase to read: "They went home beating their breasts *in sorrow.*" If we had done this, we would not have included a textual footnote, since the literal Greek clearly appears in translation.

- Metaphorical language is sometimes difficult for contemporary readers to understand, so at times we have chosen to translate or illuminate the meaning of a metaphor. For example, the ancient poet writes, "Your neck is *like* the tower of David" (Song of Songs 4:4). We have rendered it "Your neck is *as beautiful as* the tower of David" to clarify the intended positive meaning of the simile. Another example comes in Ecclesiastes 12:3, which can be literally rendered: "Remember him . . . when the grinding women cease because they are few, and the women who look through the windows see dimly." We have rendered it: "Remember him before your teeth—your few remaining servants—stop grinding; and before your eyes—the women looking through the windows—see dimly." We clarified such metaphors only when we believed a typical reader might be confused by the literal text.

- When the content of the original language text is poetic in character, we have rendered it in English poetic form. We sought to break lines in ways that clarify and highlight the relationships between phrases of the text. Hebrew poetry often uses parallelism, a literary form where a second phrase (or in some instances a third or fourth) echoes the initial phrase in some way. In Hebrew parallelism, the subsequent parallel phrases continue, while also furthering and sharpening, the thought expressed in the initial line or phrase. Whenever possible, we sought to represent these parallel phrases in natural poetic English.

- The Greek term *hoi Ioudaioi* is literally translated "the Jews" in many English translations. In the Gospel of John, however, this term doesn't always refer to the Jewish people generally. In some contexts, it refers more particularly to the Jewish religious leaders. We have attempted to capture the meaning in these different contexts by using terms such as "the people" (with a footnote: Greek *the Jewish people*) or "the religious leaders," where appropriate.

- One challenge we faced was how to translate accurately the ancient biblical text that was originally written in a context where male-oriented terms were used to refer to humanity generally. We needed to respect the nature of the ancient context while also trying to make the translation clear to a modern audience that tends to read male-oriented language as applying only to males. Often the original text, though using masculine nouns and pronouns, clearly intends that the message be applied to both men and women. A typical example is found in the New Testament letters, where the believers are called "brothers" (*adelphoi*). Yet it is clear from the content of these letters that they were addressed to all the believers—male and female. Thus, we have usually translated this Greek word as "brothers and sisters" in order to represent the historical situation more accurately.

   We have also been sensitive to passages where the text applies generally to human beings or to the human condition. In some instances we have used plural pronouns (they, them) in place of the masculine singular (he, him). For example, a traditional rendering of Proverbs 22:6 is: "Train up a child in the way he should go, and when he is old he will not turn from it." We have rendered it: "Direct your children onto the right path, and when they are older, they will not leave it." At times, we have also replaced third person pronouns with the second person to ensure clarity. A traditional rendering of Proverbs 26:27 is: "He who digs a pit will fall into it, and he who rolls a stone, it will come back on him." We have rendered it: "If you set a trap for others, you will get caught in it yourself. If you roll a boulder down on others, it will crush you instead."

   We should emphasize, however, that all masculine nouns and pronouns used to represent God (for example, "Father") have been maintained without exception. All decisions of this kind have been driven by the concern to reflect accurately the intended meaning of the original texts of Scripture.

*Lexical Consistency in Terminology.*   For the sake of clarity, we have translated certain original-language terms consistently, especially within synoptic passages and for commonly repeated rhetorical phrases, and within certain word categories such as divine names and non-theological technical terminology (e.g., liturgical, legal, cultural, zoological, and botanical terms). For theological terms, we have allowed a greater semantic range of acceptable English words or phrases for a single Hebrew or Greek word. We have avoided some theological terms that are not readily understood by many modern readers. For example, we avoided using words such as "justification," "sanctification," and "regeneration," which are carryovers from Latin translations. In place of these words, we have provided renderings such as "we are made right with God," "we are made holy," and "we are born anew."

*The Spelling of Proper Names.* Many individuals in the Bible, especially the Old Testament, are known by more than one name (e.g., Uzziah/Azariah). For the sake of clarity, we have tried to use a single spelling for any one individual, footnoting the literal spelling whenever we differ from it. This is especially helpful in delineating the kings of Israel and Judah. King Joash/Jehoash of Israel has been consistently called Jehoash, while King Joash/Jehoash of Judah is called Joash. A similar distinction has been used to distinguish between Joram/Jehoram of Israel and Joram/Jehoram of Judah. All such decisions were made with the goal of clarifying the text for the reader. When the ancient biblical writers clearly had a theological purpose in their choice of a variant name (e.g., Eshbaal/Ishbosheth), the different names have been maintained with an explanatory footnote.

For the names Jacob and Israel, which are used interchangeably for both the individual patriarch and the nation, we generally render it "Israel" when it refers to the nation and "Jacob" when it refers to the individual. When our rendering of the name differs from the underlying Hebrew text, we provide a textual footnote, which includes this explanation: "The names 'Jacob' and 'Israel' are often interchanged throughout the Old Testament, referring sometimes to the individual patriarch and sometimes to the nation."

*The Rendering of Divine Names.* All appearances of *'el, 'elohim,* or *'eloah* have been translated "God," except where the context demands the translation "god(s)." We have generally rendered the tetragrammaton (*YHWH*) consistently as "the Lord," utilizing a form with small capitals that is common among English translations. This will distinguish it from the name *'adonai,* which we render "Lord." When *'adonai* and *YHWH* appear together, we have rendered it "Sovereign Lord." This also distinguishes *'adonai YHWH* from cases where *YHWH* appears with *'elohim,* which is rendered "Lord God." When *YH* (the short form of *YHWH*) and *YHWH* appear together, we have rendered it "Lord God." When *YHWH* appears with the term *tseba'oth,* we have rendered it "Lord of Heaven's Armies" to translate the meaning of the name. In a few cases, we have utilized the transliteration, *Yahweh,* when the personal character of the name is being invoked in contrast to another divine name or the name of some other god (for example, see Exod 3:15; 6:2-3).

In the New Testament, the Greek word *christos* has been translated as "Messiah" when the context assumes a Jewish audience. When a Gentile audience can be assumed, *christos* has been translated as "Christ." The Greek word *kurios* is consistently translated "Lord," except that it is translated "Lord" wherever the New Testament text explicitly quotes from the Old Testament, and the text there has it in small capitals.

*Textual Footnotes.* The New Living Translation provides several kinds of textual footnotes, all designated in the text with an asterisk:

- When for the sake of clarity the NLT renders a difficult or potentially confusing phrase dynamically, we generally give the literal rendering in a textual footnote. This allows the reader to see the literal source of our dynamic rendering and how our translation relates to other more literal translations. These notes are prefaced with "Hebrew," "Aramaic," or "Greek," identifying the language of the underlying source text. For example, in Acts 2:42 we translated the literal "breaking of bread" (from the Greek) as "the Lord's Supper" to clarify that this verse refers to the ceremonial practice of the church rather than just an ordinary meal. Then we attached a footnote to "the Lord's Supper," which reads: "Greek *the breaking of bread.*"
- Textual footnotes are also used to show alternative renderings, prefaced with the word "Or." These normally occur for passages where an aspect of the meaning is debated. On occasion, we also provide notes on words or phrases that represent a departure from long-standing tradition. These notes are prefaced with "Traditionally rendered." For example, the footnote to the translation "serious skin disease" at Leviticus 13:2 says:

"Traditionally rendered *leprosy*. The Hebrew word used throughout this passage is used to describe various skin diseases."

- When our translators follow a textual variant that differs significantly from our standard Hebrew or Greek texts (listed earlier), we document that difference with a footnote. We also footnote cases when the NLT excludes a passage that is included in the Greek text known as the *Textus Receptus* (and familiar to readers through its translation in the King James Version). In such cases, we offer a translation of the excluded text in a footnote, even though it is generally recognized as a later addition to the Greek text and not part of the original Greek New Testament.

- All Old Testament passages that are quoted in the New Testament are identified by a textual footnote at the New Testament location. When the New Testament clearly quotes from the Greek translation of the Old Testament, and when it differs significantly in wording from the Hebrew text, we also place a textual footnote at the Old Testament location. This note includes a rendering of the Greek version, along with a cross-reference to the New Testament passage(s) where it is cited (for example, see notes on Proverbs 3:12; Psalms 8:2; 53:3).

- Some textual footnotes provide cultural and historical information on places, things, and people in the Bible that are probably obscure to modern readers. Such notes should aid the reader in understanding the message of the text. For example, in Acts 12:1, "King Herod" is named in this translation as "King Herod Agrippa" and is identified in a footnote as being "the nephew of Herod Antipas and a grandson of Herod the Great."

- When the meaning of a proper name (or a wordplay inherent in a proper name) is relevant to the meaning of the text, it is either illuminated with a textual footnote or included within parentheses in the text itself. For example, the footnote concerning the name "Eve" at Genesis 3:20 reads: "Eve sounds like a Hebrew term that means 'to give life.'" This wordplay in the Hebrew illuminates the meaning of the text, which goes on to say that Eve "would be the mother of all who live."

AS WE SUBMIT this translation for publication, we recognize that any translation of the Scriptures is subject to limitations and imperfections. Anyone who has attempted to communicate the richness of God's Word into another language will realize it is impossible to make a perfect translation. Recognizing these limitations, we sought God's guidance and wisdom throughout this project. Now we pray that he will accept our efforts and use this translation for the benefit of the church and of all people.

We pray that the New Living Translation will overcome some of the barriers of history, culture, and language that have kept people from reading and understanding God's Word. We hope that readers unfamiliar with the Bible will find the words clear and easy to understand and that readers well versed in the Scriptures will gain a fresh perspective. We pray that readers will gain insight and wisdom for living, but most of all that they will meet the God of the Bible and be forever changed by knowing him.

*The Bible Translation Committee*
*July 2004*

# JANUARY
# 1

GENESIS 1:1–2:25

In the beginning God created the heavens and the earth.* ²The earth was formless and empty, and darkness covered the deep waters. And the Spirit of God was hovering over the surface of the waters.

³Then God said, "Let there be light," and there was light. ⁴And God saw that the light was good. Then he separated the light from the darkness. ⁵God called the light "day" and the darkness "night."

And evening passed and morning came, marking the first day.

⁶Then God said, "Let there be a space between the waters, to separate the waters of the heavens from the waters of the earth." ⁷And that is what happened. God made this space to separate the waters of the earth from the waters of the heavens. ⁸God called the space "sky."

And evening passed and morning came, marking the second day.

⁹Then God said, "Let the waters beneath the sky flow together into one place, so dry ground may appear." And that is what happened. ¹⁰God called the dry ground "land" and the waters "seas." And God saw that it was good. ¹¹Then God said, "Let the land sprout with vegetation—every sort of seed-bearing plant, and trees that grow seed-bearing fruit. These seeds will then produce the kinds of plants and trees from which they came." And that is what happened. ¹²The land produced vegetation—all sorts of seed-bearing plants, and trees with seed-bearing fruit. Their seeds produced plants and trees of the same kind. And God saw that it was good.

¹³And evening passed and morning came, marking the third day.

¹⁴Then God said, "Let great lights appear in the sky to separate the day from the night. Let them mark off the seasons, days, and years. ¹⁵Let these lights in the sky shine down on the earth." And that is what happened. ¹⁶God made two great lights, the sun and the moon—the larger one to govern the day, and the smaller one to govern the night. He also made the stars. ¹⁷God set these lights in the sky to light the earth, ¹⁸to govern the day and night, and to separate the light from the darkness. And God saw that it was good.

¹⁹And evening passed and morning came, marking the fourth day.

²⁰Then God said, "Let the waters swarm with fish and other life. Let the skies be filled with birds of every kind." ²¹So God created great sea creatures and every living thing that scurries and swarms in the water, and every sort of bird—each producing offspring of the same kind. And God saw that it was good. ²²Then God blessed them, saying, "Be fruitful and multiply. Let the fish fill the seas, and let the birds multiply on the earth."

²³And evening passed and morning came, marking the fifth day.

²⁴Then God said, "Let the earth produce every sort of animal, each producing offspring of the same kind—livestock, small animals that scurry

along the ground, and wild animals."
And that is what happened. ²⁵God
made all sorts of wild animals,
livestock, and small animals, each
able to produce offspring of the
same kind. And God saw that it
was good.

²⁶Then God said, "Let us make
human beings* in our image, to
be like ourselves. They will reign
over the fish in the sea, the birds
in the sky, the livestock, all the wild
animals on the earth, and the small
animals that scurry along the
ground."

²⁷ **So God created human beings***
   **in his own image.**
   **In the image of God he**
      **created them;**
   **male and female he created**
      **them.**

²⁸Then God blessed them and
said, "Be fruitful and multiply. Fill
the earth and govern it. Reign over
the fish in the sea, the birds in the
sky, and all the animals that scurry
along the ground."

²⁹Then God said, "Look! I have
given you every seed-bearing plant
throughout the earth and all the
fruit trees for your food. ³⁰And I
have given every green plant as food
for all the wild animals, the birds in
the sky, and the small animals that
scurry along the ground—everything
that has life." And that is what
happened.

³¹Then God looked over all he had
made, and he saw that it was very good!

And evening passed and morning
came, marking the sixth day.

²:¹So the creation of the heavens and
the earth and everything in them
was completed. ²On the seventh
day God had finished his work of
creation, so he rested* from all his
work. ³And God blessed the seventh
day and declared it holy, because it
was the day when he rested from all
his work of creation.

⁴This is the account of the creation of
the heavens and the earth.

When the LORD God made the earth
and the heavens, ⁵neither wild plants
nor grains were growing on the earth.
The LORD God had not yet sent rain to
water the earth, and there were no
people to cultivate the soil. ⁶Instead,
springs* came up from the ground and
watered all the land. ⁷Then the LORD
God formed the man from the dust of
the ground. He breathed the breath of
life into the man's nostrils, and the man
became a living person.

⁸Then the LORD God planted a garden
in Eden in the east, and there he placed
the man he had made. ⁹The LORD God
made all sorts of trees grow up from the
ground—trees that were beautiful and
that produced delicious fruit. In the
middle of the garden he placed the tree
of life and the tree of the knowledge of
good and evil.

¹⁰A river watered the garden and
then flowed out of Eden and divided
into four branches. ¹¹The first branch,
called the Pishon, flowed around the
entire land of Havilah, where gold is
found. ¹²The gold of that land is excep-
tionally pure; aromatic resin and onyx
stone are also found there. ¹³The second branch, called the Gihon, flowed
around the entire land of Cush. ¹⁴The
third branch, called the Tigris, flowed
east of the land of Asshur. The fourth
branch is called the Euphrates.

¹⁵The LORD God placed the man in
the Garden of Eden to tend and watch
over it. ¹⁶But the LORD God warned him,
"You may freely eat the fruit of every
tree in the garden—¹⁷except the tree of
the knowledge of good and evil. If you
eat its fruit, you are sure to die."

¹⁸Then the LORD God said, "It is not
good for the man to be alone. I will
make a helper who is just right for him."
¹⁹So the LORD God formed from the
ground all the wild animals and all
the birds of the sky. He brought them to
the man* to see what he would call
them, and the man chose a name for

each one. [20]He gave names to all the livestock, all the birds of the sky, and all the wild animals. But still there was no helper just right for him.

[21]So the LORD God caused the man to fall into a deep sleep. While the man slept, the LORD God took out one of the man's ribs* and closed up the opening. [22]Then the LORD God made a woman from the rib, and he brought her to the man.

[23]"At last!" the man exclaimed.

"This one is bone from my bone,
    and flesh from my flesh!
She will be called 'woman,'
    because she was taken from
    'man.'"

[24]This explains why a man leaves his father and mother and is joined to his wife, and the two are united into one.

[25]Now the man and his wife were both naked, but they felt no shame.

1:1 Or *In the beginning when God created the heavens and the earth, . . .* Or *When God began to create the heavens and the earth, . . .*   1:26 Or *man;* Hebrew reads *adam.*
1:27 Or *the man;* Hebrew reads *ha-adam.*   2:2 Or *ceased;* also in 2:3.   2:6 Or *mist.*   2:19 Or *Adam,* and so throughout the chapter.   2:21 Or *took a part of the man's side.*

## MATTHEW 1:1–2:12

**T**his is a record of the ancestors of Jesus the Messiah, a descendant of David* and of Abraham:

² Abraham was the father of Isaac.
    Isaac was the father of Jacob.
    Jacob was the father of Judah and
    his brothers.
³ Judah was the father of Perez and
    Zerah (whose mother was Tamar).
    Perez was the father of Hezron.
    Hezron was the father of Ram.*
⁴ Ram was the father of Amminadab.
    Amminadab was the father of
    Nahshon.
    Nahshon was the father of Salmon.
⁵ Salmon was the father of Boaz
    (whose mother was Rahab).
    Boaz was the father of Obed (whose
    mother was Ruth).
    Obed was the father of Jesse.
⁶ Jesse was the father of King David.
    David was the father of Solomon

(whose mother was Bathsheba,
    the widow of Uriah).
⁷ Solomon was the father of
    Rehoboam.
    Rehoboam was the father of Abijah.
    Abijah was the father of Asa.*
⁸ Asa was the father of
    Jehoshaphat.
    Jehoshaphat was the father
    of Jehoram.*
    Jehoram was the father* of Uzziah.
⁹ Uzziah was the father of Jotham.
    Jotham was the father of Ahaz.
    Ahaz was the father of Hezekiah.
¹⁰ Hezekiah was the father of
    Manasseh.
    Manasseh was the father of Amon.*
    Amon was the father of Josiah.
¹¹ Josiah was the father of Jehoiachin*
    and his brothers (born at the time
    of the exile to Babylon).
¹² After the Babylonian exile:
    Jehoiachin was the father of Shealtiel.
    Shealtiel was the father of
    Zerubbabel.
¹³ Zerubbabel was the father of Abiud.
    Abiud was the father of Eliakim.
    Eliakim was the father of Azor.
¹⁴ Azor was the father of Zadok.
    Zadok was the father of Akim.
    Akim was the father of Eliud.
¹⁵ Eliud was the father of Eleazar.
    Eleazar was the father of Matthan.
    Matthan was the father of Jacob.
¹⁶ Jacob was the father of Joseph, the
    husband of Mary.
    Mary gave birth to Jesus, who is
    called the Messiah.

[17]All those listed above include fourteen generations from Abraham to David, fourteen from David to the Babylonian exile, and fourteen from the Babylonian exile to the Messiah.

[18]This is how Jesus the Messiah was born. His mother, Mary, was engaged to be married to Joseph. But before the marriage took place, while she was still a virgin, she became pregnant through the power of the Holy Spirit. [19]Joseph, her fiancé, was a good man and did not

want to disgrace her publicly, so he decided to break the engagement* quietly.

20As he considered this, an angel of the Lord appeared to him in a dream. "Joseph, son of David," the angel said, "do not be afraid to take Mary as your wife. For the child within her was conceived by the Holy Spirit. 21And she will have a son, and you are to name him Jesus,* for he will save his people from their sins."

22All of this occurred to fulfill the Lord's message through his prophet:

23 "Look! The virgin will conceive
      a child!
    She will give birth to a son,
  and they will call him Immanuel,*
    which means 'God is with us.'"

24When Joseph woke up, he did as the angel of the Lord commanded and took Mary as his wife. 25But he did not have sexual relations with her until her son was born. And Joseph named him Jesus.

2:1 JESUS was born in Bethlehem in Judea, during the reign of King Herod. About that time some wise men* from eastern lands arrived in Jerusalem, asking, 2"Where is the newborn king of the Jews? We saw his star as it rose,* and we have come to worship him."

3King Herod was deeply disturbed when he heard this, as was everyone in Jerusalem. 4He called a meeting of the leading priests and teachers of religious law and asked, "Where is the Messiah supposed to be born?"

5"In Bethlehem in Judea," they said, "for this is what the prophet wrote:

6 'And you, O Bethlehem in the land
      of Judah,
    are not least among the ruling
      cities* of Judah,
  for a ruler will come from you
    who will be the shepherd for my
      people Israel.'*"

7Then Herod called for a private meeting with the wise men, and he learned from them the time when the star first appeared. 8Then he told them, "Go to Bethlehem and search carefully for the child. And when you find him, come back and tell me so that I can go and worship him, too!"

9After this interview the wise men went their way. And the star they had seen in the east guided them to Bethlehem. It went ahead of them and stopped over the place where the child was. 10When they saw the star, they were filled with joy! 11They entered the house and saw the child with his mother, Mary, and they bowed down and worshiped him. Then they opened their treasure chests and gave him gifts of gold, frankincense, and myrrh.

12When it was time to leave, they returned to their own country by another route, for God had warned them in a dream not to return to Herod.

1:1 Greek *Jesus the Messiah, son of David.*   1:3 Greek *Aram,* a variant spelling of Ram; also in 1:4. See 1 Chr 2:9-10.   1:7 Greek *Asaph,* a variant spelling of Asa; also in 1:8. See 1 Chr 3:10.   1:8a Greek *Joram,* a variant spelling of Jehoram; also in 1:8b. See 1 Kgs 22:50 and note at 1 Chr 3:11.   1:8b Or *ancestor;* also in 1:11.   1:10 Greek *Amos,* a variant spelling of Amon; also in 1:10b. See 1 Chr 3:14. 1:11 Greek *Jeconiah,* a variant spelling of Jehoiachin; also in 1:12. See 2 Kgs 24:6 and note at 1 Chr 3:16.   1:19 Greek *to divorce her.*   1:21 *Jesus* means "The LORD saves." 1:23 Isa 7:14; 8:8, 10 (Greek version).   2:1 Or *royal astrologers;* Greek reads *magi;* also in 2:7, 16.   2:2 Or *star in the east.*   2:6a Greek *the rulers.*   2:6b Mic 5:2; 2 Sam 5:2.

## PSALM 1:1-6

  Oh, the joys of those who do not
      follow the advice of the wicked,
    or stand around with sinners,
    or join in with mockers.
2 But they delight in the law
      of the LORD,
    meditating on it day and night.
3 They are like trees planted along
      the riverbank,
    bearing fruit each season.
  Their leaves never wither,
    and they prosper in all they do.

4 But not the wicked!
    They are like worthless chaff,
      scattered by the wind.
5 They will be condemned at the time
      of judgment.

Sinners will have no place among
the godly.
6 For the LORD watches over the path
of the godly,
but the path of the wicked leads
to destruction.

## PROVERBS 1:1-6

These are the proverbs of Solomon, David's son, king of Israel. □ Their purpose is to teach people wisdom and discipline, to help them understand the insights of the wise. Their purpose is to teach people to live disciplined and successful lives, to help them do what is right, just, and fair. These proverbs will give insight to the simple, knowledge and discernment to the young. □ Let the wise listen to these proverbs and become even wiser. Let those with understanding receive guidance by exploring the meaning in these proverbs and parables, the words of the wise and their riddles.

# JANUARY 2

## GENESIS 3:1-4:26

The serpent was the shrewdest of all the wild animals the LORD God had made. One day he asked the woman, "Did God really say you must not eat the fruit from any of the trees in the garden?"

2"Of course we may eat fruit from the trees in the garden," the woman replied. 3"It's only the fruit from the tree in the middle of the garden that we are not allowed to eat. God said, 'You must not eat it or even touch it; if you do, you will die.'"

4"You won't die!" the serpent replied to the woman. 5"God knows that your eyes will be opened as soon as you eat it, and you will be like God, knowing both good and evil."

6The woman was convinced. She saw that the tree was beautiful and its fruit looked delicious, and she wanted the wisdom it would give her. So she took some of the fruit and ate it. Then she gave some to her husband, who was with her, and he ate it, too. 7At that moment their eyes were opened, and they suddenly felt shame at their nakedness. So they sewed fig leaves together to cover themselves.

8When the cool evening breezes were blowing, the man* and his wife heard the LORD God walking about in the garden. So they hid from the LORD God among the trees. 9Then the LORD God called to the man, "Where are you?"

10He replied, "I heard you walking in the garden, so I hid. I was afraid because I was naked."

11"Who told you that you were naked?" the LORD God asked. "Have you eaten from the tree whose fruit I commanded you not to eat?"

12The man replied, "It was the woman you gave me who gave me the fruit, and I ate it."

13Then the LORD God asked the woman, "What have you done?"

"The serpent deceived me," she replied. "That's why I ate it."

14Then the LORD God said to the serpent,

"Because you have done this,
you are cursed
more than all animals, domestic
and wild.
You will crawl on your belly,
groveling in the dust as long as
you live.
15 And I will cause hostility between
you and the woman,
and between your offspring and
her offspring.
He will strike* your head,
and you will strike his heel."

16Then he said to the woman,

"I will sharpen the pain of your
pregnancy,
and in pain you will give birth.
And you will desire to control your
husband,
but he will rule over you.*"

17And to the man he said,

"Since you listened to your wife and
    ate from the tree
  whose fruit I commanded you
    not to eat,
the ground is cursed because of you.
  All your life you will struggle to
    scratch a living from it.
18 It will grow thorns and thistles
    for you,
  though you will eat of its grains.
19 By the sweat of your brow
    will you have food to eat
  until you return to the ground
    from which you were made.
  For you were made from dust,
    and to dust you will return."

20Then the man—Adam—named his
wife Eve, because she would be the
mother of all who live.* 21And the LORD
God made clothing from animal skins
for Adam and his wife.

22Then the LORD God said, "Look, the
human beings* have become like us,
knowing both good and evil. What if
they reach out, take fruit from the tree
of life, and eat it? Then they will live forever!" 23So the LORD God banished
them from the Garden of Eden, and he
sent Adam out to cultivate the ground
from which he had been made. 24After
sending them out, the LORD God stationed mighty cherubim to the east of
the Garden of Eden. And he placed a
flaming sword that flashed back and
forth to guard the way to the tree of life.

4:1Now Adam* had sexual relations
with his wife, Eve, and she became pregnant. When she gave birth to Cain, she
said, "With the LORD's help, I have produced* a man!" 2Later she gave birth to
his brother and named him Abel.

When they grew up, Abel became a
shepherd, while Cain cultivated the
ground. 3When it was time for the harvest, Cain presented some of his crops
as a gift to the LORD. 4Abel also brought
a gift—the best of the firstborn lambs
from his flock. The LORD accepted Abel
and his gift, 5but he did not accept Cain

and his gift. This made Cain very angry,
and he looked dejected.

6"Why are you so angry?" the LORD
asked Cain. "Why do you look so dejected? 7You will be accepted if you do
what is right. But if you refuse to do what
is right, then watch out! Sin is crouching
at the door, eager to control you. But you
must subdue it and be its master."

8One day Cain suggested to his
brother, "Let's go out into the fields."*
And while they were in the field, Cain attacked his brother, Abel, and killed him.

9Afterward the LORD asked Cain,
"Where is your brother? Where is Abel?"

"I don't know," Cain responded. "Am
I my brother's guardian?"

10But the LORD said, "What have you
done? Listen! Your brother's blood cries
out to me from the ground! 11Now you are
cursed and banished from the ground,
which has swallowed your brother's
blood. 12No longer will the ground yield
good crops for you, no matter how hard
you work! From now on you will be a
homeless wanderer on the earth."

13Cain replied to the LORD, "My punishment* is too great for me to bear!
14You have banished me from the land
and from your presence; you have made
me a homeless wanderer. Anyone who
finds me will kill me!"

15The LORD replied, "No, for I will
give a sevenfold punishment to anyone
who kills you." Then the LORD put a
mark on Cain to warn anyone who
might try to kill him. 16So Cain left the
LORD's presence and settled in the land
of Nod,* east of Eden.

17Cain had sexual relations with his
wife, and she became pregnant and gave
birth to Enoch. Then Cain founded a city,
which he named Enoch, after his son.
18Enoch had a son named Irad. Irad became the father of* Mehujael. Mehujael
became the father of Methushael.
Methushael became the father of Lamech.

19Lamech married two women. The
first was named Adah, and the second
was Zillah. 20Adah gave birth to Jabal,
who was the first of those who raise livestock and live in tents. 21His brother's

name was Jubal, the first of all who play the harp and flute. [22]Lamech's other wife, Zillah, gave birth to a son named Tubal-cain. He became an expert in forging tools of bronze and iron. Tubal-cain had a sister named Naamah. [23]One day Lamech said to his wives,

"Adah and Zillah, hear my voice;
    listen to me, you wives of Lamech.
I have killed a man who attacked me,
    a young man who wounded me.
[24] If someone who kills Cain is
        punished seven times,
    then the one who kills me will be
        punished seventy-seven times!"

[25]Adam had sexual relations with his wife again, and she gave birth to another son. She named him Seth,* for she said, "God has granted me another son in place of Abel, whom Cain killed." [26]When Seth grew up, he had a son and named him Enosh. At that time people first began to worship the LORD by name.

**3:8** Or *Adam,* and so throughout the chapter.   **3:15** Or *bruise;* also in 3:15b.   **3:16** Or *And though you will have desire for your husband, / he will rule over you.*   **3:20** *Eve* sounds like a Hebrew term that means "to give life."   **3:22** Or *the man;* Hebrew reads *ha-adam.*   **4:1a** Or *the man;* also in 4:25.   **4:1b** Or *I have acquired. Cain* sounds like a Hebrew term that can mean "produce" or "acquire."   **4:8** As in Samaritan Pentateuch, Greek and Syriac versions, and Latin Vulgate; Masoretic Text lacks *"Let's go out into the fields."*   **4:13** Or *My sin.*   **4:16** *Nod* means "wandering."   **4:18** Or *the ancestor of,* and so throughout the verse.   **4:25** *Seth* probably means "granted"; the name may also mean "appointed."

## MATTHEW 2:13–3:6

**A**fter the wise men were gone, an angel of the Lord appeared to Joseph in a dream. "Get up! Flee to Egypt with the child and his mother," the angel said. "Stay there until I tell you to return, because Herod is going to search for the child to kill him."

[14]That night Joseph left for Egypt with the child and Mary, his mother, [15]and they stayed there until Herod's death. This fulfilled what the Lord had spoken through the prophet: "I called my Son out of Egypt."*

[16]Herod was furious when he realized that the wise men had outwitted him. He sent soldiers to kill all the boys in and around Bethlehem who were two years old and under, based on the wise men's report of the star's first appearance. [17]Herod's brutal action fulfilled what God had spoken through the prophet Jeremiah:

[18] "A cry was heard in Ramah—
        weeping and great mourning.
    Rachel weeps for her children,
        refusing to be comforted,
        for they are dead."*

[19]When Herod died, an angel of the Lord appeared in a dream to Joseph in Egypt. [20]"Get up!" the angel said. "Take the child and his mother back to the land of Israel, because those who were trying to kill the child are dead."

[21]So Joseph got up and returned to the land of Israel with Jesus and his mother. [22]But when he learned that the new ruler of Judea was Herod's son Archelaus, he was afraid to go there. Then, after being warned in a dream, he left for the region of Galilee. [23]So the family went and lived in a town called Nazareth. This fulfilled what the prophets had said: "He will be called a Nazarene."

[3:1]**I**N those days John the Baptist came to the Judean wilderness and began preaching. His message was, [2]"Repent of your sins and turn to God, for the Kingdom of Heaven is near.*" [3]The prophet Isaiah was speaking about John when he said,

"He is a voice shouting in the
        wilderness,
    'Prepare the way for the LORD's
        coming!
    Clear the road for him!'"*

[4]John's clothes were woven from coarse camel hair, and he wore a leather belt around his waist. For food he ate locusts and wild honey. [5]People from Jerusalem and from all of Judea and all over the Jordan Valley went out to see and hear John. [6]And when they confessed their sins, he baptized them in the Jordan River.

**2:15** Hos 11:1.   **2:18** Jer 31:15.   **3:2** Or *has come,* or *is coming soon.*   **3:3** Isa 40:3 (Greek version).

PSALM 2:1-12

**W**hy are the nations so angry?
Why do they waste their time
with futile plans?
[2] The kings of the earth prepare
for battle;
the rulers plot together
against the LORD
and against his anointed one.
[3] "Let us break their chains," they cry,
"and free ourselves from slavery
to God."

[4] But the one who rules in heaven
laughs.
The Lord scoffs at them.
[5] Then in anger he rebukes them,
terrifying them with his fierce
fury.
[6] For the Lord declares, "I have placed
my chosen king on the throne
in Jerusalem,* on my holy
mountain."

[7] The king proclaims the LORD's
decree:
"The LORD said to me, 'You are
my son.*
Today I have become your
Father.*
[8] Only ask, and I will give you the
nations as your inheritance,
the whole earth as your
possession.
[9] You will break* them with an
iron rod
and smash them like clay pots.'"

[10] Now then, you kings, act wisely!
Be warned, you rulers of the earth!
[11] Serve the LORD with reverent fear,
and rejoice with trembling.
[12] Submit to God's royal son,* or he
will become angry,
and you will be destroyed in the
midst of all your activities—
for his anger flares up in an instant.
But what joy for all who take
refuge in him!

2:6 Hebrew *on Zion.*   2:7a Or *Son;* also in 2:12.   2:7b Or
*Today I reveal you as my son.*   2:9 Greek version reads
*rule.* Compare Rev 2:27.   2:12 The meaning of the Hebrew
is uncertain.

PROVERBS 1:7-9

**F**ear of the LORD is the foundation of
true knowledge, but fools despise wisdom and discipline. □ My child,* listen
when your father corrects you. Don't
neglect your mother's instruction.
What you learn from them will crown
you with grace and be a chain of honor
around your neck.

1:8 Hebrew *My son;* also in 1:10, 15.

JANUARY
**3**

GENESIS 5:1–7:24

**T**his is the written account of the descendants of Adam. When God created
human beings,* he made them to be
like himself. [2] He created them male
and female, and he blessed them and
called them "human."

[3] When Adam was 130 years old, he
became the father of a son who was
just like him—in his very image. He
named his son Seth. [4] After the birth
of Seth, Adam lived another
800 years, and he had other sons
and daughters. [5] Adam lived
930 years, and then he died.
[6] When Seth was 105 years old, he
became the father of* Enosh. [7] After
the birth of* Enosh, Seth lived
another 807 years, and he had other
sons and daughters. [8] Seth lived
912 years, and then he died.
[9] When Enosh was 90 years old, he
became the father of Kenan. [10] After
the birth of Kenan, Enosh lived
another 815 years, and he had other
sons and daughters. [11] Enosh lived
905 years, and then he died.
[12] When Kenan was 70 years old, he
became the father of Mahalalel.
[13] After the birth of Mahalalel,
Kenan lived another 840 years, and
he had other sons and daughters.

¹⁴Kenan lived 910 years, and then he died.

¹⁵When Mahalalel was 65 years old, he became the father of Jared. ¹⁶After the birth of Jared, Mahalalel lived another 830 years, and he had other sons and daughters. ¹⁷Mahalalel lived 895 years, and then he died.

¹⁸When Jared was 162 years old, he became the father of Enoch. ¹⁹After the birth of Enoch, Jared lived another 800 years, and he had other sons and daughters. ²⁰Jared lived 962 years, and then he died.

²¹When Enoch was 65 years old, he became the father of Methuselah. ²²After the birth of Methuselah, Enoch lived in close fellowship with God for another 300 years, and he had other sons and daughters. ²³Enoch lived 365 years, ²⁴walking in close fellowship with God. Then one day he disappeared, because God took him.

²⁵When Methuselah was 187 years old, he became the father of Lamech. ²⁶After the birth of Lamech, Methuselah lived another 782 years, and he had other sons and daughters. ²⁷Methuselah lived 969 years, and then he died.

²⁸When Lamech was 182 years old, he became the father of a son. ²⁹Lamech named his son Noah, for he said, "May he bring us relief* from our work and the painful labor of farming this ground that the LORD has cursed." ³⁰After the birth of Noah, Lamech lived another 595 years, and he had other sons and daughters. ³¹Lamech lived 777 years, and then he died.

³²By the time Noah was 500 years old, he was the father of Shem, Ham, and Japheth.

⁶:¹THEN the people began to multiply on the earth, and daughters were born to them. ²The sons of God saw the beautiful women* and took any they wanted as their wives. ³Then the LORD said, "My Spirit will not put up with* humans for such a long time, for they are only mortal flesh. In the future, their normal lifespan will be no more than 120 years."

⁴In those days, and for some time after, giant Nephilites lived on the earth, for whenever the sons of God had intercourse with women, they gave birth to children who became the heroes and famous warriors of ancient times.

⁵The LORD observed the extent of human wickedness on the earth, and he saw that everything they thought or imagined was consistently and totally evil. ⁶So the LORD was sorry he had ever made them and put them on the earth. It broke his heart. ⁷And the LORD said, "I will wipe this human race I have created from the face of the earth. Yes, and I will destroy every living thing—all the people, the large animals, the small animals that scurry along the ground, and even the birds of the sky. I am sorry I ever made them." ⁸But Noah found favor with the LORD.

⁹This is the account of Noah and his family. Noah was a righteous man, the only blameless person living on earth at the time, and he walked in close fellowship with God. ¹⁰Noah was the father of three sons: Shem, Ham, and Japheth.

¹¹Now God saw that the earth had become corrupt and was filled with violence. ¹²God observed all this corruption in the world, for everyone on earth was corrupt. ¹³So God said to Noah, "I have decided to destroy all living creatures, for they have filled the earth with violence. Yes, I will wipe them all out along with the earth!

¹⁴"Build a large boat* from cypress wood* and waterproof it with tar, inside and out. Then construct decks and stalls throughout its interior. ¹⁵Make the boat 450 feet long, 75 feet wide, and 45 feet high.* ¹⁶Leave an 18-inch opening* below the roof all the way around the boat. Put the door on the side, and build three decks inside the boat—lower, middle, and upper.

¹⁷"Look! I am about to cover the earth with a flood that will destroy every living thing that breathes. Everything on earth

will die. [18]But I will confirm my covenant with you. So enter the boat—you and your wife and your sons and their wives. [19]Bring a pair of every kind of animal—a male and a female—into the boat with you to keep them alive during the flood. [20]Pairs of every kind of bird, and every kind of animal, and every kind of small animal that scurries along the ground, will come to you to be kept alive. [21]And be sure to take on board enough food for your family and for all the animals."

[22]So Noah did everything exactly as God had commanded him.

[7:1]WHEN everything was ready, the LORD said to Noah, "Go into the boat with all your family, for among all the people of the earth, I can see that you alone are righteous. [2]Take with you seven pairs—male and female—of each animal I have approved for eating and for sacrifice,* and take one pair of each of the others. [3]Also take seven pairs of every kind of bird. There must be a male and a female in each pair to ensure that all life will survive on the earth after the flood. [4]Seven days from now I will make the rains pour down on the earth. And it will rain for forty days and forty nights, until I have wiped from the earth all the living things I have created."

[5]So Noah did everything as the LORD commanded him.

[6]Noah was 600 years old when the flood covered the earth. [7]He went on board the boat to escape the flood—he and his wife and his sons and their wives. [8]With them were all the various kinds of animals—those approved for eating and for sacrifice and those that were not—along with all the birds and the small animals that scurry along the ground. [9]They entered the boat in pairs, male and female, just as God had commanded Noah. [10]After seven days, the waters of the flood came and covered the earth.

[11]When Noah was 600 years old, on the seventeenth day of the second month, all the underground waters erupted from the earth, and the rain fell in mighty torrents from the sky. [12]The rain continued to fall for forty days and forty nights.

[13]That very day Noah had gone into the boat with his wife and his sons—Shem, Ham, and Japheth—and their wives. [14]With them in the boat were pairs of every kind of animal—domestic and wild, large and small—along with birds of every kind. [15]Two by two they came into the boat, representing every living thing that breathes. [16]A male and female of each kind entered, just as God had commanded Noah. Then the LORD closed the door behind them.

[17]For forty days the floodwaters grew deeper, covering the ground and lifting the boat high above the earth. [18]As the waters rose higher and higher above the ground, the boat floated safely on the surface. [19]Finally, the water covered even the highest mountains on the earth, [20]rising more than twenty-two feet* above the highest peaks. [21]All the living things on earth died—birds, domestic animals, wild animals, small animals that scurry along the ground, and all the people. [22]Everything that breathed and lived on dry land died. [23]God wiped out every living thing on the earth—people, livestock, small animals that scurry along the ground, and the birds of the sky. All were destroyed. The only people who survived were Noah and those with him in the boat. [24]And the floodwaters covered the earth for 150 days.

5:1 Or *man;* Hebrew reads *adam;* similarly in 5:2.   5:6 Or *the ancestor of;* also in 5:9, 12, 15, 18, 21, 25.   5:7 Or *the birth of this ancestor of;* also in 5:10, 13, 16, 19, 22, 26. 5:29 *Noah* sounds like a Hebrew term that can mean "relief" or "comfort."   6:2 Hebrew *daughters of men;* also in 6:4.   6:3 Greek version reads *will not remain in.* 6:14a Traditionally rendered *an ark.*   6:14b Or *gopher wood.*   6:15 Hebrew *300 cubits* [138 meters] *long, 50 cubits* [23 meters] *wide, and 30 cubits* [13.8 meters] *high.*   6:16 Hebrew *an opening of 1 cubit* [46 centimeters]. 7:2 Hebrew *of each clean animal;* similarly in 7:8. 7:20 Hebrew *15 cubits* [6.9 meters].

## MATTHEW 3:7–4:11

**B**ut when he [John] saw many Pharisees and Sadducees coming to watch him baptize,* he denounced them. "You brood of snakes!" he exclaimed. "Who warned you to flee God's coming wrath? [8]Prove by the way you live that you have repented of your sins and turned to God. ⁹Don't just say to each other, 'We're safe, for we are descendants of Abraham.' That means nothing, for I tell you, God can create children of Abraham from these very stones. ¹⁰Even now the ax of God's judgment is poised, ready to sever the roots of the trees. Yes, every tree that does not produce good fruit will be chopped down and thrown into the fire.

¹¹"I baptize with* water those who repent of their sins and turn to God. But someone is coming soon who is greater than I am—so much greater that I'm not worthy even to be his slave and carry his sandals. He will baptize you with the Holy Spirit and with fire.* ¹²He is ready to separate the chaff from the wheat with his winnowing fork. Then he will clean up the threshing area, gathering the wheat into his barn but burning the chaff with never-ending fire."

¹³Then Jesus went from Galilee to the Jordan River to be baptized by John. ¹⁴But John tried to talk him out of it. "I am the one who needs to be baptized by you," he said, "so why are you coming to me?"

¹⁵But Jesus said, "It should be done, for we must carry out all that God requires.*" So John agreed to baptize him.

¹⁶After his baptism, as Jesus came up out of the water, the heavens were opened* and he saw the Spirit of God descending like a dove and settling on him. ¹⁷And a voice from heaven said, "This is my dearly loved Son, who brings me great joy."

⁴:¹THEN Jesus was led by the Spirit into the wilderness to be tempted there by the devil. ²For forty days and forty nights he fasted and became very hungry. ³During that time the devil* came and said to him, "If you are the Son of God, tell these stones to become loaves of bread."

⁴But Jesus told him, "No! The Scriptures say,

'People do not live by bread
    alone,
but by every word that comes
    from the mouth of God.'*"

⁵Then the devil took him to the holy city, Jerusalem, to the highest point of the Temple, ⁶and said, "If you are the Son of God, jump off! For the Scriptures say,

'He will order his angels to protect
    you.
And they will hold you up with their
    hands
    so you won't even hurt your foot
        on a stone.'*"

⁷Jesus responded, "The Scriptures also say, 'You must not test the LORD your God.'*"

⁸Next the devil took him to the peak of a very high mountain and showed him the kingdoms of the world and all their glory. ⁹"I will give it all to you," he said, "if you will kneel down and worship me."

¹⁰"Get out of here, Satan," Jesus told him. "For the Scriptures say,

'You must worship the LORD
    your God
    and serve only him.'*"

¹¹Then the devil went away, and angels came and took care of Jesus.

3:7 Or *coming to be baptized.*   3:11a Or *in.*   3:11b Or *in the Holy Spirit and in fire.*   3:15 Or *for we must fulfill all righteousness.*   3:16 Some manuscripts read *opened to him.*   4:3 Greek *the tempter.*   4:4 Deut 8:3.   4:6 Ps 91:11-12.   4:7 Deut 6:16.   4:10 Deut 6:13.

## PSALM 3:1-8
*A psalm of David, regarding the time David fled from his son Absalom.*

¹ **O** LORD, I have so many enemies;
    so many are against me.
² So many are saying,
    "God will never rescue him!"
                                    *Interlude**

³ But you, O LORD, are a shield
        around me;
    you are my glory, the one who
        holds my head high.

⁴ I cried out to the LORD,
    and he answered me from his
        holy mountain.          *Interlude*

⁵ I lay down and slept,
    yet I woke up in safety,
    for the LORD was watching
        over me.
⁶ I am not afraid of ten thousand
        enemies
    who surround me on every side.

⁷ Arise, O LORD!
    Rescue me, my God!
  Slap all my enemies in the face!
    Shatter the teeth of the
        wicked!
⁸ Victory comes from you,
        O LORD.
    May you bless your people.
                                *Interlude*

3:2 Hebrew *Selah*. The meaning of this word is uncertain, though it is probably a musical or literary term. It is rendered *Interlude* throughout the Psalms.

## PROVERBS 1:10-19

**M**y child, if sinners entice you, turn your back on them! They may say, "Come and join us. Let's hide and kill someone! Just for fun, let's ambush the innocent! Let's swallow them alive, like the grave*; let's swallow them whole, like those who go down to the pit of death. Think of the great things we'll get! We'll fill our houses with all the stuff we take. Come, throw in your lot with us; we'll all share the loot." ☐ My child, don't go along with them! Stay far away from their paths. They rush to commit evil deeds. They hurry to commit murder. If a bird sees a trap being set, it knows to stay away. But these people set an ambush for themselves; they are trying to get themselves killed. Such is the fate of all who are greedy for money; it robs them of life.

1:12 Hebrew *like Sheol*.

# JANUARY 4

## GENESIS 8:1-10:32

**B**ut God remembered Noah and all the wild animals and livestock with him in the boat. He sent a wind to blow across the earth, and the floodwaters began to recede. ²The underground waters stopped flowing, and the torrential rains from the sky were stopped. ³So the floodwaters gradually receded from the earth. After 150 days, ⁴exactly five months from the time the flood began,* the boat came to rest on the mountains of Ararat. ⁵Two and a half months later,* as the waters continued to go down, other mountain peaks became visible.

⁶After another forty days, Noah opened the window he had made in the boat ⁷and released a raven. The bird flew back and forth until the floodwaters on the earth had dried up. ⁸He also released a dove to see if the water had receded and it could find dry ground. ⁹But the dove could find no place to land because the water still covered the ground. So it returned to the boat, and Noah held out his hand and drew the dove back inside. ¹⁰After waiting another seven days, Noah released the dove again. ¹¹This time the dove returned to him in the evening with a fresh olive leaf in its beak. Then Noah knew that the floodwaters were almost gone. ¹²He waited another seven days and then released the dove again. This time it did not come back.

¹³Noah was now 601 years old. On the first day of the new year, ten and a half months after the flood began,* the floodwaters had almost dried up from the earth. Noah lifted back the covering of the boat and saw that the surface of the ground was drying. ¹⁴Two more months went by,* and at last the earth was dry!

¹⁵Then God said to Noah, ¹⁶"Leave the boat, all of you—you and your wife, and your sons and their wives. ¹⁷Release all the animals—the birds, the livestock,

and the small animals that scurry along the ground—so they can be fruitful and multiply throughout the earth."

18So Noah, his wife, and his sons and their wives left the boat. 19And all of the large and small animals and birds came out of the boat, pair by pair.

20Then Noah built an altar to the LORD, and there he sacrificed as burnt offerings the animals and birds that had been approved for that purpose.* 21And the LORD was pleased with the aroma of the sacrifice and said to himself, "I will never again curse the ground because of the human race, even though everything they think or imagine is bent toward evil from childhood. I will never again destroy all living things. 22As long as the earth remains, there will be planting and harvest, cold and heat, summer and winter, day and night."

9:1THEN God blessed Noah and his sons and told them, "Be fruitful and multiply. Fill the earth. 2All the animals of the earth, all the birds of the sky, all the small animals that scurry along the ground, and all the fish in the sea will look on you with fear and terror. I have placed them in your power. 3I have given them to you for food, just as I have given you grain and vegetables. 4But you must never eat any meat that still has the life-blood in it.

5"And I will require the blood of anyone who takes another person's life. If a wild animal kills a person, it must die. And anyone who murders a fellow human must die. 6If anyone takes a human life, that person's life will also be taken by human hands. For God made human beings* in his own image. 7Now be fruitful and multiply, and repopulate the earth."

8Then God told Noah and his sons, 9"I hereby confirm my covenant with you and your descendants, 10and with all the animals that were on the boat with you— the birds, the livestock, and all the wild animals—every living creature on earth. 11Yes, I am confirming my covenant with you. Never again will floodwaters kill all

living creatures; never again will a flood destroy the earth."

12Then God said, "I am giving you a sign of my covenant with you and with all living creatures, for all generations to come. 13I have placed my rainbow in the clouds. It is the sign of my covenant with you and with all the earth. 14When I send clouds over the earth, the rainbow will appear in the clouds, 15and I will remember my covenant with you and with all living creatures. Never again will the floodwaters destroy all life. 16When I see the rainbow in the clouds, I will remember the eternal covenant between God and every living creature on earth." 17Then God said to Noah, "Yes, this rainbow is the sign of the covenant I am confirming with all the creatures on earth."

18The sons of Noah who came out of the boat with their father were Shem, Ham, and Japheth. (Ham is the father of Canaan.) 19From these three sons of Noah came all the people who now populate the earth.

20After the flood, Noah began to cultivate the ground, and he planted a vineyard. 21One day he drank some wine he had made, and he became drunk and lay naked inside his tent. 22Ham, the father of Canaan, saw that his father was naked and went outside and told his brothers. 23Then Shem and Japheth took a robe, held it over their shoulders, and backed into the tent to cover their father. As they did this, they looked the other way so they would not see him naked.

24When Noah woke up from his stupor, he learned what Ham, his youngest son, had done. 25Then he cursed Canaan, the son of Ham:

"May Canaan be cursed!
    May he be the lowest of servants
        to his relatives."

26Then Noah said,

"May the LORD, the God of Shem,
        be blessed,
    and may Canaan be his servant!
27 May God expand the territory
        of Japheth!

May Japheth share the prosperity
     of Shem,*
     and may Canaan be his servant."

28Noah lived another 350 years after
the great flood. 29He lived 950 years,
and then he died.

10:1THIS is the account of the families of
Shem, Ham, and Japheth, the three sons
of Noah. Many children were born to
them after the great flood.

2The descendants of Japheth were
     Gomer, Magog, Madai, Javan, Tubal,
     Meshech, and Tiras.
3The descendants of Gomer were
     Ashkenaz, Riphath, and Togarmah.
4The descendants of Javan were
     Elishah, Tarshish, Kittim, and
     Rodanim.* 5Their descendants
     became the seafaring peoples that
     spread out to various lands, each
     identified by its own language, clan,
     and national identity.

6The descendants of Ham were Cush,
     Mizraim, Put, and Canaan.
7The descendants of Cush were Seba,
     Havilah, Sabtah, Raamah, and
     Sabteca. The descendants of
     Raamah were Sheba and Dedan.
     8Cush was also the ancestor of
Nimrod, who was the first heroic
warrior on earth. 9Since he was the
greatest hunter in the world,* his
name became proverbial. People
would say, "This man is like Nimrod,
the greatest hunter in the world."
10He built his kingdom in the land
of Babylonia,* with the cities of
Babylon, Erech, Akkad, and Calneh.
11From there he expanded his
territory to Assyria,* building the
cities of Nineveh, Rehoboth-ir,
Calah, 12and Resen (the great city
located between Nineveh and
Calah).
13Mizraim was the ancestor of the
     Ludites, Anamites, Lehabites,
     Naphtuhites, 14Pathrusites,
     Casluhites, and the Caphtorites,
     from whom the Philistines came.*

15Canaan's oldest son was Sidon, the
     ancestor of the Sidonians. Canaan
     was also the ancestor of the Hittites,
     16Jebusites, Amorites, Girgashites,
     17Hivites, Arkites, Sinites,
     18Arvadites, Zemarites, and
     Hamathites. The Canaanite clans
     eventually spread out, 19and the
     territory of Canaan extended from
     Sidon in the north to Gerar and Gaza
     in the south, and east as far as
     Sodom, Gomorrah, Admah, and
     Zeboiim, near Lasha.
20These were the descendants of Ham,
identified by clan, language, territory,
and national identity.

21Sons were also born to Shem, the
     older brother of Japheth.* Shem
     was the ancestor of all the
     descendants of Eber.
22The descendants of Shem were
     Elam, Asshur, Arphaxad, Lud, and
     Aram.
23The descendants of Aram were Uz,
     Hul, Gether, and Mash.
24Arphaxad was the father of
     Shelah,* and Shelah was the father
     of Eber.
25Eber had two sons. The first was
     named Peleg (which means
     "division"), for during his lifetime
     the people of the world were divided
     into different language groups. His
     brother's name was Joktan.
26Joktan was the ancestor of Almodad,
     Sheleph, Hazarmaveth, Jerah,
     27Hadoram, Uzal, Diklah, 28Obal,
     Abimael, Sheba, 29Ophir, Havilah,
     and Jobab. All these were
     descendants of Joktan. 30The
     territory they occupied extended
     from Mesha all the way to Sephar in
     the eastern mountains.
31These were the descendants of Shem,
identified by clan, language, territory,
and national identity.

32These are the clans that descended
from Noah's sons, arranged by nation
according to their lines of descent. All

the nations of the earth descended from these clans after the great flood.

8:4 Hebrew *on the seventeenth day of the seventh month;* see 7:11.   8:5 Hebrew *On the first day of the tenth month;* see 7:11 and note on 8:4.   8:13 Hebrew *On the first day of the first month;* see 7:11.   8:14 Hebrew *The twenty-seventh day of the second month arrived;* see note on 8:13.   8:20 Hebrew *every clean animal and every clean bird.*   9:6 Or *man;* Hebrew reads *ha-adam.*   9:27 Hebrew *May he live in the tents of Shem.*   10:4 As in some Hebrew manuscripts and Greek version (see also 1 Chr 1:7); most Hebrew manuscripts read *Dodanim.*   10:9 Hebrew *a great hunter before the* Lord; also in 10:9b.   10:10 Hebrew *Shinar.*   10:11 Or *From that land Assyria went out.*   10:14 Hebrew *Casluhites, from whom the Philistines came, and Caphtorites.* Compare Jer 47:4; Amos 9:7.   10:21 Or *Shem, whose older brother was Japheth.*   10:24 Greek version reads *Arphaxad was the father of Cainan, Cainan was the father of Shelah.* Compare Luke 3:36.

## MATTHEW 4:12-25

**W**hen Jesus heard that John had been arrested, he left Judea and returned to Galilee. [13]He went first to Nazareth, then left there and moved to Capernaum, beside the Sea of Galilee, in the region of Zebulun and Naphtali. [14]This fulfilled what God said through the prophet Isaiah:

[15] "In the land of Zebulun and
 of Naphtali,
  beside the sea, beyond the
   Jordan River,
  in Galilee where so many Gentiles
   live,
[16] the people who sat in darkness
  have seen a great light.
 And for those who lived in the land
  where death casts its shadow,
  a light has shined."*

[17]From then on Jesus began to preach, "Repent of your sins and turn to God, for the Kingdom of Heaven is near.*"

[18]One day as Jesus was walking along the shore of the Sea of Galilee, he saw two brothers—Simon, also called Peter, and Andrew—throwing a net into the water, for they fished for a living. [19]**Jesus called out to them, "Come, follow me, and I will show you how to fish for people!"** [20]**And they left their nets at once and followed him.**

[21]A little farther up the shore he saw two other brothers, James and John, sitting in a boat with their father, Zebedee, repairing their nets. And he called them

to come, too. [22]They immediately followed him, leaving the boat and their father behind.

[23]Jesus traveled throughout the region of Galilee, teaching in the synagogues and announcing the Good News about the Kingdom. And he healed every kind of disease and illness. [24]News about him spread as far as Syria, and people soon began bringing to him all who were sick. And whatever their sickness or disease, or if they were demon-possessed or epileptic or paralyzed—he healed them all. [25]Large crowds followed him wherever he went—people from Galilee, the Ten Towns,* Jerusalem, from all over Judea, and from east of the Jordan River.

4:15-16 Isa 9:1-2 (Greek version).   4:17 Or *has come,* or *is coming soon.*   4:25 Greek *Decapolis.*

## PSALM 4:1-8

*For the choir director: A psalm of David, to be accompanied by stringed instruments.*

[1] **A**nswer me when I call to you,
  O God who declares me innocent.
 Free me from my troubles.
  Have mercy on me and hear
   my prayer.

[2] How long will you people ruin my
   reputation?
  How long will you make
   groundless accusations?
  How long will you continue your
   lies?          *Interlude*

[3] You can be sure of this:
  The Lord set apart the godly
   for himself.
  The Lord will answer when I call
   to him.

[4] Don't sin by letting anger control
   you.
  Think about it overnight and
   remain silent.     *Interlude*

[5] Offer sacrifices in the right spirit,
  and trust the Lord.

[6] Many people say, "Who will show us
   better times?"
  Let your face smile on us, Lord.

[7] You have given me greater joy

than those who have abundant harvests of grain and new wine.
⁸ In peace I will lie down and sleep, for you alone, O LORD, will keep me safe.

PROVERBS 1:20-23

**W**isdom shouts in the streets. She cries out in the public square. She calls to the crowds along the main street, to those gathered in front of the city gate: "How long, you simpletons, will you insist on being simpleminded? How long will you mockers relish your mocking? How long will you fools hate knowledge? Come and listen to my counsel. I'll share my heart with you and make you wise.

# JANUARY 5

GENESIS 11:1-13:4

**A**t one time all the people of the world spoke the same language and used the same words. ²As the people migrated to the east, they found a plain in the land of Babylonia* and settled there.

³They began saying to each other, "Let's make bricks and harden them with fire." (In this region bricks were used instead of stone, and tar was used for mortar.) ⁴Then they said, "Come, let's build a great city for ourselves with a tower that reaches into the sky. This will make us famous and keep us from being scattered all over the world."

⁵But the LORD came down to look at the city and the tower the people were building. ⁶"Look!" he said. "The people are united, and they all speak the same language. After this, nothing they set out to do will be impossible for them! ⁷Come, let's go down and confuse the people with different languages. Then they won't be able to understand each other."

⁸In that way, the LORD scattered them all over the world, and they stopped building the city. ⁹That is why the city was called Babel,* because that is where the LORD confused the people with different languages. In this way he scattered them all over the world.

¹⁰This is the account of Shem's family.

Two years after the great flood, when Shem was 100 years old, he became the father of* Arphaxad. ¹¹After the birth of* Arphaxad, Shem lived another 500 years and had other sons and daughters.

¹²When Arphaxad was 35 years old, he became the father of Shelah. ¹³After the birth of Shelah, Arphaxad lived another 403 years and had other sons and daughters.*

¹⁴When Shelah was 30 years old, he became the father of Eber. ¹⁵After the birth of Eber, Shelah lived another 403 years and had other sons and daughters.

¹⁶When Eber was 34 years old, he became the father of Peleg. ¹⁷After the birth of Peleg, Eber lived another 430 years and had other sons and daughters.

¹⁸When Peleg was 30 years old, he became the father of Reu. ¹⁹After the birth of Reu, Peleg lived another 209 years and had other sons and daughters.

²⁰When Reu was 32 years old, he became the father of Serug. ²¹After the birth of Serug, Reu lived another 207 years and had other sons and daughters.

²²When Serug was 30 years old, he became the father of Nahor. ²³After the birth of Nahor, Serug lived another 200 years and had other sons and daughters.

²⁴When Nahor was 29 years old, he became the father of Terah. ²⁵After the birth of Terah, Nahor lived another 119 years and had other sons and daughters.

²⁶When Terah was 70 years old, he

had become the father of Abram, Nahor, and Haran.

27 This is the account of Terah's family. Terah was the father of Abram, Nahor, and Haran; and Haran was the father of Lot. 28 But Haran died in Ur of the Chaldeans, the land of his birth, while his father, Terah, was still living. 29 Meanwhile, Abram and Nahor both married. The name of Abram's wife was Sarai, and the name of Nahor's wife was Milcah. (Milcah and her sister Iscah were daughters of Nahor's brother Haran.) 30 But Sarai was unable to become pregnant and had no children.

31 One day Terah took his son Abram, his daughter-in-law Sarai (his son Abram's wife), and his grandson Lot (his son Haran's child) and moved away from Ur of the Chaldeans. He was headed for the land of Canaan, but they stopped at Haran and settled there. 32 Terah lived for 205 years* and died while still in Haran.

12:1 THE LORD had said to Abram, "Leave your native country, your relatives, and your father's family, and go to the land that I will show you. 2 I will make you into a great nation. I will bless you and make you famous, and you will be a blessing to others. 3 I will bless those who bless you and curse those who treat you with contempt. All the families on earth will be blessed through you."

4 So Abram departed as the LORD had instructed, and Lot went with him. Abram was seventy-five years old when he left Haran. 5 He took his wife, Sarai, his nephew Lot, and all his wealth—his livestock and all the people he had taken into his household at Haran—and headed for the land of Canaan. When they arrived in Canaan, 6 Abram traveled through the land as far as Shechem. There he set up camp beside the oak of Moreh. At that time, the area was inhabited by Canaanites.

7 Then the LORD appeared to Abram and said, "I will give this land to your descendants.*" And Abram built an altar there and dedicated it to the LORD, who had appeared to him. 8 After that, Abram traveled south and set up camp in the hill country, with Bethel to the west and Ai to the east. There he built another altar and dedicated it to the LORD, and he worshiped the LORD. 9 Then Abram continued traveling south by stages toward the Negev.

10 At that time a severe famine struck the land of Canaan, forcing Abram to go down to Egypt, where he lived as a foreigner. 11 As he was approaching the border of Egypt, Abram said to his wife, Sarai, "Look, you are a very beautiful woman. 12 When the Egyptians see you, they will say, 'This is his wife. Let's kill him; then we can have her!' 13 So please tell them you are my sister. Then they will spare my life and treat me well because of their interest in you."

14 And sure enough, when Abram arrived in Egypt, everyone spoke of Sarai's beauty. 15 When the palace officials saw her, they sang her praises to Pharaoh, their king, and Sarai was taken into his palace. 16 Then Pharaoh gave Abram many gifts because of her—sheep, goats, cattle, male and female donkeys, male and female servants, and camels.

17 But the LORD sent terrible plagues upon Pharaoh and his household because of Sarai, Abram's wife. 18 So Pharaoh summoned Abram and accused him sharply. "What have you done to me?" he demanded. "Why didn't you tell me she was your wife? 19 Why did you say, 'She is my sister,' and allow me to take her as my wife? Now then, here is your wife. Take her and get out of here!" 20 Pharaoh ordered some of his men to escort them, and he sent Abram out of the country, along with his wife and all his possessions.

13:1 So Abram left Egypt and traveled north into the Negev, along with his wife and Lot and all that they owned. 2 (Abram was very rich in livestock, silver, and gold.) 3 From the Negev, they continued traveling by stages toward Bethel, and they pitched their tents between Bethel and Ai, where they had camped before. ⁴This was the same place where Abram had built the altar, and there he worshiped the LORD again.

11:2 Hebrew *Shinar*.   11:9 Or *Babylon. Babel* sounds like a Hebrew term that means "confusion."   11:10 Or *the ancestor of;* also in 11:12, 14, 16, 18, 20, 22, 24.   11:11 Or *the birth of this ancestor of;* also in 11:13, 15, 17, 19, 21, 23, 25.   11:12-13 Greek version reads ¹²*When Arphaxad was 135 years old, he became the father of Cainan. ¹³After the birth of Cainan, Arphaxad lived another 430 years and had other sons and daughters, and then he died. When Cainan was 130 years old, he became the father of Shelah. After the birth of Shelah, Cainan lived another 330 years and had other sons and daughters, and then he died.* Compare Luke 3:35-36.   11:32 Some ancient versions read *145 years;* compare 11:26 and 12:4.   12:7 Hebrew *seed*.

## MATTHEW 5:1-26

❶ne day as he saw the crowds gathering, Jesus went up on the mountainside and sat down. His disciples gathered around him, ²and he began to teach them.

³ "God blesses those who are poor
    and realize their need for
    him,*
  for the Kingdom of Heaven
    is theirs.
⁴ God blesses those who mourn,
  for they will be comforted.
⁵ God blesses those who are humble,
  for they will inherit the whole
    earth.
⁶ God blesses those who hunger and
    thirst for justice,*
  for they will be satisfied.
⁷ God blesses those who are merciful,
  for they will be shown mercy.
⁸ God blesses those whose hearts
    are pure,
  for they will see God.
⁹ God blesses those who work for peace,
  for they will be called the children
    of God.
¹⁰ God blesses those who are
    persecuted for doing right,
  for the Kingdom of Heaven is
    theirs.

¹¹"God blesses you when people mock you and persecute you and lie about you* and say all sorts of evil things against you because you are my followers. ¹²Be happy about it! Be very glad! For a great reward awaits you in heaven.

And remember, the ancient prophets were persecuted in the same way.

¹³"You are the salt of the earth. But what good is salt if it has lost its flavor? Can you make it salty again? It will be thrown out and trampled underfoot as worthless.

¹⁴"You are the light of the world—like a city on a hilltop that cannot be hidden. ¹⁵No one lights a lamp and then puts it under a basket. Instead, a lamp is placed on a stand, where it gives light to everyone in the house. **¹⁶In the same way, let your good deeds shine out for all to see, so that everyone will praise your heavenly Father.**

¹⁷"Don't misunderstand why I have come. I did not come to abolish the law of Moses or the writings of the prophets. No, I came to accomplish their purpose. ¹⁸I tell you the truth, until heaven and earth disappear, not even the smallest detail of God's law will disappear until its purpose is achieved. ¹⁹So if you ignore the least commandment and teach others to do the same, you will be called the least in the Kingdom of Heaven. But anyone who obeys God's laws and teaches them will be called great in the Kingdom of Heaven.

²⁰"But I warn you—unless your righteousness is better than the righteousness of the teachers of religious law and the Pharisees, you will never enter the Kingdom of Heaven!

²¹"You have heard that our ancestors were told, 'You must not murder. If you commit murder, you are subject to judgment.'* ²²But I say, if you are even angry with someone,* you are subject to judgment! If you call someone an idiot,* you are in danger of being brought before the court. And if you curse someone,* you are in danger of the fires of hell.*

²³"So if you are presenting a sacrifice at the altar in the Temple and you suddenly remember that someone has something against you, ²⁴leave your sacrifice there at the altar. Go and be reconciled to that person. Then come and offer your sacrifice to God.

²⁵"When you are on the way to court

with your adversary, settle your differences quickly. Otherwise, your accuser may hand you over to the judge, who will hand you over to an officer, and you will be thrown into prison. ²⁶And if that happens, you surely won't be free again until you have paid the last penny.*

5:3 Greek *poor in spirit.*    5:6 Or *for righteousness.*
5:11 Some manuscripts omit *and lie about you.*
5:21 Exod 20:13; Deut 5:17.    5:22a Some manuscripts add *without cause.*    5:22b Greek uses an Aramaic term of contempt: *If you say to your brother, 'Raca.'*    5:22c Greek *if you say, 'You fool.'*    5:22d Greek *Gehenna;* also in 5:29, 30.    5:26 Greek *the last kodrantes* [i.e., quadrans].

## PSALM 5:1-12
*For the choir director: A psalm of David, to be accompanied by the flute.*

¹ **O** LORD, hear me as I pray;
    pay attention to my groaning.
² Listen to my cry for help, my King
        and my God,
    for I pray to no one but you.
³ Listen to my voice in the morning,
        LORD.
    Each morning I bring my requests
        to you and wait expectantly.

⁴ O God, you take no pleasure in
        wickedness;
    you cannot tolerate the sins
        of the wicked.
⁵ Therefore, the proud may not stand
        in your presence,
    for you hate all who do evil.
⁶ You will destroy those who tell lies.
    The LORD detests murderers and
        deceivers.

⁷ Because of your unfailing love, I can
        enter your house;
    I will worship at your Temple with
        deepest awe.
⁸ Lead me in the right path, O LORD,
        or my enemies will conquer me.
    Make your way plain for me
        to follow.

⁹ My enemies cannot speak a truthful
        word.
    Their deepest desire is to destroy
        others.
    Their talk is foul, like the stench
        from an open grave.

    Their tongues are filled with
        flattery.*
¹⁰ O God, declare them guilty.
    Let them be caught in their
        own traps.
    Drive them away because of their
        many sins,
        for they have rebelled against you.

¹¹ But let all who take refuge in you
        rejoice;
    let them sing joyful praises
        forever.
    Spread your protection over them,
        that all who love your name may
        be filled with joy.
¹² For you bless the godly, O LORD;
    you surround them with your
        shield of love.

5:9 Greek version reads *with lies.* Compare Rom 3:12.

## PROVERBS 1:24-28
"**I** [Wisdom] called you so often, but you wouldn't come. I reached out to you, but you paid no attention. You ignored my advice and rejected the correction I offered. So I will laugh when you are in trouble! I will mock you when disaster overtakes you—when calamity overtakes you like a storm, when disaster engulfs you like a cyclone, and anguish and distress overwhelm you. □"When they cry for help, I will not answer. Though they anxiously search for me, they will not find me.

# JANUARY 6

## GENESIS 13:5–15:21
**L**ot, who was traveling with Abram, had also become very wealthy with flocks of sheep and goats, herds of cattle, and many tents. ⁶But the land could not support both Abram and Lot with all their flocks and herds living so close together. ⁷So disputes broke out between the

herdsmen of Abram and Lot. (At that time Canaanites and Perizzites were also living in the land.)

⁸Finally Abram said to Lot, "Let's not allow this conflict to come between us or our herdsmen. After all, we are close relatives! ⁹The whole countryside is open to you. Take your choice of any section of the land you want, and we will separate. If you want the land to the left, then I'll take the land on the right. If you prefer the land on the right, then I'll go to the left."

¹⁰Lot took a long look at the fertile plains of the Jordan Valley in the direction of Zoar. The whole area was well watered everywhere, like the garden of the LORD or the beautiful land of Egypt. (This was before the LORD destroyed Sodom and Gomorrah.) ¹¹Lot chose for himself the whole Jordan Valley to the east of them. He went there with his flocks and servants and parted company with his uncle Abram. ¹²So Abram settled in the land of Canaan, and Lot moved his tents to a place near Sodom and settled among the cities of the plain. ¹³But the people of this area were extremely wicked and constantly sinned against the LORD.

¹⁴After Lot had gone, the LORD said to Abram, "Look as far as you can see in every direction—north and south, east and west. ¹⁵I am giving all this land, as far as you can see, to you and your descendants* as a permanent possession. ¹⁶And I will give you so many descendants that, like the dust of the earth, they cannot be counted! ¹⁷Go and walk through the land in every direction, for I am giving it to you."

¹⁸So Abram moved his camp to Hebron and settled near the oak grove belonging to Mamre. There he built another altar to the LORD.

¹⁴:¹ABOUT this time war broke out in the region. King Amraphel of Babylonia,* King Arioch of Ellasar, King Kedorlaomer of Elam, and King Tidal of Goiim ²fought against King Bera of Sodom, King Birsha of Gomorrah, King Shinab

of Admah, King Shemeber of Zeboiim, and the king of Bela (also called Zoar).

³This second group of kings joined forces in Siddim Valley (that is, the valley of the Dead Sea*). ⁴For twelve years they had been subject to King Kedorlaomer, but in the thirteenth year they rebelled against him.

⁵One year later Kedorlaomer and his allies arrived and defeated the Rephaites at Ashteroth-karnaim, the Zuzites at Ham, the Emites at Shaveh-kiriathaim, ⁶and the Horites at Mount Seir, as far as El-paran at the edge of the wilderness. ⁷Then they turned back and came to En-mishpat (now called Kadesh) and conquered all the territory of the Amalekites, and also the Amorites living in Hazazon-tamar.

⁸Then the rebel kings of Sodom, Gomorrah, Admah, Zeboiim, and Bela (also called Zoar) prepared for battle in the valley of the Dead Sea.* ⁹They fought against King Kedorlaomer of Elam, King Tidal of Goiim, King Amraphel of Babylonia, and King Arioch of Ellasar—four kings against five. ¹⁰As it happened, the valley of the Dead Sea was filled with tar pits. And as the army of the kings of Sodom and Gomorrah fled, some fell into the tar pits, while the rest escaped into the mountains. ¹¹The victorious invaders then plundered Sodom and Gomorrah and headed for home, taking with them all the spoils of war and the food supplies. ¹²They also captured Lot—Abram's nephew who lived in Sodom—and carried off everything he owned.

¹³But one of Lot's men escaped and reported everything to Abram the Hebrew, who was living near the oak grove belonging to Mamre the Amorite. Mamre and his relatives, Eshcol and Aner, were Abram's allies.

¹⁴When Abram heard that his nephew Lot had been captured, he mobilized the 318 trained men who had been born into his household. Then he pursued Kedorlaomer's army until he caught up with them at Dan. ¹⁵There he divided his men and attacked during the night. Kedorlaomer's army fled, but Abram

chased them as far as Hobah, north of Damascus. ¹⁶Abram recovered all the goods that had been taken, and he brought back his nephew Lot with his possessions and all the women and other captives.

¹⁷After Abram returned from his victory over Kedorlaomer and all his allies, the king of Sodom went out to meet him in the valley of Shaveh (that is, the King's Valley).

¹⁸And Melchizedek, the king of Salem and a priest of God Most High,* brought Abram some bread and wine. ¹⁹Melchizedek blessed Abram with this blessing:

"Blessed be Abram by God Most High,
    Creator of heaven and earth.
²⁰ And blessed be God Most High,
    who has defeated your enemies
        for you."

Then Abram gave Melchizedek a tenth of all the goods he had recovered.

²¹The king of Sodom said to Abram, "Give back my people who were captured. But you may keep for yourself all the goods you have recovered."

²²Abram replied to the king of Sodom, "I solemnly swear to the LORD, God Most High, Creator of heaven and earth, ²³that I will not take so much as a single thread or sandal thong from what belongs to you. Otherwise you might say, 'I am the one who made Abram rich.' ²⁴I will accept only what my young warriors have already eaten, and I request that you give a fair share of the goods to my allies—Aner, Eshcol, and Mamre."

¹⁵:¹SOME time later, the LORD spoke to Abram in a vision and said to him, "Do not be afraid, Abram, for I will protect you, and your reward will be great."

²But Abram replied, "O Sovereign LORD, what good are all your blessings when I don't even have a son? Since you've given me no children, Eliezer of Damascus, a servant in my household, will inherit all my wealth. ³You have given me no descendants of my own, so one of my servants will be my heir."

⁴Then the LORD said to him, "No, your servant will not be your heir, for you will have a son of your own who will be your heir." ⁵Then the LORD took Abram outside and said to him, "Look up into the sky and count the stars if you can. That's how many descendants you will have!"

⁶And Abram believed the LORD, and the LORD counted him as righteous because of his faith.

⁷Then the LORD told him, "I am the LORD who brought you out of Ur of the Chaldeans to give you this land as your possession."

⁸But Abram replied, "O Sovereign LORD, how can I be sure that I will actually possess it?"

⁹The LORD told him, "Bring me a three-year-old heifer, a three-year-old female goat, a three-year-old ram, a turtledove, and a young pigeon." ¹⁰So Abram presented all these to him and killed them. Then he cut each animal down the middle and laid the halves side by side; he did not, however, cut the birds in half. ¹¹Some vultures swooped down to eat the carcasses, but Abram chased them away.

¹²As the sun was going down, Abram fell into a deep sleep, and a terrifying darkness came down over him. ¹³Then the LORD said to Abram, "You can be sure that your descendants will be strangers in a foreign land, where they will be oppressed as slaves for 400 years. ¹⁴But I will punish the nation that enslaves them, and in the end they will come away with great wealth. ¹⁵(As for you, you will die in peace and be buried at a ripe old age.) ¹⁶After four generations your descendants will return here to this land, for the sins of the Amorites do not yet warrant their destruction."

¹⁷After the sun went down and darkness fell, Abram saw a smoking firepot and a flaming torch pass between the halves of the carcasses. ¹⁸So the LORD made a covenant with Abram that day and said, "I have given this land to your descendants, all the way from the border of Egypt* to the great Euphrates River—¹⁹the land now occupied by the

Kenites, Kenizzites, Kadmonites, 20Hittites, Perizzites, Rephaites, 21Amorites, Canaanites, Girgashites, and Jebusites."

13:15 Hebrew *seed*.   14:1 Hebrew *Shinar;* also in 14:9.
14:3 Hebrew *Salt Sea*.   14:8 Hebrew *Siddim Valley*
(see 14:3); also in 14:10.   14:18 Hebrew *El-Elyon;* also in
14:19, 20, 22.   15:18 Hebrew *the river of Egypt,* referring
either to an eastern branch of the Nile River or to the Brook
of Egypt in the Sinai (see Num 34:5).

MATTHEW 5:27-48
"You have heard the commandment that says, 'You must not commit adultery.'* 28But I say, anyone who even looks at a woman with lust has already committed adultery with her in his heart. 29So if your eye—even your good eye*—causes you to lust, gouge it out and throw it away. It is better for you to lose one part of your body than for your whole body to be thrown into hell. 30And if your hand—even your stronger hand*—causes you to sin, cut it off and throw it away. It is better for you to lose one part of your body than for your whole body to be thrown into hell.

31"You have heard the law that says, 'A man can divorce his wife by merely giving her a written notice of divorce.'* 32But I say that a man who divorces his wife, unless she has been unfaithful, causes her to commit adultery. And anyone who marries a divorced woman also commits adultery.

33"You have also heard that our ancestors were told, 'You must not break your vows; you must carry out the vows you make to the Lord.'* 34But I say, do not make any vows! Do not say, 'By heaven!' because heaven is God's throne. 35And do not say, 'By the earth!' because the earth is his footstool. And do not say, 'By Jerusalem!' for Jerusalem is the city of the great King. 36Do not even say, 'By my head!' for you can't turn one hair white or black. 37Just say a simple, 'Yes, I will,' or 'No, I won't.' Anything beyond this is from the evil one.

38"You have heard the law that says the punishment must match the injury: 'An eye for an eye, and a tooth for a tooth.'* 39But I say, do not resist an evil person! If someone slaps you on the

right cheek, offer the other cheek also. 40If you are sued in court and your shirt is taken from you, give your coat, too. 41If a soldier demands that you carry his gear for a mile,* carry it two miles. 42Give to those who ask, and don't turn away from those who want to borrow.

43"You have heard the law that says, 'Love your neighbor'* and hate your enemy. 44But I say, love your enemies!* Pray for those who persecute you! 45In that way, you will be acting as true children of your Father in heaven. For he gives his sunlight to both the evil and the good, and he sends rain on the just and the unjust alike. 46If you love only those who love you, what reward is there for that? Even corrupt tax collectors do that much. 47If you are kind only to your friends,* how are you different from anyone else? Even pagans do that. 48But you are to be perfect, even as your Father in heaven is perfect.

5:27 Exod 20:14; Deut 5:18.   5:29 Greek *your right
eye*.   5:30 Greek *your right hand*.   5:31 Deut 24:1.
5:33 Num 30:2.   5:38 Greek *the law that says: 'An eye
for an eye and a tooth for a tooth.'* Exod 21:24; Lev 24:20;
Deut 19:21.   5:41 Greek *milion* [4,854 feet or 1,478
meters].   5:43 Lev 19:18.   5:44 Some manuscripts add
*Bless those who curse you. Do good to those who hate you.*
Compare Luke 6:27-28.   5:47 Greek *your brothers*.

PSALM 6:1-10
*For the choir director: A psalm of David,
to be accompanied by an eight-stringed
instrument.*

¹ **O** Lord, don't rebuke me in
       your anger
   or discipline me in your rage.
² Have compassion on me, Lord,
       for I am weak.
   Heal me, Lord, for my bones are
       in agony.
³ I am sick at heart.
   How long, O Lord, until you
       restore me?

⁴ Return, O Lord, and rescue me.
   Save me because of your unfailing
       love.
⁵ For the dead do not remember
       you.
   Who can praise you from
       the grave?*

⁶ I am worn out from sobbing.
  All night I flood my bed with
    weeping,
  drenching it with my tears.
⁷ My vision is blurred by grief;
  my eyes are worn out because
    of all my enemies.

⁸ Go away, all you who do evil,
  for the LORD has heard my
    weeping.
⁹ The LORD has heard my plea;
  the LORD will answer my prayer.
¹⁰ May all my enemies be disgraced
    and terrified.
  May they suddenly turn back
    in shame.

6:TITLE Hebrew *with stringed instruments; according to the sheminith.*   **6:5** Hebrew *from Sheol?*

## PROVERBS 1:29-33

For they hated knowledge and chose not to fear the LORD. They rejected my advice and paid no attention when I corrected them. Therefore, they must eat the bitter fruit of living their own way, choking on their own schemes. For simpletons turn away from me—to death. Fools are destroyed by their own complacency. But all who listen to me will live in peace, untroubled by fear of harm.

# JANUARY 7

## GENESIS 16:1-18:15

Now Sarai, Abram's wife, had not been able to bear children for him. But she had an Egyptian servant named Hagar. ²So Sarai said to Abram, "The LORD has prevented me from having children. Go and sleep with my servant. Perhaps I can have children through her." And Abram agreed with Sarai's proposal. ³So Sarai, Abram's wife, took Hagar the Egyptian servant and gave her to Abram as a wife.

(This happened ten years after Abram had settled in the land of Canaan.)

⁴So Abram had sexual relations with Hagar, and she became pregnant. But when Hagar knew she was pregnant, she began to treat her mistress, Sarai, with contempt. ⁵Then Sarai said to Abram, "This is all your fault! I put my servant into your arms, but now that she's pregnant she treats me with contempt. The LORD will show who's wrong—you or me!"

⁶Abram replied, "Look, she is your servant, so deal with her as you see fit." Then Sarai treated Hagar so harshly that she finally ran away.

⁷The angel of the LORD found Hagar beside a spring of water in the wilderness, along the road to Shur. ⁸The angel said to her, "Hagar, Sarai's servant, where have you come from, and where are you going?"

"I'm running away from my mistress, Sarai," she replied.

⁹The angel of the LORD said to her, "Return to your mistress, and submit to her authority." ¹⁰Then he added, "I will give you more descendants than you can count."

¹¹And the angel also said, "You are now pregnant and will give birth to a son. You are to name him Ishmael (which means 'God hears'), for the LORD has heard your cry of distress. ¹²This son of yours will be a wild man, as untamed as a wild donkey! He will raise his fist against everyone, and everyone will be against him. Yes, he will live in open hostility against all his relatives."

¹³Thereafter, Hagar used another name to refer to the LORD, who had spoken to her. She said, "You are the God who sees me."* She also said, "Have I truly seen the One who sees me?" ¹⁴So that well was named Beer-lahai-roi (which means "well of the Living One who sees me"). It can still be found between Kadesh and Bered.

¹⁵So Hagar gave Abram a son, and Abram named him Ishmael. ¹⁶Abram was eighty-six years old when Ishmael was born.

17:1WHEN Abram was ninety-nine years old, the LORD appeared to him and said, "I am El-Shaddai—'God Almighty.' Serve me faithfully and live a blameless life. 2I will make a covenant with you, by which I will guarantee to give you countless descendants."

3At this, Abram fell face down on the ground. Then God said to him, 4"This is my covenant with you: I will make you the father of a multitude of nations! 5What's more, I am changing your name. It will no longer be Abram. Instead, you will be called Abraham,* for you will be the father of many nations. 6I will make you extremely fruitful. Your descendants will become many nations, and kings will be among them!

7"I will confirm my covenant with you and your descendants after you, from generation to generation. This is the everlasting covenant: I will always be your God and the God of your descendants after you. 8And I will give the entire land of Canaan, where you now live as a foreigner, to you and your descendants. It will be their possession forever, and I will be their God."

9Then God said to Abraham, "Your responsibility is to obey the terms of the covenant. You and all your descendants have this continual responsibility. 10This is the covenant that you and your descendants must keep: Each male among you must be circumcised. 11You must cut off the flesh of your foreskin as a sign of the covenant between me and you. 12From generation to generation, every male child must be circumcised on the eighth day after his birth. This applies not only to members of your family but also to the servants born in your household and the foreign-born servants whom you have purchased. 13All must be circumcised. Your bodies will bear the mark of my everlasting covenant. 14Any male who fails to be circumcised will be cut off from the covenant family for breaking the covenant."

15Then God said to Abraham, "Regarding Sarai, your wife—her name will no longer be Sarai. From now on her name will be Sarah.* 16And I will bless her and give you a son from her! Yes, I will bless her richly, and she will become the mother of many nations. Kings of nations will be among her descendants."

17Then Abraham bowed down to the ground, but he laughed to himself in disbelief. "How could I become a father at the age of 100?" he thought. "And how can Sarah have a baby when she is ninety years old?" 18So Abraham said to God, "May Ishmael live under your special blessing!"

19But God replied, "No—Sarah, your wife, will give birth to a son for you. You will name him Isaac,* and I will confirm my covenant with him and his descendants as an everlasting covenant. 20As for Ishmael, I will bless him also, just as you have asked. I will make him extremely fruitful and multiply his descendants. He will become the father of twelve princes, and I will make him a great nation. 21But my covenant will be confirmed with Isaac, who will be born to you and Sarah about this time next year." 22When God had finished speaking, he left Abraham.

23On that very day Abraham took his son, Ishmael, and every male in his household, including those born there and those he had bought. Then he circumcised them, cutting off their foreskins, just as God had told him. 24Abraham was ninety-nine years old when he was circumcised, 25and Ishmael, his son, was thirteen. 26Both Abraham and his son, Ishmael, were circumcised on that same day, 27along with all the other men and boys of the household, whether they were born there or bought as servants. All were circumcised with him.

18:1THE LORD appeared again to Abraham near the oak grove belonging to Mamre. One day Abraham was sitting at the entrance to his tent during the hottest part of the day. 2He looked up and noticed three men standing nearby. When he saw them, he ran to meet them and welcomed them, bowing low to the ground.

³"My lord," he said, "if it pleases you, stop here for a while. ⁴Rest in the shade of this tree while water is brought to wash your feet. ⁵And since you've honored your servant with this visit, let me prepare some food to refresh you before you continue on your journey."

"All right," they said. "Do as you have said."

⁶So Abraham ran back to the tent and said to Sarah, "Hurry! Get three large measures* of your best flour, knead it into dough, and bake some bread." ⁷Then Abraham ran out to the herd and chose a tender calf and gave it to his servant, who quickly prepared it. ⁸When the food was ready, Abraham took some yogurt and milk and the roasted meat, and he served it to the men. As they ate, Abraham waited on them in the shade of the trees.

⁹"Where is Sarah, your wife?" the visitors asked.

"She's inside the tent," Abraham replied.

¹⁰Then one of them said, "I will return to you about this time next year, and your wife, Sarah, will have a son!"

Sarah was listening to this conversation from the tent. ¹¹Abraham and Sarah were both very old by this time, and Sarah was long past the age of having children. ¹²So she laughed silently to herself and said, "How could a worn-out woman like me enjoy such pleasure, especially when my master—my husband—is also so old?"

¹³Then the LORD said to Abraham, "Why did Sarah laugh? Why did she say, 'Can an old woman like me have a baby?' ¹⁴Is anything too hard for the LORD? I will return about this time next year, and Sarah will have a son."

¹⁵Sarah was afraid, so she denied it, saying, "I didn't laugh."

But the LORD said, "No, you did laugh."

16:13 Hebrew *El-roi*.   17:5 *Abram* means "exalted father"; *Abraham* sounds like a Hebrew term that means "father of many."   17:15 *Sarai* and *Sarah* both mean "princess." 17:19 *Isaac* means "he laughs."   18:6 Hebrew 3 *seahs*, about 15 quarts or 18 liters.

## MATTHEW 6:1-24

"**W**atch out! Don't do your good deeds publicly, to be admired by others, for you will lose the reward from your Father in heaven. ²When you give to someone in need, don't do as the hypocrites do—blowing trumpets in the synagogues and streets to call attention to their acts of charity! I tell you the truth, they have received all the reward they will ever get. ³But when you give to someone in need, don't let your left hand know what your right hand is doing. ⁴Give your gifts in private, and your Father, who sees everything, will reward you.

⁵"When you pray, don't be like the hypocrites who love to pray publicly on street corners and in the synagogues where everyone can see them. I tell you the truth, that is all the reward they will ever get. ⁶But when you pray, go away by yourself, shut the door behind you, and pray to your Father in private. Then your Father, who sees everything, will reward you.

⁷"When you pray, don't babble on and on as people of other religions do. They think their prayers are answered merely by repeating their words again and again. ⁸Don't be like them, for your Father knows exactly what you need even before you ask him! ⁹**Pray like this:**

**Our Father in heaven,
    may your name be kept holy.**
¹⁰ **May your Kingdom come soon.
    May your will be done on earth,
        as it is in heaven.**
¹¹ **Give us today the food we need,***
¹² **and forgive us our sins,
        as we have forgiven those who
            sin against us.**
¹³ **And don't let us yield to temptation,* but rescue us from
        the evil one.***

¹⁴"If you forgive those who sin against you, your heavenly Father will forgive you. ¹⁵But if you refuse to forgive others, your Father will not forgive your sins.

¹⁶"And when you fast, don't make it

obvious, as the hypocrites do, for they try to look miserable and disheveled so people will admire them for their fasting. I tell you the truth, that is the only reward they will ever get. ¹⁷But when you fast, comb your hair and wash your face. ¹⁸Then no one will notice that you are fasting, except your Father, who knows what you do in private. And your Father, who sees everything, will reward you.

¹⁹"Don't store up treasures here on earth, where moths eat them and rust destroys them, and where thieves break in and steal. ²⁰Store your treasures in heaven, where moths and rust cannot destroy, and thieves do not break in and steal. ²¹Wherever your treasure is, there the desires of your heart will also be.

²²"Your eye is a lamp that provides light for your body. When your eye is good, your whole body is filled with light. ²³But when your eye is bad, your whole body is filled with darkness. And if the light you think you have is actually darkness, how deep that darkness is!

²⁴"No one can serve two masters. For you will hate one and love the other; you will be devoted to one and despise the other. You cannot serve both God and money."

6:11 Or *Give us today our food for the day;* or *Give us today our food for tomorrow.*    6:13a Or *And keep us from being tested.*    6:13b Or *from evil.* Some manuscripts add *For yours is the kingdom and the power and the glory forever. Amen.*

## PSALM 7:1-17

*A psalm of David, which he sang to the LORD concerning Cush of the tribe of Benjamin.*

¹ I come to you for protection,
    O LORD my God.
  Save me from my persecutors—
    rescue me!
² If you don't, they will maul me like
    a lion,
    tearing me to pieces with no one
      to rescue me.
³ O LORD my God, if I have done
      wrong
    or am guilty of injustice,
⁴ if I have betrayed a friend

or plundered my enemy without
    cause,
⁵ then let my enemies capture me.
  Let them trample me into the
    ground
  and drag my honor in the dust.
                              *Interlude*

⁶ Arise, O LORD, in anger!
  Stand up against the fury of my
    enemies!
  Wake up, my God, and bring
    justice!
⁷ Gather the nations before you.
  Rule over them from on high.
⁸   The LORD judges the nations.
  Declare me righteous, O LORD,
    for I am innocent, O Most High!
⁹ End the evil of those who are
    wicked,
    and defend the righteous.
  For you look deep within the mind
    and heart,
    O righteous God.

¹⁰ God is my shield,
    saving those whose hearts are true
      and right.
¹¹ God is an honest judge.
  He is angry with the wicked every
    day.

¹² If a person does not repent,
    God* will sharpen his sword;
  he will bend and string his bow.
¹³ He will prepare his deadly weapons
    and shoot his flaming arrows.

¹⁴ The wicked conceive evil;
    they are pregnant with trouble
      and give birth to lies.
¹⁵ They dig a deep pit to trap others,
    then fall into it themselves.
¹⁶ The trouble they make for others
      backfires on them.
  The violence they plan falls on
    their own heads.

¹⁷ I will thank the LORD because
      he is just;
  I will sing praise to the name of
    the LORD Most High.

7:12 Hebrew *he.*

**PROVERBS 2:1-5**

**M**y child,* listen to what I say, and treasure my commands. Tune your ears to wisdom, and concentrate on understanding. Cry out for insight, and ask for understanding. Search for them as you would for silver; seek them like hidden treasures. Then you will understand what it means to fear the LORD, and you will gain knowledge of God.

2:1 Hebrew *My son.*

# JANUARY
# 8

**GENESIS 18:16–19:38**

**T**hen the men got up from their meal and looked out toward Sodom. As they left, Abraham went with them to send them on their way.

¹⁷"Should I hide my plan from Abraham?" the LORD asked. ¹⁸"For Abraham will certainly become a great and mighty nation, and all the nations of the earth will be blessed through him. ¹⁹I have singled him out so that he will direct his sons and their families to keep the way of the LORD by doing what is right and just. Then I will do for Abraham all that I have promised."

²⁰So the LORD told Abraham, "I have heard a great outcry from Sodom and Gomorrah, because their sin is so flagrant. ²¹I am going down to see if their actions are as wicked as I have heard. If not, I want to know."

²²The other men turned and headed toward Sodom, but the LORD remained with Abraham. ²³Abraham approached him and said, "Will you sweep away both the righteous and the wicked? ²⁴Suppose you find fifty righteous people living there in the city—will you still sweep it away and not spare it for their sakes? ²⁵Surely you wouldn't do such a thing, destroying the righteous along with the wicked. Why, you would be treating the righteous and the wicked exactly the same! Surely you wouldn't do that! Should not the Judge of all the earth do what is right?"

²⁶And the LORD replied, "If I find fifty righteous people in Sodom, I will spare the entire city for their sake."

²⁷Then Abraham spoke again. "Since I have begun, let me speak further to my Lord, even though I am but dust and ashes. ²⁸Suppose there are only forty-five righteous people rather than fifty? Will you destroy the whole city for lack of five?"

And the LORD said, "I will not destroy it if I find forty-five righteous people there."

²⁹Then Abraham pressed his request further. "Suppose there are only forty?"

And the LORD replied, "I will not destroy it for the sake of the forty."

³⁰"Please don't be angry, my Lord," Abraham pleaded. "Let me speak—suppose only thirty righteous people are found?"

And the LORD replied, "I will not destroy it if I find thirty."

³¹Then Abraham said, "Since I have dared to speak to the Lord, let me continue—suppose there are only twenty?"

And the LORD replied, "Then I will not destroy it for the sake of the twenty."

³²Finally, Abraham said, "Lord, please don't be angry with me if I speak one more time. Suppose only ten are found there?"

And the LORD replied, "Then I will not destroy it for the sake of the ten."

³³When the LORD had finished his conversation with Abraham, he went on his way, and Abraham returned to his tent.

¹⁹:¹THAT evening the two angels came to the entrance of the city of Sodom. Lot was sitting there, and when he saw them, he stood up to meet them. Then he welcomed them and bowed with his face to the ground. ²"My lords," he said, "come to my home to wash your feet, and be my guests for the night. You may

then get up early in the morning and be on your way again."

"Oh no," they replied. "We'll just spend the night out here in the city square."

³But Lot insisted, so at last they went home with him. Lot prepared a feast for them, complete with fresh bread made without yeast, and they ate. ⁴But before they retired for the night, all the men of Sodom, young and old, came from all over the city and surrounded the house. ⁵They shouted to Lot, "Where are the men who came to spend the night with you? Bring them out to us so we can have sex with them!"

⁶So Lot stepped outside to talk to them, shutting the door behind him. ⁷"Please, my brothers," he begged, "don't do such a wicked thing. ⁸Look, I have two virgin daughters. Let me bring them out to you, and you can do with them as you wish. But please, leave these men alone, for they are my guests and are under my protection."

⁹"Stand back!" they shouted. "This fellow came to town as an outsider, and now he's acting like our judge! We'll treat you far worse than those other men!" And they lunged toward Lot to break down the door.

¹⁰But the two angels* reached out, pulled Lot into the house, and bolted the door. ¹¹Then they blinded all the men, young and old, who were at the door of the house, so they gave up trying to get inside.

¹²Meanwhile, the angels questioned Lot. "Do you have any other relatives here in the city?" they asked. "Get them out of this place—your sons-in-law, sons, daughters, or anyone else. ¹³For we are about to destroy this city completely. The outcry against this place is so great it has reached the LORD, and he has sent us to destroy it."

¹⁴So Lot rushed out to tell his daughters' fiancés, "Quick, get out of the city! The LORD is about to destroy it." But the young men thought he was only joking.

¹⁵At dawn the next morning the angels became insistent. "Hurry," they said to Lot. "Take your wife and your two daughters who are here. Get out right now, or you will be swept away in the destruction of the city!"

¹⁶When Lot still hesitated, the angels seized his hand and the hands of his wife and two daughters and rushed them to safety outside the city, for the LORD was merciful. ¹⁷When they were safely out of the city, one of the angels ordered, "Run for your lives! And don't look back or stop anywhere in the valley! Escape to the mountains, or you will be swept away!"

¹⁸"Oh no, my lord!" Lot begged. ¹⁹"You have been so gracious to me and saved my life, and you have shown such great kindness. But I cannot go to the mountains. Disaster would catch up to me there, and I would soon die. ²⁰See, there is a small village nearby. Please let me go there instead; don't you see how small it is? Then my life will be saved."

²¹"All right," the angel said, "I will grant your request. I will not destroy the little village. ²²But hurry! Escape to it, for I can do nothing until you arrive there." (This explains why that village was known as Zoar, which means "little place.")

²³Lot reached the village just as the sun was rising over the horizon. ²⁴Then the LORD rained down fire and burning sulfur from the sky on Sodom and Gomorrah. ²⁵He utterly destroyed them, along with the other cities and villages of the plain, wiping out all the people and every bit of vegetation. ²⁶But Lot's wife looked back as she was following behind him, and she turned into a pillar of salt.

²⁷Abraham got up early that morning and hurried out to the place where he had stood in the LORD's presence. ²⁸He looked out across the plain toward Sodom and Gomorrah and watched as columns of smoke rose from the cities like smoke from a furnace.

²⁹But God had listened to Abraham's request and kept Lot safe, removing him from the disaster that engulfed the cities on the plain.

³⁰Afterward Lot left Zoar because he was afraid of the people there, and he went to live in a cave in the mountains with his two daughters. ³¹One day the older daughter said to her sister, "There are no men left anywhere in this entire area, so we can't get married like everyone else. And our father will soon be too old to have children. ³²Come, let's get him drunk with wine, and then we will have sex with him. That way we will preserve our family line through our father."

³³So that night they got him drunk with wine, and the older daughter went in and had intercourse with her father. He was unaware of her lying down or getting up again.

³⁴The next morning the older daughter said to her younger sister, "I had sex with our father last night. Let's get him drunk with wine again tonight, and you go in and have sex with him. That way we will preserve our family line through our father." ³⁵So that night they got him drunk with wine again, and the younger daughter went in and had intercourse with him. As before, he was unaware of her lying down or getting up again.

³⁶As a result, both of Lot's daughters became pregnant by their own father. ³⁷When the older daughter gave birth to a son, she named him Moab.* He became the ancestor of the nation now known as the Moabites. ³⁸When the younger daughter gave birth to a son, she named him Ben-ammi.* He became the ancestor of the nation now known as the Ammonites.

19:10 Hebrew *men;* also in 19:12, 16.    19:37 *Moab* sounds like a Hebrew term that means "from father." 19:38 *Ben-ammi* means "son of my kinsman."

## MATTHEW 6:25–7:14

"**T**hat is why I tell you not to worry about everyday life—whether you have enough food and drink, or enough clothes to wear. Isn't life more than food, and your body more than clothing? ²⁶Look at the birds. They don't plant or harvest or store food in barns, for your heavenly Father feeds them. And aren't you far more valuable to him than they are? ²⁷Can all your worries add a single moment to your life?

²⁸"And why worry about your clothing? Look at the lilies of the field and how they grow. They don't work or make their clothing, ²⁹yet Solomon in all his glory was not dressed as beautifully as they are. ³⁰And if God cares so wonderfully for wildflowers that are here today and thrown into the fire tomorrow, he will certainly care for you. Why do you have so little faith?

³¹"So don't worry about these things, saying, 'What will we eat? What will we drink? What will we wear?' ³²These things dominate the thoughts of unbelievers, but your heavenly Father already knows all your needs. ³³Seek the Kingdom of God* above all else, and live righteously, and he will give you everything you need.

³⁴"So don't worry about tomorrow, for tomorrow will bring its own worries. Today's trouble is enough for today.

⁷:¹"Do not judge others, and you will not be judged. ²For you will be treated as you treat others.* The standard you use in judging is the standard by which you will be judged.*

³"And why worry about a speck in your friend's eye* when you have a log in your own? ⁴How can you think of saying to your friend,* 'Let me help you get rid of that speck in your eye,' when you can't see past the log in your own eye? ⁵Hypocrite! First get rid of the log in your own eye; then you will see well enough to deal with the speck in your friend's eye.

⁶"Don't waste what is holy on people who are unholy.* Don't throw your pearls to pigs! They will trample the pearls, then turn and attack you.

⁷"Keep on asking, and you will receive what you ask for. Keep on seeking, and you will find. Keep on knocking, and the door will be opened to you. ⁸For everyone who asks, receives. Everyone who seeks, finds. And to everyone who knocks, the door will be opened.

⁹"You parents—if your children ask

for a loaf of bread, do you give them a stone instead? [10]Or if they ask for a fish, do you give them a snake? Of course not! [11]So if you sinful people know how to give good gifts to your children, how much more will your heavenly Father give good gifts to those who ask him.

[12]**"Do to others whatever you would like them to do to you. This is the essence of all that is taught in the law and the prophets.**

[13]"You can enter God's Kingdom only through the narrow gate. The highway to hell* is broad, and its gate is wide for the many who choose that way. [14]But the gateway to life is very narrow and the road is difficult, and only a few ever find it."

6:33 Some manuscripts do not include *of God.*    7:2a Or *For God will judge you as you judge others.*    7:2b Or *The measure you give will be the measure you get back.*    7:3 Greek *your brother's eye;* also in 7:5.    7:4 Greek *your brother.*    7:6 Greek *Don't give the sacred to dogs.*    7:13 Greek *The road that leads to destruction.*

## PSALM 8:1-9

*For the choir director: A psalm of David, to be accompanied by a stringed instrument.**

¹ **O** LORD, our Lord, your majestic
    name fills the earth!
  Your glory is higher than the
    heavens.
² You have taught children and
    infants
  to tell of your strength,*
  silencing your enemies
  and all who oppose you.

³ When I look at the night sky and
    see the work of your fingers—
  the moon and the stars you
    set in place—
⁴ what are people that you should
    think about them,
  mere mortals that you should care
    for them?*
⁵ Yet you made them only a little
    lower than God*
  and crowned them* with glory
    and honor.
⁶ You gave them charge of everything
    you made,

putting all things under their
    authority—
⁷ the flocks and the herds
  and all the wild animals,
⁸ the birds in the sky, the fish
    in the sea,
  and everything that swims the
    ocean currents.

⁹ O LORD, our Lord, your majestic
    name fills the earth!

8:TITLE Hebrew *according to the gittith.*    8:2 Greek version reads *to give you praise.* Compare Matt 21:16.    8:4 Hebrew *what is man that you should think of him, / the son of man that you should care for him?*    8:5a Or *Yet you made them only a little lower than the angels;* Hebrew reads *Yet you made him* [i.e., man] *a little lower than Elohim.*    8:5b Hebrew *him* [i.e., man]; similarly in 8:6.

## PROVERBS 2:6-15

**F**or the LORD grants wisdom! From his mouth come knowledge and understanding. He grants a treasure of common sense to the honest. He is a shield to those who walk with integrity. He guards the paths of the just and protects those who are faithful to him. □ Then you will understand what is right, just, and fair, and you will find the right way to go. For wisdom will enter your heart, and knowledge will fill you with joy. Wise choices will watch over you. Understanding will keep you safe. □ Wisdom will save you from evil people, from those whose words are twisted. These men turn from the right way to walk down dark paths. They take pleasure in doing wrong, and they enjoy the twisted ways of evil. Their actions are crooked, and their ways are wrong.

# JANUARY 9

GENESIS 20:1–22:24

**A**braham moved south to the Negev and lived for a while between Kadesh and Shur, and then he moved on to

Gerar. While living there as a foreigner, [2]Abraham introduced his wife, Sarah, by saying, "She is my sister." So King Abimelech of Gerar sent for Sarah and had her brought to him at his palace.

[3]But that night God came to Abimelech in a dream and told him, "You are a dead man, for that woman you have taken is already married!"

[4]But Abimelech had not slept with her yet, so he said, "Lord, will you destroy an innocent nation? [5]Didn't Abraham tell me, 'She is my sister'? And she herself said, 'Yes, he is my brother.' I acted in complete innocence! My hands are clean."

[6]In the dream God responded, "Yes, I know you are innocent. That's why I kept you from sinning against me, and why I did not let you touch her. [7]Now return the woman to her husband, and he will pray for you, for he is a prophet. Then you will live. But if you don't return her to him, you can be sure that you and all your people will die."

[8]Abimelech got up early the next morning and quickly called all his servants together. When he told them what had happened, his men were terrified. [9]Then Abimelech called for Abraham. "What have you done to us?" he demanded. "What crime have I committed that deserves treatment like this, making me and my kingdom guilty of this great sin? No one should ever do what you have done! [10]Whatever possessed you to do such a thing?"

[11]Abraham replied, "I thought, 'This is a godless place. They will want my wife and will kill me to get her.' [12]And she really is my sister, for we both have the same father, but different mothers. And I married her. [13]When God called me to leave my father's home and to travel from place to place, I told her, 'Do me a favor. Wherever we go, tell the people that I am your brother.'"

[14]Then Abimelech took some of his sheep and goats, cattle, and male and female servants, and he presented them to Abraham. He also returned his wife, Sarah, to him. [15]Then Abimelech said, "Look over my land and choose any place where you would like to live." [16]And he said to Sarah, "Look, I am giving your 'brother' 1,000 pieces of silver* in the presence of all these witnesses. This is to compensate you for any wrong I may have done to you. This will settle any claim against me, and your reputation is cleared."

[17]Then Abraham prayed to God, and God healed Abimelech, his wife, and his female servants, so they could have children. [18]For the LORD had caused all the women to be infertile because of what happened with Abraham's wife, Sarah.

21:1THE LORD kept his word and did for Sarah exactly what he had promised. [2]She became pregnant, and she gave birth to a son for Abraham in his old age. This happened at just the time God had said it would. [3]And Abraham named their son Isaac. [4]Eight days after Isaac was born, Abraham circumcised him as God had commanded. [5]Abraham was 100 years old when Isaac was born.

[6]And Sarah declared, "God has brought me laughter.* All who hear about this will laugh with me. [7]Who would have said to Abraham that Sarah would nurse a baby? Yet I have given Abraham a son in his old age!"

[8]When Isaac grew up and was about to be weaned, Abraham prepared a huge feast to celebrate the occasion. [9]But Sarah saw Ishmael—the son of Abraham and her Egyptian servant Hagar—making fun of her son, Isaac.* [10]So she turned to Abraham and demanded, "Get rid of that slave-woman and her son. He is not going to share the inheritance with my son, Isaac. I won't have it!"

[11]This upset Abraham very much because Ishmael was his son. [12]But God told Abraham, "Do not be upset over the boy and your servant. Do whatever Sarah tells you, for Isaac is the son through whom your descendants will be counted. [13]But I will also make a nation of the descendants of Hagar's son because he is your son, too."

[14]So Abraham got up early the next morning, prepared food and a container of water, and strapped them on Hagar's shoulders. Then he sent her away with their son, and she wandered aimlessly in the wilderness of Beersheba.

[15]When the water was gone, she put the boy in the shade of a bush. [16]Then she went and sat down by herself about a hundred yards* away. "I don't want to watch the boy die," she said, as she burst into tears.

[17]But God heard the boy crying, and the angel of God called to Hagar from heaven, "Hagar, what's wrong? Do not be afraid! God has heard the boy crying as he lies there. [18]Go to him and comfort him, for I will make a great nation from his descendants."

[19]Then God opened Hagar's eyes, and she saw a well full of water. She quickly filled her water container and gave the boy a drink.

[20]And God was with the boy as he grew up in the wilderness. He became a skillful archer, [21]and he settled in the wilderness of Paran. His mother arranged for him to marry a woman from the land of Egypt.

[22]About this time, Abimelech came with Phicol, his army commander, to visit Abraham. "God is obviously with you, helping you in everything you do," Abimelech said. [23]"Swear to me in God's name that you will never deceive me, my children, or any of my descendants. I have been loyal to you, so now swear that you will be loyal to me and to this country where you are living as a foreigner."

[24]Abraham replied, "Yes, I swear to it!" [25]Then Abraham complained to Abimelech about a well that Abimelech's servants had taken by force from Abraham's servants.

[26]"This is the first I've heard of it," Abimelech answered. "I have no idea who is responsible. You have never complained about this before."

[27]Abraham then gave some of his sheep, goats, and cattle to Abimelech, and they made a treaty. [28]But Abraham also took seven additional female lambs and set them off by themselves. [29]Abimelech asked, "Why have you set these seven apart from the others?"

[30]Abraham replied, "Please accept these seven lambs to show your agreement that I dug this well." [31]Then he named the place Beersheba (which means "well of the oath"), because that was where they had sworn the oath.

[32]After making their covenant at Beersheba, Abimelech left with Phicol, the commander of his army, and they returned home to the land of the Philistines. [33]Then Abraham planted a tamarisk tree at Beersheba, and there he worshiped the LORD, the Eternal God.* [34]And Abraham lived as a foreigner in Philistine country for a long time.

22:1SOME time later, God tested Abraham's faith. "Abraham!" God called.

"Yes," he replied. "Here I am."

[2]"Take your son, your only son—yes, Isaac, whom you love so much—and go to the land of Moriah. Go and sacrifice him as a burnt offering on one of the mountains, which I will show you."

[3]The next morning Abraham got up early. He saddled his donkey and took two of his servants with him, along with his son, Isaac. Then he chopped wood for a fire for a burnt offering and set out for the place God had told him about. [4]On the third day of their journey, Abraham looked up and saw the place in the distance. [5]"Stay here with the donkey," Abraham told the servants. "The boy and I will travel a little farther. We will worship there, and then we will come right back."

[6]So Abraham placed the wood for the burnt offering on Isaac's shoulders, while he himself carried the fire and the knife. As the two of them walked on together, [7]Isaac turned to Abraham and said, "Father?"

"Yes, my son?" Abraham replied.

"We have the fire and the wood," the boy said, "but where is the sheep for the burnt offering?"

8"God will provide a sheep for the burnt offering, my son," Abraham answered. And they both walked on together.

9When they arrived at the place where God had told him to go, Abraham built an altar and arranged the wood on it. Then he tied his son, Isaac, and laid him on the altar on top of the wood. 10And Abraham picked up the knife to kill his son as a sacrifice. 11At that moment the angel of the LORD called to him from heaven, "Abraham! Abraham!"

"Yes," Abraham replied. "Here I am!"

12"Don't lay a hand on the boy!" the angel said. "Do not hurt him in any way, for now I know that you truly fear God. You have not withheld from me even your son, your only son."

13Then Abraham looked up and saw a ram caught by its horns in a thicket. So he took the ram and sacrificed it as a burnt offering in place of his son. 14Abraham named the place Yahweh-Yireh (which means "the LORD will provide"). To this day, people still use that name as a proverb: "On the mountain of the LORD it will be provided."

15Then the angel of the LORD called again to Abraham from heaven. 16"This is what the LORD says: Because you have obeyed me and have not withheld even your son, your only son, I swear by my own name that 17I will certainly bless you. I will multiply your descendants beyond number, like the stars in the sky and the sand on the seashore. Your descendants will conquer the cities of their enemies. 18And through your descendants all the nations of the earth will be blessed—all because you have obeyed me."

19Then they returned to the servants and traveled back to Beersheba, where Abraham continued to live.

20Soon after this, Abraham heard that Milcah, his brother Nahor's wife, had borne Nahor eight sons. 21The oldest was named Uz, the next oldest was Buz, followed by Kemuel (the ancestor of the Arameans), 22Kesed, Hazo, Pildash,

Jidlaph, and Bethuel. 23(Bethuel became the father of Rebekah.) In addition to these eight sons from Milcah, 24Nahor had four other children from his concubine Reumah. Their names were Tebah, Gaham, Tahash, and Maacah.

20:16 Hebrew *1,000 shekels of silver*, about 25 pounds or 11.4 kilograms in weight.   21:6 The name *Isaac* means "he laughs."   21:9 As in Greek version and Latin Vulgate; Hebrew omits *of her son, Isaac*.   21:16 Hebrew *a bowshot*. 21:33 Hebrew *El-Olam*.

## MATTHEW 7:15-29

"Beware of false prophets who come disguised as harmless sheep but are really vicious wolves. 16You can identify them by their fruit, that is, by the way they act. Can you pick grapes from thornbushes, or figs from thistles? 17A good tree produces good fruit, and a bad tree produces bad fruit. 18A good tree can't produce bad fruit, and a bad tree can't produce good fruit. 19So every tree that does not produce good fruit is chopped down and thrown into the fire. 20Yes, just as you can identify a tree by its fruit, so you can identify people by their actions.

21"Not everyone who calls out to me, 'Lord! Lord!' will enter the Kingdom of Heaven. Only those who actually do the will of my Father in heaven will enter. 22On judgment day many will say to me, 'Lord! Lord! We prophesied in your name and cast out demons in your name and performed many miracles in your name.' 23But I will reply, 'I never knew you. Get away from me, you who break God's laws.'

24"Anyone who listens to my teaching and follows it is wise, like a person who builds a house on solid rock. 25Though the rain comes in torrents and the floodwaters rise and the winds beat against that house, it won't collapse because it is built on bedrock. 26But anyone who hears my teaching and ignores it is foolish, like a person who builds a house on sand. 27When the rains and floods come and the winds beat against that house, it will collapse with a mighty crash."

28When Jesus had finished saying these things, the crowds were amazed at his teaching, ²⁹for he taught with real authority—quite unlike their teachers of religious law.

## PSALM 9:1-12

*For the choir director: A psalm of David, to be sung to the tune "Death of the Son."*

¹ I will praise you, LORD, with all my heart;
    I will tell of all the marvelous things you have done.
² I will be filled with joy because of you.
    I will sing praises to your name, O Most High.

³ My enemies retreated;
    they staggered and died when you appeared.
⁴ For you have judged in my favor;
    from your throne you have judged with fairness.
⁵ You have rebuked the nations and destroyed the wicked;
    you have erased their names forever.
⁶ The enemy is finished, in endless ruins;
    the cities you uprooted are now forgotten.

⁷ But the LORD reigns forever,
    executing judgment from his throne.
⁸ He will judge the world with justice and rule the nations with fairness.
⁹ **The LORD is a shelter for the oppressed,**
    **a refuge in times of trouble.**
¹⁰ **Those who know your name trust in you,**
    **for you, O LORD, do not abandon those who search for you.**

¹¹ Sing praises to the LORD who reigns in Jerusalem.*
    Tell the world about his unforgettable deeds.
¹² For he who avenges murder cares for the helpless.
    He does not ignore the cries of those who suffer.

9:11 Hebrew *Zion;* also in 9:14.

## PROVERBS 2:16-22

**W**isdom will save you from the immoral woman, from the seductive words of the promiscuous woman. She has abandoned her husband and ignores the covenant she made before God. Entering her house leads to death; it is the road to the grave.* The man who visits her is doomed. He will never reach the paths of life. □Follow the steps of good men instead, and stay on the paths of the righteous. For only the godly will live in the land, and those with integrity will remain in it. But the wicked will be removed from the land, and the treacherous will be uprooted.

2:18 Hebrew *to the spirits of the dead.*

# JANUARY 10

## GENESIS 23:1–24:51

**W**hen Sarah was 127 years old, ²she died at Kiriath-arba (now called Hebron) in the land of Canaan. There Abraham mourned and wept for her.

³Then, leaving her body, he said to the Hittite elders, ⁴"Here I am, a stranger and a foreigner among you. Please sell me a piece of land so I can give my wife a proper burial."

⁵The Hittites replied to Abraham, ⁶"Listen, my lord, you are an honored prince among us. Choose the finest of our tombs and bury her there. No one here will refuse to help you in this way."

⁷Then Abraham bowed low before the Hittites and said, ⁸"Since you are willing to help me in this way, be so kind as to ask Ephron son of Zohar ⁹to let me buy his cave at Machpelah, down at the end of his field. I will pay the full price in the presence of witnesses, so I will have a permanent burial place for my family."

¹⁰Ephron was sitting there among the others, and he answered Abraham as

the others listened, speaking publicly before all the Hittite elders of the town. ¹¹"No, my lord," he said to Abraham, "please listen to me. I will give you the field and the cave. Here in the presence of my people, I give it to you. Go and bury your dead."

¹²Abraham again bowed low before the citizens of the land, ¹³and he replied to Ephron as everyone listened. "No, listen to me. I will buy it from you. Let me pay the full price for the field so I can bury my dead there."

¹⁴Ephron answered Abraham, ¹⁵"My lord, please listen to me. The land is worth 400 pieces* of silver, but what is that between friends? Go ahead and bury your dead."

¹⁶So Abraham agreed to Ephron's price and paid the amount he had suggested—400 pieces of silver, weighed according to the market standard. The Hittite elders witnessed the transaction.

¹⁷So Abraham bought the plot of land belonging to Ephron at Machpelah, near Mamre. This included the field itself, the cave that was in it, and all the surrounding trees. ¹⁸It was transferred to Abraham as his permanent possession in the presence of the Hittite elders at the city gate. ¹⁹Then Abraham buried his wife, Sarah, there in Canaan, in the cave of Machpelah, near Mamre (also called Hebron). ²⁰So the field and the cave were transferred from the Hittites to Abraham for use as a permanent burial place.

²⁴:¹ABRAHAM was now a very old man, and the LORD had blessed him in every way. ²One day Abraham said to his oldest servant, the man in charge of his household, "Take an oath by putting your hand under my thigh. ³Swear by the LORD, the God of heaven and earth, that you will not allow my son to marry one of these local Canaanite women. ⁴Go instead to my homeland, to my relatives, and find a wife there for my son Isaac."

⁵The servant asked, "But what if I can't find a young woman who is willing to travel so far from home? Should I

then take Isaac there to live among your relatives in the land you came from?"

⁶"No!" Abraham responded. "Be careful never to take my son there. ⁷For the LORD, the God of heaven, who took me from my father's house and my native land, solemnly promised to give this land to my descendants. He will send his angel ahead of you, and he will see to it that you find a wife there for my son. ⁸If she is unwilling to come back with you, then you are free from this oath of mine. But under no circumstances are you to take my son there."

⁹So the servant took an oath by putting his hand under the thigh of his master, Abraham. He swore to follow Abraham's instructions. ¹⁰Then he loaded ten of Abraham's camels with all kinds of expensive gifts from his master, and he traveled to distant Aramnaharaim. There he went to the town where Abraham's brother Nahor had settled. ¹¹He made the camels kneel beside a well just outside the town. It was evening, and the women were coming out to draw water.

¹²"O LORD, God of my master, Abraham," he prayed. "Please give me success today, and show unfailing love to my master, Abraham. ¹³See, I am standing here beside this spring, and the young women of the town are coming out to draw water. ¹⁴This is my request. I will ask one of them, 'Please give me a drink from your jug.' If she says, 'Yes, have a drink, and I will water your camels, too!'—let her be the one you have selected as Isaac's wife. This is how I will know that you have shown unfailing love to my master."

¹⁵Before he had finished praying, he saw a young woman named Rebekah coming out with her water jug on her shoulder. She was the daughter of Bethuel, who was the son of Abraham's brother Nahor and his wife, Milcah. ¹⁶Rebekah was very beautiful and old enough to be married, but she was still a virgin. She went down to the spring, filled her jug, and came up again. ¹⁷Running over to her, the servant said,

"Please give me a little drink of water from your jug."

¹⁸"Yes, my lord," she answered, "have a drink." And she quickly lowered her jug from her shoulder and gave him a drink. ¹⁹When she had given him a drink, she said, "I'll draw water for your camels, too, until they have had enough to drink." ²⁰So she quickly emptied her jug into the watering trough and ran back to the well to draw water for all his camels.

²¹The servant watched her in silence, wondering whether or not the LORD had given him success in his mission. ²²Then at last, when the camels had finished drinking, he took out a gold ring for her nose and two large gold bracelets* for her wrists.

²³"Whose daughter are you?" he asked. "And please tell me, would your father have any room to put us up for the night?"

²⁴"I am the daughter of Bethuel," she replied. "My grandparents are Nahor and Milcah. ²⁵Yes, we have plenty of straw and feed for the camels, and we have room for guests."

²⁶The man bowed low and worshiped the LORD. ²⁷"Praise the LORD, the God of my master, Abraham," he said. "The LORD has shown unfailing love and faithfulness to my master, for he has led me straight to my master's relatives."

²⁸The young woman ran home to tell her family everything that had happened. ²⁹Now Rebekah had a brother named Laban, who ran out to meet the man at the spring. ³⁰He had seen the nose-ring and the bracelets on his sister's wrists, and had heard Rebekah tell what the man had said. So he rushed out to the spring, where the man was still standing beside his camels. Laban said to him, ³¹"Come and stay with us, you who are blessed by the LORD! Why are you standing here outside the town when I have a room all ready for you and a place prepared for the camels?"

³²So the man went home with Laban, and Laban unloaded the camels, gave him straw for their bedding, fed them, and provided water for the man and the camel drivers to wash their feet. ³³Then food was served. But Abraham's servant said, "I don't want to eat until I have told you why I have come."

"All right," Laban said, "tell us."

³⁴"I am Abraham's servant," he explained. ³⁵"And the LORD has greatly blessed my master; he has become a wealthy man. The LORD has given him flocks of sheep and goats, herds of cattle, a fortune in silver and gold, and many male and female servants and camels and donkeys.

³⁶"When Sarah, my master's wife, was very old, she gave birth to my master's son, and my master has given him everything he owns. ³⁷And my master made me take an oath. He said, 'Do not allow my son to marry one of these local Canaanite women. ³⁸Go instead to my father's house, to my relatives, and find a wife there for my son.'

³⁹"But I said to my master, 'What if I can't find a young woman who is willing to go back with me?' ⁴⁰He responded, 'The LORD, in whose presence I have lived, will send his angel with you and will make your mission successful. Yes, you must find a wife for my son from among my relatives, from my father's family. ⁴¹Then you will have fulfilled your obligation. But if you go to my relatives and they refuse to let her go with you, you will be free from my oath.'

⁴²"So today when I came to the spring, I prayed this prayer: 'O LORD, God of my master, Abraham, please give me success on this mission. ⁴³See, I am standing here beside this spring. This is my request. When a young woman comes to draw water, I will say to her, "Please give me a little drink of water from your jug." ⁴⁴If she says, "Yes, have a drink, and I will draw water for your camels, too," let her be the one you have selected to be the wife of my master's son.'

⁴⁵"Before I had finished praying in my heart, I saw Rebekah coming out with her water jug on her shoulder. She went down to the spring and drew water. So I said to her, 'Please give me a drink.' ⁴⁶She quickly lowered her jug

from her shoulder and said, 'Yes, have a drink, and I will water your camels, too!' So I drank, and then she watered the camels.

⁴⁷"Then I asked, 'Whose daughter are you?' She replied, 'I am the daughter of Bethuel, and my grandparents are Nahor and Milcah.' So I put the ring on her nose, and the bracelets on her wrists.

⁴⁸"Then I bowed low and worshiped the Lord. I praised the Lord, the God of my master, Abraham, because he had led me straight to my master's niece to be his son's wife. ⁴⁹So tell me—will you or won't you show unfailing love and faithfulness to my master? Please tell me yes or no, and then I'll know what to do next."

⁵⁰Then Laban and Bethuel replied, "The Lord has obviously brought you here, so there is nothing we can say. ⁵¹Here is Rebekah; take her and go. Yes, let her be the wife of your master's son, as the Lord has directed."

23:15 Hebrew *400 shekels*, about 10 pounds or 4.6 kilograms in weight; also in 23:16.    24:22 Hebrew *a gold nose-ring weighing a half shekel* [0.2 ounces or 6 grams] *and two gold bracelets weighing 10 shekels* [4 ounces or 114 grams].

## MATTHEW 8:1-17

Large crowds followed Jesus as he came down the mountainside. ²Suddenly, a man with leprosy approached him and knelt before him. "Lord," the man said, "if you are willing, you can heal me and make me clean."

³Jesus reached out and touched him. "I am willing," he said. "Be healed!" And instantly the leprosy disappeared. ⁴Then Jesus said to him, "Don't tell anyone about this. Instead, go to the priest and let him examine you. Take along the offering required in the law of Moses for those who have been healed of leprosy.* This will be a public testimony that you have been cleansed."

⁵When Jesus returned to Capernaum, a Roman officer* came and pleaded with him, ⁶"Lord, my young servant* lies in bed, paralyzed and in terrible pain."

⁷Jesus said, "I will come and heal him."

⁸But the officer said, "Lord, I am not worthy to have you come into my home. Just say the word from where you are, and my servant will be healed. ⁹I know this because I am under the authority of my superior officers, and I have authority over my soldiers. I only need to say, 'Go,' and they go, or 'Come,' and they come. And if I say to my slaves, 'Do this,' they do it."

¹⁰When Jesus heard this, he was amazed. Turning to those who were following him, he said, "I tell you the truth, I haven't seen faith like this in all Israel! ¹¹**And I tell you this, that many Gentiles will come from all over the world—from east and west—and sit down with Abraham, Isaac, and Jacob at the feast in the Kingdom of Heaven.** ¹²But many Israelites—those for whom the Kingdom was prepared—will be thrown into outer darkness, where there will be weeping and gnashing of teeth."

¹³Then Jesus said to the Roman officer, "Go back home. Because you believed, it has happened." And the young servant was healed that same hour.

¹⁴When Jesus arrived at Peter's house, Peter's mother-in-law was sick in bed with a high fever. ¹⁵But when Jesus touched her hand, the fever left her. Then she got up and prepared a meal for him.

¹⁶That evening many demon-possessed people were brought to Jesus. He cast out the evil spirits with a simple command, and he healed all the sick. ¹⁷This fulfilled the word of the Lord through the prophet Isaiah, who said,

"He took our sicknesses
   and removed our diseases."*

8:4 See Lev 14:2-32.    8:5 Greek *a centurion;* similarly in 8:8, 13.    8:6 Or *child;* also in 8:13.    8:17 Isa 53:4.

## PSALM 9:13-20

Lord, have mercy on me.
   See how my enemies torment me.
   Snatch me back from the jaws
      of death.

[14] Save me so I can praise you publicly
        at Jerusalem's gates,
    so I can rejoice that you have
        rescued me.

[15] The nations have fallen into the pit
        they dug for others.
    Their own feet have been caught
        in the trap they set.
[16] The LORD is known for his justice.
    The wicked are trapped by their
        own deeds.      *Quiet Interlude**

[17] The wicked will go down to the
        grave.*
    This is the fate of all the nations
        who ignore God.
[18] But the needy will not be ignored
        forever;
    the hopes of the poor will not
        always be crushed.

[19] Arise, O LORD!
    Do not let mere mortals defy you!
    Judge the nations!
[20] Make them tremble in fear, O LORD.
    Let the nations know they are
        merely human.      *Interlude*

9:16 Hebrew *Higgaion Selah.* The meaning of this phrase
is uncertain.   9:17 Hebrew *to Sheol.*

## PROVERBS 3:1-6

**M**y child,* never forget the things I have
taught you. Store my commands in your
heart. If you do this, you will live many
years, and your life will be satisfying.
Never let loyalty and kindness leave
you! Tie them around your neck as a reminder. Write them deep within your
heart. Then you will find favor with both
God and people, and you will earn a good
reputation. □ Trust in the LORD with all
your heart; do not depend on your own
understanding. Seek his will in all you
do, and he will show you which path to
take.

3:1 Hebrew *My son;* also in 3:11, 21.

# JANUARY 11

## GENESIS 24:52–26:16

**W**hen Abraham's servant heard their
answer, he bowed down to the ground
and worshiped the LORD. [53] Then he
brought out silver and gold jewelry and
clothing and presented them to Rebekah. He also gave expensive presents
to her brother and mother. [54] Then they
ate their meal, and the servant and the
men with him stayed there overnight.

But early the next morning, Abraham's servant said, "Send me back to
my master."

[55] "But we want Rebekah to stay with
us at least ten days," her brother and
mother said. "Then she can go."

[56] But he said, "Don't delay me. The
LORD has made my mission successful;
now send me back so I can return to my
master."

[57] "Well," they said, "we'll call Rebekah and ask her what she thinks." [58] So
they called Rebekah. "Are you willing to
go with this man?" they asked her.

And she replied, "Yes, I will go."

[59] So they said good-bye to Rebekah
and sent her away with Abraham's servant and his men. The woman who had
been Rebekah's childhood nurse went
along with her. [60] They gave her this
blessing as she parted:

"Our sister, may you become
    the mother of many millions!
May your descendants be strong
    and conquer the cities of their
        enemies."

[61] Then Rebekah and her servant girls
mounted the camels and followed the
man. So Abraham's servant took Rebekah and went on his way.

[62] Meanwhile, Isaac, whose home was
in the Negev, had returned from Beer-
lahai-roi. [63] One evening as he was walking and meditating in the fields, he
looked up and saw the camels coming.

⁶⁴When Rebekah looked up and saw Isaac, she quickly dismounted from her camel. ⁶⁵"Who is that man walking through the fields to meet us?" she asked the servant.

And he replied, "It is my master." So Rebekah covered her face with her veil. ⁶⁶Then the servant told Isaac everything he had done.

⁶⁷And Isaac brought Rebekah into his mother Sarah's tent, and she became his wife. He loved her deeply, and she was a special comfort to him after the death of his mother.

25:1ABRAHAM married another wife, whose name was Keturah. ²She gave birth to Zimran, Jokshan, Medan, Midian, Ishbak, and Shuah. ³Jokshan was the father of Sheba and Dedan. Dedan's descendants were the Asshurites, Letushites, and Leummites. ⁴Midian's sons were Ephah, Epher, Hanoch, Abida, and Eldaah. These were all descendants of Abraham through Keturah.

⁵Abraham gave everything he owned to his son Isaac. ⁶But before he died, he gave gifts to the sons of his concubines and sent them off to a land in the east, away from Isaac.

⁷Abraham lived for 175 years, ⁸and he died at a ripe old age, having lived a long and satisfying life. He breathed his last and joined his ancestors in death. ⁹His sons Isaac and Ishmael buried him in the cave of Machpelah, near Mamre, in the field of Ephron son of Zohar the Hittite. ¹⁰This was the field Abraham had purchased from the Hittites and where he had buried his wife Sarah. ¹¹After Abraham's death, God blessed his son Isaac, who settled near Beer-lahai-roi in the Negev.

¹²This is the account of the family of Ishmael, the son of Abraham through Hagar, Sarah's Egyptian servant. ¹³Here is a list, by their names and clans, of Ishmael's descendants: The oldest was Nebaioth, followed by Kedar, Adbeel, Mibsam, ¹⁴Mishma, Dumah, Massa, ¹⁵Hadad, Tema, Jetur, Naphish, and Kedemah. ¹⁶These twelve sons of Ishmael became the founders of twelve tribes named after them, listed according to the places they settled and camped. ¹⁷Ishmael lived for 137 years. Then he breathed his last and joined his ancestors in death. ¹⁸Ishmael's descendants occupied the region from Havilah to Shur, which is east of Egypt in the direction of Asshur. There they lived in open hostility toward all their relatives.*

¹⁹This is the account of the family of Isaac, the son of Abraham. ²⁰When Isaac was forty years old, he married Rebekah, the daughter of Bethuel the Aramean from Paddan-aram and the sister of Laban the Aramean.

²¹Isaac pleaded with the LORD on behalf of his wife, because she was unable to have children. The LORD answered Isaac's prayer, and Rebekah became pregnant with twins. ²²But the two children struggled with each other in her womb. So she went to ask the LORD about it. "Why is this happening to me?" she asked.

²³And the LORD told her, "The sons in your womb will become two nations. From the very beginning, the two nations will be rivals. One nation will be stronger than the other; and your older son will serve your younger son."

²⁴And when the time came to give birth, Rebekah discovered that she did indeed have twins! ²⁵The first one was very red at birth and covered with thick hair like a fur coat. So they named him Esau.* ²⁶Then the other twin was born with his hand grasping Esau's heel. So they named him Jacob.* Isaac was sixty years old when the twins were born.

²⁷As the boys grew up, Esau became a skillful hunter. He was an outdoorsman, but Jacob had a quiet temperament, preferring to stay at home. ²⁸Isaac loved Esau because he enjoyed eating the wild game Esau brought home, but Rebekah loved Jacob.

²⁹One day when Jacob was cooking some stew, Esau arrived home from the wilderness exhausted and hungry. ³⁰Esau said to Jacob, "I'm starved! Give

me some of that red stew!" (This is how Esau got his other name, Edom, which means "red.")

³¹"All right," Jacob replied, "but trade me your rights as the firstborn son."

³²"Look, I'm dying of starvation!" said Esau. "What good is my birthright to me now?"

³³But Jacob said, "First you must swear that your birthright is mine." So Esau swore an oath, thereby selling all his rights as the firstborn to his brother, Jacob.

³⁴Then Jacob gave Esau some bread and lentil stew. Esau ate the meal, then got up and left. He showed contempt for his rights as the firstborn.

²⁶:¹A SEVERE famine now struck the land, as had happened before in Abraham's time. So Isaac moved to Gerar, where Abimelech, king of the Philistines, lived.

²The LORD appeared to Isaac and said, "Do not go down to Egypt, but do as I tell you. ³Live here as a foreigner in this land, and I will be with you and bless you. I hereby confirm that I will give all these lands to you and your descendants, just as I solemnly promised Abraham, your father. ⁴**I will cause your descendants to become as numerous as the stars of the sky, and I will give them all these lands. And through your descendants all the nations of the earth will be blessed. ⁵I will do this because Abraham listened to me and obeyed all my requirements, commands, decrees, and instructions."** ⁶So Isaac stayed in Gerar.

⁷When the men who lived there asked Isaac about his wife, Rebekah, he said, "She is my sister." He was afraid to say, "She is my wife." He thought, "They will kill me to get her, because she is so beautiful." ⁸But some time later, Abimelech, king of the Philistines, looked out his window and saw Isaac caressing Rebekah.

⁹Immediately, Abimelech called for Isaac and exclaimed, "She is obviously your wife! Why did you say, 'She is my sister'?"

"Because I was afraid someone would kill me to get her from me," Isaac replied.

¹⁰"How could you do this to us?" Abimelech exclaimed. "One of my people might easily have taken your wife and slept with her, and you would have made us guilty of great sin."

¹¹Then Abimelech issued a public proclamation: "Anyone who touches this man or his wife will be put to death!"

¹²When Isaac planted his crops that year, he harvested a hundred times more grain than he planted, for the LORD blessed him. ¹³He became a very rich man, and his wealth continued to grow. ¹⁴He acquired so many flocks of sheep and goats, herds of cattle, and servants that the Philistines became jealous of him. ¹⁵So the Philistines filled up all of Isaac's wells with dirt. These were the wells that had been dug by the servants of his father, Abraham.

¹⁶Finally, Abimelech ordered Isaac to leave the country. "Go somewhere else," he said, "for you have become too powerful for us."

25:18 The meaning of the Hebrew is uncertain.
25:25 *Esau* sounds like a Hebrew term that means "hair."
25:26 *Jacob* sounds like the Hebrew words for "heel" and "deceiver."

## MATTHEW 8:18-34

**W**hen Jesus saw the crowd around him, he instructed his disciples to cross to the other side of the lake.

¹⁹Then one of the teachers of religious law said to him, "Teacher, I will follow you wherever you go."

²⁰But Jesus replied, "Foxes have dens to live in, and birds have nests, but the Son of Man* has no place even to lay his head."

²¹Another of his disciples said, "Lord, first let me return home and bury my father."

²²But Jesus told him, "Follow me now. Let the spiritually dead bury their own dead.*"

²³Then Jesus got into the boat and started across the lake with his disci-

ples. 24Suddenly, a fierce storm struck the lake, with waves breaking into the boat. But Jesus was sleeping. 25The disciples went and woke him up, shouting, "Lord, save us! We're going to drown!"

26Jesus responded, "Why are you afraid? You have so little faith!" Then he got up and rebuked the wind and waves, and suddenly all was calm.

27The disciples were amazed. "Who is this man?" they asked. "Even the winds and waves obey him!"

28When Jesus arrived on the other side of the lake, in the region of the Gadarenes,* two men who were possessed by demons met him. They lived in a cemetery and were so violent that no one could go through that area.

29They began screaming at him, "Why are you interfering with us, Son of God? Have you come here to torture us before God's appointed time?"

30There happened to be a large herd of pigs feeding in the distance. 31So the demons begged, "If you cast us out, send us into that herd of pigs."

32"All right, go!" Jesus commanded them. So the demons came out of the men and entered the pigs, and the whole herd plunged down the steep hillside into the lake and drowned in the water.

33The herdsmen fled to the nearby town, telling everyone what happened to the demon-possessed men. 34Then the entire town came out to meet Jesus, but they begged him to go away and leave them alone.

8:20 "Son of Man" is a title Jesus used for himself.
8:22 Greek *Let the dead bury their own dead.*   8:28 Other manuscripts read *Gerasenes;* still others read *Gergesenes.* Compare Mark 5:1; Luke 8:26.

PSALM 10:1-15
   O Lord, why do you stand so far away?
      Why do you hide when I am in trouble?
 2 The wicked arrogantly hunt down the poor.
      Let them be caught in the evil they plan for others.
 3 For they brag about their evil desires;

they praise the greedy and curse the Lord.

 4 The wicked are too proud to seek God.
      They seem to think that God is dead.
 5 Yet they succeed in everything they do.
      They do not see your punishment awaiting them.
      They sneer at all their enemies.
 6 They think, "Nothing bad will ever happen to us!
      We will be free of trouble forever!"

 7 Their mouths are full of cursing, lies, and threats.*
      Trouble and evil are on the tips of their tongues.
 8 They lurk in ambush in the villages, waiting to murder innocent people.
      They are always searching for helpless victims.
 9 Like lions crouched in hiding, they wait to pounce on the helpless.
      Like hunters they capture the helpless
      and drag them away in nets.
10 Their helpless victims are crushed; they fall beneath the strength of the wicked.
11 The wicked think, "God isn't watching us!
      He has closed his eyes and won't even see what we do!"

12 Arise, O Lord!
      Punish the wicked, O God!
      Do not ignore the helpless!
13 Why do the wicked get away with despising God?
      They think, "God will never call us to account."
14 But you see the trouble and grief they cause.
      You take note of it and punish them.
      The helpless put their trust in you.
      You defend the orphans.

¹⁵ Break the arms of these wicked,
    evil people!
Go after them until the last one
    is destroyed.

**10:7** Greek version reads *cursing and bitterness.*
Compare Rom 3:14.

### PROVERBS 3:7-8

**D**on't be impressed with your own wisdom. Instead, fear the Lᴏʀᴅ and turn away from evil. Then you will have healing for your body and strength for your bones.

# JANUARY
# 12

### GENESIS 26:17–27:46

**S**o Isaac moved away to the Gerar Valley, where he set up their tents and settled down. ¹⁸He reopened the wells his father had dug, which the Philistines had filled in after Abraham's death. Isaac also restored the names Abraham had given them.

¹⁹Isaac's servants also dug in the Gerar Valley and discovered a well of fresh water. ²⁰But then the shepherds from Gerar came and claimed the spring. "This is our water," they said, and they argued over it with Isaac's herdsmen. So Isaac named the well Esek (which means "argument"). ²¹Isaac's men then dug another well, but again there was a dispute over it. So Isaac named it Sitnah (which means "hostility"). ²²Abandoning that one, Isaac moved on and dug another well. This time there was no dispute over it, so Isaac named the place Rehoboth (which means "open space"), for he said, "At last the Lᴏʀᴅ has created enough space for us to prosper in this land."

²³From there Isaac moved to Beersheba, ²⁴where the Lᴏʀᴅ appeared to him on the night of his arrival. "I am the God of your father, Abraham," he said. "Do not be afraid, for I am with you and will bless you. I will multiply your descendants, and they will become a great nation. I will do this because of my promise to Abraham, my servant."

²⁵Then Isaac built an altar there and worshiped the Lᴏʀᴅ. He set up his camp at that place, and his servants dug another well.

²⁶One day King Abimelech came from Gerar with his adviser, Ahuzzath, and also Phicol, his army commander. ²⁷"Why have you come here?" Isaac asked. "You obviously hate me, since you kicked me off your land."

²⁸They replied, "We can plainly see that the Lᴏʀᴅ is with you. So we want to enter into a sworn treaty with you. Let's make a covenant. ²⁹Swear that you will not harm us, just as we have never troubled you. We have always treated you well, and we sent you away from us in peace. And now look how the Lᴏʀᴅ has blessed you!"

³⁰So Isaac prepared a covenant feast to celebrate the treaty, and they ate and drank together. ³¹Early the next morning, they each took a solemn oath not to interfere with each other. Then Isaac sent them home again, and they left him in peace.

³²That very day Isaac's servants came and told him about a new well they had dug. "We've found water!" they exclaimed. ³³So Isaac named the well Shibah (which means "oath"). And to this day the town that grew up there is called Beersheba (which means "well of the oath").

³⁴At the age of forty, Esau married two Hittite wives: Judith, the daughter of Beeri, and Basemath, the daughter of Elon. ³⁵But Esau's wives made life miserable for Isaac and Rebekah.

²⁷:¹Oɴᴇ day when Isaac was old and turning blind, he called for Esau, his older son, and said, "My son."

"Yes, Father?" Esau replied.

²"I am an old man now," Isaac said, "and I don't know when I may die. ³Take your bow and a quiver full of arrows, and go out into the open country

to hunt some wild game for me. [4]Prepare my favorite dish, and bring it here for me to eat. Then I will pronounce the blessing that belongs to you, my firstborn son, before I die."

[5]But Rebekah overheard what Isaac had said to his son Esau. So when Esau left to hunt for the wild game, [6]she said to her son Jacob, "Listen. I overheard your father say to Esau, [7]'Bring me some wild game and prepare me a delicious meal. Then I will bless you in the LORD's presence before I die.' [8]Now, my son, listen to me. Do exactly as I tell you. [9]Go out to the flocks, and bring me two fine young goats. I'll use them to prepare your father's favorite dish. [10]Then take the food to your father so he can eat it and bless you before he dies."

[11]"But look," Jacob replied to Rebekah, "my brother, Esau, is a hairy man, and my skin is smooth. [12]What if my father touches me? He'll see that I'm trying to trick him, and then he'll curse me instead of blessing me."

[13]But his mother replied, "Then let the curse fall on me, my son! Just do what I tell you. Go out and get the goats for me!"

[14]So Jacob went out and got the young goats for his mother. Rebekah took them and prepared a delicious meal, just the way Isaac liked it. [15]Then she took Esau's favorite clothes, which were there in the house, and gave them to her younger son, Jacob. [16]She covered his arms and the smooth part of his neck with the skin of the young goats. [17]Then she gave Jacob the delicious meal, including freshly baked bread.

[18]So Jacob took the food to his father. "My father?" he said.

"Yes, my son," Isaac answered. "Who are you—Esau or Jacob?"

[19]Jacob replied, "It's Esau, your firstborn son. I've done as you told me. Here is the wild game. Now sit up and eat it so you can give me your blessing."

[20]Isaac asked, "How did you find it so quickly, my son?"

"The LORD your God put it in my path!" Jacob replied.

[21]Then Isaac said to Jacob, "Come closer so I can touch you and make sure that you really are Esau." [22]So Jacob went closer to his father, and Isaac touched him. "The voice is Jacob's, but the hands are Esau's," Isaac said. [23]But he did not recognize Jacob, because Jacob's hands felt hairy just like Esau's. So Isaac prepared to bless Jacob. [24]"But are you really my son Esau?" he asked.

"Yes, I am," Jacob replied.

[25]Then Isaac said, "Now, my son, bring me the wild game. Let me eat it, and then I will give you my blessing." So Jacob took the food to his father, and Isaac ate it. He also drank the wine that Jacob served him. Then Isaac said to Jacob, [26]"Please come a little closer and kiss me, my son."

[27]So Jacob went over and kissed him. And when Isaac caught the smell of his clothes, he was finally convinced, and he blessed his son. He said, "Ah! The smell of my son is like the smell of the outdoors, which the LORD has blessed!

[28] "From the dew of heaven
and the richness of the earth,
may God always give you abundant
harvests of grain
and bountiful new wine.
[29] May many nations become your
servants,
and may they bow down to you.
May you be the master over your
brothers,
and may your mother's sons bow
down to you.
All who curse you will be cursed,
and all who bless you will be
blessed."

[30]As soon as Isaac had finished blessing Jacob, and almost before Jacob had left his father, Esau returned from his hunt. [31]Esau prepared a delicious meal and brought it to his father. Then he said, "Sit up, my father, and eat my wild game so you can give me your blessing."

[32]But Isaac asked him, "Who are you?"

Esau replied, "It's your son, your first-born son, Esau."

33Isaac began to tremble uncontrollably and said, "Then who just served me wild game? I have already eaten it, and I blessed him just before you came. And yes, that blessing must stand!"

34When Esau heard his father's words, he let out a loud and bitter cry. "Oh my father, what about me? Bless me, too!" he begged.

35But Isaac said, "Your brother was here, and he tricked me. He has taken away your blessing."

36Esau exclaimed, "No wonder his name is Jacob, for now he has cheated me twice.* First he took my rights as the firstborn, and now he has stolen my blessing. Oh, haven't you saved even one blessing for me?"

37Isaac said to Esau, "I have made Jacob your master and have declared that all his brothers will be his servants. I have guaranteed him an abundance of grain and wine—what is left for me to give you, my son?"

38Esau pleaded, "But do you have only one blessing? Oh my father, bless me, too!" Then Esau broke down and wept.

39Finally, his father, Isaac, said to him,

"You will live away from the
    richness of the earth,
    and away from the dew of the
        heaven above.
40 You will live by your sword,
    and you will serve your brother.
But when you decide to break free,
    you will shake his yoke from
        your neck."

41From that time on, Esau hated Jacob because their father had given Jacob the blessing. And Esau began to scheme: "I will soon be mourning my father's death. Then I will kill my brother, Jacob."

42But Rebekah heard about Esau's plans. So she sent for Jacob and told him, "Listen, Esau is consoling himself by plotting to kill you. 43So listen carefully, my son. Get ready and flee to my brother, Laban, in Haran. 44Stay there with him until your brother cools off. 45When he calms down and forgets what you have done to him, I will send for you to come back. Why should I lose both of you in one day?"

46Then Rebekah said to Isaac, "I'm sick and tired of these local Hittite women! I would rather die than see Jacob marry one of them."

27:36 *Jacob* sounds like the Hebrew words for "heel" and "deceiver."

## MATTHEW 9:1-17

Jesus climbed into a boat and went back across the lake to his own town. 2Some people brought to him a paralyzed man on a mat. Seeing their faith, Jesus said to the paralyzed man, "Be encouraged, my child! Your sins are forgiven."

3But some of the teachers of religious law said to themselves, "That's blasphemy! Does he think he's God?"

4Jesus knew* what they were thinking, so he asked them, "Why do you have such evil thoughts in your hearts? 5Is it easier to say 'Your sins are forgiven,' or 'Stand up and walk'? 6So I will prove to you that the Son of Man* has the authority on earth to forgive sins." Then Jesus turned to the paralyzed man and said, "Stand up, pick up your mat, and go home!"

7And the man jumped up and went home! 8Fear swept through the crowd as they saw this happen. And they praised God for sending a man with such great authority.*

9As Jesus was walking along, he saw a man named Matthew sitting at his tax collector's booth. "Follow me and be my disciple," Jesus said to him. So Matthew got up and followed him.

10Later, Matthew invited Jesus and his disciples to his home as dinner guests, along with many tax collectors and other disreputable sinners. 11But when the Pharisees saw this, they asked his disciples, "Why does your teacher eat with such scum?*"

12When Jesus heard this, he said,

"Healthy people don't need a doctor—sick people do." [13]Then he added, "Now go and learn the meaning of this Scripture: 'I want you to show mercy, not offer sacrifices.'* For I have come to call not those who think they are righteous, but those who know they are sinners."

[14]One day the disciples of John the Baptist came to Jesus and asked him, "Why don't your disciples fast* like we do and the Pharisees do?"

[15]Jesus replied, "Do wedding guests mourn while celebrating with the groom? Of course not. But someday the groom will be taken away from them, and then they will fast.

[16]"Besides, who would patch old clothing with new cloth? For the new patch would shrink and rip away from the old cloth, leaving an even bigger tear than before.

[17]"And no one puts new wine into old wineskins. For the old skins would burst from the pressure, spilling the wine and ruining the skins. New wine is stored in new wineskins so that both are preserved."

**9:4** Some manuscripts read *saw.* **9:6** "Son of Man" is a title Jesus used for himself. **9:8** Greek *for giving such authority to human beings.* **9:11** Greek *with tax collectors and sinners?* **9:13** Hos 6:6 (Greek version). **9:14** Some manuscripts read *fast often.*

PSALM 10:16-18

The LORD is king forever and ever!
  The godless nations will vanish
    from the land.
[17] LORD, you know the hopes of the
      helpless.
  Surely you will hear their cries
    and comfort them.
[18] You will bring justice to the orphans
    and the oppressed,
  so mere people can no longer
    terrify them.

PROVERBS 3:9-10

Honor the LORD with your wealth and with the best part of everything you produce. Then he will fill your barns with grain, and your vats will overflow with good wine.

JANUARY
13

GENESIS 28:1–29:35

So Isaac called for Jacob, blessed him, and said, "You must not marry any of these Canaanite women. [2]Instead, go at once to Paddan-aram, to the house of your grandfather Bethuel, and marry one of your uncle Laban's daughters. [3]May God Almighty* bless you and give you many children. And may your descendants multiply and become many nations! [4]May God pass on to you and your descendants the blessings he promised to Abraham. May you own this land where you are now living as a foreigner, for God gave this land to Abraham."

[5]So Isaac sent Jacob away, and he went to Paddan-aram to stay with his uncle Laban, his mother's brother, the son of Bethuel the Aramean.

[6]Esau knew that his father, Isaac, had blessed Jacob and sent him to Paddan-aram to find a wife, and that he had warned Jacob, "You must not marry a Canaanite woman." [7]He also knew that Jacob had obeyed his parents and gone to Paddan-aram. [8]It was now very clear to Esau that his father did not like the local Canaanite women. [9]So Esau visited his uncle Ishmael's family and married one of Ishmael's daughters, in addition to the wives he already had. His new wife's name was Mahalath. She was the sister of Nebaioth and the daughter of Ishmael, Abraham's son.

[10]Meanwhile, Jacob left Beersheba and traveled toward Haran. [11]At sundown he arrived at a good place to set up camp and stopped there for the night. Jacob found a stone to rest his head against and lay down to sleep. [12]As he slept, he dreamed of a stairway that reached from the earth up to heaven. And he saw the angels of God going up and down the stairway.

[13]At the top of the stairway stood the

LORD, and he said, "I am the LORD, the God of your grandfather Abraham, and the God of your father, Isaac. The ground you are lying on belongs to you. I am giving it to you and your descendants. 14Your descendants will be as numerous as the dust of the earth! They will spread out in all directions—to the west and the east, to the north and the south. And all the families of the earth will be blessed through you and your descendants. 15What's more, I am with you, and I will protect you wherever you go. One day I will bring you back to this land. I will not leave you until I have finished giving you everything I have promised you."

16Then Jacob awoke from his sleep and said, "Surely the LORD is in this place, and I wasn't even aware of it!" 17But he was also afraid and said, "What an awesome place this is! It is none other than the house of God, the very gateway to heaven!"

18The next morning Jacob got up very early. He took the stone he had rested his head against, and he set it upright as a memorial pillar. Then he poured olive oil over it. 19He named that place Bethel (which means "house of God"), although the name of the nearby village was Luz.

20Then Jacob made this vow: "If God will indeed be with me and protect me on this journey, and if he will provide me with food and clothing, 21and if I return safely to my father's home, then the LORD will certainly be my God. 22And this memorial pillar I have set up will become a place for worshiping God, and I will present to God a tenth of everything he gives me."

29:1THEN Jacob hurried on, finally arriving in the land of the east. 2He saw a well in the distance. Three flocks of sheep and goats lay in an open field beside it, waiting to be watered. But a heavy stone covered the mouth of the well. 3It was the custom there to wait for all the flocks to arrive before removing the stone and watering the animals.

Afterward the stone would be placed back over the mouth of the well. 4Jacob went over to the shepherds and asked, "Where are you from, my friends?"

"We are from Haran," they answered.

5"Do you know a man there named Laban, the grandson of Nahor?" he asked.

"Yes, we do," they replied.

6"Is he doing well?" Jacob asked.

"Yes, he's well," they answered. "Look, here comes his daughter Rachel with the flock now."

7Jacob said, "Look, it's still broad daylight—too early to round up the animals. Why don't you water the sheep and goats so they can get back out to pasture?"

8"We can't water the animals until all the flocks have arrived," they replied. "Then the shepherds move the stone from the mouth of the well, and we water all the sheep and goats."

9Jacob was still talking with them when Rachel arrived with her father's flock, for she was a shepherd. 10And because Rachel was his cousin—the daughter of Laban, his mother's brother—and because the sheep and goats belonged to his uncle Laban, Jacob went over to the well and moved the stone from its mouth and watered his uncle's flock. 11Then Jacob kissed Rachel, and he wept aloud. 12He explained to Rachel that he was her cousin on her father's side—the son of her aunt Rebekah. So Rachel quickly ran and told her father, Laban.

13As soon as Laban heard that his nephew Jacob had arrived, he ran out to meet him. He embraced and kissed him and brought him home. When Jacob had told him his story, 14Laban exclaimed, "You really are my own flesh and blood!"

After Jacob had stayed with Laban for about a month, 15Laban said to him, "You shouldn't work for me without pay just because we are relatives. Tell me how much your wages should be."

16Now Laban had two daughters. The older daughter was named Leah, and the younger one was Rachel. 17There was no sparkle in Leah's eyes,* but Rachel had a beautiful figure and a lovely face. [18]Since Jacob was in love with Rachel, he told her father, "I'll work for you for seven years if you'll give me Rachel, your younger daughter, as my wife."

[19]"Agreed!" Laban replied. "I'd rather give her to you than to anyone else. Stay and work with me." [20]So Jacob worked seven years to pay for Rachel. But his love for her was so strong that it seemed to him but a few days.

[21]Finally, the time came for him to marry her. "I have fulfilled my agreement," Jacob said to Laban. "Now give me my wife so I can marry her."

[22]So Laban invited everyone in the neighborhood and prepared a wedding feast. [23]But that night, when it was dark, Laban took Leah to Jacob, and he slept with her. [24](Laban had given Leah a servant, Zilpah, to be her maid.)

[25]But when Jacob woke up in the morning—it was Leah! "What have you done to me?" Jacob raged at Laban. "I worked seven years for Rachel! Why have you tricked me?"

[26]"It's not our custom here to marry off a younger daughter ahead of the firstborn," Laban replied. [27]"But wait until the bridal week is over, then we'll give you Rachel, too—provided you promise to work another seven years for me."

[28]So Jacob agreed to work seven more years. A week after Jacob had married Leah, Laban gave him Rachel, too. [29](Laban gave Rachel a servant, Bilhah, to be her maid.) [30]So Jacob slept with Rachel, too, and he loved her much more than Leah. He then stayed and worked for Laban the additional seven years.

[31]When the LORD saw that Leah was unloved, he enabled her to have children, but Rachel could not conceive. [32]So Leah became pregnant and gave birth to a son. She named him Reuben,* for she said, "The LORD has noticed my misery, and now my husband will love me."

[33]She soon became pregnant again and gave birth to another son. She named him Simeon,* for she said, "The LORD heard that I was unloved and has given me another son."

[34]Then she became pregnant a third time and gave birth to another son. She named him Levi,* for she said, "Surely this time my husband will feel affection for me, since I have given him three sons!"

[35]Once again Leah became pregnant and gave birth to another son. She named him Judah,* for she said, "Now I will praise the LORD!" And then she stopped having children.

28:3 Hebrew *El-Shaddai.*    29:17 Or *Leah had dull eyes,* or *Leah had soft eyes.* The meaning of the Hebrew is uncertain.    29:32 *Reuben* means "Look, a son!" It also sounds like the Hebrew for "He has seen my misery."    29:33 *Simeon* probably means "one who hears."    29:34 *Levi* sounds like a Hebrew term that means "being attached" or "feeling affection for."    29:35 *Judah* sounds like the Hebrew term for "praise."

## MATTHEW 9:18-38

**A**s Jesus was saying this, the leader of a synagogue came and knelt before him. "My daughter has just died," he said, "but you can bring her back to life again if you just come and lay your hand on her."

[19]So Jesus and his disciples got up and went with him. [20]Just then a woman who had suffered for twelve years with constant bleeding came up behind him. She touched the fringe of his robe, [21]for she thought, "If I can just touch his robe, I will be healed."

[22]Jesus turned around, and when he saw her he said, "Daughter, be encouraged! Your faith has made you well." And the woman was healed at that moment.

[23]When Jesus arrived at the official's home, he saw the noisy crowd and heard the funeral music. [24]"Get out!" he told them. "The girl isn't dead; she's only asleep." But the crowd laughed at him. [25]After the crowd was put outside, however, Jesus went in and took the girl by the hand, and she stood up! [26]The report of this miracle swept through the entire countryside.

[27]After Jesus left the girl's home, two blind men followed along behind him,

shouting, "Son of David, have mercy on us!"

28They went right into the house where he was staying, and Jesus asked them, "Do you believe I can make you see?"

"Yes, Lord," they told him, "we do."

29Then he touched their eyes and said, "Because of your faith, it will happen." 30Then their eyes were opened, and they could see! Jesus sternly warned them, "Don't tell anyone about this." 31But instead, they went out and spread his fame all over the region.

32When they left, a demon-possessed man who couldn't speak was brought to Jesus. 33So Jesus cast out the demon, and then the man began to speak. The crowds were amazed. "Nothing like this has ever happened in Israel!" they exclaimed.

34But the Pharisees said, "He can cast out demons because he is empowered by the prince of demons."

35Jesus traveled through all the towns and villages of that area, teaching in the synagogues and announcing the Good News about the Kingdom. And he healed every kind of disease and illness. 36When he saw the crowds, he had compassion on them because they were confused and helpless, like sheep without a shepherd. 37**He said to his disciples, "The harvest is great, but the workers are few. 38So pray to the Lord who is in charge of the harvest; ask him to send more workers into his fields."**

PSALM 11:1-7
*For the choir director: A psalm of David.*

1 I trust in the LORD for protection.
   So why do you say to me,
      "Fly like a bird to the mountains
         for safety!
2 The wicked are stringing their bows
      and fitting their arrows on the
         bowstrings.
   They shoot from the shadows
      at those whose hearts are right.
3 The foundations of law and order
      have collapsed.
   What can the righteous do?"

4 But the LORD is in his holy Temple;
      the LORD still rules from heaven.
   He watches everyone closely,
      examining every person on earth.
5 The LORD examines both the
      righteous and the wicked.
   He hates those who love violence.
6 He will rain down blazing coals and
      burning sulfur on the wicked,
      punishing them with scorching
         winds.
7 For the righteous LORD loves justice.
   The virtuous will see his face.

PROVERBS 3:11-12
My child, don't reject the LORD's discipline, and don't be upset when he corrects you. For the LORD corrects those he loves, just as a father corrects a child in whom he delights.*

3:12 Greek version reads *And he punishes those he accepts as his children.* Compare Heb 12:6.

# JANUARY
# 14

GENESIS 30:1–31:16
When Rachel saw that she wasn't having any children for Jacob, she became jealous of her sister. She pleaded with Jacob, "Give me children, or I'll die!"

2Then Jacob became furious with Rachel. "Am I God?" he asked. "He's the one who has kept you from having children!"

3Then Rachel told him, "Take my maid, Bilhah, and sleep with her. She will bear children for me,* and through her I can have a family, too." 4So Rachel gave her servant, Bilhah, to Jacob as a wife, and he slept with her. 5Bilhah became pregnant and presented him with a son. 6Rachel named him Dan,* for she said, "God has vindicated me! He has heard my request and given me a son." 7Then Bilhah became pregnant again and gave Jacob a second son. 8Rachel named him Naphtali,* for she said, "I have struggled hard with my sister, and I'm winning!"

⁹Meanwhile, Leah realized that she wasn't getting pregnant anymore, so she took her servant, Zilpah, and gave her to Jacob as a wife. ¹⁰Soon Zilpah presented him with a son. ¹¹Leah named him Gad,* for she said, "How fortunate I am!" ¹²Then Zilpah gave Jacob a second son. ¹³And Leah named him Asher,* for she said, "What joy is mine! Now the other women will celebrate with me."

¹⁴One day during the wheat harvest, Reuben found some mandrakes growing in a field and brought them to his mother, Leah. Rachel begged Leah, "Please give me some of your son's mandrakes."

¹⁵But Leah angrily replied, "Wasn't it enough that you stole my husband? Now will you steal my son's mandrakes, too?"

Rachel answered, "I will let Jacob sleep with you tonight if you give me some of the mandrakes."

¹⁶So that evening, as Jacob was coming home from the fields, Leah went out to meet him. "You must come and sleep with me tonight!" she said. "I have paid for you with some mandrakes that my son found." So that night he slept with Leah. ¹⁷And God answered Leah's prayers. She became pregnant again and gave birth to a fifth son for Jacob. ¹⁸She named him Issachar,* for she said, "God has rewarded me for giving my servant to my husband as a wife." ¹⁹Then Leah became pregnant again and gave birth to a sixth son for Jacob. ²⁰She named him Zebulun,* for she said, "God has given me a good reward. Now my husband will treat me with respect, for I have given him six sons." ²¹Later she gave birth to a daughter and named her Dinah.

²²Then God remembered Rachel's plight and answered her prayers by enabling her to have children. ²³She became pregnant and gave birth to a son. "God has removed my disgrace," she said. ²⁴And she named him Joseph,* for

she said, "May the LORD add yet another son to my family."

²⁵Soon after Rachel had given birth to Joseph, Jacob said to Laban, "Please release me so I can go home to my own country. ²⁶Let me take my wives and children, for I have earned them by serving you, and let me be on my way. You certainly know how hard I have worked for you."

²⁷"Please listen to me," Laban replied. "I have become wealthy, for* the LORD has blessed me because of you. ²⁸Tell me how much I owe you. Whatever it is, I'll pay it."

²⁹Jacob replied, "You know how hard I've worked for you, and how your flocks and herds have grown under my care. ³⁰You had little indeed before I came, but your wealth has increased enormously. The LORD has blessed you through everything I've done. But now, what about me? When can I start providing for my own family?"

³¹"What wages do you want?" Laban asked again.

Jacob replied, "Don't give me anything. Just do this one thing, and I'll continue to tend and watch over your flocks. ³²Let me inspect your flocks today and remove all the sheep and goats that are speckled or spotted, along with all the black sheep. Give these to me as my wages. ³³In the future, when you check on the animals you have given me as my wages, you'll see that I have been honest. If you find in my flock any goats without speckles or spots, or any sheep that are not black, you will know that I have stolen them from you."

³⁴"All right," Laban replied. "It will be as you say." ³⁵But that very day Laban went out and removed the male goats that were streaked and spotted, all the female goats that were speckled and spotted or had white patches, and all the black sheep. He placed them in the care of his own sons, ³⁶who took them a three-days' journey from where Jacob was. Meanwhile, Jacob stayed and cared for the rest of Laban's flock.

³⁷Then Jacob took some fresh branches

from poplar, almond, and plane trees and peeled off strips of bark, making white streaks on them. ³⁸Then he placed these peeled branches in the watering troughs where the flocks came to drink, for that was where they mated. ³⁹And when they mated in front of the white-streaked branches, they gave birth to young that were streaked, speckled, and spotted. ⁴⁰Jacob separated those lambs from Laban's flock. And at mating time he turned the flock to face Laban's animals that were streaked or black. This is how he built his own flock instead of increasing Laban's.

⁴¹Whenever the stronger females were ready to mate, Jacob would place the peeled branches in the watering troughs in front of them. Then they would mate in front of the branches. ⁴²But he didn't do this with the weaker ones, so the weaker lambs belonged to Laban, and the stronger ones were Jacob's. ⁴³As a result, Jacob became very wealthy, with large flocks of sheep and goats, male and female servants, and many camels and donkeys.

³¹:¹But Jacob soon learned that Laban's sons were grumbling about him. "Jacob has robbed our father of everything!" they said. "He has gained all his wealth at our father's expense." ²And Jacob began to notice a change in Laban's attitude toward him.

³Then the Lord said to Jacob, "Return to the land of your father and grandfather and to your relatives there, and I will be with you."

⁴So Jacob called Rachel and Leah out to the field where he was watching his flock. ⁵He said to them, "I have noticed that your father's attitude toward me has changed. But the God of my father has been with me. ⁶You know how hard I have worked for your father, ⁷but he has cheated me, changing my wages ten times. But God has not allowed him to do me any harm. ⁸For if he said, 'The speckled animals will be your wages,' the whole flock began to produce speckled young. And when he changed

his mind and said, 'The striped animals will be your wages,' then the whole flock produced striped young. ⁹In this way, God has taken your father's animals and given them to me.

¹⁰"One time during the mating season, I had a dream and saw that the male goats mating with the females were streaked, speckled, and spotted. ¹¹Then in my dream, the angel of God said to me, 'Jacob!' And I replied, 'Yes, here I am.'

¹²"The angel said, 'Look up, and you will see that only the streaked, speckled, and spotted males are mating with the females of your flock. For I have seen how Laban has treated you. ¹³I am the God who appeared to you at Bethel,* the place where you anointed the pillar of stone and made your vow to me. Now get ready and leave this country and return to the land of your birth.'"

¹⁴Rachel and Leah responded, "That's fine with us! We won't inherit any of our father's wealth anyway. ¹⁵He has reduced our rights to those of foreign women. And after he sold us, he wasted the money you paid him for us. ¹⁶All the wealth God has given you from our father legally belongs to us and our children. So go ahead and do whatever God has told you."

30:3 Hebrew *bear children on my knees.*   30:6 *Dan* means "he judged" or "he vindicated."   30:8 *Naphtali* means "my struggle."   30:11 *Gad* means "good fortune." 30:13 *Asher* means "happy."   30:18 *Issachar* sounds like a Hebrew term that means "reward."   30:20 *Zebulun* probably means "honor."   30:24 *Joseph* means "may he add."   30:27 Or *I have learned by divination that.* 31:13 As in Greek version and an Aramaic Targum; Hebrew reads *the God of Bethel.*

## MATTHEW 10:1-23

Jesus called his twelve disciples together and gave them authority to cast out evil* spirits and to heal every kind of disease and illness. ²Here are the names of the twelve apostles:

first, Simon (also called Peter),
then Andrew (Peter's brother),
James (son of Zebedee),
John (James's brother),
³ Philip,
Bartholomew,

Thomas,
Matthew (the tax collector),
James (son of Alphaeus),
Thaddaeus,*
4 Simon (the zealot*),
Judas Iscariot (who later betrayed him).

5 Jesus sent out the twelve apostles with these instructions: "Don't go to the Gentiles or the Samaritans, 6 but only to the people of Israel—God's lost sheep. 7 Go and announce to them that the Kingdom of Heaven is near.* 8 Heal the sick, raise the dead, cure those with leprosy, and cast out demons. Give as freely as you have received!

9 "Don't take any money in your money belts—no gold, silver, or even copper coins. 10 Don't carry a traveler's bag with a change of clothes and sandals or even a walking stick. Don't hesitate to accept hospitality, because those who work deserve to be fed.

11 "Whenever you enter a city or village, search for a worthy person and stay in his home until you leave town. 12 When you enter the home, give it your blessing. 13 If it turns out to be a worthy home, let your blessing stand; if it is not, take back the blessing. 14 If any household or town refuses to welcome you or listen to your message, shake its dust from your feet as you leave. 15 I tell you the truth, the wicked cities of Sodom and Gomorrah will be better off than such a town on the judgment day.

16 "Look, I am sending you out as sheep among wolves. So be as shrewd as snakes and harmless as doves. 17 But beware! For you will be handed over to the courts and will be flogged with whips in the synagogues. 18 You will stand trial before governors and kings because you are my followers. But this will be your opportunity to tell the rulers and other unbelievers about me.* 19 When you are arrested, don't worry about how to respond or what to say. God will give you the right words at the right time. 20 For it is not you who will be speaking—it will be the Spirit of your Father speaking through you.

21 "A brother will betray his brother to death, a father will betray his own child, and children will rebel against their parents and cause them to be killed. 22 And all nations will hate you because you are my followers.* But everyone who endures to the end will be saved. 23 When you are persecuted in one town, flee to the next. I tell you the truth, the Son of Man* will return before you have reached all the towns of Israel."

10:1 Greek *unclean.*   10:3 Other manuscripts read *Lebbaeus;* still others read *Lebbaeus who is called Thaddaeus.*   10:4 Greek *the Cananean,* an Aramaic term for Jewish nationalists.   10:7 Or *has come,* or *is coming soon.*   10:18 Or *But this will be your testimony against the rulers and other unbelievers.*   10:22 Greek *on account of my name.*   10:23 "Son of Man" is a title Jesus used for himself.

PSALM 12:1-8

*For the choir director: A psalm of David, to be accompanied by an eight-stringed instrument.**

1 **H**elp, O LORD, for the godly are fast disappearing!
   The faithful have vanished from the earth!
2 Neighbors lie to each other,
   speaking with flattering lips and deceitful hearts.
3 May the LORD cut off their flattering lips
   and silence their boastful tongues.
4 They say, "We will lie to our hearts' content.
   Our lips are our own—who can stop us?"

5 The LORD replies, "I have seen violence done to the helpless,
   and I have heard the groans of the poor.
   Now I will rise up to rescue them,
   as they have longed for me to do."
6 The LORD's promises are pure,
   like silver refined in a furnace,
   purified seven times over.
7 Therefore, LORD, we know you will protect the oppressed,

preserving them forever from this
lying generation,
⁸ even though the wicked strut about,
and evil is praised throughout
the land.

12:TITLE Hebrew *according to the sheminith.*

PROVERBS 3:13-15
Joyful is the person who finds wisdom,
the one who gains understanding. For
wisdom is more profitable than silver,
and her wages are better than gold.
Wisdom is more precious than rubies;
nothing you desire can compare with
her.

# JANUARY
# 15

GENESIS 31:17–32:12
So Jacob put his wives and children on
camels, ¹⁸and he drove all his livestock
in front of him. He packed all the belongings he had acquired in Paddan-
aram and set out for the land of Canaan,
where his father, Isaac, lived. ¹⁹At the
time they left, Laban was some distance
away, shearing his sheep. Rachel stole
her father's household idols and took
them with her. ²⁰Jacob outwitted Laban
the Aramean, for they set out secretly
and never told Laban they were leaving.
²¹So Jacob took all his possessions with
him, and crossed the Euphrates River,*
heading for the hill country of Gilead.

²²Three days later, Laban was told
that Jacob had fled. ²³So he gathered a
group of his relatives and set out in hot
pursuit. He caught up with Jacob seven
days later in the hill country of Gilead.
²⁴But the previous night God had appeared to Laban the Aramean in a
dream and told him, "I'm warning you—
leave Jacob alone!"

²⁵Laban caught up with Jacob as he
was camped in the hill country of Gilead,

and he set up his camp not far from
Jacob's. ²⁶"What do you mean by stealing away like this?" Laban demanded.
"How dare you drag my daughters away
like prisoners of war? ²⁷Why did you
slip away secretly? Why did you steal
away? And why didn't you say you
wanted to leave? I would have given you
a farewell feast, with singing and music,
accompanied by tambourines and
harps. ²⁸Why didn't you let me kiss my
daughters and grandchildren and tell
them good-bye? You have acted very
foolishly! ²⁹I could destroy you, but the
God of your father appeared to me last
night and warned me, 'Leave Jacob alone!'
³⁰I can understand your feeling that you
must go, and your intense longing for
your father's home. But why have you
stolen my gods?"

³¹"I rushed away because I was
afraid," Jacob answered. "I thought you
would take your daughters from me by
force. ³²But as for your gods, see if you
can find them, and let the person who
has taken them die! And if you find anything else that belongs to you, identify it
before all these relatives of ours, and I
will give it back!" But Jacob did not
know that Rachel had stolen the household idols.

³³Laban went first into Jacob's tent to
search there, then into Leah's, and then
the tents of the two servant wives—but
he found nothing. Finally, he went into
Rachel's tent. ³⁴But Rachel had taken
the household idols and hidden them
in her camel saddle, and now she was
sitting on them. When Laban had thoroughly searched her tent without finding them, ³⁵she said to her father,
"Please, sir, forgive me if I don't get up
for you. I'm having my monthly period."
So Laban continued his search, but he
could not find the household idols.

³⁶Then Jacob became very angry, and
he challenged Laban. "What's my
crime?" he demanded. "What have I
done wrong to make you chase after me
as though I were a criminal? ³⁷You have
rummaged through everything I own.
Now show me what you found that be-

longs to you! Set it out here in front of us, before our relatives, for all to see. Let them judge between us!

³⁸"For twenty years I have been with you, caring for your flocks. In all that time your sheep and goats never miscarried. In all those years I never used a single ram of yours for food. ³⁹If any were attacked and killed by wild animals, I never showed you the carcass and asked you to reduce the count of your flock. No, I took the loss myself! You made me pay for every stolen animal, whether it was taken in broad daylight or in the dark of night.

⁴⁰"I worked for you through the scorching heat of the day and through cold and sleepless nights. ⁴¹Yes, for twenty years I slaved in your house! I worked for fourteen years earning your two daughters, and then six more years for your flock. And you changed my wages ten times! ⁴²In fact, if the God of my father had not been on my side—the God of Abraham and the fearsome God of Isaac*—you would have sent me away empty-handed. But God has seen your abuse and my hard work. That is why he appeared to you last night and rebuked you!"

⁴³Then Laban replied to Jacob, "These women are my daughters, these children are my grandchildren, and these flocks are my flocks—in fact, everything you see is mine. But what can I do now about my daughters and their children? ⁴⁴So come, let's make a covenant, you and I, and it will be a witness to our commitment."

⁴⁵So Jacob took a stone and set it up as a monument. ⁴⁶Then he told his family members, "Gather some stones." So they gathered stones and piled them in a heap. Then Jacob and Laban sat down beside the pile of stones to eat a covenant meal. ⁴⁷To commemorate the event, Laban called the place Jegar-sahadutha (which means "witness pile" in Aramaic), and Jacob called it Galeed (which means "witness pile" in Hebrew).

⁴⁸Then Laban declared, "This pile of stones will stand as a witness to remind us of the covenant we have made today." This explains why it was called Galeed— "Witness Pile." ⁴⁹But it was also called Mizpah (which means "watchtower"), for Laban said, "May the LORD keep watch between us to make sure that we keep this covenant when we are out of each other's sight. ⁵⁰If you mistreat my daughters or if you marry other wives, God will see it even if no one else does. He is a witness to this covenant between us.

⁵¹"See this pile of stones," Laban continued, "and see this monument I have set between us. ⁵²They stand between us as witnesses of our vows. I will never pass this pile of stones to harm you, and you must never pass these stones or this monument to harm me. ⁵³I call on the God of our ancestors—the God of your grandfather Abraham and the God of my grandfather Nahor—to serve as a judge between us."

So Jacob took an oath before the fearsome God of his father, Isaac,* to respect the boundary line. ⁵⁴Then Jacob offered a sacrifice to God there on the mountain and invited everyone to a covenant feast. After they had eaten, they spent the night on the mountain.

⁵⁵*Laban got up early the next morning, and he kissed his grandchildren and his daughters and blessed them. Then he left and returned home.

³²:¹*As Jacob started on his way again, angels of God came to meet him. ²When Jacob saw them, he exclaimed, "This is God's camp!" So he named the place Mahanaim.*

³Then Jacob sent messengers ahead to his brother, Esau, who was living in the region of Seir in the land of Edom. ⁴He told them, "Give this message to my master Esau: 'Humble greetings from your servant Jacob. Until now I have been living with Uncle Laban, ⁵and now I own cattle, donkeys, flocks of sheep and goats, and many servants, both men and women. I have sent these messengers to inform my lord of my coming, hoping that you will be friendly to me.'"

⁶After delivering the message, the messengers returned to Jacob and reported, "We met your brother, Esau, and he is already on his way to meet you—with an army of 400 men!" ⁷Jacob was terrified at the news. He divided his household, along with the flocks and herds and camels, into two groups. ⁸He thought, "If Esau meets one group and attacks it, perhaps the other group can escape."

⁹Then Jacob prayed, "O God of my grandfather Abraham, and God of my father, Isaac—O LORD, you told me, 'Return to your own land and to your relatives.' And you promised me, 'I will treat you kindly.' ¹⁰I am not worthy of all the unfailing love and faithfulness you have shown to me, your servant. When I left home and crossed the Jordan River, I owned nothing except a walking stick. Now my household fills two large camps! ¹¹O LORD, please rescue me from the hand of my brother, Esau. I am afraid that he is coming to attack me, along with my wives and children. ¹²But you promised me, 'I will surely treat you kindly, and I will multiply your descendants until they become as numerous as the sands along the seashore—too many to count.'"

31:21 Hebrew *the river.*   31:42 Or *and the Fear of Isaac.* 31:53 Or *the Fear of his father, Isaac.*   31:55 Verse 31:55 is numbered 32:1 in Hebrew text.   32:1 Verses 32:1-32 are numbered 32:2-33 in Hebrew text.   32:2 *Mahanaim* means "two camps."

## MATTHEW 10:24–11:6

"**S**tudents* are not greater than their teacher, and slaves are not greater than their master. ²⁵Students are to be like their teacher, and slaves are to be like their master. And since I, the master of the household, have been called the prince of demons,* the members of my household will be called by even worse names!

²⁶"But don't be afraid of those who threaten you. For the time is coming when everything that is covered will be revealed, and all that is secret will be made known to all. ²⁷What I tell you now in the darkness, shout abroad when daybreak comes. What I whisper in your ear, shout from the housetops for all to hear!

²⁸"Don't be afraid of those who want to kill your body; they cannot touch your soul. Fear only God, who can destroy both soul and body in hell.* ²⁹**What is the price of two sparrows— one copper coin*? But not a single sparrow can fall to the ground without your Father knowing it. ³⁰And the very hairs on your head are all numbered. ³¹So don't be afraid; you are more valuable to God than a whole flock of sparrows.**

³²"Everyone who acknowledges me publicly here on earth, I will also acknowledge before my Father in heaven. ³³But everyone who denies me here on earth, I will also deny before my Father in heaven.

³⁴"Don't imagine that I came to bring peace to the earth! I came not to bring peace, but a sword.

³⁵ 'I have come to set a man against his father,
    a daughter against her mother,
and a daughter-in-law against her
    mother-in-law.
³⁶    Your enemies will be right in
        your own household!'*

³⁷"If you love your father or mother more than you love me, you are not worthy of being mine; or if you love your son or daughter more than me, you are not worthy of being mine. ³⁸If you refuse to take up your cross and follow me, you are not worthy of being mine. ³⁹If you cling to your life, you will lose it; but if you give up your life for me, you will find it.

⁴⁰"Anyone who receives you receives me, and anyone who receives me receives the Father who sent me. ⁴¹If you receive a prophet as one who speaks for God,* you will be given the same reward as a prophet. And if you receive righteous people because of their righteousness, you will be given a reward like theirs. ⁴²And if you give

even a cup of cold water to one of the least of my followers, you will surely be rewarded."

11:1WHEN Jesus had finished giving these instructions to his twelve disciples, he went out to teach and preach in towns throughout the region.

2John the Baptist, who was in prison, heard about all the things the Messiah was doing. So he sent his disciples to ask Jesus, 3"Are you the Messiah we've been expecting,* or should we keep looking for someone else?"

4Jesus told them, "Go back to John and tell him what you have heard and seen—5the blind see, the lame walk, the lepers are cured, the deaf hear, the dead are raised to life, and the Good News is being preached to the poor. 6And tell him, 'God blesses those who do not turn away because of me.*'"

10:24 Or Disciples.    10:25 Greek Beelzeboul; other manuscripts read Beezeboul; Latin version reads Beelzebub.
10:28 Greek Gehenna.    10:29 Greek one assarion [i.e., one "as," a Roman coin equal to 1/16 of a denarius].
10:35-36 Mic 7:6.    10:41 Greek receive a prophet in the name of a prophet.    11:3 Greek Are you the one who is coming?    11:6 Or who are not offended by me.

PSALM 13:1-6
*For the choir director: A psalm of David.*

1 O LORD, how long will you forget
    me? Forever?
  How long will you look the
    other way?
2 How long must I struggle with
    anguish in my soul,
  with sorrow in my heart every
    day?
  How long will my enemy have
    the upper hand?

3 Turn and answer me, O LORD
    my God!
  Restore the sparkle to my eyes,
    or I will die.
4 Don't let my enemies gloat, saying,
    "We have defeated him!"
  Don't let them rejoice at my
    downfall.

5 But I trust in your unfailing love.
  I will rejoice because you have
    rescued me.

6 I will sing to the LORD
    because he is good to me.

PROVERBS 3:16-18
She [Wisdom] offers you long life in her right hand, and riches and honor in her left. She will guide you down delightful paths; all her ways are satisfying. Wisdom is a tree of life to those who embrace her; happy are those who hold her tightly.

# JANUARY 16

GENESIS 32:13–34:31
Jacob stayed where he was for the night. Then he selected these gifts from his possessions to present to his brother, Esau: 14200 female goats, 20 male goats, 200 ewes, 20 rams, 1530 female camels with their young, 40 cows, 10 bulls, 20 female donkeys, and 10 male donkeys. 16He divided these animals into herds and assigned each to different servants. Then he told his servants, "Go ahead of me with the animals, but keep some distance between the herds."

17He gave these instructions to the men leading the first group: "When my brother, Esau, meets you, he will ask, 'Whose servants are you? Where are you going? Who owns these animals?' 18You must reply, 'They belong to your servant Jacob, but they are a gift for his master Esau. Look, he is coming right behind us.'"

19Jacob gave the same instructions to the second and third herdsmen and to all who followed behind the herds: "You must say the same thing to Esau when you meet him. 20And be sure to say, 'Look, your servant Jacob is right behind us.'"

Jacob thought, "I will try to appease him by sending gifts ahead of me.

When I see him in person, perhaps he will be friendly to me." ²¹So the gifts were sent on ahead, while Jacob himself spent that night in the camp.

²²During the night Jacob got up and took his two wives, his two servant wives, and his eleven sons and crossed the Jabbok River with them. ²³After taking them to the other side, he sent over all his possessions.

²⁴This left Jacob all alone in the camp, and a man came and wrestled with him until the dawn began to break. ²⁵When the man saw that he would not win the match, he touched Jacob's hip and wrenched it out of its socket. ²⁶Then the man said, "Let me go, for the dawn is breaking!"

But Jacob said, "I will not let you go unless you bless me."

²⁷"What is your name?" the man asked.

He replied, "Jacob."

²⁸"Your name will no longer be Jacob," the man told him. "From now on you will be called Israel,* because you have fought with God and with men and have won."

²⁹"Please tell me your name," Jacob said.

"Why do you want to know my name?" the man replied. Then he blessed Jacob there.

³⁰Jacob named the place Peniel (which means "face of God"), for he said, "I have seen God face to face, yet my life has been spared." ³¹The sun was rising as Jacob left Peniel,* and he was limping because of the injury to his hip. ³²(Even today the people of Israel don't eat the tendon near the hip socket because of what happened that night when the man strained the tendon of Jacob's hip.)

³³:¹THEN Jacob looked up and saw Esau coming with his 400 men. So he divided the children among Leah, Rachel, and his two servant wives. ²He put the servant wives and their children at the front, Leah and her children next, and Rachel and Joseph last. ³Then Jacob went on ahead. As he approached his brother, he bowed to the ground seven times before him. ⁴Then Esau ran to meet him and embraced him, threw his arms around his neck, and kissed him. And they both wept.

⁵Then Esau looked at the women and children and asked, "Who are these people with you?"

"These are the children God has graciously given to me, your servant," Jacob replied. ⁶Then the servant wives came forward with their children and bowed before him. ⁷Next came Leah with her children, and they bowed before him. Finally, Joseph and Rachel came forward and bowed before him.

⁸"And what were all the flocks and herds I met as I came?" Esau asked.

Jacob replied, "They are a gift, my lord, to ensure your friendship."

⁹"My brother, I have plenty," Esau answered. "Keep what you have for yourself."

¹⁰But Jacob insisted, "No, if I have found favor with you, please accept this gift from me. And what a relief to see your friendly smile. It is like seeing the face of God! ¹¹Please take this gift I have brought you, for God has been very gracious to me. I have more than enough." And because Jacob insisted, Esau finally accepted the gift.

¹²"Well," Esau said, "let's be going. I will lead the way."

¹³But Jacob replied, "You can see, my lord, that some of the children are very young, and the flocks and herds have their young, too. If they are driven too hard, even for one day, all the animals could die. ¹⁴Please, my lord, go ahead of your servant. We will follow slowly, at a pace that is comfortable for the livestock and the children. I will meet you at Seir."

¹⁵"All right," Esau said, "but at least let me assign some of my men to guide and protect you."

Jacob responded, "That's not necessary. It's enough that you've received me warmly, my lord!"

¹⁶So Esau turned around and started back to Seir that same day. ¹⁷Jacob, on

the other hand, traveled on to Succoth. There he built himself a house and made shelters for his livestock. That is why the place was named Succoth (which means "shelters").

<sup>18</sup>Later, having traveled all the way from Paddan-aram, Jacob arrived safely at the town of Shechem, in the land of Canaan. There he set up camp outside the town. <sup>19</sup>Jacob bought the plot of land where he camped from the family of Hamor, the father of Shechem, for 100 pieces of silver.* <sup>20</sup>And there he built an altar and named it El-Elohe-Israel.*

<sup>34:1</sup>ONE day Dinah, the daughter of Jacob and Leah, went to visit some of the young women who lived in the area. <sup>2</sup>But when the local prince, Shechem son of Hamor the Hivite, saw Dinah, he seized her and raped her. <sup>3</sup>But then he fell in love with her, and he tried to win her affection with tender words. <sup>4</sup>He said to his father, Hamor, "Get me this young girl. I want to marry her."

<sup>5</sup>Soon Jacob heard that Shechem had defiled his daughter, Dinah. But since his sons were out in the fields herding his livestock, he said nothing until they returned. <sup>6</sup>Hamor, Shechem's father, came to discuss the matter with Jacob. <sup>7</sup>Meanwhile, Jacob's sons had come in from the field as soon as they heard what had happened. They were shocked and furious that their sister had been raped. Shechem had done a disgraceful thing against Jacob's family,* something that should never be done.

<sup>8</sup>Hamor tried to speak with Jacob and his sons. "My son Shechem is truly in love with your daughter," he said. "Please let him marry her. <sup>9</sup>In fact, let's arrange other marriages, too. You give us your daughters for our sons, and we will give you our daughters for your sons. <sup>10</sup>And you may live among us; the land is open to you! Settle here and trade with us. And feel free to buy property in the area."

<sup>11</sup>Then Shechem himself spoke to Dinah's father and brothers. "Please be kind to me, and let me marry her," he begged. "I will give you whatever you ask. <sup>12</sup>No matter what dowry or gift you demand, I will gladly pay it—just give me the girl as my wife."

<sup>13</sup>But since Shechem had defiled their sister, Dinah, Jacob's sons responded deceitfully to Shechem and his father, Hamor. <sup>14</sup>They said to them, "We couldn't possibly allow this, because you're not circumcised. It would be a disgrace for our sister to marry a man like you! <sup>15</sup>But here is a solution. If every man among you will be circumcised like we are, <sup>16</sup>then we will give you our daughters, and we'll take your daughters for ourselves. We will live among you and become one people. <sup>17</sup>But if you don't agree to be circumcised, we will take her and be on our way."

<sup>18</sup>Hamor and his son Shechem agreed to their proposal. <sup>19</sup>Shechem wasted no time in acting on this request, for he wanted Jacob's daughter desperately. Shechem was a highly respected member of his family, <sup>20</sup>and he went with his father, Hamor, to present this proposal to the leaders at the town gate.

<sup>21</sup>"These men are our friends," they said. "Let's invite them to live here among us and trade freely. Look, the land is large enough to hold them. We can take their daughters as wives and let them marry ours. <sup>22</sup>But they will consider staying here and becoming one people with us only if all of our men are circumcised, just as they are. <sup>23</sup>But if we do this, all their livestock and possessions will eventually be ours. Come, let's agree to their terms and let them settle here among us."

<sup>24</sup>So all the men in the town council agreed with Hamor and Shechem, and every male in the town was circumcised. <sup>25</sup>But three days later, when their wounds were still sore, two of Jacob's sons, Simeon and Levi, who were Dinah's full brothers, took their swords and entered the town without opposition. Then they slaughtered every male there, <sup>26</sup>including Hamor and his son Shechem. They killed them with their swords, then took

Dinah from Shechem's house and returned to their camp.

27Meanwhile, the rest of Jacob's sons arrived. Finding the men slaughtered, they plundered the town because their sister had been defiled there. 28They seized all the flocks and herds and donkeys—everything they could lay their hands on, both inside the town and outside in the fields. 29They looted all their wealth and plundered their houses. They also took all their little children and wives and led them away as captives.

30Afterward Jacob said to Simeon and Levi, "You have ruined me! You've made me stink among all the people of this land—among all the Canaanites and Perizzites. We are so few that they will join forces and crush us. I will be ruined, and my entire household will be wiped out!"

31"But why should we let him treat our sister like a prostitute?" they retorted angrily.

32:28 *Jacob* sounds like the Hebrew words for "heel" and "deceiver." *Israel* means "God fights." 32:31 Hebrew *Penuel*, a variant spelling of Peniel. 33:19 Hebrew *100 kesitahs*; the value or weight of the kesitah is no longer known. 33:20 *El-Elohe-Israel* means "God, the God of Israel." 34:7 Hebrew *a disgraceful thing in Israel.*

## MATTHEW 11:7-30

As John's disciples were leaving, Jesus began talking about him to the crowds. "What kind of man did you go into the wilderness to see? Was he a weak reed, swayed by every breath of wind? 8Or were you expecting to see a man dressed in expensive clothes? No, people with expensive clothes live in palaces. 9Were you looking for a prophet? Yes, and he is more than a prophet. 10John is the man to whom the Scriptures refer when they say,

'Look, I am sending my messenger
    ahead of you,
and he will prepare your way
    before you.'*

11"I tell you the truth, of all who have ever lived, none is greater than John the Baptist. Yet even the least person in the Kingdom of Heaven is greater than he is!

12And from the time John the Baptist began preaching until now, the Kingdom of Heaven has been forcefully advancing, and violent people are attacking it.* 13For before John came, all the prophets and the law of Moses looked forward to this present time. 14And if you are willing to accept what I say, he is Elijah, the one the prophets said would come.* 15Anyone with ears to hear should listen and understand!

16"To what can I compare this generation? It is like children playing a game in the public square. They complain to their friends,

17 'We played wedding songs,
        and you didn't dance,
    so we played funeral songs,
        and you didn't mourn.'

18For John didn't spend his time eating and drinking, and you say, 'He's possessed by a demon.' 19The Son of Man,* on the other hand, feasts and drinks, and you say, 'He's a glutton and a drunkard, and a friend of tax collectors and other sinners!' But wisdom is shown to be right by its results."

20Then Jesus began to denounce the towns where he had done so many of his miracles, because they hadn't repented of their sins and turned to God. 21"What sorrow awaits you, Korazin and Bethsaida! For if the miracles I did in you had been done in wicked Tyre and Sidon, their people would have repented of their sins long ago, clothing themselves in burlap and throwing ashes on their heads to show their remorse. 22I tell you, Tyre and Sidon will be better off on judgment day than you.

23"And you people of Capernaum, will you be honored in heaven? No, you will go down to the place of the dead.* For if the miracles I did for you had been done in wicked Sodom, it would still be here today. 24I tell you, even Sodom will be better off on judgment day than you."

25At that time Jesus prayed this prayer: "O Father, Lord of heaven and earth, thank you for hiding these things from those who think themselves wise and clever, and for revealing them to the childlike. 26Yes, Father, it pleased you to do it this way!

27"My Father has entrusted everything to me. No one truly knows the Son except the Father, and no one truly knows the Father except the Son and those to whom the Son chooses to reveal him."

28Then Jesus said, "Come to me, all of you who are weary and carry heavy burdens, and I will give you rest. 29Take my yoke upon you. Let me teach you, because I am humble and gentle at heart, and you will find rest for your souls. 30For my yoke is easy to bear, and the burden I give you is light."

11:10 Mal 3:1.   11:12 Or *until now, eager multitudes have been pressing into the Kingdom of Heaven.* 11:14 See Mal 4:5.   11:19 "Son of Man" is a title Jesus used for himself.   11:23 Greek *to Hades.*

## PSALM 14:1-7
*For the choir director: A psalm of David.*

1 **O**nly fools say in their hearts,
    "There is no God."
  They are corrupt, and their actions
      are evil;
    not one of them does good!

2 The LORD looks down from heaven
      on the entire human race;
  he looks to see if anyone is truly
      wise,
    if anyone seeks God.

3 But no, all have turned away;
    all have become corrupt.*
  No one does good,
    not a single one!

4 Will those who do evil never learn?
    They eat up my people like bread
    and wouldn't think of praying
      to the LORD.

5 Terror will grip them,
    for God is with those who
      obey him.

6 The wicked frustrate the plans
    of the oppressed,

  but the LORD will protect
    his people.

7 Who will come from Mount Zion
      to rescue Israel?
  When the LORD restores his
      people,
  Jacob will shout with joy, and
    Israel will rejoice.

14:3 Greek version reads *have become useless.* Compare Rom 3:12.

## PROVERBS 3:19-20
**B**y wisdom the LORD founded the earth; by understanding he created the heavens. By his knowledge the deep fountains of the earth burst forth, and the dew settles beneath the night sky.

# JANUARY
# 17

## GENESIS 35:1–36:43
**T**hen God said to Jacob, "Get ready and move to Bethel and settle there. Build an altar there to the God who appeared to you when you fled from your brother, Esau."

2So Jacob told everyone in his household, "Get rid of all your pagan idols, purify yourselves, and put on clean clothing. 3We are now going to Bethel, where I will build an altar to the God who answered my prayers when I was in distress. He has been with me wherever I have gone."

4So they gave Jacob all their pagan idols and earrings, and he buried them under the great tree near Shechem. 5As they set out, a terror from God spread over the people in all the towns of that area, so no one attacked Jacob's family.

6Eventually, Jacob and his household arrived at Luz (also called Bethel) in Canaan. 7Jacob built an altar there and named the place El-bethel (which means "God of Bethel"), because God had appeared to him there when he was fleeing from his brother, Esau.

[8] Soon after this, Rebekah's old nurse, Deborah, died. She was buried beneath the oak tree in the valley below Bethel. Ever since, the tree has been called Allon-bacuth (which means "oak of weeping").

[9] Now that Jacob had returned from Paddan-aram, God appeared to him again at Bethel. God blessed him, [10] saying, "Your name is Jacob, but you will not be called Jacob any longer. From now on your name will be Israel."* So God renamed him Israel.

[11] Then God said, "I am El-Shaddai— 'God Almighty.' Be fruitful and multiply. You will become a great nation, even many nations. Kings will be among your descendants! [12] And I will give you the land I once gave to Abraham and Isaac. Yes, I will give it to you and your descendants after you." [13] Then God went up from the place where he had spoken to Jacob.

[14] Jacob set up a stone pillar to mark the place where God had spoken to him. Then he poured wine over it as an offering to God and anointed the pillar with olive oil. [15] And Jacob named the place Bethel (which means "house of God"), because God had spoken to him there.

[16] Leaving Bethel, Jacob and his clan moved on toward Ephrath. But Rachel went into labor while they were still some distance away. Her labor pains were intense. [17] After a very hard delivery, the midwife finally exclaimed, "Don't be afraid—you have another son!" [18] Rachel was about to die, but with her last breath she named the baby Benoni (which means "son of my sorrow"). The baby's father, however, called him Benjamin (which means "son of my right hand"). [19] So Rachel died and was buried on the way to Ephrath (that is, Bethlehem). [20] Jacob set up a stone monument over Rachel's grave, and it can be seen there to this day.

[21] Then Jacob* traveled on and camped beyond Migdal-eder. [22] While he was living there, Reuben had intercourse with Bilhah, his father's concubine, and Jacob soon heard about it.

These are the names of the twelve sons of Jacob:

[23] The sons of Leah were Reuben (Jacob's oldest son), Simeon, Levi, Judah, Issachar, and Zebulun.

[24] The sons of Rachel were Joseph and Benjamin.

[25] The sons of Bilhah, Rachel's servant, were Dan and Naphtali.

[26] The sons of Zilpah, Leah's servant, were Gad and Asher.

These are the names of the sons who were born to Jacob at Paddan-aram.

[27] So Jacob returned to his father, Isaac, in Mamre, which is near Kiriath-arba (now called Hebron), where Abraham and Isaac had both lived as foreigners. [28] Isaac lived for 180 years. [29] Then he breathed his last and died at a ripe old age, joining his ancestors in death. And his sons, Esau and Jacob, buried him.

36:1 THIS is the account of the descendants of Esau (also known as Edom). [2] Esau married two young women from Canaan: Adah, the daughter of Elon the Hittite; and Oholibamah, the daughter of Anah and granddaughter of Zibeon the Hivite. [3] He also married his cousin Basemath, who was the daughter of Ishmael and the sister of Nebaioth. [4] Adah gave birth to a son named Eliphaz for Esau. Basemath gave birth to a son named Reuel. [5] Oholibamah gave birth to sons named Jeush, Jalam, and Korah. All these sons were born to Esau in the land of Canaan.

[6] Esau took his wives, his children, and his entire household, along with his livestock and cattle—all the wealth he had acquired in the land of Canaan— and moved away from his brother, Jacob. [7] There was not enough land to support them both because of all the livestock and possessions they had acquired. [8] So Esau (also known as Edom) settled in the hill country of Seir.

⁹This is the account of Esau's descendants, the Edomites, who lived in the hill country of Seir.

¹⁰These are the names of Esau's sons: Eliphaz, the son of Esau's wife Adah; and Reuel, the son of Esau's wife Basemath.

¹¹The descendants of Eliphaz were Teman, Omar, Zepho, Gatam, and Kenaz. ¹²Timna, the concubine of Esau's son Eliphaz, gave birth to a son named Amalek. These are the descendants of Esau's wife Adah.

¹³The descendants of Reuel were Nahath, Zerah, Shammah, and Mizzah. These are the descendants of Esau's wife Basemath.

¹⁴Esau also had sons through Oholibamah, the daughter of Anah and granddaughter of Zibeon. Their names were Jeush, Jalam, and Korah.

¹⁵These are the descendants of Esau who became the leaders of various clans:

The descendants of Esau's oldest son, Eliphaz, became the leaders of the clans of Teman, Omar, Zepho, Kenaz, ¹⁶Korah, Gatam, and Amalek. These are the clan leaders in the land of Edom who descended from Eliphaz. All these were descendants of Esau's wife Adah.

¹⁷The descendants of Esau's son Reuel became the leaders of the clans of Nahath, Zerah, Shammah, and Mizzah. These are the clan leaders in the land of Edom who descended from Reuel. All these were descendants of Esau's wife Basemath.

¹⁸The descendants of Esau and his wife Oholibamah became the leaders of the clans of Jeush, Jalam, and Korah. These are the clan leaders who descended from Esau's wife Oholibamah, the daughter of Anah.

¹⁹These are the clans descended from Esau (also known as Edom), identified by their clan leaders.

²⁰These are the names of the tribes that descended from Seir the Horite. They lived in the land of Edom: Lotan, Shobal, Zibeon, Anah, ²¹Dishon, Ezer, and Dishan. These were the Horite clan leaders, the descendants of Seir, who lived in the land of Edom.

²²The descendants of Lotan were Hori and Heman. Lotan also had a sister named Timna.

²³The descendants of Shobal were Alvan, Manahath, Ebal, Shepho, and Onam.

²⁴The descendants of Zibeon were Aiah and Anah. (This is the Anah who discovered the hot springs in the wilderness while he was grazing his father's donkeys.)

²⁵The descendants of Anah were his son, Dishon, and his daughter, Oholibamah.

²⁶The descendants of Dishon* were Hemdan, Eshban, Ithran, and Keran.

²⁷The descendants of Ezer were Bilhan, Zaavan, and Akan.

²⁸The descendants of Dishan were Uz and Aran.

²⁹So these were the leaders of the Horite clans: Lotan, Shobal, Zibeon, Anah, ³⁰Dishon, Ezer, and Dishan. The Horite clans are named after their clan leaders, who lived in the land of Seir.

³¹These are the kings who ruled in the land of Edom before any king ruled over the Israelites*:

³²Bela son of Beor, who ruled in Edom from the city of Dinhabah.

³³After Bela died, Jobab son of Zerah from Bozrah became king in his place.

³⁴After Jobab died, Husham from the land of the Temanites became king in his place.

³⁵After Husham died, Hadad son of Bedad became king in his place and ruled from the city of Avith. He was the one who defeated the Midianites in the land of Moab.

³⁶After Hadad died, Samlah from the

city of Masrekah became king in his place.

[37] After Samlah died, Shaul from the city of Rehoboth-on-the-River became king in his place.

[38] After Shaul died, Baal-hanan son of Acbor became king in his place.

[39] After Baal-hanan son of Acbor died, Hadad* became king in his place and ruled from the city of Pau. Hadad's wife was Mehetabel, the daughter of Matred and granddaughter of Me-zahab.

[40] These are the names of the leaders of the clans descended from Esau, who lived in the places named for them: Timna, Alvah, Jetheth, [41] Oholibamah, Elah, Pinon, [42] Kenaz, Teman, Mibzar, [43] Magdiel, and Iram. These are the leaders of the clans of Edom, listed according to their settlements in the land they occupied. They all descended from Esau, the ancestor of the Edomites.

35:10 *Jacob* sounds like the Hebrew words for "heel" and "deceiver." *Israel* means "God fights."   35:21 Hebrew *Israel;* also in 35:22a. The names "Jacob" and "Israel" are often interchanged throughout the Old Testament, referring sometimes to the individual patriarch and sometimes to the nation.   36:26 Hebrew *Dishan,* a variant spelling of Dishon; compare 36:21, 28.   36:31 Or *before an Israelite king ruled over them.*   36:39 As in some Hebrew manuscripts, Samaritan Pentateuch, and Syriac version (see also 1 Chr 1:50); most Hebrew manuscripts read *Hadar.*

## MATTHEW 12:1-21

**A**t about that time Jesus was walking through some grainfields on the Sabbath. His disciples were hungry, so they began breaking off some heads of grain and eating them. [2] But some Pharisees saw them do it and protested, "Look, your disciples are breaking the law by harvesting grain on the Sabbath."

[3] Jesus said to them, "Haven't you read in the Scriptures what David did when he and his companions were hungry? [4] He went into the house of God, and they broke the law by eating the sacred loaves of bread that only the priests are allowed to eat. [5] And haven't you read in the law of Moses that the priests on duty in the Temple may work on the Sabbath? [6] **I tell you, there is one here who is even greater than the Temple! [7] But you would not have condemned my innocent disciples if you knew the meaning of this Scripture: 'I want you to show mercy, not offer sacrifices.'\* [8] For the Son of Man\* is Lord, even over the Sabbath!"**

[9] Then Jesus went over to their synagogue, [10] where he noticed a man with a deformed hand. The Pharisees asked Jesus, "Does the law permit a person to work by healing on the Sabbath?" (They were hoping he would say yes, so they could bring charges against him.)

[11] And he answered, "If you had a sheep that fell into a well on the Sabbath, wouldn't you work to pull it out? Of course you would. [12] And how much more valuable is a person than a sheep! Yes, the law permits a person to do good on the Sabbath."

[13] Then he said to the man, "Hold out your hand." So the man held out his hand, and it was restored, just like the other one! [14] Then the Pharisees called a meeting to plot how to kill Jesus.

[15] But Jesus knew what they were planning. So he left that area, and many people followed him. He healed all the sick among them, [16] but he warned them not to reveal who he was. [17] This fulfilled the prophecy of Isaiah concerning him:

[18] "Look at my Servant, whom
     I have chosen.
   He is my Beloved, who
     pleases me.
 I will put my Spirit upon him,
   and he will proclaim justice
     to the nations.
[19] He will not fight or shout
   or raise his voice in public.
[20] He will not crush the weakest
     reed
   or put out a flickering
     candle.
   Finally he will cause justice
     to be victorious.
[21] And his name will be the hope
   of all the world."*

12:7 Hos 6:6 (Greek version).   12:8 "Son of Man" is a title Jesus used for himself.   12:18-21 Isa 42:1-4 (Greek version for 42:4).

PSALM 15:1-5
*A psalm of David.*

¹ **W**ho may worship in your
    sanctuary, L ORD?
Who may enter your presence
    on your holy hill?
² Those who lead blameless lives and
    do what is right,
speaking the truth from sincere
    hearts.
³ Those who refuse to gossip
    or harm their neighbors
    or speak evil of their friends.
⁴ Those who despise flagrant sinners,
    and honor the faithful followers
    of the L ORD,
and keep their promises even
    when it hurts.
⁵ Those who lend money without
    charging interest,
and who cannot be bribed to lie
    about the innocent.
Such people will stand firm forever.

PROVERBS 3:21-26
**M**y child, don't lose sight of common
sense and discernment. Hang on to
them, for they will refresh your soul.
They are like jewels on a necklace. They
keep you safe on your way, and your feet
will not stumble. You can go to bed
without fear; you will lie down and sleep
soundly. You need not be afraid of sudden disaster or the destruction that
comes upon the wicked, for the L ORD is
your security. He will keep your foot
from being caught in a trap.

# JANUARY
# 18

GENESIS 37:1–38:30
**S**o Jacob settled again in the land of
Canaan, where his father had lived as a
foreigner.

²This is the account of Jacob and his
family. When Joseph was seventeen
years old, he often tended his father's
flocks. He worked for his half brothers,
the sons of his father's wives Bilhah and
Zilpah. But Joseph reported to his father some of the bad things his brothers
were doing.

³Jacob* loved Joseph more than any
of his other children because Joseph
had been born to him in his old age. So
one day Jacob had a special gift made
for Joseph—a beautiful robe.* ⁴But his
brothers hated Joseph because their father loved him more than the rest of
them. They couldn't say a kind word to
him.

⁵One night Joseph had a dream, and
when he told his brothers about it, they
hated him more than ever. ⁶"Listen to
this dream," he said. ⁷"We were out in
the field, tying up bundles of grain. Suddenly my bundle stood up, and your
bundles all gathered around and bowed
low before mine!"

⁸His brothers responded, "So you
think you will be our king, do you? Do
you actually think you will reign over
us?" And they hated him all the more
because of his dreams and the way he
talked about them.

⁹Soon Joseph had another dream,
and again he told his brothers about it.
"Listen, I have had another dream," he
said. "The sun, moon, and eleven stars
bowed low before me!"

¹⁰This time he told the dream to his
father as well as to his brothers, but
his father scolded him. "What kind
of dream is that?" he asked. "Will your
mother and I and your brothers actually come and bow to the ground before
you?" ¹¹But while his brothers were
jealous of Joseph, his father wondered
what the dreams meant.

¹²Soon after this, Joseph's brothers
went to pasture their father's flocks at
Shechem. ¹³When they had been gone
for some time, Jacob said to Joseph,
"Your brothers are pasturing the sheep
at Shechem. Get ready, and I will send
you to them."

"I'm ready to go," Joseph replied.

[14]"Go and see how your brothers and the flocks are getting along," Jacob said. "Then come back and bring me a report." So Jacob sent him on his way, and Joseph traveled to Shechem from their home in the valley of Hebron.

[15]When he arrived there, a man from the area noticed him wandering around the countryside. "What are you looking for?" he asked.

[16]"I'm looking for my brothers," Joseph replied. "Do you know where they are pasturing their sheep?"

[17]"Yes," the man told him. "They have moved on from here, but I heard them say, 'Let's go on to Dothan.'" So Joseph followed his brothers to Dothan and found them there.

[18]When Joseph's brothers saw him coming, they recognized him in the distance. As he approached, they made plans to kill him. [19]"Here comes the dreamer!" they said. [20]"Come on, let's kill him and throw him into one of these cisterns. We can tell our father, 'A wild animal has eaten him.' Then we'll see what becomes of his dreams!"

[21]But when Reuben heard of their scheme, he came to Joseph's rescue. "Let's not kill him," he said. [22]"Why should we shed any blood? Let's just throw him into this empty cistern here in the wilderness. Then he'll die without our laying a hand on him." Reuben was secretly planning to rescue Joseph and return him to his father.

[23]So when Joseph arrived, his brothers ripped off the beautiful robe he was wearing. [24]Then they grabbed him and threw him into the cistern. Now the cistern was empty; there was no water in it. [25]Then, just as they were sitting down to eat, they looked up and saw a caravan of camels in the distance coming toward them. It was a group of Ishmaelite traders taking a load of gum, balm, and aromatic resin from Gilead down to Egypt.

[26]Judah said to his brothers, "What will we gain by killing our brother? His blood would just give us a guilty conscience. [27]Instead of hurting him, let's sell him to those Ishmaelite traders. Af-

ter all, he is our brother—our own flesh and blood!" And his brothers agreed. [28]So when the Ishmaelites, who were Midianite traders, came by, Joseph's brothers pulled him out of the cistern and sold him to them for twenty pieces* of silver. And the traders took him to Egypt.

[29]Some time later, Reuben returned to get Joseph out of the cistern. When he discovered that Joseph was missing, he tore his clothes in grief. [30]Then he went back to his brothers and lamented, "The boy is gone! What will I do now?"

[31]Then the brothers killed a young goat and dipped Joseph's robe in its blood. [32]They sent the beautiful robe to their father with this message: "Look at what we found. Doesn't this robe belong to your son?"

[33]Their father recognized it immediately. "Yes," he said, "it is my son's robe. A wild animal must have eaten him. Joseph has clearly been torn to pieces!" [34]Then Jacob tore his clothes and dressed himself in burlap. He mourned deeply for his son for a long time. [35]His family all tried to comfort him, but he refused to be comforted. "I will go to my grave* mourning for my son," he would say, and then he would weep.

[36]Meanwhile, the Midianite traders* arrived in Egypt, where they sold Joseph to Potiphar, an officer of Pharaoh, the king of Egypt. Potiphar was captain of the palace guard.

[38:1]ABOUT this time, Judah left home and moved to Adullam, where he stayed with a man named Hirah. [2]There he saw a Canaanite woman, the daughter of Shua, and he married her. When he slept with her, [3]she became pregnant and gave birth to a son, and he named the boy Er. [4]Then she became pregnant again and gave birth to another son, and she named him Onan. [5]And when she gave birth to a third son, she named him Shelah. At the time of Shelah's birth, they were living at Kezib.

[6]In the course of time, Judah ar-

ranged for his firstborn son, Er, to marry a young woman named Tamar. [7] But Er was a wicked man in the LORD's sight, so the LORD took his life. [8] Then Judah said to Er's brother Onan, "Go and marry Tamar, as our law requires of the brother of a man who has died. You must produce an heir for your brother."

[9] But Onan was not willing to have a child who would not be his own heir. So whenever he had intercourse with his brother's wife, he spilled the semen on the ground. This prevented her from having a child who would belong to his brother. [10] But the LORD considered it evil for Onan to deny a child to his dead brother. So the LORD took Onan's life, too.

[11] Then Judah said to Tamar, his daughter-in-law, "Go back to your parents' home and remain a widow until my son Shelah is old enough to marry you." (But Judah didn't really intend to do this because he was afraid Shelah would also die, like his two brothers.) So Tamar went back to live in her father's home.

[12] Some years later Judah's wife died. After the time of mourning was over, Judah and his friend Hirah the Adullamite went up to Timnah to supervise the shearing of his sheep. [13] Someone told Tamar, "Look, your father-in-law is going up to Timnah to shear his sheep."

[14] Tamar was aware that Shelah had grown up, but no arrangements had been made for her to come and marry him. So she changed out of her widow's clothing and covered herself with a veil to disguise herself. Then she sat beside the road at the entrance to the village of Enaim, which is on the road to Timnah. [15] Judah noticed her and thought she was a prostitute, since she had covered her face. [16] So he stopped and propositioned her. "Let me have sex with you," he said, not realizing that she was his own daughter-in-law.

"How much will you pay to have sex with me?" Tamar asked.

[17] "I'll send you a young goat from my flock," Judah promised.

"But what will you give me to guarantee that you will send the goat?" she asked.

[18] "What kind of guarantee do you want?" he replied.

She answered, "Leave me your identification seal and its cord and the walking stick you are carrying." So Judah gave them to her. Then he had intercourse with her, and she became pregnant. [19] Afterward she went back home, took off her veil, and put on her widow's clothing as usual.

[20] Later Judah asked his friend Hirah the Adullamite to take the young goat to the woman and to pick up the things he had given her as his guarantee. But Hirah couldn't find her. [21] So he asked the men who lived there, "Where can I find the shrine prostitute who was sitting beside the road at the entrance to Enaim?"

"We've never had a shrine prostitute here," they replied.

[22] So Hirah returned to Judah and told him, "I couldn't find her anywhere, and the men of the village claim they've never had a shrine prostitute there."

[23] "Then let her keep the things I gave her," Judah said. "I sent the young goat as we agreed, but you couldn't find her. We'd be the laughingstock of the village if we went back again to look for her."

[24] About three months later, Judah was told, "Tamar, your daughter-in-law, has acted like a prostitute. And now, because of this, she's pregnant."

"Bring her out, and let her be burned!" Judah demanded.

[25] But as they were taking her out to kill her, she sent this message to her father-in-law: "The man who owns these things made me pregnant. Look closely. Whose seal and cord and walking stick are these?"

[26] Judah recognized them immediately and said, "She is more righteous than I am, because I didn't arrange for her to marry my son Shelah." And Judah never slept with Tamar again.

[27] When the time came for Tamar to give birth, it was discovered that she

was carrying twins. ²⁸While she was in labor, one of the babies reached out his hand. The midwife grabbed it and tied a scarlet string around the child's wrist, announcing, "This one came out first." ²⁹But then he pulled back his hand, and out came his brother! "What!" the midwife exclaimed. "How did you break out first?" So he was named Perez.* ³⁰Then the baby with the scarlet string on his wrist was born, and he was named Zerah.*

37:3a Hebrew *Israel;* also in 37:13. See note on 35:21.
37:3b Traditionally rendered *a coat of many colors.* The exact meaning of the Hebrew is uncertain.  37:28 Hebrew *20 shekels,* about 8 ounces or 228 grams in weight.
37:35 Hebrew *go down to Sheol.*  37:36 Hebrew *Medanites,* a variant spelling of *Midianites;* compare 37:28.
38:29 *Perez* means "breaking out."  38:30 *Zerah* means "scarlet" or "brightness."

## MATTHEW 12:22-45

Then a demon-possessed man, who was blind and couldn't speak, was brought to Jesus. He healed the man so that he could both speak and see. ²³The crowd was amazed and asked, "Could it be that Jesus is the Son of David, the Messiah?"

²⁴But when the Pharisees heard about the miracle, they said, "No wonder he can cast out demons. He gets his power from Satan,* the prince of demons."

²⁵Jesus knew their thoughts and replied, "Any kingdom divided by civil war is doomed. A town or family splintered by feuding will fall apart. ²⁶And if Satan is casting out Satan, he is divided and fighting against himself. His own kingdom will not survive. ²⁷And if I am empowered by Satan, what about your own exorcists? They cast out demons, too, so they will condemn you for what you have said. ²⁸But if I am casting out demons by the Spirit of God, then the Kingdom of God has arrived among you. ²⁹For who is powerful enough to enter the house of a strong man like Satan and plunder his goods? Only someone even stronger—someone who could tie him up and then plunder his house.

³⁰"Anyone who isn't with me opposes me, and anyone who isn't working with me is actually working against me.

³¹"Every sin and blasphemy can be forgiven—except blasphemy against the Holy Spirit, which will never be forgiven. ³²Anyone who speaks against the Son of Man can be forgiven, but anyone who speaks against the Holy Spirit will never be forgiven, either in this world or in the world to come.

³³"A tree is identified by its fruit. If a tree is good, its fruit will be good. If a tree is bad, its fruit will be bad. ³⁴You brood of snakes! How could evil men like you speak what is good and right? For whatever is in your heart determines what you say. ³⁵**A good person produces good things from the treasury of a good heart, and an evil person produces evil things from the treasury of an evil heart.** ³⁶And I tell you this, you must give an account on judgment day for every idle word you speak. ³⁷The words you say will either acquit you or condemn you."

³⁸One day some teachers of religious law and Pharisees came to Jesus and said, "Teacher, we want you to show us a miraculous sign to prove your authority."

³⁹But Jesus replied, "Only an evil, adulterous generation would demand a miraculous sign; but the only sign I will give them is the sign of the prophet Jonah. ⁴⁰For as Jonah was in the belly of the great fish for three days and three nights, so will the Son of Man be in the heart of the earth for three days and three nights.

⁴¹"The people of Nineveh will stand up against this generation on judgment day and condemn it, for they repented of their sins at the preaching of Jonah. Now someone greater than Jonah is here—but you refuse to repent. ⁴²The queen of Sheba* will also stand up against this generation on judgment day and condemn it, for she came from a distant land to hear the wisdom of Solomon. Now someone greater than Solomon is here—but you refuse to listen.

⁴³"When an evil* spirit leaves a per-

son, it goes into the desert, seeking rest but finding none. ⁴⁴Then it says, 'I will return to the person I came from.' So it returns and finds its former home empty, swept, and in order. ⁴⁵Then the spirit finds seven other spirits more evil than itself, and they all enter the person and live there. And so that person is worse off than before. That will be the experience of this evil generation."

12:24 Greek *Beelzeboul;* also in 12:27. Other manuscripts read *Beezeboul;* Latin version reads *Beelzebub.* 12:42 Greek *The queen of the south.* 12:43 Greek *unclean.*

## PSALM 16:1-11
*A psalm of David.*

¹ **K**eep me safe, O God,
   for I have come to you for refuge.

² I said to the LORD, "You are my Master!
   Every good thing I have comes from you."
³ The godly people in the land are my true heroes!
   I take pleasure in them!
⁴ Troubles multiply for those who chase after other gods.
   I will not take part in their sacrifices of blood
   or even speak the names of their gods.

⁵ LORD, you alone are my inheritance, my cup of blessing.
   You guard all that is mine.
⁶ The land you have given me is a pleasant land.
   What a wonderful inheritance!

⁷ I will bless the LORD who guides me;
   even at night my heart instructs me.
⁸ I know the LORD is always with me.
   I will not be shaken, for he is right beside me.

⁹ No wonder my heart is glad, and I rejoice.*
   My body rests in safety.
¹⁰ For you will not leave my soul among the dead*

or allow your holy one* to rot in the grave.
¹¹ You will show me the way of life, granting me the joy of your presence
   and the pleasures of living with you forever.*

16:9 Greek version reads *and my tongue shouts his praises.* Compare Acts 2:26.   16:10a Hebrew *in Sheol.* 16:10b Or *your Holy One.*   16:11 Greek version reads *You have shown me the way of life, / and you will fill me with the joy of your presence.* Compare Acts 2:28.

## PROVERBS 3:27-32
**D**o not withhold good from those who deserve it when it's in your power to help them. If you can help your neighbor now, don't say, "Come back tomorrow, and then I'll help you." □ Don't plot harm against your neighbor, for those who live nearby trust you. Don't pick a fight without reason, when no one has done you harm. □ Don't envy violent people or copy their ways. Such wicked people are detestable to the LORD, but he offers his friendship to the godly.

# JANUARY 19

GENESIS 39:1-41:16
**W**hen Joseph was taken to Egypt by the Ishmaelite traders, he was purchased by Potiphar, an Egyptian officer. Potiphar was captain of the guard for Pharaoh, the king of Egypt.

²The LORD was with Joseph, so he succeeded in everything he did as he served in the home of his Egyptian master. ³Potiphar noticed this and realized that the LORD was with Joseph, giving him success in everything he did. ⁴This pleased Potiphar, so he soon made Joseph his personal attendant. He put him in charge of his entire household and everything he owned. ⁵From the day Joseph was put in charge of his master's household and property, the LORD began

to bless Potiphar's household for Joseph's sake. All his household affairs ran smoothly, and his crops and livestock flourished. ⁶So Potiphar gave Joseph complete administrative responsibility over everything he owned. With Joseph there, he didn't worry about a thing—except what kind of food to eat!

Joseph was a very handsome and well-built young man, ⁷and Potiphar's wife soon began to look at him lustfully. "Come and sleep with me," she demanded.

⁸But Joseph refused. "Look," he told her, "my master trusts me with everything in his entire household. ⁹No one here has more authority than I do. He has held back nothing from me except you, because you are his wife. How could I do such a wicked thing? It would be a great sin against God."

¹⁰She kept putting pressure on Joseph day after day, but he refused to sleep with her, and he kept out of her way as much as possible. ¹¹One day, however, no one else was around when he went in to do his work. ¹²She came and grabbed him by his cloak, demanding, "Come on, sleep with me!" Joseph tore himself away, but he left his cloak in her hand as he ran from the house.

¹³When she saw that she was holding his cloak and he had fled, ¹⁴she called out to her servants. Soon all the men came running. "Look!" she said. "My husband has brought this Hebrew slave here to make fools of us! He came into my room to rape me, but I screamed. ¹⁵When he heard me scream, he ran outside and got away, but he left his cloak behind with me."

¹⁶She kept the cloak with her until her husband came home. ¹⁷Then she told him her story. "That Hebrew slave you've brought into our house tried to come in and fool around with me," she said. ¹⁸"But when I screamed, he ran outside, leaving his cloak with me!"

¹⁹Potiphar was furious when he heard his wife's story about how Joseph had treated her. ²⁰So he took Joseph and threw him into the prison where the king's prisoners were held, and there he remained. ²¹But the LORD was with Joseph in the prison and showed him his faithful love. And the LORD made Joseph a favorite with the prison warden. ²²Before long, the warden put Joseph in charge of all the other prisoners and over everything that happened in the prison. ²³The warden had no more worries, because Joseph took care of everything. The LORD was with him and caused everything he did to succeed.

⁴⁰:¹SOME time later, Pharaoh's chief cup-bearer and chief baker offended their royal master. ²Pharaoh became angry with these two officials, ³and he put them in the prison where Joseph was, in the palace of the captain of the guard. ⁴They remained in prison for quite some time, and the captain of the guard assigned them to Joseph, who looked after them.

⁵While they were in prison, Pharaoh's cup-bearer and baker each had a dream one night, and each dream had its own meaning. ⁶When Joseph saw them the next morning, he noticed that they both looked upset. ⁷"Why do you look so worried today?" he asked them.

⁸And they replied, "We both had dreams last night, but no one can tell us what they mean."

"Interpreting dreams is God's business," Joseph replied. "Go ahead and tell me your dreams."

⁹So the chief cup-bearer told Joseph his dream first. "In my dream," he said, "I saw a grapevine in front of me. ¹⁰The vine had three branches that began to bud and blossom, and soon it produced clusters of ripe grapes. ¹¹I was holding Pharaoh's wine cup in my hand, so I took a cluster of grapes and squeezed the juice into the cup. Then I placed the cup in Pharaoh's hand."

¹²"This is what the dream means," Joseph said. "The three branches represent three days. ¹³Within three days Pharaoh will lift you up and restore you

to your position as his chief cup-bearer. [14]And please remember me and do me a favor when things go well for you. Mention me to Pharaoh, so he might let me out of this place. [15]For I was kidnapped from my homeland, the land of the Hebrews, and now I'm here in prison, but I did nothing to deserve it."

[16]When the chief baker saw that Joseph had given the first dream such a positive interpretation, he said to Joseph, "I had a dream, too. In my dream there were three baskets of white pastries stacked on my head. [17]The top basket contained all kinds of pastries for Pharaoh, but the birds came and ate them from the basket on my head."

[18]"This is what the dream means," Joseph told him. "The three baskets also represent three days. [19]Three days from now Pharaoh will lift you up and impale your body on a pole. Then birds will come and peck away at your flesh."

[20]Pharaoh's birthday came three days later, and he prepared a banquet for all his officials and staff. He summoned* his chief cup-bearer and chief baker to join the other officials. [21]He then restored the chief cup-bearer to his former position, so he could again hand Pharaoh his cup. [22]But Pharaoh impaled the chief baker, just as Joseph had predicted when he interpreted his dream. [23]Pharaoh's chief cup-bearer, however, forgot all about Joseph, never giving him another thought.

[41:1]Two full years later, Pharaoh dreamed that he was standing on the bank of the Nile River. [2]In his dream he saw seven fat, healthy cows come up out of the river and begin grazing in the marsh grass. [3]Then he saw seven more cows come up behind them from the Nile, but these were scrawny and thin. These cows stood beside the fat cows on the riverbank. [4]Then the scrawny, thin cows ate the seven healthy, fat cows! At this point in the dream, Pharaoh woke up.

[5]But he fell asleep again and had a second dream. This time he saw seven heads of grain, plump and beautiful, growing on a single stalk. [6]Then seven more heads of grain appeared, but these were shriveled and withered by the east wind. [7]And these thin heads swallowed up the seven plump, well-formed heads! Then Pharaoh woke up again and realized it was a dream.

[8]The next morning Pharaoh was very disturbed by the dreams. So he called for all the magicians and wise men of Egypt. When Pharaoh told them his dreams, not one of them could tell him what they meant.

[9]Finally, the king's chief cup-bearer spoke up. "Today I have been reminded of my failure," he told Pharaoh. [10]"Some time ago, you were angry with the chief baker and me, and you imprisoned us in the palace of the captain of the guard. [11]One night the chief baker and I each had a dream, and each dream had its own meaning. [12]There was a young Hebrew man with us in the prison who was a slave of the captain of the guard. We told him our dreams, and he told us what each of our dreams meant. [13]And everything happened just as he had predicted. I was restored to my position as cup-bearer, and the chief baker was executed and impaled on a pole."

[14]Pharaoh sent for Joseph at once, and he was quickly brought from the prison. After he shaved and changed his clothes, he went in and stood before Pharaoh. [15]Then Pharaoh said to Joseph, "I had a dream last night, and no one here can tell me what it means. But I have heard that when you hear about a dream you can interpret it."

[16]"It is beyond my power to do this," Joseph replied. "But God can tell you what it means and set you at ease."

40:20 Hebrew *He lifted up the head of.*

MATTHEW 12:46–13:23

**A**s Jesus was speaking to the crowd, his mother and brothers stood outside, asking to speak to him. [47]Someone told Jesus, "Your mother and your brothers are outside, and they want to speak to you."*

[48]Jesus asked, "Who is my mother?

Who are my brothers?" [49]Then he pointed to his disciples and said, "Look, these are my mother and brothers. [50]Anyone who does the will of my Father in heaven is my brother and sister and mother!"

[13:1]LATER that same day Jesus left the house and sat beside the lake. [2]A large crowd soon gathered around him, so he got into a boat. Then he sat there and taught as the people stood on the shore. [3]He told many stories in the form of parables, such as this one:

"Listen! A farmer went out to plant some seeds. [4]As he scattered them across his field, some seeds fell on a footpath, and the birds came and ate them. [5]Other seeds fell on shallow soil with underlying rock. The seeds sprouted quickly because the soil was shallow. [6]But the plants soon wilted under the hot sun, and since they didn't have deep roots, they died. [7]Other seeds fell among thorns that grew up and choked out the tender plants. [8]Still other seeds fell on fertile soil, and they produced a crop that was thirty, sixty, and even a hundred times as much as had been planted! [9]Anyone with ears to hear should listen and understand."

[10]His disciples came and asked him, "Why do you use parables when you talk to the people?"

[11]He replied, "You are permitted to understand the secrets* of the Kingdom of Heaven, but others are not. [12]To those who listen to my teaching, more understanding will be given, and they will have an abundance of knowledge. But for those who are not listening, even what little understanding they have will be taken away from them. [13]That is why I use these parables,

For they look, but they don't really
  see.
They hear, but they don't really
  listen or understand.

[14]This fulfills the prophecy of Isaiah that says,

'When you hear what I say,
  you will not understand.
When you see what I do,
  you will not comprehend.
[15] For the hearts of these people are
  hardened,
  and their ears cannot hear,
and they have closed their
    eyes—
  so their eyes cannot see,
and their ears cannot hear,
  and their hearts cannot
    understand,
and they cannot turn to me
  and let me heal them.'*

[16]"But blessed are your eyes, because they see; and your ears, because they hear. [17]I tell you the truth, many prophets and righteous people longed to see what you see, but they didn't see it. And they longed to hear what you hear, but they didn't hear it.

[18]"Now listen to the explanation of the parable about the farmer planting seeds: [19]The seed that fell on the footpath represents those who hear the message about the Kingdom and don't understand it. Then the evil one comes and snatches away the seed that was planted in their hearts. [20]The seed on the rocky soil represents those who hear the message and immediately receive it with joy. [21]But since they don't have deep roots, they don't last long. They fall away as soon as they have problems or are persecuted for believing God's word. [22]The seed that fell among the thorns represents those who hear God's word, but all too quickly the message is crowded out by the worries of this life and the lure of wealth, so no fruit is produced. [23]The seed that fell on good soil represents those who truly hear and understand God's word and produce a harvest of thirty, sixty, or even a hundred times as much as had been planted!"

12:47 Some manuscripts do not include verse 47. Compare Mark 3:32 and Luke 8:20.   13:11 Greek *the mysteries.*   13:14-15 Isa 6:9-10 (Greek version).

## PSALM 17:1-15
*A prayer of David.*

1 O LORD, hear my plea for justice.
Listen to my cry for help.
Pay attention to my prayer,
for it comes from honest lips.
2 Declare me innocent,
for you see those who do right.

3 You have tested my thoughts and
examined my heart in the
night.
You have scrutinized me and
found nothing wrong.
I am determined not to sin in
what I say.
4 I have followed your commands,
which keep me from following
cruel and evil people.
5 My steps have stayed on your path;
I have not wavered from
following you.

6 I am praying to you because I know
you will answer, O God.
Bend down and listen as I pray.
7 Show me your unfailing love in
wonderful ways.
By your mighty power you rescue
those who seek refuge from their
enemies.
8 Guard me as you would guard your
own eyes.*
Hide me in the shadow of your
wings.
9 Protect me from wicked people who
attack me,
from murderous enemies who
surround me.
10 They are without pity.
Listen to their boasting!
11 They track me down and
surround me,
watching for the chance to throw
me to the ground.
12 They are like hungry lions, eager
to tear me apart—
like young lions hiding in
ambush.

13 Arise, O LORD!
Stand against them, and bring
them to their knees!

Rescue me from the wicked with
your sword!
14 By the power of your hand, O LORD,
destroy those who look to this
world for their reward.
But satisfy the hunger of your
treasured ones.
May their children have plenty,
leaving an inheritance for their
descendants.
15 Because I am righteous, I will see
you.
When I awake, I will see you face
to face and be satisfied.

17:8 Hebrew *as the pupil of your eye.*

## PROVERBS 3:33-35
The LORD curses the house of the
wicked, but he blesses the home of the
upright. □ The LORD mocks the mockers but is gracious to the humble.*
□ The wise inherit honor, but fools are
put to shame!

3:34 Greek version reads *The LORD opposes the proud /
but favors the humble.* Compare Jas 4:6; 1 Pet 5:5.

# JANUARY
# 20

## GENESIS 41:17–42:17
So Pharaoh told Joseph his dream. "In
my dream," he said, "I was standing on
the bank of the Nile River, 18 and I saw
seven fat, healthy cows come up out of
the river and begin grazing in the
marsh grass. 19 But then I saw seven sick-
looking cows, scrawny and thin, come
up after them. I've never seen such
sorry-looking animals in all the land of
Egypt. 20 These thin, scrawny cows ate
the seven fat cows. 21 But afterward you
wouldn't have known it, for they were
still as thin and scrawny as before!
Then I woke up.

22 "Then I fell asleep again, and I had
another dream. This time I saw seven
heads of grain, full and beautiful,

growing on a single stalk. [23] Then seven more heads of grain appeared, but these were blighted, shriveled, and withered by the east wind. [24] And the shriveled heads swallowed the seven healthy heads. I told these dreams to the magicians, but no one could tell me what they mean."

[25] Joseph responded, "Both of Pharaoh's dreams mean the same thing. God is telling Pharaoh in advance what he is about to do. [26] The seven healthy cows and the seven healthy heads of grain both represent seven years of prosperity. [27] The seven thin, scrawny cows that came up later and the seven thin heads of grain, withered by the east wind, represent seven years of famine.

[28] "This will happen just as I have described it, for God has revealed to Pharaoh in advance what he is about to do. [29] The next seven years will be a period of great prosperity throughout the land of Egypt. [30] But afterward there will be seven years of famine so great that all the prosperity will be forgotten in Egypt. Famine will destroy the land. [31] This famine will be so severe that even the memory of the good years will be erased. [32] As for having two similar dreams, it means that these events have been decreed by God, and he will soon make them happen.

[33] "Therefore, Pharaoh should find an intelligent and wise man and put him in charge of the entire land of Egypt. [34] Then Pharaoh should appoint supervisors over the land and let them collect one-fifth of all the crops during the seven good years. [35] Have them gather all the food produced in the good years that are just ahead and bring it to Pharaoh's storehouses. Store it away, and guard it so there will be food in the cities. [36] That way there will be enough to eat when the seven years of famine come to the land of Egypt. Otherwise this famine will destroy the land."

[37] Joseph's suggestions were well received by Pharaoh and his officials. [38] So Pharaoh asked his officials, "Can we find anyone else like this man so obviously filled with the spirit of God?"

[39] Then Pharaoh said to Joseph, "Since God has revealed the meaning of the dreams to you, clearly no one else is as intelligent or wise as you are. [40] You will be in charge of my court, and all my people will take orders from you. Only I, sitting on my throne, will have a rank higher than yours."

[41] Pharaoh said to Joseph, "I hereby put you in charge of the entire land of Egypt." [42] Then Pharaoh removed his signet ring from his hand and placed it on Joseph's finger. He dressed him in fine linen clothing and hung a gold chain around his neck. [43] Then he had Joseph ride in the chariot reserved for his second-in-command. And wherever Joseph went, the command was shouted, "Kneel down!" So Pharaoh put Joseph in charge of all Egypt. [44] And Pharaoh said to him, "I am Pharaoh, but no one will lift a hand or foot in the entire land of Egypt without your approval."

[45] Then Pharaoh gave Joseph a new Egyptian name, Zaphenath-paneah.* He also gave him a wife, whose name was Asenath. She was the daughter of Potiphera, the priest of On.* So Joseph took charge of the entire land of Egypt. [46] He was thirty years old when he began serving in the court of Pharaoh, the king of Egypt. And when Joseph left Pharaoh's presence, he inspected the entire land of Egypt.

[47] As predicted, for seven years the land produced bumper crops. [48] During those years, Joseph gathered all the crops grown in Egypt and stored the grain from the surrounding fields in the cities. [49] He piled up huge amounts of grain like sand on the seashore. Finally, he stopped keeping records because there was too much to measure.

[50] During this time, before the first of the famine years, two sons were born to Joseph and his wife, Asenath, the daughter of Potiphera, the priest of On. [51] Joseph named his older son Manasseh,* for he said, "God has made me forget all my troubles and everyone in my father's family." [52] Joseph named his second son Ephraim,* for he said, "God

has made me fruitful in this land of my grief."

⁵³At last the seven years of bumper crops throughout the land of Egypt came to an end. ⁵⁴Then the seven years of famine began, just as Joseph had predicted. The famine also struck all the surrounding countries, but throughout Egypt there was plenty of food. ⁵⁵Eventually, however, the famine spread throughout the land of Egypt as well. And when the people cried out to Pharaoh for food, he told them, "Go to Joseph, and do whatever he tells you." ⁵⁶So with severe famine everywhere, Joseph opened up the storehouses and distributed grain to the Egyptians, for the famine was severe throughout the land of Egypt. ⁵⁷And people from all around came to Egypt to buy grain from Joseph because the famine was severe throughout the world.

⁴²:¹WHEN Jacob heard that grain was available in Egypt, he said to his sons, "Why are you standing around looking at one another? ²I have heard there is grain in Egypt. Go down there, and buy enough grain to keep us alive. Otherwise we'll die."

³So Joseph's ten older brothers went down to Egypt to buy grain. ⁴But Jacob wouldn't let Joseph's younger brother, Benjamin, go with them, for fear some harm might come to him. ⁵So Jacob's* sons arrived in Egypt along with others to buy food, for the famine was in Canaan as well.

⁶Since Joseph was governor of all Egypt and in charge of selling grain to all the people, it was to him that his brothers came. When they arrived, they bowed before him with their faces to the ground. ⁷Joseph recognized his brothers instantly, but he pretended to be a stranger and spoke harshly to them. "Where are you from?" he demanded.

"From the land of Canaan," they replied. "We have come to buy food."

⁸Although Joseph recognized his brothers, they didn't recognize him. ⁹And he remembered the dreams he'd had about them many years before. He said to them, "You are spies! You have come to see how vulnerable our land has become."

¹⁰"No, my lord!" they exclaimed. "Your servants have simply come to buy food. ¹¹We are all brothers—members of the same family. We are honest men, sir! We are not spies!"

¹²"Yes, you are!" Joseph insisted. "You have come to see how vulnerable our land has become."

¹³"Sir," they said, "there are actually twelve of us. We, your servants, are all brothers, sons of a man living in the land of Canaan. Our youngest brother is back there with our father right now, and one of our brothers is no longer with us."

¹⁴But Joseph insisted, "As I said, you are spies! ¹⁵This is how I will test your story. I swear by the life of Pharaoh that you will never leave Egypt unless your youngest brother comes here! ¹⁶One of you must go and get your brother. I'll keep the rest of you here in prison. Then we'll find out whether or not your story is true. By the life of Pharaoh, if it turns out that you don't have a younger brother, then I'll know you are spies."

¹⁷So Joseph put them all in prison for three days.

41:45a *Zaphenath-paneah* probably means "God speaks and lives."    41:45b Greek version reads *of Heliopolis;* also in 41:50.    41:51 *Manasseh* sounds like a Hebrew term that means "causing to forget."    41:52 *Ephraim* sounds like a Hebrew term that means "fruitful."    42:5 Hebrew *Israel's.* See note on 35:21.

## MATTHEW 13:24-46

Here is another story Jesus told: "The Kingdom of Heaven is like a farmer who planted good seed in his field. ²⁵But that night as the workers slept, his enemy came and planted weeds among the wheat, then slipped away. ²⁶When the crop began to grow and produce grain, the weeds also grew.

²⁷"The farmer's workers went to him and said, 'Sir, the field where you planted that good seed is full of weeds! Where did they come from?'

²⁸" 'An enemy has done this!' the farmer exclaimed.

"'Should we pull out the weeds?' they asked.

29"'No,' he replied, 'you'll uproot the wheat if you do. 30Let both grow together until the harvest. Then I will tell the harvesters to sort out the weeds, tie them into bundles, and burn them, and to put the wheat in the barn.'"

31Here is another illustration Jesus used: "The Kingdom of Heaven is like a mustard seed planted in a field. 32It is the smallest of all seeds, but it becomes the largest of garden plants; it grows into a tree, and birds come and make nests in its branches."

33Jesus also used this illustration: "The Kingdom of Heaven is like the yeast a woman used in making bread. Even though she put only a little yeast in three measures of flour, it permeated every part of the dough."

34Jesus always used stories and illustrations like these when speaking to the crowds. In fact, he never spoke to them without using such parables. 35This fulfilled what God had spoken through the prophet:

"I will speak to you in parables.
I will explain things hidden since
the creation of the world.*"

36Then, leaving the crowds outside, Jesus went into the house. His disciples said, "Please explain to us the story of the weeds in the field."

37Jesus replied, "The Son of Man* is the farmer who plants the good seed. 38The field is the world, and the good seed represents the people of the Kingdom. The weeds are the people who belong to the evil one. 39The enemy who planted the weeds among the wheat is the devil. The harvest is the end of the world,* and the harvesters are the angels.

40"Just as the weeds are sorted out and burned in the fire, so it will be at the end of the world. 41The Son of Man will send his angels, and they will remove from his Kingdom everything that causes sin and all who do evil. 42And the angels will throw them into the fiery furnace, where there will be weeping and gnashing of teeth. 43Then the righteous will shine like the sun in their Father's Kingdom. Anyone with ears to hear should listen and understand!

44"The Kingdom of Heaven is like a treasure that a man discovered hidden in a field. In his excitement, he hid it again and sold everything he owned to get enough money to buy the field.

45"**Again, the Kingdom of Heaven is like a merchant on the lookout for choice pearls. 46When he discovered a pearl of great value, he sold everything he owned and bought it!**"

**13:35** Some manuscripts do not include *of the world.* Ps 78:2. **13:37** "Son of Man" is a title Jesus used for himself. **13:39** Or *the age;* also in 13:40, 49.

PSALM 18:1-15
*For the choir director: A psalm of David, the servant of the LORD. He sang this song to the LORD on the day the LORD rescued him from all his enemies and from Saul. He sang:*

1 I love you, LORD;
      you are my strength.
2 The LORD is my rock, my fortress,
      and my savior;
   my God is my rock, in whom
      I find protection.
   He is my shield, the power that
      saves me,
      and my place of safety.
3 I called on the LORD, who is worthy
      of praise,
   and he saved me from my
      enemies.

4 The ropes of death entangled me;
   floods of destruction swept
      over me.
5 The grave* wrapped its ropes
      around me;
   death laid a trap in my path.
6 But in my distress I cried out
      to the LORD;
   yes, I prayed to my God for help.
   He heard me from his sanctuary;
      my cry to him reached his ears.

7 Then the earth quaked and
      trembled.

The foundations of the
  mountains shook;
they quaked because of his
  anger.
8 Smoke poured from his nostrils;
  fierce flames leaped from
    his mouth.
  Glowing coals blazed forth
    from him.
9 He opened the heavens and came
    down;
  dark storm clouds were beneath
    his feet.
10 Mounted on a mighty angelic
    being,* he flew,
  soaring on the wings of the wind.
11 He shrouded himself in darkness,
    veiling his approach with dark
    rain clouds.
12 Thick clouds shielded the
    brightness around him
  and rained down hail and burning
    coals.*
13 The LORD thundered from heaven;
  the voice of the Most High
    resounded
  amid the hail and burning coals.
14 He shot his arrows and scattered
    his enemies;
  his lightning flashed, and they
    were greatly confused.
15 Then at your command, O LORD,
  at the blast of your breath,
  the bottom of the sea could be
    seen,
  and the foundations of the earth
    were laid bare.

**18:5** Hebrew *Sheol.*   **18:10** Hebrew *a cherub.*   **18:12** Or
*and lightning bolts;* also in 18:13.

## PROVERBS 4:1-6

**M**y children,* listen when your father
corrects you. Pay attention and learn
good judgment, for I am giving you good
guidance. Don't turn away from my instructions. For I, too, was once my father's son, tenderly loved as my mother's
only child. □ My father taught me, "Take
my words to heart. Follow my commands, and you will live. Get wisdom; develop good judgment. Don't forget my
words or turn away from them. Don't

turn your back on wisdom, for she will
protect you. Love her, and she will guard
you.

**4:1** Hebrew *My sons.*

# JANUARY 21

## GENESIS 42:18–43:34

**O**n the third day Joseph said to them, "I
am a God-fearing man. If you do as I say,
you will live. 19If you really are honest
men, choose one of your brothers to remain in prison. The rest of you may go
home with grain for your starving families. 20But you must bring your youngest
brother back to me. This will prove that
you are telling the truth, and you will
not die." To this they agreed.

21Speaking among themselves, they
said, "Clearly we are being punished because of what we did to Joseph long ago.
We saw his anguish when he pleaded
for his life, but we wouldn't listen.
That's why we're in this trouble."

22"Didn't I tell you not to sin against
the boy?" Reuben asked. "But you
wouldn't listen. And now we have to answer for his blood!"

23Of course, they didn't know that Joseph understood them, for he had been
speaking to them through an inter-
preter. 24Now he turned away from
them and began to weep. When he re-
gained his composure, he spoke to
them again. Then he chose Simeon
from among them and had him tied up
right before their eyes.

25Joseph then ordered his servants to
fill the men's sacks with grain, but he
also gave secret instructions to return
each brother's payment at the top of his
sack. He also gave them supplies for
their journey home. 26So the brothers
loaded their donkeys with the grain and
headed for home.

<sup>27</sup> But when they stopped for the night and one of them opened his sack to get grain for his donkey, he found his money in the top of his sack. <sup>28</sup>"Look!" he exclaimed to his brothers. "My money has been returned; it's here in my sack!" Then their hearts sank. Trembling, they said to each other, "What has God done to us?"

<sup>29</sup>When the brothers came to their father, Jacob, in the land of Canaan, they told him everything that had happened to them. <sup>30</sup>"The man who is governor of the land spoke very harshly to us," they told him. "He accused us of being spies scouting the land. <sup>31</sup>But we said, 'We are honest men, not spies. <sup>32</sup>We are twelve brothers, sons of one father. One brother is no longer with us, and the youngest is at home with our father in the land of Canaan.'

<sup>33</sup>"Then the man who is governor of the land told us, 'This is how I will find out if you are honest men. Leave one of your brothers here with me, and take grain for your starving families and go on home. <sup>34</sup>But you must bring your youngest brother back to me. Then I will know you are honest men and not spies. Then I will give you back your brother, and you may trade freely in the land.'"

<sup>35</sup>As they emptied out their sacks, there in each man's sack was the bag of money he had paid for the grain! The brothers and their father were terrified when they saw the bags of money. <sup>36</sup>Jacob exclaimed, "You are robbing me of my children! Joseph is gone! Simeon is gone! And now you want to take Benjamin, too. Everything is going against me!"

<sup>37</sup>Then Reuben said to his father, "You may kill my two sons if I don't bring Benjamin back to you. I'll be responsible for him, and I promise to bring him back."

<sup>38</sup>But Jacob replied, "My son will not go down with you. His brother Joseph is dead, and he is all I have left. If anything should happen to him on your journey, you would send this grieving, white-haired man to his grave.*"

<sup>43:1</sup>BUT the famine continued to ravage the land of Canaan. <sup>2</sup>When the grain they had brought from Egypt was almost gone, Jacob said to his sons, "Go back and buy us a little more food."

<sup>3</sup>But Judah said, "The man was serious when he warned us, 'You won't see my face again unless your brother is with you.' <sup>4</sup>If you send Benjamin with us, we will go down and buy more food. <sup>5</sup>But if you don't let Benjamin go, we won't go either. Remember, the man said, 'You won't see my face again unless your brother is with you.'"

<sup>6</sup>"Why were you so cruel to me?" Jacob* moaned. "Why did you tell him you had another brother?"

<sup>7</sup>"The man kept asking us questions about our family," they replied. "He asked, 'Is your father still alive? Do you have another brother?' So we answered his questions. How could we know he would say, 'Bring your brother down here'?"

<sup>8</sup>Judah said to his father, "Send the boy with me, and we will be on our way. Otherwise we will all die of starvation—and not only we, but you and our little ones. <sup>9</sup>I personally guarantee his safety. You may hold me responsible if I don't bring him back to you. Then let me bear the blame forever. <sup>10</sup>If we hadn't wasted all this time, we could have gone and returned twice by now."

<sup>11</sup>So their father, Jacob, finally said to them, "If it can't be avoided, then at least do this. Pack your bags with the best products of this land. Take them down to the man as gifts—balm, honey, gum, aromatic resin, pistachio nuts, and almonds. <sup>12</sup>Also take double the money that was put back in your sacks, as it was probably someone's mistake. <sup>13</sup>Then take your brother, and go back to the man. <sup>14</sup>May God Almighty* give you mercy as you go before the man, so that he will release Simeon and let Benjamin return. But if I must lose my children, so be it."

<sup>15</sup>So the men packed Jacob's gifts and double the money and headed off with Benjamin. They finally arrived in

Egypt and presented themselves to Joseph. [16]When Joseph saw Benjamin with them, he said to the manager of his household, "These men will eat with me this noon. Take them inside the palace. Then go slaughter an animal, and prepare a big feast." [17]So the man did as Joseph told him and took them into Joseph's palace.

[18]The brothers were terrified when they saw that they were being taken into Joseph's house. "It's because of the money someone put in our sacks last time we were here," they said. "He plans to pretend that we stole it. Then he will seize us, make us slaves, and take our donkeys."

[19]The brothers approached the manager of Joseph's household and spoke to him at the entrance to the palace. [20]"Sir," they said, "we came to Egypt once before to buy food. [21]But as we were returning home, we stopped for the night and opened our sacks. Then we discovered that each man's money—the exact amount paid—was in the top of his sack! Here it is; we have brought it back with us. [22]We also have additional money to buy more food. We have no idea who put our money in our sacks."

[23]"Relax. Don't be afraid," the household manager told them. "Your God, the God of your father, must have put this treasure into your sacks. I know I received your payment." Then he released Simeon and brought him out to them.

[24]The manager then led the men into Joseph's palace. He gave them water to wash their feet and provided food for their donkeys. [25]They were told they would be eating there, so they prepared their gifts for Joseph's arrival at noon.

[26]When Joseph came home, they gave him the gifts they had brought him, then bowed low to the ground before him. [27]After greeting them, he asked, "How is your father, the old man you spoke about? Is he still alive?"

[28]"Yes," they replied. "Our father, your servant, is alive and well." And they bowed low again.

[29]Then Joseph looked at his brother Benjamin, the son of his own mother. "Is this your youngest brother, the one you told me about?" Joseph asked. "May God be gracious to you, my son." [30]Then Joseph hurried from the room because he was overcome with emotion for his brother. He went into his private room, where he broke down and wept. [31]After washing his face, he came back out, keeping himself under control. Then he ordered, "Bring out the food!"

[32]The waiters served Joseph at his own table, and his brothers were served at a separate table. The Egyptians who ate with Joseph sat at their own table, because Egyptians despise Hebrews and refuse to eat with them. [33]Joseph told each of his brothers where to sit, and to their amazement, he seated them according to age, from oldest to youngest. [34]And Joseph filled their plates with food from his own table, giving Benjamin five times as much as he gave the others. So they feasted and drank freely with him.

42:38 Hebrew *to Sheol.*  43:6 Hebrew *Israel;* also in 43:11. See note on 35:21.  43:14 Hebrew *El-Shaddai.*

MATTHEW 13:47–14:12

"**A**gain, the Kingdom of Heaven is like a fishing net that was thrown into the water and caught fish of every kind. [48]When the net was full, they dragged it up onto the shore, sat down, and sorted the good fish into crates, but threw the bad ones away. [49]That is the way it will be at the end of the world. The angels will come and separate the wicked people from the righteous, [50]throwing the wicked into the fiery furnace, where there will be weeping and gnashing of teeth. [51]Do you understand all these things?"

"Yes," they said, "we do."

[52]Then he added, "Every teacher of religious law who becomes a disciple in the Kingdom of Heaven is like a homeowner who brings from his storeroom new gems of truth as well as old."

[53]When Jesus had finished telling these stories and illustrations, he left that part of the country. [54]He returned

to Nazareth, his hometown. When he taught there in the synagogue, everyone was amazed and said, "Where does he get this wisdom and the power to do miracles?" 55Then they scoffed, "He's just the carpenter's son, and we know Mary, his mother, and his brothers— James, Joseph,* Simon, and Judas. 56All his sisters live right here among us. Where did he learn all these things?" 57And they were deeply offended and refused to believe in him.

Then Jesus told them, "A prophet is honored everywhere except in his own hometown and among his own family." 58And so he did only a few miracles there because of their unbelief.

14:1WHEN Herod Antipas, the ruler of Galilee,* heard about Jesus, 2he said to his advisers, "This must be John the Baptist raised from the dead! That is why he can do such miracles."

3For Herod had arrested and imprisoned John as a favor to his wife Herodias (the former wife of Herod's brother Philip). 4John had been telling Herod, "It is against God's law for you to marry her." 5Herod wanted to kill John, but he was afraid of a riot, because all the people believed John was a prophet.

6But at a birthday party for Herod, Herodias's daughter performed a dance that greatly pleased him, 7so he promised with a vow to give her anything she wanted. 8At her mother's urging, the girl said, "I want the head of John the Baptist on a tray!" 9Then the king regretted what he had said; but because of the vow he had made in front of his guests, he issued the necessary orders. 10So John was beheaded in the prison, 11and his head was brought on a tray and given to the girl, who took it to her mother. 12Later, John's disciples came for his body and buried it. Then they went and told Jesus what had happened.

13:55 Other manuscripts read *Joses;* still others read *John.*
14:1 Greek *Herod the tetrarch.* Herod Antipas was a son of King Herod and was ruler over Galilee.

PSALM 18:16-36

He reached down from heaven and rescued me;
he drew me out of deep waters.
17 He rescued me from my powerful enemies,
from those who hated me and were too strong for me.
18 They attacked me at a moment when I was in distress,
but the LORD supported me.
19 He led me to a place of safety;
he rescued me because he delights in me.
20 The LORD rewarded me for doing right;
he restored me because of my innocence.
21 For I have kept the ways of the LORD;
I have not turned from my God to follow evil.
22 I have followed all his regulations;
I have never abandoned his decrees.
23 I am blameless before God;
I have kept myself from sin.
24 The LORD rewarded me for doing right.
He has seen my innocence.

25 To the faithful you show yourself faithful;
to those with integrity you show integrity.
26 To the pure you show yourself pure,
but to the wicked you show yourself hostile.
27 You rescue the humble,
but you humiliate the proud.
28 You light a lamp for me.
The LORD, my God, lights up my darkness.
29 In your strength I can crush an army;
with my God I can scale any wall.

30 God's way is perfect.
All the LORD's promises prove true.
He is a shield for all who look to him for protection.
31 For who is God except the LORD?
Who but our God is a solid rock?

[32] God arms me with strength,
and he makes my way perfect.
[33] He makes me as surefooted
as a deer,
enabling me to stand on
mountain heights.
[34] He trains my hands for battle;
he strengthens my arm to draw
a bronze bow.
[35] You have given me your shield
of victory.
Your right hand supports me;
your help has made me great.
[36] You have made a wide path for
my feet
to keep them from slipping.

PROVERBS 4:7-10

Getting wisdom is the wisest thing you can do! And whatever else you do, develop good judgment. If you prize wisdom, she will make you great. Embrace her, and she will honor you. She will place a lovely wreath on your head; she will present you with a beautiful crown. □ My child,* listen to me and do as I say, and you will have a long, good life.

4:10 Hebrew *My son;* also in 4:20.

# JANUARY
## 22

GENESIS 44:1-45:28

When his brothers were ready to leave, Joseph gave these instructions to his palace manager: "Fill each of their sacks with as much grain as they can carry, and put each man's money back into his sack. [2] Then put my personal silver cup at the top of the youngest brother's sack, along with the money for his grain." So the manager did as Joseph instructed him.

[3] The brothers were up at dawn and were sent on their journey with their loaded donkeys. [4] But when they had gone only a short distance and were barely out of the city, Joseph said to his palace manager, "Chase after them and stop them. When you catch up with them, ask them, 'Why have you repaid my kindness with such evil? [5] Why have you stolen my master's silver cup,* which he uses to predict the future? What a wicked thing you have done!'"

[6] When the palace manager caught up with the men, he spoke to them as he had been instructed.

[7] "What are you talking about?" the brothers responded. "We are your servants and would never do such a thing! [8] Didn't we return the money we found in our sacks? We brought it back all the way from the land of Canaan. Why would we steal silver or gold from your master's house? [9] If you find his cup with any one of us, let that man die. And all the rest of us, my lord, will be your slaves."

[10] "That's fair," the man replied. "But only the one who stole the cup will be my slave. The rest of you may go free."

[11] They all quickly took their sacks from the backs of their donkeys and opened them. [12] The palace manager searched the brothers' sacks, from the oldest to the youngest. And the cup was found in Benjamin's sack! [13] When the brothers saw this, they tore their clothing in despair. Then they loaded their donkeys again and returned to the city.

[14] Joseph was still in his palace when Judah and his brothers arrived, and they fell to the ground before him. [15] "What have you done?" Joseph demanded. "Don't you know that a man like me can predict the future?"

[16] Judah answered, "Oh, my lord, what can we say to you? How can we explain this? How can we prove our innocence? God is punishing us for our sins. My lord, we have all returned to be your slaves—all of us, not just our brother who had your cup in his sack."

[17] "No," Joseph said. "I would never do such a thing! Only the man who stole the cup will be my slave. The rest of you may go back to your father in peace."

[18] Then Judah stepped forward and said, "Please, my lord, let your servant

say just one word to you. Please, do not be angry with me, even though you are as powerful as Pharaoh himself.

¹⁹"My lord, previously you asked us, your servants, 'Do you have a father or a brother?' ²⁰And we responded, 'Yes, my lord, we have a father who is an old man, and his youngest son is a child of his old age. His full brother is dead, and he alone is left of his mother's children, and his father loves him very much.'

²¹"And you said to us, 'Bring him here so I can see him with my own eyes.' ²²But we said to you, 'My lord, the boy cannot leave his father, for his father would die.' ²³But you told us, 'Unless your youngest brother comes with you, you will never see my face again.'

²⁴"So we returned to your servant, our father, and told him what you had said. ²⁵Later, when he said, 'Go back again and buy us more food,' ²⁶we replied, 'We can't go unless you let our youngest brother go with us. We'll never get to see the man's face unless our youngest brother is with us.'

²⁷"Then my father said to us, 'As you know, my wife had two sons, ²⁸and one of them went away and never returned. Doubtless he was torn to pieces by some wild animal. I have never seen him since. ²⁹Now if you take his brother away from me, and any harm comes to him, you will send this grieving, white-haired man to his grave.*'

³⁰"And now, my lord, I cannot go back to my father without the boy. Our father's life is bound up in the boy's life. ³¹If he sees that the boy is not with us, our father will die. We, your servants, will indeed be responsible for sending that grieving, white-haired man to his grave. ³²My lord, I guaranteed to my father that I would take care of the boy. I told him, 'If I don't bring him back to you, I will bear the blame forever.'

³³"So please, my lord, let me stay here as a slave instead of the boy, and let the boy return with his brothers. ³⁴For how can I return to my father if the boy is not with me? I couldn't bear to see the anguish this would cause my father!"

⁴⁵:¹JOSEPH could stand it no longer. There were many people in the room, and he said to his attendants, "Out, all of you!" So he was alone with his brothers when he told them who he was. ²Then he broke down and wept. He wept so loudly the Egyptians could hear him, and word of it quickly carried to Pharaoh's palace.

³"I am Joseph!" he said to his brothers. "Is my father still alive?" But his brothers were speechless! They were stunned to realize that Joseph was standing there in front of them. ⁴"Please, come closer," he said to them. So they came closer. And he said again, "I am Joseph, your brother, whom you sold into slavery in Egypt. ⁵**But don't be upset, and don't be angry with yourselves for selling me to this place. It was God who sent me here ahead of you to preserve your lives.** ⁶This famine that has ravaged the land for two years will last five more years, and there will be neither plowing nor harvesting. ⁷God has sent me ahead of you to keep you and your families alive and to preserve many survivors.* ⁸So it was God who sent me here, not you! And he is the one who made me an adviser* to Pharaoh—the manager of his entire palace and the governor of all Egypt.

⁹"Now hurry back to my father and tell him, 'This is what your son Joseph says: God has made me master over all the land of Egypt. So come down to me immediately! ¹⁰You can live in the region of Goshen, where you can be near me with all your children and grandchildren, your flocks and herds, and everything you own. ¹¹I will take care of you there, for there are still five years of famine ahead of us. Otherwise you, your household, and all your animals will starve.'"

¹²Then Joseph added, "Look! You can see for yourselves, and so can my brother Benjamin, that I really am Joseph! ¹³Go tell my father of my honored position here in Egypt. Describe for him everything you have seen, and then bring my father here quickly." ¹⁴Weeping with

joy, he embraced Benjamin, and Benjamin did the same. [15]Then Joseph kissed each of his brothers and wept over them, and after that they began talking freely with him.

[16]The news soon reached Pharaoh's palace: "Joseph's brothers have arrived!" Pharaoh and his officials were all delighted to hear this.

[17]Pharaoh said to Joseph, "Tell your brothers, 'This is what you must do: Load your pack animals, and hurry back to the land of Canaan. [18]Then get your father and all of your families, and return here to me. I will give you the very best land in Egypt, and you will eat from the best that the land produces.'"

[19]Then Pharaoh said to Joseph, "Tell your brothers, 'Take wagons from the land of Egypt to carry your little children and your wives, and bring your father here. [20]Don't worry about your personal belongings, for the best of all the land of Egypt is yours.'"

[21]So the sons of Jacob* did as they were told. Joseph provided them with wagons, as Pharaoh had commanded, and he gave them supplies for the journey. [22]And he gave each of them new clothes—but to Benjamin he gave five changes of clothes and 300 pieces* of silver. [23]He also sent his father ten male donkeys loaded with the finest products of Egypt, and ten female donkeys loaded with grain and bread and other supplies he would need on his journey.

[24]So Joseph sent his brothers off, and as they left, he called after them, "Don't quarrel about all this along the way!"

[25]And they left Egypt and returned to their father, Jacob, in the land of Canaan.

[26]"Joseph is still alive!" they told him. "And he is governor of all the land of Egypt!" Jacob was stunned at the news—he couldn't believe it. [27]But when they repeated to Jacob everything Joseph had told them, and when he saw the wagons Joseph had sent to carry him, their father's spirits revived.

[28]Then Jacob exclaimed, "It must be true! My son Joseph is alive! I must go and see him before I die."

44:5 As in Greek version; Hebrew lacks this phrase. 44:29 Hebrew *to Sheol;* also in 44:31. 45:7 Or *and to save you with an extraordinary rescue.* The meaning of the Hebrew is uncertain. 45:8 Hebrew *a father.* 45:21 Hebrew *Israel;* also in 45:28. See note on 35:21. 45:22 Hebrew *300 shekels,* about 7.5 pounds or 3.4 kilograms in weight.

## MATTHEW 14:13-36

**A**s soon as Jesus heard the news, he left in a boat to a remote area to be alone. But the crowds heard where he was headed and followed on foot from many towns. [14]Jesus saw the huge crowd as he stepped from the boat, and he had compassion on them and healed their sick.

[15]That evening the disciples came to him and said, "This is a remote place, and it's already getting late. Send the crowds away so they can go to the villages and buy food for themselves."

[16]But Jesus said, "That isn't necessary—you feed them."

[17]"But we have only five loaves of bread and two fish!" they answered.

[18]"Bring them here," he said. [19]Then he told the people to sit down on the grass. Jesus took the five loaves and two fish, looked up toward heaven, and blessed them. Then, breaking the loaves into pieces, he gave the bread to the disciples, who distributed it to the people. [20]They all ate as much as they wanted, and afterward, the disciples picked up twelve baskets of leftovers. [21]About 5,000 men were fed that day, in addition to all the women and children!

[22]Immediately after this, Jesus insisted that his disciples get back into the boat and cross to the other side of the lake, while he sent the people home. [23]After sending them home, he went up into the hills by himself to pray. Night fell while he was there alone.

[24]Meanwhile, the disciples were in trouble far away from land, for a strong wind had risen, and they were fighting heavy waves. [25]About three o'clock in the morning* Jesus came toward them, walking on the water. [26]When the disciples saw him walking on the water, they

were terrified. In their fear, they cried out, "It's a ghost!"

27 But Jesus spoke to them at once. "Don't be afraid," he said. "Take courage. I am here!*"

28 Then Peter called to him, "Lord, if it's really you, tell me to come to you, walking on the water."

29 "Yes, come," Jesus said.

So Peter went over the side of the boat and walked on the water toward Jesus. 30 But when he saw the strong* wind and the waves, he was terrified and began to sink. "Save me, Lord!" he shouted.

31 Jesus immediately reached out and grabbed him. "You have so little faith," Jesus said. "Why did you doubt me?"

32 When they climbed back into the boat, the wind stopped. 33 Then the disciples worshiped him. "You really are the Son of God!" they exclaimed.

34 After they had crossed the lake, they landed at Gennesaret. 35 When the people recognized Jesus, the news of his arrival spread quickly throughout the whole area, and soon people were bringing all their sick to be healed. 36 They begged him to let the sick touch at least the fringe of his robe, and all who touched him were healed.

**14:25** Greek *In the fourth watch of the night.*   **14:27** Or *The 'I AM' is here;* Greek reads *I am.* See Exod 3:14. **14:30** Some manuscripts do not include *strong.*

PSALM 18:37-50

I chased my enemies and caught them;
    I did not stop until they were conquered.
38 I struck them down so they could not get up;
    they fell beneath my feet.
39 You have armed me with strength for the battle;
    you have subdued my enemies under my feet.
40 You placed my foot on their necks.
    I have destroyed all who hated me.
41 They called for help, but no one came to their rescue.

They even cried to the LORD, but he refused to answer.
42 I ground them as fine as dust in the wind.
    I swept them into the gutter like dirt.
43 You gave me victory over my accusers.
    You appointed me ruler over nations;
    people I don't even know now serve me.
44 As soon as they hear of me, they submit;
    foreign nations cringe before me.
45 They all lose their courage
    and come trembling from their strongholds.

46 The LORD lives! Praise to my Rock! May the God of my salvation be exalted!
47 He is the God who pays back those who harm me;
    he subdues the nations under me
48 and rescues me from my enemies.
    You hold me safe beyond the reach of my enemies;
    you save me from violent opponents.
49 For this, O LORD, I will praise you among the nations;
    I will sing praises to your name.
50 You give great victories to your king;
    you show unfailing love to your anointed,
    to David and all his descendants forever.

PROVERBS 4:11-13

I will teach you wisdom's ways and lead you in straight paths. When you walk, you won't be held back; when you run, you won't stumble. Take hold of my instructions; don't let them go. Guard them, for they are the key to life.

# JANUARY
# 23

GENESIS 46:1–47:31

**S**o Jacob* set out for Egypt with all his possessions. And when he came to Beersheba, he offered sacrifices to the God of his father, Isaac. ²During the night God spoke to him in a vision. "Jacob! Jacob!" he called.

"Here I am," Jacob replied.

³"I am God,* the God of your father," the voice said. "Do not be afraid to go down to Egypt, for there I will make your family into a great nation. ⁴I will go with you down to Egypt, and I will bring you back again. But you will die in Egypt with Joseph attending to you."

⁵So Jacob left Beersheba, and his sons took him to Egypt. They carried him and their little ones and their wives in the wagons Pharaoh had provided for them. ⁶They also took all their livestock and all the personal belongings they had acquired in the land of Canaan. So Jacob and his entire family went to Egypt—⁷sons and grandsons, daughters and granddaughters—all his descendants.

⁸These are the names of the descendants of Israel—the sons of Jacob—who went to Egypt:

Reuben was Jacob's oldest son. ⁹The sons of Reuben were Hanoch, Pallu, Hezron, and Carmi.

¹⁰The sons of Simeon were Jemuel, Jamin, Ohad, Jakin, Zohar, and Shaul. (Shaul's mother was a Canaanite woman.)

¹¹The sons of Levi were Gershon, Kohath, and Merari.

¹²The sons of Judah were Er, Onan, Shelah, Perez, and Zerah (though Er and Onan had died in the land of Canaan). The sons of Perez were Hezron and Hamul.

¹³The sons of Issachar were Tola, Puah,* Jashub,* and Shimron.

¹⁴The sons of Zebulun were Sered, Elon, and Jahleel.

¹⁵These were the sons of Leah and Jacob who were born in Paddan-aram, in addition to their daughter, Dinah. The number of Jacob's descendants (male and female) through Leah was thirty-three.

¹⁶The sons of Gad were Zephon,* Haggi, Shuni, Ezbon, Eri, Arodi, and Areli.

¹⁷The sons of Asher were Imnah, Ishvah, Ishvi, and Beriah. Their sister was Serah. Beriah's sons were Heber and Malkiel.

¹⁸These were the sons of Zilpah, the servant given to Leah by her father, Laban. The number of Jacob's descendants through Zilpah was sixteen.

¹⁹The sons of Jacob's wife Rachel were Joseph and Benjamin.

²⁰Joseph's sons, born in the land of Egypt, were Manasseh and Ephraim. Their mother was Asenath, daughter of Potiphera, the priest of On.*

²¹Benjamin's sons were Bela, Beker, Ashbel, Gera, Naaman, Ehi, Rosh, Muppim, Huppim, and Ard.

²²These were the sons of Rachel and Jacob. The number of Jacob's descendants through Rachel was fourteen.

²³The son of Dan was Hushim.

²⁴The sons of Naphtali were Jahzeel, Guni, Jezer, and Shillem.

²⁵These were the sons of Bilhah, the servant given to Rachel by her father, Laban. The number of Jacob's descendants through Bilhah was seven.

²⁶The total number of Jacob's direct descendants who went with him to Egypt, not counting his sons' wives, was sixty-six. ²⁷In addition, Joseph had two sons* who were born in Egypt. So altogether, there were seventy* members of Jacob's family in the land of Egypt.

²⁸As they neared their destination, Jacob sent Judah ahead to meet Joseph

and get directions to the region of Goshen. And when they finally arrived there, 29Joseph prepared his chariot and traveled to Goshen to meet his father, Jacob. When Joseph arrived, he embraced his father and wept, holding him for a long time. 30Finally, Jacob said to Joseph, "Now I am ready to die, since I have seen your face again and know you are still alive."

31And Joseph said to his brothers and to his father's entire family, "I will go to Pharaoh and tell him, 'My brothers and my father's entire family have come to me from the land of Canaan. 32These men are shepherds, and they raise livestock. They have brought with them their flocks and herds and everything they own.'"

33Then he said, "When Pharaoh calls for you and asks you about your occupation, 34you must tell him, 'We, your servants, have raised livestock all our lives, as our ancestors have always done.' When you tell him this, he will let you live here in the region of Goshen, for the Egyptians despise shepherds."

47:1THEN Joseph went to see Pharaoh and told him, "My father and my brothers have arrived from the land of Canaan. They have come with all their flocks and herds and possessions, and they are now in the region of Goshen."

2Joseph took five of his brothers with him and presented them to Pharaoh. 3And Pharaoh asked the brothers, "What is your occupation?"

They replied, "We, your servants, are shepherds, just like our ancestors. 4We have come to live here in Egypt for a while, for there is no pasture for our flocks in Canaan. The famine is very severe there. So please, we request permission to live in the region of Goshen."

5Then Pharaoh said to Joseph, "Now that your father and brothers have joined you here, 6choose any place in the entire land of Egypt for them to live. Give them the best land of Egypt. Let them live in the region of Goshen. And if any of them have special skills, put them in charge of my livestock, too."

7Then Joseph brought in his father, Jacob, and presented him to Pharaoh. And Jacob blessed Pharaoh.

8"How old are you?" Pharaoh asked him.

9Jacob replied, "I have traveled this earth for 130 hard years. But my life has been short compared to the lives of my ancestors." 10Then Jacob blessed Pharaoh again before leaving his court.

11So Joseph assigned the best land of Egypt—the region of Rameses—to his father and his brothers, and he settled them there, just as Pharaoh had commanded. 12And Joseph provided food for his father and his brothers in amounts appropriate to the number of their dependents, including the smallest children.

13Meanwhile, the famine became so severe that all the food was used up, and people were starving throughout the lands of Egypt and Canaan. 14By selling grain to the people, Joseph eventually collected all the money in Egypt and Canaan, and he put the money in Pharaoh's treasury. 15When the people of Egypt and Canaan ran out of money, all the Egyptians came to Joseph. "Our money is gone!" they cried. "But please give us food, or we will die before your very eyes!"

16Joseph replied, "Since your money is gone, bring me your livestock. I will give you food in exchange for your livestock." 17So they brought their livestock to Joseph in exchange for food. In exchange for their horses, flocks of sheep and goats, herds of cattle, and donkeys, Joseph provided them with food for another year.

18But that year ended, and the next year they came again and said, "We cannot hide the truth from you, my lord. Our money is gone, and all our livestock and cattle are yours. We have nothing left to give but our bodies and our land. 19Why should we die before your very eyes? Buy us and our land in exchange for food; we offer our land and ourselves as slaves for Pharaoh. Just give us grain so we may live and not die, and so the land does not become empty and desolate."

<sup>20</sup>So Joseph bought all the land of Egypt for Pharaoh. All the Egyptians sold him their fields because the famine was so severe, and soon all the land belonged to Pharaoh. <sup>21</sup>As for the people, he made them all slaves,* from one end of Egypt to the other. <sup>22</sup>The only land he did not buy was the land belonging to the priests. They received an allotment of food directly from Pharaoh, so they didn't need to sell their land.

<sup>23</sup>Then Joseph said to the people, "Look, today I have bought you and your land for Pharaoh. I will provide you with seed so you can plant the fields. <sup>24</sup>Then when you harvest it, one-fifth of your crop will belong to Pharaoh. You may keep the remaining four-fifths as seed for your fields and as food for you, your households, and your little ones."

<sup>25</sup>"You have saved our lives!" they exclaimed. "May it please you, my lord, to let us be Pharaoh's servants." <sup>26</sup>Joseph then issued a decree still in effect in the land of Egypt, that Pharaoh should receive one-fifth of all the crops grown on his land. Only the land belonging to the priests was not given to Pharaoh.

<sup>27</sup>Meanwhile, the people of Israel settled in the region of Goshen in Egypt. There they acquired property, and they were fruitful, and their population grew rapidly. <sup>28</sup>Jacob lived for seventeen years after his arrival in Egypt, so he lived 147 years in all.

<sup>29</sup>As the time of his death drew near, Jacob* called for his son Joseph and said to him, "Please do me this favor. Put your hand under my thigh and swear that you will treat me with unfailing love by honoring this last request: Do not bury me in Egypt. <sup>30</sup>When I die, please take my body out of Egypt and bury me with my ancestors."

So Joseph promised, "I will do as you ask."

<sup>31</sup>"Swear that you will do it," Jacob in-

sisted. So Joseph gave his oath, and Jacob bowed humbly at the head of his bed.*

**46:1** Hebrew *Israel;* also in 46:29, 30. See note on 35:21.
**46:3** Hebrew *I am El.*    **46:13a** As in Syriac version and Samaritan Pentateuch (see also 1 Chr 7:1); Hebrew reads *Puvah.*    **46:13b** As in some Greek manuscripts and Samaritan Pentateuch (see also Num 26:24; 1 Chr 7:1); Hebrew reads *Iob.*    **46:16** As in Greek version and Samaritan Pentateuch (see also Num 26:15); Hebrew reads *Ziphion.*    **46:20** Greek version reads *of Heliopolis.*
**46:27a** Greek version reads *nine sons,* probably including Joseph's grandsons through Ephraim and Manasseh (see 1 Chr 7:14-20).    **46:27b** Greek version reads *seventy-five;* see note on Exod 1:5.    **47:21** As in Greek version and Samaritan Pentateuch; Hebrew reads *he moved them all into the towns.*    **47:29** Hebrew *Israel;* also in 47:31b. See note on 35:21.    **47:31** Greek version reads *and Israel bowed in worship as he leaned on his staff.* Compare Heb 11:21.

## MATTHEW 15:1-28

**S**ome Pharisees and teachers of religious law now arrived from Jerusalem to see Jesus. <sup>2</sup>"Why do your disciples disobey our age-old tradition?" they demanded. "They ignore our tradition of ceremonial hand washing before they eat."

<sup>3</sup>Jesus replied, "And why do you, by your traditions, violate the direct commandments of God? <sup>4</sup>For instance, God says, 'Honor your father and mother,'* and 'Anyone who speaks disrespectfully of father or mother must be put to death.'* <sup>5</sup>But you say it is all right for people to say to their parents, 'Sorry, I can't help you. For I have vowed to give to God what I would have given to you.' <sup>6</sup>In this way, you say they don't need to honor their parents.* And so you cancel the word of God for the sake of your own tradition. <sup>7</sup>You hypocrites! Isaiah was right when he prophesied about you, for he wrote,

<sup>8</sup> 'These people honor me with their
       lips,
    but their hearts are far from me.
<sup>9</sup> Their worship is a farce,
    for they teach man-made ideas
       as commands from God.'*"

<sup>10</sup>Then Jesus called to the crowd to come and hear. "Listen," he said, "and try to understand. <sup>11</sup>It's not what goes into your mouth that defiles you; you are defiled by the words that come out of your mouth."

<sup>12</sup>Then the disciples came to him and

asked, "Do you realize you offended the Pharisees by what you just said?"

¹³Jesus replied, "Every plant not planted by my heavenly Father will be uprooted, ¹⁴so ignore them. They are blind guides leading the blind, and if one blind person guides another, they will both fall into a ditch."

¹⁵Then Peter said to Jesus, "Explain to us the parable that says people aren't defiled by what they eat."

¹⁶"Don't you understand yet?" Jesus asked. ¹⁷"Anything you eat passes through the stomach and then goes into the sewer. ¹⁸But the words you speak come from the heart—that's what defiles you. ¹⁹For from the heart come evil thoughts, murder, adultery, all sexual immorality, theft, lying, and slander. ²⁰These are what defile you. Eating with unwashed hands will never defile you."

²¹Then Jesus left Galilee and went north to the region of Tyre and Sidon. ²²A Gentile* woman who lived there came to him, pleading, "Have mercy on me, O Lord, Son of David! For my daughter is possessed by a demon that torments her severely."

²³But Jesus gave her no reply, not even a word. Then his disciples urged him to send her away. "Tell her to go away," they said. "She is bothering us with all her begging."

²⁴Then Jesus said to the woman, "I was sent only to help God's lost sheep— the people of Israel."

²⁵But she came and worshiped him, pleading again, "Lord, help me!"

²⁶Jesus responded, "It isn't right to take food from the children and throw it to the dogs."

²⁷She replied, "That's true, Lord, but even dogs are allowed to eat the scraps that fall beneath their master's table."

²⁸"Dear woman," Jesus said to her, "your faith is great. Your request is granted." And her daughter was instantly healed.

15:4a Exod 20:12; Deut 5:16.   15:4b Exod 21:17 (Greek version); Lev 20:9 (Greek version).   15:6 Greek *their father;* other manuscripts read *their father or their mother.* 15:8-9 Isa 29:13 (Greek version).   15:22 Greek *Canaanite.*

## PSALM 19:1-14
*For the choir director: A psalm of David.*

¹ The heavens proclaim the glory of God.
   The skies display his craftsmanship.
² Day after day they continue to speak;
   night after night they make him known.
³ They speak without a sound or word;
   their voice is never heard.*
⁴ Yet their message has gone throughout the earth,
   and their words to all the world.

God has made a home in the heavens for the sun.
⁵ It bursts forth like a radiant bridegroom after his wedding.
   It rejoices like a great athlete eager to run the race.
⁶ The sun rises at one end of the heavens
   and follows its course to the other end.
   Nothing can hide from its heat.

⁷ The instructions of the LORD are perfect,
   reviving the soul.
   The decrees of the LORD are trustworthy,
   making wise the simple.
⁸ The commandments of the LORD are right,
   bringing joy to the heart.
   The commands of the LORD are clear,
   giving insight for living.
⁹ Reverence for the LORD is pure,
   lasting forever.
   The laws of the LORD are true;
   each one is fair.
¹⁰ They are more desirable than gold,
   even the finest gold.
   They are sweeter than honey,
   even honey dripping from the comb.
¹¹ They are a warning to your servant,
   a great reward for those who obey them.

<sup>12</sup> How can I know all the sins lurking
        in my heart?
   Cleanse me from these hidden
        faults.
<sup>13</sup> Keep your servant from deliberate
        sins!
   Don't let them control me.
   Then I will be free of guilt
        and innocent of great sin.

**<sup>14</sup> May the words of my mouth
        and the meditation of my heart
   be pleasing to you,
        O L<small>ORD</small>, my rock and my
        redeemer.**

**19:3** Or *There is no speech or language where their voice is
not heard.*

PROVERBS 4:14-19

Don't do as the wicked do, and don't
follow the path of evildoers. Don't even
think about it; don't go that way. Turn
away and keep moving. For evil people
can't sleep until they've done their evil
deed for the day. They can't rest until
they've caused someone to stumble.
They eat the food of wickedness and
drink the wine of violence! □ The way
of the righteous is like the first gleam
of dawn, which shines ever brighter
until the full light of day. But the way of
the wicked is like total darkness. They
have no idea what they are stumbling
over.

# JANUARY
# 24

GENESIS 48:1–49:33

One day not long after this, word came
to Joseph, "Your father is failing rapidly." So Joseph went to visit his father,
and he took with him his two sons,
Manasseh and Ephraim.

<sup>2</sup> When Joseph arrived, Jacob was
told, "Your son Joseph has come to see
you." So Jacob* gathered his strength
and sat up in his bed.

<sup>3</sup> Jacob said to Joseph, "God Almighty*
appeared to me at Luz in the land of
Canaan and blessed me. <sup>4</sup> He said to me,
'I will make you fruitful, and I will multiply your descendants. I will make you
a multitude of nations. And I will give
this land of Canaan to your descendants
after you as an everlasting possession.'

<sup>5</sup> "Now I am claiming as my own sons
these two boys of yours, Ephraim and
Manasseh, who were born here in the
land of Egypt before I arrived. They
will be my sons, just as Reuben and
Simeon are. <sup>6</sup> But any children born to
you in the future will be your own, and
they will inherit land within the territories of their brothers Ephraim and
Manasseh.

<sup>7</sup> "Long ago, as I was returning from
Paddan-aram, Rachel died in the land of
Canaan. We were still on the way, some
distance from Ephrath (that is, Bethlehem). So with great sorrow I buried her
there beside the road to Ephrath."

<sup>8</sup> Then Jacob looked over at the two
boys. "Are these your sons?" he asked.

<sup>9</sup> "Yes," Joseph told him, "these are the
sons God has given me here in Egypt."

And Jacob said, "Bring them closer to
me, so I can bless them."

<sup>10</sup> Jacob was half blind because of his
age and could hardly see. So Joseph
brought the boys close to him, and
Jacob kissed and embraced them.
<sup>11</sup> Then Jacob said to Joseph, "I never
thought I would see your face again,
but now God has let me see your children, too!"

<sup>12</sup> Joseph moved the boys, who were at
their grandfather's knees, and he bowed
with his face to the ground. <sup>13</sup> Then he
positioned the boys in front of Jacob.
With his right hand he directed Ephraim
toward Jacob's left hand, and with his
left hand he put Manasseh at Jacob's
right hand. <sup>14</sup> But Jacob crossed his arms
as he reached out to lay his hands on
the boys' heads. He put his right hand on
the head of Ephraim, though he was the
younger boy, and his left hand on the

head of Manasseh, though he was the firstborn. ¹⁵Then he blessed Joseph and said,

"May the God before whom my
    grandfather Abraham
and my father, Isaac, walked—
the God who has been my
    shepherd
all my life, to this very day,
¹⁶ the Angel who has redeemed me
    from all harm—
may he bless these boys.
May they preserve my name
    and the names of Abraham and
    Isaac.
And may their descendants multiply
    greatly
    throughout the earth."

¹⁷But Joseph was upset when he saw that his father placed his right hand on Ephraim's head. So Joseph lifted it to move it from Ephraim's head to Manasseh's head. ¹⁸"No, my father," he said. "This one is the firstborn. Put your right hand on his head."

¹⁹But his father refused. "I know, my son; I know," he replied. "Manasseh will also become a great people, but his younger brother will become even greater. And his descendants will become a multitude of nations."

²⁰So Jacob blessed the boys that day with this blessing: "The people of Israel will use your names when they give a blessing. They will say, 'May God make you as prosperous as Ephraim and Manasseh.'" In this way, Jacob put Ephraim ahead of Manasseh.

²¹Then Jacob said to Joseph, "Look, I am about to die, but God will be with you and will take you back to Canaan, the land of your ancestors. ²²And beyond what I have given your brothers, I am giving you an extra portion of the land* that I took from the Amorites with my sword and bow."

⁴⁹:¹THEN Jacob called together all his sons and said, "Gather around me, and I will tell you what will happen to each of you in the days to come.

² "Come and listen, you sons of Jacob;
    listen to Israel, your father.

³ "Reuben, you are my firstborn, my
    strength,
    the child of my vigorous youth.
    You are first in rank and first in
    power.
⁴ But you are as unruly as a flood,
    and you will be first no longer.
For you went to bed with my wife;
    you defiled my marriage couch.

⁵ "Simeon and Levi are two of a kind;
    their weapons are instruments of
    violence.
⁶ May I never join in their meetings;
    may I never be a party to their
    plans.
For in their anger they murdered
    men,
    and they crippled oxen just for
    sport.
⁷ A curse on their anger, for it is
    fierce;
    a curse on their wrath, for
    it is cruel.
I will scatter them among the
    descendants of Jacob;
    I will disperse them throughout
    Israel.

⁸ "Judah, your brothers will praise
    you.
    You will grasp your enemies
    by the neck.
    All your relatives will bow before
    you.
⁹ Judah, my son, is a young lion
    that has finished eating its prey.
Like a lion he crouches and lies
    down;
    like a lioness—who dares to rouse
    him?
¹⁰ The scepter will not depart from
    Judah,
    nor the ruler's staff from his
    descendants,*
until the coming of the one to whom
    it belongs,*
    the one whom all nations
    will honor.
¹¹ He ties his foal to a grapevine,

the colt of his donkey to a choice
vine.
He washes his clothes in wine,
his robes in the blood of grapes.
¹² His eyes are darker than wine,
and his teeth are whiter than
milk.

¹³ "Zebulun will settle by the seashore
and will be a harbor for ships;
his borders will extend to Sidon.

¹⁴ "Issachar is a sturdy donkey,
resting between two
saddlepacks.*
¹⁵ When he sees how good the
countryside is
and how pleasant the land,
he will bend his shoulder to the load
and submit himself to hard labor.

¹⁶ "Dan will govern his people,
like any other tribe in Israel.
¹⁷ Dan will be a snake beside the road,
a poisonous viper along the path
that bites the horse's hooves
so its rider is thrown off.
¹⁸ I trust in you for salvation, O LORD!

¹⁹ "Gad will be attacked by marauding
bands,
but he will attack them when they
retreat.

²⁰ "Asher will dine on rich foods
and produce food fit for kings.

²¹ "Naphtali is a doe set free
that bears beautiful fawns.

²² "Joseph is the foal of a wild donkey,
the foal of a wild donkey at a
spring—
one of the wild donkeys on the
ridge.*
²³ Archers attacked him savagely;
they shot at him and harassed
him.
²⁴ But his bow remained taut,
and his arms were strengthened
by the hands of the Mighty One
of Jacob,
by the Shepherd, the Rock of
Israel.
²⁵ May the God of your father help you;

May the Almighty bless you
with the blessings of the heavens
above,
and blessings of the watery
depths below,
and blessings of the breasts and
womb.
²⁶ May the blessings of your father
surpass the blessings of the
ancient mountains,*
reaching to the heights of the
eternal hills.
May these blessings rest on the
head of Joseph,
who is a prince among his
brothers.

²⁷ "Benjamin is a ravenous wolf,
devouring his enemies in the
morning
and dividing his plunder in the
evening."

²⁸These are the twelve tribes of Israel,
and this is what their father said as he
told his sons good-bye. He blessed each
one with an appropriate message.

²⁹Then Jacob instructed them, "Soon
I will die and join my ancestors. Bury me
with my father and grandfather in the
cave in the field of Ephron the Hittite.
³⁰This is the cave in the field of Machpelah, near Mamre in Canaan, that Abraham bought from Ephron the Hittite as
a permanent burial site. ³¹There Abraham and his wife Sarah are buried.
There Isaac and his wife, Rebekah, are
buried. And there I buried Leah. ³²It is
the plot of land and the cave that my
grandfather Abraham bought from the
Hittites."

³³When Jacob had finished this
charge to his sons, he drew his feet into
the bed, breathed his last, and joined his
ancestors in death.

48:2 Hebrew *Israel;* also in 48:8, 10, 11, 13, 14, 21. See
note on 35:21.    48:3 Hebrew *El-Shaddai.*    48:22 Or
*giving you the ridge of land.* The meaning of the Hebrew
is uncertain.    49:10a Hebrew *from between his feet.*
49:10b Or *until tribute is brought to him and the peoples
obey;* traditionally rendered *until Shiloh comes.*    49:14 Or
*sheepfolds,* or *hearths.*    49:22 Or *Joseph is a fruitful tree,
/ a fruitful tree beside a spring. / His branches reach over
the wall.* The meaning of the Hebrew is uncertain.
49:26 Or *of my ancestors.*

## MATTHEW 15:29–16:12

Jesus returned to the Sea of Galilee and climbed a hill and sat down. [30]A vast crowd brought to him people who were lame, blind, crippled, those who couldn't speak, and many others. They laid them before Jesus, and he healed them all. [31]The crowd was amazed! Those who hadn't been able to speak were talking, the crippled were made well, the lame were walking, and the blind could see again! And they praised the God of Israel.

[32]Then Jesus called his disciples and told them, "I feel sorry for these people. They have been here with me for three days, and they have nothing left to eat. I don't want to send them away hungry, or they will faint along the way."

[33]The disciples replied, "Where would we get enough food here in the wilderness for such a huge crowd?"

[34]Jesus asked, "How much bread do you have?"

They replied, "Seven loaves, and a few small fish."

[35]So Jesus told all the people to sit down on the ground. [36]Then he took the seven loaves and the fish, thanked God for them, and broke them into pieces. He gave them to the disciples, who distributed the food to the crowd.

[37]They all ate as much as they wanted. Afterward, the disciples picked up seven large baskets of leftover food. [38]There were 4,000 men who were fed that day, in addition to all the women and children. [39]Then Jesus sent the people home, and he got into a boat and crossed over to the region of Magadan.

[16:1]ONE day the Pharisees and Sadducees came to test Jesus, demanding that he show them a miraculous sign from heaven to prove his authority.

[2]He replied, "You know the saying, 'Red sky at night means fair weather tomorrow; [3]red sky in the morning means foul weather all day.' You know how to interpret the weather signs in the sky, but you don't know how to interpret the signs of the times!* [4]Only an evil, adulterous generation would demand a miraculous sign, but the only sign I will give them is the sign of the prophet Jonah.*" Then Jesus left them and went away.

[5]Later, after they crossed to the other side of the lake, the disciples discovered they had forgotten to bring any bread. [6]"Watch out!" Jesus warned them. "Beware of the yeast of the Pharisees and Sadducees."

[7]At this they began to argue with each other because they hadn't brought any bread. [8]Jesus knew what they were saying, so he said, "You have so little faith! Why are you arguing with each other about having no bread? [9]Don't you understand even yet? Don't you remember the 5,000 I fed with five loaves, and the baskets of leftovers you picked up? [10]Or the 4,000 I fed with seven loaves, and the large baskets of leftovers you picked up? [11]Why can't you understand that I'm not talking about bread? So again I say, 'Beware of the yeast of the Pharisees and Sadducees.'"

[12]Then at last they understood that he wasn't speaking about the yeast in bread, but about the deceptive teaching of the Pharisees and Sadducees.

16:2-3 Several manuscripts do not include any of the words in 16:2-3 after *He replied.*   16:4 Greek *the sign of Jonah.*

## PSALM 20:1-9

*For the choir director: A psalm of David.*

[1] In times of trouble, may the LORD
        answer your cry.
    May the name of the God
        of Jacob keep you safe from
        all harm.
[2] May he send you help from his
        sanctuary
    and strengthen you from
        Jerusalem.*
[3] May he remember all your gifts
        and look favorably on your burnt
        offerings.            *Interlude*

[4] May he grant your heart's desires
        and make all your plans succeed.
[5] May we shout for joy when we hear
        of your victory
    and raise a victory banner in the
        name of our God.

May the Lᴏʀᴅ answer all your
prayers.

⁶ Now I know that the Lᴏʀᴅ rescues
his anointed king.
He will answer him from his holy
heaven
and rescue him by his great
power.
⁷ **Some nations boast of their
chariots and horses,
but we boast in the name of the
Lᴏʀᴅ our God.**
⁸ **Those nations will fall down and
collapse,
but we will rise up and stand
firm.**

⁹ Give victory to our king, O Lᴏʀᴅ!
Answer our cry for help.

20:2 Hebrew *Zion.*

PROVERBS 4:20-27

**M**y child, pay attention to what I say.
Listen carefully to my words. Don't lose
sight of them. Let them penetrate deep
into your heart, for they bring life to
those who find them, and healing to
their whole body. □ Guard your heart
above all else, for it determines the
course of your life. □ Avoid all perverse
talk; stay away from corrupt speech.
□ Look straight ahead, and fix your eyes
on what lies before you. Mark out a
straight path for your feet; stay on the
safe path. Don't get sidetracked; keep
your feet from following evil.

# JANUARY
# 25

GENESIS 50:1—EXODUS 2:10
**J**oseph threw himself on his father and
wept over him and kissed him. ²Then
Joseph told the physicians who served
him to embalm his father's body; so Jacob* was embalmed. ³The embalming
process took the usual forty days. And

the Egyptians mourned his death for
seventy days.

⁴When the period of mourning was
over, Joseph approached Pharaoh's advisers and said, "Please do me this favor
and speak to Pharaoh on my behalf. ⁵Tell
him that my father made me swear an
oath. He said to me, 'Listen, I am about to
die. Take my body back to the land of
Canaan, and bury me in the tomb I prepared for myself.' So please allow me to
go and bury my father. After his burial, I
will return without delay."

⁶Pharaoh agreed to Joseph's request.
"Go and bury your father, as he made you
promise," he said. ⁷So Joseph went up to
bury his father. He was accompanied by
all of Pharaoh's officials, all the senior
members of Pharaoh's household, and
all the senior officers of Egypt. ⁸Joseph
also took his entire household and his
brothers and their households. But they
left their little children and flocks and
herds in the land of Goshen. ⁹A great
number of chariots and charioteers accompanied Joseph.

¹⁰When they arrived at the threshing
floor of Atad, near the Jordan River, they
held a very great and solemn memorial
service, with a seven-day period of
mourning for Joseph's father. ¹¹The local
residents, the Canaanites, watched them
mourning at the threshing floor of Atad.
Then they renamed that place (which is
near the Jordan) Abel-mizraim,* for they
said, "This is a place of deep mourning
for these Egyptians."

¹²So Jacob's sons did as he had commanded them. ¹³They carried his body
to the land of Canaan and buried him in
the cave in the field of Machpelah, near
Mamre. This is the cave that Abraham
had bought as a permanent burial site
from Ephron the Hittite.

¹⁴After burying Jacob, Joseph returned to Egypt with his brothers and
all who had accompanied him to his father's burial. ¹⁵But now that their father
was dead, Joseph's brothers became
fearful. "Now Joseph will show his anger
and pay us back for all the wrong we did
to him," they said.

16So they sent this message to Joseph: "Before your father died, he instructed us 17to say to you: 'Please forgive your brothers for the great wrong they did to you—for their sin in treating you so cruelly.' So we, the servants of the God of your father, beg you to forgive our sin." When Joseph received the message, he broke down and wept. 18Then his brothers came and threw themselves down before Joseph. "Look, we are your slaves!" they said.

19But Joseph replied, "Don't be afraid of me. Am I God, that I can punish you? 20You intended to harm me, but God intended it all for good. He brought me to this position so I could save the lives of many people. 21No, don't be afraid. I will continue to take care of you and your children." So he reassured them by speaking kindly to them.

22So Joseph and his brothers and their families continued to live in Egypt. Joseph lived to the age of 110. 23He lived to see three generations of descendants of his son Ephraim, and he lived to see the birth of the children of Manasseh's son Makir, whom he claimed as his own.*

24"Soon I will die," Joseph told his brothers, "but God will surely come to help you and lead you out of this land of Egypt. He will bring you back to the land he solemnly promised to give to Abraham, to Isaac, and to Jacob."

25Then Joseph made the sons of Israel swear an oath, and he said, "When God comes to help you and lead you back, you must take my bones with you." 26So Joseph died at the age of 110. The Egyptians embalmed him, and his body was placed in a coffin in Egypt.

1:1THESE are the names of the sons of Israel (that is, Jacob) who moved to Egypt with their father, each with his family: 2Reuben, Simeon, Levi, Judah, 3Issachar, Zebulun, Benjamin, 4Dan, Naphtali, Gad, and Asher. 5In all, Jacob had seventy* descendants in Egypt, including Joseph, who was already there.

6In time, Joseph and all of his brothers died, ending that entire generation.

7But their descendants, the Israelites, had many children and grandchildren. In fact, they multiplied so greatly that they became extremely powerful and filled the land.

8Eventually, a new king came to power in Egypt who knew nothing about Joseph or what he had done. 9He said to his people, "Look, the people of Israel now outnumber us and are stronger than we are. 10We must make a plan to keep them from growing even more. If we don't, and if war breaks out, they will join our enemies and fight against us. Then they will escape from the country.*"

11So the Egyptians made the Israelites their slaves. They appointed brutal slave drivers over them, hoping to wear them down with crushing labor. They forced them to build the cities of Pithom and Rameses as supply centers for the king. 12But the more the Egyptians oppressed them, the more the Israelites multiplied and spread, and the more alarmed the Egyptians became. 13So the Egyptians worked the people of Israel without mercy. 14They made their lives bitter, forcing them to mix mortar and make bricks and do all the work in the fields. They were ruthless in all their demands.

15Then Pharaoh, the king of Egypt, gave this order to the Hebrew midwives, Shiphrah and Puah: 16"When you help the Hebrew women as they give birth, watch as they deliver.* If the baby is a boy, kill him; if it is a girl, let her live." 17But because the midwives feared God, they refused to obey the king's orders. They allowed the boys to live, too.

18So the king of Egypt called for the midwives. "Why have you done this?" he demanded. "Why have you allowed the boys to live?"

19"The Hebrew women are not like the Egyptian women," the midwives replied. "They are more vigorous and have their babies so quickly that we cannot get there in time."

20So God was good to the midwives, and the Israelites continued to multiply, growing more and more powerful. 21And because the midwives feared God, he gave them families of their own.

²²Then Pharaoh gave this order to all his people: "Throw every newborn Hebrew boy into the Nile River. But you may let the girls live."

²:¹ABOUT this time, a man and woman from the tribe of Levi got married. ²The woman became pregnant and gave birth to a son. She saw that he was a special baby and kept him hidden for three months. ³But when she could no longer hide him, she got a basket made of papyrus reeds and waterproofed it with tar and pitch. She put the baby in the basket and laid it among the reeds along the bank of the Nile River. ⁴The baby's sister then stood at a distance, watching to see what would happen to him.

⁵Soon Pharaoh's daughter came down to bathe in the river, and her attendants walked along the riverbank. When the princess saw the basket among the reeds, she sent her maid to get it for her. ⁶When the princess opened it, she saw the baby. The little boy was crying, and she felt sorry for him. "This must be one of the Hebrew children," she said.

⁷Then the baby's sister approached the princess. "Should I go and find one of the Hebrew women to nurse the baby for you?" she asked.

⁸"Yes, do!" the princess replied. So the girl went and called the baby's mother.

⁹"Take this baby and nurse him for me," the princess told the baby's mother. "I will pay you for your help." So the woman took her baby home and nursed him.

¹⁰Later, when the boy was older, his mother brought him back to Pharaoh's daughter, who adopted him as her own son. The princess named him Moses,* for she explained, "I lifted him out of the water."

50:2 Hebrew *Israel*. See note on 35:21.   50:11 *Abelmizraim* means "mourning of the Egyptians."
50:23 Hebrew *who were born on Joseph's knees.*
1:5 Dead Sea Scrolls and Greek version read *seventy-five;* see notes on Gen 46:27.   1:10 Or *will take the country.*
1:16 Hebrew *look upon the two stones;* perhaps the reference is to a birthstool.   2:10 *Moses* sounds like a Hebrew term that means "to lift out."

MATTHEW 16:13–17:9

**W**hen Jesus came to the region of Caesarea Philippi, he asked his disciples, "Who do people say that the Son of Man is?"*

¹⁴"Well," they replied, "some say John the Baptist, some say Elijah, and others say Jeremiah or one of the other prophets."

¹⁵Then he asked them, "But who do you say I am?"

¹⁶Simon Peter answered, "You are the Messiah,* the Son of the living God."

¹⁷Jesus replied, "You are blessed, Simon son of John,* because my Father in heaven has revealed this to you. You did not learn this from any human being. ¹⁸Now I say to you that you are Peter (which means 'rock'),* and upon this rock I will build my church, and all the powers of hell* will not conquer it. ¹⁹And I will give you the keys of the Kingdom of Heaven. Whatever you forbid* on earth will be forbidden in heaven, and whatever you permit* on earth will be permitted in heaven."

²⁰Then he sternly warned the disciples not to tell anyone that he was the Messiah.

²¹From then on Jesus* began to tell his disciples plainly that it was necessary for him to go to Jerusalem, and that he would suffer many terrible things at the hands of the elders, the leading priests, and the teachers of religious law. He would be killed, but on the third day he would be raised from the dead.

²²But Peter took him aside and began to reprimand him* for saying such things. "Heaven forbid, Lord," he said. "This will never happen to you!"

²³Jesus turned to Peter and said, "Get away from me, Satan! You are a dangerous trap to me. You are seeing things merely from a human point of view, not from God's."

²⁴**Then Jesus said to his disciples, "If any of you wants to be my follower, you must turn from your selfish ways, take up your cross, and follow me. ²⁵If you try to hang on to your life, you will lose it. But if you**

**give up your life for my sake, you will save it.** 26And what do you benefit if you gain the whole world but lose your own soul?* Is anything worth more than your soul? 27For the Son of Man will come with his angels in the glory of his Father and will judge all people according to their deeds. 28And I tell you the truth, some standing here right now will not die before they see the Son of Man coming in his Kingdom."

17:1Six days later Jesus took Peter and the two brothers, James and John, and led them up a high mountain to be alone. 2As the men watched, Jesus' appearance was transformed so that his face shone like the sun, and his clothes became as white as light. 3Suddenly, Moses and Elijah appeared and began talking with Jesus.

4Peter blurted out, "Lord, it's wonderful for us to be here! If you want, I'll make three shelters as memorials*—one for you, one for Moses, and one for Elijah."

5But even as he spoke, a bright cloud came over them, and a voice from the cloud said, "This is my dearly loved Son, who brings me great joy. Listen to him." 6The disciples were terrified and fell face down on the ground.

7Then Jesus came over and touched them. "Get up," he said. "Don't be afraid." 8And when they looked, they saw only Jesus.

9As they went back down the mountain, Jesus commanded them, "Don't tell anyone what you have seen until the Son of Man* has been raised from the dead."

16:13 "Son of Man" is a title Jesus used for himself.
16:16 Or *the Christ. Messiah* (a Hebrew term) and *Christ* (a Greek term) both mean "the anointed one."    16:17 Greek *Simon bar-Jonah;* see John 1:42; 21:15-17.    16:18a Greek *that you are Peter.*    16:18b Greek *and the gates of Hades.*
16:19a Or *bind,* or *lock.*    16:19b Or *loose,* or *open.*
16:21 Some manuscripts read *Jesus the Messiah.*
16:22 Or *began to correct him.*    16:26 Or *your self?* also in 16:26b.    17:4 Greek *three tabernacles.*    17:9 "Son of Man" is a title Jesus used for himself.

## PSALM 21:1-13
*For the choir director: A psalm of David.*

1 **H**ow the king rejoices in your
    strength, O Lord!

He shouts with joy because you
    give him victory.
2 For you have given him his heart's
    desire;
    you have withheld nothing he
    requested.              *Interlude*

3 You welcomed him back with
    success and prosperity.
    You placed a crown of finest gold
    on his head.
4 He asked you to preserve his life,
    and you granted his request.
    The days of his life stretch on
    forever.
5 Your victory brings him great
    honor,
    and you have clothed him with
    splendor and majesty.
6 You have endowed him with eternal
    blessings
    and given him the joy of your
    presence.
7 For the king trusts in the Lord.
    The unfailing love of the Most
    High will keep him from
    stumbling.

8 You will capture all your enemies.
    Your strong right hand will seize
    all who hate you.
9 You will throw them in a flaming
    furnace
    when you appear.
    The Lord will consume them in
    his anger;
    fire will devour them.
10 You will wipe their children from
    the face of the earth;
    they will never have descendants.
11 Although they plot against you,
    their evil schemes will never succeed.
12 For they will turn and run
    when they see your arrows aimed
    at them.
13 Rise up, O Lord, in all your power.
    With music and singing we
    celebrate your mighty acts.

## PROVERBS 5:1-6
**M**y son, pay attention to my wisdom; listen carefully to my wise counsel. Then you will show discernment, and your lips

will express what you've learned. For the lips of an immoral woman are as sweet as honey, and her mouth is smoother than oil. But in the end she is as bitter as poison, as dangerous as a double-edged sword. Her feet go down to death; her steps lead straight to the grave.* For she cares nothing about the path to life. She staggers down a crooked trail and doesn't realize it.

5:5 Hebrew *to Sheol.*

# JANUARY 26

## EXODUS 2:11–3:22

**M**any years later, when Moses had grown up, he went out to visit his own people, the Hebrews, and he saw how hard they were forced to work. During his visit, he saw an Egyptian beating one of his fellow Hebrews. ¹²After looking in all directions to make sure no one was watching, Moses killed the Egyptian and hid the body in the sand.

¹³The next day, when Moses went out to visit his people again, he saw two Hebrew men fighting. "Why are you beating up your friend?" Moses said to the one who had started the fight.

¹⁴The man replied, "Who appointed you to be our prince and judge? Are you going to kill me as you killed that Egyptian yesterday?"

Then Moses was afraid, thinking, "Everyone knows what I did." ¹⁵And sure enough, Pharaoh heard what had happened, and he tried to kill Moses. But Moses fled from Pharaoh and went to live in the land of Midian.

When Moses arrived in Midian, he sat down beside a well. ¹⁶Now the priest of Midian had seven daughters who came as usual to draw water and fill the water troughs for their father's flocks. ¹⁷But some other shepherds came and

chased them away. So Moses jumped up and rescued the girls from the shepherds. Then he drew water for their flocks.

¹⁸When the girls returned to Reuel, their father, he asked, "Why are you back so soon today?"

¹⁹"An Egyptian rescued us from the shepherds," they answered. "And then he drew water for us and watered our flocks."

²⁰"Then where is he?" their father asked. "Why did you leave him there? Invite him to come and eat with us."

²¹Moses accepted the invitation, and he settled there with him. In time, Reuel gave Moses his daughter Zipporah to be his wife. ²²Later she gave birth to a son, and Moses named him Gershom,* for he explained, "I have been a foreigner in a foreign land."

²³Years passed, and the king of Egypt died. But the Israelites continued to groan under their burden of slavery. They cried out for help, and their cry rose up to God. ²⁴God heard their groaning, and he remembered his covenant promise to Abraham, Isaac, and Jacob. ²⁵He looked down on the people of Israel and knew it was time to act.*

³:¹ONE day Moses was tending the flock of his father-in-law, Jethro,* the priest of Midian. He led the flock far into the wilderness and came to Sinai,* the mountain of God. ²There the angel of the LORD appeared to him in a blazing fire from the middle of a bush. Moses stared in amazement. Though the bush was engulfed in flames, it didn't burn up. ³"This is amazing," Moses said to himself. "Why isn't that bush burning up? I must go see it."

⁴When the LORD saw Moses coming to take a closer look, God called to him from the middle of the bush, "Moses! Moses!"

"Here I am!" Moses replied.

⁵"Do not come any closer," the LORD warned. "Take off your sandals, for you are standing on holy ground. ⁶I am the God of your father*—the God of

Abraham, the God of Isaac, and the God of Jacob." When Moses heard this, he covered his face because he was afraid to look at God.

⁷Then the LORD told him, "I have certainly seen the oppression of my people in Egypt. I have heard their cries of distress because of their harsh slave drivers. Yes, I am aware of their suffering. ⁸So I have come down to rescue them from the power of the Egyptians and lead them out of Egypt into their own fertile and spacious land. It is a land flowing with milk and honey—the land where the Canaanites, Hittites, Amorites, Perizzites, Hivites, and Jebusites now live. ⁹Look! The cry of the people of Israel has reached me, and I have seen how harshly the Egyptians abuse them. ¹⁰Now go, for I am sending you to Pharaoh. You must lead my people Israel out of Egypt."

¹¹But Moses protested to God, "Who am I to appear before Pharaoh? Who am I to lead the people of Israel out of Egypt?"

¹²God answered, "I will be with you. And this is your sign that I am the one who has sent you: When you have brought the people out of Egypt, you will worship God at this very mountain."

¹³But Moses protested, "If I go to the people of Israel and tell them, 'The God of your ancestors has sent me to you,' they will ask me, 'What is his name?' Then what should I tell them?"

¹⁴God replied to Moses, "I AM WHO I AM.* Say this to the people of Israel: I AM has sent me to you." ¹⁵God also said to Moses, "Say this to the people of Israel: Yahweh,* the God of your ancestors—the God of Abraham, the God of Isaac, and the God of Jacob—has sent me to you.

This is my eternal name,
    my name to remember for all
        generations.

¹⁶"Now go and call together all the elders of Israel. Tell them, 'The LORD, the God of your ancestors—the God of Abra-

ham, Isaac, and Jacob—has appeared to me. He told me, "I have been watching closely, and I see how the Egyptians are treating you. ¹⁷I have promised to rescue you from your oppression in Egypt. I will lead you to a land flowing with milk and honey—the land where the Canaanites, Hittites, Amorites, Perizzites, Hivites, and Jebusites now live."'

¹⁸"The elders of Israel will accept your message. Then you and the elders must go to the king of Egypt and tell him, 'The LORD, the God of the Hebrews, has met with us. So please let us take a three-day journey into the wilderness to offer sacrifices to the LORD, our God.'

¹⁹"But I know that the king of Egypt will not let you go unless a mighty hand forces him.* ²⁰So I will raise my hand and strike the Egyptians, performing all kinds of miracles among them. Then at last he will let you go. ²¹And I will cause the Egyptians to look favorably on you. They will give you gifts when you go so you will not leave empty-handed. ²²Every Israelite woman will ask for articles of silver and gold and fine clothing from her Egyptian neighbors and from the foreign women in their houses. You will dress your sons and daughters with these, stripping the Egyptians of their wealth."

2:22 *Gershom* sounds like a Hebrew term that means "a foreigner there."   2:25 Or *and acknowledged his obligation to help them.*   3:1a Moses' father-in-law went by two names, Jethro and Reuel.   3:1b Hebrew *Horeb,* another name for Sinai.   3:6 Greek version reads *your fathers.*   3:14 Or *I WILL BE WHAT I WILL BE.*   3:15 *Yahweh* is a transliteration of the proper name *YHWH* that is sometimes rendered "Jehovah"; in this translation it is usually rendered "the LORD" (note the use of small capitals).   3:19 As in Greek and Latin versions; Hebrew reads *will not let you go, not by a mighty hand.*

## MATTHEW 17:10-27

Then his disciples asked him, "Why do the teachers of religious law insist that Elijah must return before the Messiah comes?*"

¹¹Jesus replied, "Elijah is indeed coming first to get everything ready for the Messiah. ¹²But I tell you, Elijah has already come, but he wasn't recognized, and they chose to abuse him. And in the same way they will also make the Son of

Man suffer." [13] Then the disciples realized he was talking about John the Baptist.

[14] At the foot of the mountain, a large crowd was waiting for them. A man came and knelt before Jesus and said, [15] "Lord, have mercy on my son. He has seizures and suffers terribly. He often falls into the fire or into the water. [16] So I brought him to your disciples, but they couldn't heal him."

[17] Jesus replied, "You faithless and corrupt people! How long must I be with you? How long must I put up with you? Bring the boy to me." [18] Then Jesus rebuked the demon in the boy, and it left him. From that moment the boy was well.

[19] Afterward the disciples asked Jesus privately, "Why couldn't we cast out that demon?"

[20] "You don't have enough faith," Jesus told them. "I tell you the truth, if you had faith even as small as a mustard seed, you could say to this mountain, 'Move from here to there,' and it would move. Nothing would be impossible.*"

[22] After they gathered again in Galilee, Jesus told them, "The Son of Man is going to be betrayed into the hands of his enemies. [23] He will be killed, but on the third day he will be raised from the dead." And the disciples were filled with grief.

[24] On their arrival in Capernaum, the collectors of the Temple tax* came to Peter and asked him, "Doesn't your teacher pay the Temple tax?"

[25] "Yes, he does," Peter replied. Then he went into the house.

But before he had a chance to speak, Jesus asked him, "What do you think, Peter?* Do kings tax their own people or the people they have conquered?*"

[26] "They tax the people they have conquered," Peter replied.

"Well, then," Jesus said, "the citizens are free! [27] However, we don't want to offend them, so go down to the lake and throw in a line. Open the mouth of the first fish you catch, and you will find a large silver coin.* Take it and pay the tax for both of us."

**17:10** Greek *that Elijah must come first?*  **17:20** Some manuscripts add verse 21, *But this kind of demon won't leave except by prayer and fasting.* Compare Mark 9:29. **17:24** Greek *the two-drachma [tax]*; also in 17:24b. See Exod 30:13-16; Neh 10:32-33. **17:25a** Greek *Simon?* **17:25b** Greek *their sons or others?* **17:27** Greek *a stater* [a Greek coin equivalent to four drachmas].

## PSALM 22:1-18

*For the choir director: A psalm of David, to be sung to the tune "Doe of the Dawn."*

[1] **M**y God, my God, why have you abandoned me?
  Why are you so far away when I groan for help?
[2] Every day I call to you, my God, but you do not answer.
  Every night you hear my voice, but I find no relief.

[3] Yet you are holy,
  enthroned on the praises of Israel.
[4] Our ancestors trusted in you,
  and you rescued them.
[5] They cried out to you and were saved.
  They trusted in you and were never disgraced.

[6] But I am a worm and not a man.
  I am scorned and despised by all!
[7] Everyone who sees me mocks me.
  They sneer and shake their heads, saying,
[8] "Is this the one who relies on the LORD?
  Then let the LORD save him!
  If the LORD loves him so much, let the LORD rescue him!"

[9] Yet you brought me safely from my mother's womb
  and led me to trust you at my mother's breast.
[10] I was thrust into your arms at my birth.
  You have been my God from the moment I was born.

[11] Do not stay so far from me,
  for trouble is near,
  and no one else can help me.

<sup>12</sup> My enemies surround me like a herd
of bulls;
fierce bulls of Bashan have
hemmed me in!
<sup>13</sup> Like lions they open their jaws
against me,
roaring and tearing into their
prey.
<sup>14</sup> My life is poured out like water,
and all my bones are out of joint.
My heart is like wax,
melting within me.
<sup>15</sup> My strength has dried up like
sunbaked clay.
My tongue sticks to the roof
of my mouth.
You have laid me in the dust and
left me for dead.
<sup>16</sup> My enemies surround me like a pack
of dogs;
an evil gang closes in on me.
They have pierced my hands
and feet.
<sup>17</sup> I can count all my bones.
My enemies stare at me and gloat.
<sup>18</sup> They divide my garments among
themselves
and throw dice* for my clothing.

**22:18** Hebrew *cast lots.*

PROVERBS 5:7-14

**S**o now, my sons, listen to me. Never stray from what I am about to say: Stay away from her! Don't go near the door of her house! If you do, you will lose your honor and will lose to merciless people all you have achieved. Strangers will consume your wealth, and someone else will enjoy the fruit of your labor. In the end you will groan in anguish when disease consumes your body. You will say, "How I hated discipline! If only I had not ignored all the warnings! Oh, why didn't I listen to my teachers? Why didn't I pay attention to my instructors? I have come to the brink of utter ruin, and now I must face public disgrace."

**JANUARY
27**

EXODUS 4:1–5:21

**B**ut Moses protested again, "What if they won't believe me or listen to me? What if they say, 'The LORD never appeared to you'?"

<sup>2</sup>Then the LORD asked him, "What is that in your hand?"

"A shepherd's staff," Moses replied.

<sup>3</sup>"Throw it down on the ground," the LORD told him. So Moses threw down the staff, and it turned into a snake! Moses jumped back.

<sup>4</sup>Then the LORD told him, "Reach out and grab its tail." So Moses reached out and grabbed it, and it turned back into a shepherd's staff in his hand.

<sup>5</sup>"Perform this sign," the LORD told him. "Then they will believe that the LORD, the God of their ancestors—the God of Abraham, the God of Isaac, and the God of Jacob—really has appeared to you."

<sup>6</sup>Then the LORD said to Moses, "Now put your hand inside your cloak." So Moses put his hand inside his cloak, and when he took it out again, his hand was white as snow with a severe skin disease.* <sup>7</sup>"Now put your hand back into your cloak," the LORD said. So Moses put his hand back in, and when he took it out again, it was as healthy as the rest of his body.

<sup>8</sup>The LORD said to Moses, "If they do not believe you and are not convinced by the first miraculous sign, they will be convinced by the second sign. <sup>9</sup>And if they don't believe you or listen to you even after these two signs, then take some water from the Nile River and pour it out on the dry ground. When you do, the water from the Nile will turn to blood on the ground."

<sup>10</sup>But Moses pleaded with the LORD, "O Lord, I'm not very good with words. I never have been, and I'm not now, even though you have spoken to me. I get tongue-tied, and my words get tangled."

<sup>11</sup>Then the LORD asked Moses, "Who makes a person's mouth? Who decides whether people speak or do not speak, hear or do not hear, see or do not see? Is it not I, the LORD? <sup>12</sup>Now go! I will be with you as you speak, and I will instruct you in what to say."

<sup>13</sup>But Moses again pleaded, "Lord, please! Send anyone else."

<sup>14</sup>Then the LORD became angry with Moses. "All right," he said. "What about your brother, Aaron the Levite? I know he speaks well. And look! He is on his way to meet you now. He will be delighted to see you. <sup>15</sup>Talk to him, and put the words in his mouth. I will be with both of you as you speak, and I will instruct you both in what to do. <sup>16</sup>Aaron will be your spokesman to the people. He will be your mouthpiece, and you will stand in the place of God for him, telling him what to say. <sup>17</sup>And take your shepherd's staff with you, and use it to perform the miraclous signs I have shown you."

<sup>18</sup>So Moses went back home to Jethro, his father-in-law. "Please let me return to my relatives in Egypt," Moses said. "I don't even know if they are still alive."

"Go in peace," Jethro replied.

<sup>19</sup>Before Moses left Midian, the LORD said to him, "Return to Egypt, for all those who wanted to kill you have died."

<sup>20</sup>So Moses took his wife and sons, put them on a donkey, and headed back to the land of Egypt. In his hand he carried the staff of God.

<sup>21</sup>And the LORD told Moses, "When you arrive back in Egypt, go to Pharaoh and perform all the miracles I have empowered you to do. But I will harden his heart so he will refuse to let the people go. <sup>22</sup>Then you will tell him, 'This is what the LORD says: Israel is my firstborn son. <sup>23</sup>I commanded you, "Let my son go, so he can worship me." But since you have refused, I will now kill your firstborn son!'"

<sup>24</sup>On the way to Egypt, at a place where Moses and his family had stopped for the night, the LORD confronted him and was about to kill him. <sup>25</sup>But Moses' wife, Zipporah, took a flint knife and circumcised her son. She touched his feet* with the foreskin and said, "Now you are a bridegroom of blood to me." <sup>26</sup>(When she said "a bridegroom of blood," she was referring to the circumcision.) After that, the LORD left him alone.

<sup>27</sup>Now the LORD had said to Aaron, "Go out into the wilderness to meet Moses." So Aaron went and met Moses at the mountain of God, and he embraced him. <sup>28</sup>Moses then told Aaron everything the LORD had commanded him to say. And he told him about the miraculous signs the LORD had commanded him to perform.

<sup>29</sup>Then Moses and Aaron returned to Egypt and called all the elders of Israel together. <sup>30</sup>Aaron told them everything the LORD had told Moses, and Moses performed the miraculous signs as they watched. <sup>31</sup>Then the people of Israel were convinced that the LORD had sent Moses and Aaron. When they heard that the LORD was concerned about them and had seen their misery, they bowed down and worshiped.

<sup>5:1</sup>AFTER this presentation to Israel's leaders, Moses and Aaron went and spoke to Pharaoh. They told him, "This is what the LORD, the God of Israel, says: Let my people go so they may hold a festival in my honor in the wilderness."

<sup>2</sup>"Is that so?" retorted Pharaoh. "And who is the LORD? Why should I listen to him and let Israel go? I don't know the LORD, and I will not let Israel go."

<sup>3</sup>But Aaron and Moses persisted. "The God of the Hebrews has met with us," they declared. "So let us take a three-day journey into the wilderness so we can offer sacrifices to the LORD our God. If we don't, he will kill us with a plague or with the sword."

<sup>4</sup>Pharaoh replied, "Moses and Aaron, why are you distracting the people from their tasks? Get back to work! <sup>5</sup>Look, there are many of your people in the land, and you are stopping them from their work."

<sup>6</sup>That same day Pharaoh sent this

order to the Egyptian slave drivers and the Israelite foremen: [7]"Do not supply any more straw for making bricks. Make the people get it themselves! [8]But still require them to make the same number of bricks as before. Don't reduce the quota. They are lazy. That's why they are crying out, 'Let us go and offer sacrifices to our God.' [9]Load them down with more work. Make them sweat! That will teach them to listen to lies!"

[10]So the slave drivers and foremen went out and told the people: "This is what Pharaoh says: I will not provide any more straw for you. [11]Go and get it yourselves. Find it wherever you can. But you must produce just as many bricks as before!" [12]So the people scattered throughout the land of Egypt in search of stubble to use as straw.

[13]Meanwhile, the Egyptian slave drivers continued to push hard. "Meet your daily quota of bricks, just as you did when we provided you with straw!" they demanded. [14]Then they whipped the Israelite foremen they had put in charge of the work crews. "Why haven't you met your quotas either yesterday or today?" they demanded.

[15]So the Israelite foremen went to Pharaoh and pleaded with him. "Please don't treat your servants like this," they begged. [16]"We are given no straw, but the slave drivers still demand, 'Make bricks!' We are being beaten, but it isn't our fault! Your own people are to blame!"

[17]But Pharaoh shouted, "You're just lazy! Lazy! That's why you're saying, 'Let us go and offer sacrifices to the LORD.' [18]Now get back to work! No straw will be given to you, but you must still produce the full quota of bricks."

[19]The Israelite foremen could see that they were in serious trouble when they were told, "You must not reduce the number of bricks you make each day." [20]As they left Pharaoh's court, they confronted Moses and Aaron, who were waiting outside for them. [21]The foremen said to them, "May the LORD judge and punish you for making us stink be-

fore Pharaoh and his officials. You have put a sword into their hands, an excuse to kill us!"

4:6 Or *with leprosy*. The Hebrew word used here can describe various skin diseases.    4:25 The Hebrew word for "feet" may refer here to the male sex organ.

## MATTHEW 18:1-20

About that time the disciples came to Jesus and asked, "Who is greatest in the Kingdom of Heaven?"

[2]Jesus called a little child to him and put the child among them. [3]Then he said, "I tell you the truth, unless you turn from your sins and become like little children, you will never get into the Kingdom of Heaven. [4]So anyone who becomes as humble as this little child is the greatest in the Kingdom of Heaven.

[5]"And anyone who welcomes a little child like this on my behalf* is welcoming me. [6]But if you cause one of these little ones who trusts in me to fall into sin, it would be better for you to have a large millstone tied around your neck and be drowned in the depths of the sea.

[7]"What sorrow awaits the world, because it tempts people to sin. Temptations are inevitable, but what sorrow awaits the person who does the tempting. [8]So if your hand or foot causes you to sin, cut it off and throw it away. It's better to enter eternal life with only one hand or one foot than to be thrown into eternal fire with both of your hands and feet. [9]And if your eye causes you to sin, gouge it out and throw it away. It's better to enter eternal life with only one eye than to have two eyes and be thrown into the fire of hell.*

[10]"Beware that you don't look down on any of these little ones. For I tell you that in heaven their angels are always in the presence of my heavenly Father.*

[12]"If a man has a hundred sheep and one of them wanders away, what will he do? Won't he leave the ninety-nine others on the hills and go out to search for the one that is lost? [13]And if he finds it, I tell you the truth, he will rejoice over it more than over the ninety-nine that didn't wander away! [14]In the same way, it

is not my heavenly Father's will that even one of these little ones should perish.

¹⁵"If another believer* sins against you,* go privately and point out the offense. If the other person listens and confesses it, you have won that person back. ¹⁶But if you are unsuccessful, take one or two others with you and go back again, so that everything you say may be confirmed by two or three witnesses. ¹⁷If the person still refuses to listen, take your case to the church. Then if he or she won't accept the church's decision, treat that person as a pagan or a corrupt tax collector.

¹⁸"I tell you the truth, whatever you forbid* on earth will be forbidden in heaven, and whatever you permit* on earth will be permitted in heaven.

¹⁹"I also tell you this: If two of you agree here on earth concerning anything you ask, my Father in heaven will do it for you. ²⁰For where two or three gather together as my followers,* I am there among them."

18:5 Greek *in my name*.   18:9 Greek *the Gehenna of fire*.   18:10 Some manuscripts add verse 11, *And the Son of Man came to save those who are lost*. Compare Luke 19:10.   18:15a Greek *If your brother*.   18:15b Some manuscripts do not include *against you*.   18:18a Or *bind*, or *lock*.   18:18b Or *loose*, or *open*.   18:20 Greek *gather together in my name*.

## PSALM 22:19-31

**◐** LORD, do not stay far away!
    You are my strength; come
        quickly to my aid!
²⁰ Save me from the sword;
    spare my precious life from
        these dogs.
²¹ Snatch me from the lion's jaws
    and from the horns of these
        wild oxen.

²² I will proclaim your name to my
        brothers and sisters.*
    I will praise you among your
        assembled people.
²³ Praise the LORD, all you who fear
        him!
    Honor him, all you descendants
        of Jacob!
    Show him reverence, all you
        descendants of Israel!

²⁴ For he has not ignored or belittled
        the suffering of the needy.
    He has not turned his back
        on them,
    but has listened to their cries
        for help.

²⁵ I will praise you in the great assembly.
    I will fulfill my vows in the
        presence of those who worship
        you.
²⁶ The poor will eat and be satisfied.
    All who seek the LORD will
        praise him.
    Their hearts will rejoice with
        everlasting joy.
²⁷ The whole earth will acknowledge
        the LORD and return to him.
    All the families of the nations will
        bow down before him.
²⁸ For royal power belongs to the LORD.
    He rules all the nations.

²⁹ Let the rich of the earth feast and
        worship.
    Bow before him, all who are
        mortal,
    all whose lives will end as dust.
³⁰ Our children will also serve him.
    Future generations will hear
        about the wonders of the Lord.
³¹ His righteous acts will be told to
        those not yet born.
    They will hear about everything
        he has done.

22:22 Hebrew *my brothers*.

## PROVERBS 5:15-21

**D**rink water from your own well—share your love only with your wife.* Why spill the water of your springs in the streets, having sex with just anyone?* You should reserve it for yourselves. Never share it with strangers. □ Let your wife be a fountain of blessing for you. Rejoice in the wife of your youth. She is a loving deer, a graceful doe. Let her breasts satisfy you always. May you always be captivated by her love. Why be captivated, my son, by an immoral woman, or fondle the breasts of a promiscuous woman? □ For the LORD sees clearly what a man does, examining every path he takes.

5:15 Hebrew *Drink water from your own cistern, / flowing water from your own well.*   5:16 Hebrew *Why spill your springs in the streets, / your streams in the city squares?*

# JANUARY
# 28

EXODUS 5:22–7:25

Then Moses went back to the LORD and protested, "Why have you brought all this trouble on your own people, Lord? Why did you send me? 23Ever since I came to Pharaoh as your spokesman, he has been even more brutal to your people. And you have done nothing to rescue them!"

6:1THEN the LORD told Moses, "Now you will see what I will do to Pharaoh. When he feels the force of my strong hand, he will let the people go. In fact, he will force them to leave his land!"

2And God said to Moses, "I am Yahweh— 'the LORD.'* 3I appeared to Abraham, to Isaac, and to Jacob as El-Shaddai—'God Almighty'*—but I did not reveal my name, Yahweh, to them. 4And I reaffirmed my covenant with them. Under its terms, I promised to give them the land of Canaan, where they were living as foreigners. 5You can be sure that I have heard the groans of the people of Israel, who are now slaves to the Egyptians. And I am well aware of my covenant with them.

6"Therefore, say to the people of Israel: 'I am the LORD. I will free you from your oppression and will rescue you from your slavery in Egypt. I will redeem you with a powerful arm and great acts of judgment. 7I will claim you as my own people, and I will be your God. Then you will know that I am the LORD your God who has freed you from your oppression in Egypt. 8I will bring you into the land I swore to give to Abraham, Isaac, and Ja-

cob. I will give it to you as your very own possession. I am the LORD!'"

9So Moses told the people of Israel what the LORD had said, but they refused to listen anymore. They had become too discouraged by the brutality of their slavery.

10Then the LORD said to Moses, 11"Go back to Pharaoh, the king of Egypt, and tell him to let the people of Israel leave his country."

12"But LORD!" Moses objected. "My own people won't listen to me anymore. How can I expect Pharaoh to listen? I'm such a clumsy speaker!*"

13But the LORD spoke to Moses and Aaron and gave them orders for the Israelites and for Pharaoh, the king of Egypt. The LORD commanded Moses and Aaron to lead the people of Israel out of Egypt.

14These are the ancestors of some of the clans of Israel:

The sons of Reuben, Israel's oldest son, were Hanoch, Pallu, Hezron, and Carmi. Their descendants became the clans of Reuben.
15The sons of Simeon were Jemuel, Jamin, Ohad, Jakin, Zohar, and Shaul. (Shaul's mother was a Canaanite woman.) Their descendants became the clans of Simeon.
16These are the descendants of Levi, as listed in their family records: The sons of Levi were Gershon, Kohath, and Merari. (Levi lived to be 137 years old.)
17The descendants of Gershon included Libni and Shimei, each of whom became the ancestor of a clan.
18The descendants of Kohath included Amram, Izhar, Hebron, and Uzziel. (Kohath lived to be 133 years old.)
19The descendants of Merari included Mahli and Mushi.

These are the clans of the Levites, as listed in their family records.

20Amram married his father's sister Jochebed, and she gave birth to his sons, Aaron and Moses. (Amram lived to be 137 years old.)

21The sons of Izhar were Korah, Nepheg, and Zicri.

22The sons of Uzziel were Mishael, Elzaphan, and Sithri.

23Aaron married Elisheba, the daughter of Amminadab and sister of Nahshon, and she gave birth to his sons, Nadab, Abihu, Eleazar, and Ithamar.

24The sons of Korah were Assir, Elkanah, and Abiasaph. Their descendants became the clans of Korah.

25Eleazar son of Aaron married one of the daughters of Putiel, and she gave birth to his son, Phinehas.

These are the ancestors of the Levite families, listed according to their clans.

26The Aaron and Moses named in this list are the same ones to whom the LORD said, "Lead the people of Israel out of the land of Egypt like an army." 27It was Moses and Aaron who spoke to Pharaoh, the king of Egypt, about leading the people of Israel out of Egypt.

28When the LORD spoke to Moses in the land of Egypt, 29he said to him, "I am the LORD! Tell Pharaoh, the king of Egypt, everything I am telling you." 30But Moses argued with the LORD, saying, "I can't do it! I'm such a clumsy speaker! Why should Pharaoh listen to me?"

7:1THEN the LORD said to Moses, "Pay close attention to this. I will make you seem like God to Pharaoh, and your brother, Aaron, will be your prophet. 2Tell Aaron everything I command you, and Aaron must command Pharaoh to let the people of Israel leave his country. 3But I will make Pharaoh's heart stubborn so I can multiply my miraculous signs and wonders in the land of Egypt. 4Even then Pharaoh will refuse to listen to you. So I will bring down my fist on Egypt. Then I will rescue my forces—my people, the Israelites—from the land of Egypt with great acts of judgment. 5When I raise my powerful hand and

bring out the Israelites, the Egyptians will know that I am the LORD."

6So Moses and Aaron did just as the LORD had commanded them. 7Moses was eighty years old, and Aaron was eighty-three when they made their demands to Pharaoh.

8Then the LORD said to Moses and Aaron, 9"Pharaoh will demand, 'Show me a miracle.' When he does this, say to Aaron, 'Take your staff and throw it down in front of Pharaoh, and it will become a serpent.*'"

10So Moses and Aaron went to Pharaoh and did what the LORD had commanded them. Aaron threw down his staff before Pharaoh and his officials, and it became a serpent! 11Then Pharaoh called in his own wise men and sorcerers, and these Egyptian magicians did the same thing with their magic. 12They threw down their staffs, which also became serpents! But then Aaron's staff swallowed up their staffs. 13Pharaoh's heart, however, remained hard. He still refused to listen, just as the LORD had predicted.

14Then the LORD said to Moses, "Pharaoh's heart is stubborn,* and he still refuses to let the people go. 15So go to Pharaoh in the morning as he goes down to the river. Stand on the bank of the Nile and meet him there. Be sure to take along the staff that turned into a snake. 16Then announce to him, 'The LORD, the God of the Hebrews, has sent me to tell you, "Let my people go, so they can worship me in the wilderness." Until now, you have refused to listen to him. 17So this is what the LORD says: "I will show you that I am the LORD." Look! I will strike the water of the Nile with this staff in my hand, and the river will turn to blood. 18The fish in it will die, and the river will stink. The Egyptians will not be able to drink any water from the Nile.'"

19Then the LORD said to Moses: "Tell Aaron, 'Take your staff and raise your hand over the waters of Egypt—all its rivers, canals, ponds, and all the reservoirs. Turn all the water to blood.

Everywhere in Egypt the water will turn to blood, even the water stored in wooden bowls and stone pots.'"

²⁰So Moses and Aaron did just as the LORD commanded them. As Pharaoh and all of his officials watched, Aaron raised his staff and struck the water of the Nile. Suddenly, the whole river turned to blood! ²¹The fish in the river died, and the water became so foul that the Egyptians couldn't drink it. There was blood everywhere throughout the land of Egypt. ²²But again the magicians of Egypt used their magic, and they, too, turned water into blood. So Pharaoh's heart remained hard. He refused to listen to Moses and Aaron, just as the LORD had predicted. ²³Pharaoh returned to his palace and put the whole thing out of his mind. ²⁴Then all the Egyptians dug along the riverbank to find drinking water, for they couldn't drink the water from the Nile.

²⁵Seven days passed from the time the LORD struck the Nile.

6:2 *Yahweh* is a transliteration of the proper name *YHWH* that is sometimes rendered "Jehovah"; in this translation it is usually rendered "the LORD" (note the use of small capitals). 6:3 *El-Shaddai*, which means "God Almighty," is the name for God used in Gen 17:1; 28:3; 35:11; 43:14; 48:3. 6:12 Hebrew *I have uncircumcised lips;* also in 6:30. 7:9 Hebrew *tannin*, which elsewhere refers to a sea monster. Greek version translates it "dragon." 7:14 Hebrew *heavy.*

## MATTHEW 18:21–19:12

Then Peter came to him and asked, "Lord, how often should I forgive someone* who sins against me? Seven times?"

²²"No, not seven times," Jesus replied, "but seventy times seven!*

²³"Therefore, the Kingdom of Heaven can be compared to a king who decided to bring his accounts up to date with servants who had borrowed money from him. ²⁴In the process, one of his debtors was brought in who owed him millions of dollars.* ²⁵He couldn't pay, so his master ordered that he be sold—along with his wife, his children, and everything he owned—to pay the debt.

²⁶"But the man fell down before his master and begged him, 'Please, be patient with me, and I will pay it all.' ²⁷Then

his master was filled with pity for him, and he released him and forgave his debt.

²⁸"But when the man left the king, he went to a fellow servant who owed him a few thousand dollars.* He grabbed him by the throat and demanded instant payment.

²⁹"His fellow servant fell down before him and begged for a little more time. 'Be patient with me, and I will pay it,' he pleaded. ³⁰But his creditor wouldn't wait. He had the man arrested and put in prison until the debt could be paid in full.

³¹"When some of the other servants saw this, they were very upset. They went to the king and told him everything that had happened. ³²Then the king called in the man he had forgiven and said, 'You evil servant! I forgave you that tremendous debt because you pleaded with me. ³³Shouldn't you have mercy on your fellow servant, just as I had mercy on you?' ³⁴Then the angry king sent the man to prison to be tortured until he had paid his entire debt.

³⁵"That's what my heavenly Father will do to you if you refuse to forgive your brothers and sisters* from your heart."

¹⁹:¹WHEN Jesus had finished saying these things, he left Galilee and went down to the region of Judea east of the Jordan River. ²Large crowds followed him there, and he healed their sick.

³Some Pharisees came and tried to trap him with this question: "Should a man be allowed to divorce his wife for just any reason?"

⁴"Haven't you read the Scriptures?" Jesus replied. "They record that from the beginning 'God made them male and female.'* ⁵And he said, 'This explains why a man leaves his father and mother and is joined to his wife, and the two are united into one.'* ⁶Since they are no longer two but one, let no one split apart what God has joined together."

⁷"Then why did Moses say in the law that a man could give his wife a written notice of divorce and send her away?"* they asked.

8 Jesus replied, "Moses permitted divorce only as a concession to your hard hearts, but it was not what God had originally intended. 9 And I tell you this, whoever divorces his wife and marries someone else commits adultery—unless his wife has been unfaithful.*"

10 Jesus' disciples then said to him, "If this is the case, it is better not to marry!"

11 "Not everyone can accept this statement," Jesus said. "Only those whom God helps. 12 Some are born as eunuchs, some have been made eunuchs by others, and some choose not to marry for the sake of the Kingdom of Heaven. Let anyone accept this who can."

18:21 Greek *my brother.*   18:22 Or *seventy-seven times.*
18:24 Greek *10,000 talents* [375 tons or 340 metric tons of silver].   18:28 Greek *100 denarii.* A denarius was equivalent to a laborer's full day's wage.   18:35 Greek *your brother.*   19:4 Gen 1:27; 5:2.   19:5 Gen 2:24.   19:7 See Deut 24:1.   19:9 Some manuscripts add *And anyone who marries a divorced woman commits adultery.* Compare Matt 5:32.

PSALM 23:1-6
*A psalm of David.*

1  **The** Lord is my shepherd;
     I have all that I need.
2  He lets me rest in green meadows;
     he leads me beside peaceful
       streams.
3    He renews my strength.
     He guides me along right paths,
       bringing honor to his name.
4  Even when I walk
       through the darkest valley,*
     I will not be afraid,
       for you are close beside me.
     Your rod and your staff
       protect and comfort me.
5  You prepare a feast for me
       in the presence of my enemies.
     You honor me by anointing my head
       with oil.
     My cup overflows with
       blessings.
6  Surely your goodness and unfailing
       love will pursue me
     all the days of my life,
     and I will live in the house
       of the Lord
     forever.

23:4 Or *the dark valley of death.*

PROVERBS 5:22-23
**A**n evil man is held captive by his own sins; they are ropes that catch and hold him. He will die for lack of self-control; he will be lost because of his great foolishness.

# JANUARY
## 29

EXODUS 8:1–9:35
1 *Then the Lord said to Moses, "Go back to Pharaoh and announce to him, 'This is what the Lord says: Let my people go, so they can worship me. 2 If you refuse to let them go, I will send a plague of frogs across your entire land. 3 The Nile River will swarm with frogs. They will come up out of the river and into your palace, even into your bedroom and onto your bed! They will enter the houses of your officials and your people. They will even jump into your ovens and your kneading bowls. 4 Frogs will jump on you, your people, and all your officials.'"

5 *Then the Lord said to Moses, "Tell Aaron, 'Raise the staff in your hand over all the rivers, canals, and ponds of Egypt, and bring up frogs over all the land.'" 6 So Aaron raised his hand over the waters of Egypt, and frogs came up and covered the whole land! 7 But the magicians were able to do the same thing with their magic. They, too, caused frogs to come up on the land of Egypt.

8 Then Pharaoh summoned Moses and Aaron and begged, "Plead with the Lord to take the frogs away from me and my people. I will let your people go, so they can offer sacrifices to the Lord."

9 "You set the time!" Moses replied. "Tell me when you want me to pray for you, your officials, and your people. Then you and your houses will be rid of

the frogs. They will remain only in the Nile River."

¹⁰"Do it tomorrow," Pharaoh said.

"All right," Moses replied, "it will be as you have said. Then you will know that there is no one like the LORD our God. ¹¹The frogs will leave you and your houses, your officials, and your people. They will remain only in the Nile River."

¹²So Moses and Aaron left Pharaoh's palace, and Moses cried out to the LORD about the frogs he had inflicted on Pharaoh. ¹³And the LORD did just what Moses had predicted. The frogs in the houses, the courtyards, and the fields all died. ¹⁴The Egyptians piled them into great heaps, and a terrible stench filled the land. ¹⁵But when Pharaoh saw that relief had come, he became stubborn.* He refused to listen to Moses and Aaron, just as the LORD had predicted.

¹⁶So the LORD said to Moses, "Tell Aaron, 'Raise your staff and strike the ground. The dust will turn into swarms of gnats throughout the land of Egypt.'" ¹⁷So Moses and Aaron did just as the LORD had commanded them. When Aaron raised his hand and struck the ground with his staff, gnats infested the entire land, covering the Egyptians and their animals. All the dust in the land of Egypt turned into gnats. ¹⁸Pharaoh's magicians tried to do the same thing with their secret arts, but this time they failed. And the gnats covered everyone, people and animals alike.

¹⁹"This is the finger of God!" the magicians exclaimed to Pharaoh. But Pharaoh's heart remained hard. He wouldn't listen to them, just as the LORD had predicted.

²⁰Then the LORD told Moses, "Get up early in the morning and stand in Pharaoh's way as he goes down to the river. Say to him, 'This is what the LORD says: Let my people go, so they can worship me. ²¹If you refuse, then I will send swarms of flies on you, your officials, your people, and all the houses. The Egyptian homes will be filled with flies, and the ground will be covered with them. ²²But this time I will spare the re-

gion of Goshen, where my people live. No flies will be found there. Then you will know that I am the LORD and that I am present even in the heart of your land. ²³I will make a clear distinction between* my people and your people. This miraculous sign will happen tomorrow.'"

²⁴And the LORD did just as he had said. A thick swarm of flies filled Pharaoh's palace and the houses of his officials. The whole land of Egypt was thrown into chaos by the flies.

²⁵Pharaoh called for Moses and Aaron. "All right! Go ahead and offer sacrifices to your God," he said. "But do it here in this land."

²⁶But Moses replied, "That wouldn't be right. The Egyptians detest the sacrifices that we offer to the LORD our God. Look, if we offer our sacrifices here where the Egyptians can see us, they will stone us. ²⁷We must take a three-day trip into the wilderness to offer sacrifices to the LORD our God, just as he has commanded us."

²⁸"All right, go ahead," Pharaoh replied. "I will let you go into the wilderness to offer sacrifices to the LORD your God. But don't go too far away. Now hurry and pray for me."

²⁹Moses answered, "As soon as I leave you, I will pray to the LORD, and tomorrow the swarms of flies will disappear from you and your officials and all your people. But I am warning you, Pharaoh, don't lie to us again and refuse to let the people go to sacrifice to the LORD."

³⁰So Moses left Pharaoh's palace and pleaded with the LORD to remove all the flies. ³¹And the LORD did as Moses asked and caused the swarms of flies to disappear from Pharaoh, his officials, and his people. Not a single fly remained. ³²But Pharaoh again became stubborn and refused to let the people go.

⁹:¹"Go back to Pharaoh," the LORD commanded Moses. "Tell him, 'This is what the LORD, the God of the Hebrews, says: Let my people go, so they can worship me. ²If you continue to hold them and

refuse to let them go, [3] the hand of the LORD will strike all your livestock—your horses, donkeys, camels, cattle, sheep, and goats—with a deadly plague. [4] But the LORD will again make a distinction between the livestock of the Israelites and that of the Egyptians. Not a single one of Israel's animals will die! [5] The LORD has already set the time for the plague to begin. He has declared that he will strike the land tomorrow.'"

[6] And the LORD did just as he had said. The next morning all the livestock of the Egyptians died, but the Israelites didn't lose a single animal. [7] Pharaoh sent his officials to investigate, and they discovered that the Israelites had not lost a single animal! But even so, Pharaoh's heart remained stubborn,* and he still refused to let the people go.

[8] Then the LORD said to Moses and Aaron, "Take handfuls of soot from a brick kiln, and have Moses toss it into the air while Pharaoh watches. [9] The ashes will spread like fine dust over the whole land of Egypt, causing festering boils to break out on people and animals throughout the land."

[10] So they took soot from a brick kiln and went and stood before Pharaoh. As Pharaoh watched, Moses threw the soot into the air, and boils broke out on people and animals alike. [11] Even the magicians were unable to stand before Moses, because the boils had broken out on them and all the Egyptians. [12] But the LORD hardened Pharaoh's heart, and just as the LORD had predicted to Moses, Pharaoh refused to listen.

[13] Then the LORD said to Moses, "Get up early in the morning and stand before Pharaoh. Tell him, 'This is what the LORD, the God of the Hebrews, says: Let my people go, so they can worship me. [14] If you don't, I will send more plagues on you* and your officials and your people. Then you will know that there is no one like me in all the earth. [15] By now I could have lifted my hand and struck you and your people with a plague to wipe you off the face of the earth. [16] But I have spared you for a purpose—to

show you my power* and to spread my fame throughout the earth. [17] But you still lord it over my people and refuse to let them go. [18] So tomorrow at this time I will send a hailstorm more devastating than any in all the history of Egypt. [19] Quick! Order your livestock and servants to come in from the fields to find shelter. Any person or animal left outside will die when the hail falls.'"

[20] Some of Pharaoh's officials were afraid because of what the LORD had said. They quickly brought their servants and livestock in from the fields. [21] But those who paid no attention to the word of the LORD left theirs out in the open.

[22] Then the LORD said to Moses, "Lift your hand toward the sky so hail may fall on the people, the livestock, and all the plants throughout the land of Egypt."

[23] So Moses lifted his staff toward the sky, and the LORD sent thunder and hail, and lightning flashed toward the earth. The LORD sent a tremendous hailstorm against all the land of Egypt. [24] Never in all the history of Egypt had there been a storm like that, with such devastating hail and continuous lightning. [25] It left all of Egypt in ruins. The hail struck down everything in the open field—people, animals, and plants alike. Even the trees were destroyed. [26] The only place without hail was the region of Goshen, where the people of Israel lived.

[27] Then Pharaoh quickly summoned Moses and Aaron. "This time I have sinned," he confessed. "The LORD is the righteous one, and my people and I are wrong. [28] Please beg the LORD to end this terrifying thunder and hail. We've had enough. I will let you go; you don't need to stay any longer."

[29] "All right," Moses replied. "As soon as I leave the city, I will lift my hands and pray to the LORD. Then the thunder and hail will stop, and you will know that the earth belongs to the LORD. [30] But I know that you and your officials still do not fear the LORD God."

[31] (All the flax and barley were ruined

by the hail, because the barley had formed heads and the flax was budding. ³²But the wheat and the emmer wheat were spared, because they had not yet sprouted from the ground.)

³³So Moses left Pharaoh's court and went out of the city. When he lifted his hands to the LORD, the thunder and hail stopped, and the downpour ceased. ³⁴But when Pharaoh saw that the rain, hail, and thunder had stopped, he and his officials sinned again, and Pharaoh again became stubborn.* ³⁵Because his heart was hard, Pharaoh refused to let the people leave, just as the LORD had predicted through Moses.

8:1 Verses 8:1-4 are numbered 7:26-29 in Hebrew text. 8:5 Verses 8:5-32 are numbered 8:1-28 in Hebrew text. 8:15 Hebrew *made his heart heavy;* also in 8:32.   8:23 As in Greek and Latin versions; Hebrew reads *I will set redemption between.*   9:7 Hebrew *heavy.*   9:14 Hebrew *on your heart.*   9:16 Greek version reads *to display my power in you;* compare Rom 9:17.   9:34 Hebrew *made his heart heavy.*

## MATTHEW 19:13-30

One day some parents brought their children to Jesus so he could lay his hands on them and pray for them. But the disciples scolded the parents for bothering him.

¹⁴**But Jesus said, "Let the children come to me. Don't stop them! For the Kingdom of Heaven belongs to those who are like these children." ¹⁵And he placed his hands on their heads and blessed them before he left.**

¹⁶Someone came to Jesus with this question: "Teacher,* what good deed must I do to have eternal life?"

¹⁷"Why ask me about what is good?" Jesus replied. "There is only One who is good. But to answer your question—if you want to receive eternal life, keep* the commandments."

¹⁸"Which ones?" the man asked.

And Jesus replied: " 'You must not murder. You must not commit adultery. You must not steal. You must not testify falsely. ¹⁹Honor your father and mother. Love your neighbor as yourself.'*"

²⁰"I've obeyed all these commandments," the young man replied. "What else must I do?"

²¹Jesus told him, "If you want to be perfect, go and sell all your possessions and give the money to the poor, and you will have treasure in heaven. Then come, follow me."

²²But when the young man heard this, he went away very sad, for he had many possessions.

²³Then Jesus said to his disciples, "I tell you the truth, it is very hard for a rich person to enter the Kingdom of Heaven. ²⁴I'll say it again—it is easier for a camel to go through the eye of a needle than for a rich person to enter the Kingdom of God!"

²⁵The disciples were astounded. "Then who in the world can be saved?" they asked.

²⁶Jesus looked at them intently and said, "Humanly speaking, it is impossible. But with God everything is possible."

²⁷Then Peter said to him, "We've given up everything to follow you. What will we get?"

²⁸"Yes," Jesus replied, "and I assure you that when the world is made new* and the Son of Man* sits upon his glorious throne, you who have been my followers will also sit on twelve thrones, judging the twelve tribes of Israel. ²⁹And everyone who has given up houses or brothers or sisters or father or mother or children or property, for my sake, will receive a hundred times as much in return and will inherit eternal life. ³⁰But many who are the greatest now will be least important then, and those who seem least important now will be the greatest then.*"

19:16 Some manuscripts read *Good Teacher.*   19:17 Some manuscripts read *continue to keep.*   19:18-19 Exod 20:12-16; Deut 5:16-20; Lev 19:18.   19:28a Or *in the regeneration.*   19:28b "Son of Man" is a title Jesus used for himself.   19:30 Greek *But many who are first will be last; and the last, first.*

## PSALM 24:1-10
*A psalm of David.*

¹ The earth is the LORD's, and
      everything in it.
   The world and all its people
      belong to him.

2 For he laid the earth's foundation
       on the seas
   and built it on the ocean depths.

3 Who may climb the mountain
       of the LORD?
   Who may stand in his holy place?
4 Only those whose hands and hearts
       are pure,
   who do not worship idols
   and never tell lies.
5 They will receive the LORD's blessing
   and have a right relationship with
       God their savior.
6 Such people may seek you
   and worship in your presence,
       O God of Jacob.        *Interlude*

7 Open up, ancient gates!
       Open up, ancient doors,
       and let the King of glory enter.
8 Who is the King of glory?
       The LORD, strong and mighty;
       the LORD, invincible in battle.
9 Open up, ancient gates!
       Open up, ancient doors,
       and let the King of glory enter.
10 Who is the King of glory?
       The LORD of Heaven's Armies—
       he is the King of glory.
                                    *Interlude*

## PROVERBS 6:1-5

**M**y child,* if you have put up security
for a friend's debt or agreed to guarantee the debt of a stranger—if you have
trapped yourself by your agreement and
are caught by what you said— follow my
advice and save yourself, for you have
placed yourself at your friend's mercy.
Now swallow your pride; go and beg to
have your name erased. Don't put it off;
do it now! Don't rest until you do. Save
yourself like a gazelle escaping from a
hunter, like a bird fleeing from a net.

6:1 Hebrew *My son.*

# JANUARY
# 30

## EXODUS 10:1–12:13

**T**hen the LORD said to Moses, "Return to
Pharaoh and make your demands
again. I have made him and his officials
stubborn* so I can display my miraculous signs among them. 2I've also done
it so you can tell your children and
grandchildren about how I made a
mockery of the Egyptians and about the
signs I displayed among them—and so
you will know that I am the LORD."

3So Moses and Aaron went to Pharaoh and said, "This is what the LORD,
the God of the Hebrews, says: How long
will you refuse to submit to me? Let my
people go, so they can worship me. 4If
you refuse, watch out! For tomorrow I
will bring a swarm of locusts on your
country. 5They will cover the land so
that you won't be able to see the ground.
They will devour what little is left of
your crops after the hailstorm, including all the trees growing in the fields.
6They will overrun your palaces and the
homes of your officials and all the
houses in Egypt. Never in the history of
Egypt have your ancestors seen a plague
like this one!" And with that, Moses
turned and left Pharaoh.

7Pharaoh's officials now came to Pharaoh and appealed to him. "How long
will you let this man hold us hostage? Let
the men go to worship the LORD their
God! Don't you realize that Egypt lies in
ruins?"

8So Moses and Aaron were brought
back to Pharaoh. "All right," he told them,
"go and worship the LORD your God. But
who exactly will be going with you?"

9Moses replied. "We will all go—
young and old, our sons and daughters,
and our flocks and herds. We must all
join together in celebrating a festival to
the LORD."

10Pharaoh retorted, "The LORD will
certainly need to be with you if I let you

take your little ones! I can see through your evil plan. ¹¹Never! Only the men may go and worship the LORD, since that is what you requested." And Pharaoh threw them out of the palace.

¹²Then the LORD said to Moses, "Raise your hand over the land of Egypt to bring on the locusts. Let them cover the land and devour every plant that survived the hailstorm."

¹³So Moses raised his staff over Egypt, and the LORD caused an east wind to blow over the land all that day and through the night. When morning arrived, the east wind had brought the locusts. ¹⁴And the locusts swarmed over the whole land of Egypt, settling in dense swarms from one end of the country to the other. It was the worst locust plague in Egyptian history, and there has never been another one like it. ¹⁵For the locusts covered the whole country and darkened the land. They devoured every plant in the fields and all the fruit on the trees that had survived the hailstorm. Not a single leaf was left on the trees and plants throughout the land of Egypt.

¹⁶Pharaoh quickly summoned Moses and Aaron. "I have sinned against the LORD your God and against you," he confessed. ¹⁷"Forgive my sin, just this once, and plead with the LORD your God to take away this death from me."

¹⁸So Moses left Pharaoh's court and pleaded with the LORD. ¹⁹The LORD responded by shifting the wind, and the strong west wind blew the locusts into the Red Sea.* Not a single locust remained in all the land of Egypt. ²⁰But the LORD hardened Pharaoh's heart again, so he refused to let the people go.

²¹Then the LORD said to Moses, "Lift your hand toward heaven, and the land of Egypt will be covered with a darkness so thick you can feel it." ²²So Moses lifted his hand to the sky, and a deep darkness covered the entire land of Egypt for three days. ²³During all that time the people could not see each other, and no one moved. But there was light as usual where the people of Israel lived.

²⁴Finally, Pharaoh called for Moses. "Go and worship the LORD," he said. "But leave your flocks and herds here. You may even take your little ones with you."

²⁵"No," Moses said, "you must provide us with animals for sacrifices and burnt offerings to the LORD our God. ²⁶All our livestock must go with us, too; not a hoof can be left behind. We must choose our sacrifices for the LORD our God from among these animals. And we won't know how we are to worship the LORD until we get there."

²⁷But the LORD hardened Pharaoh's heart once more, and he would not let them go. ²⁸"Get out of here!" Pharaoh shouted at Moses. "I'm warning you. Never come back to see me again! The day you see my face, you will die!"

²⁹"Very well," Moses replied. "I will never see your face again."

¹¹:¹THEN the LORD said to Moses, "I will strike Pharaoh and the land of Egypt with one more blow. After that, Pharaoh will let you leave this country. In fact, he will be so eager to get rid of you that he will force you all to leave. ²Tell all the Israelite men and women to ask their Egyptian neighbors for articles of silver and gold." ³(Now the LORD had caused the Egyptians to look favorably on the people of Israel. And Moses was considered a very great man in the land of Egypt, respected by Pharaoh's officials and the Egyptian people alike.)

⁴Moses had announced to Pharaoh, "This is what the LORD says: At midnight tonight I will pass through the heart of Egypt. ⁵All the firstborn sons will die in every family in Egypt, from the oldest son of Pharaoh, who sits on his throne, to the oldest son of his lowliest servant girl who grinds the flour. Even the firstborn of all the livestock will die. ⁶Then a loud wail will rise throughout the land of Egypt, a wail like no one has heard before or will ever hear again. ⁷But among the Israelites it will be so peaceful that not even a dog will bark. Then you will

know that the LORD makes a distinction between the Egyptians and the Israelites. [8]All the officials of Egypt will run to me and fall to the ground before me. 'Please leave!' they will beg. 'Hurry! And take all your followers with you.' Only then will I go!" Then, burning with anger, Moses left Pharaoh.

[9]Now the LORD had told Moses earlier, "Pharaoh will not listen to you, but then I will do even more mighty miracles in the land of Egypt." [10]Moses and Aaron performed these miracles in Pharaoh's presence, but the LORD hardened Pharaoh's heart, and he wouldn't let the Israelites leave the country.

[12:1]WHILE the Israelites were still in the land of Egypt, the LORD gave the following instructions to Moses and Aaron: [2]"From now on, this month will be the first month of the year for you. [3]Announce to the whole community of Israel that on the tenth day of this month each family must choose a lamb or a young goat for a sacrifice, one animal for each household. [4]If a family is too small to eat a whole animal, let them share with another family in the neighborhood. Divide the animal according to the size of each family and how much they can eat. [5]The animal you select must be a one-year-old male, either a sheep or a goat, with no defects.

[6]"Take special care of this chosen animal until the evening of the fourteenth day of this first month. Then the whole assembly of the community of Israel must slaughter their lamb or young goat at twilight. [7]They are to take some of the blood and smear it on the sides and top of the doorframes of the houses where they eat the animal. [8]That same night they must roast the meat over a fire and eat it along with bitter salad greens and bread made without yeast. [9]Do not eat any of the meat raw or boiled in water. The whole animal—including the head, legs, and internal organs—must be roasted over a fire. [10]Do not leave any of it until the next morning. Burn whatever is not eaten before morning.

[11]"These are your instructions for eating this meal: Be fully dressed,* wear your sandals, and carry your walking stick in your hand. Eat the meal with urgency, for this is the LORD's Passover. [12]On that night I will pass through the land of Egypt and strike down every firstborn son and firstborn male animal in the land of Egypt. I will execute judgment against all the gods of Egypt, for I am the LORD! [13]But the blood on your doorposts will serve as a sign, marking the houses where you are staying. When I see the blood, I will pass over you. This plague of death will not touch you when I strike the land of Egypt."

10:1 Hebrew *have made his heart and his officials' hearts heavy.*   10:19 Hebrew *sea of reeds.*   12:11 Hebrew *Bind up your loins.*

## MATTHEW 20:1-28

"For the Kingdom of Heaven is like the landowner who went out early one morning to hire workers for his vineyard. [2]He agreed to pay the normal daily wage* and sent them out to work.

[3]"At nine o'clock in the morning he was passing through the marketplace and saw some people standing around doing nothing. [4]So he hired them, telling them he would pay them whatever was right at the end of the day. [5]So they went to work in the vineyard. At noon and again at three o'clock he did the same thing.

[6]"At five o'clock that afternoon he was in town again and saw some more people standing around. He asked them, 'Why haven't you been working today?'

[7]"They replied, 'Because no one hired us.'

"The landowner told them, 'Then go out and join the others in my vineyard.'

[8]"That evening he told the foreman to call the workers in and pay them, beginning with the last workers first. [9]When those hired at five o'clock were paid, each received a full day's wage. [10]When those hired first came to get their pay, they assumed they would receive more. But they, too, were paid a day's wage. [11]When they received their pay, they protested to

the owner, ¹²"Those people worked only one hour, and yet you've paid them just as much as you paid us who worked all day in the scorching heat.'

¹³"He answered one of them, 'Friend, I haven't been unfair! Didn't you agree to work all day for the usual wage? ¹⁴Take your money and go. I wanted to pay this last worker the same as you. ¹⁵Is it against the law for me to do what I want with my money? Should you be jealous because I am kind to others?'

¹⁶"So those who are last now will be first then, and those who are first will be last."

¹⁷As Jesus was going up to Jerusalem, he took the twelve disciples aside privately and told them what was going to happen to him. ¹⁸"Listen," he said, "we're going up to Jerusalem, where the Son of Man* will be betrayed to the leading priests and the teachers of religious law. They will sentence him to die. ¹⁹Then they will hand him over to the Romans* to be mocked, flogged with a whip, and crucified. But on the third day he will be raised from the dead."

²⁰Then the mother of James and John, the sons of Zebedee, came to Jesus with her sons. She knelt respectfully to ask a favor. ²¹"What is your request?" he asked.

She replied, "In your Kingdom, please let my two sons sit in places of honor next to you, one on your right and the other on your left."

²²But Jesus answered by saying to them, "You don't know what you are asking! Are you able to drink from the bitter cup of suffering I am about to drink?"

"Oh yes," they replied, "we are able!"

²³Jesus told them, "You will indeed drink from my bitter cup. But I have no right to say who will sit on my right or my left. My Father has prepared those places for the ones he has chosen."

²⁴When the ten other disciples heard what James and John had asked, they were indignant. ²⁵But Jesus called them together and said, "You know that the rulers in this world lord it over their people, and officials flaunt their authority over those under them. ²⁶**But among you it will be different. Whoever wants to be a leader among you must be your servant, ²⁷and whoever wants to be first among you must become your slave. ²⁸For even the Son of Man came not to be served but to serve others and to give his life as a ransom for many."**

20:2 Greek *a denarius*, the payment for a full day's labor; similarly in 20:9, 10, 13.   **20:18** "Son of Man" is a title Jesus used for himself.   **20:19** Greek *the Gentiles*.

## PSALM 25:1-15*
*A psalm of David.*

¹ ● LORD, I give my life to you.
²   I trust in you, my God!
 Do not let me be disgraced,
   or let my enemies rejoice
     in my defeat.
³ No one who trusts in you will ever
   be disgraced,
   but disgrace comes to those who
     try to deceive others.

⁴ Show me the right path, O LORD;
   point out the road for me
     to follow.
⁵ Lead me by your truth and teach me,
   for you are the God who saves me.
   All day long I put my hope in you.
⁶ Remember, O LORD, your
   compassion and unfailing love,
   which you have shown from long
     ages past.
⁷ Do not remember the rebellious sins
   of my youth.
   Remember me in the light of your
     unfailing love,
   for you are merciful, O LORD.

⁸ The LORD is good and does what is
   right;
   he shows the proper path to those
     who go astray.
⁹ He leads the humble in doing right,
   teaching them his way.
¹⁰ The LORD leads with unfailing love
   and faithfulness
   all who keep his covenant and
     obey his demands.

¹¹ For the honor of your name, O LORD,
   forgive my many, many sins.

¹² Who are those who fear the LORD?
He will show them the path they
should choose.
¹³ They will live in prosperity,
and their children will inherit
the land.
¹⁴ The LORD is a friend to those who
fear him.
He teaches them his covenant.
¹⁵ My eyes are always on the LORD,
for he rescues me from the traps
of my enemies.

25 This psalm is a Hebrew acrostic poem; each verse
begins with a successive letter of the Hebrew alphabet.

## PROVERBS 6:6-11

**T**ake a lesson from the ants, you lazybones. Learn from their ways and become wise! Though they have no prince
or governor or ruler to make them work,
they labor hard all summer, gathering
food for the winter. But you, lazybones,
how long will you sleep? When will you
wake up? A little extra sleep, a little more
slumber, a little folding of the hands to
rest— then poverty will pounce on you
like a bandit; scarcity will attack you like
an armed robber.

# JANUARY
# 31

## EXODUS 12:14–13:16

"**T**his is a day to remember. Each year,
from generation to generation, you
must celebrate it as a special festival to
the LORD. This is a law for all time.
¹⁵For seven days the bread you eat
must be made without yeast. On the
first day of the festival, remove every
trace of yeast from your homes. Anyone who eats bread made with yeast
during the seven days of the festival
will be cut off from the community of
Israel. ¹⁶On the first day of the festival
and again on the seventh day, all the
people must observe an official day for

holy assembly. No work of any kind
may be done on these days except in
the preparation of food.

¹⁷"Celebrate this Festival of Unleavened
Bread, for it will remind you that I brought
your forces out of the land of Egypt on
this very day. This festival will be a permanent law for you; celebrate this day
from generation to generation. ¹⁸The
bread you eat must be made without
yeast from the evening of the fourteenth
day of the first month until the evening
of the twenty-first day of that month.
¹⁹During those seven days, there must be
no trace of yeast in your homes. Anyone
who eats anything made with yeast during this week will be cut off from the
community of Israel. These regulations
apply both to the foreigners living
among you and to the native-born Israelites. ²⁰During those days you must not
eat anything made with yeast. Wherever
you live, eat only bread made without
yeast."

²¹Then Moses called all the elders of
Israel together and said to them, "Go,
pick out a lamb or young goat for each of
your families, and slaughter the Passover
animal. ²²Drain the blood into a basin.
Then take a bundle of hyssop branches
and dip it into the blood. Brush the hyssop across the top and sides of the
doorframes of your houses. And no one
may go out through the door until morning. ²³For the LORD will pass through the
land to strike down the Egyptians. But
when he sees the blood on the top and
sides of the doorframe, the LORD will
pass over your home. He will not permit
his death angel to enter your house and
strike you down.

²⁴"Remember, these instructions are
a permanent law that you and your
descendants must observe forever.
²⁵When you enter the land the LORD
has promised to give you, you will continue to observe this ceremony. ²⁶Then
your children will ask, 'What does this
ceremony mean?' ²⁷And you will reply,
'It is the Passover sacrifice to the LORD,
for he passed over the houses of the Israelites in Egypt. And though he struck

the Egyptians, he spared our families.'"
When Moses had finished speaking, all
the people bowed down to the ground
and worshiped.

28So the people of Israel did just as the
LORD had commanded through Moses
and Aaron. 29And that night at midnight,
the LORD struck down all the firstborn
sons in the land of Egypt, from the firstborn son of Pharaoh, who sat on his
throne, to the firstborn son of the prisoner in the dungeon. Even the firstborn
of their livestock were killed. 30Pharaoh
and all his officials and all the people of
Egypt woke up during the night, and
loud wailing was heard throughout the
land of Egypt. There was not a single
house where someone had not died.

31Pharaoh sent for Moses and Aaron
during the night. "Get out!" he ordered.
"Leave my people—and take the rest of
the Israelites with you! Go and worship
the LORD as you have requested. 32Take
your flocks and herds, as you said, and be
gone. Go, but bless me as you leave." 33All
the Egyptians urged the people of Israel
to get out of the land as quickly as possible, for they thought, "We will all die!"

34The Israelites took their bread
dough before yeast was added. They
wrapped their kneading boards in their
cloaks and carried them on their shoulders. 35And the people of Israel did as
Moses had instructed; they asked the
Egyptians for clothing and articles of
silver and gold. 36The LORD caused the
Egyptians to look favorably on the Israelites, and they gave the Israelites whatever they asked for. So they stripped the
Egyptians of their wealth!

37That night the people of Israel left
Rameses and started for Succoth. There
were about 600,000 men,* plus all the
women and children. 38A rabble of non-
Israelites went with them, along with
great flocks and herds of livestock.
39For bread they baked flat cakes from
the dough without yeast they had
brought from Egypt. It was made without yeast because the people were
driven out of Egypt in such a hurry that

they had no time to prepare the bread
or other food.

40The people of Israel had lived in
Egypt* for 430 years. 41In fact, it was on
the last day of the 430th year that all the
LORD's forces left the land. 42On this
night the LORD kept his promise to bring
his people out of the land of Egypt. So
this night belongs to him, and it must be
commemorated every year by all the Israelites, from generation to generation.

43Then the LORD said to Moses and
Aaron, "These are the instructions for
the festival of Passover. No outsiders
are allowed to eat the Passover meal.
44But any slave who has been purchased
may eat it if he has been circumcised.
45Temporary residents and hired servants may not eat it. 46Each Passover
lamb must be eaten in one house. Do
not carry any of its meat outside, and do
not break any of its bones. 47The whole
community of Israel must celebrate this
Passover festival.

48"If there are foreigners living among
you who want to celebrate the LORD's
Passover, let all their males be circumcised. Only then may they celebrate the
Passover with you like any native-born
Israelite. But no uncircumcised male
may ever eat the Passover meal. 49This
instruction applies to everyone, whether
a native-born Israelite or a foreigner living among you."

50So all the people of Israel followed
all the LORD's commands to Moses and
Aaron. 51On that very day the LORD
brought the people of Israel out of the
land of Egypt like an army.

13:1Then the LORD said to Moses, 2"Dedicate to me every firstborn among the
Israelites. The first offspring to be born,
of both humans and animals, belongs to
me."

3So Moses said to the people, "This is a
day to remember forever—the day you
left Egypt, the place of your slavery. Today the LORD has brought you out by the
power of his mighty hand. (Remember,
eat no food containing yeast.) 4On this
day in early spring, in the month of

Abib,* you have been set free. [5] You must celebrate this event in this month each year after the LORD brings you into the land of the Canaanites, Hittites, Amorites, Hivites, and Jebusites. (He swore to your ancestors that he would give you this land—a land flowing with milk and honey.) [6] For seven days the bread you eat must be made without yeast. Then on the seventh day, celebrate a feast to the LORD. [7] Eat bread without yeast during those seven days. In fact, there must be no yeast bread or any yeast at all found within the borders of your land during this time.

[8] "On the seventh day you must explain to your children, 'I am celebrating what the LORD did for me when I left Egypt.' [9] This annual festival will be a visible sign to you, like a mark branded on your hand or your forehead. Let it remind you always to recite this teaching of the LORD: 'With a strong hand, the LORD rescued you from Egypt.'* [10] So observe the decree of this festival at the appointed time each year.

[11] "This is what you must do when the LORD fulfills the promise he swore to you and to your ancestors. When he gives you the land where the Canaanites now live, [12] you must present all firstborn sons and firstborn male animals to the LORD, for they belong to him. [13] A firstborn donkey may be bought back from the LORD by presenting a lamb or young goat in its place. But if you do not buy it back, you must break its neck. However, you must buy back every firstborn son.

[14] "And in the future, your children will ask you, 'What does all this mean?' Then you will tell them, 'With the power of his mighty hand, the LORD brought us out of Egypt, the place of our slavery. [15] Pharaoh stubbornly refused to let us go, so the LORD killed all the firstborn males throughout the land of Egypt, both people and animals. That is why I now sacrifice all the firstborn males to the LORD—except that the firstborn sons are always bought back.' [16] This ceremony will be like a mark branded on your hand or your forehead. It is a reminder that

the power of the LORD's mighty hand brought us out of Egypt."

12:37 Or *fighting men;* Hebrew reads *men on foot.*
12:40 Samaritan Pentateuch reads *in Canaan and Egypt;* Greek version reads *in Egypt and Canaan.*   13:4 Hebrew *On this day in the month of Abib.* This first month of the ancient Hebrew lunar calendar usually occurs within the months of March and April.   13:9 Or *Let it remind you always to keep the instructions of the LORD on the tip of your tongue, because with a strong hand, the LORD rescued you from Egypt.*

## MATTHEW 20:29–21:22

**A**s Jesus and the disciples left the town of Jericho, a large crowd followed behind. [30] Two blind men were sitting beside the road. When they heard that Jesus was coming that way, they began shouting, "Lord, Son of David, have mercy on us!"

[31] "Be quiet!" the crowd yelled at them.

But they only shouted louder, "Lord, Son of David, have mercy on us!"

[32] When Jesus heard them, he stopped and called, "What do you want me to do for you?"

[33] "Lord," they said, "we want to see!" [34] Jesus felt sorry for them and touched their eyes. Instantly they could see! Then they followed him.

[21:1] As Jesus and the disciples approached Jerusalem, they came to the town of Bethphage on the Mount of Olives. Jesus sent two of them on ahead. [2] "Go into the village over there," he said. "As soon as you enter it, you will see a donkey tied there, with its colt beside it. Untie them and bring them to me. [3] If anyone asks what you are doing, just say, 'The Lord needs them,' and he will immediately let you take them."

[4] This took place to fulfill the prophecy that said,

[5] "Tell the people of Israel,*
      'Look, your King is coming to you.
   He is humble, riding on a donkey—
      riding on a donkey's colt.'"*

[6] The two disciples did as Jesus commanded. [7] They brought the donkey and the colt to him and threw their garments over the colt, and he sat on it.* [8] Most of the crowd spread their garments on the road ahead of him, and

others cut branches from the trees and spread them on the road. ⁹Jesus was in the center of the procession, and the people all around him were shouting,

"Praise God* for the Son of David!
Blessings on the one who comes
    in the name of the LORD!
Praise God in highest heaven!"*

¹⁰The entire city of Jerusalem was in an uproar as he entered. "Who is this?" they asked.

¹¹And the crowds replied, "It's Jesus, the prophet from Nazareth in Galilee."

¹²Jesus entered the Temple and began to drive out all the people buying and selling animals for sacrifice. He knocked over the tables of the money changers and the chairs of those selling doves. ¹³He said to them, "The Scriptures declare, 'My Temple will be called a house of prayer,' but you have turned it into a den of thieves!"*

¹⁴The blind and the lame came to him in the Temple, and he healed them. ¹⁵The leading priests and the teachers of religious law saw these wonderful miracles and heard even the children in the Temple shouting, "Praise God for the Son of David."

But the leaders were indignant. ¹⁶They asked Jesus, "Do you hear what these children are saying?"

"Yes," Jesus replied. "Haven't you ever read the Scriptures? For they say, 'You have taught children and infants to give you praise.'*" ¹⁷Then he returned to Bethany, where he stayed overnight.

¹⁸In the morning, as Jesus was returning to Jerusalem, he was hungry, ¹⁹and he noticed a fig tree beside the road. He went over to see if there were any figs, but there were only leaves. Then he said to it, "May you never bear fruit again!" And immediately the fig tree withered up.

²⁰The disciples were amazed when they saw this and asked, "How did the fig tree wither so quickly?"

²¹Then Jesus told them, "I tell you the truth, if you have faith and don't doubt, you can do things like this and much more. You can even say to this mountain, 'May you be lifted up and thrown into the sea,' and it will happen. ²²You can pray for anything, and if you have faith, you will receive it."

21:5a Greek *Tell the daughter of Zion.* Isa 62:11.
21:5b Zech 9:9.   21:7 Greek *over them, and he sat on them.*   21:9a Greek *Hosanna,* an exclamation of praise that literally means "save now"; also in 21:9b, 15.
21:9b Pss 118:25-26; 148:1.   21:13 Isa 56:7; Jer 7:11.
21:16 Ps 8:2.

PSALM 25:16-22

**Turn to me and have mercy,
    for I am alone and in deep
        distress.**
¹⁷ **My problems go from bad to worse.
    Oh, save me from them all!**
¹⁸ Feel my pain and see my trouble.
    Forgive all my sins.
¹⁹ See how many enemies I have
    and how viciously they hate me!
²⁰ Protect me! Rescue my life from
        them!
    Do not let me be disgraced,
        for in you I take refuge.
²¹ May integrity and honesty
        protect me,
    for I put my hope in you.

²² O God, ransom Israel
    from all its troubles.

PROVERBS 6:12-15

**W**hat are worthless and wicked people like? They are constant liars, signaling their deceit with a wink of the eye, a nudge of the foot, or the wiggle of fingers. Their perverted hearts plot evil, and they constantly stir up trouble. But they will be destroyed suddenly, broken in an instant beyond all hope of healing.

# FEBRUARY 1

EXODUS 13:17–15:18

**W**hen Pharaoh finally let the people go, God did not lead them along the main road that runs through Philistine territory, even though that was the shortest route to the Promised Land. God said, "If the people are faced with a battle, they might change their minds and return to Egypt." ¹⁸So God led them in a roundabout way through the wilderness toward the Red Sea.* Thus the Israelites left Egypt like an army ready for battle.*

¹⁹Moses took the bones of Joseph with him, for Joseph had made the sons of Israel swear to do this. He said, "God will certainly come to help you. When he does, you must take my bones with you from this place."

²⁰The Israelites left Succoth and camped at Etham on the edge of the wilderness. ²¹The Lord went ahead of them. He guided them during the day with a pillar of cloud, and he provided light at night with a pillar of fire. This allowed them to travel by day or by night. ²²And the Lord did not remove the pillar of cloud or pillar of fire from its place in front of the people.

¹⁴:¹Then the Lord gave these instructions to Moses: ²"Order the Israelites to turn back and camp by Pi-hahiroth between Migdol and the sea. Camp there along the shore, across from Baalzephon. ³Then Pharaoh will think, 'The Israelites are confused. They are trapped in the wilderness!' ⁴And once again I will harden Pharaoh's heart, and he will chase after you.* I have planned this in order to display my glory through Pharaoh and his whole army. After this the Egyptians will know that I am the Lord!"

So the Israelites camped there as they were told.

⁵When word reached the king of Egypt that the Israelites had fled, Pharaoh and his officials changed their minds. "What have we done, letting all those Israelite slaves get away?" they asked. ⁶So Pharaoh harnessed his chariot and called up his troops. ⁷He took with him 600 of Egypt's best chariots, along with the rest of the chariots of Egypt, each with its commander. ⁸The Lord hardened the heart of Pharaoh, the king of Egypt, so he chased after the people of Israel, who had left with fists raised in defiance. ⁹The Egyptians chased after them with all the forces in Pharaoh's army—all his horses and chariots, his charioteers, and his troops. The Egyptians caught up with the people of Israel as they were camped beside the shore near Pi-hahiroth, across from Baal-zephon.

¹⁰As Pharaoh approached, the people of Israel looked up and panicked when they saw the Egyptians overtaking them. They cried out to the Lord, ¹¹and they said to Moses, "Why did you bring us out here to die in the wilderness? Weren't there enough graves for us in Egypt? What have you done to us? Why did you make us leave Egypt? ¹²Didn't we tell you this would happen while we were still in Egypt? We said, 'Leave us alone! Let us be slaves to the Egyptians. It's better to be a slave in Egypt than a corpse in the wilderness!'"

¹³**But Moses told the people, "Don't be afraid. Just stand still and watch the Lord rescue you today. The Egyptians you see today will never be seen again. ¹⁴The Lord himself will fight for you. Just stay calm."**

¹⁵Then the Lord said to Moses, "Why are you crying out to me? Tell the people to get moving! ¹⁶Pick up your staff and raise your hand over the sea. Divide

the water so the Israelites can walk through the middle of the sea on dry ground. ¹⁷And I will harden the hearts of the Egyptians, and they will charge in after the Israelites. My great glory will be displayed through Pharaoh and his troops, his chariots, and his charioteers. ¹⁸When my glory is displayed through them, all Egypt will see my glory and know that I am the Lord!"

¹⁹Then the angel of God, who had been leading the people of Israel, moved to the rear of the camp. The pillar of cloud also moved from the front and stood behind them. ²⁰The cloud settled between the Egyptian and Israelite camps. As darkness fell, the cloud turned to fire, lighting up the night. But the Egyptians and Israelites did not approach each other all night.

²¹Then Moses raised his hand over the sea, and the Lord opened up a path through the water with a strong east wind. The wind blew all that night, turning the seabed into dry land. ²²So the people of Israel walked through the middle of the sea on dry ground, with walls of water on each side!

²³Then the Egyptians—all of Pharaoh's horses, chariots, and charioteers—chased them into the middle of the sea. ²⁴But just before dawn the Lord looked down on the Egyptian army from the pillar of fire and cloud, and he threw their forces into total confusion. ²⁵He twisted* their chariot wheels, making their chariots difficult to drive. "Let's get out of here—away from these Israelites!" the Egyptians shouted. "The Lord is fighting for them against Egypt!"

²⁶When all the Israelites had reached the other side, the Lord said to Moses, "Raise your hand over the sea again. Then the waters will rush back and cover the Egyptians and their chariots and charioteers." ²⁷So as the sun began to rise, Moses raised his hand over the sea, and the water rushed back into its usual place. The Egyptians tried to escape, but the Lord swept them into the sea. ²⁸Then the waters returned and covered all the chariots and chari-

oteers—the entire army of Pharaoh. Of all the Egyptians who had chased the Israelites into the sea, not a single one survived.

²⁹But the people of Israel had walked through the middle of the sea on dry ground, as the water stood up like a wall on both sides. ³⁰That is how the Lord rescued Israel from the hand of the Egyptians that day. And the Israelites saw the bodies of the Egyptians washed up on the seashore. ³¹When the people of Israel saw the mighty power that the Lord had unleashed against the Egyptians, they were filled with awe before him. They put their faith in the Lord and in his servant Moses.

¹⁵:¹Then Moses and the people of Israel sang this song to the Lord:

"I will sing to the Lord,
    for he has triumphed gloriously;
he has hurled both horse and rider
    into the sea.
² The Lord is my strength and
        my song;
    he has given me victory.
This is my God, and I will praise
        him—
    my father's God, and I will
        exalt him!
³ The Lord is a warrior;
    Yahweh* is his name!
⁴ Pharaoh's chariots and army
    he has hurled into the sea.
The finest of Pharaoh's officers
    are drowned in the Red Sea.*
⁵ The deep waters gushed over
        them;
    they sank to the bottom like
        a stone.

⁶ "Your right hand, O Lord,
    is glorious in power.
Your right hand, O Lord,
    smashes the enemy.
⁷ In the greatness of your majesty,
    you overthrow those who rise
        against you.
You unleash your blazing
        fury;
    it consumes them like straw.

⁸ At the blast of your breath,
  the waters piled up!
The surging waters stood straight
    like a wall;
  in the heart of the sea the deep
    waters became hard.

⁹ "The enemy boasted, 'I will
      chase them
    and catch up with them.
  I will plunder them
    and consume them.
  I will flash my sword;
    my powerful hand will
      destroy them.'
¹⁰ But you blew with your breath,
    and the sea covered them.
  They sank like lead
    in the mighty waters.

¹¹ "Who is like you among the gods,
      O Lord—
    glorious in holiness,
  awesome in splendor,
    performing great wonders?
¹² You raised your right hand,
    and the earth swallowed
      our enemies.

¹³ "With your unfailing love
      you lead
    the people you have redeemed.
  In your might, you guide them
    to your sacred home.
¹⁴ The peoples hear and tremble;
    anguish grips those who live
      in Philistia.
¹⁵ The leaders of Edom are
      terrified;
    the nobles of Moab tremble.
  All who live in Canaan melt away;
¹⁶    terror and dread fall upon
        them.
  The power of your arm
    makes them lifeless as stone
  until your people pass by, O Lord,
    until the people you purchased
      pass by.
¹⁷ You will bring them in and plant
      them on your own mountain—
    the place, O Lord, reserved for
      your own dwelling,

the sanctuary, O Lord, that your
  hands have established.
¹⁸ The Lord will reign forever and
      ever!"

13:18a Hebrew *sea of reeds.*   13:18b Greek version reads *left Egypt in the fifth generation.*   14:4 Hebrew *after them.*   14:25 As in Greek version, Samaritan Pentateuch, and Syriac version; Hebrew reads *He removed.* 15:3 *Yahweh* is a transliteration of the proper name *YHWH* that is sometimes rendered "Jehovah"; in this translation it is usually rendered "the Lord" (note the use of small capitals).   15:4 Hebrew *sea of reeds;* also in 15:22.

## MATTHEW 21:23-46

**W**hen Jesus returned to the Temple and began teaching, the leading priests and elders came up to him. They demanded, "By what authority are you doing all these things? Who gave you the right?"

²⁴"I'll tell you by what authority I do these things if you answer one question," Jesus replied. ²⁵"Did John's authority to baptize come from heaven, or was it merely human?"

They talked it over among themselves. "If we say it was from heaven, he will ask us why we didn't believe John. ²⁶But if we say it was merely human, we'll be mobbed because the people believe John was a prophet." ²⁷So they finally replied, "We don't know."

And Jesus responded, "Then I won't tell you by what authority I do these things.

²⁸"But what do you think about this? A man with two sons told the older boy, 'Son, go out and work in the vineyard today.' ²⁹The son answered, 'No, I won't go,' but later he changed his mind and went anyway. ³⁰Then the father told the other son, 'You go,' and he said, 'Yes, sir, I will.' But he didn't go.

³¹"Which of the two obeyed his father?"

They replied, "The first."*

Then Jesus explained his meaning: "I tell you the truth, corrupt tax collectors and prostitutes will get into the Kingdom of God before you do. ³²For John the Baptist came and showed you the right way to live, but you didn't believe him, while tax collectors and prostitutes did. And even when you saw this happening, you refused to believe him and repent of your sins.

³³"Now listen to another story. A certain landowner planted a vineyard, built a wall around it, dug a pit for pressing out the grape juice, and built a lookout tower. Then he leased the vineyard to tenant farmers and moved to another country. ³⁴At the time of the grape harvest, he sent his servants to collect his share of the crop. ³⁵But the farmers grabbed his servants, beat one, killed one, and stoned another. ³⁶So the landowner sent a larger group of his servants to collect for him, but the results were the same.

³⁷"Finally, the owner sent his son, thinking, 'Surely they will respect my son.'

³⁸"But when the tenant farmers saw his son coming, they said to one another, 'Here comes the heir to this estate. Come on, let's kill him and get the estate for ourselves!' ³⁹So they grabbed him, dragged him out of the vineyard, and murdered him.

⁴⁰"When the owner of the vineyard returns," Jesus asked, "what do you think he will do to those farmers?"

⁴¹The religious leaders replied, "He will put the wicked men to a horrible death and lease the vineyard to others who will give him his share of the crop after each harvest."

⁴²Then Jesus asked them, "Didn't you ever read this in the Scriptures?

'The stone that the builders rejected
    has now become the cornerstone.
This is the LORD's doing,
    and it is wonderful to see.'*

⁴³I tell you, the Kingdom of God will be taken away from you and given to a nation that will produce the proper fruit. ⁴⁴Anyone who stumbles over that stone will be broken to pieces, and it will crush anyone it falls on.*"

⁴⁵When the leading priests and Pharisees heard this parable, they realized he was telling the story against them—they were the wicked farmers. ⁴⁶They wanted to arrest him, but they were afraid of the crowds, who considered Jesus to be a prophet.

21:29-31 Other manuscripts read *"The second."* In still other manuscripts the first son says "Yes" but does nothing, the second son says "No" but then repents and goes, and the answer to Jesus' question is that the second son obeyed his father.    21:42 Ps 118:22-23.    21:44 This verse is omitted in some early manuscripts. Compare Luke 20:18.

## PSALM 26:1-12
*A psalm of David.*

¹ **D**eclare me innocent, O LORD,
        for I have acted with integrity;
    I have trusted in the LORD
        without wavering.
² Put me on trial, LORD, and
        cross-examine me.
    Test my motives and my heart.
³ For I am always aware of your
        unfailing love,
    and I have lived according
        to your truth.
⁴ I do not spend time with liars
    or go along with hypocrites.
⁵ I hate the gatherings of those
        who do evil,
    and I refuse to join in with
        the wicked.
⁶ I wash my hands to declare my
        innocence.
    I come to your altar, O LORD,
⁷ singing a song of thanksgiving
    and telling of all your wonders.
⁸ I love your sanctuary, LORD,
    the place where your glorious
        presence dwells.

⁹ Don't let me suffer the fate
        of sinners.
    Don't condemn me along
        with murderers.
¹⁰ Their hands are dirty with evil
        schemes,
    and they constantly take
        bribes.
¹¹ But I am not like that; I live
        with integrity.
    So redeem me and show
        me mercy.
¹² Now I stand on solid ground,
    and I will publicly praise
        the LORD.

PROVERBS 6:16-19

There are six things the LORD hates—no, seven things he detests: haughty eyes, a lying tongue, hands that kill the innocent, a heart that plots evil, feet that race to do wrong, a false witness who pours out lies, a person who sows discord in a family.

# FEBRUARY 2

EXODUS 15:19–17:7

When Pharaoh's horses, chariots, and charioteers rushed into the sea, the LORD brought the water crashing down on them. But the people of Israel had walked through the middle of the sea on dry ground!

²⁰Then Miriam the prophet, Aaron's sister, took a tambourine and led all the women as they played their tambourines and danced. ²¹And Miriam sang this song:

"Sing to the LORD,
    for he has triumphed gloriously;
he has hurled both horse and rider
    into the sea."

²²Then Moses led the people of Israel away from the Red Sea, and they moved out into the desert of Shur. They traveled in this desert for three days without finding any water. ²³When they came to the oasis of Marah, the water was too bitter to drink. So they called the place Marah (which means "bitter").

²⁴Then the people complained and turned against Moses. "What are we going to drink?" they demanded. ²⁵So Moses cried out to the LORD for help, and the LORD showed him a piece of wood. Moses threw it into the water, and this made the water good to drink.

It was there at Marah that the LORD set before them the following decree as a standard to test their faithfulness to him. ²⁶He said, "If you will listen carefully to the voice of the LORD your God and do what is right in his sight, obeying his commands and keeping all his decrees, then I will not make you suffer any of the diseases I sent on the Egyptians; for I am the LORD who heals you."

²⁷After leaving Marah, the Israelites traveled on to the oasis of Elim, where they found twelve springs and seventy palm trees. They camped there beside the water.

16:1THEN the whole community of Israel set out from Elim and journeyed into the wilderness of Sin,* between Elim and Mount Sinai. They arrived there on the fifteenth day of the second month, one month after leaving the land of Egypt.* ²There, too, the whole community of Israel complained about Moses and Aaron.

³"If only the LORD had killed us back in Egypt," they moaned. "There we sat around pots filled with meat and ate all the bread we wanted. But now you have brought us into this wilderness to starve us all to death."

⁴Then the LORD said to Moses, "Look, I'm going to rain down food from heaven for you. Each day the people can go out and pick up as much food as they need for that day. I will test them in this to see whether or not they will follow my instructions. ⁵On the sixth day they will gather food, and when they prepare it, there will be twice as much as usual."

⁶So Moses and Aaron said to all the people of Israel, "By evening you will realize it was the LORD who brought you out of the land of Egypt. ⁷In the morning you will see the glory of the LORD, because he has heard your complaints, which are against him, not against us. What have we done that you should complain about us?" ⁸Then Moses added, "The LORD will give you meat to eat in the evening and bread to satisfy you in the morning, for he has heard all your complaints against him. What

have we done? Yes, your complaints are against the LORD, not against us."

⁹Then Moses said to Aaron, "Announce this to the entire community of Israel: 'Present yourselves before the LORD, for he has heard your complaining.' " ¹⁰And as Aaron spoke to the whole community of Israel, they looked out toward the wilderness. There they could see the awesome glory of the LORD in the cloud.

¹¹Then the LORD said to Moses, ¹²"I have heard the Israelites' complaints. Now tell them, 'In the evening you will have meat to eat, and in the morning you will have all the bread you want. Then you will know that I am the LORD your God.'"

¹³That evening vast numbers of quail flew in and covered the camp. And the next morning the area around the camp was wet with dew. ¹⁴When the dew evaporated, a flaky substance as fine as frost blanketed the ground. ¹⁵The Israelites were puzzled when they saw it. "What is it?" they asked each other. They had no idea what it was.

And Moses told them, "It is the food the LORD has given you to eat. ¹⁶These are the LORD's instructions: Each household should gather as much as it needs. Pick up two quarts* for each person in your tent."

¹⁷So the people of Israel did as they were told. Some gathered a lot, some only a little. ¹⁸But when they measured it out,* everyone had just enough. Those who gathered a lot had nothing left over, and those who gathered only a little had enough. Each family had just what it needed.

¹⁹Then Moses told them, "Do not keep any of it until morning." ²⁰But some of them didn't listen and kept some of it until morning. But by then it was full of maggots and had a terrible smell. Moses was very angry with them.

²¹After this the people gathered the food morning by morning, each family according to its need. And as the sun became hot, the flakes they had not picked up melted and disappeared.

²²On the sixth day, they gathered twice as much as usual—four quarts* for each person instead of two. Then all the leaders of the community came and asked Moses for an explanation. ²³He told them, "This is what the LORD commanded: Tomorrow will be a day of complete rest, a holy Sabbath day set apart for the LORD. So bake or boil as much as you want today, and set aside what is left for tomorrow."

²⁴So they put some aside until morning, just as Moses had commanded. And in the morning the leftover food was wholesome and good, without maggots or odor. ²⁵Moses said, "Eat this food today, for today is a Sabbath day dedicated to the LORD. There will be no food on the ground today. ²⁶You may gather the food for six days, but the seventh day is the Sabbath. There will be no food on the ground that day."

²⁷Some of the people went out anyway on the seventh day, but they found no food. ²⁸The LORD asked Moses, "How long will these people refuse to obey my commands and instructions? ²⁹They must realize that the Sabbath is the LORD's gift to you. That is why he gives you a two-day supply on the sixth day, so there will be enough for two days. On the Sabbath day you must each stay in your place. Do not go out to pick up food on the seventh day." ³⁰So the people did not gather any food on the seventh day.

³¹The Israelites called the food manna.* It was white like coriander seed, and it tasted like honey wafers.

³²Then Moses said, "This is what the LORD has commanded: Fill a two-quart container with manna to preserve it for your descendants. Then later generations will be able to see the food I gave you in the wilderness when I set you free from Egypt."

³³Moses said to Aaron, "Get a jar and fill it with two quarts of manna. Then put it in a sacred place before the LORD to preserve it for all future generations." ³⁴Aaron did just as the LORD had commanded Moses. He eventually placed it

in the Ark of the Covenant—in front of the stone tablets inscribed with the terms of the covenant.* [35]So the people of Israel ate manna for forty years until they arrived at the land where they would settle. They ate manna until they came to the border of the land of Canaan.

[36]The container used to measure the manna was an omer, which was one tenth of an ephah; it held about two quarts.*

[17:1]At the LORD's command, the whole community of Israel left the wilderness of Sin* and moved from place to place. Eventually they camped at Rephidim, but there was no water there for the people to drink. [2]So once more the people complained against Moses. "Give us water to drink!" they demanded.

"Quiet!" Moses replied. "Why are you complaining against me? And why are you testing the LORD?"

[3]But tormented by thirst, they continued to argue with Moses. "Why did you bring us out of Egypt? Are you trying to kill us, our children, and our livestock with thirst?"

[4]Then Moses cried out to the LORD, "What should I do with these people? They are ready to stone me!"

[5]The LORD said to Moses, "Walk out in front of the people. Take your staff, the one you used when you struck the water of the Nile, and call some of the elders of Israel to join you. [6]I will stand before you on the rock at Mount Sinai.* Strike the rock, and water will come gushing out. Then the people will be able to drink." So Moses struck the rock as he was told, and water gushed out as the elders looked on.

[7]Moses named the place Massah (which means "test") and Meribah (which means "arguing") because the people of Israel argued with Moses and tested the LORD by saying, "Is the LORD here with us or not?"

16:1a The geographical name *Sin* is related to *Sinai* and should not be confused with the English word *sin*.
16:1b The Exodus had occurred on the fifteenth day of the first month (see Num 33:3).    16:16 Hebrew *1 omer* [2 liters]; also in 16:32, 33.    16:18 Hebrew *measured it with an omer*.    16:22 Hebrew *2 omers* [4 liters].

16:31 *Manna* means "What is it?" See 16:15.
16:34 Hebrew *He placed it in front of the Testimony;* see note on 25:16.    16:36 Hebrew *An omer is one tenth of an ephah*.    17:1 The geographical name *Sin* is related to *Sinai* and should not be confused with the English word *sin*.
17:6 Hebrew *Horeb*, another name for Sinai.

## MATTHEW 22:1-33

**J**esus also told them other parables. He said, [2]"The Kingdom of Heaven can be illustrated by the story of a king who prepared a great wedding feast for his son. [3]When the banquet was ready, he sent his servants to notify those who were invited. But they all refused to come!

[4]"So he sent other servants to tell them, 'The feast has been prepared. The bulls and fattened cattle have been killed, and everything is ready. Come to the banquet!' [5]But the guests he had invited ignored them and went their own way, one to his farm, another to his business. [6]Others seized his messengers and insulted them and killed them.

[7]"The king was furious, and he sent out his army to destroy the murderers and burn their town. [8]And he said to his servants, 'The wedding feast is ready, and the guests I invited aren't worthy of the honor. [9]Now go out to the street corners and invite everyone you see.' [10]So the servants brought in everyone they could find, good and bad alike, and the banquet hall was filled with guests.

[11]"But when the king came in to meet the guests, he noticed a man who wasn't wearing the proper clothes for a wedding. [12]'Friend,' he asked, 'how is it that you are here without wedding clothes?' But the man had no reply. [13]Then the king said to his aides, 'Bind his hands and feet and throw him into the outer darkness, where there will be weeping and gnashing of teeth.'

[14]"For many are called, but few are chosen."

[15]Then the Pharisees met together to plot how to trap Jesus into saying something for which he could be arrested. [16]They sent some of their disciples, along with the supporters of Herod, to meet with him. "Teacher,"

they said, "we know how honest you are. You teach the way of God truthfully. You are impartial and don't play favorites. ¹⁷Now tell us what you think about this: Is it right to pay taxes to Caesar or not?"

¹⁸But Jesus knew their evil motives. "You hypocrites!" he said. "Why are you trying to trap me? ¹⁹Here, show me the coin used for the tax." When they handed him a Roman coin,* ²⁰he asked, "Whose picture and title are stamped on it?"

²¹"Caesar's," they replied.

"Well, then," he said, "give to Caesar what belongs to Caesar, and give to God what belongs to God."

²²His reply amazed them, and they went away.

²³That same day Jesus was approached by some Sadducees—religious leaders who say there is no resurrection from the dead. They posed this question: ²⁴"Teacher, Moses said, 'If a man dies without children, his brother should marry the widow and have a child who will carry on the brother's name.'* ²⁵Well, suppose there were seven brothers. The oldest one married and then died without children, so his brother married the widow. ²⁶But the second brother also died, and the third brother married her. This continued with all seven of them. ²⁷Last of all, the woman also died. ²⁸So tell us, whose wife will she be in the resurrection? For all seven were married to her."

²⁹Jesus replied, "Your mistake is that you don't know the Scriptures, and you don't know the power of God. ³⁰For when the dead rise, they will neither marry nor be given in marriage. In this respect they will be like the angels in heaven.

³¹"But now, as to whether there will be a resurrection of the dead—haven't you ever read about this in the Scriptures? Long after Abraham, Isaac, and Jacob had died, God said,* ³²'I am the God of Abraham, the God of Isaac, and the God of Jacob.'* So he is the God of the living, not the dead."

³³When the crowds heard him, they were astounded at his teaching.

22:19 Greek *a denarius.*    22:24 Deut 25:5-6.
22:31 Greek *read about this? God said.*    22:32 Exod 3:6.

## PSALM 27:1-6
*A psalm of David.*

¹ **The** LORD is my light and my
        salvation—
    so why should I be afraid?
The LORD is my fortress,
        protecting me from danger,
    so why should I tremble?
² When evil people come to
        devour me,
    when my enemies and foes
        attack me,
    they will stumble and fall.
³ Though a mighty army
        surrounds me,
    my heart will not be afraid.
    Even if I am attacked,
    I will remain confident.

⁴ The one thing I ask of the LORD—
        the thing I seek most—
    is to live in the house of the LORD
        all the days of my life,
    delighting in the LORD's
        perfections
    and meditating in his Temple.
⁵ For he will conceal me there when
        troubles come;
    he will hide me in his sanctuary.
    He will place me out of reach
        on a high rock.
⁶ Then I will hold my head high
        above my enemies who
        surround me.
    At his sanctuary I will offer
        sacrifices with shouts of joy,
    singing and praising the LORD
        with music.

## PROVERBS 6:20-26
**M**y son, obey your father's commands, and don't neglect your mother's instruction. Keep their words always in your heart. Tie them around your neck. When you walk, their counsel will lead you. When you sleep, they will protect you. When you wake up, they will advise you. For their command is a lamp

and their instruction a light; their corrective discipline is the way to life. It will keep you from the immoral woman, from the smooth tongue of a promiscuous woman. Don't lust for her beauty. Don't let her coy glances seduce you. For a prostitute will bring you to poverty,* but sleeping with another man's wife will cost you your life.

**6:26** Hebrew *to a loaf of bread.*

# FEBRUARY
# 3

### EXODUS 17:8–19:15

**W**hile the people of Israel were still at Rephidim, the warriors of Amalek attacked them. ⁹Moses commanded Joshua, "Choose some men to go out and fight the army of Amalek for us. Tomorrow, I will stand at the top of the hill, holding the staff of God in my hand."

¹⁰So Joshua did what Moses had commanded and fought the army of Amalek. Meanwhile, Moses, Aaron, and Hur climbed to the top of a nearby hill. ¹¹As long as Moses held up the staff in his hand, the Israelites had the advantage. But whenever he dropped his hand, the Amalekites gained the advantage. ¹²Moses' arms soon became so tired he could no longer hold them up. So Aaron and Hur found a stone for him to sit on. Then they stood on each side of Moses, holding up his hands. So his hands held steady until sunset. ¹³As a result, Joshua overwhelmed the army of Amalek in battle.

¹⁴After the victory, the LORD instructed Moses, "Write this down on a scroll as a permanent reminder, and read it aloud to Joshua: I will erase the memory of Amalek from under heaven." ¹⁵Moses built an altar there and named it Yahweh-nissi (which means "the LORD is my banner"). ¹⁶He said, "They have raised

their fist against the LORD's throne, so now* the LORD will be at war with Amalek generation after generation."

¹⁸:¹MOSES' father-in-law, Jethro, the priest of Midian, heard about everything God had done for Moses and his people, the Israelites. He heard especially about how the LORD had rescued them from Egypt.

²Earlier, Moses had sent his wife, Zipporah, and his two sons back to Jethro, who had taken them in. ³(Moses' first son was named Gershom,* for Moses had said when the boy was born, "I have been a foreigner in a foreign land." ⁴His second son was named Eliezer,* for Moses had said, "The God of my ancestors was my helper; he rescued me from the sword of Pharaoh.") ⁵Jethro, Moses' father-in-law, now came to visit Moses in the wilderness. He brought Moses' wife and two sons with him, and they arrived while Moses and the people were camped near the mountain of God. ⁶Jethro had sent a message to Moses, saying, "I, Jethro, your father-in-law, am coming to see you with your wife and your two sons."

⁷So Moses went out to meet his father-in-law. He bowed low and kissed him. They asked about each other's welfare and then went into Moses' tent. ⁸Moses told his father-in-law everything the LORD had done to Pharaoh and Egypt on behalf of Israel. He also told about all the hardships they had experienced along the way and how the LORD had rescued his people from all their troubles. ⁹Jethro was delighted when he heard about all the good things the LORD had done for Israel as he rescued them from the hand of the Egyptians.

¹⁰"Praise the LORD," Jethro said, "for he has rescued you from the Egyptians and from Pharaoh. Yes, he has rescued Israel from the powerful hand of Egypt! ¹¹I know now that the LORD is greater than all other gods, because he rescued his people from the oppression of the proud Egyptians."

¹²Then Jethro, Moses' father-in-law,

brought a burnt offering and sacrifices to God. Aaron and all the elders of Israel came out and joined him in a sacrificial meal in God's presence.

¹³The next day, Moses took his seat to hear the people's disputes against each other. They waited before him from morning till evening.

¹⁴When Moses' father-in-law saw all that Moses was doing for the people, he asked, "What are you really accomplishing here? Why are you trying to do all this alone while everyone stands around you from morning till evening?"

¹⁵Moses replied, "Because the people come to me to get a ruling from God. ¹⁶When a dispute arises, they come to me, and I am the one who settles the case between the quarreling parties. I inform the people of God's decrees and give them his instructions."

¹⁷"This is not good!" Moses' father-in-law exclaimed. ¹⁸"You're going to wear yourself out—and the people, too. This job is too heavy a burden for you to handle all by yourself. ¹⁹Now listen to me, and let me give you a word of advice, and may God be with you. You should continue to be the people's representative before God, bringing their disputes to him. ²⁰Teach them God's decrees, and give them his instructions. Show them how to conduct their lives. ²¹But select from all the people some capable, honest men who fear God and hate bribes. Appoint them as leaders over groups of one thousand, one hundred, fifty, and ten. ²²They should always be available to solve the people's common disputes, but have them bring the major cases to you. Let the leaders decide the smaller matters themselves. They will help you carry the load, making the task easier for you. ²³If you follow this advice, and if God commands you to do so, then you will be able to endure the pressures, and all these people will go home in peace."

²⁴Moses listened to his father-in-law's advice and followed his suggestions. ²⁵He chose capable men from all over Israel and appointed them as leaders over the people. He put them in charge of groups of one thousand, one hundred, fifty, and ten. ²⁶These men were always available to solve the people's common disputes. They brought the major cases to Moses, but they took care of the smaller matters themselves.

²⁷Soon after this, Moses said goodbye to his father-in-law, who returned to his own land.

¹⁹:¹EXACTLY two months after the Israelites left Egypt,* they arrived in the wilderness of Sinai. ²After breaking camp at Rephidim, they came to the wilderness of Sinai and set up camp there at the base of Mount Sinai.

³Then Moses climbed the mountain to appear before God. The LORD called to him from the mountain and said, "Give these instructions to the family of Jacob; announce it to the descendants of Israel: ⁴'You have seen what I did to the Egyptians. You know how I carried you on eagles' wings and brought you to myself. ⁵Now if you will obey me and keep my covenant, you will be my own special treasure from among all the peoples on earth; for all the earth belongs to me. ⁶And you will be my kingdom of priests, my holy nation.' This is the message you must give to the people of Israel."

⁷So Moses returned from the mountain and called together the elders of the people and told them everything the LORD had commanded him. ⁸And all the people responded together, "We will do everything the LORD has commanded." So Moses brought the people's answer back to the LORD.

⁹Then the LORD said to Moses, "I will come to you in a thick cloud, Moses, so the people themselves can hear me when I speak with you. Then they will always trust you."

Moses told the LORD what the people had said. ¹⁰Then the LORD told Moses, "Go down and prepare the people for my arrival. Consecrate them today and tomorrow, and have them wash their clothing. ¹¹Be sure they are ready on the third day, for on that day the LORD will come down on Mount Sinai as all the people watch. [12]Mark off a boundary all around the mountain. Warn the people, 'Be careful! Do not go up on the mountain or even touch its boundaries. Anyone who touches the mountain will certainly be put to death. [13]No hand may touch the person or animal that crosses the boundary; instead, stone them or shoot them with arrows. They must be put to death.' However, when the ram's horn sounds a long blast, then the people may go up on the mountain.*"

[14]So Moses went down to the people. He consecrated them for worship, and they washed their clothes. [15]He told them, "Get ready for the third day, and until then abstain from having sexual intercourse."

17:16 Or *Hands have been lifted up to the LORD's throne, and now.*   18:3 *Gershom* sounds like a Hebrew term that means "a foreigner there."   18:4 *Eliezer* means "God is my helper."   19:1 Hebrew *In the third month after the Israelites left Egypt, on the very day,* i.e., two lunar months to the day after leaving Egypt. Compare Num 33:3.   19:13 Or *up to the mountain.*

## MATTHEW 22:34–23:12

**B**ut when the Pharisees heard that he [Jesus] had silenced the Sadducees with his reply, they met together to question him again. [35]One of them, an expert in religious law, tried to trap him with this question: [36]"Teacher, which is the most important commandment in the law of Moses?"

[37]**Jesus replied, "'You must love the LORD your God with all your heart, all your soul, and all your mind.'*** [38]**This is the first and greatest commandment. [39]A second is equally important: 'Love your neighbor as yourself.'*** [40]The entire law and all the demands of the prophets are based on these two commandments."

[41]Then, surrounded by the Pharisees, Jesus asked them a question: [42]"What do you think about the Messiah? Whose son is he?"

They replied, "He is the son of David."

[43]Jesus responded, "Then why does David, speaking under the inspiration of the Spirit, call the Messiah 'my Lord'? For David said,

[44] 'The LORD said to my Lord,
    Sit in the place of honor at my
        right hand
    until I humble your enemies
        beneath your feet.'*

[45]Since David called the Messiah 'my Lord,' how can the Messiah be his son?"

[46]No one could answer him. And after that, no one dared to ask him any more questions.

23:1THEN Jesus said to the crowds and to his disciples, [2]"The teachers of religious law and the Pharisees are the official interpreters of the law of Moses.* [3]So practice and obey whatever they tell you, but don't follow their example. For they don't practice what they teach. [4]They crush people with impossible religious demands and never lift a finger to ease the burden.

[5]"Everything they do is for show. On their arms they wear extra wide prayer boxes with Scripture verses inside, and they wear robes with extra long tassels.* [6]And they love to sit at the head table at banquets and in the seats of honor in the synagogues. [7]They love to receive respectful greetings as they walk in the marketplaces, and to be called 'Rabbi.'*

[8]"Don't let anyone call you 'Rabbi,' for you have only one teacher, and all of you are equal as brothers and sisters.* [9]And don't address anyone here on earth as 'Father,' for only God in heaven is your spiritual Father. [10]And don't let anyone call you 'Teacher,' for you have only one teacher, the Messiah. [11]The greatest among you must be a servant. [12]But those who exalt themselves will be humbled, and those who humble themselves will be exalted."

22:37 Deut 6:5.   22:39 Lev 19:18.   22:44 Ps 110:1.
23:2 Greek *and the Pharisees sit in the seat of Moses.*
23:5 Greek *They enlarge their phylacteries and lengthen their tassels.*   23:7 *Rabbi,* from Aramaic, means "master" or "teacher."   23:8 Greek *brothers.*

## PSALM 27:7-14

**H**ear me as I pray, O LORD.
    Be merciful and answer me!
[8] My heart has heard you say, "Come
    and talk with me."

And my heart responds, "LORD,
I am coming."
9 Do not turn your back on me.
Do not reject your servant
in anger.
You have always been my
helper.
Don't leave me now; don't
abandon me,
O God of my salvation!
10 Even if my father and mother
abandon me,
the LORD will hold me close.

11 Teach me how to live, O LORD.
Lead me along the right path,
for my enemies are waiting
for me.
12 Do not let me fall into their hands.
For they accuse me of things
I've never done;
with every breath they threaten
me with violence.
13 Yet I am confident I will see the
LORD's goodness
while I am here in the land
of the living.

14 Wait patiently for the LORD.
Be brave and courageous.
Yes, wait patiently for the LORD.

## PROVERBS 6:27-35

Can a man scoop a flame into his lap
and not have his clothes catch on fire?
Can he walk on hot coals and not blister
his feet? So it is with the man who
sleeps with another man's wife. He who
embraces her will not go unpunished.
□ Excuses might be found for a thief
who steals because he is starving. But if
he is caught, he must pay back seven
times what he stole, even if he has to sell
everything in his house. But the man
who commits adultery is an utter fool,
for he destroys himself. He will be
wounded and disgraced. His shame will
never be erased. For the woman's jealous husband will be furious, and he will
show no mercy when he takes revenge.
He will accept no compensation, nor be
satisfied with a payoff of any size.

# FEBRUARY
# 4

## EXODUS 19:16–21:21

On the morning of the third day, thunder roared and lightning flashed, and a
dense cloud came down on the mountain. There was a long, loud blast from
a ram's horn, and all the people trembled. 17Moses led them out from the
camp to meet with God, and they stood
at the foot of the mountain. 18All of
Mount Sinai was covered with smoke
because the LORD had descended on it
in the form of fire. The smoke billowed
into the sky like smoke from a brick
kiln, and the whole mountain shook violently. 19As the blast of the ram's horn
grew louder and louder, Moses spoke,
and God thundered his reply. 20The
LORD came down on the top of Mount
Sinai and called Moses to the top of the
mountain. So Moses climbed the
mountain.

21Then the LORD told Moses, "Go
back down and warn the people not to
break through the boundaries to see
the LORD, or they will die. 22Even the
priests who regularly come near to the
LORD must purify themselves so that
the LORD does not break out and destroy them."

23"But LORD," Moses protested, "the
people cannot come up to Mount Sinai.
You already warned us. You told me,
'Mark off a boundary all around the
mountain to set it apart as holy.'"

24But the LORD said, "Go down and
bring Aaron back up with you. In the
meantime, do not let the priests or the
people break through to approach
the LORD, or he will break out and destroy them."

25So Moses went down to the people
and told them what the LORD had said.

20:1THEN God gave the people all these
instructions*:

²"I am the LORD your God, who rescued you from the land of Egypt, the place of your slavery. ³"You must not have any other god but me.

⁴"You must not make for yourself an idol of any kind or an image of anything in the heavens or on the earth or in the sea. ⁵You must not bow down to them or worship them, for I, the LORD your God, am a jealous God who will not tolerate your affection for any other gods. I lay the sins of the parents upon their children; the entire family is affected—even children in the third and fourth generations of those who reject me. ⁶But I lavish unfailing love for a thousand generations on those* who love me and obey my commands.

⁷"You must not misuse the name of the LORD your God. The LORD will not let you go unpunished if you misuse his name.

⁸"Remember to observe the Sabbath day by keeping it holy. ⁹You have six days each week for your ordinary work, ¹⁰but the seventh day is a Sabbath day of rest dedicated to the LORD your God. On that day no one in your household may do any work. This includes you, your sons and daughters, your male and female servants, your livestock, and any foreigners living among you. ¹¹For in six days the LORD made the heavens, the earth, the sea, and everything in them; but on the seventh day he rested. That is why the LORD blessed the Sabbath day and set it apart as holy.

¹²"Honor your father and mother. Then you will live a long, full life in the land the LORD your God is giving you.

¹³"You must not murder.

¹⁴"You must not commit adultery.

¹⁵"You must not steal.

¹⁶"You must not testify falsely against your neighbor.

¹⁷"You must not covet your neighbor's house. You must not covet your neighbor's wife, male or female servant, ox or donkey, or anything else that belongs to your neighbor."

¹⁸When the people heard the thunder and the loud blast of the ram's horn, and when they saw the flashes of lightning and the smoke billowing from the mountain, they stood at a distance, trembling with fear.

¹⁹And they said to Moses, "You speak to us, and we will listen. But don't let God speak directly to us, or we will die!"

²⁰"Don't be afraid," Moses answered them, "for God has come in this way to test you, and so that your fear of him will keep you from sinning!"

²¹As the people stood in the distance, Moses approached the dark cloud where God was.

²²And the LORD said to Moses, "Say this to the people of Israel: You saw for yourselves that I spoke to you from heaven. ²³Remember, you must not make any idols of silver or gold to rival me.

²⁴"Build for me an altar made of earth, and offer your sacrifices to me—your burnt offerings and peace offerings, your sheep and goats, and your cattle. Build my altar wherever I cause my name to be remembered, and I will come to you and bless you. ²⁵If you use stones to build my altar, use only natural, uncut stones. Do not shape the stones with a tool, for that would make the altar unfit for holy use. ²⁶And do not approach my altar by going up steps. If you do, someone might look up under your clothing and see your nakedness.

²¹:¹"THESE are the regulations you must present to Israel.

²"If you buy a Hebrew slave, he may serve for no more than six years. Set him free in the seventh year, and he will owe you nothing for his freedom. ³If he was single when he became your slave, he shall leave single. But if he was married

before he became a slave, then his wife must be freed with him.

4"If his master gave him a wife while he was a slave and they had sons or daughters, then only the man will be free in the seventh year, but his wife and children will still belong to his master. 5But the slave may declare, 'I love my master, my wife, and my children. I don't want to go free.' 6If he does this, his master must present him before God.* Then his master must take him to the door or doorpost and publicly pierce his ear with an awl. After that, the slave will serve his master for life.

7"When a man sells his daughter as a slave, she will not be freed at the end of six years as the men are. 8If she does not satisfy her owner, he must allow her to be bought back again. But he is not allowed to sell her to foreigners, since he is the one who broke the contract with her. 9But if the slave's owner arranges for her to marry his son, he may no longer treat her as a slave but as a daughter.

10"If a man who has married a slave wife takes another wife for himself, he must not neglect the rights of the first wife to food, clothing, and sexual intimacy. 11If he fails in any of these three obligations, she may leave as a free woman without making any payment.

12"Anyone who assaults and kills another person must be put to death. 13But if it was simply an accident permitted by God, I will appoint a place of refuge where the slayer can run for safety. 14However, if someone deliberately kills another person, then the slayer must be dragged even from my altar and be put to death.

15"Anyone who strikes father or mother must be put to death.

16"Kidnappers must be put to death, whether they are caught in possession of their victims or have already sold them as slaves.

17"Anyone who dishonors* father or mother must be put to death.

18"Now suppose two men quarrel, and one hits the other with a stone or fist, and the injured person does not die but

is confined to bed. 19If he is later able to walk outside again, even with a crutch, the assailant will not be punished but must compensate his victim for lost wages and provide for his full recovery.

20"If a man beats his male or female slave with a club and the slave dies as a result, the owner must be punished. 21But if the slave recovers within a day or two, then the owner shall not be punished, since the slave is his property."

20:1 Hebrew *all these words.* 20:6 Hebrew *for thousands of those.* 21:6 Or *before the judges.* 21:17 Greek version reads *Anyone who speaks disrespectfully of.* Compare Matt 15:4; Mark 7:10.

## MATTHEW 23:13-39

"What sorrow awaits you teachers of religious law and you Pharisees. Hypocrites! For you shut the door of the Kingdom of Heaven in people's faces. You won't go in yourselves, and you don't let others enter either.*

15"What sorrow awaits you teachers of religious law and you Pharisees. Hypocrites! For you cross land and sea to make one convert, and then you turn that person into twice the child of hell* you yourselves are!

16"Blind guides! What sorrow awaits you! For you say that it means nothing to swear 'by God's Temple,' but that it is binding to swear 'by the gold in the Temple.' 17Blind fools! Which is more important—the gold or the Temple that makes the gold sacred? 18And you say that to swear 'by the altar' is not binding, but to swear 'by the gifts on the altar' is binding. 19How blind! For which is more important—the gift on the altar or the altar that makes the gift sacred? 20When you swear 'by the altar,' you are swearing by it and by everything on it. 21And when you swear 'by the Temple,' you are swearing by it and by God, who lives in it. 22And when you swear 'by heaven,' you are swearing by the throne of God and by God, who sits on the throne.

23"What sorrow awaits you teachers of religious law and you Pharisees. Hypocrites! For you are careful to tithe even the tiniest income from your herb gardens,* but you ignore the more important aspects of the law—justice, mercy, and faith. You should tithe, yes, but do not neglect the more important things. [24]Blind guides! You strain your water so you won't accidentally swallow a gnat, but you swallow a camel!*

[25]"What sorrow awaits you teachers of religious law and you Pharisees. Hypocrites! For you are so careful to clean the outside of the cup and the dish, but inside you are filthy—full of greed and self-indulgence! [26]You blind Pharisee! First wash the inside of the cup and the dish,* and then the outside will become clean, too.

[27]"What sorrow awaits you teachers of religious law and you Pharisees. Hypocrites! For you are like whitewashed tombs—beautiful on the outside but filled on the inside with dead people's bones and all sorts of impurity. [28]Outwardly you look like righteous people, but inwardly your hearts are filled with hypocrisy and lawlessness.

[29]"What sorrow awaits you teachers of religious law and you Pharisees. Hypocrites! For you build tombs for the prophets your ancestors killed, and you decorate the monuments of the godly people your ancestors destroyed. [30]Then you say, 'If we had lived in the days of our ancestors, we would never have joined them in killing the prophets.'

[31]"But in saying that, you testify against yourselves that you are indeed the descendants of those who murdered the prophets. [32]Go ahead and finish what your ancestors started. [33]Snakes! Sons of vipers! How will you escape the judgment of hell?

[34]"Therefore, I am sending you prophets and wise men and teachers of religious law. But you will kill some by crucifixion, and you will flog others with whips in your synagogues, chasing them from city to city. [35]As a result, you will be held responsible for the murder of all godly people of all time—from the murder of righteous Abel to the murder of Zechariah son of Barachiah, whom you killed in the Temple between the sanctuary and the altar. [36]I tell you the truth, this judgment will fall on this very generation.

[37]"O Jerusalem, Jerusalem, the city that kills the prophets and stones God's messengers! How often I have wanted to gather your children together as a hen protects her chicks beneath her wings, but you wouldn't let me. [38]And now, look, your house is abandoned and desolate.* [39]For I tell you this, you will never see me again until you say, 'Blessings on the one who comes in the name of the LORD!'*"

23:13 Some manuscripts add verse 14, *What sorrow awaits you teachers of religious law and you Pharisees. Hypocrites! You shamelessly cheat widows out of their property and then pretend to be pious by making long prayers in public. Because of this, you will be severely punished.* Compare Mark 12:40 and Luke 20:47.    23:15 Greek *of Gehenna;* also in 23:33.    23:23 Greek *tithe the mint, the dill, and the cumin.*    23:24 See Lev 11:4, 23, where gnats and camels are both forbidden as food.    23:26 Some manuscripts do not include *and the dish.*    23:38 Some manuscripts do not include *and desolate.*    23:39 Ps 118:26.

## PSALM 28:1-9
*A psalm of David.*

[1] I pray to you, O LORD, my rock.
   Do not turn a deaf ear to me.
For if you are silent,
   I might as well give up and die.
[2] Listen to my prayer for mercy
   as I cry out to you for help,
   as I lift my hands toward your
      holy sanctuary.

[3] Do not drag me away with
      the wicked—
   with those who do evil—
those who speak friendly words
      to their neighbors
   while planning evil in their hearts.
[4] Give them the punishment they
      so richly deserve!
   Measure it out in proportion
      to their wickedness.
Pay them back for all their evil
      deeds!
   Give them a taste of what they
      have done to others.
[5] They care nothing for what the
      LORD has done
   or for what his hands have made.
So he will tear them down,
   and they will never be rebuilt!

6 Praise the LORD!
For he has heard my cry
for mercy.
7 The LORD is my strength and shield.
I trust him with all my heart.
He helps me, and my heart is filled
with joy.
I burst out in songs of
thanksgiving.

8 The LORD gives his people strength.
He is a safe fortress for his
anointed king.
9 Save your people!
Bless Israel, your special
possession.*
Lead them like a shepherd,
and carry them in your
arms forever.

28:9 Hebrew *Bless your inheritance.*

## PROVERBS 7:1-5

Follow my advice, my son; always treasure my commands. Obey my commands and live! Guard my instructions
as you guard your own eyes.* Tie them
on your fingers as a reminder. Write
them deep within your heart. □ Love wisdom like a sister; make insight a beloved
member of your family. Let them protect you from an affair with an immoral
woman, from listening to the flattery of a
promiscuous woman.

7:2 Hebrew *as the pupil of your eye.*

# FEBRUARY 5

## EXODUS 21:22–23:13

"Now suppose two men are fighting,
and in the process they accidentally
strike a pregnant woman so she gives
birth prematurely.* If no further injury
results, the man who struck the woman
must pay the amount of compensation
the woman's husband demands and the
judges approve. 23 But if there is further

injury, the punishment must match the
injury: a life for a life, 24 an eye for an eye,
a tooth for a tooth, a hand for a hand, a
foot for a foot, 25 a burn for a burn, a
wound for a wound, a bruise for a bruise.

26 "If a man hits his male or female
slave in the eye and the eye is blinded,
he must let the slave go free to compensate for the eye. 27 And if a man knocks
out the tooth of his male or female
slave, he must let the slave go free to
compensate for the tooth.

28 "If an ox* gores a man or woman to
death, the ox must be stoned, and its
flesh may not be eaten. In such a case,
however, the owner will not be held
liable. 29 But suppose the ox had a reputation for goring, and the owner had
been informed but failed to keep it
under control. If the ox then kills
someone, it must be stoned, and the
owner must also be put to death.
30 However, the dead person's relatives
may accept payment to compensate
for the loss of life. The owner of the ox
may redeem his life by paying whatever is demanded.

31 "The same regulation applies if the
ox gores a boy or a girl. 32 But if the ox
gores a slave, either male or female, the
animal's owner must pay the slave's
owner thirty silver coins,* and the ox
must be stoned.

33 "Suppose someone digs or uncovers
a pit and fails to cover it, and then an ox
or a donkey falls into it. 34 The owner of
the pit must pay full compensation to
the owner of the animal, but then he gets
to keep the dead animal.

35 "If someone's ox injures a neighbor's
ox and the injured ox dies, then the two
owners must sell the live ox and divide
the price equally between them. They
must also divide the dead animal. 36 But if
the ox had a reputation for goring, yet its
owner failed to keep it under control, he
must pay full compensation—a live ox
for the dead one—but he may keep the
dead ox.

22:1*"IF someone steals an ox* or sheep
and then kills or sells it, the thief must

pay back five oxen for each ox stolen, and four sheep for each sheep stolen.

2*"If a thief is caught in the act of breaking into a house and is struck and killed in the process, the person who killed the thief is not guilty of murder. 3But if it happens in daylight, the one who killed the thief is guilty of murder.

"A thief who is caught must pay in full for everything he stole. If he cannot pay, he must be sold as a slave to pay for his theft. 4If someone steals an ox or a donkey or a sheep and it is found in the thief's possession, then the thief must pay double the value of the stolen animal.

5"If an animal is grazing in a field or vineyard and the owner lets it stray into someone else's field to graze, then the animal's owner must pay compensation from the best of his own grain or grapes.

6"If you are burning thornbushes and the fire gets out of control and spreads into another person's field, destroying the sheaves or the uncut grain or the whole crop, the one who started the fire must pay for the lost crop.

7"Suppose someone leaves money or goods with a neighbor for safekeeping, and they are stolen from the neighbor's house. If the thief is caught, the compensation is double the value of what was stolen. 8But if the thief is not caught, the neighbor must appear before God,* who will determine if he stole the property.

9"Suppose there is a dispute between two people who both claim to own a particular ox, donkey, sheep, article of clothing, or any lost property. Both parties must come before God, and the person whom God declares* guilty must pay double compensation to the other.

10"Now suppose someone leaves a donkey, ox, sheep, or any other animal with a neighbor for safekeeping, but it dies or is injured or gets away, and no one sees what happened. 11The neighbor must then take an oath in the presence of the Lord. If the Lord confirms that the neighbor did not steal the prop-

erty, the owner must accept the verdict, and no payment will be required. 12But if the animal was indeed stolen, the guilty person must pay compensation to the owner. 13If it was torn to pieces by a wild animal, the remains of the carcass must be shown as evidence, and no compensation will be required.

14"If someone borrows an animal from a neighbor and it is injured or dies when the owner is absent, the person who borrowed it must pay full compensation. 15But if the owner was present, no compensation is required. And no compensation is required if the animal was rented, for this loss is covered by the rental fee.

16"If a man seduces a virgin who is not engaged to anyone and has sex with her, he must pay the customary bride price and marry her. 17But if her father refuses to let him marry her, the man must still pay him an amount equal to the bride price of a virgin.

18"You must not allow a sorceress to live.

19"Anyone who has sexual relations with an animal must certainly be put to death.

20"Anyone who sacrifices to any god other than the Lord must be destroyed.*

21"You must not mistreat or oppress foreigners in any way. Remember, you yourselves were once foreigners in the land of Egypt.

22**"You must not exploit a widow or an orphan. 23If you exploit them in any way and they cry out to me, then I will certainly hear their cry. 24My** anger will blaze against you, and I will kill you with the sword. Then your wives will be widows and your children fatherless.

25"If you lend money to any of my people who are in need, do not charge interest as a money lender would. 26If you take your neighbor's cloak as security for a loan, you must return it before sunset. 27This coat may be the only blanket your neighbor has. How can a person sleep without it? If you do not return it and your neighbor cries out to me for help, then I will hear, for I am merciful.

²⁸"You must not dishonor God or curse any of your rulers.

²⁹"You must not hold anything back when you give me offerings from your crops and your wine.

"You must give me your firstborn sons.

³⁰"You must also give me the first-born of your cattle, sheep, and goats. But leave the newborn animal with its mother for seven days; then give it to me on the eighth day.

³¹"You must be my holy people. Therefore, do not eat any animal that has been torn up and killed by wild animals. Throw it to the dogs.

²³:¹"You must not pass along false rumors. You must not cooperate with evil people by lying on the witness stand.

²"You must not follow the crowd in doing wrong. When you are called to testify in a dispute, do not be swayed by the crowd to twist justice. ³And do not slant your testimony in favor of a person just because that person is poor.

⁴"If you come upon your enemy's ox or donkey that has strayed away, take it back to its owner. ⁵If you see that the donkey of someone who hates you has collapsed under its load, do not walk by. Instead, stop and help.

⁶"In a lawsuit, you must not deny justice to the poor.

⁷"Be sure never to charge anyone falsely with evil. Never sentence an innocent or blameless person to death, for I never declare a guilty person to be innocent.

⁸"Take no bribes, for a bribe makes you ignore something that you clearly see. A bribe makes even a righteous person twist the truth.

⁹"You must not oppress foreigners. You know what it's like to be a foreigner, for you yourselves were once foreigners in the land of Egypt.

¹⁰"Plant and harvest your crops for six years, ¹¹but let the land be renewed

and lie uncultivated during the seventh year. Then let the poor among you harvest whatever grows on its own. Leave the rest for wild animals to eat. The same applies to your vineyards and olive groves.

¹²"You have six days each week for your ordinary work, but on the seventh day you must stop working. This gives your ox and your donkey a chance to rest. It also allows your slaves and the foreigners living among you to be refreshed.

¹³"Pay close attention to all my instructions. You must not call on the name of any other gods. Do not even speak their names."

**21:22** Or *so she has a miscarriage;* Hebrew reads *so her children come out.* **21:28** Or *bull,* or *cow;* also in 21:29-36. **21:32** Hebrew *30 shekels of silver,* about 12 ounces or 342 grams in weight. **22:1a** Verse 22:1 is numbered 21:37 in Hebrew text. **22:1b** Or *bull,* or *cow;* also in 22:4, 9, 10. **22:2** Verses 22:2-31 are numbered 22:1-30 in Hebrew text. **22:8** Or *before the judges.* **22:9** Or *before the judges, and the person whom the judges declare.* **22:20** The Hebrew term used here refers to the complete consecration of things or people to the LORD, either by destroying them or by giving them as an offering.

## MATTHEW 24:1-28

As Jesus was leaving the Temple grounds, his disciples pointed out to him the various Temple buildings. ²But he responded, "Do you see all these buildings? I tell you the truth, they will be completely demolished. Not one stone will be left on top of another!"

³Later, Jesus sat on the Mount of Olives. His disciples came to him privately and said, "Tell us, when will all this happen? What sign will signal your return and the end of the world?*"

⁴Jesus told them, "Don't let anyone mislead you, ⁵for many will come in my name, claiming, 'I am the Messiah.' They will deceive many. ⁶And you will hear of wars and threats of wars, but don't panic. Yes, these things must take place, but the end won't follow immediately. ⁷Nation will go to war against nation, and kingdom against kingdom. There will be famines and earthquakes in many parts of the world. ⁸But all this is only the first of the birth pains, with more to come.

9"Then you will be arrested, persecuted, and killed. You will be hated all over the world because you are my followers.* 10And many will turn away from me and betray and hate each other. 11And many false prophets will appear and will deceive many people. 12Sin will be rampant everywhere, and the love of many will grow cold. 13But the one who endures to the end will be saved. 14And the Good News about the Kingdom will be preached throughout the whole world, so that all nations* will hear it; and then the end will come.

15"The day is coming when you will see what Daniel the prophet spoke about—the sacrilegious object that causes desecration* standing in the Holy Place." (Reader, pay attention!) 16"Then those in Judea must flee to the hills. 17A person out on the deck of a roof must not go down into the house to pack. 18A person out in the field must not return even to get a coat. 19How terrible it will be for pregnant women and for nursing mothers in those days. 20And pray that your flight will not be in winter or on the Sabbath. 21For there will be greater anguish than at any time since the world began. And it will never be so great again. 22In fact, unless that time of calamity is shortened, not a single person will survive. But it will be shortened for the sake of God's chosen ones.

23"Then if anyone tells you, 'Look, here is the Messiah,' or 'There he is,' don't believe it. 24For false messiahs and false prophets will rise up and perform great signs and wonders so as to deceive, if possible, even God's chosen ones. 25See, I have warned you about this ahead of time.

26"So if someone tells you, 'Look, the Messiah is out in the desert,' don't bother to go and look. Or, 'Look, he is hiding here,' don't believe it! 27For as the lightning flashes in the east and shines to the west, so it will be when the Son of Man* comes. 28Just as the gathering of vultures shows there is a car-cass nearby, so these signs indicate that the end is near.*"

24:3 Or the age? 24:9 Greek on account of my name. 24:14 Or all peoples. 24:15 Greek the abomination of desolation. See Dan 9:27; 11:31; 12:11. 24:27 "Son of Man" is a title Jesus used for himself. 24:28 Greek Wherever the carcass is, the vultures gather.

## PSALM 29:1-11
*A psalm of David.*

1 Honor the LORD, you heavenly beings*;
  honor the LORD for his glory and strength.
2 Honor the LORD for the glory of his name.
  Worship the LORD in the splendor of his holiness.

3 The voice of the LORD echoes above the sea.
  The God of glory thunders.
  The LORD thunders over the mighty sea.
4 The voice of the LORD is powerful;
  the voice of the LORD is majestic.
5 The voice of the LORD splits the mighty cedars;
  the LORD shatters the cedars of Lebanon.
6 He makes Lebanon's mountains skip like a calf;
  he makes Mount Hermon* leap like a young wild ox.
7 The voice of the LORD strikes with bolts of lightning.
8 The voice of the LORD makes the barren wilderness quake;
  the LORD shakes the wilderness of Kadesh.
9 The voice of the LORD twists mighty oaks*
  and strips the forests bare.
  In his Temple everyone shouts, "Glory!"

10 The LORD rules over the floodwaters.
  The LORD reigns as king forever.
11 The LORD gives his people strength.
  The LORD blesses them with peace.

29:1 Hebrew you sons of God. 29:6 Hebrew Sirion, another name for Mount Hermon. 29:9 Or causes the deer to writhe in labor.

PROVERBS 7:6-23

While I was at the window of my house, looking through the curtain, I saw some naive young men, and one in particular who lacked common sense. He was crossing the street near the house of an immoral woman, strolling down the path by her house. It was at twilight, in the evening, as deep darkness fell. The woman approached him, seductively dressed and sly of heart. She was the brash, rebellious type, never content to stay at home. She is often in the streets and markets, soliciting at every corner. She threw her arms around him and kissed him, and with a brazen look she said, "I've just made my peace offerings and fulfilled my vows. You're the one I was looking for! I came out to find you, and here you are! My bed is spread with beautiful blankets, with colored sheets of Egyptian linen. I've perfumed my bed with myrrh, aloes, and cinnamon. Come, let's drink our fill of love until morning. Let's enjoy each other's caresses, for my husband is not home. He's away on a long trip. He has taken a wallet full of money with him and won't return until later this month.*" □So she seduced him with her pretty speech and enticed him with her flattery. He followed her at once, like an ox going to the slaughter. He was like a stag caught in a trap, awaiting the arrow that would pierce its heart. He was like a bird flying into a snare, little knowing it would cost him his life.

7:20 Hebrew *until the moon is full.*

# FEBRUARY
# 6

EXODUS 23:14–25:40

"Each year you must celebrate three festivals in my honor. 15First, celebrate the Festival of Unleavened Bread. For seven days the bread you eat must be made without yeast, just as I commanded you. Celebrate this festival annually at the appointed time in early spring, in the month of Abib,* for that is the anniversary of your departure from Egypt. No one may appear before me without an offering.

16"Second, celebrate the Festival of Harvest,* when you bring me the first crops of your harvest.

"Finally, celebrate the Festival of the Final Harvest* at the end of the harvest season, when you have harvested all the crops from your fields. 17At these three times each year, every man in Israel must appear before the Sovereign, the LORD.

18"You must not offer the blood of my sacrificial offerings together with any baked goods containing yeast. And do not leave the fat from the festival offerings until the next morning.

19"As you harvest your crops, bring the very best of the first harvest to the house of the LORD your God.

"You must not cook a young goat in its mother's milk.

20"See, I am sending an angel before you to protect you on your journey and lead you safely to the place I have prepared for you. 21Pay close attention to him, and obey his instructions. Do not rebel against him, for he is my representative, and he will not forgive your rebellion. 22But if you are careful to obey him, following all my instructions, then I will be an enemy to your enemies, and I will oppose those who oppose you. 23For my angel will go before you and bring you into the land of the Amorites, Hittites, Perizzites, Canaanites, Hivites, and Jebusites, so you may live there. And I will destroy them completely. 24You must not worship the gods of these nations or serve them in any way or imitate their evil practices. Instead, you must utterly destroy them and smash their sacred pillars.

25"You must serve only the LORD your God. If you do, I* will bless you with food and water, and I will protect you from illness. ²⁶There will be no mis-carriages or infertility in your land, and I will give you long, full lives.

²⁷"I will send my terror ahead of you and create panic among all the people whose lands you invade. I will make all your enemies turn and run. ²⁸I will send terror* ahead of you to drive out the Hivites, Canaanites, and Hittites. ²⁹But I will not drive them out in a single year, because the land would become deso-late and the wild animals would multi-ply and threaten you. ³⁰I will drive them out a little at a time until your popula-tion has increased enough to take pos-session of the land. ³¹And I will fix your boundaries from the Red Sea to the Mediterranean Sea,* and from the east-ern wilderness to the Euphrates River.* I will hand over to you the people now liv-ing in the land, and you will drive them out ahead of you.

³²"Make no treaties with them or their gods. ³³They must not live in your land, or they will cause you to sin against me. If you serve their gods, you will be caught in the trap of idolatry."

24:1THEN the LORD instructed Moses: "Come up here to me, and bring along Aaron, Nadab, Abihu, and seventy of Is-rael's elders. All of you must worship from a distance. ²Only Moses is allowed to come near to the LORD. The others must not come near, and none of the other people are allowed to climb up the mountain with him."

³Then Moses went down to the peo-ple and repeated all the instructions and regulations the LORD had given him. All the people answered with one voice, "We will do everything the LORD has commanded."

⁴Then Moses carefully wrote down all the LORD's instructions. Early the next morning Moses got up and built an altar at the foot of the mountain. He also set up twelve pillars, one for each of the twelve tribes of Israel. ⁵Then he sent some of the young Israelite men to pre-sent burnt offerings and to sacrifice bulls as peace offerings to the LORD. ⁶Moses

drained half the blood from these animals into basins. The other half he splattered against the altar.

⁷Then he took the Book of the Cov-enant and read it aloud to the people. Again they all responded, "We will do everything the LORD has commanded. We will obey."

⁸Then Moses took the blood from the basins and splattered it over the people, declaring, "Look, this blood confirms the covenant the LORD has made with you in giving you these instructions."

⁹Then Moses, Aaron, Nadab, Abihu, and the seventy elders of Israel climbed up the mountain again. ¹⁰There they saw the God of Israel. Under his feet there seemed to be a surface of brilliant blue lapis lazuli, as clear as the sky itself. ¹¹And though these nobles of Israel gazed upon God, he did not destroy them. In fact, they ate a covenant meal, eating and drinking in his presence!

¹²Then the LORD said to Moses, "Come up to me on the mountain. Stay there, and I will give you the tablets of stone on which I have inscribed the instructions and commands so you can teach the people." ¹³So Moses and his assistant Joshua set out, and Moses climbed up the mountain of God.

¹⁴Moses told the elders, "Stay here and wait for us until we come back. Aaron and Hur are here with you. If any-one has a dispute while I am gone, con-sult with them."

¹⁵Then Moses climbed up the moun-tain, and the cloud covered it. ¹⁶And the glory of the LORD settled down on Mount Sinai, and the cloud covered it for six days. On the seventh day the LORD called to Moses from inside the cloud. ¹⁷To the Israelites at the foot of the mountain, the glory of the LORD ap-peared at the summit like a consuming fire. ¹⁸Then Moses disappeared into the cloud as he climbed higher up the mountain. He remained on the moun-tain forty days and forty nights.

25:1THE LORD said to Moses, ²"Tell the people of Israel to bring me their sacred offerings. Accept the contributions from all whose hearts are moved to offer them. ³Here is a list of sacred offerings you may accept from them:

gold, silver, and bronze;

⁴ blue, purple, and scarlet thread; fine linen and goat hair for cloth;

⁵ tanned ram skins and fine goatskin leather;

acacia wood;

⁶ olive oil for the lamps; spices for the anointing oil and the fragrant incense;

⁷ onyx stones, and other gemstones to be set in the ephod and the priest's chestpiece.

⁸"Have the people of Israel build me a holy sanctuary so I can live among them. ⁹You must build this Tabernacle and its furnishings exactly according to the pattern I will show you.

¹⁰"Have the people make an Ark of acacia wood—a sacred chest 45 inches long, 27 inches wide, and 27 inches high.* ¹¹Overlay it inside and outside with pure gold, and run a molding of gold all around it. ¹²Cast four gold rings and attach them to its four feet, two rings on each side. ¹³Make poles from acacia wood, and overlay them with gold. ¹⁴Insert the poles into the rings at the sides of the Ark to carry it. ¹⁵These carrying poles must stay inside the rings; never remove them. ¹⁶When the Ark is finished, place inside it the stone tablets inscribed with the terms of the covenant,* which I will give to you.

¹⁷"Then make the Ark's cover—the place of atonement—from pure gold. It must be 45 inches long and 27 inches wide.* ¹⁸Then make two cherubim from hammered gold, and place them on the two ends of the atonement cover. ¹⁹Mold the cherubim on each end of the atonement cover, making it all of one piece of gold. ²⁰The cherubim will face each other and look down on the atonement cover. With their wings spread above it, they will protect it. ²¹Place inside the Ark the stone tablets inscribed with the terms of the covenant, which I will give to you. Then put the atonement cover on top of the Ark. ²²I will meet with you there and talk to you from above the atonement cover between the gold cherubim that hover over the Ark of the Covenant.* From there I will give you my commands for the people of Israel.

²³"Then make a table of acacia wood, 36 inches long, 18 inches wide, and 27 inches high.* ²⁴Overlay it with pure gold and run a gold molding around the edge. ²⁵Decorate it with a 3-inch border* all around, and run a gold molding along the border. ²⁶Make four gold rings for the table and attach them at the four corners next to the four legs. ²⁷Attach the rings near the border to hold the poles that are used to carry the table. ²⁸Make these poles from acacia wood, and overlay them with gold. ²⁹Make special containers of pure gold for the table—bowls, pans, pitchers, and jars—to be used in pouring out liquid offerings. ³⁰Place the Bread of the Presence on the table to remain before me at all times.

³¹"Make a lampstand of pure, hammered gold. Make the entire lampstand and its decorations of one piece—the base, center stem, lamp cups, buds, and petals. ³²Make it with six branches going out from the center stem, three on each side. ³³Each of the six branches will have three lamp cups shaped like almond blossoms, complete with buds and petals. ³⁴Craft the center stem of the lampstand with four lamp cups shaped like almond blossoms, complete with buds and petals. ³⁵There will also be an almond bud beneath each pair of branches where the six branches extend from the center stem. ³⁶The almond buds and branches must all be of one piece with the center stem, and they must be hammered from pure gold. ³⁷Then make the seven lamps for the lampstand, and set them so they reflect their light forward. ³⁸The lamp snuffers and trays must also be made of pure gold. ³⁹You will need seventy-five pounds* of pure gold for the lampstand and its accessories.

40"Be sure that you make everything according to the pattern I have shown you here on the mountain."

23:15 Hebrew *appointed time in the month of Abib*. This first month of the ancient Hebrew lunar calendar usually occurs within the months of March and April.   23:16a Or *Festival of Weeks*. This was later called the Festival of Pentecost (see Acts 2:1). It is celebrated today as Shavuat (or Shabuoth).   23:16b Or *Festival of Ingathering*. This was later called the Festival of Shelters or Festival of Tabernacles (see Lev 23:33-36). It is celebrated today as Sukkot (or Succoth).   23:25 As in Greek and Latin versions; Hebrew reads *he*.   23:28 Often rendered *the hornet*. The meaning of the Hebrew is uncertain. 23:31a Hebrew *from the sea of reeds to the sea of the Philistines*.   23:31b Hebrew *from the wilderness to the river*.   25:10 Hebrew *2.5 cubits* [115 centimeters] *long, 1.5 cubits* [69 centimeters] *wide, and 1.5 cubits high*. 25:16 Hebrew *Place inside the Ark the Testimony*; similarly in 25:21. The Hebrew word for "testimony" refers to the terms of the LORD's covenant with Israel as written on stone tablets, and also to the covenant itself.   25:17 Hebrew *2.5 cubits* [115 centimeters] *long and 1.5 cubits* [69 centimeters] *wide*.   25:22 Or *Ark of the Testimony*. 25:23 Hebrew *2 cubits* [92 centimeters] *long, 1 cubit* [46 centimeters] *wide, and 1.5 cubits* [69 centimeters] *high*.   25:25 Hebrew *a border of a handbreadth* [8 centimeters].   25:39 Hebrew *1 talent* [34 kilograms].

## MATTHEW 24:29-51

"Immediately after the anguish of those days,

the sun will be darkened,
    the moon will give no light,
the stars will fall from the sky,
    and the powers in the heavens
        will be shaken.*

30And then at last, the sign that the Son of Man is coming will appear in the heavens, and there will be deep mourning among all the peoples of the earth. And they will see the Son of Man coming on the clouds of heaven with power and great glory.*  31And he will send out his angels with the mighty blast of a trumpet, and they will gather his chosen ones from all over the world*— from the farthest ends of the earth and heaven.

32"Now learn a lesson from the fig tree. When its branches bud and its leaves begin to sprout, you know that summer is near. 33In the same way, when you see all these things, you can know his return is very near, right at the door. 34I tell you the truth, this generation* will not pass from the scene until all these things take place. 35Heaven and earth will disappear, but my words will never disappear.

36"However, no one knows the day or hour when these things will happen, not even the angels in heaven or the Son himself.* Only the Father knows.

37"When the Son of Man returns, it will be like it was in Noah's day. 38In those days before the flood, the people were enjoying banquets and parties and weddings right up to the time Noah entered his boat. 39People didn't realize what was going to happen until the flood came and swept them all away. That is the way it will be when the Son of Man comes.

40"Two men will be working together in the field; one will be taken, the other left. 41Two women will be grinding flour at the mill; one will be taken, the other left.

42"So you, too, must keep watch! For you don't know what day your Lord is coming. 43Understand this: If a homeowner knew exactly when a burglar was coming, he would keep watch and not permit his house to be broken into. 44You also must be ready all the time, for the Son of Man will come when least expected.

45"A faithful, sensible servant is one to whom the master can give the responsibility of managing his other household servants and feeding them. 46If the master returns and finds that the servant has done a good job, there will be a reward. 47I tell you the truth, the master will put that servant in charge of all he owns. 48But what if the servant is evil and thinks, 'My master won't be back for a while,' 49and he begins beating the other servants, partying, and getting drunk? 50The master will return unannounced and unexpected, 51and he will cut the servant to pieces and assign him a place with the hypocrites. In that place there will be weeping and gnashing of teeth."

24:29 See Isa 13:10; 34:4; Joel 2:10.   24:30 See Dan 7:13. 24:31 Greek *from the four winds*.   24:34 Or *this age*, or *this nation*.   24:36 Some manuscripts do not include *or the Son himself*.

## PSALM 30:1-12

*A psalm of David. A song for the dedication of the Temple.*

1 I will exalt you, LORD, for you
   rescued me.
   You refused to let my enemies
   triumph over me.
2 O LORD my God, I cried to you
   for help,
   and you restored my health.
3 You brought me up from the
   grave,* O LORD.
   You kept me from falling into
   the pit of death.

4 Sing to the LORD, all you godly ones!
   Praise his holy name.
5 For his anger lasts only a moment,
   but his favor lasts a lifetime!
   Weeping may last through the night,
   but joy comes with the morning.

6 When I was prosperous, I said,
   "Nothing can stop me now!"
7 Your favor, O LORD, made me as
   secure as a mountain.
   Then you turned away from me,
   and I was shattered.

8 I cried out to you, O LORD.
   I begged the Lord for mercy,
   saying,
9 "What will you gain if I die,
   if I sink into the grave?
   Can my dust praise you?
   Can it tell of your faithfulness?
10 Hear me, LORD, and have mercy
   on me.
   Help me, O LORD."

11 You have turned my mourning into
   joyful dancing.
   You have taken away my clothes
   of mourning and clothed me
   with joy,
12 that I might sing praises to you
   and not be silent.
   O LORD my God, I will give you
   thanks forever!

30:3 Hebrew *from Sheol.*

## PROVERBS 7:24-27

So listen to me, my sons, and pay attention to my words. Don't let your hearts stray away toward her. Don't wander down her wayward path. For she has been the ruin of many; many men have been her victims. Her house is the road to the grave.* Her bedroom is the den of death.

7:27 Hebrew *to Sheol.*

# FEBRUARY 7

## EXODUS 26:1–27:21

"Make the Tabernacle from ten curtains of finely woven linen. Decorate the curtains with blue, purple, and scarlet thread and with skillfully embroidered cherubim. 2These ten curtains must all be exactly the same size— 42 feet long and 6 feet wide.* 3Join five of these curtains together to make one long curtain, then join the other five into a second long curtain. 4Put loops of blue yarn along the edge of the last curtain in each set. 5The fifty loops along the edge of one curtain are to match the fifty loops along the edge of the other curtain. 6Then make fifty gold clasps and fasten the long curtains together with the clasps. In this way, the Tabernacle will be made of one continuous piece.

7"Make eleven curtains of goat-hair cloth to serve as a tent covering for the Tabernacle. 8These eleven curtains must all be exactly the same size— 45 feet long and 6 feet wide.* 9Join five of these curtains together to make one long curtain, and join the other six into a second long curtain. Allow 3 feet of material from the second set of curtains to hang over the front* of the sacred tent. 10Make fifty loops for one edge of each large curtain. 11Then make fifty bronze clasps, and fasten the loops of the long curtains with the clasps. In this way, the tent covering will be made of one continuous piece. [12]The remaining 3 feet* of this tent covering will be left to hang over the back of the Tabernacle. [13]Allow 18 inches* of remaining material to hang down over each side, so the Tabernacle is completely covered. [14]Complete the tent covering with a protective layer of tanned ram skins and a layer of fine goatskin leather.

[15]"For the framework of the Tabernacle, construct frames of acacia wood. [16]Each frame must be 15 feet high and 27 inches wide,* [17]with two pegs under each frame. Make all the frames identical. [18]Make twenty of these frames to support the curtains on the south side of the Tabernacle. [19]Also make forty silver bases—two bases under each frame, with the pegs fitting securely into the bases. [20]For the north side of the Tabernacle, make another twenty frames, [21]with their forty silver bases, two bases under each frame. [22]Make six frames for the rear—the west side of the Tabernacle—[23]along with two additional frames to reinforce the rear corners of the Tabernacle. [24]These corner frames will be matched at the bottom and firmly attached at the top with a single ring, forming a single corner unit. Make both of these corner units the same way. [25]So there will be eight frames at the rear of the Tabernacle, set in sixteen silver bases—two bases under each frame.

[26]"Make crossbars of acacia wood to link the frames, five crossbars for the north side of the Tabernacle [27]and five for the south side. Also make five crossbars for the rear of the Tabernacle, which will face west. [28]The middle crossbar, attached halfway up the frames, will run all the way from one end of the Tabernacle to the other. [29]Overlay the frames with gold, and make gold rings to hold the crossbars. Overlay the crossbars with gold as well.

[30]"Set up this Tabernacle according to the pattern you were shown on the mountain.

[31]"For the inside of the Tabernacle, make a special curtain of finely woven linen. Decorate it with blue, purple, and scarlet thread and with skillfully embroidered cherubim. [32]Hang this curtain on gold hooks attached to four posts of acacia wood. Overlay the posts with gold, and set them in four silver bases. [33]Hang the inner curtain from clasps, and put the Ark of the Covenant* in the room behind it. This curtain will separate the Holy Place from the Most Holy Place.

[34]"Then put the Ark's cover—the place of atonement—on top of the Ark of the Covenant inside the Most Holy Place. [35]Place the table outside the inner curtain on the north side of the Tabernacle, and place the lampstand across the room on the south side.

[36]"Make another curtain for the entrance to the sacred tent. Make it of finely woven linen and embroider it with exquisite designs, using blue, purple, and scarlet thread. [37]Craft five posts from acacia wood. Overlay them with gold, and hang the curtain from them with gold hooks. Cast five bronze bases for the posts.

[27:1]"USING acacia wood, construct a square altar 7½ feet wide, 7½ feet long, and 4½ feet high.* [2]Make horns for each of its four corners so that the horns and altar are all one piece. Overlay the altar with bronze. [3]Make ash buckets, shovels, basins, meat forks, and firepans, all of bronze. [4]Make a bronze grating for it, and attach four bronze rings at its four corners. [5]Install the grating halfway down the side of the altar, under the ledge. [6]For carrying the altar, make poles from acacia wood, and overlay them with bronze. [7]Insert the poles through the rings on the two sides of the altar. [8]The altar must be hollow, made from planks. Build it just as you were shown on the mountain.

[9]"Then make the courtyard for the Tabernacle, enclosed with curtains made of finely woven linen. On the south side, make the curtains 150 feet long.* [10]They will be held up by twenty posts set securely in twenty bronze bases. Hang the curtains with silver

hooks and rings. ¹¹Make the curtains the same on the north side—150 feet of curtains held up by twenty posts set securely in bronze bases. Hang the curtains with silver hooks and rings. ¹²The curtains on the west end of the courtyard will be 75 feet long,* supported by ten posts set into ten bases. ¹³The east end of the courtyard, the front, will also be 75 feet long. ¹⁴The courtyard entrance will be on the east end, flanked by two curtains. The curtain on the right side will be 22½ feet long,* supported by three posts set into three bases. ¹⁵The curtain on the left side will also be 22½ feet long, supported by three posts set into three bases.

¹⁶"For the entrance to the courtyard, make a curtain that is 30 feet long.* Make it from finely woven linen, and decorate it with beautiful embroidery in blue, purple, and scarlet thread. Support it with four posts, each securely set in its own base. ¹⁷All the posts around the courtyard must have silver rings and hooks and bronze bases. ¹⁸So the entire courtyard will be 150 feet long and 75 feet wide, with curtain walls 7½ feet high,* made from finely woven linen. The bases for the posts will be made of bronze.

¹⁹"All the articles used in the rituals of the Tabernacle, including all the tent pegs used to support the Tabernacle and the courtyard curtains, must be made of bronze.

²⁰"Command the people of Israel to bring you pure oil of pressed olives for the light, to keep the lamps burning continually. ²¹The lampstand will stand in the Tabernacle, in front of the inner curtain that shields the Ark of the Covenant.* Aaron and his sons must keep the lamps burning in the LORD's presence all night. This is a permanent law for the people of Israel, and it must be observed from generation to generation."

26:2 Hebrew *28 cubits* [12.9 meters] *long and 4 cubits* [1.8 meters] *wide.*   26:8 Hebrew *30 cubits* [13.8 meters] *long and 4 cubits* [1.8 meters] *wide.*   26:9 Hebrew *Double over the sixth sheet at the front.*   26:12 Hebrew *The half sheet that is left over.*   26:13 Hebrew *1 cubit* [46 centimeters].   26:16 Hebrew *10 cubits* [4.6 meters] *high and 1.5 cubits* [69 centimeters] *wide.*

26:33 Or *Ark of the Testimony;* also in 26:34.
27:1 Hebrew *5 cubits* [2.3 meters] *wide, 5 cubits long, a square, and 3 cubits* [1.4 meters] *high.*   27:9 Hebrew *100 cubits* [46 meters]; also in 27:11.   27:12 Hebrew *50 cubits* [23 meters]; also in 27:13.   27:14 Hebrew *15 cubits* [6.9 meters]; also in 27:15.   27:16 Hebrew *20 cubits* [9.2 meters].   27:18 Hebrew *100 cubits* [46 meters] *long and 50 cubits* [23 meters] *wide and 5 cubits* [2.3 meters] *high.*   27:21 Hebrew *in the Tent of Meeting, outside the inner curtain that is in front of the Testimony.* See note on 25:16.

## MATTHEW 25:1-30

"The Kingdom of Heaven can be illustrated by the story of ten bridesmaids* who took their lamps and went to meet the bridegroom. ²Five of them were foolish, and five were wise. ³The five who were foolish didn't take enough olive oil for their lamps, ⁴but the other five were wise enough to take along extra oil. ⁵When the bridegroom was delayed, they all became drowsy and fell asleep.

⁶"At midnight they were roused by the shout, 'Look, the bridegroom is coming! Come out and meet him!'

⁷"All the bridesmaids got up and prepared their lamps. ⁸Then the five foolish ones asked the others, 'Please give us some of your oil because our lamps are going out.'

⁹"But the others replied, 'We don't have enough for all of us. Go to a shop and buy some for yourselves.'

¹⁰"But while they were gone to buy oil, the bridegroom came. Then those who were ready went in with him to the marriage feast, and the door was locked. ¹¹Later, when the other five bridesmaids returned, they stood outside, calling, 'Lord! Lord! Open the door for us!'

¹²"But he called back, 'Believe me, I don't know you!'

¹³"So you, too, must keep watch! For you do not know the day or hour of my return.

¹⁴"Again, the Kingdom of Heaven can be illustrated by the story of a man going on a long trip. He called together his servants and entrusted his money to them while he was gone. ¹⁵He gave five bags of silver* to one, two bags of silver to another, and one bag of silver to the

last—dividing it in proportion to their abilities. He then left on his trip.

16"The servant who received the five bags of silver began to invest the money and earned five more. 17The servant with two bags of silver also went to work and earned two more. 18But the servant who received the one bag of silver dug a hole in the ground and hid the master's money.

19"After a long time their master returned from his trip and called them to give an account of how they had used his money. 20The servant to whom he had entrusted the five bags of silver came forward with five more and said, 'Master, you gave me five bags of silver to invest, and I have earned five more.'

21"The master was full of praise. 'Well done, my good and faithful servant. You have been faithful in handling this small amount, so now I will give you many more responsibilities. Let's celebrate together!*'

22"The servant who had received the two bags of silver came forward and said, 'Master, you gave me two bags of silver to invest, and I have earned two more.'

23"The master said, 'Well done, my good and faithful servant. You have been faithful in handling this small amount, so now I will give you many more responsibilities. Let's celebrate together!'

24"Then the servant with the one bag of silver came and said, 'Master, I knew you were a harsh man, harvesting crops you didn't plant and gathering crops you didn't cultivate. 25I was afraid I would lose your money, so I hid it in the earth. Look, here is your money back.'

26"But the master replied, 'You wicked and lazy servant! If you knew I harvested crops I didn't plant and gathered crops I didn't cultivate, 27why didn't you deposit my money in the bank? At least I could have gotten some interest on it.'

28"Then he ordered, 'Take the money from this servant, and give it to the one with the ten bags of silver. 29To those who use well what they are given, even more will be given, and they will have an abundance. But from those who do nothing, even what little they have will be taken away. 30Now throw this useless servant into outer darkness, where there will be weeping and gnashing of teeth.'"

25:1 Or *virgins;* also in 25:7, 11.   25:15 Greek *talents;* also throughout the story. A talent is equal to 75 pounds or 34 kilograms.   25:21 Greek *Enter into the joy of your master* (or *your Lord*); also in 25:23.

## PSALM 31:1-8
*For the choir director: A psalm of David.*

1 O LORD, I have come to you for protection;
   don't let me be disgraced.
   Save me, for you do what
      is right.
2 Turn your ear to listen to me;
   rescue me quickly.
  Be my rock of protection,
   a fortress where I will be safe.
3 You are my rock and my fortress.
   For the honor of your name, lead
      me out of this danger.
4 Pull me from the trap my enemies
      set for me,
   for I find protection in you alone.
5 I entrust my spirit into your hand.
   Rescue me, LORD, for you are
      a faithful God.

6 I hate those who worship
      worthless idols.
   I trust in the LORD.
7 I will be glad and rejoice in your
      unfailing love,
   for you have seen my troubles,
   and you care about the anguish
      of my soul.
8 You have not handed me over
      to my enemies
   but have set me in a safe place.

## PROVERBS 8:1-11
Listen as Wisdom calls out! Hear as understanding raises her voice! On the hilltop along the road, she takes her stand at the crossroads. By the gates at the entrance to the town, on the road leading in, she cries aloud, "I call to you, to all of you! I raise my voice to all people. You simple people, use good judgment. You foolish people, show some understanding.

Listen to me! For I have important things to tell you. Everything I say is right, for I speak the truth and detest every kind of deception. My advice is wholesome. There is nothing devious or crooked in it. My words are plain to anyone with understanding, clear to those with knowledge. Choose my instruction rather than silver, and knowledge rather than pure gold. For wisdom is far more valuable than rubies. Nothing you desire can compare with it."

# FEBRUARY 8

EXODUS 28:1-43

"Call for your [Moses'] brother, Aaron, and his sons, Nadab, Abihu, Eleazar, and Ithamar. Set them apart from the rest of the people of Israel so they may minister to me and be my priests. ²Make sacred garments for Aaron that are glorious and beautiful. ³Instruct all the skilled craftsmen whom I have filled with the spirit of wisdom. Have them make garments for Aaron that will distinguish him as a priest set apart for my service. ⁴These are the garments they are to make: a chestpiece, an ephod, a robe, a patterned tunic, a turban, and a sash. They are to make these sacred garments for your brother, Aaron, and his sons to wear when they serve me as priests. ⁵So give them fine linen cloth, gold thread, and blue, purple, and scarlet thread.

⁶"The craftsmen must make the ephod of finely woven linen and skillfully embroider it with gold and with blue, purple, and scarlet thread. ⁷It will consist of two pieces, front and back, joined at the shoulders with two shoulder-pieces. ⁸The decorative sash will be made of the same materials: finely woven linen embroidered with gold and with blue, purple, and scarlet thread.

⁹"Take two onyx stones, and engrave on them the names of the tribes of Israel. ¹⁰Six names will be on each stone, arranged in the order of the births of the original sons of Israel. ¹¹Engrave these names on the two stones in the same way a jeweler engraves a seal. Then mount the stones in settings of gold filigree. ¹²Fasten the two stones on the shoulder-pieces of the ephod as a reminder that Aaron represents the people of Israel. Aaron will carry these names on his shoulders as a constant reminder whenever he goes before the LORD. ¹³Make the settings of gold filigree, ¹⁴then braid two cords of pure gold and attach them to the filigree settings on the shoulders of the ephod.

¹⁵"Then, with great skill and care, make a chestpiece to be worn for seeking a decision from God.* Make it to match the ephod, using finely woven linen embroidered with gold and with blue, purple, and scarlet thread. ¹⁶Make the chestpiece of a single piece of cloth folded to form a pouch nine inches* square. ¹⁷Mount four rows of gemstones* on it. The first row will contain a red carnelian, a pale green peridot, and an emerald. ¹⁸The second row will contain a turquoise, a blue lapis lazuli, and a white moonstone. ¹⁹The third row will contain an orange jacinth, an agate, and a purple amethyst. ²⁰The fourth row will contain a blue-green beryl, an onyx, and a green jasper. All these stones will be set in gold filigree. ²¹Each stone will represent one of the twelve sons of Israel, and the name of that tribe will be engraved on it like a seal.

²²"To attach the chestpiece to the ephod, make braided cords of pure gold thread. ²³Then make two gold rings and attach them to the top corners of the chestpiece. ²⁴Tie the two gold cords to the two rings on the chestpiece. ²⁵Tie the other ends of the cords to the gold settings on the shoulder-pieces of the ephod. ²⁶Then make two more gold rings and attach them to the inside edges of the chestpiece next to the ephod. ²⁷And make two more gold rings and at-

tach them to the front of the ephod, below the shoulder-pieces, just above the knot where the decorative sash is fastened to the ephod. [28]Then attach the bottom rings of the chestpiece to the rings on the ephod with blue cords. This will hold the chestpiece securely to the ephod above the decorative sash.

[29]"In this way, Aaron will carry the names of the tribes of Israel on the sacred chestpiece* over his heart when he goes into the Holy Place. This will be a continual reminder that he represents the people when he comes before the LORD. [30]Insert the Urim and Thummim into the sacred chestpiece so they will be carried over Aaron's heart when he goes into the LORD's presence. In this way, Aaron will always carry over his heart the objects used to determine the LORD's will for his people whenever he goes in before the LORD.

[31]"Make the robe that is worn with the ephod from a single piece of blue cloth, [32]with an opening for Aaron's head in the middle of it. Reinforce the opening with a woven collar* so it will not tear. [33]Make pomegranates out of blue, purple, and scarlet yarn, and attach them to the hem of the robe, with gold bells between them. [34]The gold bells and pomegranates are to alternate all around the hem. [35]Aaron will wear this robe whenever he ministers before the LORD, and the bells will tinkle as he goes in and out of the LORD's presence in the Holy Place. If he wears it, he will not die.

[36]"Next make a medallion of pure gold, and engrave it like a seal with these words: HOLY TO THE LORD. [37]Attach the medallion with a blue cord to the front of Aaron's turban, where it must remain. [38]Aaron must wear it on his forehead so he may take on himself any guilt of the people of Israel when they consecrate their sacred offerings. He must always wear it on his forehead so the LORD will accept the people.

[39]"Weave Aaron's patterned tunic from fine linen cloth. Fashion the turban from this linen as well. Also make a sash, and decorate it with colorful embroidery.

[40]"For Aaron's sons, make tunics, sashes, and special head coverings that are glorious and beautiful. [41]Clothe your brother, Aaron, and his sons with these garments, and then anoint and ordain them. Consecrate them so they can serve as my priests. [42]Also make linen undergarments for them, to be worn next to their bodies, reaching from their hips to their thighs. [43]These must be worn whenever Aaron and his sons enter the Tabernacle* or approach the altar in the Holy Place to perform their priestly duties. Then they will not incur guilt and die. This is a permanent law for Aaron and all his descendants after him."

28:15 Hebrew *a chestpiece for decision.*   28:16 Hebrew *1 span* [23 centimeters].   28:17 The identification of some of these gemstones is uncertain.   28:29 Hebrew *the chestpiece for decision;* also in 28:30. See 28:15.   28:32 The meaning of the Hebrew is uncertain.   28:43 Hebrew *Tent of Meeting.*

## MATTHEW 25:31–26:13

"**B**ut when the Son of Man* comes in his glory, and all the angels with him, then he will sit upon his glorious throne. [32]All the nations* will be gathered in his presence, and he will separate the people as a shepherd separates the sheep from the goats. [33]He will place the sheep at his right hand and the goats at his left.

[34]"Then the King will say to those on his right, 'Come, you who are blessed by my Father, inherit the Kingdom prepared for you from the creation of the world. [35]For I was hungry, and you fed me. I was thirsty, and you gave me a drink. I was a stranger, and you invited me into your home. [36]I was naked, and you gave me clothing. I was sick, and you cared for me. I was in prison, and you visited me.'

[37]"Then these righteous ones will reply, 'Lord, when did we ever see you hungry and feed you? Or thirsty and give you something to drink? [38]Or a stranger and show you hospitality? Or naked and give you clothing? [39]When did we ever see you sick or in prison and visit you?'

⁴⁰"And the King will say, 'I tell you the truth, when you did it to one of the least of these my brothers and sisters,* you were doing it to me!'

⁴¹"Then the King will turn to those on the left and say, 'Away with you, you cursed ones, into the eternal fire prepared for the devil and his demons.* ⁴²For I was hungry, and you didn't feed me. I was thirsty, and you didn't give me a drink. ⁴³I was a stranger, and you didn't invite me into your home. I was naked, and you didn't give me clothing. I was sick and in prison, and you didn't visit me.'

⁴⁴"Then they will reply, 'Lord, when did we ever see you hungry or thirsty or a stranger or naked or sick or in prison, and not help you?'

⁴⁵"And he will answer, 'I tell you the truth, when you refused to help the least of these my brothers and sisters, you were refusing to help me.'

⁴⁶"And they will go away into eternal punishment, but the righteous will go into eternal life."

²⁶:¹WHEN Jesus had finished saying all these things, he said to his disciples, ²"As you know, Passover begins in two days, and the Son of Man* will be handed over to be crucified."

³At that same time the leading priests and elders were meeting at the residence of Caiaphas, the high priest, ⁴plotting how to capture Jesus secretly and kill him. ⁵"But not during the Passover celebration," they agreed, "or the people may riot."

⁶Meanwhile, Jesus was in Bethany at the home of Simon, a man who had previously had leprosy. ⁷While he was eating,* a woman came in with a beautiful alabaster jar of expensive perfume and poured it over his head.

⁸The disciples were indignant when they saw this. "What a waste of money," they said. ⁹"It could have been sold for a high price and the money given to the poor."

¹⁰But Jesus, aware of this, replied, "Why criticize this woman for doing such a good thing to me? ¹¹You will always have the poor among you, but you will not always have me. ¹²She has poured this perfume on me to prepare my body for burial. ¹³I tell you the truth, wherever the Good News is preached throughout the world, this woman's deed will be remembered and discussed."

25:31 "Son of Man" is a title Jesus used for himself. 25:32 Or *peoples.* 25:40 Greek *my brothers.* 25:41 Greek *his angels.* 26:2 "Son of Man" is a title Jesus used for himself. 26:7 Or *reclining.*

PSALM 31:9-18

**H**ave mercy on me, LORD, for I am
    in distress.
  Tears blur my eyes.
  My body and soul are withering
    away.
¹⁰ I am dying from grief;
    my years are shortened by
      sadness.
  Sin has drained my strength;
    I am wasting away from within.
¹¹ I am scorned by all my enemies
    and despised by my neighbors—
    even my friends are afraid to
      come near me.
  When they see me on the street,
    they run the other way.
¹² I am ignored as if I were dead,
    as if I were a broken pot.
¹³ I have heard the many rumors
    about me,
    and I am surrounded by terror.
  My enemies conspire against me,
    plotting to take my life.
¹⁴ But I am trusting you, O LORD,
    saying, "You are my God!"
¹⁵ My future is in your hands.
    Rescue me from those who hunt
      me down relentlessly.
¹⁶ Let your favor shine on your servant.
    In your unfailing love, rescue me.
¹⁷ Don't let me be disgraced, O LORD,
    for I call out to you for help.
  Let the wicked be disgraced;
    let them lie silent in the grave.*
¹⁸ Silence their lying lips—
    those proud and arrogant lips that
      accuse the godly.

31:17 Hebrew *in Sheol.*

PROVERBS 8:12-13

**I**, Wisdom, live together with good judgment. I know where to discover knowledge and discernment. All who fear the LORD will hate evil. Therefore, I hate pride and arrogance, corruption and perverse speech.

# FEBRUARY 9

EXODUS 29:1-30:10

"This is the ceremony you must follow when you consecrate Aaron and his sons to serve me as priests: Take a young bull and two rams with no defects. ²Then, using choice wheat flour and no yeast, make loaves of bread, thin cakes mixed with olive oil, and wafers spread with oil. ³Place them all in a single basket, and present them at the entrance of the Tabernacle, along with the young bull and the two rams.

⁴"Present Aaron and his sons at the entrance of the Tabernacle,* and wash them with water. ⁵Dress Aaron in his priestly garments—the tunic, the robe worn with the ephod, the ephod itself, and the chestpiece. Then wrap the decorative sash of the ephod around him. ⁶Place the turban on his head, and fasten the sacred medallion to the turban. ⁷Then anoint him by pouring the anointing oil over his head. ⁸Next present his sons, and dress them in their tunics. ⁹Wrap the sashes around the waists of Aaron and his sons, and put their special head coverings on them. Then the right to the priesthood will be theirs by law forever. In this way, you will ordain Aaron and his sons.

¹⁰"Bring the young bull to the entrance of the Tabernacle, where Aaron and his sons will lay their hands on its head. ¹¹Then slaughter the bull in the LORD's presence at the entrance of the Tabernacle. ¹²Put some of its blood on the horns of the altar with your finger, and pour out the rest at the base of the altar. ¹³Take all the fat around the internal organs, the long lobe of the liver, and the two kidneys and the fat around them, and burn it all on the altar. ¹⁴Then take the rest of the bull, including its hide, meat, and dung, and burn it outside the camp as a sin offering.

¹⁵"Next Aaron and his sons must lay their hands on the head of one of the rams. ¹⁶Then slaughter the ram, and splatter its blood against all sides of the altar. ¹⁷Cut the ram into pieces, and wash off the internal organs and the legs. Set them alongside the head and the other pieces of the body, ¹⁸then burn the entire animal on the altar. This is a burnt offering to the LORD; it is a pleasing aroma, a special gift presented to the LORD.

¹⁹"Now take the other ram, and have Aaron and his sons lay their hands on its head. ²⁰Then slaughter it, and apply some of its blood to the right earlobes of Aaron and his sons. Also put it on the thumbs of their right hands and the big toes of their right feet. Splatter the rest of the blood against all sides of the altar. ²¹Then take some of the blood from the altar and some of the anointing oil, and sprinkle it on Aaron and his sons and on their garments. In this way, they and their garments will be set apart as holy.

²²"Since this is the ram for the ordination of Aaron and his sons, take the fat of the ram, including the fat of the broad tail, the fat around the internal organs, the long lobe of the liver, and the two kidneys and the fat around them, along with the right thigh. ²³Then take one round loaf of bread, one thin cake mixed with olive oil, and one wafer from the basket of bread without yeast that was placed in the LORD's presence. ²⁴Put all these in the hands of Aaron and his sons to be lifted up as a special offering to the LORD. ²⁵Afterward take the various breads from their hands, and burn them on the altar along with the burnt offering. It is a pleasing aroma to

the LORD, a special gift for him. ²⁶Then take the breast of Aaron's ordination ram, and lift it up in the LORD's presence as a special offering to him. Then keep it as your own portion.

²⁷"Set aside the portions of the ordination ram that belong to Aaron and his sons. This includes the breast and the thigh that were lifted up before the LORD as a special offering. ²⁸In the future, whenever the people of Israel lift up a peace offering, a portion of it must be set aside for Aaron and his descendants. This is their permanent right, and it is a sacred offering from the Israelites to the LORD.

²⁹"Aaron's sacred garments must be preserved for his descendants who succeed him, and they will wear them when they are anointed and ordained. ³⁰The descendant who succeeds him as high priest will wear these clothes for seven days as he ministers in the Tabernacle and the Holy Place.

³¹"Take the ram used in the ordination ceremony, and boil its meat in a sacred place. ³²Then Aaron and his sons will eat this meat, along with the bread in the basket, at the Tabernacle entrance. ³³They alone may eat the meat and bread used for their purification* in the ordination ceremony. No one else may eat them, for these things are set apart and holy. ³⁴If any of the ordination meat or bread remains until the morning, it must be burned. It may not be eaten, for it is holy.

³⁵"This is how you will ordain Aaron and his sons to their offices, just as I have commanded you. The ordination ceremony will go on for seven days. ³⁶Each day you must sacrifice a young bull as a sin offering to purify them, making them right with the LORD.* Afterward, cleanse the altar by purifying it*; make it holy by anointing it with oil. ³⁷Purify the altar, and consecrate it every day for seven days. After that, the altar will be absolutely holy, and whatever touches it will become holy.

³⁸"These are the sacrifices you are to offer regularly on the altar. Each day, offer two lambs that are a year old, ³⁹one in the morning and the other in the evening. ⁴⁰With one of them, offer two quarts of choice flour mixed with one quart of pure oil of pressed olives; also, offer one quart of wine* as a liquid offering. ⁴¹Offer the other lamb in the evening, along with the same offerings of flour and wine as in the morning. It will be a pleasing aroma, a special gift presented to the LORD.

⁴²"These burnt offerings are to be made each day from generation to generation. Offer them in the LORD's presence at the Tabernacle entrance; there I will meet with you and speak with you. ⁴³I will meet the people of Israel there, in the place made holy by my glorious presence. ⁴⁴Yes, I will consecrate the Tabernacle and the altar, and I will consecrate Aaron and his sons to serve me as priests. ⁴⁵Then I will live among the people of Israel and be their God, ⁴⁶and they will know that I am the LORD their God. I am the one who brought them out of the land of Egypt so that I could live among them. I am the LORD their God.

30:1"THEN make another altar of acacia wood for burning incense. ²Make it 18 inches square and 36 inches high,* with horns at the corners carved from the same piece of wood as the altar itself. ³Overlay the top, sides, and horns of the altar with pure gold, and run a gold molding around the entire altar. ⁴Make two gold rings, and attach them on opposite sides of the altar below the gold molding to hold the carrying poles. ⁵Make the poles of acacia wood and overlay them with gold. ⁶Place the incense altar just outside the inner curtain that shields the Ark of the Covenant,* in front of the Ark's cover—the place of atonement—that covers the tablets inscribed with the terms of the covenant.* I will meet with you there.

⁷"Every morning when Aaron maintains the lamps, he must burn fragrant incense on the altar. ⁸And each evening when he lights the lamps, he must again burn incense in the LORD's presence.

This must be done from generation to generation. 9Do not offer any unholy incense on this altar, or any burnt offerings, grain offerings, or liquid offerings.

10"Once a year Aaron must purify* the altar by smearing its horns with blood from the offering made to purify the people from their sin. This will be a regular, annual event from generation to generation, for this is the LORD's most holy altar."

29:4 Hebrew *Tent of Meeting;* also in 29:10, 11, 30, 32, 42, 44.    29:33 Or *their atonement.*    29:36a Or *to make atonement.*    29:36b Or *by making atonement for it;* similarly in 29:37.    29:40 Hebrew *¹⁄₁₀ of an ephah* [2.2 liters] *of choice flour . . . ¼ of a hin* [1 liter] *of pure oil . . . ¼ of a hin of wine.*    30:2 Hebrew *1 cubit* [46 centimeters] *long and 1 cubit wide, a square, and 2 cubits* [92 centimeters] *high.*    30:6a Or *Ark of the Testimony;* also in 30:26.    30:6b Hebrew *that covers the Testimony;* see note on 25:16.    30:10 Or *make atonement for;* also in 30:10b.

## MATTHEW 26:14-46

**T**hen Judas Iscariot, one of the twelve disciples, went to the leading priests 15and asked, "How much will you pay me to betray Jesus to you?" And they gave him thirty pieces of silver. 16From that time on, Judas began looking for an opportunity to betray Jesus.

17On the first day of the Festival of Unleavened Bread, the disciples came to Jesus and asked, "Where do you want us to prepare the Passover meal for you?"

18"As you go into the city," he told them, "you will see a certain man. Tell him, 'The Teacher says: My time has come, and I will eat the Passover meal with my disciples at your house.'" 19So the disciples did as Jesus told them and prepared the Passover meal there.

20When it was evening, Jesus sat down at the table* with the twelve disciples.* 21While they were eating, he said, "I tell you the truth, one of you will betray me."

22Greatly distressed, each one asked in turn, "Am I the one, Lord?"

23He replied, "One of you who has just eaten from this bowl with me will betray me. 24For the Son of Man must die, as the Scriptures declared long ago. But how terrible it will be for the one who betrays him. It would be far better for that man if he had never been born!"

25Judas, the one who would betray him, also asked, "Rabbi, am I the one?"

And Jesus told him, "You have said it."

26As they were eating, Jesus took some bread and blessed it. Then he broke it in pieces and gave it to the disciples, saying, "Take this and eat it, for this is my body."

27And he took a cup of wine and gave thanks to God for it. He gave it to them and said, "Each of you drink from it, 28for this is my blood, which confirms the covenant* between God and his people. It is poured out as a sacrifice to forgive the sins of many. 29Mark my words—I will not drink wine again until the day I drink it new with you in my Father's Kingdom."

30Then they sang a hymn and went out to the Mount of Olives.

31On the way, Jesus told them, "Tonight all of you will desert me. For the Scriptures say,

'God will strike* the Shepherd,
    and the sheep of the flock
        will be scattered.'

32But after I have been raised from the dead, I will go ahead of you to Galilee and meet you there."

33Peter declared, "Even if everyone else deserts you, I will never desert you."

34Jesus replied, "I tell you the truth, Peter—this very night, before the rooster crows, you will deny three times that you even know me."

35"No!" Peter insisted. "Even if I have to die with you, I will never deny you!" And all the other disciples vowed the same.

36Then Jesus went with them to the olive grove called Gethsemane, and he said, "Sit here while I go over there to pray." 37He took Peter and Zebedee's two sons, James and John, and he became anguished and distressed. 38He told them, "My soul is crushed with grief to the point of death. Stay here and keep watch with me."

39He went on a little farther and bowed with his face to the ground, praying, "My Father! If it is possible, let this cup of suffering be taken away from me. Yet I want your will to be done, not mine."

⁴⁰Then he returned to the disciples and found them asleep. He said to Peter, "Couldn't you watch with me even one hour? ⁴¹Keep watch and pray, so that you will not give in to temptation. For the spirit is willing, but the body is weak!"

⁴²Then Jesus left them a second time and prayed, "My Father! If this cup cannot be taken away* unless I drink it, your will be done." ⁴³When he returned to them again, he found them sleeping, for they couldn't keep their eyes open.

⁴⁴So he went to pray a third time, saying the same things again. ⁴⁵Then he came to the disciples and said, "Go ahead and sleep. Have your rest. But look—the time has come. The Son of Man is betrayed into the hands of sinners. ⁴⁶Up, let's be going. Look, my betrayer is here!"

26:20a Or *Jesus reclined.*  26:20b Some manuscripts read *the Twelve.*  26:28 Some manuscripts read *the new covenant.*  26:31 Greek *I will strike.* Zech 13:7. 26:42 Greek *If this cannot pass.*

## PSALM 31:19-24

**H**ow great is the goodness
    you have stored up for those
    who fear you.
You lavish it on those who come
    to you for protection,
    blessing them before the
    watching world.
²⁰ You hide them in the shelter
    of your presence,
    safe from those who conspire
    against them.
You shelter them in your presence,
    far from accusing tongues.

²¹ Praise the LORD,
    for he has shown me the wonders
    of his unfailing love.
    He kept me safe when my city
    was under attack.
²² In panic I cried out,
    "I am cut off from the LORD!"
But you heard my cry for mercy
    and answered my call for help.

²³ Love the LORD, all you godly ones!
    For the LORD protects those
    who are loyal to him,
    but he harshly punishes
    the arrogant.
²⁴ So be strong and courageous,
    all you who put your hope
    in the LORD!

## PROVERBS 8:14-26

**C**ommon sense and success belong to me. Insight and strength are mine. Because of me, kings reign, and rulers make just decrees. Rulers lead with my help, and nobles make righteous judgments. □ "I love all who love me. Those who search will surely find me. I have riches and honor, as well as enduring wealth and justice. My gifts are better than gold, even the purest gold, my wages better than sterling silver! I walk in righteousness, in paths of justice. Those who love me inherit wealth. I will fill their treasuries. □ "The LORD formed me from the beginning, before he created anything else. I was appointed in ages past, at the very first, before the earth began. I was born before the oceans were created, before the springs bubbled forth their waters. Before the mountains were formed, before the hills, I was born—before he had made the earth and fields and the first handfuls of soil.

# FEBRUARY 10

## EXODUS 30:11-31:18

**T**hen the LORD said to Moses, ¹²"Whenever you take a census of the people of Israel, each man who is counted must pay a ransom for himself to the LORD. Then no plague will strike the people as you count them. ¹³Each person who is counted must give a small piece of silver as a sacred offering to the LORD.

(This payment is half a shekel,* based on the sanctuary shekel, which equals twenty gerahs.) [14]All who have reached their twentieth birthday must give this sacred offering to the LORD. [15]When this offering is given to the LORD to purify your lives, making you right with him,* the rich must not give more than the specified amount, and the poor must not give less. [16]Receive this ransom money from the Israelites, and use it for the care of the Tabernacle.* It will bring the Israelites to the LORD's attention, and it will purify your lives."

[17]Then the LORD said to Moses, [18]"Make a bronze washbasin with a bronze stand. Place it between the Tabernacle and the altar, and fill it with water. [19]Aaron and his sons will wash their hands and feet there. [20]They must wash with water whenever they go into the Tabernacle to appear before the LORD and when they approach the altar to burn up their special gifts to the LORD— or they will die! [21]They must always wash their hands and feet, or they will die. This is a permanent law for Aaron and his descendants, to be observed from generation to generation."

[22]Then the LORD said to Moses, [23]"Collect choice spices—12½ pounds of pure myrrh, 6¼ pounds of fragrant cinnamon, 6¼ pounds of fragrant calamus* [24]and 12½ pounds of cassia*—as measured by the weight of the sanctuary shekel. Also get one gallon of olive oil.* [25]Like a skilled incense maker, blend these ingredients to make a holy anointing oil. [26]Use this sacred oil to anoint the Tabernacle, the Ark of the Covenant, [27]the table and all its utensils, the lampstand and all its accessories, the incense altar, [28]the altar of burnt offering and all its utensils, and the washbasin with its stand. [29]Consecrate them to make them absolutely holy. After this, whatever touches them will also become holy.

[30]"Anoint Aaron and his sons also, consecrating them to serve me as priests. [31]And say to the people of Israel, 'This holy anointing oil is reserved for me from generation to generation. [32]It must never be used to anoint anyone else, and you must never make any blend like it for yourselves. It is holy, and you must treat it as holy. [33]Anyone who makes a blend like it or anoints someone other than a priest will be cut off from the community.'"

[34]Then the LORD said to Moses, "Gather fragrant spices—resin droplets, mollusk shell, and galbanum—and mix these fragrant spices with pure frankincense, weighed out in equal amounts. [35]Using the usual techniques of the incense maker, blend the spices together and sprinkle them with salt to produce a pure and holy incense. [36]Grind some of the mixture into a very fine powder and put it in front of the Ark of the Covenant,* where I will meet with you in the Tabernacle. You must treat this incense as most holy. [37]Never use this formula to make this incense for yourselves. It is reserved for the LORD, and you must treat it as holy. [38]Anyone who makes incense like this for personal use will be cut off from the community."

[31:1]THEN the LORD said to Moses, [2]"Look, I have specifically chosen Bezalel son of Uri, grandson of Hur, of the tribe of Judah. [3]I have filled him with the Spirit of God, giving him great wisdom, ability, and expertise in all kinds of crafts. [4]He is a master craftsman, expert in working with gold, silver, and bronze. [5]He is skilled in engraving and mounting gemstones and in carving wood. He is a master at every craft!

[6]"And I have personally appointed Oholiab son of Ahisamach, of the tribe of Dan, to be his assistant. Moreover, I have given special skill to all the gifted craftsmen so they can make all the things I have commanded you to make:

[7] the Tabernacle;*
    the Ark of the Covenant;*
    the Ark's cover—the place
       of atonement;
    all the furnishings of the Tabernacle;
[8] the table and its utensils;

the pure gold lampstand with
all its accessories;
the incense altar;
⁹ the altar of burnt offering with
all its utensils;
the washbasin with its stand;
¹⁰ the beautifully stitched garments—
the sacred garments for Aaron
the priest, and the garments for
his sons to wear as they minister
as priests;
¹¹ the anointing oil;
the fragrant incense for the
Holy Place.

The craftsmen must make everything
as I have commanded you."

¹²The Lord then gave these instructions to Moses: ¹³"Tell the people of Israel: 'Be careful to keep my Sabbath day,
for the Sabbath is a sign of the covenant
between me and you from generation to
generation. It is given so you may know
that I am the Lord, who makes you holy.
¹⁴You must keep the Sabbath day, for it
is a holy day for you. Anyone who dese-
crates it must be put to death; anyone
who works on that day will be cut off
from the community. ¹⁵You have six
days each week for your ordinary work,
but the seventh day must be a Sabbath
day of complete rest, a holy day dedicated to the Lord. Anyone who works on
the Sabbath must be put to death. ¹⁶The
people of Israel must keep the Sabbath
day by observing it from generation to
generation. This is a covenant obligation
for all time. ¹⁷It is a permanent sign of
my covenant with the people of Israel.
For in six days the Lord made heaven
and earth, but on the seventh day he
stopped working and was refreshed.'"
¹⁸When the Lord finished speaking
with Moses on Mount Sinai, he gave him
the two stone tablets inscribed with the
terms of the covenant,* written by the
finger of God.

30:13 Or 0.2 ounces, or 6 grams.   30:15 Or to
make atonement for your lives; similarly in 30:16.
30:16 Hebrew Tent of Meeting; also in 30:18, 20, 26, 36.
30:23 Hebrew 500 shekels [5.7 kilograms] of pure myrrh,
250 shekels [2.9 kilograms] of fragrant cinnamon,
250 shekels of fragrant calamus.   30:24a Hebrew

500 shekels [5.7 kilograms] of cassia.   30:24b Hebrew
1 hin [3.8 liters] of olive oil.   30:36 Hebrew in front of the
Testimony; see note on 25:16.   31:7a Hebrew the Tent
of Meeting.   31:7b Hebrew the Ark of the Testimony.
31:18 Hebrew the two tablets of the Testimony; see
note on 25:16.

## MATTHEW 26:47-68

And even as Jesus said this, Judas, one of
the twelve disciples, arrived with a crowd
of men armed with swords and clubs.
They had been sent by the leading priests
and elders of the people. ⁴⁸The traitor,
Judas, had given them a prearranged signal: "You will know which one to arrest
when I greet him with a kiss." ⁴⁹So Judas
came straight to Jesus. "Greetings, Rabbi!" he exclaimed and gave him the kiss.
⁵⁰Jesus said, "My friend, go ahead
and do what you have come for."
Then the others grabbed Jesus and arrested him. ⁵¹But one of the men with
Jesus pulled out his sword and struck the
high priest's slave, slashing off his ear.
⁵²"Put away your sword," Jesus told
him. "Those who use the sword will die
by the sword. ⁵³Don't you realize that I
could ask my Father for thousands* of
angels to protect us, and he would send
them instantly? ⁵⁴But if I did, how
would the Scriptures be fulfilled that
describe what must happen now?"
⁵⁵Then Jesus said to the crowd, "Am I
some dangerous revolutionary, that you
come with swords and clubs to arrest
me? Why didn't you arrest me in the
Temple? I was there teaching every day.
⁵⁶But this is all happening to fulfill the
words of the prophets as recorded in
the Scriptures." At that point, all the disciples deserted him and fled.
⁵⁷Then the people who had arrested
Jesus led him to the home of Caiaphas,
the high priest, where the teachers of
religious law and the elders had gathered. ⁵⁸Meanwhile, Peter followed him
at a distance and came to the high
priest's courtyard. He went in and sat
with the guards and waited to see how it
would all end.
⁵⁹Inside, the leading priests and the
entire high council* were trying to find
witnesses who would lie about Jesus, so

they could put him to death. ⁶⁰But even though they found many who agreed to give false witness, they could not use anyone's testimony. Finally, two men came forward ⁶¹who declared, "This man said, 'I am able to destroy the Temple of God and rebuild it in three days.'"

⁶²Then the high priest stood up and said to Jesus, "Well, aren't you going to answer these charges? What do you have to say for yourself?" ⁶³But Jesus remained silent. Then the high priest said to him, "I demand in the name of the living God—tell us if you are the Messiah, the Son of God."

⁶⁴Jesus replied, "You have said it. And in the future you will see the Son of Man seated in the place of power at God's right hand* and coming on the clouds of heaven."*

⁶⁵Then the high priest tore his clothing to show his horror and said, "Blasphemy! Why do we need other witnesses? You have all heard his blasphemy. ⁶⁶What is your verdict?"

"Guilty!" they shouted. "He deserves to die!"

⁶⁷Then they began to spit in Jesus' face and beat him with their fists. And some slapped him, ⁶⁸jeering, "Prophesy to us, you Messiah! Who hit you that time?"

26:53 Greek *twelve legions.*   26:59 Greek *the Sanhedrin.*
26:64a Greek *seated at the right hand of the power.*
See Ps 110:1.   26:64b See Dan 7:13.

## PSALM 32:1-11
*A psalm* of David.

¹ **Oh, what joy for those**
  **whose disobedience is forgiven,**
  **whose sin is put out of sight!**
² **Yes, what joy for those**
  **whose record the LORD has**
    **cleared of guilt,***
  **whose lives are lived in**
    **complete honesty!**
³ When I refused to confess my sin,
  my body wasted away,
  and I groaned all day long.
⁴ Day and night your hand of
    discipline was heavy on me.

My strength evaporated like water
  in the summer heat.                 *Interlude*

⁵ Finally, I confessed all my sins to you
  and stopped trying to hide my
    guilt.
I said to myself, "I will confess my
    rebellion to the LORD."
And you forgave me! All my guilt
    is gone.                          *Interlude*

⁶ Therefore, let all the godly pray to
    you while there is still time,
  that they may not drown in the
    floodwaters of judgment.
⁷ For you are my hiding place;
  you protect me from trouble.
  You surround me with songs
    of victory.                       *Interlude*

⁸ The LORD says, "I will guide you
    along the best pathway
    for your life.
I will advise you and watch
    over you.
⁹ Do not be like a senseless horse
    or mule
  that needs a bit and bridle
    to keep it under control."

¹⁰ Many sorrows come to the wicked,
  but unfailing love surrounds
    those who trust the LORD.
¹¹ So rejoice in the LORD and be glad,
    all you who obey him!
  Shout for joy, all you whose hearts
    are pure!

32:TITLE Hebrew *maskil.* This may be a literary or musical
term.   32:2 Greek version reads *of sin.* Compare Rom 4:7.

## PROVERBS 8:27-32
❚ [Wisdom] was there when he established the heavens, when he drew the horizon on the oceans. I was there when he set the clouds above, when he established springs deep in the earth. I was there when he set the limits of the seas, so they would not spread beyond their boundaries. And when he marked off the earth's foundations, I was the architect at his side. I was his constant delight, rejoicing always in his presence. And how happy I was with the world he

created; how I rejoiced with the human family!  And so, my children,* listen to me, for all who follow my ways are joyful.

8:32 Hebrew *my sons.*

# FEBRUARY 11

EXODUS 32:1–33:23

**W**hen the people saw how long it was taking Moses to come back down the mountain, they gathered around Aaron. "Come on," they said, "make us some gods who can lead us. We don't know what happened to this fellow Moses, who brought us here from the land of Egypt."

²So Aaron said, "Take the gold rings from the ears of your wives and sons and daughters, and bring them to me."

³All the people took the gold rings from their ears and brought them to Aaron. ⁴Then Aaron took the gold, melted it down, and molded it into the shape of a calf. When the people saw it, they exclaimed, "O Israel, these are the gods who brought you out of the land of Egypt!"

⁵Aaron saw how excited the people were, so he built an altar in front of the calf. Then he announced, "Tomorrow will be a festival to the Lᴏʀᴅ!"

⁶The people got up early the next morning to sacrifice burnt offerings and peace offerings. After this, they celebrated with feasting and drinking, and they indulged in pagan revelry.

⁷The Lᴏʀᴅ told Moses, "Quick! Go down the mountain! Your people whom you brought from the land of Egypt have corrupted themselves. ⁸How quickly they have turned away from the way I commanded them to live! They have melted down gold and made a calf, and they have bowed down and sacrificed to

it. They are saying, 'These are your gods, O Israel, who brought you out of the land of Egypt.'"

⁹Then the Lᴏʀᴅ said, "I have seen how stubborn and rebellious these people are. ¹⁰Now leave me alone so my fierce anger can blaze against them, and I will destroy them. Then I will make you, Moses, into a great nation."

¹¹But Moses tried to pacify the Lᴏʀᴅ his God. "O Lᴏʀᴅ!" he said. "Why are you so angry with your own people whom you brought from the land of Egypt with such great power and such a strong hand? ¹²Why let the Egyptians say, 'Their God rescued them with the evil intention of slaughtering them in the mountains and wiping them from the face of the earth'? Turn away from your fierce anger. Change your mind about this terrible disaster you have threatened against your people! ¹³Remember your servants Abraham, Isaac, and Jacob.* You bound yourself with an oath to them, saying, 'I will make your descendants as numerous as the stars of heaven. And I will give them all of this land that I have promised to your descendants, and they will possess it forever.'"

¹⁴So the Lᴏʀᴅ changed his mind about the terrible disaster he had threatened to bring on his people.

¹⁵Then Moses turned and went down the mountain. He held in his hands the two stone tablets inscribed with the terms of the covenant.* They were inscribed on both sides, front and back. ¹⁶These tablets were God's work; the words on them were written by God himself.

¹⁷When Joshua heard the boisterous noise of the people shouting below them, he exclaimed to Moses, "It sounds like war in the camp!"

¹⁸But Moses replied, "No, it's not a shout of victory nor the wailing of defeat. I hear the sound of a celebration."

¹⁹When they came near the camp, Moses saw the calf and the dancing, and he burned with anger. He threw the stone tablets to the ground, smashing them at the foot of the mountain. ²⁰He

took the calf they had made and burned it. Then he ground it into powder, threw it into the water, and forced the people to drink it.

21Finally, he turned to Aaron and demanded, "What did these people do to you to make you bring such terrible sin upon them?"

22"Don't get so upset, my lord," Aaron replied. "You yourself know how evil these people are. 23They said to me, 'Make us gods who will lead us. We don't know what happened to this fellow Moses, who brought us here from the land of Egypt.' 24So I told them, 'Whoever has gold jewelry, take it off.' When they brought it to me, I simply threw it into the fire—and out came this calf!"

25Moses saw that Aaron had let the people get completely out of control, much to the amusement of their enemies.* 26So he stood at the entrance to the camp and shouted, "All of you who are on the LORD's side, come here and join me." And all the Levites gathered around him.

27Moses told them, "This is what the LORD, the God of Israel, says: Each of you, take your swords and go back and forth from one end of the camp to the other. Kill everyone—even your brothers, friends, and neighbors." 28The Levites obeyed Moses' command, and about 3,000 people died that day.

29Then Moses told the Levites, "Today you have ordained yourselves* for the service of the LORD, for you obeyed him even though it meant killing your own sons and brothers. Today you have earned a blessing."

30The next day Moses said to the people, "You have committed a terrible sin, but I will go back up to the LORD on the mountain. Perhaps I will be able to obtain forgiveness* for your sin."

31So Moses returned to the LORD and said, "Oh, what a terrible sin these people have committed. They have made gods of gold for themselves. 32But now, if you will only forgive their sin—but if not, erase my name from the record you have written!"

33But the LORD replied to Moses, "No, I will erase the name of everyone who has sinned against me. 34Now go, lead the people to the place I told you about. Look! My angel will lead the way before you. And when I come to call the people to account, I will certainly hold them responsible for their sins."

35Then the LORD sent a great plague upon the people because they had worshiped the calf Aaron had made.

33:1THE LORD said to Moses, "Get going, you and the people you brought up from the land of Egypt. Go up to the land I swore to give to Abraham, Isaac, and Jacob. I told them, 'I will give this land to your descendants.' 2And I will send an angel before you to drive out the Canaanites, Amorites, Hittites, Perizzites, Hivites, and Jebusites. 3Go up to this land that flows with milk and honey. But I will not travel among you, for you are a stubborn and rebellious people. If I did, I would surely destroy you along the way."

4When the people heard these stern words, they went into mourning and stopped wearing their jewelry and fine clothes. 5For the LORD had told Moses to tell them, "You are a stubborn and rebellious people. If I were to travel with you for even a moment, I would destroy you. Remove your jewelry and fine clothes while I decide what to do with you." 6So from the time they left Mount Sinai,* the Israelites wore no more jewelry or fine clothes.

7It was Moses' practice to take the Tent of Meeting* and set it up some distance from the camp. Everyone who wanted to make a request of the LORD would go to the Tent of Meeting outside the camp.

8Whenever Moses went out to the Tent of Meeting, all the people would get up and stand in the entrances of their own tents. They would all watch Moses until he disappeared inside. 9As he went into the tent, the pillar of cloud would come down and hover at its entrance while the LORD spoke with Moses.

¹⁰When the people saw the cloud standing at the entrance of the tent, they would stand and bow down in front of their own tents. ¹¹Inside the Tent of Meeting, the LORD would speak to Moses face to face, as one speaks to a friend. Afterward Moses would return to the camp, but the young man who assisted him, Joshua son of Nun, would remain behind in the Tent of Meeting.

¹²One day Moses said to the LORD, "You have been telling me, 'Take these people up to the Promised Land.' But you haven't told me whom you will send with me. You have told me, 'I know you by name, and I look favorably on you.' ¹³If it is true that you look favorably on me, let me know your ways so I may understand you more fully and continue to enjoy your favor. And remember that this nation is your very own people."

¹⁴The LORD replied, "I will personally go with you, Moses, and I will give you rest—everything will be fine for you."

¹⁵Then Moses said, "If you don't personally go with us, don't make us leave this place. ¹⁶How will anyone know that you look favorably on me—on me and on your people—if you don't go with us? For your presence among us sets your people and me apart from all other people on the earth."

¹⁷The LORD replied to Moses, "I will indeed do what you have asked, for I look favorably on you, and I know you by name."

¹⁸Moses responded, "Then show me your glorious presence."

¹⁹**The LORD replied, "I will make all my goodness pass before you, and I will call out my name, Yahweh,\* before you. For I will show mercy to anyone I choose, and I will show compassion to anyone I choose.** ²⁰But you may not look directly at my face, for no one may see me and live." ²¹The LORD continued, "Look, stand near me on this rock. ²²As my glorious presence passes by, I will hide you in the crevice of the rock and cover you with my hand until I have passed by. ²³Then I will re-

move my hand and let you see me from behind. But my face will not be seen."

32:13 Hebrew *Israel*. The names "Jacob" and "Israel" are often interchanged throughout the Old Testament, referring sometimes to the individual patriarch and sometimes to the nation. 32:15 Hebrew *the two tablets of the Testimony;* see note on 25:16. 32:25 Or *out of control, and they mocked anyone who opposed them.* The meaning of the Hebrew is unclear. 32:29 As in Greek and Latin versions; Hebrew reads *Today ordain yourselves.* 32:30 Or *to make atonement.* 33:6 Hebrew *Horeb,* another name for Sinai. 33:7 This "Tent of Meeting" is different from the Tabernacle described in chapters 26 and 36. 33:19 *Yahweh* is a transliteration of the proper name YHWH that is sometimes rendered "Jehovah"; in this translation it is usually rendered "the LORD" (note the use of small capitals).

## MATTHEW 26:69–27:14

**M**eanwhile, Peter was sitting outside in the courtyard. A servant girl came over and said to him, "You were one of those with Jesus the Galilean."

⁷⁰But Peter denied it in front of everyone. "I don't know what you're talking about," he said.

⁷¹Later, out by the gate, another servant girl noticed him and said to those standing around, "This man was with Jesus of Nazareth.\*"

⁷²Again Peter denied it, this time with an oath. "I don't even know the man," he said.

⁷³A little later some of the other bystanders came over to Peter and said, "You must be one of them; we can tell by your Galilean accent."

⁷⁴Peter swore, "A curse on me if I'm lying—I don't know the man!" And immediately the rooster crowed.

⁷⁵Suddenly, Jesus' words flashed through Peter's mind: "Before the rooster crows, you will deny three times that you even know me." And he went away, weeping bitterly.

²⁷:¹VERY early in the morning the leading priests and the elders met again to lay plans for putting Jesus to death. ²Then they bound him, led him away, and took him to Pilate, the Roman governor.

³When Judas, who had betrayed him, realized that Jesus had been condemned to die, he was filled with remorse. So he took the thirty pieces of silver back to the leading priests and the elders. ⁴"I

have sinned," he declared, "for I have betrayed an innocent man."

"What do we care?" they retorted. "That's your problem."

5 Then Judas threw the silver coins down in the Temple and went out and hanged himself.

6 The leading priests picked up the coins. "It wouldn't be right to put this money in the Temple treasury," they said, "since it was payment for murder."* 7 After some discussion they finally decided to buy the potter's field, and they made it into a cemetery for foreigners. 8 That is why the field is still called the Field of Blood. 9 This fulfilled the prophecy of Jeremiah that says,

"They took* the thirty pieces
of silver—
the price at which he was valued
by the people of Israel,
10 and purchased the potter's field,
as the LORD directed.*"

11 Now Jesus was standing before Pilate, the Roman governor. "Are you the king of the Jews?" the governor asked him.

Jesus replied, "You have said it."

12 But when the leading priests and the elders made their accusations against him, Jesus remained silent. 13 "Don't you hear all these charges they are bringing against you?" Pilate demanded. 14 But Jesus made no response to any of the charges, much to the governor's surprise.

26:71 Or Jesus the Nazarene.   27:6 Greek since it is the price for blood.   27:9 Or I took.   27:9-10 Greek as the LORD directed me. Zech 11:12-13; Jer 32:6-9.

PSALM 33:1-11
Let the godly sing for joy
to the LORD;
it is fitting for the pure
to praise him.
2 Praise the LORD with melodies
on the lyre;
make music for him on the
ten-stringed harp.
3 Sing a new song of praise to him;

play skillfully on the harp, and
sing with joy.
4 For the word of the LORD holds true,
and we can trust everything
he does.
5 He loves whatever is just and good;
the unfailing love of the LORD
fills the earth.

6 The LORD merely spoke,
and the heavens were created.
He breathed the word,
and all the stars were born.
7 He assigned the sea its boundaries
and locked the oceans in vast
reservoirs.
8 Let the whole world fear the LORD,
and let everyone stand in awe
of him.
9 For when he spoke, the world began!
It appeared at his command.

10 The LORD frustrates the plans
of the nations
and thwarts all their schemes.
11 But the LORD's plans stand firm
forever;
his intentions can never
be shaken.

PROVERBS 8:33-36
Listen to my [Wisdom's] instruction and be wise. Don't ignore it. Joyful are those who listen to me, watching for me daily at my gates, waiting for me outside my home! For whoever finds me finds life and receives favor from the LORD. But those who miss me injure themselves. All who hate me love death.

# FEBRUARY
## 12

EXODUS 34:1–35:9
Then the LORD told Moses, "Chisel out two stone tablets like the first ones. I will write on them the same words that were on the tablets you smashed. 2 Be

ready in the morning to climb up Mount Sinai and present yourself to me on the top of the mountain. ³No one else may come with you. In fact, no one is to appear anywhere on the mountain. Do not even let the flocks or herds graze near the mountain."

⁴So Moses chiseled out two tablets of stone like the first ones. Early in the morning he climbed Mount Sinai as the LORD had commanded him, and he carried the two stone tablets in his hands.

⁵Then the LORD came down in a cloud and stood there with him; and he called out his own name, Yahweh.* ⁶The LORD passed in front of Moses, calling out,

"Yaweh!* The LORD!
   The God of compassion and
      mercy!
I am slow to anger
   and filled with unfailing love
      and faithfulness.
⁷ I lavish unfailing love to a thousand
      generations.*
   I forgive iniquity, rebellion,
      and sin.
But I do not excuse the guilty.
   I lay the sins of the parents upon
      their children and
      grandchildren;
   the entire family is affected—
      even children in the third and
      fourth generations."

⁸Moses immediately threw himself to the ground and worshiped. ⁹And he said, "O Lord, if it is true that I have found favor with you, then please travel with us. Yes, this is a stubborn and rebellious people, but please forgive our iniquity and our sins. Claim us as your own special possession."

¹⁰The LORD replied, "Listen, I am making a covenant with you in the presence of all your people. I will perform miracles that have never been performed anywhere in all the earth or in any nation. And all the people around you will see the power of the LORD—the awesome power I will display for you. ¹¹But listen carefully to everything I command you today. Then I will go ahead of

you and drive out the Amorites, Canaanites, Hittites, Perizzites, Hivites, and Jebusites.

¹²"Be very careful never to make a treaty with the people who live in the land where you are going. If you do, you will follow their evil ways and be trapped. ¹³Instead, you must break down their pagan altars, smash their sacred pillars, and cut down their Asherah poles. ¹⁴You must worship no other gods, for the LORD, whose very name is Jealous, is a God who is jealous about his relationship with you.

¹⁵"You must not make a treaty of any kind with the people living in the land. They lust after their gods, offering sacrifices to them. They will invite you to join them in their sacrificial meals, and you will go with them. ¹⁶Then you will accept their daughters, who sacrifice to other gods, as wives for your sons. And they will seduce your sons to commit adultery against me by worshiping other gods. ¹⁷You must not make any gods of molten metal for yourselves.

¹⁸"You must celebrate the Festival of Unleavened Bread. For seven days the bread you eat must be made without yeast, just as I commanded you. Celebrate this festival annually at the appointed time in early spring, in the month of Abib,* for that is the anniversary of your departure from Egypt.

¹⁹"The firstborn of every animal belongs to me, including the firstborn males from your herds of cattle and your flocks of sheep and goats. ²⁰A firstborn donkey may be bought back from the LORD by presenting a lamb or young goat in its place. But if you do not buy it back, you must break its neck. However, you must buy back every firstborn son.

"No one may appear before me without an offering.

²¹"You have six days each week for your ordinary work, but on the seventh day you must stop working, even during the seasons of plowing and harvest.

²²"You must celebrate the Festival of Harvest* with the first crop of the wheat harvest, and celebrate the Festi-

val of the Final Harvest* at the end of the harvest season. ²³Three times each year every man in Israel must appear before the Sovereign, the LORD, the God of Israel. ²⁴I will drive out the other nations ahead of you and expand your territory, so no one will covet and conquer your land while you appear before the LORD your God three times each year.

²⁵"You must not offer the blood of my sacrificial offerings together with any baked goods containing yeast. And none of the meat of the Passover sacrifice may be kept over until the next morning.

²⁶"As you harvest your crops, bring the very best of the first harvest to the house of the LORD your God.

"You must not cook a young goat in its mother's milk."

²⁷Then the LORD said to Moses, "Write down all these instructions, for they represent the terms of the covenant I am making with you and with Israel."

²⁸Moses remained there on the mountain with the LORD forty days and forty nights. In all that time he ate no bread and drank no water. And the LORD* wrote the terms of the covenant—the Ten Commandments*—on the stone tablets.

²⁹When Moses came down Mount Sinai carrying the two stone tablets inscribed with the terms of the covenant,* he wasn't aware that his face had become radiant because he had spoken to the LORD. ³⁰So when Aaron and the people of Israel saw the radiance of Moses' face, they were afraid to come near him.

³¹But Moses called out to them and asked Aaron and all the leaders of the community to come over, and he talked with them. ³²Then all the people of Israel approached him, and Moses gave them all the instructions the LORD had given him on Mount Sinai. ³³When Moses finished speaking with them, he covered his face with a veil. ³⁴But whenever he went into the Tent of Meeting to speak with the LORD, he would remove the veil until he came out again. Then he would give the people whatever instructions the LORD had given him, ³⁵and the

people of Israel would see the radiant glow of his face. So he would put the veil over his face until he returned to speak with the LORD.

³⁵:¹THEN Moses called together the whole community of Israel and told them, "These are the instructions the LORD has commanded you to follow. ²You have six days each week for your ordinary work, but the seventh day must be a Sabbath day of complete rest, a holy day dedicated to the LORD. Anyone who works on that day must be put to death. ³You must not even light a fire in any of your homes on the Sabbath."

⁴Then Moses said to the whole community of Israel, "This is what the LORD has commanded: ⁵Take a sacred offering for the LORD. Let those with generous hearts present the following gifts to the LORD:

gold, silver, and bronze;
⁶ blue, purple, and scarlet thread;
    fine linen and goat hair for cloth;
⁷ tanned ram skins and fine goatskin
    leather;
    acacia wood;
⁸ olive oil for the lamps;
    spices for the anointing oil and the
    fragrant incense;
⁹ onyx stones, and other gemstones
    to be set in the ephod and the
    priest's chestpiece."

34:5 *Yahweh* is a transliteration of the proper name *YHWH* that is sometimes rendered "Jehovah"; in this translation it is usually rendered "the LORD (note the use of small capitals). 34:6 See note on 34:5. 34:7 Hebrew *for thousands.* 34:18 Hebrew *appointed time in the month of Abib.* This first month of the ancient Hebrew lunar calendar usually occurs within the months of March and April. 34:22a Hebrew *Festival of Weeks;* compare 23:16. This was later called the Festival of Pentecost. It is celebrated today as Shavuat (or Shabuoth). 34:22b Or *Festival of Ingathering.* This was later called the Festival of Shelters or Festival of Tabernacles (see Lev 23:33-36). It is celebrated today as Sukkot (or Succoth). 34:28a Hebrew *he.* 34:28b Hebrew *the ten words.* 34:29 Hebrew *the two tablets of the Testimony;* see note on 25:16.

## MATTHEW 27:15-31

Now it was the governor's custom each year during the Passover celebration to release one prisoner to the crowd—anyone they wanted. ¹⁶This year there was a notorious prisoner, a man named

Barabbas.* [17]As the crowds gathered before Pilate's house that morning, he asked them, "Which one do you want me to release to you—Barabbas, or Jesus who is called the Messiah?" [18](He knew very well that the religious leaders had arrested Jesus out of envy.)

[19]Just then, as Pilate was sitting on the judgment seat, his wife sent him this message: "Leave that innocent man alone. I suffered through a terrible nightmare about him last night."

[20]Meanwhile, the leading priests and the elders persuaded the crowd to ask for Barabbas to be released and for Jesus to be put to death. [21]So the governor asked again, "Which of these two do you want me to release to you?"

The crowd shouted back, "Barabbas!"

[22]Pilate responded, "Then what should I do with Jesus who is called the Messiah?"

They shouted back, "Crucify him!"

[23]"Why?" Pilate demanded. "What crime has he committed?"

But the mob roared even louder, "Crucify him!"

[24]Pilate saw that he wasn't getting anywhere and that a riot was developing. So he sent for a bowl of water and washed his hands before the crowd, saying, "I am innocent of this man's blood. The responsibility is yours!"

[25]And all the people yelled back, "We will take responsibility for his death— we and our children!"*

[26]So Pilate released Barabbas to them. He ordered Jesus flogged with a lead-tipped whip, then turned him over to the Roman soldiers to be crucified.

[27]Some of the governor's soldiers took Jesus into their headquarters* and called out the entire regiment. [28]They stripped him and put a scarlet robe on him. [29]They wove thorn branches into a crown and put it on his head, and they placed a reed stick in his right hand as a scepter. Then they knelt before him in mockery and taunted, "Hail! King of the Jews!" [30]And they spit on him and grabbed the stick and struck him on the head with it. [31]When they were finally tired of mocking him, they took off the robe and put his own clothes on him again. Then they led him away to be crucified.

27:16 Some manuscripts read *Jesus Barabbas;* also in 27:17.   27:25 Greek *"His blood be on us and on our children."*   27:27 Or *into the Praetorium.*

## PSALM 33:12-22

What joy for the nation whose God
is the LORD,
  whose people he has chosen as
  his inheritance.

[13] The LORD looks down from heaven
  and sees the whole human race.
[14] From his throne he observes
  all who live on the earth.
[15] He made their hearts,
  so he understands everything
  they do.
[16] The best-equipped army cannot
  save a king,
  nor is great strength enough to
  save a warrior.
[17] Don't count on your warhorse to
  give you victory—
  for all its strength, it cannot save
  you.

[18] **But the LORD watches over those**
  **who fear him,**
  **those who rely on his unfailing**
  **love.**
[19] **He rescues them from death**
  **and keeps them alive in times**
  **of famine.**

[20] We put our hope in the LORD.
  He is our help and our shield.
[21] In him our hearts rejoice,
  for we trust in his holy name.
[22] Let your unfailing love surround
  us, LORD,
  for our hope is in you alone.

## PROVERBS 9:1-6

Wisdom has built her house; she has carved its seven columns. She has prepared a great banquet, mixed the wines, and set the table. She has sent her servants to invite everyone to come. She calls out from the heights overlooking the city. "Come in with me," she urges the simple. To those who lack good judgment, she says, "Come, eat my food, and drink the wine I have mixed. Leave your simple ways behind, and begin to live; learn to use good judgment."

# FEBRUARY
# 13

EXODUS 35:10–36:38

"**C**ome, all of you who are gifted craftsmen. Construct everything that the LORD has commanded:

11 the Tabernacle and its sacred tent, its covering, clasps, frames, crossbars, posts, and bases;
12 the Ark and its carrying poles; the Ark's cover—the place of atonement; the inner curtain to shield the Ark;
13 the table, its carrying poles, and all its utensils; the Bread of the Presence;
14 for light, the lampstand, its accessories, the lamp cups, and the olive oil for lighting;
15 the incense altar and its carrying poles; the anointing oil and fragrant incense; the curtain for the entrance of the Tabernacle;
16 the altar of burnt offering; the bronze grating of the altar and its carrying poles and utensils; the washbasin with its stand;
17 the curtains for the walls of the courtyard; the posts and their bases; the curtain for the entrance to the courtyard;
18 the tent pegs of the Tabernacle and courtyard and their ropes;
19 the beautifully stitched garments for the priests to wear while ministering in the Holy Place—the

sacred garments for Aaron the priest, and the garments for his sons to wear as they minister as priests."

20So the whole community of Israel left Moses and returned to their tents. 21All whose hearts were stirred and whose spirits were moved came and brought their sacred offerings to the LORD. They brought all the materials needed for the Tabernacle,* for the performance of its rituals, and for the sacred garments. 22Both men and women came, all whose hearts were willing. They brought to the LORD their offerings of gold—brooches, earrings, rings from their fingers, and necklaces. They presented gold objects of every kind as a special offering to the LORD. 23All those who owned the following items willingly brought them: blue, purple, and scarlet thread; fine linen and goat hair for cloth; and tanned ram skins and fine goatskin leather. 24And all who had silver and bronze objects gave them as a sacred offering to the LORD. And those who had acacia wood brought it for use in the project.

25All the women who were skilled in sewing and spinning prepared blue, purple, and scarlet thread, and fine linen cloth. 26All the women who were willing used their skills to spin the goat hair into yarn. 27The leaders brought onyx stones and the special gemstones to be set in the ephod and the priest's chestpiece. 28They also brought spices and olive oil for the light, the anointing oil, and the fragrant incense. 29So the people of Israel—every man and woman who was eager to help in the work the LORD had given them through Moses—brought their gifts and gave them freely to the LORD.

30Then Moses told the people of Israel, "The LORD has specifically chosen Bezalel son of Uri, grandson of Hur, of the tribe of Judah. 31The LORD has filled Bezalel with the Spirit of God, giving him great wisdom, ability, and expertise in all kinds of crafts. 32He is a master craftsman, expert in working with gold, silver, and bronze. ³³He is skilled in engraving and mounting gemstones and in carving wood. He is a master at every craft. ³⁴And the LORD has given both him and Oholiab son of Ahisamach, of the tribe of Dan, the ability to teach their skills to others. ³⁵The LORD has given them special skills as engravers, designers, embroiderers in blue, purple, and scarlet thread on fine linen cloth, and weavers. They excel as craftsmen and as designers.

36:1"THE LORD has gifted Bezalel, Oholiab, and the other skilled craftsmen with wisdom and ability to perform any task involved in building the sanctuary. Let them construct and furnish the Tabernacle, just as the LORD has commanded."

²So Moses summoned Bezalel and Oholiab and all the others who were specially gifted by the LORD and were eager to get to work. ³Moses gave them the materials donated by the people of Israel as sacred offerings for the completion of the sanctuary. But the people continued to bring additional gifts each morning. ⁴Finally the craftsmen who were working on the sanctuary left their work. ⁵They went to Moses and reported, "The people have given more than enough materials to complete the job the LORD has commanded us to do!"

⁶So Moses gave the command, and this message was sent throughout the camp: "Men and women, don't prepare any more gifts for the sanctuary. We have enough!" So the people stopped bringing their sacred offerings. ⁷Their contributions were more than enough to complete the whole project.

⁸The skilled craftsmen made ten curtains of finely woven linen for the Tabernacle. Then Bezalel* decorated the curtains with blue, purple, and scarlet thread and with skillfully embroidered cherubim. ⁹All ten curtains were exactly the same size—42 feet long and 6 feet wide.* ¹⁰Five of these curtains were joined together to make one long curtain, and the other five were joined to make a second long curtain. ¹¹He made fifty

loops of blue yarn and put them along the edge of the last curtain in each set. ¹²The fifty loops along the edge of one curtain matched the fifty loops along the edge of the other curtain. ¹³Then he made fifty gold clasps and fastened the long curtains together with the clasps. In this way, the Tabernacle was made of one continuous piece.

¹⁴He made eleven curtains of goat-hair cloth to serve as a tent covering for the Tabernacle. ¹⁵These eleven curtains were all exactly the same size—45 feet long and 6 feet wide.* ¹⁶Bezalel joined five of these curtains together to make one long curtain, and the other six were joined to make a second long curtain. ¹⁷He made fifty loops for the edge of each large curtain. ¹⁸He also made fifty bronze clasps to fasten the long curtains together. In this way, the tent covering was made of one continuous piece. ¹⁹He completed the tent covering with a layer of tanned ram skins and a layer of fine goatskin leather.

²⁰For the framework of the Tabernacle, Bezalel constructed frames of acacia wood. ²¹Each frame was 15 feet high and 27 inches wide,* ²²with two pegs under each frame. All the frames were identical. ²³He made twenty of these frames to support the curtains on the south side of the Tabernacle. ²⁴He also made forty silver bases—two bases under each frame, with the pegs fitting securely into the bases. ²⁵For the north side of the Tabernacle, he made another twenty frames, ²⁶with their forty silver bases, two bases under each frame. ²⁷He made six frames for the rear—the west side of the Tabernacle—²⁸along with two additional frames to reinforce the rear corners of the Tabernacle. ²⁹These corner frames were matched at the bottom and firmly attached at the top with a single ring, forming a single corner unit. Both of these corner units were made the same way. ³⁰So there were eight frames at the rear of the Tabernacle, set in sixteen silver bases—two bases under each frame.

³¹Then he made crossbars of acacia

wood to link the frames, five crossbars for the north side of the Tabernacle [32]and five for the south side. He also made five crossbars for the rear of the Tabernacle, which faced west. [33]He made the middle crossbar to attach halfway up the frames; it ran all the way from one end of the Tabernacle to the other. [34]He overlaid the frames with gold and made gold rings to hold the crossbars. Then he overlaid the crossbars with gold as well.

[35]For the inside of the Tabernacle, Bezalel made a special curtain of finely woven linen. He decorated it with blue, purple, and scarlet thread and with skillfully embroidered cherubim. [36]For the curtain, he made four posts of acacia wood and four gold hooks. He overlaid the posts with gold and set them in four silver bases.

[37]Then he made another curtain for the entrance to the sacred tent. He made it of finely woven linen and embroidered it with exquisite designs using blue, purple, and scarlet thread. [38]This curtain was hung on gold hooks attached to five posts. The posts with their decorated tops and hooks were overlaid with gold, and the five bases were cast from bronze.

35:21 Hebrew *Tent of Meeting.*    36:8 Hebrew *he;* also in 36:16, 20, 35. See 37:1.    36:9 Hebrew *28 cubits* [12.9 meters] *long and 4 cubits* [1.8 meters] *wide.* 36:15 Hebrew *30 cubits* [13.8 meters] *long and 4 cubits* [1.8 meters] *wide.*    36:21 Hebrew *10 cubits* [4.6 meters] *high and 1.5 cubits* [69 centimeters] *wide.*

## MATTHEW 27:32-66

Along the way, they came across a man named Simon, who was from Cyrene,* and the soldiers forced him to carry Jesus' cross. [33]And they went out to a place called Golgotha (which means "Place of the Skull"). [34]The soldiers gave him wine mixed with bitter gall, but when he had tasted it, he refused to drink it.

[35]After they had nailed him to the cross, the soldiers gambled for his clothes by throwing dice.* [36]Then they sat around and kept guard as he hung there. [37]A sign was fastened to the cross above Jesus' head, announcing the charge against him. It read: "This is Jesus, the King of the Jews." [38]Two revolutionaries* were crucified with him, one on his right and one on his left.

[39]The people passing by shouted abuse, shaking their heads in mockery. [40]"Look at you now!" they yelled at him. "You said you were going to destroy the Temple and rebuild it in three days. Well then, if you are the Son of God, save yourself and come down from the cross!"

[41]The leading priests, the teachers of religious law, and the elders also mocked Jesus. [42]"He saved others," they scoffed, "but he can't save himself! So he is the King of Israel, is he? Let him come down from the cross right now, and we will believe in him! [43]He trusted God, so let God rescue him now if he wants him! For he said, 'I am the Son of God.' " [44]Even the revolutionaries who were crucified with him ridiculed him in the same way.

[45]At noon, darkness fell across the whole land until three o'clock. [46]At about three o'clock, Jesus called out with a loud voice, *"Eli, Eli,\* lema sabachthani?"* which means "My God, my God, why have you abandoned me?"*

[47]Some of the bystanders misunderstood and thought he was calling for the prophet Elijah. [48]One of them ran and filled a sponge with sour wine, holding it up to him on a reed stick so he could drink. [49]But the rest said, "Wait! Let's see whether Elijah comes to save him."*

[50]Then Jesus shouted out again, and he released his spirit. [51]At that moment the curtain in the sanctuary of the Temple was torn in two, from top to bottom. The earth shook, rocks split apart, [52]and tombs opened. The bodies of many godly men and women who had died were raised from the dead. [53]They left the cemetery after Jesus' resurrection, went into the holy city of Jerusalem, and appeared to many people.

**[54]The Roman officer\* and the other soldiers at the crucifixion were terrified by the earthquake and all**

that had happened. They said, "This man truly was the Son of God!"

⁵⁵And many women who had come from Galilee with Jesus to care for him were watching from a distance. ⁵⁶Among them were Mary Magdalene, Mary (the mother of James and Joseph), and the mother of James and John, the sons of Zebedee.

⁵⁷As evening approached, Joseph, a rich man from Arimathea who had become a follower of Jesus, ⁵⁸went to Pilate and asked for Jesus' body. And Pilate issued an order to release it to him. ⁵⁹Joseph took the body and wrapped it in a long sheet of clean linen cloth. ⁶⁰He placed it in his own new tomb, which had been carved out of the rock. Then he rolled a great stone across the entrance and left. ⁶¹Both Mary Magdalene and the other Mary were sitting across from the tomb and watching.

⁶²The next day, on the Sabbath,* the leading priests and Pharisees went to see Pilate. ⁶³They told him, "Sir, we remember what that deceiver once said while he was still alive: 'After three days I will rise from the dead.' ⁶⁴So we request that you seal the tomb until the third day. This will prevent his disciples from coming and stealing his body and then telling everyone he was raised from the dead! If that happens, we'll be worse off than we were at first."

⁶⁵Pilate replied, "Take guards and secure it the best you can." ⁶⁶So they sealed the tomb and posted guards to protect it.

27:32 *Cyrene* was a city in northern Africa.    27:35 Greek *by casting lots.* A few late manuscripts add *This fulfilled the word of the prophet: "They divided my garments among themselves and cast lots for my robe."* See Ps 22:18.
27:38 Or *criminals;* also in 27:44.    27:46a Some manuscripts read *Eloi, Eloi.*    27:46b Ps 22:1.
27:49 Some manuscripts add *And another took a spear and pierced his side, and out flowed water and blood.* Compare John 19:34.    27:54 Greek *The centurion.*
27:62 Or *On the next day, which is after the Preparation.*

PSALM 34:1-10*

*A psalm of David, regarding the time he pretended to be insane in front of Abimelech, who sent him away.*

¹ I will praise the LORD at all times.
   I will constantly speak his praises.

² I will boast only in the LORD;
   let all who are helpless take heart.
³ Come, let us tell of the LORD's greatness;
   let us exalt his name together.

⁴ I prayed to the LORD, and he answered me.
   He freed me from all my fears.
⁵ Those who look to him for help will be radiant with joy;
   no shadow of shame will darken their faces.
⁶ In my desperation I prayed, and the LORD listened;
   he saved me from all my troubles.
⁷ For the angel of the LORD is a guard;
   he surrounds and defends all who fear him.

⁸ Taste and see that the LORD is good.
   Oh, the joys of those who take refuge in him!
⁹ Fear the LORD, you his godly people,
   for those who fear him will have all they need.
¹⁰ Even strong young lions sometimes go hungry,
   but those who trust in the LORD will lack no good thing.

34 This psalm is a Hebrew acrostic poem; each verse begins with a successive letter of the Hebrew alphabet.

PROVERBS 9:7-8

Anyone who rebukes a mocker will get an insult in return. Anyone who corrects the wicked will get hurt. So don't bother correcting mockers; they will only hate you. But correct the wise, and they will love you.

FEBRUARY
14

EXODUS 37:1-38:31

Next Bezalel made the Ark of acacia wood—a sacred chest 45 inches long, 27 inches wide, and 27 inches high.*

²He overlaid it inside and outside with pure gold, and he ran a molding of gold all around it. ³He cast four gold rings and attached them to its four feet, two rings on each side. ⁴Then he made poles from acacia wood and overlaid them with gold. ⁵He inserted the poles into the rings at the sides of the Ark to carry it.

⁶Then he made the Ark's cover—the place of atonement—from pure gold. It was 45 inches long and 27 inches wide.* ⁷He made two cherubim from hammered gold and placed them on the two ends of the atonement cover. ⁸He molded the cherubim on each end of the atonement cover, making it all of one piece of gold. ⁹The cherubim faced each other and looked down on the atonement cover. With their wings spread above it, they protected it.

¹⁰Then Bezalel* made the table of acacia wood, 36 inches long, 18 inches wide, and 27 inches high.* ¹¹He overlaid it with pure gold and ran a gold molding around the edge. ¹²He decorated it with a 3-inch border* all around, and he ran a gold molding along the border. ¹³Then he cast four gold rings for the table and attached them at the four corners next to the four legs. ¹⁴The rings were attached near the border to hold the poles that were used to carry the table. ¹⁵He made these poles from acacia wood and overlaid them with gold. ¹⁶Then he made special containers of pure gold for the table—bowls, pans, jars, and pitchers—to be used in pouring out liquid offerings.

¹⁷Then Bezalel made the lampstand of pure, hammered gold. He made the entire lampstand and its decorations of one piece—the base, center stem, lamp cups, buds, and petals. ¹⁸The lampstand had six branches going out from the center stem, three on each side. ¹⁹Each of the six branches had three lamp cups shaped like almond blossoms, complete with buds and petals. ²⁰The center stem of the lampstand was crafted with four lamp cups shaped like almond blossoms, complete with buds and petals. ²¹There was an almond bud beneath each pair of branches where the six branches extended from the center stem, all made of one piece. ²²The almond buds and branches were all of one piece with the center stem, and they were hammered from pure gold.

²³He also made seven lamps for the lampstand, lamp snuffers, and trays, all of pure gold. ²⁴The entire lampstand, along with its accessories, was made from seventy-five pounds* of pure gold.

²⁵Then Bezalel made the incense altar of acacia wood. It was 18 inches square and 36 inches high,* with horns at the corners carved from the same piece of wood as the altar itself. ²⁶He overlaid the top, sides, and horns of the altar with pure gold, and he ran a gold molding around the entire altar. ²⁷He made two gold rings and attached them on opposite sides of the altar below the gold molding to hold the carrying poles. ²⁸He made the poles of acacia wood and overlaid them with gold.

²⁹Then he made the sacred anointing oil and the fragrant incense, using the techniques of a skilled incense maker.

38:1Next Bezalel* used acacia wood to construct the square altar of burnt offering. It was 7½ feet wide, 7½ feet long, and 4½ feet high.* ²He made horns for each of its four corners so that the horns and altar were all one piece. He overlaid the altar with bronze. ³Then he made all the altar utensils of bronze—the ash buckets, shovels, basins, meat forks, and firepans. ⁴Next he made a bronze grating and installed it halfway down the side of the altar, under the ledge. ⁵He cast four rings and attached them to the corners of the bronze grating to hold the carrying poles. ⁶He made the poles from acacia wood and overlaid them with bronze. ⁷He inserted the poles through the rings on the sides of the altar. The altar was hollow and was made from planks.

⁸Bezalel made the bronze washbasin and its bronze stand from bronze mirrors donated by the women who served at the entrance of the Tabernacle.*

⁹Then Bezalel made the courtyard, which was enclosed with curtains made of finely woven linen. On the south side the curtains were 150 feet long.* ¹⁰They were held up by twenty posts set securely in twenty bronze bases. He hung the curtains with silver hooks and rings. ¹¹He made a similar set of curtains for the north side—150 feet of curtains held up by twenty posts set securely in bronze bases. He hung the curtains with silver hooks and rings. ¹²The curtains on the west end of the courtyard were 75 feet long,* hung with silver hooks and rings and supported by ten posts set into ten bases. ¹³The east end, the front, was also 75 feet long.

¹⁴The courtyard entrance was on the east end, flanked by two curtains. The curtain on the right side was 22½ feet long* and was supported by three posts set into three bases. ¹⁵The curtain on the left side was also 22½ feet long and was supported by three posts set into three bases. ¹⁶All the curtains used in the courtyard were made of finely woven linen. ¹⁷Each post had a bronze base, and all the hooks and rings were silver. The tops of the posts of the courtyard were overlaid with silver, and the rings to hold up the curtains were made of silver.

¹⁸He made the curtain for the entrance to the courtyard of finely woven linen, and he decorated it with beautiful embroidery in blue, purple, and scarlet thread. It was 30 feet long, and its height was 7½ feet,* just like the curtains of the courtyard walls. ¹⁹It was supported by four posts, each set securely in its own bronze base. The tops of the posts were overlaid with silver, and the hooks and rings were also made of silver.

²⁰All the tent pegs used in the Tabernacle and courtyard were made of bronze.

²¹This is an inventory of the materials used in building the Tabernacle of the Covenant.* The Levites compiled the figures, as Moses directed, and Ithamar son of Aaron the priest served as re-

corder. ²²Bezalel son of Uri, grandson of Hur, of the tribe of Judah, made everything just as the LORD had commanded Moses. ²³He was assisted by Oholiab son of Ahisamach, of the tribe of Dan, a craftsman expert at engraving, designing, and embroidering with blue, purple, and scarlet thread on fine linen cloth.

²⁴The people brought special offerings of gold totaling 2,193 pounds,* as measured by the weight of the sanctuary shekel. This gold was used throughout the Tabernacle.

²⁵The whole community of Israel gave 7,545 pounds* of silver, as measured by the weight of the sanctuary shekel. ²⁶This silver came from the tax collected from each man registered in the census. (The tax is one beka, which is half a shekel,* based on the sanctuary shekel.) The tax was collected from 603,550 men who had reached their twentieth birthday. ²⁷The hundred bases for the frames of the sanctuary walls and for the posts supporting the inner curtain required 7,500 pounds of silver, about 75 pounds for each base.* ²⁸The remaining 45 pounds* of silver was used to make the hooks and rings and to overlay the tops of the posts.

²⁹The people also brought as special offerings 5,310 pounds* of bronze, ³⁰which was used for casting the bases for the posts at the entrance to the Tabernacle, and for the bronze altar with its bronze grating and all the altar utensils. ³¹Bronze was also used to make the bases for the posts that supported the curtains around the courtyard, the bases for the curtain at the entrance of the courtyard, and all the tent pegs for the Tabernacle and the courtyard.

37:1 Hebrew 2.5 cubits [115 centimeters] long, 1.5 cubits [69 centimeters] wide, and 1.5 cubits high.   37:6 Hebrew 2.5 cubits [115 centimeters] long and 1.5 cubits [69 centimeters] wide.   37:10a Hebrew he; also in 37:17, 25.   37:10b Hebrew 2 cubits [92 centimeters] long, 1 cubit [46 centimeters] wide, and 1.5 cubits [69 centimeters] high.   37:12 Hebrew a border of a handbreadth [8 centimeters].   37:24 Hebrew 1 talent [34 kilograms].   37:25 Hebrew 1 cubit [46 centimeters] long and 1 cubit wide, a square, and 2 cubits [92 centimeters] high.   38:1a Hebrew he; also in 38:8, 9.   38:1b Hebrew 5 cubits [2.3 meters] wide, 5 cubits long, a square, and 3 cubits [1.4 meters] high.   38:8 Hebrew

*Tent of Meeting;* also in 38:30. **38:9** Hebrew *100 cubits* [46 meters]; also in 38:11. **38:12** Hebrew *50 cubits* [23 meters]; also in 38:13. **38:14** Hebrew *15 cubits* [6.9 meters]; also in 38:15. **38:18** Hebrew *20 cubits* [9.2 meters] *long and 5 cubits* [2.3 meters] *high.* **38:21** Hebrew *the Tabernacle, the Tabernacle of the Testimony.* **38:24** Hebrew *29 talents and 730 shekels* [994 kilograms]. Each shekel weighed about 0.4 ounces. **38:25** Hebrew *100 talents and 1,775 shekels* [3,420 kilograms]. **38:26** Or *0.2 ounces or 6 grams.* **38:27** Hebrew *100 talents* [3,400 kilograms] *of silver, 1 talent* [34 kilograms] *for each base.* **38:28** Hebrew *1,775 shekels* [20.2 kilograms]. **38:29** Hebrew *70 talents and 2,400 shekels* [2,407 kilograms].

## MATTHEW 28:1-20

Early on Sunday morning,* as the new day was dawning, Mary Magdalene and the other Mary went out to visit the tomb.

²Suddenly there was a great earthquake! For an angel of the Lord came down from heaven, rolled aside the stone, and sat on it. ³His face shone like lightning, and his clothing was as white as snow. ⁴The guards shook with fear when they saw him, and they fell into a dead faint.

⁵Then the angel spoke to the women. "Don't be afraid!" he said. "I know you are looking for Jesus, who was crucified. ⁶He isn't here! He is risen from the dead, just as he said would happen. Come, see where his body was lying. ⁷And now, go quickly and tell his disciples that he has risen from the dead, and he is going ahead of you to Galilee. You will see him there. Remember what I have told you."

⁸The women ran quickly from the tomb. They were very frightened but also filled with great joy, and they rushed to give the disciples the angel's message. ⁹And as they went, Jesus met them and greeted them. And they ran to him, grasped his feet, and worshiped him. ¹⁰Then Jesus said to them, "Don't be afraid! Go tell my brothers to leave for Galilee, and they will see me there."

¹¹As the women were on their way, some of the guards went into the city and told the leading priests what had happened. ¹²A meeting with the elders was called, and they decided to give the soldiers a large bribe. ¹³They told the soldiers, "You must say, 'Jesus' disciples came during the night while we were sleeping, and they stole his body.' ¹⁴If the governor hears about it, we'll stand up for you so you won't get in trouble." ¹⁵So the guards accepted the bribe and said what they were told to say. Their story spread widely among the Jews, and they still tell it today.

¹⁶Then the eleven disciples left for Galilee, going to the mountain where Jesus had told them to go. ¹⁷When they saw him, they worshiped him—but some of them doubted!

¹⁸**Jesus came and told his disciples, "I have been given all authority in heaven and on earth. ¹⁹Therefore, go and make disciples of all the nations,* baptizing them in the name of the Father and the Son and the Holy Spirit. ²⁰Teach these new disciples to obey all the commands I have given you. And be sure of this: I am with you always, even to the end of the age."**

**28:1** Greek *After the Sabbath, on the first day of the week.* **28:19** Or *all peoples.*

## PSALM 34:11-22

Come, my children, and listen to me,
    and I will teach you to fear the Lord.
¹² Does anyone want to live a life
    that is long and prosperous?
¹³ Then keep your tongue from
        speaking evil
    and your lips from telling lies!
¹⁴ Turn away from evil and do good.
    Search for peace, and work
        to maintain it.

¹⁵ The eyes of the Lord watch over
        those who do right;
    his ears are open to their cries
        for help.
¹⁶ But the Lord turns his face against
        those who do evil;
    he will erase their memory from
        the earth.
¹⁷ The Lord hears his people when
        they call to him for help.
    He rescues them from all their
        troubles.
¹⁸ The Lord is close to the
        brokenhearted;

he rescues those whose spirits
are crushed.

¹⁹ The righteous person faces many
troubles,
but the LORD comes to the rescue
each time.
²⁰ For the LORD protects the bones
of the righteous;
not one of them is broken!
²¹ Calamity will surely overtake the
wicked,
and those who hate the righteous
will be punished.
²² But the LORD will redeem those
who serve him.
No one who takes refuge in him
will be condemned.

PROVERBS 9:9-10
Instruct the wise, and they will be even
wiser. Teach the righteous, and they will
learn even more. □ Fear of the LORD is
the foundation of wisdom. Knowledge
of the Holy One results in good judgment.

FEBRUARY
15

EXODUS 39:1-40:38
The craftsmen made beautiful sacred
garments of blue, purple, and scarlet
cloth—clothing for Aaron to wear while
ministering in the Holy Place, just as the
LORD had commanded Moses.
²Bezalel* made the ephod of finely
woven linen and embroidered it with
gold and with blue, purple, and scarlet
thread. ³He made gold thread by ham-
mering out thin sheets of gold and cutting it into fine strands. With great skill
and care, he worked it into the fine
linen with the blue, purple, and scarlet
thread.
⁴The ephod consisted of two pieces,
front and back, joined at the shoulders

with two shoulder-pieces. ⁵The decorative sash was made of the same materials:
finely woven linen embroidered with
gold and with blue, purple, and scarlet
thread, just as the LORD had commanded
Moses. ⁶They mounted the two onyx
stones in settings of gold filigree. The
stones were engraved with the names of
the tribes of Israel, just as a seal is engraved. ⁷He fastened these stones on the
shoulder-pieces of the ephod as a reminder that the priest represents the
people of Israel. All this was done just as
the LORD had commanded Moses.
⁸Bezalel made the chestpiece with
great skill and care. He made it to match
the ephod, using finely woven linen embroidered with gold and with blue, purple, and scarlet thread. ⁹He made the
chestpiece of a single piece of cloth
folded to form a pouch nine inches*
square. ¹⁰They mounted four rows of
gemstones* on it. The first row contained a red carnelian, a pale green
peridot, and an emerald. ¹¹The second
row contained a turquoise, a blue lapis
lazuli, and a white moonstone. ¹²The
third row contained an orange jacinth,
an agate, and a purple amethyst. ¹³The
fourth row contained a blue-green
beryl, an onyx, and a green jasper. All
these stones were set in gold filigree.
¹⁴Each stone represented one of the
twelve sons of Israel, and the name of
that tribe was engraved on it like a seal.
¹⁵To attach the chestpiece to the
ephod, they made braided cords of pure
gold thread. ¹⁶They also made two settings of gold filigree and two gold rings
and attached them to the top corners of
the chestpiece. ¹⁷They tied the two gold
cords to the rings on the chestpiece.
¹⁸They tied the other ends of the cords
to the gold settings on the shoulder-
pieces of the ephod. ¹⁹Then they made
two more gold rings and attached them
to the inside edges of the chestpiece
next to the ephod. ²⁰Then they made
two more gold rings and attached them
to the front of the ephod, below the
shoulder-pieces, just above the knot
where the decorative sash was fastened

to the ephod. 21They attached the bottom rings of the chestpiece to the rings on the ephod with blue cords. In this way, the chestpiece was held securely to the ephod above the decorative sash. All this was done just as the Lord had commanded Moses.

22Bezalel made the robe that is worn with the ephod from a single piece of blue woven cloth, 23with an opening for Aaron's head in the middle of it. The opening was reinforced with a woven collar* so it would not tear. 24They made pomegranates of blue, purple, and scarlet yarn, and attached them to the hem of the robe. 25They also made bells of pure gold and placed them between the pomegranates along the hem of the robe, 26with bells and pomegranates alternating all around the hem. This robe was to be worn whenever the priest ministered before the Lord, just as the Lord had commanded Moses.

27They made tunics for Aaron and his sons from fine linen cloth. 28The turban and the special head coverings were made of fine linen, and the undergarments were also made of finely woven linen. 29The sashes were made of finely woven linen and embroidered with blue, purple, and scarlet thread, just as the Lord had commanded Moses.

30Finally, they made the sacred medallion—the badge of holiness—of pure gold. They engraved it like a seal with these words: Holy to the Lord. 31They attached the medallion with a blue cord to Aaron's turban, just as the Lord had commanded Moses.

32And so at last the Tabernacle* was finished. The Israelites had done everything just as the Lord had commanded Moses. 33And they brought the entire Tabernacle to Moses:

the sacred tent with all its furnishings, clasps, frames, crossbars, posts, and bases;
34 the tent coverings of tanned ram skins and fine goatskin leather;
the inner curtain to shield the Ark;

35 the Ark of the Covenant* and its carrying poles;
the Ark's cover—the place of atonement;
36 the table and all its utensils;
the Bread of the Presence;
37 the pure gold lampstand with its symmetrical lamp cups, all its accessories, and the olive oil for lighting;
38 the gold altar;
the anointing oil and fragrant incense;
the curtain for the entrance of the sacred tent;
39 the bronze altar;
the bronze grating and its carrying poles and utensils;
the washbasin with its stand;
40 the curtains for the walls of the courtyard;
the posts and their bases;
the curtain for the entrance to the courtyard;
the ropes and tent pegs;
all the furnishings to be used in worship at the Tabernacle;
41 the beautifully stitched garments for the priests to wear while ministering in the Holy Place— the sacred garments for Aaron the priest, and the garments for his sons to wear as they minister as priests.

42So the people of Israel followed all of the Lord's instructions to Moses. 43Then Moses inspected all their work. When he found it had been done just as the Lord had commanded him, he blessed them.

40:1Then the Lord said to Moses, 2"Set up the Tabernacle* on the first day of the new year.* 3Place the Ark of the Covenant* inside, and install the inner curtain to enclose the Ark within the Most Holy Place. 4Then bring in the table, and arrange the utensils on it. And bring in the lampstand, and set up the lamps.

5"Place the gold incense altar in front of the Ark of the Covenant. Then hang the curtain at the entrance of the Tabernacle. [6]Place the altar of burnt offering in front of the Tabernacle entrance. [7]Set the washbasin between the Tabernacle* and the altar, and fill it with water. [8]Then set up the courtyard around the outside of the tent, and hang the curtain for the courtyard entrance.

[9]"Take the anointing oil and anoint the Tabernacle and all its furnishings to consecrate them and make them holy. [10]Anoint the altar of burnt offering and its utensils to consecrate them. Then the altar will become absolutely holy. [11]Next anoint the washbasin and its stand to consecrate them.

[12]"Present Aaron and his sons at the entrance of the Tabernacle, and wash them with water. [13]Dress Aaron with the sacred garments and anoint him, consecrating him to serve me as a priest. [14]Then present his sons and dress them in their tunics. [15]Anoint them as you did their father, so they may also serve me as priests. With their anointing, Aaron's descendants are set apart for the priesthood forever, from generation to generation."

[16]Moses proceeded to do everything just as the LORD had commanded him. [17]So the Tabernacle was set up on the first day of the first month of the second year. [18]Moses erected the Tabernacle by setting down its bases, inserting the frames, attaching the crossbars, and setting up the posts. [19]Then he spread the coverings over the Tabernacle framework and put on the protective layers, just as the LORD had commanded him.

[20]He took the stone tablets inscribed with the terms of the covenant and placed them* inside the Ark. Then he attached the carrying poles to the Ark, and he set the Ark's cover—the place of atonement—on top of it. [21]Then he brought the Ark of the Covenant into the Tabernacle and hung the inner curtain to shield it from view, just as the LORD had commanded him.

[22]Next Moses placed the table in the Tabernacle, along the north side of the

Holy Place, just outside the inner curtain. [23]And he arranged the Bread of the Presence on the table before the LORD, just as the LORD had commanded him.

[24]He set the lampstand in the Tabernacle across from the table on the south side of the Holy Place. [25]Then he lit the lamps in the LORD's presence, just as the LORD had commanded him. [26]He also placed the gold incense altar in the Tabernacle, in the Holy Place in front of the inner curtain. [27]On it he burned the fragrant incense, just as the LORD had commanded him.

[28]He hung the curtain at the entrance of the Tabernacle, [29]and he placed the altar of burnt offering near the Tabernacle entrance. On it he offered a burnt offering and a grain offering, just as the LORD had commanded him.

[30]Next Moses placed the washbasin between the Tabernacle and the altar. He filled it with water so the priests could wash themselves. [31]Moses and Aaron and Aaron's sons used water from it to wash their hands and feet. [32]Whenever they approached the altar and entered the Tabernacle, they washed themselves, just as the LORD had commanded Moses.

[33]Then he hung the curtains forming the courtyard around the Tabernacle and the altar. And he set up the curtain at the entrance of the courtyard. So at last Moses finished the work.

[34]Then the cloud covered the Tabernacle, and the glory of the LORD filled the Tabernacle. [35]Moses could no longer enter the Tabernacle because the cloud had settled down over it, and the glory of the LORD filled the Tabernacle.

[36]Now whenever the cloud lifted from the Tabernacle, the people of Israel would set out on their journey, following it. [37]But if the cloud did not rise, they remained where they were until it lifted. [38]The cloud of the LORD hovered over the Tabernacle during the day, and at night fire glowed inside the cloud so the whole family of Israel

could see it. This continued throughout all their journeys.

39:2 Hebrew *He;* also in 39:8, 22.　39:9 Hebrew *1 span*
[23 centimeters].　39:10 The identification of some of
these gemstones is uncertain.　39:23 The meaning of the
Hebrew is uncertain.　39:32 Hebrew *the Tabernacle, the
Tent of Meeting;* also in 39:40.　39:35 Or *Ark of the
Testimony.*　40:2a Hebrew *the Tabernacle, the Tent of
Meeting;* also in 40:6, 29.　40:2b Hebrew *the first day
of the first month.* This day of the ancient Hebrew lunar
calendar occurred in March or April.　40:3 Or *Ark of
the Testimony;* also in 40:5, 21.　40:7 Hebrew *Tent of
Meeting;* also in 40:12, 22, 24, 26, 30, 32, 34, 35.
40:20 Hebrew *He placed the Testimony;* see note on 25:16.

## MARK 1:1-28

**T**his is the Good News about Jesus the
Messiah, the Son of God.* It began ²just
as the prophet Isaiah had written:

"Look, I am sending my messenger
　　ahead of you,
　and he will prepare your way.*
³ He is a voice shouting in the
　　wilderness,
　'Prepare the way for the LORD's
　　coming!
　Clear the road for him!'*"

⁴This messenger was John the Baptist.
He was in the wilderness and preached
that people should be baptized to show
that they had turned to God to receive
forgiveness for their sins. ⁵All of Judea,
including all the people of Jerusalem,
went out to see and hear John. And
when they confessed their sins, he
baptized them in the Jordan River. ⁶His
clothes were woven from coarse camel
hair, and he wore a leather belt around
his waist. For food he ate locusts and
wild honey.

⁷John announced: "Someone is coming soon who is greater than I am—so
much greater that I'm not even worthy
to stoop down like a slave and untie the
straps of his sandals. ⁸I baptize you
with* water, but he will baptize you
with the Holy Spirit!"

⁹One day Jesus came from Nazareth
in Galilee, and John baptized him in the
Jordan River. ¹⁰**As Jesus came up out of
the water, he saw the heavens split-
ting apart and the Holy Spirit descending on him* like a dove. ¹¹And a
voice from heaven said, "You are my
dearly loved Son, and you bring me
great joy."**

¹²The Spirit then compelled Jesus to
go into the wilderness, ¹³where he was
tempted by Satan for forty days. He was
out among the wild animals, and angels
took care of him.

¹⁴Later on, after John was arrested,
Jesus went into Galilee, where he
preached God's Good News.* ¹⁵"The
time promised by God has come at last!"
he announced. "The Kingdom of God is
near! Repent of your sins and believe
the Good News!"

¹⁶One day as Jesus was walking along
the shore of the Sea of Galilee, he saw
Simon* and his brother Andrew throwing a net into the water, for they fished
for a living. ¹⁷Jesus called out to them,
"Come, follow me, and I will show you
how to fish for people!" ¹⁸And they left
their nets at once and followed him.

¹⁹A little farther up the shore Jesus
saw Zebedee's sons, James and John, in a
boat repairing their nets. ²⁰He called
them at once, and they also followed
him, leaving their father, Zebedee, in
the boat with the hired men.

²¹Jesus and his companions went to
the town of Capernaum. When the Sabbath day came, he went into the synagogue and began to teach. ²²The people
were amazed at his teaching, for he
taught with real authority—quite unlike
the teachers of religious law.

²³Suddenly, a man in the synagogue
who was possessed by an evil* spirit
began shouting, ²⁴"Why are you interfering with us, Jesus of Nazareth? Have
you come to destroy us? I know
who you are—the Holy One sent from
God!"

²⁵Jesus cut him short. "Be quiet!
Come out of the man," he ordered. ²⁶At
that, the evil spirit screamed, threw the
man into a convulsion, and then came
out of him.

²⁷Amazement gripped the audience,
and they began to discuss what had
happened. "What sort of new teaching
is this?" they asked excitedly. "It has
such authority! Even evil spirits obey his

orders!" ²⁸The news about Jesus spread quickly throughout the entire region of Galilee.

1:1 Some manuscripts do not include *the Son of God*.
1:2 Mal 3:1.    1:3 Isa 40:3 (Greek version).    1:8 Or *in;* also in 1:8b.    1:10 Or *toward him,* or *into him*.
1:14 Some manuscripts read *the Good News of the Kingdom of God*.    1:16 *Simon* is called "Peter" in 3:16 and thereafter.    1:23 Greek *unclean;* also in 1:26, 27.

## PSALM 35:1-16
*A psalm of David.*

¹ O Lord, oppose those who oppose me.
Fight those who fight against me.
² Put on your armor, and take up your shield.
Prepare for battle, and come to my aid.
³ Lift up your spear and javelin against those who pursue me.
Let me hear you say,
"I will give you victory!"
⁴ Bring shame and disgrace on those trying to kill me;
turn them back and humiliate those who want to harm me.
⁵ Blow them away like chaff in the wind—
a wind sent by the angel of the Lord.
⁶ Make their path dark and slippery, with the angel of the Lord pursuing them.
⁷ I did them no wrong, but they laid a trap for me.
I did them no wrong, but they dug a pit to catch me.
⁸ So let sudden ruin come upon them!
Let them be caught in the trap they set for me!
Let them be destroyed in the pit they dug for me.

⁹ Then I will rejoice in the Lord.
I will be glad because he rescues me.
¹⁰ With every bone in my body I will praise him:
"Lord, who can compare with you?
Who else rescues the helpless from the strong?

Who else protects the helpless and poor from those who rob them?"

¹¹ Malicious witnesses testify against me.
They accuse me of crimes I know nothing about.
¹² They repay me evil for good.
I am sick with despair.
¹³ Yet when they were ill, I grieved for them.
I denied myself by fasting for them,
but my prayers returned unanswered.
¹⁴ I was sad, as though they were my friends or family,
as if I were grieving for my own mother.
¹⁵ But they are glad now that I am in trouble;
they gleefully join together against me.
I am attacked by people I don't even know;
they slander me constantly.
¹⁶ They mock me and call me names;
they snarl at me.

## PROVERBS 9:11-12
Wisdom will multiply your days and add years to your life. If you become wise, you will be the one to benefit. If you scorn wisdom, you will be the one to suffer.

# FEBRUARY 16

## LEVITICUS 1:1–3:17
The Lord called to Moses from the Tabernacle* and said to him, ²"Give the following instructions to the people of Israel. When you present an animal as an offering to the Lord, you may take it from your herd of cattle or your flock of sheep and goats.

³"If the animal you present as a burnt offering is from the herd, it must be a male with no defects. Bring it to the entrance of the Tabernacle so you* may be accepted by the LORD. ⁴Lay your hand on the animal's head, and the LORD will accept its death in your place to purify you, making you right with him.* ⁵Then slaughter the young bull in the LORD's presence, and Aaron's sons, the priests, will present the animal's blood by splattering it against all sides of the altar that stands at the entrance to the Tabernacle. ⁶Then skin the animal and cut it into pieces. ⁷The sons of Aaron the priest will build a wood fire on the altar. ⁸They will arrange the pieces of the offering, including the head and fat, on the wood burning on the altar. ⁹But the internal organs and the legs must first be washed with water. Then the priest will burn the entire sacrifice on the altar as a burnt offering. It is a special gift, a pleasing aroma to the LORD.

¹⁰"If the animal you present as a burnt offering is from the flock, it may be either a sheep or a goat, but it must be a male with no defects. ¹¹Slaughter the animal on the north side of the altar in the LORD's presence, and Aaron's sons, the priests, will splatter its blood against all sides of the altar. ¹²Then cut the animal in pieces, and the priests will arrange the pieces of the offering, including the head and fat, on the wood burning on the altar. ¹³But the internal organs and the legs must first be washed with water. Then the priest will burn the entire sacrifice on the altar as a burnt offering. It is a special gift, a pleasing aroma to the LORD.

¹⁴"If you present a bird as a burnt offering to the LORD, choose either a turtledove or a young pigeon. ¹⁵The priest will take the bird to the altar, wring off its head, and burn it on the altar. But first he must drain its blood against the side of the altar. ¹⁶The priest must also remove the crop and the feathers* and throw them in the ashes on the east side of the altar. ¹⁷Then, grasping the bird by its wings, the priest will tear the bird

open, but without tearing it apart. Then he will burn it as a burnt offering on the wood burning on the altar. It is a special gift, a pleasing aroma to the LORD.

2:1"WHEN you present grain as an offering to the LORD, the offering must consist of choice flour. You are to pour olive oil on it, sprinkle it with frankincense, ²and bring it to Aaron's sons, the priests. The priest will scoop out a handful of the flour moistened with oil, together with all the frankincense, and burn this representative portion on the altar. It is a special gift, a pleasing aroma to the LORD. ³The rest of the grain offering will then be given to Aaron and his sons. This offering will be considered a most holy part of the special gifts presented to the LORD.

⁴"If your offering is a grain offering baked in an oven, it must be made of choice flour, but without any yeast. It may be presented in the form of thin cakes mixed with olive oil or wafers spread with olive oil. ⁵If your grain offering is cooked on a griddle, it must be made of choice flour mixed with olive oil but without any yeast. ⁶Break it in pieces and pour olive oil on it; it is a grain offering. ⁷If your grain offering is prepared in a pan, it must be made of choice flour and olive oil.

⁸"No matter how a grain offering for the LORD has been prepared, bring it to the priest, who will present it at the altar. ⁹The priest will take a representative portion of the grain offering and burn it on the altar. It is a special gift, a pleasing aroma to the LORD. ¹⁰The rest of the grain offering will then be given to Aaron and his sons as their food. This offering will be considered a most holy part of the special gifts presented to the LORD.

¹¹"Do not use yeast in preparing any of the grain offerings you present to the LORD, because no yeast or honey may be burned as a special gift presented to the LORD. ¹²You may add yeast and honey to an offering of the first crops of your harvest, but these must never be offered

on the altar as a pleasing aroma to the LORD. [13]Season all your grain offerings with salt to remind you of God's eternal covenant. Never forget to add salt to your grain offerings.

[14]"If you present a grain offering to the LORD from the first portion of your harvest, bring fresh grain that is coarsely ground and roasted on a fire. [15]Put olive oil on this grain offering, and sprinkle it with frankincense. [16]The priest will take a representative portion of the grain moistened with oil, together with all the frankincense, and burn it as a special gift presented to the LORD.

[3:1]"IF you present an animal from the herd as a peace offering to the LORD, it may be a male or a female, but it must have no defects. [2]Lay your hand on the animal's head, and slaughter it at the entrance of the Tabernacle.* Then Aaron's sons, the priests, will splatter its blood against all sides of the altar. [3]The priest must present part of this peace offering as a special gift to the LORD. This includes all the fat around the internal organs, [4]the two kidneys and the fat around them near the loins, and the long lobe of the liver. These must be removed with the kidneys, [5]and Aaron's sons will burn them on top of the burnt offering on the wood burning on the altar. It is a special gift, a pleasing aroma to the LORD.

[6]"If you present an animal from the flock as a peace offering to the LORD, it may be a male or a female, but it must have no defects. [7]If you present a sheep as your offering, bring it to the LORD, [8]lay your hand on its head, and slaughter it in front of the Tabernacle. Aaron's sons will then splatter the sheep's blood against all sides of the altar. [9]The priest must present the fat of this peace offering as a special gift to the LORD. This includes the fat of the broad tail cut off near the backbone, all the fat around the internal organs, [10]the two kidneys and the fat around them near the loins, and the long lobe of the liver. These must be removed with the kidneys,

[11]and the priest will burn them on the altar. It is a special gift of food presented to the LORD.

[12]"If you present a goat as your offering, bring it to the LORD, [13]lay your hand on its head, and slaughter it in front of the Tabernacle. Aaron's sons will then splatter the goat's blood against all sides of the altar. [14]The priest must present part of this offering as a special gift to the LORD. This includes all the fat around the internal organs, [15]the two kidneys and the fat around them near the loins, and the long lobe of the liver. These must be removed with the kidneys, [16]and the priest will burn them on the altar. It is a special gift of food, a pleasing aroma to the LORD. All the fat belongs to the LORD.

[17]"You must never eat any fat or blood. This is a permanent law for you, and it must be observed from generation to generation, wherever you live."

1:1 Hebrew *Tent of Meeting;* also in 1:3, 5.   1:3 Or *it.*
1:4 Or *to make atonement for you.*   1:16 Or *the crop and its contents.* The meaning of the Hebrew is uncertain.
3:2 Hebrew *Tent of Meeting;* also in 3:8, 13.

## MARK 1:29–2:12

After Jesus left the synagogue with James and John, they went to Simon and Andrew's home. [30]Now Simon's mother-in-law was sick in bed with a high fever. They told Jesus about her right away. [31]So he went to her bedside, took her by the hand, and helped her sit up. Then the fever left her, and she prepared a meal for them.

[32]That evening after sunset, many sick and demon-possessed people were brought to Jesus. [33]The whole town gathered at the door to watch. [34]So Jesus healed many people who were sick with various diseases, and he cast out many demons. But because the demons knew who he was, he did not allow them to speak.

[35]Before daybreak the next morning, Jesus got up and went out to an isolated place to pray. [36]Later Simon and the others went out to find him. [37]When they found him, they said, "Everyone is looking for you."

[38]But Jesus replied, "We must go on to other towns as well, and I will preach to them, too. That is why I came." [39]So he traveled throughout the region of Galilee, preaching in the synagogues and casting out demons.

[40]**A man with leprosy came and knelt in front of Jesus, begging to be healed. "If you are willing, you can heal me and make me clean," he said.** [41]**Moved with compassion,\* Jesus reached out and touched him. "I am willing," he said. "Be healed!"** [42]**Instantly the leprosy disappeared, and the man was healed.** [43]Then Jesus sent him on his way with a stern warning: [44]"Don't tell anyone about this. Instead, go to the priest and let him examine you. Take along the offering required in the law of Moses for those who have been healed of leprosy.\* This will be a public testimony that you have been cleansed."

[45]But the man went and spread the word, proclaiming to everyone what had happened. As a result, large crowds soon surrounded Jesus, and he couldn't publicly enter a town anywhere. He had to stay out in the secluded places, but people from everywhere kept coming to him.

[2:1]WHEN Jesus returned to Capernaum several days later, the news spread quickly that he was back home. [2]Soon the house where he was staying was so packed with visitors that there was no more room, even outside the door. While he was preaching God's word to them, [3]four men arrived carrying a paralyzed man on a mat. [4]They couldn't bring him to Jesus because of the crowd, so they dug a hole through the roof above his head. Then they lowered the man on his mat, right down in front of Jesus. [5]Seeing their faith, Jesus said to the paralyzed man, "My child, your sins are forgiven."

[6]But some of the teachers of religious law who were sitting there thought to themselves, [7]"What is he saying? This is blasphemy! Only God can forgive sins!"

[8]Jesus knew immediately what they were thinking, so he asked them, "Why do you question this in your hearts? [9]Is it easier to say to the paralyzed man 'Your sins are forgiven,' or 'Stand up, pick up your mat, and walk'? [10]So I will prove to you that the Son of Man\* has the authority on earth to forgive sins." Then Jesus turned to the paralyzed man and said, [11]"Stand up, pick up your mat, and go home!"

[12]And the man jumped up, grabbed his mat, and walked out through the stunned onlookers. They were all amazed and praised God, exclaiming, "We've never seen anything like this before!"

1:41 Some manuscripts read *Moved with anger.*    1:44 See Lev 14:2-32.    2:10 "Son of Man" is a title Jesus used for himself.

## PSALM 35:17-28

How long, O Lord, will you look on
    and do nothing?
    Rescue me from their fierce
        attacks.
    Protect my life from these lions!
[18] Then I will thank you in front of the
        great assembly.
    I will praise you before all the
        people.
[19] Don't let my treacherous enemies
        rejoice over my defeat.
    Don't let those who hate me
        without cause gloat over
        my sorrow.
[20] They don't talk of peace;
        they plot against innocent people
        who mind their own business.
[21] They shout, "Aha! Aha!
    With our own eyes we saw him
        do it!"

[22] O LORD, you know all about this.
    Do not stay silent.
    Do not abandon me now, O Lord.
[23] Wake up! Rise to my defense!
    Take up my case, my God and
        my Lord.
[24] Declare me not guilty, O LORD my
        God, for you give justice.
    Don't let my enemies laugh
        about me in my troubles.

²⁵ Don't let them say, "Look, we got
   what we wanted!
   Now we will eat him alive!"

²⁶ May those who rejoice at my
   troubles
   be humiliated and disgraced.
   May those who triumph over me
   be covered with shame and
   dishonor.
²⁷ But give great joy to those who came
   to my defense.
   Let them continually say, "Great
   is the LORD,
   who delights in blessing his
   servant with peace!"
²⁸ Then I will proclaim your justice,
   and I will praise you all day long.

PROVERBS 9:13-18

The woman named Folly is brash. She is
ignorant and doesn't know it. She sits in
her doorway on the heights overlooking
the city. She calls out to men going by
who are minding their own business.
"Come in with me," she urges the simple. To those who lack good judgment,
she says, "Stolen water is refreshing;
food eaten in secret tastes the best!" But
little do they know that the dead are
there. Her guests are in the depths of
the grave.*

9:18 Hebrew *in Sheol*.

# FEBRUARY 17

LEVITICUS 4:1–5:19

Then the LORD said to Moses, ²"Give the
following instructions to the people of
Israel. This is how you are to deal with
those who sin unintentionally by doing
anything that violates one of the LORD's
commands.

³"If the high priest* sins, bringing
guilt upon the entire community, he
must give a sin offering for the sin he

has committed. He must present to the
LORD a young bull with no defects. ⁴He
must bring the bull to the LORD at the
entrance of the Tabernacle,* lay his
hand on the bull's head, and slaughter it
before the LORD. ⁵The high priest will
then take some of the bull's blood into
the Tabernacle, ⁶dip his finger in the
blood, and sprinkle it seven times before the LORD in front of the inner curtain of the sanctuary. ⁷The priest will
then put some of the blood on the horns
of the altar for fragrant incense that
stands in the LORD's presence inside the
Tabernacle. He will pour out the rest of
the bull's blood at the base of the altar
for burnt offerings at the entrance of
the Tabernacle. ⁸Then the priest must
remove all the fat of the bull to be offered as a sin offering. This includes all
the fat around the internal organs, ⁹the
two kidneys and the fat around them
near the loins, and the long lobe of the
liver. He must remove these along with
the kidneys, ¹⁰just as he does with cattle
offered as a peace offering, and burn
them on the altar of burnt offerings.
¹¹But he must take whatever is left of the
bull—its hide, meat, head, legs, internal
organs, and dung—¹²and carry it away
to a place outside the camp that is ceremonially clean, the place where the
ashes are dumped. There, on the ash
heap, he will burn it on a wood fire.

¹³"If the entire Israelite community
sins by violating one of the LORD's commands, but the people don't realize it,
they are still guilty. ¹⁴When they become aware of their sin, the people
must bring a young bull as an offering
for their sin and present it before the
Tabernacle. ¹⁵The elders of the community must then lay their hands on the
bull's head and slaughter it before the
LORD. ¹⁶The high priest will then take
some of the bull's blood into the Tabernacle, ¹⁷dip his finger in the blood, and
sprinkle it seven times before the LORD
in front of the inner curtain. ¹⁸He will
then put some of the blood on the horns
of the altar for fragrant incense that
stands in the LORD's presence inside the

Tabernacle. He will pour out the rest of the blood at the base of the altar for burnt offerings at the entrance of the Tabernacle. [19]Then the priest must remove all the animal's fat and burn it on the altar, [20]just as he does with the bull offered as a sin offering for the high priest. Through this process, the priest will purify the people, making them right with the LORD,* and they will be forgiven. [21]Then the priest must take what is left of the bull and carry it outside the camp and burn it there, just as is done with the sin offering for the high priest. This offering is for the sin of the entire congregation of Israel.

[22]"If one of Israel's leaders sins by violating one of the commands of the LORD his God but doesn't realize it, he is still guilty. [23]When he becomes aware of his sin, he must bring as his offering a male goat with no defects. [24]He must lay his hand on the goat's head and slaughter it at the place where burnt offerings are slaughtered before the LORD. This is an offering for his sin. [25]Then the priest will dip his finger in the blood of the sin offering and put it on the horns of the altar for burnt offerings. He will pour out the rest of the blood at the base of the altar. [26]Then he must burn all the goat's fat on the altar, just as he does with the peace offering. Through this process, the priest will purify the leader from his sin, making him right with the LORD, and he will be forgiven.

[27]"If any of the common people sin by violating one of the LORD's commands, but they don't realize it, they are still guilty. [28]When they become aware of their sin, they must bring as an offering for their sin a female goat with no defects. [29]They must lay a hand on the head of the sin offering and slaughter it at the place where burnt offerings are slaughtered. [30]Then the priest will dip his finger in the blood and put it on the horns of the altar for burnt offerings. He will pour out the rest of the blood at the base of the altar. [31]Then he must remove all the goat's fat, just as he does with the

fat of the peace offering. He will burn the fat on the altar, and it will be a pleasing aroma to the LORD. Through this process, the priest will purify the people, making them right with the LORD, and they will be forgiven.

[32]"If the people bring a sheep as their sin offering, it must be a female with no defects. [33]They must lay a hand on the head of the sin offering and slaughter it at the place where burnt offerings are slaughtered. [34]Then the priest will dip his finger in the blood of the sin offering and put it on the horns of the altar for burnt offerings. He will pour out the rest of the blood at the base of the altar. [35]Then he must remove all the sheep's fat, just as he does with the fat of a sheep presented as a peace offering. He will burn the fat on the altar on top of the special gifts presented to the LORD. Through this process, the priest will purify the people from their sin, making them right with the LORD, and they will be forgiven.

[5:1]"IF you are called to testify about something you have seen or that you know about, it is sinful to refuse to testify, and you will be punished for your sin.

[2]"Or suppose you unknowingly touch something that is ceremonially unclean, such as the carcass of an unclean animal. When you realize what you have done, you must admit your defilement and your guilt. This is true whether it is a wild animal, a domestic animal, or an animal that scurries along the ground.

[3]"Or suppose you unknowingly touch something that makes a person unclean. When you realize what you have done, you must admit your guilt.

[4]"Or suppose you make a foolish vow of any kind, whether its purpose is for good or for bad. When you realize its foolishness, you must admit your guilt.

[5]"When you become aware of your guilt in any of these ways, you must confess your sin. [6]Then you must bring to the LORD as the penalty for your sin a female from the flock, either a sheep or a

goat. This is a sin offering with which the priest will purify you from your sin, making you right with the LORD.*

7"But if you cannot afford to bring a sheep, you may bring to the LORD two turtledoves or two young pigeons as the penalty for your sin. One of the birds will be for a sin offering, and the other for a burnt offering. 8You must bring them to the priest, who will present the first bird as the sin offering. He will wring its neck but without severing its head from the body. 9Then he will sprinkle some of the blood of the sin offering against the sides of the altar, and the rest of the blood will be drained out at the base of the altar. This is an offering for sin. 10The priest will then prepare the second bird as a burnt offering, following all the procedures that have been prescribed. Through this process the priest will purify you from your sin, making you right with the LORD, and you will be forgiven.

11"If you cannot afford to bring two turtledoves or two young pigeons, you may bring two quarts* of choice flour for your sin offering. Since it is an offering for sin, you must not moisten it with olive oil or put any frankincense on it. 12Take the flour to the priest, who will scoop out a handful as a representative portion. He will burn it on the altar on top of the special gifts presented to the LORD. It is an offering for sin. 13Through this process, the priest will purify those who are guilty of any of these sins, making them right with the LORD, and they will be forgiven. The rest of the flour will belong to the priest, just as with the grain offering."

14Then the LORD said to Moses, 15"If one of you commits a sin by unintentionally defiling the LORD's sacred property, you must bring a guilt offering to the LORD. The offering must be your own ram with no defects, or you may buy one of equal value with silver, as measured by the weight of the sanctuary shekel.* 16You must make restitution for the sacred property you have harmed by paying for the loss, plus an additional

20 percent. When you give the payment to the priest, he will purify you with the ram sacrificed as a guilt offering, making you right with the LORD, and you will be forgiven.

17"Suppose you sin by violating one of the LORD's commands. Even if you are unaware of what you have done, you are guilty and will be punished for your sin. 18For a guilt offering, you must bring to the priest your own ram with no defects, or you may buy one of equal value. Through this process the priest will purify you from your unintentional sin, making you right with the LORD, and you will be forgiven. 19This is a guilt offering, for you have been guilty of an offense against the LORD."

4:3 Hebrew *the anointed priest;* also in 4:5, 16.
4:4 Hebrew *Tent of Meeting;* also in 4:5, 7, 14, 16, 18.
4:20 Or *will make atonement for the people;* similarly in 4:26, 31, 35.   5:6 Or *will make atonement for you;* similarly in 5:10, 13, 16, 18.   5:11 Hebrew ⅒ *of an ephah* [2.2 liters].   5:15 Each shekel was about 0.4 ounces or 11 grams in weight.

## MARK 2:13–3:6

**T**hen Jesus went out to the lakeshore again and taught the crowds that were coming to him. 14As he walked along, he saw Levi son of Alphaeus sitting at his tax collector's booth. "Follow me and be my disciple," Jesus said to him. So Levi got up and followed him.

15Later, Levi invited Jesus and his disciples to his home as dinner guests, along with many tax collectors and other disreputable sinners. (There were many people of this kind among Jesus' followers.) 16But when the teachers of religious law who were Pharisees* saw him eating with tax collectors and other sinners, they asked his disciples, "Why does he eat with such scum?*"

17When Jesus heard this, he told them, "Healthy people don't need a doctor—sick people do. I have come to call not those who think they are righteous, but those who know they are sinners."

18Once when John's disciples and the Pharisees were fasting, some people came to Jesus and asked, "Why don't your disciples fast like John's disciples and the Pharisees do?"

[19]Jesus replied, "Do wedding guests fast while celebrating with the groom? Of course not. They can't fast while the groom is with them. [20]But someday the groom will be taken away from them, and then they will fast.

[21]"Besides, who would patch old clothing with new cloth? For the new patch would shrink and rip away from the old cloth, leaving an even bigger tear than before.

[22]"And no one puts new wine into old wineskins. For the wine would burst the wineskins, and the wine and the skins would both be lost. New wine calls for new wineskins."

[23]One Sabbath day as Jesus was walking through some grainfields, his disciples began breaking off heads of grain to eat. [24]But the Pharisees said to Jesus, "Look, why are they breaking the law by harvesting grain on the Sabbath?"

[25]Jesus said to them, "Haven't you ever read in the Scriptures what David did when he and his companions were hungry? [26]He went into the house of God (during the days when Abiathar was high priest) and broke the law by eating the sacred loaves of bread that only the priests are allowed to eat. He also gave some to his companions."

[27]Then Jesus said to them, "The Sabbath was made to meet the needs of people, and not people to meet the requirements of the Sabbath. [28]So the Son of Man is Lord, even over the Sabbath!"

[3:1]Jesus went into the synagogue again and noticed a man with a deformed hand. [2]Since it was the Sabbath, Jesus' enemies watched him closely. If he healed the man's hand, they planned to accuse him of working on the Sabbath.

[3]Jesus said to the man, "Come and stand in front of everyone." [4]Then he turned to his critics and asked, "Does the law permit good deeds on the Sabbath, or is it a day for doing evil? Is this a day to save life or to destroy it?" But they wouldn't answer him.

[5]He looked around at them angrily and was deeply saddened by their hard hearts. Then he said to the man, "Hold out your hand." So the man held out his hand, and it was restored! [6]At once the Pharisees went away and met with the supporters of Herod to plot how to kill Jesus.

2:16a Greek *the scribes of the Pharisees.*    2:16b Greek *with tax collectors and sinners?*

## PSALM 36:1-12

*For the choir director: A psalm of David, the servant of the LORD.*

[1] **S**in whispers to the wicked, deep
      within their hearts.
   They have no fear of God at all.
[2] In their blind conceit,
      they cannot see how wicked they
      really are.
[3] Everything they say is crooked and
      deceitful.
   They refuse to act wisely or
      do good.
[4] They lie awake at night, hatching
      sinful plots.
   Their actions are never good.
   They make no attempt to turn
      from evil.

[5] **Your unfailing love, O LORD, is as
      vast as the heavens;
   your faithfulness reaches
      beyond the clouds.**
[6] **Your righteousness is like the
      mighty mountains,
   your justice like the ocean
      depths.
   You care for people and animals
      alike, O LORD.**
[7]  How precious is your unfailing
      love, O God!
   All humanity finds shelter
      in the shadow of your wings.
[8] You feed them from the abundance
      of your own house,
   letting them drink from your river
      of delights.
[9] For you are the fountain of life,
   the light by which we see.

[10] Pour out your unfailing love on
      those who love you;
   give justice to those with honest
      hearts.

¹¹ Don't let the proud trample me
  or the wicked push me around.
¹² Look! Those who do evil have fallen!
  They are thrown down, never to
  rise again.

PROVERBS 10:1-2
The proverbs of Solomon: A wise child*
brings joy to a father; a foolish child
brings grief to a mother. □ Tainted
wealth has no lasting value, but right living can save your life.

10:1 Hebrew *son;* also in 10:1b.

# FEBRUARY
# 18

LEVITICUS 6:1-7:27
¹*Then the LORD said to Moses, ²"Suppose one of you sins against your asso-
ciate and is unfaithful to the LORD.
Suppose you cheat in a deal involving a
security deposit, or you steal or commit fraud, ³or you find lost property
and lie about it, or you lie while swearing to tell the truth, or you commit any
other such sin. ⁴If you have sinned in
any of these ways, you are guilty. You
must give back whatever you stole, or
the money you took by extortion, or the
security deposit, or the lost property
you found, ⁵or anything obtained by
swearing falsely. You must make restitution by paying the full price plus an
additional 20 percent to the person
you have harmed. On the same day you
must present a guilt offering. ⁶As a
guilt offering to the LORD, you must
bring to the priest your own ram with
no defects, or you may buy one of equal
value. ⁷Through this process, the
priest will purify you before the LORD,
making you right with him,* and you
will be forgiven for any of these sins
you have committed."

⁸*Then the LORD said to Moses,
⁹"Give Aaron and his sons the following
instructions regarding the burnt offering. The burnt offering must be left on
top of the altar until the next morning,
and the fire on the altar must be kept
burning all night. ¹⁰In the morning,
after the priest on duty has put on his official linen clothing and linen undergarments, he must clean out the ashes
of the burnt offering and put them beside the altar. ¹¹Then he must take off
these garments, change back into his
regular clothes, and carry the ashes outside the camp to a place that is ceremonially clean. ¹²Meanwhile, the fire on
the altar must be kept burning; it must
never go out. Each morning the priest
will add fresh wood to the fire and arrange the burnt offering on it. He will
then burn the fat of the peace offerings
on it. ¹³Remember, the fire must be
kept burning on the altar at all times. It
must never go out.

¹⁴"These are the instructions regarding the grain offering. Aaron's sons must
present this offering to the LORD in front
of the altar. ¹⁵The priest on duty will take
from the grain offering a handful of the
choice flour moistened with olive oil, together with all the frankincense. He will
burn this representative portion on the
altar as a pleasing aroma to the LORD.
¹⁶Aaron and his sons may eat the rest of
the flour, but it must be baked without
yeast and eaten in a sacred place within
the courtyard of the Tabernacle.* ¹⁷Re-
member, it must never be prepared with
yeast. I have given it to the priests as their
share of the special gifts presented to
me. Like the sin offering and the guilt offering, it is most holy. ¹⁸Any of Aaron's
male descendants may eat from the special gifts presented to the LORD. This is
their permanent right from generation
to generation. Anyone or anything that
touches these offerings will become
holy."

¹⁹Then the LORD said to Moses, ²⁰"On
the day Aaron and his sons are anointed,
they must present to the LORD a grain
offering of two quarts* of choice flour,
half to be offered in the morning and
half to be offered in the evening. ²¹It

must be carefully mixed with olive oil and cooked on a griddle. Then slice* this grain offering and present it as a pleasing aroma to the LORD. 22In each generation, the high priest* who succeeds Aaron must prepare this same offering. It belongs to the LORD and must be burned up completely. This is a permanent law. 23All such grain offerings of a priest must be burned up entirely. None of it may be eaten."

24Then the LORD said to Moses, 25"Give Aaron and his sons the following instructions regarding the sin offering. The animal given as an offering for sin is a most holy offering, and it must be slaughtered in the LORD's presence at the place where the burnt offerings are slaughtered. 26The priest who offers the sacrifice as a sin offering must eat his portion in a sacred place within the courtyard of the Tabernacle. 27Anyone or anything that touches the sacrificial meat will become holy. If any of the sacrificial blood spatters on a person's clothing, the soiled garment must be washed in a sacred place. 28If a clay pot is used to boil the sacrificial meat, it must then be broken. If a bronze pot is used, it must be scoured and thoroughly rinsed with water. 29Only males from a priest's family may eat from this offering, for it is most holy. 30But the offering for sin may not be eaten if its blood was brought into the Tabernacle as an offering for purification* in the Holy Place. It must be completely burned with fire.

7:1"THESE are the instructions for the guilt offering. It is most holy. 2The animal sacrificed as a guilt offering must be slaughtered at the place where the burnt offerings are slaughtered, and its blood must be splattered against all sides of the altar. 3The priest will then offer all its fat on the altar, including the fat of the broad tail, the fat around the internal organs, 4the two kidneys and the fat around them near the loins, and the long lobe of the liver. These are to be removed with the kidneys, 5and the priests will burn them on the altar as a special gift presented to the LORD. This is the guilt offering. 6All males from a priest's family may eat the meat. It must be eaten in a sacred place, for it is most holy.

7"The same instructions apply to both the guilt offering and the sin offering. Both belong to the priest who uses them to purify someone, making that person right with the LORD.* 8In the case of the burnt offering, the priest may keep the hide of the sacrificed animal. 9Any grain offering that has been baked in an oven, prepared in a pan, or cooked on a griddle belongs to the priest who presents it. 10All other grain offerings, whether made of dry flour or flour moistened with olive oil, are to be shared equally among all the priests, the descendants of Aaron.

11"These are the instructions regarding the different kinds of peace offerings that may be presented to the LORD. 12If you present your peace offering as an expression of thanksgiving, the usual animal sacrifice must be accompanied by various kinds of bread made without yeast—thin cakes mixed with olive oil, wafers spread with oil, and cakes made of choice flour mixed with olive oil. 13This peace offering of thanksgiving must also be accompanied by loaves of bread made with yeast. 14One of each kind of bread must be presented as a gift to the LORD. It will then belong to the priest who splatters the blood of the peace offering against the altar. 15The meat of the peace offering of thanksgiving must be eaten on the same day it is offered. None of it may be saved for the next morning.

16"If you bring an offering to fulfill a vow or as a voluntary offering, the meat must be eaten on the same day the sacrifice is offered, but whatever is left over may be eaten on the second day. 17Any meat left over until the third day must be completely burned up. 18If any of the meat from the peace offering is eaten on the third day, the person who presented it will not be accepted by the LORD. You will receive no credit for offering it. By then the meat will be contaminated; if you eat it, you will be punished for your sin.

[19] "Meat that touches anything ceremonially unclean may not be eaten; it must be completely burned up. The rest of the meat may be eaten, but only by people who are ceremonially clean. [20] If you are ceremonially unclean and you eat meat from a peace offering that was presented to the LORD, you will be cut off from the community. [21] If you touch anything that is unclean (whether it is human defilement or an unclean animal or any other unclean, detestable thing) and then eat meat from a peace offering presented to the LORD, you will be cut off from the community."

[22] Then the LORD said to Moses, [23] "Give the following instructions to the people of Israel. You must never eat fat, whether from cattle, sheep, or goats. [24] The fat of an animal found dead or torn to pieces by wild animals must never be eaten, though it may be used for any other purpose. [25] Anyone who eats fat from an animal presented as a special gift to the LORD will be cut off from the community. [26] No matter where you live, you must never consume the blood of any bird or animal. [27] Anyone who consumes blood will be cut off from the community."

**6:1** Verses 6:1-7 are numbered 5:20-26 in Hebrew text. **6:7** Or *will make atonement for you before the LORD.* **6:8** Verses 6:8-30 are numbered 6:1-23 in Hebrew text. **6:16** Hebrew *Tent of Meeting;* also in 6:26, 30. **6:20** Hebrew *1/10 of an ephah* [2.2 liters]. **6:21** The meaning of this Hebrew term is uncertain. **6:22** Hebrew *the anointed priest.* **6:30** Or *an offering to make atonement.* **7:7** Or *to make atonement.*

## MARK 3:7-30

Jesus went out to the lake with his disciples, and a large crowd followed him. They came from all over Galilee, Judea, [8] Jerusalem, Idumea, from east of the Jordan River, and even from as far north as Tyre and Sidon. The news about his miracles had spread far and wide, and vast numbers of people came to see him.

[9] Jesus instructed his disciples to have a boat ready so the crowd would not crush him. [10] He had healed many people

that day, so all the sick people eagerly pushed forward to touch him. [11] And whenever those possessed by evil* spirits caught sight of him, the spirits would throw them to the ground in front of him shrieking, "You are the Son of God!" [12] But Jesus sternly commanded the spirits not to reveal who he was.

[13] Afterward Jesus went up on a mountain and called out the ones he wanted to go with him. And they came to him. [14] Then he appointed twelve of them and called them his apostles.* They were to accompany him, and he would send them out to preach, [15] giving them authority to cast out demons. [16] Here are their names:

Simon (whom he named Peter),
[17] James and John (the sons of
    Zebedee, but Jesus nicknamed
    them "Sons of Thunder"*),
[18] Andrew,
    Philip,
    Bartholomew,
    Matthew,
    Thomas,
    James (son of Alphaeus),
    Thaddaeus,
    Simon (the zealot*),
[19] Judas Iscariot (who later
    betrayed him).

[20] One time Jesus entered a house, and the crowds began to gather again. Soon he and his disciples couldn't even find time to eat. [21] When his family heard what was happening, they tried to take him away. "He's out of his mind," they said.

[22] But the teachers of religious law who had arrived from Jerusalem said, "He's possessed by Satan,* the prince of demons. That's where he gets the power to cast out demons."

[23] Jesus called them over and responded with an illustration. "How can Satan cast out Satan?" he asked. [24] "A kingdom divided by civil war will collapse. [25] Similarly, a family splintered by feuding will fall apart. [26] And if Satan is divided and fights against himself, how

can he stand? He would never survive. [27]Let me illustrate this further. Who is powerful enough to enter the house of a strong man like Satan and plunder his goods? Only someone even stronger—someone who could tie him up and then plunder his house.

[28]"I tell you the truth, all sin and blasphemy can be forgiven, [29]but anyone who blasphemes the Holy Spirit will never be forgiven. This is a sin with eternal consequences." [30]He told them this because they were saying, "He's possessed by an evil spirit."

3:11 Greek *unclean;* also in 3:30.    3:14 Some manuscripts do not include *and called them his apostles.*    3:17 Greek *whom he named Boanerges, which means Sons of Thunder.* 3:18 Greek *the Cananean,* an Aramaic term for Jewish nationalists.    3:22 Greek *Beelzeboul;* other manuscripts read *Beezeboul;* Latin version reads *Beelzebub.*

PSALM 37:1-11*
*A psalm of David.*

[1] **D**on't worry about the wicked
   or envy those who do wrong.
[2] For like grass, they soon fade away.
   Like spring flowers, they soon
      wither.

[3] **Trust in the LORD and do good.
   Then you will live safely in
      the land and prosper.**
[4] **Take delight in the LORD,
   and he will give you your
      heart's desires.**

[5] Commit everything you do to
   the LORD.
   Trust him, and he will help you.
[6] He will make your innocence radiate
   like the dawn,
   and the justice of your cause will
      shine like the noonday sun.

[7] Be still in the presence of the LORD,
   and wait patiently for him to act.
   Don't worry about evil people
      who prosper
   or fret about their wicked
      schemes.

[8] Stop being angry!
   Turn from your rage!
   Do not lose your temper—
      it only leads to harm.

[9] For the wicked will be destroyed,
   but those who trust in the LORD
      will possess the land.

[10] Soon the wicked will disappear.
   Though you look for them, they
      will be gone.
[11] The lowly will possess the land
   and will live in peace and
      prosperity.

37 This psalm is a Hebrew acrostic poem; each stanza begins with a successive letter of the Hebrew alphabet.

PROVERBS 10:3-4
**T**he LORD will not let the godly go hungry, but he refuses to satisfy the craving of the wicked. □ Lazy people are soon poor; hard workers get rich.

# FEBRUARY
# 19

LEVITICUS 7:28–9:6
**T**hen the LORD said to Moses, [29]"Give the following instructions to the people of Israel. When you present a peace offering to the LORD, bring part of it as a gift to the LORD. [30]Present it to the LORD with your own hands as a special gift to the LORD. Bring the fat of the animal, together with the breast, and lift up the breast as a special offering to the LORD. [31]Then the priest will burn the fat on the altar, but the breast will belong to Aaron and his descendants. [32]Give the right thigh of your peace offering to the priest as a gift. [33]The right thigh must always be given to the priest who offers the blood and the fat of the peace offering. [34]For I have reserved the breast of the special offering and the right thigh of the sacred offering for the priests. It is the permanent right of Aaron and his descendants to share in the peace offerings brought by the people of Israel. [35]This is their rightful share. The special gifts

presented to the LORD have been reserved for Aaron and his descendants from the time they were set apart to serve the LORD as priests. [36] On the day they were anointed, the LORD commanded the Israelites to give these portions to the priests as their permanent share from generation to generation."

[37] These are the instructions for the burnt offering, the grain offering, the sin offering, and the guilt offering, as well as the ordination offering and the peace offering. [38] The LORD gave these instructions to Moses on Mount Sinai when he commanded the Israelites to present their offerings to the LORD in the wilderness of Sinai.

[8:1] THEN the LORD said to Moses, [2] "Bring Aaron and his sons, along with their sacred garments, the anointing oil, the bull for the sin offering, the two rams, and the basket of bread made without yeast, [3] and call the entire community of Israel together at the entrance of the Tabernacle.*"

[4] So Moses followed the LORD's instructions, and the whole community assembled at the Tabernacle entrance. [5] Moses announced to them, "This is what the LORD has commanded us to do!" [6] Then he presented Aaron and his sons and washed them with water. [7] He put the official tunic on Aaron and tied the sash around his waist. He dressed him in the robe, placed the ephod on him, and attached the ephod securely with its decorative sash. [8] Then Moses placed the chestpiece on Aaron and put the Urim and the Thummim inside it. [9] He placed the turban on Aaron's head and attached the gold medallion—the badge of holiness—to the front of the turban, just as the LORD had commanded him.

[10] Then Moses took the anointing oil and anointed the Tabernacle and everything in it, making them holy. [11] He sprinkled the oil on the altar seven times, anointing it and all its utensils, as well as the washbasin and its stand, making them holy. [12] Then he poured some of the anointing oil on Aaron's head, anointing him and making him holy for his work. [13] Next Moses presented Aaron's sons. He clothed them in their tunics, tied their sashes around them, and put their special head coverings on them, just as the LORD had commanded him.

[14] Then Moses presented the bull for the sin offering. Aaron and his sons laid their hands on the bull's head, [15] and Moses slaughtered it. Moses took some of the blood, and with his finger he put it on the four horns of the altar to purify it. He poured out the rest of the blood at the base of the altar. Through this process, he made the altar holy by purifying it.* [16] Then Moses took all the fat around the internal organs, the long lobe of the liver, and the two kidneys and the fat around them, and he burned it all on the altar. [17] He took the rest of the bull, including its hide, meat, and dung, and burned it on a fire outside the camp, just as the LORD had commanded him.

[18] Then Moses presented the ram for the burnt offering. Aaron and his sons laid their hands on the ram's head, [19] and Moses slaughtered it. Then Moses took the ram's blood and splattered it against all sides of the altar. [20] Then he cut the ram into pieces, and he burned the head, some of its pieces, and the fat on the altar. [21] After washing the internal organs and the legs with water, Moses burned the entire ram on the altar as a burnt offering. It was a pleasing aroma, a special gift presented to the LORD, just as the LORD had commanded him.

[22] Then Moses presented the other ram, which was the ram of ordination. Aaron and his sons laid their hands on the ram's head, [23] and Moses slaughtered it. Then Moses took some of its blood and applied it to the lobe of Aaron's right ear, the thumb of his right hand, and the big toe of his right foot. [24] Next Moses presented Aaron's sons and applied some of the blood to the lobes of their right ears, the thumbs of their right hands, and the big toes of their right feet. He then splattered the

rest of the blood against all sides of the altar.

25Next Moses took the fat, including the fat of the broad tail, the fat around the internal organs, the long lobe of the liver, and the two kidneys and the fat around them, along with the right thigh. 26On top of these he placed a thin cake of bread made without yeast, a cake of bread mixed with olive oil, and a wafer spread with olive oil. All these were taken from the basket of bread made without yeast that was placed in the LORD's presence. 27He put all these in the hands of Aaron and his sons, and he lifted them up as a special offering to the LORD. 28Moses then took all the offerings back from them and burned them on the altar on top of the burnt offering. This was the ordination offering. It was a pleasing aroma, a special gift presented to the LORD. 29Then Moses took the breast and lifted it up as a special offering to the LORD. This was Moses' portion of the ram of ordination, just as the LORD had commanded him.

30Next Moses took some of the anointing oil and some of the blood that was on the altar, and he sprinkled them on Aaron and his garments and on his sons and their garments. In this way, he made Aaron and his sons and their garments holy.

31Then Moses said to Aaron and his sons, "Boil the remaining meat of the offerings at the Tabernacle entrance, and eat it there, along with the bread that is in the basket of offerings for the ordination, just as I commanded when I said, 'Aaron and his sons will eat it.' 32Any meat or bread that is left over must then be burned up. 33You must not leave the Tabernacle entrance for seven days, for that is when the ordination ceremony will be completed. 34Everything we have done today was commanded by the LORD in order to purify you, making you right with him.* 35Now stay at the entrance of the Tabernacle day and night for seven days, and do everything the LORD requires. If you fail to do this, you will die, for this is

what the LORD has commanded." 36So Aaron and his sons did everything the LORD had commanded through Moses.

9:1AFTER the ordination ceremony, on the eighth day, Moses called together Aaron and his sons and the elders of Israel. 2He said to Aaron, "Take a young bull for a sin offering and a ram for a burnt offering, both without defects, and present them to the LORD. 3Then tell the Israelites, 'Take a male goat for a sin offering, and take a calf and a lamb, both a year old and without defects, for a burnt offering. 4Also take a bull* and a ram for a peace offering and flour moistened with olive oil for a grain offering. Present all these offerings to the LORD because the LORD will appear to you today.'"

5So the people presented all these things at the entrance of the Tabernacle,* just as Moses had commanded. Then the whole community came forward and stood before the LORD. 6And Moses said, "This is what the LORD has commanded you to do so that the glory of the LORD may appear to you."

8:3 Hebrew *Tent of Meeting;* also in 8:4, 31, 33, 35.
8:15 Or *by making atonement for it;* or *that offerings for purification might be made on it.* 8:34 Or *to make atonement for you.* 9:4 Or *cow;* also in 9:18, 19.
9:5 Hebrew *Tent of Meeting;* also in 9:23.

MARK 3:31–4:25

Then Jesus' mother and brothers came to see him. They stood outside and sent word for him to come out and talk with them. 32There was a crowd sitting around Jesus, and someone said, "Your mother and your brothers* are outside asking for you."

33Jesus replied, "Who is my mother? Who are my brothers?" 34Then he looked at those around him and said, "Look, these are my mother and brothers. 35Anyone who does God's will is my brother and sister and mother."

4:1ONCE again Jesus began teaching by the lakeshore. A very large crowd soon gathered around him, so he got into a boat. Then he sat in the boat while all the people remained on the shore. [2]He taught them by telling many stories in the form of parables, such as this one:

[3]"Listen! A farmer went out to plant some seed. [4]As he scattered it across his field, some of the seed fell on a footpath, and the birds came and ate it. [5]Other seed fell on shallow soil with underlying rock. The seed sprouted quickly because the soil was shallow. [6]But the plant soon wilted under the hot sun, and since it didn't have deep roots, it died. [7]Other seed fell among thorns that grew up and choked out the tender plants so they produced no grain. [8]Still other seeds fell on fertile soil, and they sprouted, grew, and produced a crop that was thirty, sixty, and even a hundred times as much as had been planted!" [9]Then he said, "Anyone with ears to hear should listen and understand."

[10]Later, when Jesus was alone with the twelve disciples and with the others who were gathered around, they asked him what the parables meant.

[11]He replied, "You are permitted to understand the secret* of the Kingdom of God. But I use parables for everything I say to outsiders, [12]so that the Scriptures might be fulfilled:

'When they see what I do,
    they will learn nothing.
When they hear what I say,
    they will not understand.
Otherwise, they will turn to me
    and be forgiven.'*"

[13]Then Jesus said to them, "If you can't understand the meaning of this parable, how will you understand all the other parables? [14]The farmer plants seed by taking God's word to others. [15]The seed that fell on the footpath represents those who hear the message, only to have Satan come at once and take it away. [16]The seed on the rocky soil represents those who hear the message and immediately receive it with joy. [17]But since they don't have deep roots, they don't last long. They fall away as soon as they have problems or are persecuted for believing God's word. [18]The seed that

fell among the thorns represents others who hear God's word, [19]but all too quickly the message is crowded out by the worries of this life, the lure of wealth, and the desire for other things, so no fruit is produced. [20]And the seed that fell on good soil represents those who hear and accept God's word and produce a harvest of thirty, sixty, or even a hundred times as much as had been planted!"

[21]Then Jesus asked them, "Would anyone light a lamp and then put it under a basket or under a bed? Of course not! A lamp is placed on a stand, where its light will shine. [22]For everything that is hidden will eventually be brought into the open, and every secret will be brought to light. [23]Anyone with ears to hear should listen and understand."

[24]Then he added, "Pay close attention to what you hear. The closer you listen, the more understanding you will be given*—and you will receive even more. [25]To those who listen to my teaching, more understanding will be given. But for those who are not listening, even what little understanding they have will be taken away from them."

3:32 Some manuscripts add *and sisters.*   4:11 Greek *mystery.*   4:12 Isa 6:9-10 (Greek version).   4:24 Or *The measure you give will be the measure you get back.*

PSALM 37:12-29

The wicked plot against the godly;
    they snarl at them in defiance.
[13] But the Lord just laughs,
    for he sees their day of judgment
        coming.

[14] The wicked draw their swords
    and string their bows
to kill the poor and the oppressed,
    to slaughter those who do right.
[15] But their swords will stab their
        own hearts,
    and their bows will be broken.

[16] It is better to be godly and have little
    than to be evil and rich.
[17] For the strength of the wicked will
        be shattered,

but the LORD takes care
   of the godly.
<sup>18</sup> Day by day the LORD takes care
   of the innocent,
   and they will receive an
      inheritance that lasts forever.
<sup>19</sup> They will not be disgraced in hard
      times;
   even in famine they will have
      more than enough.

<sup>20</sup> But the wicked will die.
   The LORD's enemies are like
      flowers in a field—
   they will disappear like smoke.

<sup>21</sup> The wicked borrow and never repay,
   but the godly are generous
      givers.
<sup>22</sup> Those the LORD blesses will possess
      the land,
   but those he curses will die.

<sup>23</sup> The LORD directs the steps
      of the godly.
   He delights in every detail of their
      lives.
<sup>24</sup> Though they stumble, they will
      never fall,
   for the LORD holds them by
      the hand.

<sup>25</sup> Once I was young, and now
      I am old.
   Yet I have never seen the godly
      abandoned
   or their children begging for
      bread.
<sup>26</sup> The godly always give generous
      loans to others,
   and their children are a blessing.

<sup>27</sup> Turn from evil and do good,
   and you will live in the land
      forever.
<sup>28</sup> For the LORD loves justice,
   and he will never abandon
      the godly.

   He will keep them safe forever,
   but the children of the wicked
      will die.
<sup>29</sup> The godly will possess the land
   and will live there forever.

PROVERBS 10:5
**A** wise youth harvests in the summer,
but one who sleeps during harvest is a
disgrace.

# FEBRUARY
# 20

LEVITICUS 9:7–10:20
**T**hen Moses said to Aaron, "Come to the
altar and sacrifice your sin offering and
your burnt offering to purify yourself
and the people. Then present the offerings of the people to purify them, making them right with the LORD,* just as he
has commanded."

<sup>8</sup>So Aaron went to the altar and
slaughtered the calf as a sin offering for
himself. <sup>9</sup>His sons brought him the
blood, and he dipped his finger in it and
put it on the horns of the altar. He
poured out the rest of the blood at the
base of the altar. <sup>10</sup>Then he burned on
the altar the fat, the kidneys, and the
long lobe of the liver from the sin offering, just as the LORD had commanded
Moses. <sup>11</sup>The meat and the hide, however, he burned outside the camp.

<sup>12</sup>Next Aaron slaughtered the animal
for the burnt offering. His sons brought
him the blood, and he splattered it
against all sides of the altar. <sup>13</sup>Then they
handed him each piece of the burnt
offering, including the head, and he
burned them on the altar. <sup>14</sup>Then he
washed the internal organs and the legs
and burned them on the altar along with
the rest of the burnt offering.

<sup>15</sup>Next Aaron presented the offer-
ings of the people. He slaughtered the
people's goat and presented it as an offering for their sin, just as he had first
done with the offering for his own sin.
<sup>16</sup>Then he presented the burnt offering
and sacrificed it in the prescribed way.
<sup>17</sup>He also presented the grain offering,

burning a handful of the flour mixture on the altar, in addition to the regular burnt offering for the morning.

18Then Aaron slaughtered the bull and the ram for the people's peace offering. His sons brought him the blood, and he splattered it against all sides of the altar. 19Then he took the fat of the bull and the ram—the fat of the broad tail and from around the internal organs—along with the kidneys and the long lobes of the livers. 20He placed these fat portions on top of the breasts of these animals and burned them on the altar. 21Aaron then lifted up the breasts and right thighs as a special offering to the LORD, just as Moses had commanded.

22After that, Aaron raised his hands toward the people and blessed them. Then, after presenting the sin offering, the burnt offering, and the peace offering, he stepped down from the altar. 23Then Moses and Aaron went into the Tabernacle, and when they came back out, they blessed the people again, and the glory of the LORD appeared to the whole community. 24Fire blazed forth from the LORD's presence and consumed the burnt offering and the fat on the altar. When the people saw this, they shouted with joy and fell face down on the ground.

10:1AARON's sons Nadab and Abihu put coals of fire in their incense burners and sprinkled incense over them. In this way, they disobeyed the LORD by burning before him the wrong kind of fire, different than he had commanded. 2So fire blazed forth from the LORD's presence and burned them up, and they died there before the LORD.

3Then Moses said to Aaron, "This is what the LORD meant when he said,

'I will display my holiness
    through those who come near me.
I will display my glory
    before all the people.'"

And Aaron was silent.

4Then Moses called for Mishael and Elzaphan, Aaron's cousins, the sons of Aaron's uncle Uzziel. He said to them, "Come forward and carry away the bodies of your relatives from in front of the sanctuary to a place outside the camp." 5So they came forward and picked them up by their garments and carried them out of the camp, just as Moses had commanded.

6Then Moses said to Aaron and his sons Eleazar and Ithamar, "Do not show grief by leaving your hair uncombed* or by tearing your clothes. If you do, you will die, and the LORD's anger will strike the whole community of Israel. However, the rest of the Israelites, your relatives, may mourn because of the LORD's fiery destruction of Nadab and Abihu. 7But you must not leave the entrance of the Tabernacle* or you will die, for you have been anointed with the LORD's anointing oil." So they did as Moses commanded.

8Then the LORD said to Aaron, 9"You and your descendants must never drink wine or any other alcoholic drink before going into the Tabernacle. If you do, you will die. This is a permanent law for you, and it must be observed from generation to generation. 10You must distinguish between what is sacred and what is common, between what is ceremonially unclean and what is clean. 11And you must teach the Israelites all the decrees that the LORD has given them through Moses."

12Then Moses said to Aaron and his remaining sons, Eleazar and Ithamar, "Take what is left of the grain offering after a portion has been presented as a special gift to the LORD, and eat it beside the altar. Make sure it contains no yeast, for it is most holy. 13You must eat it in a sacred place, for it has been given to you and your descendants as your portion of the special gifts presented to the LORD. These are the commands I have been given. 14But the breast and thigh that were lifted up as a special offering may be eaten in any place that is ceremonially clean. These parts have been given to you and your descendants as your portion of the peace offerings presented by the people of Israel. [15]You must lift up the thigh and breast as a special offering to the LORD, along with the fat of the special gifts. These parts will belong to you and your descendants as your permanent right, just as the LORD has commanded."

[16]Moses then asked them what had happened to the goat of the sin offering. When he discovered it had been burned up, he became very angry with Eleazar and Ithamar, Aaron's remaining sons. [17]"Why didn't you eat the sin offering in the sacred area?" he demanded. "It is a holy offering! The LORD has given it to you to remove the guilt of the community and to purify the people, making them right with the LORD.* [18]Since the animal's blood was not brought into the Holy Place, you should have eaten the meat in the sacred area as I ordered you."

[19]Then Aaron answered Moses, "Today my sons presented both their sin offering and their burnt offering to the LORD. And yet this tragedy has happened to me. If I had eaten the people's sin offering on such a tragic day as this, would the LORD have been pleased?" [20]And when Moses heard this, he was satisfied.

9:7 Or to make atonement for them.   10:6 Or by uncovering your heads.   10:7 Hebrew Tent of Meeting; also in 10:9.   10:17 Or to make atonement for the people before the LORD.

MARK 4:26–5:20

Jesus also said, "The Kingdom of God is like a farmer who scatters seed on the ground. [27]Night and day, while he's asleep or awake, the seed sprouts and grows, but he does not understand how it happens. [28]The earth produces the crops on its own. First a leaf blade pushes through, then the heads of wheat are formed, and finally the grain ripens. [29]And as soon as the grain is ready, the farmer comes and harvests it with a sickle, for the harvest time has come."

[30]Jesus said, "How can I describe the Kingdom of God? What story should I use to illustrate it? [31]It is like a mustard seed planted in the ground. It is the smallest of all seeds, [32]but it becomes the largest of all garden plants; it grows long branches, and birds can make nests in its shade."

[33]Jesus used many similar stories and illustrations to teach the people as much as they could understand. [34]In fact, in his public ministry he never taught without using parables; but afterward, when he was alone with his disciples, he explained everything to them.

[35]As evening came, Jesus said to his disciples, "Let's cross to the other side of the lake." [36]So they took Jesus in the boat and started out, leaving the crowds behind (although other boats followed). [37]But soon a fierce storm came up. High waves were breaking into the boat, and it began to fill with water.

[38]Jesus was sleeping at the back of the boat with his head on a cushion. The disciples woke him up, shouting, "Teacher, don't you care that we're going to drown?"

[39]When Jesus woke up, he rebuked the wind and said to the water, "Silence! Be still!" Suddenly the wind stopped, and there was a great calm. [40]Then he asked them, "Why are you afraid? Do you still have no faith?"

[41]The disciples were absolutely terrified. "Who is this man?" they asked each other. "Even the wind and waves obey him!"

[5:1]So they arrived at the other side of the lake, in the region of the Gerasenes.* [2]When Jesus climbed out of the boat, a man possessed by an evil* spirit came out from a cemetery to meet him. [3]This man lived among the burial caves and could no longer be restrained, even with a chain. [4]Whenever he was put into chains and shackles—as he often was—he snapped the chains from his wrists and smashed the shackles. No one was strong enough to subdue him. [5]Day and night he wandered among the burial caves and in the hills, howling and cutting himself with sharp stones.

[6]When Jesus was still some distance away, the man saw him, ran to meet him,

and bowed low before him. [7]With a shriek, he screamed, "Why are you interfering with me, Jesus, Son of the Most High God? In the name of God, I beg you, don't torture me!" [8]For Jesus had already said to the spirit, "Come out of the man, you evil spirit."

[9]Then Jesus demanded, "What is your name?"

And he replied, "My name is Legion, because there are many of us inside this man." [10]Then the evil spirits begged him again and again not to send them to some distant place.

[11]There happened to be a large herd of pigs feeding on the hillside nearby. [12]"Send us into those pigs," the spirits begged. "Let us enter them."

[13]So Jesus gave them permission. The evil spirits came out of the man and entered the pigs, and the entire herd of 2,000 pigs plunged down the steep hillside into the lake and drowned in the water.

[14]The herdsmen fled to the nearby town and the surrounding countryside, spreading the news as they ran. People rushed out to see what had happened. [15]A crowd soon gathered around Jesus, and they saw the man who had been possessed by the legion of demons. He was sitting there fully clothed and perfectly sane, and they were all afraid. [16]Then those who had seen what happened told the others about the demon-possessed man and the pigs. [17]And the crowd began pleading with Jesus to go away and leave them alone.

[18]As Jesus was getting into the boat, the man who had been demon possessed begged to go with him. [19]But Jesus said, "No, go home to your family, and tell them everything the Lord has done for you and how merciful he has been." [20]So the man started off to visit the Ten Towns* of that region and began to proclaim the great things Jesus had done for him; and everyone was amazed at what he told them.

5:1 Other manuscripts read *Gadarenes;* still others read *Gergesenes.* See Matt 8:28; Luke 8:26.   5:2 Greek *unclean;* also in 5:8, 13.   5:20 Greek *Decapolis.*

## PSALM 37:30-40

The godly offer good counsel;
  they teach right from wrong.
[31] They have made God's law their
    own,
  so they will never slip from
    his path.

[32] The wicked wait in ambush for
    the godly,
  looking for an excuse to kill them.
[33] But the Lord will not let the wicked
    succeed
  or let the godly be condemned
    when they are put on trial.

[34] Put your hope in the Lord.
  Travel steadily along his path.
  He will honor you by giving you
    the land.
  You will see the wicked destroyed.

[35] I have seen wicked and ruthless
    people
  flourishing like a tree in its
    native soil.
[36] But when I looked again, they
    were gone!
  Though I searched for them,
    I could not find them!

[37] Look at those who are honest
    and good,
  for a wonderful future awaits
    those who love peace.
[38] But the rebellious will be destroyed;
  they have no future.

[39] **The Lord rescues the godly;**
  **he is their fortress in times**
    **of trouble.**
[40] **The Lord helps them,**
  **rescuing them from the**
    **wicked.**
  **He saves them,**
    **and they find shelter**
      **in him.**

## PROVERBS 10:6-7

The godly are showered with blessings; the words of the wicked conceal violent intentions. □ We have happy memories of the godly, but the name of a wicked person rots away.

# FEBRUARY
# 21

LEVITICUS 11:1–12:8

**T**hen the LORD said to Moses and Aaron, [2]"Give the following instructions to the people of Israel.

"Of all the land animals, these are the ones you may use for food. [3] You may eat any animal that has completely split hooves and chews the cud. [4] You may not, however, eat the following animals* that have split hooves or that chew the cud, but not both. The camel chews the cud but does not have split hooves, so it is ceremonially unclean for you. [5] The hyrax* chews the cud but does not have split hooves, so it is unclean. [6] The hare chews the cud but does not have split hooves, so it is unclean. [7] The pig has evenly split hooves but does not chew the cud, so it is unclean. [8] You may not eat the meat of these animals or even touch their carcasses. They are ceremonially unclean for you.

[9]"Of all the marine animals, these are ones you may use for food. You may eat anything from the water if it has both fins and scales, whether taken from salt water or from streams. [10] But you must never eat animals from the sea or from rivers that do not have both fins and scales. They are detestable to you. This applies both to little creatures that live in shallow water and to all creatures that live in deep water. [11] They will always be detestable to you. You must never eat their meat or even touch their dead bodies. [12] Any marine animal that does not have both fins and scales is detestable to you.

[13]"These are the birds that are detestable to you. You must never eat them: the griffon vulture, the bearded vulture, the black vulture, [14] the kite, falcons of all kinds, [15] ravens of all kinds, [16] the eagle owl, the short-eared owl, the seagull, hawks of all kinds, [17] the little owl, the cormorant, the great owl, [18] the barn owl,

the desert owl, the Egyptian vulture, [19] the stork, herons of all kinds, the hoopoe, and the bat.

[20]"You must not eat winged insects that walk along the ground; they are detestable to you. [21] You may, however, eat winged insects that walk along the ground and have jointed legs so they can jump. [22] The insects you are permitted to eat include all kinds of locusts, bald locusts, crickets, and grasshoppers. [23] All other winged insects that walk along the ground are detestable to you.

[24]"The following creatures will make you ceremonially unclean. If any of you touch their carcasses, you will be defiled until evening. [25] If you pick up their carcasses, you must wash your clothes, and you will remain defiled until evening.

[26]"Any animal that has split hooves that are not evenly divided or that does not chew the cud is unclean for you. If you touch the carcass of such an animal, you will be defiled. [27] Of the animals that walk on all fours, those that have paws are unclean. If you touch the carcass of such an animal, you will be defiled until evening. [28] If you pick up its carcass, you must wash your clothes, and you will remain defiled until evening. These animals are unclean for you.

[29]"Of the small animals that scurry along the ground, these are unclean for you: the mole rat, the rat, large lizards of all kinds, [30] the gecko, the monitor lizard, the common lizard, the sand lizard, and the chameleon. [31] All these small animals are unclean for you. If any of you touch the dead body of such an animal, you will be defiled until evening. [32] If such an animal dies and falls on something, that object will be unclean. This is true whether the object is made of wood, cloth, leather, or burlap. Whatever its use, you must dip it in water, and it will remain defiled until evening. After that, it will be ceremonially clean and may be used again.

[33]"If such an animal falls into a clay pot, everything in the pot will be defiled, and the pot must be smashed. [34] If the water from such a container spills on

any food, the food will be defiled. And any beverage in such a container will be defiled. [35]Any object on which the carcass of such an animal falls will be defiled. If it is an oven or hearth, it must be destroyed, for it is defiled, and you must treat it accordingly.

[36]"However, if the carcass of such an animal falls into a spring or a cistern, the water will still be clean. But anyone who touches the carcass will be defiled. [37]If the carcass falls on seed grain to be planted in the field, the seed will still be considered clean. [38]But if the seed is wet when the carcass falls on it, the seed will be defiled.

[39]"If an animal you are permitted to eat dies and you touch its carcass, you will be defiled until evening. [40]If you eat any of its meat or carry away its carcass, you must wash your clothes, and you will remain defiled until evening.

[41]"All small animals that scurry along the ground are detestable, and you must never eat them. [42]This includes all animals that slither along on their bellies, as well as those with four legs and those with many feet. All such animals that scurry along the ground are detestable, and you must never eat them. [43]Do not defile yourselves by touching them. You must not make yourselves ceremonially unclean because of them. [44]For I am the LORD your God. You must consecrate yourselves and be holy, because I am holy. So do not defile yourselves with any of these small animals that scurry along the ground. [45]**For I, the LORD, am the one who brought you up from the land of Egypt, that I might be your God. Therefore, you must be holy because I am holy.**

[46]"These are the instructions regarding land animals, birds, marine creatures, and animals that scurry along the ground. [47]By these instructions you will know what is unclean and clean, and which animals may be eaten and which may not be eaten."

[12:1]THE LORD said to Moses, "Give the following instructions to the people of Israel. [2]If a woman becomes pregnant and gives birth to a son, she will be ceremonially unclean for seven days, just as she is unclean during her menstrual period. [3]On the eighth day the boy's foreskin must be circumcised. [4]After waiting thirty-three days, she will be purified from the bleeding of childbirth. During this time of purification, she must not touch anything that is set apart as holy. And she must not enter the sanctuary until her time of purification is over. [5]If a woman gives birth to a daughter, she will be ceremonially unclean for two weeks, just as she is unclean during her menstrual period. After waiting sixty-six days, she will be purified from the bleeding of childbirth.

[6]"When the time of purification is completed for either a son or a daughter, the woman must bring a one-year-old lamb for a burnt offering and a young pigeon or turtledove for a purification offering. She must bring her offerings to the priest at the entrance of the Tabernacle.* [7]The priest will then present them to the LORD to purify her.* Then she will be ceremonially clean again after her bleeding at childbirth. These are the instructions for a woman after the birth of a son or a daughter.

[8]"If a woman cannot afford to bring a lamb, she must bring two turtledoves or two young pigeons. One will be for the burnt offering and the other for the purification offering. The priest will sacrifice them to purify her, and she will be ceremonially clean."

11:4 The identification of some of the animals, birds, and insects in this chapter is uncertain.    11:5 Or *coney*, or *rock badger*.    12:6 Hebrew *Tent of Meeting*.    12:7 Or *to make atonement for her*; also in 12:8.

## MARK 5:21-43

**J**esus got into the boat again and went back to the other side of the lake, where a large crowd gathered around him on the shore. [22]Then a leader of the local synagogue, whose name was Jairus, arrived. When he saw Jesus, he fell at his feet, [23]pleading fervently with him. "My little daughter is dying," he said. "Please come and lay your hands on her; heal her so she can live."

²⁴Jesus went with him, and all the people followed, crowding around him. ²⁵A woman in the crowd had suffered for twelve years with constant bleeding. ²⁶She had suffered a great deal from many doctors, and over the years she had spent everything she had to pay them, but she had gotten no better. In fact, she had gotten worse. ²⁷She had heard about Jesus, so she came up behind him through the crowd and touched his robe. ²⁸For she thought to herself, "If I can just touch his robe, I will be healed." ²⁹Immediately the bleeding stopped, and she could feel in her body that she had been healed of her terrible condition.

³⁰Jesus realized at once that healing power had gone out from him, so he turned around in the crowd and asked, "Who touched my robe?"

³¹His disciples said to him, "Look at this crowd pressing around you. How can you ask, 'Who touched me?'"

³²But he kept on looking around to see who had done it. ³³Then the frightened woman, trembling at the realization of what had happened to her, came and fell at his feet and told him what she had done. ³⁴And he said to her, "Daughter, your faith has made you well. Go in peace. Your suffering is over."

³⁵While he was still speaking to her, messengers arrived from the home of Jairus, the leader of the synagogue. They told him, "Your daughter is dead. There's no use troubling the Teacher now."

³⁶But Jesus overheard them and said to Jairus, "Don't be afraid. Just have faith."

³⁷Then Jesus stopped the crowd and wouldn't let anyone go with him except Peter, James, and John (the brother of James). ³⁸When they came to the home of the synagogue leader, Jesus saw much commotion and weeping and wailing. ³⁹He went inside and asked,

"Why all this commotion and weeping? The child isn't dead; she's only asleep."

⁴⁰The crowd laughed at him. But he made them all leave, and he took the girl's father and mother and his three disciples into the room where the girl was lying. ⁴¹Holding her hand, he said to her, *"Talitha koum,"* which means "Little girl, get up!" ⁴²And the girl, who was twelve years old, immediately stood up and walked around! They were overwhelmed and totally amazed. ⁴³Jesus gave them strict orders not to tell anyone what had happened, and then he told them to give her something to eat.

## PSALM 38:1-22
*A psalm of David, asking God to remember him.*

¹ 〇 LORD, don't rebuke me in your
    anger
    or discipline me in your rage!
² Your arrows have struck deep,
    and your blows are crushing me.
³ Because of your anger, my whole
    body is sick;
    my health is broken because
    of my sins.
⁴ My guilt overwhelms me—
    it is a burden too heavy to bear.
⁵ My wounds fester and stink
    because of my foolish sins.
⁶ I am bent over and racked with pain.
    All day long I walk around filled
    with grief.
⁷ A raging fever burns within me,
    and my health is broken.
⁸ I am exhausted and completely
    crushed.
    My groans come from an
    anguished heart.

⁹ You know what I long for, Lord;
    you hear my every sigh.
¹⁰ My heart beats wildly, my strength
    fails,
    and I am going blind.
¹¹ My loved ones and friends stay away,
    fearing my disease.
    Even my own family stands at
    a distance.
¹² Meanwhile, my enemies lay traps
    to kill me.

Those who wish me harm make
plans to ruin me.
All day long they plan their
treachery.

¹³ But I am deaf to all their threats.
I am silent before them as one
who cannot speak.
¹⁴ I choose to hear nothing,
and I make no reply.
¹⁵ For I am waiting for you, O LORD.
You must answer for me, O Lord
my God.
¹⁶ I prayed, "Don't let my enemies
gloat over me
or rejoice at my downfall."

¹⁷ I am on the verge of collapse,
facing constant pain.
¹⁸ But I confess my sins;
I am deeply sorry for what
I have done.
¹⁹ I have many aggressive enemies;
they hate me without reason.
²⁰ They repay me evil for good
and oppose me for pursuing
good.
²¹ Do not abandon me, O LORD.
Do not stand at a distance,
my God.
²² Come quickly to help me,
O Lord my savior.

PROVERBS 10:8-9
The wise are glad to be instructed, but
babbling fools fall flat on their faces.
□ People with integrity walk safely, but
those who follow crooked paths will
slip and fall.

# FEBRUARY
# 22

LEVITICUS 13:1-59
The LORD said to Moses and Aaron, ²"If
anyone has a swelling or a rash or discolored skin that might develop into a
serious skin disease,* that person must

be brought to Aaron the priest or to one
of his sons.* ³The priest will examine
the affected area of the skin. If the hair
in the affected area has turned white
and the problem appears to be more
than skin-deep, it is a serious skin disease, and the priest who examines it
must pronounce the person ceremonially unclean.

⁴"But if the affected area of the skin is
only a white discoloration and does not
appear to be more than skin-deep, and if
the hair on the spot has not turned white,
the priest will quarantine the person for
seven days. ⁵On the seventh day the
priest will make another examination. If
he finds the affected area has not
changed and the problem has not spread
on the skin, the priest will quarantine the
person for seven more days. ⁶On the seventh day the priest will make another examination. If he finds the affected area
has faded and has not spread, the priest
will pronounce the person ceremonially
clean. It was only a rash. The person's
clothing must be washed, and the person
will be ceremonially clean. ⁷But if the
rash continues to spread after the person has been examined by the priest and
has been pronounced clean, the infected
person must return to be examined
again. ⁸If the priest finds that the rash
has spread, he must pronounce the person ceremonially unclean, for it is indeed a skin disease.

⁹"Anyone who develops a serious skin
disease must go to the priest for an examination. ¹⁰If the priest finds a white
swelling on the skin, and some hair on
the spot has turned white, and there is an
open sore in the affected area, ¹¹it is a
chronic skin disease, and the priest must
pronounce the person ceremonially unclean. In such cases the person need not
be quarantined, for it is obvious that the
skin is defiled by the disease.

¹²"Now suppose the disease has
spread all over the person's skin, covering the body from head to foot. ¹³When
the priest examines the infected person
and finds that the disease covers the entire body, he will pronounce the person

ceremonially clean. Since the skin has turned completely white, the person is clean. [14]But if any open sores appear, the infected person will be pronounced ceremonially unclean. [15]The priest must make this pronouncement as soon as he sees an open sore, since open sores indicate the presence of a skin disease. [16]However, if the open sores heal and turn white like the rest of the skin, the person must return to the priest [17]for another examination. If the affected areas have indeed turned white, the priest will then pronounce the person ceremonially clean by declaring, 'You are clean!'

[18]"If anyone has a boil on the skin that has started to heal, [19]but a white swelling or a reddish white spot develops in its place, that person must go to the priest to be examined. [20]If the priest examines it and finds it to be more than skin-deep, and if the hair in the affected area has turned white, the priest must pronounce the person ceremonially unclean. The boil has become a serious skin disease. [21]But if the priest finds no white hair on the affected area and the problem appears to be no more than skin-deep and has faded, the priest must quarantine the person for seven days. [22]If during that time the affected area spreads on the skin, the priest must pronounce the person ceremonially unclean, because it is a serious disease. [23]But if the area grows no larger and does not spread, it is merely the scar from the boil, and the priest will pronounce the person ceremonially clean.

[24]"If anyone has suffered a burn on the skin and the burned area changes color, becoming either reddish white or shiny white, [25]the priest must examine it. If he finds that the hair in the affected area has turned white and the problem appears to be more than skin-deep, a skin disease has broken out in the burn. The priest must then pronounce the person ceremonially unclean, for it is clearly a serious skin disease. [26]But if the priest finds no white hair on the affected area and the problem appears to be no more than skin-deep and has faded, the priest

must quarantine the infected person for seven days. [27]On the seventh day the priest must examine the person again. If the affected area has spread on the skin, the priest must pronounce that person ceremonially unclean, for it is clearly a serious skin disease. [28]But if the affected area has not changed or spread on the skin and has faded, it is simply a swelling from the burn. The priest will then pronounce the person ceremonially clean, for it is only the scar from the burn.

[29]"If anyone, either a man or woman, has a sore on the head or chin, [30]the priest must examine it. If he finds it is more than skin-deep and has fine yellow hair on it, the priest must pronounce the person ceremonially unclean. It is a scabby sore of the head or chin. [31]If the priest examines the scabby sore and finds that it is only skin-deep but there is no black hair on it, he must quarantine the person for seven days. [32]On the seventh day the priest must examine the sore again. If he finds that the scabby sore has not spread, and there is no yellow hair on it, and it appears to be only skin-deep, [33]the person must shave off all hair except the hair on the affected area. Then the priest must quarantine the person for another seven days. [34]On the seventh day he will examine the sore again. If it has not spread and appears to be no more than skin-deep, the priest will pronounce the person ceremonially clean. The person's clothing must be washed, and the person will be ceremonially clean. [35]But if the scabby sore begins to spread after the person is pronounced clean, [36]the priest must do another examination. If he finds that the sore has spread, the priest does not need to look for yellow hair. The infected person is ceremonially unclean. [37]But if the color of the scabby sore does not change and black hair has grown on it, it has healed. The priest will then pronounce the person ceremonially clean.

[38]"If anyone, either a man or woman, has shiny white patches on the skin, [39]the priest must examine the affected area. If he finds that the shiny patches

are only pale white, this is a harmless skin rash, and the person is ceremonially clean.

⁴⁰"If a man loses his hair and his head becomes bald, he is still ceremonially clean. ⁴¹And if he loses hair on his forehead, he simply has a bald forehead; he is still clean. ⁴²However, if a reddish white sore appears on the bald area at the top or back of his head, this is a skin disease. ⁴³The priest must examine him, and if he finds swelling around the reddish white sore anywhere on the man's head and it looks like a skin disease, ⁴⁴the man is indeed infected with a skin disease and is unclean. The priest must pronounce him ceremonially unclean because of the sore on his head.

⁴⁵"Those who suffer from a serious skin disease must tear their clothing and leave their hair uncombed.* They must cover their mouth and call out, 'Unclean! Unclean!' ⁴⁶As long as the serious disease lasts, they will be ceremonially unclean. They must live in isolation in their place outside the camp.

⁴⁷"Now suppose mildew* contaminates some woolen or linen clothing, ⁴⁸woolen or linen fabric, the hide of an animal, or anything made of leather. ⁴⁹If the contaminated area in the clothing, the animal hide, the fabric, or the leather article has turned greenish or reddish, it is contaminated with mildew and must be shown to the priest. ⁵⁰After examining the affected spot, the priest will put the article in quarantine for seven days. ⁵¹On the seventh day the priest must inspect it again. If the contaminated area has spread, the clothing or fabric or leather is clearly contaminated by a serious mildew and is ceremonially unclean. ⁵²The priest must burn the item—the clothing, the woolen or linen fabric, or piece of leather—for it has been contaminated by a serious mildew. It must be completely destroyed by fire.

⁵³"But if the priest examines it and finds that the contaminated area has not spread in the clothing, the fabric, or the leather, ⁵⁴the priest will order the object to be washed and then quarantined for

seven more days. ⁵⁵Then the priest must examine the object again. If he finds that the contaminated area has not changed color after being washed, even if it did not spread, the object is defiled. It must be completely burned up, whether the contaminated spot* is on the inside or outside. ⁵⁶But if the priest examines it and finds that the contaminated area has faded after being washed, he must cut the spot from the clothing, the fabric, or the leather. ⁵⁷If the spot later reappears on the clothing, the fabric, or the leather article, the mildew is clearly spreading, and the contaminated object must be burned up. ⁵⁸But if the spot disappears from the clothing, the fabric, or the leather article after it has been washed, it must be washed again; then it will be ceremonially clean.

⁵⁹"These are the instructions for dealing with mildew that contaminates woolen or linen clothing or fabric or anything made of leather. This is how the priest will determine whether these items are ceremonially clean or unclean."

13:2a Traditionally rendered *leprosy*. The Hebrew word used throughout this passage is used to describe various skin diseases.   13:2b Or *one of his descendants*.
13:45 Or *and uncover their heads*.   13:47 Traditionally rendered *leprosy*. The Hebrew term used throughout this passage is the same term used for the various skin diseases described in 13:1-46.   13:55 The meaning of the Hebrew is uncertain.

## MARK 6:1-29

Jesus left that part of the country and returned with his disciples to Nazareth, his hometown. ²The next Sabbath he began teaching in the synagogue, and many who heard him were amazed. They asked, "Where did he get all this wisdom and the power to perform such miracles?" ³Then they scoffed, "He's just a carpenter, the son of Mary* and the brother of James, Joseph,* Judas, and Simon. And his sisters live right here among us." They were deeply offended and refused to believe in him.

⁴Then Jesus told them, "A prophet is honored everywhere except in his own hometown and among his relatives and his own family." ⁵And because of their

unbelief, he couldn't do any mighty miracles among them except to place his hands on a few sick people and heal them. ⁶And he was amazed at their unbelief.

Then Jesus went from village to village, teaching the people. ⁷And he called his twelve disciples together and began sending them out two by two, giving them authority to cast out evil* spirits. ⁸He told them to take nothing for their journey except a walking stick—no food, no traveler's bag, no money.* ⁹He allowed them to wear sandals but not to take a change of clothes.

¹⁰"Wherever you go," he said, "stay in the same house until you leave town. ¹¹But if any place refuses to welcome you or listen to you, shake its dust from your feet as you leave to show that you have abandoned those people to their fate."

¹²So the disciples went out, telling everyone they met to repent of their sins and turn to God. ¹³And they cast out many demons and healed many sick people, anointing them with olive oil.

¹⁴Herod Antipas, the king, soon heard about Jesus, because everyone was talking about him. Some were saying,* "This must be John the Baptist raised from the dead. That is why he can do such miracles." ¹⁵Others said, "He's the prophet Elijah." Still others said, "He's a prophet like the other great prophets of the past."

¹⁶When Herod heard about Jesus, he said, "John, the man I beheaded, has come back from the dead."

¹⁷For Herod had sent soldiers to arrest and imprison John as a favor to Herodias. She had been his brother Philip's wife, but Herod had married her. ¹⁸John had been telling Herod, "It is against God's law for you to marry your brother's wife." ¹⁹So Herodias bore a grudge against John and wanted to kill him. But without Herod's approval she was powerless, ²⁰for Herod respected John; and knowing that he was a good and holy man, he protected him. Herod was greatly disturbed whenever he talked with John, but even so, he liked to listen to him.

²¹Herodias's chance finally came on Herod's birthday. He gave a party for his high government officials, army officers, and the leading citizens of Galilee. ²²Then his daughter, also named Herodias,* came in and performed a dance that greatly pleased Herod and his guests. "Ask me for anything you like," the king said to the girl, "and I will give it to you." ²³He even vowed, "I will give you whatever you ask, up to half my kingdom!"

²⁴She went out and asked her mother, "What should I ask for?"

Her mother told her, "Ask for the head of John the Baptist!"

²⁵So the girl hurried back to the king and told him, "I want the head of John the Baptist, right now, on a tray!"

²⁶Then the king deeply regretted what he had said; but because of the vows he had made in front of his guests, he couldn't refuse her. ²⁷So he immediately sent an executioner to the prison to cut off John's head and bring it to him. The soldier beheaded John in the prison, ²⁸brought his head on a tray, and gave it to the girl, who took it to her mother. ²⁹When John's disciples heard what had happened, they came to get his body and buried it in a tomb.

6:3a Some manuscripts read *He's just the son of the carpenter and of Mary.*   6:3b Most manuscripts read *Joses;* see Matt 13:55.   6:7 Greek *unclean.*   6:8 Greek *no copper coins in their money belts.*   6:14 Some manuscripts read *He was saying.*   6:22 Some manuscripts read *the daughter of Herodias herself.*

## PSALM 39:1-13
*For Jeduthun, the choir director: A psalm of David.*

¹ **I** said to myself, "I will watch
    what I do
    and not sin in what I say.
  I will hold my tongue
    when the ungodly are
    around me."
² But as I stood there in silence—
    not even speaking of good
    things—
  the turmoil within me
    grew worse.
³ The more I thought about it,

the hotter I got,
igniting a fire of words:
⁴ "LORD, remind me how brief my
time on earth will be.
Remind me that my days are
numbered—
how fleeting my life is.
⁵ You have made my life no longer
than the width of my hand.
My entire lifetime is just a
moment to you;
at best, each of us is but
a breath."                    *Interlude*

⁶ We are merely moving shadows,
and all our busy rushing ends in
nothing.
We heap up wealth,
not knowing who will spend it.
⁷ And so, Lord, where do I put my
hope?
My only hope is in you.
⁸ Rescue me from my rebellion.
Do not let fools mock me.
⁹ I am silent before you; I won't
say a word,
for my punishment is from you.
¹⁰ But please stop striking me!
I am exhausted by the blows
from your hand.
¹¹ When you discipline us for our sins,
you consume like a moth what is
precious to us.
Each of us is but a breath.
                              *Interlude*

¹² Hear my prayer, O LORD!
Listen to my cries for help!
Don't ignore my tears.
For I am your guest—
a traveler passing through,
as my ancestors were before me.
¹³ Leave me alone so I can smile again
before I am gone and exist
no more.

PROVERBS 10:10

People who wink at wrong cause trouble, but a bold reproof promotes peace.*

10:10 As in Greek version; Hebrew reads *but babbling fools
fall flat on their faces.*

# FEBRUARY
# 23

LEVITICUS 14:1-57

And the LORD said to Moses, ²"The following instructions are for those seeking ceremonial purification from a skin disease.* Those who have been healed must be brought to the priest, ³who will examine them at a place outside the camp. If the priest finds that someone has been healed of a serious skin disease, ⁴he will perform a purification ceremony, using two live birds that are ceremonially clean, a stick of cedar,* some scarlet yarn, and a hyssop branch. ⁵The priest will order that one bird be slaughtered over a clay pot filled with fresh water. ⁶He will take the live bird, the cedar stick, the scarlet yarn, and the hyssop branch, and dip them into the blood of the bird that was slaughtered over the fresh water. ⁷The priest will then sprinkle the blood of the dead bird seven times on the person being purified of the skin disease. When the priest has purified the person, he will release the live bird in the open field to fly away.

⁸"The persons being purified must then wash their clothes, shave off all their hair, and bathe themselves in water. Then they will be ceremonially clean and may return to the camp. However, they must remain outside their tents for seven days. ⁹On the seventh day they must again shave all the hair from their heads, including the hair of the beard and eyebrows. They must also wash their clothes and bathe themselves in water. Then they will be ceremonially clean.

¹⁰"On the eighth day each person being purified must bring two male lambs and a one-year-old female lamb, all with no defects, along with a grain offering of six quarts* of choice flour moistened with olive oil, and a cup* of olive oil. ¹¹Then the officiating priest will present that person for purification, along with the offerings, before the LORD at

the entrance of the Tabernacle.* [12] The priest will take one of the male lambs and the olive oil and present them as a guilt offering, lifting them up as a special offering before the LORD. [13] He will then slaughter the male lamb in the sacred area where sin offerings and burnt offerings are slaughtered. As with the sin offering, the guilt offering belongs to the priest. It is a most holy offering. [14] The priest will then take some of the blood of the guilt offering and apply it to the lobe of the right ear, the thumb of the right hand, and the big toe of the right foot of the person being purified.

[15] "Then the priest will pour some of the olive oil into the palm of his own left hand. [16] He will dip his right finger into the oil in his palm and sprinkle some of it with his finger seven times before the LORD. [17] The priest will then apply some of the oil in his palm over the blood from the guilt offering that is on the lobe of the right ear, the thumb of the right hand, and the big toe of the right foot of the person being purified. [18] The priest will apply the oil remaining in his hand to the head of the person being purified. Through this process, the priest will purify* the person before the LORD.

[19] "Then the priest must present the sin offering to purify the person who was cured of the skin disease. After that, the priest will slaughter the burnt offering [20] and offer it on the altar along with the grain offering. Through this process, the priest will purify the person who was healed, and the person will be ceremonially clean.

[21] "But anyone who is too poor and cannot afford these offerings may bring one male lamb for a guilt offering, to be lifted up as a special offering for purification. The person must also bring two quarts* of choice flour moistened with olive oil for the grain offering and a cup of olive oil. [22] The offering must also include two turtledoves or two young pigeons, whichever the person can afford. One of the pair must be used for the sin offering and the other for a burnt offering. [23] On the eighth day of the purifica-

tion ceremony, the person being purified must bring the offerings to the priest in the LORD's presence at the entrance of the Tabernacle. [24] The priest will take the lamb for the guilt offering, along with the olive oil, and lift them up as a special offering to the LORD. [25] Then the priest will slaughter the lamb for the guilt offering. He will take some of its blood and apply it to the lobe of the right ear, the thumb of the right hand, and the big toe of the right foot of the person being purified.

[26] "The priest will also pour some of the olive oil into the palm of his own left hand. [27] He will dip his right finger into the oil in his palm and sprinkle some of it seven times before the LORD. [28] The priest will then apply some of the oil in his palm over the blood from the guilt offering that is on the lobe of the right ear, the thumb of the right hand, and the big toe of the right foot of the person being purified. [29] The priest will apply the oil remaining in his hand to the head of the person being purified. Through this process, the priest will purify the person before the LORD.

[30] "Then the priest will offer the two turtledoves or the two young pigeons, whichever the person can afford. [31] One of them is for a sin offering and the other for a burnt offering, to be presented along with the grain offering. Through this process, the priest will purify the person before the LORD. [32] These are the instructions for purification for those who have recovered from a serious skin disease but who cannot afford to bring the offerings normally required for the ceremony of purification."

[33] Then the LORD said to Moses and Aaron, [34] "When you arrive in Canaan, the land I am giving you as your own possession, I may contaminate some of the houses in your land with mildew.* [35] The owner of such a house must then go to the priest and say, 'It appears that my house has some kind of mildew.' [36] Before the priest goes in to inspect the house, he must have the house emptied so nothing inside will be pronounced ceremonially unclean. [37] Then the priest

will go in and examine the mildew on the walls. If he finds greenish or reddish streaks and the contamination appears to go deeper than the wall's surface, [38] the priest will step outside the door and put the house in quarantine for seven days. [39] On the seventh day the priest must return for another inspection. If he finds that the mildew on the walls of the house has spread, [40] the priest must order that the stones from those areas be removed. The contaminated material will then be taken outside the town to an area designated as ceremonially unclean. [41] Next the inside walls of the entire house must be scraped thoroughly and the scrapings dumped in the unclean place outside the town. [42] Other stones will be brought in to replace the ones that were removed, and the walls will be replastered.

[43] "But if the mildew reappears after all the stones have been replaced and the house has been scraped and replastered, [44] the priest must return and inspect the house again. If he finds that the mildew has spread, the walls are clearly contaminated with a serious mildew, and the house is defiled. [45] It must be torn down, and all its stones, timbers, and plaster must be carried out of town to the place designated as ceremonially unclean. [46] Those who enter the house during the period of quarantine will be ceremonially unclean until evening, [47] and all who sleep or eat in the house must wash their clothing.

[48] "But if the priest returns for his inspection and finds that the mildew has not reappeared in the house after the fresh plastering, he will pronounce it clean because the mildew is clearly gone. [49] To purify the house the priest must take two birds, a stick of cedar, some scarlet yarn, and a hyssop branch. [50] He will slaughter one of the birds over a clay pot filled with fresh water. [51] He will take the cedar stick, the hyssop branch, the scarlet yarn, and the live bird, and dip them into the blood of the slaughtered bird and into the fresh water. Then he will sprinkle the house seven times. [52] When the priest has purified the

house in exactly this way, [53] he will release the live bird in the open fields outside the town. Through this process, the priest will purify the house, and it will be ceremonially clean.

[54] "These are the instructions for dealing with serious skin diseases,* including scabby sores; [55] and mildew,* whether on clothing or in a house; [56] and a swelling on the skin, a rash, or discolored skin. [57] This procedure will determine whether a person or object is ceremonially clean or unclean.

"These are the instructions regarding skin diseases and mildew."

14:2 Traditionally rendered *leprosy;* see note on 13:2a. 14:4 Or *juniper;* also in 14:6, 49, 51.   14:10a Hebrew ³⁄₁₀ *of an ephah* (6.6 liters).   14:10b Hebrew *1 log* (0.3 liters); also in 14:21.   14:11 Hebrew *Tent of Meeting;* also in 14:23.   14:18 Or *will make atonement for;* similarly in 14:19, 20, 21, 29, 31, 53.   14:21 Hebrew ¹⁄₁₀ *of an ephah* (2.2 liters).   14:34 Traditionally rendered *leprosy;* see note on 13:47.   14:54 Traditionally rendered *leprosy;* see note on 13:2a.   14:55 Traditionally rendered *leprosy;* see note on 13:47.

## MARK 6:30-56

The apostles returned to Jesus from their ministry tour and told him all they had done and taught. [31] Then Jesus said, "Let's go off by ourselves to a quiet place and rest awhile." He said this because there were so many people coming and going that Jesus and his apostles didn't even have time to eat.

[32] So they left by boat for a quiet place, where they could be alone. [33] But many people recognized them and saw them leaving, and people from many towns ran ahead along the shore and got there ahead of them. [34] Jesus saw the huge crowd as he stepped from the boat, and he had compassion on them because they were like sheep without a shepherd. So he began teaching them many things.

[35] Late in the afternoon his disciples came to him and said, "This is a remote place, and it's already getting late. [36] Send the crowds away so they can go to the nearby farms and villages and buy something to eat."

[37] But Jesus said, "You feed them."

"With what?" they asked. "We'd have to work for months to earn enough money* to buy food for all these people!"

<sup>38</sup>"How much bread do you have?" he asked. "Go and find out."

They came back and reported, "We have five loaves of bread and two fish."

<sup>39</sup>Then Jesus told the disciples to have the people sit down in groups on the green grass. <sup>40</sup>So they sat down in groups of fifty or a hundred.

<sup>41</sup>Jesus took the five loaves and two fish, looked up toward heaven, and blessed them. Then, breaking the loaves into pieces, he kept giving the bread to the disciples so they could distribute it to the people. He also divided the fish for everyone to share. <sup>42</sup>They all ate as much as they wanted, <sup>43</sup>and afterward, the disciples picked up twelve baskets of leftover bread and fish. <sup>44</sup>A total of 5,000 men and their families were fed from those loaves!

<sup>45</sup>Immediately after this, Jesus insisted that his disciples get back into the boat and head across the lake to Bethsaida, while he sent the people home. <sup>46</sup>After telling everyone good-bye, he went up into the hills by himself to pray.

<sup>47</sup>Late that night, the disciples were in their boat in the middle of the lake, and Jesus was alone on land. <sup>48</sup>He saw that they were in serious trouble, rowing hard and struggling against the wind and waves. About three o'clock in the morning* Jesus came toward them, walking on the water. He intended to go past them, <sup>49</sup>but when they saw him walking on the water, they cried out in terror, thinking he was a ghost. <sup>50</sup>They were all terrified when they saw him.

But Jesus spoke to them at once. "Don't be afraid," he said. "Take courage! I am here!*" <sup>51</sup>Then he climbed into the boat, and the wind stopped. They were totally amazed, <sup>52</sup>for they still didn't understand the significance of the miracle of the loaves. Their hearts were too hard to take it in.

<sup>53</sup>After they had crossed the lake, they landed at Gennesaret. They brought the boat to shore <sup>54</sup>and climbed out. The people recognized Jesus at once, <sup>55</sup>and they ran throughout the whole area, carrying sick people on mats to wherever they heard he was. <sup>56</sup>Wherever he went—in villages, cities, or the countryside—they brought the sick out to the marketplaces. They begged him to let the sick touch at least the fringe of his robe, and all who touched him were healed.

6:37 Greek *It would take 200 denarii.* A denarius was equivalent to a laborer's full day's wage. 6:48 Greek *About the fourth watch of the night.* 6:50 Or *The 'I Am' is here;* Greek reads *I am.* See Exod 3:14.

## PSALM 40:1-10
*For the choir director: A psalm of David.*

<sup>1</sup> I waited patiently for the LORD
  to help me,
  and he turned to me and heard
  my cry.
<sup>2</sup> He lifted me out of the pit
  of despair,
  out of the mud and the mire.
He set my feet on solid ground
  and steadied me as I walked
  along.
<sup>3</sup> He has given me a new song to sing,
  a hymn of praise to our God.
Many will see what he has done and
  be amazed.
  They will put their trust in
  the LORD.

<sup>4</sup> Oh, the joys of those who trust
  the LORD,
  who have no confidence in
  the proud
  or in those who worship idols.
<sup>5</sup> O LORD my God, you have
  performed many wonders
  for us.
Your plans for us are too
  numerous to list.
  You have no equal.
If I tried to recite all your wonderful
  deeds,
  I would never come to the
  end of them.

<sup>6</sup> You take no delight in sacrifices
  or offerings.
Now that you have made me
  listen, I finally understand*—
you don't require burnt offerings
  or sin offerings.
<sup>7</sup> Then I said, "Look, I have come.

As is written about me in the Scriptures:

⁸ I take joy in doing your will, my God,
for your instructions are written
on my heart."

⁹ I have told all your people about
your justice.
I have not been afraid to
speak out,
as you, O LORD, well know.
¹⁰ I have not kept the good news of
your justice hidden in my heart;
I have talked about your
faithfulness and saving power.
I have told everyone in the great
assembly
of your unfailing love and
faithfulness.

**40:6** Greek text reads *You have given me a body.*
Compare Heb 10:5.

## PROVERBS 10:11-12

The words of the godly are a life-giving fountain; the words of the wicked conceal violent intentions. □ Hatred stirs up quarrels, but love makes up for all offenses.

# FEBRUARY
# 24

## LEVITICUS 15:1–16:28

The LORD said to Moses and Aaron, ²"Give the following instructions to the people of Israel.

"Any man who has a bodily discharge is ceremonially unclean. ³This defilement is caused by his discharge, whether the discharge continues or stops. In either case the man is unclean. ⁴Any bed on which the man with the discharge lies and anything on which he sits will be ceremonially unclean. ⁵So if you touch the man's bed, you must wash your clothes and bathe yourself in water, and you will remain unclean until evening.

⁶If you sit where the man with the discharge has sat, you must wash your clothes and bathe yourself in water, and you will remain unclean until evening. ⁷If you touch the man with the discharge, you must wash your clothes and bathe yourself in water, and you will remain unclean until evening. ⁸If the man spits on you, you must wash your clothes and bathe yourself in water, and you will remain unclean until evening. ⁹Any saddle blanket on which the man rides will be ceremonially unclean. ¹⁰If you touch anything that was under the man, you will be unclean until evening. You must wash your clothes and bathe yourself in water, and you will remain unclean until evening. ¹¹If the man touches you without first rinsing his hands, you must wash your clothes and bathe yourself in water, and you will remain unclean until evening. ¹²Any clay pot the man touches must be broken, and any wooden utensil he touches must be rinsed with water.

¹³"When the man with the discharge is healed, he must count off seven days for the period of purification. Then he must wash his clothes and bathe himself in fresh water, and he will be ceremonially clean. ¹⁴On the eighth day he must get two turtledoves or two young pigeons and come before the LORD at the entrance of the Tabernacle* and give his offerings to the priest. ¹⁵The priest will offer one bird for a sin offering and the other for a burnt offering. Through this process, the priest will purify* the man before the LORD for his discharge.

¹⁶"Whenever a man has an emission of semen, he must bathe his entire body in water, and he will remain ceremonially unclean until the next evening.* ¹⁷Any clothing or leather with semen on it must be washed in water, and it will remain unclean until evening. ¹⁸After a man and a woman have sexual intercourse, they must each bathe in water, and they will remain unclean until the next evening.

¹⁹"Whenever a woman has her menstrual period, she will be ceremonially unclean for seven days. Anyone who

touches her during that time will be unclean until evening. ²⁰Anything on which the woman lies or sits during the time of her period will be unclean. ²¹If any of you touch her bed, you must wash your clothes and bathe yourself in water, and you will remain unclean until evening. ²²If you touch any object she has sat on, you must wash your clothes and bathe yourself in water, and you will remain unclean until evening. ²³This includes her bed or any other object she has sat on; you will be unclean until evening if you touch it. ²⁴If a man has sexual intercourse with her and her blood touches him, her menstrual impurity will be transmitted to him. He will remain unclean for seven days, and any bed on which he lies will be unclean.

²⁵"If a woman has a flow of blood for many days that is unrelated to her menstrual period, or if the blood continues beyond the normal period, she is ceremonially unclean. As during her menstrual period, the woman will be unclean as long as the discharge continues. ²⁶Any bed she lies on and any object she sits on during that time will be unclean, just as during her normal menstrual period. ²⁷If any of you touch these things, you will be ceremonially unclean. You must wash your clothes and bathe yourself in water, and you will remain unclean until evening.

²⁸"When the woman's bleeding stops, she must count off seven days. Then she will be ceremonially clean. ²⁹On the eighth day she must bring two turtledoves or two young pigeons and present them to the priest at the entrance of the Tabernacle. ³⁰The priest will offer one for a sin offering and the other for a burnt offering. Through this process, the priest will purify her before the LORD for the ceremonial impurity caused by her bleeding.

³¹"This is how you will guard the people of Israel from ceremonial uncleanness. Otherwise they would die, for their impurity would defile my Tabernacle that stands among them. ³²These are the instructions for dealing with anyone who has a bodily discharge—a man who is unclean because of an emission of semen ³³or a woman during her menstrual period. It applies to any man or woman who has a bodily discharge, and to a man who has sexual intercourse with a woman who is ceremonially unclean."

¹⁶:¹THE LORD spoke to Moses after the death of Aaron's two sons, who died after they entered the LORD's presence and burned the wrong kind of fire before him. ²The LORD said to Moses, "Warn your brother, Aaron, not to enter the Most Holy Place behind the inner curtain whenever he chooses; if he does, he will die. For the Ark's cover—the place of atonement—is there, and I myself am present in the cloud above the atonement cover.

³"When Aaron enters the sanctuary area, he must follow these instructions fully. He must bring a young bull for a sin offering and a ram for a burnt offering. ⁴He must put on his linen tunic and the linen undergarments worn next to his body. He must tie the linen sash around his waist and put the linen turban on his head. These are sacred garments, so he must bathe himself in water before he puts them on. ⁵Aaron must take from the community of Israel two male goats for a sin offering and a ram for a burnt offering.

⁶"Aaron will present his own bull as a sin offering to purify himself and his family, making them right with the LORD.* ⁷Then he must take the two male goats and present them to the LORD at the entrance of the Tabernacle.* ⁸He is to cast sacred lots to determine which goat will be reserved as an offering to the LORD and which will carry the sins of the people to the wilderness of Azazel. ⁹Aaron will then present as a sin offering the goat chosen by lot for the LORD. ¹⁰The other goat, the scapegoat chosen by lot to be sent away, will be kept alive, standing before the LORD. When it is sent away to Azazel in the wilderness, the people will be purified and made right with the LORD.*

[11]"Aaron will present his own bull as a sin offering to purify himself and his family, making them right with the LORD. After he has slaughtered the bull as a sin offering, [12]he will fill an incense burner with burning coals from the altar that stands before the LORD. Then he will take two handfuls of fragrant powdered incense and will carry the burner and the incense behind the inner curtain. [13]There in the LORD's presence he will put the incense on the burning coals so that a cloud of incense will rise over the Ark's cover—the place of atonement—that rests on the Ark of the Covenant.* If he follows these instructions, he will not die. [14]Then he must take some of the blood of the bull, dip his finger in it, and sprinkle it on the east side of the atonement cover. He must sprinkle blood seven times with his finger in front of the atonement cover.

[15]"Then Aaron must slaughter the first goat as a sin offering for the people and carry its blood behind the inner curtain. There he will sprinkle the goat's blood over the atonement cover and in front of it, just as he did with the bull's blood. [16]Through this process, he will purify* the Most Holy Place, and he will do the same for the entire Tabernacle, because of the defiling sin and rebellion of the Israelites. [17]No one else is allowed inside the Tabernacle when Aaron enters it for the purification ceremony in the Most Holy Place. No one may enter until he comes out again after purifying himself, his family, and all the congregation of Israel, making them right with the LORD.

[18]"Then Aaron will come out to purify the altar that stands before the LORD. He will do this by taking some of the blood from the bull and the goat and putting it on each of the horns of the altar. [19]Then he must sprinkle the blood with his finger seven times over the altar. In this way, he will cleanse it from Israel's defilement and make it holy.

[20]"When Aaron has finished purifying the Most Holy Place and the Tabernacle and the altar, he must present the live goat. [21]He will lay both of his hands on the goat's head and confess over it all the wickedness, rebellion, and sins of the people of Israel. In this way, he will transfer the people's sins to the head of the goat. Then a man specially chosen for the task will drive the goat into the wilderness. [22]As the goat goes into the wilderness, it will carry all the people's sins upon itself into a desolate land.

[23]"When Aaron goes back into the Tabernacle, he must take off the linen garments he was wearing when he entered the Most Holy Place, and he must leave the garments there. [24]Then he must bathe himself with water in a sacred place, put on his regular garments, and go out to sacrifice a burnt offering for himself and a burnt offering for the people. Through this process, he will purify himself and the people, making them right with the LORD. [25]He must then burn all the fat of the sin offering on the altar.

[26]"The man chosen to drive the scapegoat into the wilderness of Azazel must wash his clothes and bathe himself in water. Then he may return to the camp.

[27]"The bull and the goat presented as sin offerings, whose blood Aaron takes into the Most Holy Place for the purification ceremony, will be carried outside the camp. The animals' hides, internal organs, and dung are all to be burned. [28]The man who burns them must wash his clothes and bathe himself in water before returning to the camp."

15:14 Hebrew Tent of Meeting; also in 15:29.   15:15 Or will make atonement for; also in 15:30.   15:16 Hebrew until evening; also in 15:18.   16:6 Or to make atonement for himself and his family; similarly in 16:11, 17b, 24, 34.   16:7 Hebrew Tent of Meeting; also in 16:16, 17, 20, 23, 33.   16:10 Or wilderness, it will make atonement for the people.   16:13 Hebrew that is above the Testimony. The Hebrew word for "testimony" refers to the terms of the LORD's covenant with Israel as written on stone tablets, which were kept in the Ark, and also to the covenant itself.   16:16 Or make atonement for; similarly in 16:17a, 18, 20, 27, 33.

## MARK 7:1-23

**O**ne day some Pharisees and teachers of religious law arrived from Jerusalem to see Jesus. [2]They noticed that some of his disciples failed to follow the Jewish ritual of hand washing before eating. 3(The Jews, especially the Pharisees, do not eat until they have poured water over their cupped hands,* as required by their ancient traditions. 4Similarly, they don't eat anything from the market until they immerse their hands* in water. This is but one of many traditions they have clung to—such as their ceremonial washing of cups, pitchers, and kettles.*)

5So the Pharisees and teachers of religious law asked him, "Why don't your disciples follow our age-old tradition? They eat without first performing the hand-washing ceremony."

6Jesus replied, "You hypocrites! Isaiah was right when he prophesied about you, for he wrote,

'These people honor me with
     their lips,
   but their hearts are far from me.
7  Their worship is a farce,
   for they teach man-made ideas
     as commands from God.'*

8For you ignore God's law and substitute your own tradition."

9Then he said, "You skillfully sidestep God's law in order to hold on to your own tradition. 10For instance, Moses gave you this law from God: 'Honor your father and mother,'* and 'Anyone who speaks disrespectfully of father or mother must be put to death.'* 11But you say it is all right for people to say to their parents, 'Sorry, I can't help you. For I have vowed to give to God what I would have given to you.'* 12In this way, you let them disregard their needy parents. 13And so you cancel the word of God in order to hand down your own tradition. And this is only one example among many others."

14**Then Jesus called to the crowd to come and hear. "All of you listen," he said, "and try to understand. 15It's not what goes into your body that defiles you; you are defiled by what comes from your heart.***"

17Then Jesus went into a house to get away from the crowd, and his disciples asked him what he meant by the parable he had just used. 18"Don't you understand either?" he asked. "Can't you see that the food you put into your body cannot defile you? 19Food doesn't go into your heart, but only passes through the stomach and then goes into the sewer." (By saying this, he declared that every kind of food is acceptable in God's eyes.)

20And then he added, "It is what comes from inside that defiles you. 21For from within, out of a person's heart, come evil thoughts, sexual immorality, theft, murder, 22adultery, greed, wickedness, deceit, lustful desires, envy, slander, pride, and foolishness. 23All these vile things come from within; they are what defile you."

7:3 Greek *have washed with the fist.*   7:4a Some manuscripts read *sprinkle themselves.*   7:4b Some manuscripts add *and dining couches.*   7:7 Isa 29:13 (Greek version).   7:10a Exod 20:12; Deut 5:16. 7:10b Exod 21:17 (Greek version); Lev 20:9 (Greek version). 7:11 Greek *'What I would have given to you is Corban' (that is, a gift).*   7:15 Some manuscripts add verse 16, *Anyone with ears to hear should listen and understand.* Compare 4:9, 23.

## PSALM 40:11-17

Lᴏʀᴅ, don't hold back your tender
     mercies from me.
   Let your unfailing love and
     faithfulness always protect me.
12 For troubles surround me—
     too many to count!
   My sins pile up so high
     I can't see my way out.
   They outnumber the hairs on
     my head.
   I have lost all courage.

13 Please, Lᴏʀᴅ, rescue me!
     Come quickly, Lᴏʀᴅ, and
     help me.
14 May those who try to destroy me
     be humiliated and put to shame.
   May those who take delight in my
     trouble
     be turned back in disgrace.
15 Let them be horrified by their shame,
     for they said, "Aha! We've got him
     now!"

¹⁶ But may all who search for you
  be filled with joy and gladness
  in you.
May those who love your salvation
  repeatedly shout, "The LORD
  is great!"
¹⁷ As for me, since I am poor and
  needy,
  let the Lord keep me in his
  thoughts.
You are my helper and my savior.
  O my God, do not delay.

PROVERBS 10:13-14

**W**ise words come from the lips of people with understanding, but those lacking sense will be beaten with a rod. □ Wise people treasure knowledge, but the babbling of a fool invites disaster.

# FEBRUARY
# 25

LEVITICUS 16:29–18:30

"**O**n the tenth day of the appointed month in early autumn,* you must deny yourselves.* Neither native-born Israelites nor foreigners living among you may do any kind of work. This is a permanent law for you. ³⁰On that day offerings of purification will be made for you,* and you will be purified in the LORD's presence from all your sins. ³¹It will be a Sabbath day of complete rest for you, and you must deny yourselves. This is a permanent law for you. ³²In future generations, the purification* ceremony will be performed by the priest who has been anointed and ordained to serve as high priest in place of his ancestor Aaron. He will put on the holy linen garments ³³and purify the Most Holy Place, the Tabernacle, the altar, the priests, and the entire congregation. ³⁴This is a permanent law for you, to purify the people of Israel from their sins, making them right with the LORD once each year."

Moses followed all these instructions exactly as the LORD had commanded him.

¹⁷:¹THEN the LORD said to Moses, ²"Give the following instructions to Aaron and his sons and all the people of Israel. This is what the LORD has commanded.

³"If any native Israelite sacrifices a bull* or a lamb or a goat anywhere inside or outside the camp ⁴instead of bringing it to the entrance of the Tabernacle* to present it as an offering to the LORD, that person will be as guilty as a murderer.* Such a person has shed blood and will be cut off from the community. ⁵The purpose of this rule is to stop the Israelites from sacrificing animals in the open fields. It will ensure that they bring their sacrifices to the priest at the entrance of the Tabernacle, so he can present them to the LORD as peace offerings. ⁶Then the priest will be able to splatter the blood against the LORD's altar at the entrance of the Tabernacle, and he will burn the fat as a pleasing aroma to the LORD. ⁷The people must no longer be unfaithful to the LORD by offering sacrifices to the goat idols.* This is a permanent law for them, to be observed from generation to generation.

⁸"Give them this command as well. If any native Israelite or foreigner living among you offers a burnt offering or a sacrifice ⁹but does not bring it to the entrance of the Tabernacle to offer it to the LORD, that person will be cut off from the community.

¹⁰"And if any native Israelite or foreigner living among you eats or drinks blood in any form, I will turn against that person and cut him off from the community of your people, ¹¹for the life of the body is in its blood. I have given you the blood on the altar to purify you, making you right with the LORD.* It is the blood, given in exchange for a life, that makes purification possible. ¹²That is why I have said to the people of Israel, 'You must never eat or drink blood—neither you nor the foreigners living among you.'

¹³"And if any native Israelite or foreigner living among you goes hunting

and kills an animal or bird that is approved for eating, he must drain its blood and cover it with earth. [14]The life of every creature is in its blood. That is why I have said to the people of Israel, 'You must never eat or drink blood, for the life of any creature is in its blood.' So whoever consumes blood will be cut off from the community.

[15]"And if any native-born Israelites or foreigners eat the meat of an animal that died naturally or was torn up by wild animals, they must wash their clothes and bathe themselves in water. They will remain ceremonially unclean until evening, but then they will be clean. [16]But if they do not wash their clothes and bathe themselves, they will be punished for their sin."

[18:1]THEN the LORD said to Moses, [2]"Give the following instructions to the people of Israel. I am the LORD your God. [3]So do not act like the people in Egypt, where you used to live, or like the people of Canaan, where I am taking you. You must not imitate their way of life. [4]You must obey all my regulations and be careful to obey my decrees, for I am the LORD your God. [5]If you obey my decrees and my regulations, you will find life through them. I am the LORD.

[6]"You must never have sexual relations with a close relative, for I am the LORD.

[7]"Do not violate your father by having sexual relations with your mother. She is your mother; you must not have sexual relations with her.

[8]"Do not have sexual relations with any of your father's wives, for this would violate your father.

[9]"Do not have sexual relations with your sister or half sister, whether she is your father's daughter or your mother's daughter, whether she was born into your household or someone else's.

[10]"Do not have sexual relations with your granddaughter, whether she is your son's daughter or your daughter's daughter, for this would violate yourself.

[11]"Do not have sexual relations with your stepsister, the daughter of any of your father's wives, for she is your sister.

[12]"Do not have sexual relations with your father's sister, for she is your father's close relative.

[13]"Do not have sexual relations with your mother's sister, for she is your mother's close relative.

[14]"Do not violate your uncle, your father's brother, by having sexual relations with his wife, for she is your aunt.

[15]"Do not have sexual relations with your daughter-in-law; she is your son's wife, so you must not have sexual relations with her.

[16]"Do not have sexual relations with your brother's wife, for this would violate your brother.

[17]"Do not have sexual relations with both a woman and her daughter. And do not take* her granddaughter, whether her son's daughter or her daughter's daughter, and have sexual relations with her. They are close relatives, and this would be a wicked act.

[18]"While your wife is living, do not marry her sister and have sexual relations with her, for they would be rivals.

[19]"Do not have sexual relations with a woman during her period of menstrual impurity.

[20]"Do not defile yourself by having sexual intercourse with your neighbor's wife.

[21]"Do not permit any of your children to be offered as a sacrifice to Molech, for you must not bring shame on the name of your God. I am the LORD.

[22]"Do not practice homosexuality, having sex with another man as with a woman. It is a detestable sin.

[23]"A man must not defile himself by having sex with an animal. And a woman must not offer herself to a male animal to have intercourse with it. This is a perverse act.

[24]"Do not defile yourselves in any of these ways, for the people I am driving out before you have defiled themselves in all these ways. [25]Because the entire land has become defiled, I am punishing the people who live there. I will cause the

land to vomit them out. ²⁶You must obey all my decrees and regulations. You must not commit any of these detestable sins. This applies both to native-born Israelites and to the foreigners living among you.

²⁷"All these detestable activities are practiced by the people of the land where I am taking you, and this is how the land has become defiled. ²⁸So do not defile the land and give it a reason to vomit you out, as it will vomit out the people who live there now. ²⁹Whoever commits any of these detestable sins will be cut off from the community of Israel. ³⁰So obey my instructions, and do not defile yourselves by committing any of these detestable practices that were committed by the people who lived in the land before you. I am the Lᴏʀᴅ your God."

16:29a Hebrew *On the tenth day of the seventh month.* This day in the ancient Hebrew lunar calendar occurred in September or October.    16:29b Or *must fast;* also in 16:31.    16:30 Or *atonement will be made for you, to purify you.*    16:32 Or *atonement.*    17:3 Or *cow.* 17:4a Hebrew *Tent of Meeting;* also in 17:5, 6, 9. 17:4b Hebrew *will be guilty of blood.*    17:7 Or *goat demons.*    17:11 Or *to make atonement for you.* 18:17 Or *do not marry.*

## MARK 7:24–8:10

Then Jesus left Galilee and went north to the region of Tyre.* He didn't want anyone to know which house he was staying in, but he couldn't keep it a secret. ²⁵Right away a woman who had heard about him came and fell at his feet. Her little girl was possessed by an evil* spirit, ²⁶and she begged him to cast out the demon from her daughter.

Since she was a Gentile, born in Syrian Phoenicia, ²⁷Jesus told her, "First I should feed the children—my own family, the Jews.* It isn't right to take food from the children and throw it to the dogs."

²⁸She replied, "That's true, Lord, but even the dogs under the table are allowed to eat the scraps from the children's plates."

²⁹"Good answer!" he said. "Now go home, for the demon has left your daughter." ³⁰And when she arrived home, she found her little girl lying quietly in bed, and the demon was gone.

³¹Jesus left Tyre and went up to Sidon before going back to the Sea of Galilee and the region of the Ten Towns.* ³²A deaf man with a speech impediment was brought to him, and the people begged Jesus to lay his hands on the man to heal him.

³³Jesus led him away from the crowd so they could be alone. He put his fingers into the man's ears. Then, spitting on his own fingers, he touched the man's tongue. ³⁴Looking up to heaven, he sighed and said, "*Ephphatha,*" which means, "Be opened!" ³⁵Instantly the man could hear perfectly, and his tongue was freed so he could speak plainly!

³⁶Jesus told the crowd not to tell anyone, but the more he told them not to, the more they spread the news. ³⁷They were completely amazed and said again and again, "Everything he does is wonderful. He even makes the deaf to hear and gives speech to those who cannot speak."

8:1Aʙᴏᴜᴛ this time another large crowd had gathered, and the people ran out of food again. Jesus called his disciples and told them, ²"I feel sorry for these people. They have been here with me for three days, and they have nothing left to eat. ³If I send them home hungry, they will faint along the way. For some of them have come a long distance."

⁴His disciples replied, "How are we supposed to find enough food to feed them out here in the wilderness?"

⁵Jesus asked, "How much bread do you have?"

"Seven loaves," they replied.

⁶So Jesus told all the people to sit down on the ground. Then he took the seven loaves, thanked God for them, and broke them into pieces. He gave them to his disciples, who distributed the bread to the crowd. ⁷A few small fish were found, too, so Jesus also blessed these and told the disciples to distribute them.

⁸They ate as much as they wanted. Afterward, the disciples picked up seven large baskets of leftover food. ⁹There were about 4,000 people in the crowd that day, and Jesus sent them home after they had

eaten. [10]Immediately after this, he got into a boat with his disciples and crossed over to the region of Dalmanutha.

7:24 Some manuscripts add *and Sidon*.    7:25 Greek *unclean*.    7:27 Greek *Let the children eat first*. 7:31 Greek *Decapolis*.

## PSALM 41:1-13
*For the choir director: A psalm of David.*

[1] **Oh, the joys of those who are kind to the poor!**
**The Lord rescues them when they are in trouble.**
[2] The Lord protects them
    and keeps them alive.
He gives them prosperity in
        the land
    and rescues them from their
        enemies.
[3] The Lord nurses them when they
        are sick
    and restores them to health.

[4] "O Lord," I prayed, "have mercy
        on me.
    Heal me, for I have sinned
        against you."
[5] But my enemies say nothing but
        evil about me.
    "How soon will he die and be
        forgotten?" they ask.
[6] They visit me as if they were
        my friends,
    but all the while they gather
        gossip,
    and when they leave, they spread
        it everywhere.
[7] All who hate me whisper about me,
    imagining the worst.
[8] "He has some fatal disease," they
        say.
    "He will never get out of that bed!"
[9] Even my best friend, the one I
        trusted completely,
    the one who shared my food,
        has turned against me.

[10] Lord, have mercy on me.
    Make me well again, so I can pay
        them back!
[11] I know you are pleased with me,
    for you have not let my enemies
        triumph over me.

[12] You have preserved my life because
        I am innocent;
    you have brought me into your
        presence forever.

[13] Praise the Lord, the God of Israel,
    who lives from everlasting to
        everlasting.
    Amen and amen!

## PROVERBS 10:15-16
The wealth of the rich is their fortress; the poverty of the poor is their destruction. □ The earnings of the godly enhance their lives, but evil people squander their money on sin.

# FEBRUARY 26

## LEVITICUS 19:1–20:21
The Lord also said to Moses, [2]"Give the following instructions to the entire community of Israel. You must be holy because I, the Lord your God, am holy.

[3]"Each of you must show great respect for your mother and father, and you must always observe my Sabbath days of rest. I am the Lord your God.

[4]"Do not put your trust in idols or make metal images of gods for yourselves. I am the Lord your God.

[5]"When you sacrifice a peace offering to the Lord, offer it properly so you* will be accepted by God. [6]The sacrifice must be eaten on the same day you offer it or on the next day. Whatever is left over until the third day must be completely burned up. [7]If any of the sacrifice is eaten on the third day, it will be contaminated, and I will not accept it. [8]Anyone who eats it on the third day will be punished for defiling what is holy to the Lord and will be cut off from the community.

[9]"When you harvest the crops of your land, do not harvest the grain along the edges of your fields, and do not pick up

what the harvesters drop. [10]It is the same with your grape crop—do not strip every last bunch of grapes from the vines, and do not pick up the grapes that fall to the ground. Leave them for the poor and the foreigners living among you. I am the LORD your God.

[11]"Do not steal.

"Do not deceive or cheat one another.

[12]"Do not bring shame on the name of your God by using it to swear falsely. I am the LORD.

[13]"Do not defraud or rob your neighbor.

"Do not make your hired workers wait until the next day to receive their pay.

[14]"Do not insult the deaf or cause the blind to stumble. You must fear your God; I am the LORD.

[15]"Do not twist justice in legal matters by favoring the poor or being partial to the rich and powerful. Always judge people fairly.

[16]"Do not spread slanderous gossip among your people.*

"Do not stand idly by when your neighbor's life is threatened. I am the LORD.

[17]"Do not nurse hatred in your heart for any of your relatives.* Confront people directly so you will not be held guilty for their sin.

[18]"Do not seek revenge or bear a grudge against a fellow Israelite, but love your neighbor as yourself. I am the LORD.

[19]"You must obey all my decrees.

"Do not mate two different kinds of animals. Do not plant your field with two different kinds of seed. Do not wear clothing woven from two different kinds of thread.

[20]"If a man has sex with a slave girl whose freedom has never been purchased but who is committed to become another man's wife, he must pay full compensation to her master. But since she is not a free woman, neither the man nor the woman will be put to death. [21]The man, however, must bring a ram as a guilt offering and present it to the LORD at the entrance of the Tabernacle.* [22]The priest will then purify him* before the

LORD with the ram of the guilt offering, and the man's sin will be forgiven.

[23]"When you enter the land and plant fruit trees, leave the fruit unharvested for the first three years and consider it forbidden.* Do not eat it. [24]In the fourth year the entire crop must be consecrated to the LORD as a celebration of praise. [25]Finally, in the fifth year you may eat the fruit. If you follow this pattern, your harvest will increase. I am the LORD your God.

[26]"Do not eat meat that has not been drained of its blood.

"Do not practice fortune-telling or witchcraft.

[27]"Do not trim off the hair on your temples or trim your beards.

[28]"Do not cut your bodies for the dead, and do not mark your skin with tattoos. I am the LORD.

[29]"Do not defile your daughter by making her a prostitute, or the land will be filled with prostitution and wickedness.

[30]"Keep my Sabbath days of rest, and show reverence toward my sanctuary. I am the LORD.

[31]"Do not defile yourselves by turning to mediums or to those who consult the spirits of the dead. I am the LORD your God.

[32]"Stand up in the presence of the elderly, and show respect for the aged. Fear your God. I am the LORD.

[33]"Do not take advantage of foreigners who live among you in your land. [34]Treat them like native-born Israelites, and love them as you love yourself. Remember that you were once foreigners living in the land of Egypt. I am the LORD your God.

[35]"Do not use dishonest standards when measuring length, weight, or volume. [36]Your scales and weights must be accurate. Your containers for measuring dry materials or liquids must be accurate.* I am the LORD your God who brought you out of the land of Egypt.

[37]"You must be careful to keep all of my decrees and regulations by putting them into practice. I am the LORD."

20:1The Lord said to Moses, 2"Give the people of Israel these instructions, which apply both to native Israelites and to the foreigners living in Israel.

"If any of them offer their children as a sacrifice to Molech, they must be put to death. The people of the community must stone them to death. 3I myself will turn against them and cut them off from the community, because they have defiled my sanctuary and brought shame on my holy name by offering their children to Molech. 4And if the people of the community ignore those who offer their children to Molech and refuse to execute them, 5I myself will turn against them and their families and will cut them off from the community. This will happen to all who commit spiritual prostitution by worshiping Molech.

6"I will also turn against those who commit spiritual prostitution by putting their trust in mediums or in those who consult the spirits of the dead. I will cut them off from the community. 7So set yourselves apart to be holy, for I am the Lord your God. 8Keep all my decrees by putting them into practice, for I am the Lord who makes you holy.

9"Anyone who dishonors* father or mother must be put to death. Such a person is guilty of a capital offense.

10"If a man commits adultery with his neighbor's wife, both the man and the woman who have committed adultery must be put to death.

11"If a man violates his father by having sex with one of his father's wives, both the man and the woman must be put to death, for they are guilty of a capital offense.

12"If a man has sex with his daughter-in-law, both must be put to death. They have committed a perverse act and are guilty of a capital offense.

13"If a man practices homosexuality, having sex with another man as with a woman, both men have committed a detestable act. They must both be put to death, for they are guilty of a capital offense.

14"If a man marries both a woman and her mother, he has committed a wicked act. The man and both women must be burned to death to wipe out such wickedness from among you.

15"If a man has sex with an animal, he must be put to death, and the animal must be killed.

16"If a woman presents herself to a male animal to have intercourse with it, she and the animal must both be put to death. You must kill both, for they are guilty of a capital offense.

17"If a man marries his sister, the daughter of either his father or his mother, and they have sexual relations, it is a shameful disgrace. They must be publicly cut off from the community. Since the man has violated his sister, he will be punished for his sin.

18"If a man has sexual relations with a woman during her menstrual period, both of them must be cut off from the community, for together they have exposed the source of her blood flow.

19"Do not have sexual relations with your aunt, whether your mother's sister or your father's sister. This would dishonor a close relative. Both parties are guilty and will be punished for their sin.

20If a man has sex with his uncle's wife, he has violated his uncle. Both the man and woman will be punished for their sin, and they will die childless.

21"If a man marries his brother's wife, it is an act of impurity. He has violated his brother, and the guilty couple will remain childless."

19:5 Or it.   19:16 Hebrew Do not act as a merchant toward your own people.   19:17 Hebrew for your brother.   19:21 Hebrew Tent of Meeting.   19:22 Or make atonement for him.   19:23 Hebrew consider it uncircumcised.   19:36 Hebrew Use an honest ephah [a dry measure] and an honest hin [a liquid measure].   20:9 Greek version reads Anyone who speaks disrespectfully of. Compare Matt 15:4; Mark 7:10.

MARK 8:11-38

When the Pharisees heard that Jesus had arrived, they came and started to argue with him. Testing him, they demanded that he show them a miraculous sign from heaven to prove his authority.

12When he heard this, he sighed deeply in his spirit and said, "Why do these people keep demanding a miraculous sign? I tell you the truth, I will not give this generation any such sign." [13]So he got back into the boat and left them, and he crossed to the other side of the lake.

[14]But the disciples had forgotten to bring any food. They had only one loaf of bread with them in the boat. [15]As they were crossing the lake, Jesus warned them, "Watch out! Beware of the yeast of the Pharisees and of Herod."

[16]At this they began to argue with each other because they hadn't brought any bread. [17]Jesus knew what they were saying, so he said, "Why are you arguing about having no bread? Don't you know or understand even yet? Are your hearts too hard to take it in? [18]'You have eyes—can't you see? You have ears—can't you hear?'* Don't you remember anything at all? [19]When I fed the 5,000 with five loaves of bread, how many baskets of leftovers did you pick up afterward?"

"Twelve," they said.

[20]"And when I fed the 4,000 with seven loaves, how many large baskets of leftovers did you pick up?"

"Seven," they said.

[21]"Don't you understand yet?" he asked them.

[22]When they arrived at Bethsaida, some people brought a blind man to Jesus, and they begged him to touch the man and heal him. [23]Jesus took the blind man by the hand and led him out of the village. Then, spitting on the man's eyes, he laid his hands on him and asked, "Can you see anything now?"

[24]The man looked around. "Yes," he said, "I see people, but I can't see them very clearly. They look like trees walking around."

[25]Then Jesus placed his hands on the man's eyes again, and his eyes were opened. His sight was completely restored, and he could see everything clearly. [26]Jesus sent him away, saying, "Don't go back into the village on your way home."

[27]Jesus and his disciples left Galilee and went up to the villages near Caesarea Philippi. As they were walking along, he asked them, "Who do people say I am?"

[28]"Well," they replied, "some say John the Baptist, some say Elijah, and others say you are one of the other prophets."

[29]Then he asked them, "But who do you say I am?"

Peter replied, "You are the Messiah.*"

[30]But Jesus warned them not to tell anyone about him.

[31]Then Jesus began to tell them that the Son of Man* must suffer many terrible things and be rejected by the elders, the leading priests, and the teachers of religious law. He would be killed, but three days later he would rise from the dead. [32]As he talked about this openly with his disciples, Peter took him aside and began to reprimand him for saying such things.*

[33]Jesus turned around and looked at his disciples, then reprimanded Peter. "Get away from me, Satan!" he said. "You are seeing things merely from a human point of view, not from God's."

[34]Then, calling the crowd to join his disciples, he said, "If any of you wants to be my follower, you must turn from your selfish ways, take up your cross, and follow me. [35]If you try to hang on to your life, you will lose it. But if you give up your life for my sake and for the sake of the Good News, you will save it. [36]And what do you benefit if you gain the whole world but lose your own soul?* [37]Is anything worth more than your soul? [38]If anyone is ashamed of me and my message in these adulterous and sinful days, the Son of Man will be ashamed of that person when he returns in the glory of his Father with the holy angels."

8:18 Jer 5:21. 8:29 Or *the Christ. Messiah* (a Hebrew term) and *Christ* (a Greek term) both mean "the anointed one." 8:31 "Son of Man" is a title Jesus used for himself. 8:32 Or *began to correct him.* 8:36 Or *your self?* also in 8:37.

## PSALM 42:1-11

*For the choir director: A psalm* of the descendants of Korah.*

[1] **As the deer longs for streams of water,**

so I long for you, O God.
² **I thirst for God, the living God.**
  **When can I go and stand**
    **before him?**
³ Day and night I have only tears
    for food,
  while my enemies continually
    taunt me, saying,
  "Where is this God of yours?"

⁴ My heart is breaking
    as I remember how it used
      to be:
  I walked among the crowds
    of worshipers,
    leading a great procession to the
      house of God,
  singing for joy and giving thanks
    amid the sound of a great
      celebration!

⁵ Why am I discouraged?
    Why is my heart so sad?
  I will put my hope in God!
    I will praise him again—
  my Savior and ⁶my God!

Now I am deeply discouraged,
    but I will remember you—
  even from distant Mount Hermon,
    the source of the Jordan,
    from the land of Mount Mizar.
⁷ I hear the tumult of the raging
    seas
    as your waves and surging tides
      sweep over me.
⁸ But each day the LORD pours his
    unfailing love upon me,
    and through each night I sing
      his songs,
    praying to God who gives me life.

⁹ "O God my rock," I cry,
    "Why have you forgotten me?
  Why must I wander around
    in grief,
    oppressed by my enemies?"
¹⁰ Their taunts break my bones.
    They scoff, "Where is this God
      of yours?"

¹¹ Why am I discouraged?
    Why is my heart so sad?
  I will put my hope in God!

I will praise him again—
    my Savior and my God!

42:TITLE Hebrew *maskil*. This may be a literary
or musical term.

PROVERBS 10:17
**P**eople who accept discipline are on the
pathway to life, but those who ignore
correction will go astray.

# FEBRUARY
# 27

LEVITICUS 20:22–22:16
"**Y**ou must keep all my decrees and regulations by putting them into practice;
otherwise the land to which I am bringing you as your new home will vomit you
out. ²³Do not live according to the customs of the people I am driving out before you. It is because they do these
shameful things that I detest them. ²⁴But I
have promised you, 'You will possess their
land because I will give it to you as your
possession—a land flowing with milk and
honey.' I am the LORD your God, who has
set you apart from all other people.
²⁵"You must therefore make a distinction between ceremonially clean and unclean animals, and between clean and
unclean birds. You must not defile yourselves by eating any unclean animal or
bird or creature that scurries along the
ground. I have identified them as being
unclean for you. ²⁶You must be holy because I, the LORD, am holy. I have set you
apart from all other people to be my very
own.
²⁷"Men and women among you who
act as mediums or who consult the spirits of the dead must be put to death by
stoning. They are guilty of a capital offense."
²¹:¹THE LORD said to Moses, "Give the
following instructions to the priests, the
descendants of Aaron.
"A priest must not make himself

ceremonially unclean by touching the dead body of a relative. ²The only exceptions are his closest relatives—his mother or father, son or daughter, brother, ³or his virgin sister who depends on him because she has no husband. ⁴But a priest must not defile himself and make himself unclean for someone who is related to him only by marriage.

⁵"The priests must not shave their heads or trim their beards or cut their bodies. ⁶They must be set apart as holy to their God and must never bring shame on the name of God. They must be holy, for they are the ones who present the special gifts to the Lord, gifts of food for their God.

⁷"Priests may not marry a woman defiled by prostitution, and they may not marry a woman who is divorced from her husband, for the priests are set apart as holy to their God. ⁸You must treat them as holy because they offer up food to your God. You must consider them holy because I, the Lord, am holy, and I make you holy.

⁹"If a priest's daughter defiles herself by becoming a prostitute, she also defiles her father's holiness, and she must be burned to death.

¹⁰"The high priest has the highest rank of all the priests. The anointing oil has been poured on his head, and he has been ordained to wear the priestly garments. He must never leave his hair uncombed* or tear his clothing. ¹¹He must not defile himself by going near a dead body. He may not make himself ceremonially unclean even for his father or mother. ¹²He must not defile the sanctuary of his God by leaving it to attend to a dead person, for he has been made holy by the anointing oil of his God. I am the Lord.

¹³"The high priest may marry only a virgin. ¹⁴He may not marry a widow, a woman who is divorced, or a woman who has defiled herself by prostitution. She must be a virgin from his own clan, ¹⁵so that he will not dishonor his descendants among his clan, for I am the Lord who makes him holy."

¹⁶Then the Lord said to Moses, ¹⁷"Give the following instructions to Aaron: In all future generations, none of your descendants who has any defect will qualify to offer food to his God. ¹⁸No one who has a defect qualifies, whether he is blind, lame, disfigured, deformed, ¹⁹or has a broken foot or arm, ²⁰or is hunchbacked or dwarfed, or has a defective eye, or skin sores or moles, or damaged testicles. ²¹No descendant of Aaron who has a defect may approach the altar to present special gifts to the Lord. Since he has a defect, he may not approach the altar to offer food to his God. ²²However, he may eat from the food offered to God, including the holy offerings and the most holy offerings. ²³Yet because of his physical defect, he may not enter the room behind the inner curtain or approach the altar, for this would defile my holy places. I am the Lord who makes them holy."

²⁴So Moses gave these instructions to Aaron and his sons and to all the Israelites.

22:1The Lord said to Moses, ²"Tell Aaron and his sons to be very careful with the sacred gifts that the Israelites set apart for me, so they do not bring shame on my holy name. I am the Lord. ³Give them the following instructions.

"In all future generations, if any of your descendants is ceremonially unclean when he approaches the sacred offerings that the people of Israel consecrate to the Lord, he must be cut off from my presence. I am the Lord.

⁴"If any of Aaron's descendants has a skin disease* or any kind of discharge that makes him ceremonially unclean, he may not eat from the sacred offerings until he has been pronounced clean. He also becomes unclean by touching a corpse, or by having an emission of semen, ⁵or by touching a small animal that is unclean, or by touching someone who is ceremonially unclean for any reason. ⁶The man who is defiled in any of these ways will remain unclean until evening. He may not eat from the sacred offerings until he has bathed himself in water. ⁷When the sun goes down, he will be cer-

emonially clean again and may eat from the sacred offerings, for this is his food. [8]He may not eat an animal that has died a natural death or has been torn apart by wild animals, for this would defile him. I am the LORD.

[9]"The priests must follow my instructions carefully. Otherwise they will be punished for their sin and will die for violating my instructions. I am the LORD who makes them holy.

[10]"No one outside a priest's family may eat the sacred offerings. Even guests and hired workers in a priest's home are not allowed to eat them. [11]However, if the priest buys a slave for himself, the slave may eat from the sacred offerings. And if his slaves have children, they also may share his food. [12]If a priest's daughter marries someone outside the priestly family, she may no longer eat the sacred offerings. [13]But if she becomes a widow or is divorced and has no children to support her, and she returns to live in her father's home as in her youth, she may eat her father's food again. Otherwise, no one outside a priest's family may eat the sacred offerings.

[14]"Any such person who eats the sacred offerings without realizing it must pay the priest for the amount eaten, plus an additional 20 percent. [15]The priests must not let the Israelites defile the sacred offerings brought to the LORD [16]by allowing unauthorized people to eat them. This would bring guilt upon them and require them to pay compensation. I am the LORD who makes them holy."

21:10 Or *never uncover his head.*   22:4 Traditionally rendered *leprosy;* see note on 13:2a.

## MARK 9:1-29

Jesus went on to say, "I tell you the truth, some standing here right now will not die before they see the Kingdom of God arrive in great power!"

[2]Six days later Jesus took Peter, James, and John, and led them up a high mountain to be alone. As the men watched, Jesus' appearance was transformed, [3]and his clothes became dazzling white, far whiter than any earthly bleach could ever make them. [4]Then Elijah and Moses appeared and began talking with Jesus.

[5]Peter exclaimed, "Rabbi, it's wonderful for us to be here! Let's make three shelters as memorials*—one for you, one for Moses, and one for Elijah." [6]He said this because he didn't really know what else to say, for they were all terrified.

[7]Then a cloud overshadowed them, and a voice from the cloud said, "This is my dearly loved Son. Listen to him." [8]Suddenly, when they looked around, Moses and Elijah were gone, and only Jesus was with them.

[9]As they went back down the mountain, he told them not to tell anyone what they had seen until the Son of Man* had risen from the dead. [10]So they kept it to themselves, but they often asked each other what he meant by "rising from the dead."

[11]Then they asked him, "Why do the teachers of religious law insist that Elijah must return before the Messiah comes?*"

[12]Jesus responded, "Elijah is indeed coming first to get everything ready for the Messiah. Yet why do the Scriptures say that the Son of Man must suffer greatly and be treated with utter contempt? [13]But I tell you, Elijah has already come, and they chose to abuse him, just as the Scriptures predicted."

[14]When they returned to the other disciples, they saw a large crowd surrounding them, and some teachers of religious law were arguing with them. [15]When the crowd saw Jesus, they were overwhelmed with awe, and they ran to greet him.

[16]"What is all this arguing about?" Jesus asked.

[17]One of the men in the crowd spoke up and said, "Teacher, I brought my son so you could heal him. He is possessed by an evil spirit that won't let him talk. [18]And whenever this spirit seizes him, it throws him violently to the ground. Then he foams at the mouth and grinds his teeth and becomes rigid.* So I asked your disciples to cast out the evil spirit, but they couldn't do it."

[19]Jesus said to them,* "You faithless

people! How long must I be with you? How long must I put up with you? Bring the boy to me."

²⁰So they brought the boy. But when the evil spirit saw Jesus, it threw the child into a violent convulsion, and he fell to the ground, writhing and foaming at the mouth.

²¹"How long has this been happening?" Jesus asked the boy's father.

He replied, "Since he was a little boy. ²²The spirit often throws him into the fire or into water, trying to kill him. Have mercy on us and help us, if you can."

²³**"What do you mean, 'If I can'?" Jesus asked. "Anything is possible if a person believes."**

²⁴**The father instantly cried out, "I do believe, but help me overcome my unbelief!"**

²⁵When Jesus saw that the crowd of onlookers was growing, he rebuked the evil* spirit. "Listen, you spirit that makes this boy unable to hear and speak," he said. "I command you to come out of this child and never enter him again!"

²⁶Then the spirit screamed and threw the boy into another violent convulsion and left him. The boy appeared to be dead. A murmur ran through the crowd as people said, "He's dead." ²⁷But Jesus took him by the hand and helped him to his feet, and he stood up.

²⁸Afterward, when Jesus was alone in the house with his disciples, they asked him, "Why couldn't we cast out that evil spirit?"

²⁹Jesus replied, "This kind can be cast out only by prayer.*"

9:5 Greek *three tabernacles.*   9:9 "Son of Man" is a title Jesus used for himself.   9:11 Greek *that Elijah must come first?*   9:18 Or *becomes weak.*   9:19 Or *said to his disciples.*   9:25 Greek *unclean.*   9:29 Some manuscripts read *by prayer and fasting.*

PSALM 43:1-5

**D**eclare me innocent, O God!
    Defend me against these
        ungodly people.
    Rescue me from these
        unjust liars.
² For you are God, my only safe haven.
    Why have you tossed me aside?

Why must I wander around in grief,
    oppressed by my enemies?
³ Send out your light and your truth;
    let them guide me.
Let them lead me to your holy
        mountain,
    to the place where you live.
⁴ There I will go to the altar of God,
    to God—the source of all my joy.
I will praise you with my harp,
    O God, my God!

⁵ Why am I discouraged?
    Why is my heart so sad?
I will put my hope in God!
    I will praise him again—
        my Savior and my God!

PROVERBS 10:18
**H**iding hatred makes you a liar; slandering others makes you a fool.

# FEBRUARY 28

LEVITICUS 22:17–23:44
**A**nd the LORD said to Moses, ¹⁸"Give Aaron and his sons and all the Israelites these instructions, which apply both to native Israelites and to the foreigners living among you.

"If you present a gift as a burnt offering to the LORD, whether it is to fulfill a vow or is a voluntary offering, ¹⁹you* will be accepted only if your offering is a male animal with no defects. It may be a bull, a ram, or a male goat. ²⁰Do not present an animal with defects, because the LORD will not accept it on your behalf.

²¹"If you present a peace offering to the LORD from the herd or the flock, whether it is to fulfill a vow or is a voluntary offering, you must offer a perfect animal. It may have no defect of any kind. ²²You must not offer an animal that is blind, crippled, or injured, or that

has an oozing sore, a skin sore, or scabs. Such animals must never be offered on the altar as special gifts to the LORD. 23If a bull* or lamb has a leg that is too long or too short, it may be offered as a voluntary offering, but it may not be offered to fulfill a vow. 24If an animal has damaged testicles or is castrated, you may not offer it to the LORD. You must never do this in your own land, 25and you must not accept such an animal from foreigners and then offer it as a sacrifice to your God. Such animals will not be accepted on your behalf, for they are mutilated or defective."

26And the LORD said to Moses, 27"When a calf or lamb or goat is born, it must be left with its mother for seven days. From the eighth day on, it will be acceptable as a special gift to the LORD. 28But you must not slaughter a mother animal and her offspring on the same day, whether from the herd or the flock. 29When you bring a thanksgiving offering to the LORD, sacrifice it properly so you will be accepted. 30Eat the entire sacrificial animal on the day it is presented. Do not leave any of it until the next morning. I am the LORD.

31"You must faithfully keep all my commands by putting them into practice, for I am the LORD. 32Do not bring shame on my holy name, for I will display my holiness among the people of Israel. I am the LORD who makes you holy. 33It was I who rescued you from the land of Egypt, that I might be your God. I am the LORD."

23:1THE LORD said to Moses, 2"Give the following instructions to the people of Israel. These are the LORD's appointed festivals, which you are to proclaim as official days for holy assembly.

3"You have six days each week for your ordinary work, but the seventh day is a Sabbath day of complete rest, an official day for holy assembly. It is the LORD's Sabbath day, and it must be observed wherever you live.

4"In addition to the Sabbath, these are the LORD's appointed festivals, the official days for holy assembly that are to be celebrated at their proper times each year.

5"The LORD's Passover begins at sundown on the fourteenth day of the first month.* 6On the next day, the fifteenth day of the month, you must begin celebrating the Festival of Unleavened Bread. This festival to the LORD continues for seven days, and during that time the bread you eat must be made without yeast. 7On the first day of the festival, all the people must stop their ordinary work and observe an official day for holy assembly. 8For seven days you must present special gifts to the LORD. On the seventh day the people must again stop all their ordinary work to observe an official day for holy assembly."

9Then the LORD said to Moses, 10"Give the following instructions to the people of Israel. When you enter the land I am giving you and you harvest its first crops, bring the priest a bundle of grain from the first cutting of your grain harvest. 11On the day after the Sabbath, the priest will lift it up before the LORD so it may be accepted on your behalf. 12On that same day you must sacrifice a one-year-old male lamb with no defects as a burnt offering to the LORD. 13With it you must present a grain offering consisting of four quarts* of choice flour moistened with olive oil. It will be a special gift, a pleasing aroma to the LORD. You must also offer one quart* of wine as a liquid offering. 14Do not eat any bread or roasted grain or fresh kernels on that day until you bring this offering to your God. This is a permanent law for you, and it must be observed from generation to generation wherever you live.

15"From the day after the Sabbath—the day you bring the bundle of grain to be lifted up as a special offering—count off seven full weeks. 16Keep counting until the day after the seventh Sabbath, fifty days later. Then present an offering of new grain to the LORD. 17From wherever you live, bring two loaves of bread to be lifted up before the LORD as a special offering. Make these loaves from four quarts of choice flour, and bake them with yeast. They will be an offering to the LORD from the first of your crops. [18]Along with the bread, present seven one-year-old male lambs with no defects, one young bull, and two rams as burnt offerings to the LORD. These burnt offerings, together with the grain offerings and liquid offerings, will be a special gift, a pleasing aroma to the LORD. [19]Then you must offer one male goat as a sin offering and two one-year-old male lambs as a peace offering.

[20]"The priest will lift up the two lambs as a special offering to the LORD, together with the loaves representing the first of your crops. These offerings, which are holy to the LORD, belong to the priests. [21]That same day will be proclaimed an official day for holy assembly, a day on which you do no ordinary work. This is a permanent law for you, and it must be observed from generation to generation wherever you live.*

[22]"When you harvest the crops of your land, do not harvest the grain along the edges of your fields, and do not pick up what the harvesters drop. Leave it for the poor and the foreigners living among you. I am the LORD your God."

[23]The LORD said to Moses, [24]"Give the following instructions to the people of Israel. On the first day of the appointed month in early autumn,* you are to observe a day of complete rest. It will be an official day for holy assembly, a day commemorated with loud blasts of a trumpet. [25]You must do no ordinary work on that day. Instead, you are to present special gifts to the LORD."

[26]Then the LORD said to Moses, [27]"Be careful to celebrate the Day of Atonement on the tenth day of that same month—nine days after the Festival of Trumpets.* You must observe it as an official day for holy assembly, a day to deny yourselves* and present special gifts to the LORD. [28]Do no work during that entire day because it is the Day of Atonement, when offerings of purification are made for you, making you right

with* the LORD your God. [29]All who do not deny themselves that day will be cut off from God's people. [30]And I will destroy anyone among you who does any work on that day. [31]You must not do any work at all! This is a permanent law for you, and it must be observed from generation to generation wherever you live. [32]This will be a Sabbath day of complete rest for you, and on that day you must deny yourselves. This day of rest will begin at sundown on the ninth day of the month and extend until sundown on the tenth day."

[33]And the LORD said to Moses, [34]"Give the following instructions to the people of Israel. Begin celebrating the Festival of Shelters* on the fifteenth day of the appointed month—five days after the Day of Atonement.* This festival to the LORD will last for seven days. [35]On the first day of the festival you must proclaim an official day for holy assembly, when you do no ordinary work. [36]For seven days you must present special gifts to the LORD. The eighth day is another holy day on which you present your special gifts to the LORD. This will be a solemn occasion, and no ordinary work may be done that day.

[37]("These are the LORD's appointed festivals. Celebrate them each year as official days for holy assembly by presenting special gifts to the LORD—burnt offerings, grain offerings, sacrifices, and liquid offerings—each on its proper day. [38]These festivals must be observed in addition to the LORD's regular Sabbath days, and the offerings are in addition to your personal gifts, the offerings you give to fulfill your vows, and the voluntary offerings you present to the LORD.)

[39]"Remember that this seven-day festival to the LORD—the Festival of Shelters—begins on the fifteenth day of the appointed month,* after you have harvested all the produce of the land. The first day and the eighth day of the festival will be days of complete rest. [40]On the first day gather branches from magnificent trees*—palm fronds, boughs

from leafy trees, and willows that grow by the streams. Then celebrate with joy before the LORD your God for seven days. ⁴¹You must observe this festival to the LORD for seven days every year. This is a permanent law for you, and it must be observed in the appointed month* from generation to generation. ⁴²For seven days you must live outside in little shelters. All native-born Israelites must live in shelters. ⁴³This will remind each new generation of Israelites that I made their ancestors live in shelters when I rescued them from the land of Egypt. I am the LORD your God."

⁴⁴So Moses gave the Israelites these instructions regarding the annual festivals of the LORD.

22:19 Or *it*.    22:23 Or *cow*.    23:5 This day in the ancient Hebrew lunar calendar occurred in late March, April, or early May.    23:13a Hebrew *²⁄₁₀ of an ephah* [4.4 liters]; also in 23:17.    23:13b Hebrew *¼ of a hin* [1 liter].    23:21 This celebration, called the Festival of Harvest or the Festival of Weeks, was later called the Festival of Pentecost (see Acts 2:1). It is celebrated today as Shavuat (or Shabuoth).    23:24 Hebrew *On the first day of the seventh month*. This day in the ancient Hebrew lunar calendar occurred in September or October. This festival is celebrated today as Rosh Hashanah, the Jewish new year.    23:27a Hebrew *on the tenth day of the seventh month;* see 23:24 and the note there. This day in the ancient Hebrew lunar calendar occurred in September or October. It is celebrated today as Yom Kippur.    23:27b Or *to fast;* similarly in 23:29, 32.    23:28 Or *when atonement is made for you before*.    23:34a Or *Festival of Booths,* or *Festival of Tabernacles*. This was earlier called the Festival of the Final Harvest or Festival of Ingathering (see Exod 23:16b). It is celebrated today as Sukkot (or Succoth).    23:34b Hebrew *on the fifteenth day of the seventh month;* see 23:27a and the note there.    23:39 Hebrew *on the fifteenth day of the seventh month*.    23:40 Or *gather fruit from majestic trees*.    23:41 Hebrew *the seventh month*.

MARK 9:30–10:12

Leaving that region, they traveled through Galilee. Jesus didn't want anyone to know he was there, ³¹for he wanted to spend more time with his disciples and teach them. He said to them, "The Son of Man is going to be betrayed into the hands of his enemies. He will be killed, but three days later he will rise from the dead." ³²They didn't understand what he was saying, however, and they were afraid to ask him what he meant.

³³After they arrived at Capernaum and settled in a house, Jesus asked his disciples, "What were you discussing out on the road?" ³⁴But they didn't an-

swer, because they had been arguing about which of them was the greatest. ³⁵**He sat down, called the twelve disciples over to him, and said, "Whoever wants to be first must take last place and be the servant of everyone else."**

³⁶Then he put a little child among them. Taking the child in his arms, he said to them, ³⁷"Anyone who welcomes a little child like this on my behalf* welcomes me, and anyone who welcomes me welcomes not only me but also my Father who sent me."

³⁸John said to Jesus, "Teacher, we saw someone using your name to cast out demons, but we told him to stop because he wasn't in our group."

³⁹"Don't stop him!" Jesus said. "No one who performs a miracle in my name will soon be able to speak evil of me. ⁴⁰Anyone who is not against us is for us. ⁴¹If anyone gives you even a cup of water because you belong to the Messiah, I tell you the truth, that person will surely be rewarded.

⁴²"But if you cause one of these little ones who trusts in me to fall into sin, it would be better for you to be thrown into the sea with a large millstone hung around your neck. ⁴³If your hand causes you to sin, cut it off. It's better to enter eternal life with only one hand than to go into the unquenchable fires of hell* with two hands.* ⁴⁵If your foot causes you to sin, cut it off. It's better to enter eternal life with only one foot than to be thrown into hell with two feet.* ⁴⁷And if your eye causes you to sin, gouge it out. It's better to enter the Kingdom of God with only one eye than to have two eyes and be thrown into hell, ⁴⁸'where the maggots never die and the fire never goes out.'*

⁴⁹"For everyone will be tested with fire.* ⁵⁰Salt is good for seasoning. But if it loses its flavor, how do you make it salty again? You must have the qualities of salt among yourselves and live in peace with each other."

¹⁰:¹THEN Jesus left Capernaum and went down to the region of Judea and

into the area east of the Jordan River. Once again crowds gathered around him, and as usual he was teaching them.

²Some Pharisees came and tried to trap him with this question: "Should a man be allowed to divorce his wife?"

³Jesus answered them with a question: "What did Moses say in the law about divorce?"

⁴"Well, he permitted it," they replied. "He said a man can give his wife a written notice of divorce and send her away."*

⁵But Jesus responded, "He wrote this commandment only as a concession to your hard hearts. ⁶But 'God made them male and female'* from the beginning of creation. ⁷This explains why a man leaves his father and mother and is joined to his wife,* ⁸and the two are united into one.'* Since they are no longer two but one, ⁹let no one split apart what God has joined together."

¹⁰Later, when he was alone with his disciples in the house, they brought up the subject again. ¹¹He told them, "Whoever divorces his wife and marries someone else commits adultery against her. ¹²And if a woman divorces her husband and marries someone else, she commits adultery."

9:37 Greek *in my name.*    9:43a Greek *Gehenna;* also in 9:45, 47.    9:43b Some manuscripts add verse 44, '*where the maggots never die and the fire never goes out.*' See 9:48.    9:45 Some manuscripts add verse 46, '*where the maggots never die and the fire never goes out.*' See 9:48.    9:48 Isa 66:24.    9:49 Greek *salted with fire;* other manuscripts add *and every sacrifice will be salted with salt.*    10:4 See Deut 24:1.    10:6 Gen 1:27; 5:2. 10:7 Some manuscripts do not include *and is joined to his wife.*    10:7-8 Gen 2:24.

## PSALM 44:1-8
*For the choir director: A psalm* of the descendants of Korah.*

¹ **O** God, we have heard it with
     our own ears—

our ancestors have told us
  of all you did in their day,
     in days long ago:
² You drove out the pagan nations
     by your power
  and gave all the land to our
     ancestors.
You crushed their enemies
  and set our ancestors free.
³ They did not conquer the land
     with their swords;
  it was not their own strong arm
     that gave them victory.
It was your right hand and strong
     arm
  and the blinding light from your
     face that helped them,
  for you loved them.

⁴ You are my King and my God.
  You command victories
     for Israel.*
⁵ Only by your power can we push
     back our enemies;
  only in your name can we trample
     our foes.
⁶ I do not trust in my bow;
  I do not count on my sword
     to save me.
⁷ You are the one who gives us victory
     over our enemies;
  you disgrace those who hate us.
⁸ O God, we give glory to you all
     day long
  and constantly praise your name.
                              *Interlude*

44:TITLE Hebrew *maskil.* This may be a literary or musical term.    44:4 Hebrew *for Jacob.* The names "Jacob" and "Israel" are often interchanged throughout the Old Testament, referring sometimes to the individual patriarch and sometimes to the nation.

## PROVERBS 10:19
**T**oo much talk leads to sin. Be sensible and keep your mouth shut.

# MARCH
# 1

## LEVITICUS 24:1–25:46

The Lord said to Moses, ²"Command the people of Israel to bring you pure oil of pressed olives for the light, to keep the lamps burning continually. ³This is the lampstand that stands in the Tabernacle, in front of the inner curtain that shields the Ark of the Covenant.* Aaron must keep the lamps burning in the Lord's presence all night. This is a permanent law for you, and it must be observed from generation to generation. ⁴Aaron and the priests must tend the lamps on the pure gold lampstand continually in the Lord's presence.

⁵"You must bake twelve loaves of bread from choice flour, using four quarts* of flour for each loaf. ⁶Place the bread before the Lord on the pure gold table, and arrange the loaves in two rows, with six loaves in each row. ⁷Put some pure frankincense near each row to serve as a representative offering, a special gift presented to the Lord. ⁸Every Sabbath day this bread must be laid out before the Lord. The bread is to be received from the people of Israel as a requirement of the eternal covenant. ⁹The loaves of bread will belong to Aaron and his descendants, who must eat them in a sacred place, for they are most holy. It is the permanent right of the priests to claim this portion of the special gifts presented to the Lord."

¹⁰One day a man who had an Israelite mother and an Egyptian father came out of his tent and got into a fight with one of the Israelite men. ¹¹During the fight, this son of an Israelite woman blasphemed the Name of the Lord* with a curse. So the man was brought to Moses for judg-

ment. His mother was Shelomith, the daughter of Dibri of the tribe of Dan. ¹²They kept the man in custody until the Lord's will in the matter should become clear to them.

¹³Then the Lord said to Moses, ¹⁴"Take the blasphemer outside the camp, and tell all those who heard the curse to lay their hands on his head. Then let the entire community stone him to death. ¹⁵Say to the people of Israel: Those who curse their God will be punished for their sin. ¹⁶Anyone who blasphemes the Name of the Lord must be stoned to death by the whole community of Israel. Any native-born Israelite or foreigner among you who blasphemes the Name of the Lord must be put to death.

¹⁷"Anyone who takes another person's life must be put to death.

¹⁸"Anyone who kills another person's animal must pay for it in full—a live animal for the animal that was killed.

¹⁹"Anyone who injures another person must be dealt with according to the injury inflicted—²⁰a fracture for a fracture, an eye for an eye, a tooth for a tooth. Whatever anyone does to injure another person must be paid back in kind.

²¹"Whoever kills an animal must pay for it in full, but whoever kills another person must be put to death.

²²"This same standard applies both to native-born Israelites and to the foreigners living among you. I am the Lord your God."

²³After Moses gave all these instructions to the Israelites, they took the blasphemer outside the camp and stoned him to death. The Israelites did just as the Lord had commanded Moses.

²⁵:¹While Moses was on Mount Sinai, the Lord said to him, ²"Give the following instructions to the people of Israel.

When you have entered the land I am giving you, the land itself must observe a Sabbath rest before the LORD every seventh year. ³For six years you may plant your fields and prune your vineyards and harvest your crops, ⁴but during the seventh year the land must have a Sabbath year of complete rest. It is the LORD's Sabbath. Do not plant your fields or prune your vineyards during that year. ⁵And don't store away the crops that grow on their own or gather the grapes from your unpruned vines. The land must have a year of complete rest. ⁶But you may eat whatever the land produces on its own during its Sabbath. This applies to you, your male and female servants, your hired workers, and the temporary residents who live with you. ⁷Your livestock and the wild animals in your land will also be allowed to eat what the land produces.

⁸"In addition, you must count off seven Sabbath years, seven sets of seven years, adding up to forty-nine years in all. ⁹Then on the Day of Atonement in the fiftieth year,* blow the ram's horn loud and long throughout the land. ¹⁰Set this year apart as holy, a time to proclaim freedom throughout the land for all who live there. It will be a jubilee year for you, when each of you may return to the land that belonged to your ancestors and return to your own clan. ¹¹This fiftieth year will be a jubilee for you. During that year you must not plant your fields or store away any of the crops that grow on their own, and don't gather the grapes from your unpruned vines. ¹²It will be a jubilee year for you, and you must keep it holy. But you may eat whatever the land produces on its own. ¹³In the Year of Jubilee each of you may return to the land that belonged to your ancestors.

¹⁴"When you make an agreement with your neighbor to buy or sell property, you must not take advantage of each other. ¹⁵When you buy land from your neighbor, the price you pay must be based on the number of years since the last jubilee. The seller must set the price by taking into account the number of years remaining until the next Year of Jubilee. ¹⁶The more years until the next jubilee, the higher the price; the fewer years, the lower the price. After all, the person selling the land is actually selling you a certain number of harvests. ¹⁷Show your fear of God by not taking advantage of each other. I am the LORD your God.

¹⁸"If you want to live securely in the land, follow my decrees and obey my regulations. ¹⁹Then the land will yield large crops, and you will eat your fill and live securely in it. ²⁰But you might ask, 'What will we eat during the seventh year, since we are not allowed to plant or harvest crops that year?' ²¹Be assured that I will send my blessing for you in the sixth year, so the land will produce a crop large enough for three years. ²²When you plant your fields in the eighth year, you will still be eating from the large crop of the sixth year. In fact, you will still be eating from that large crop when the new crop is harvested in the ninth year.

²³"The land must never be sold on a permanent basis, for the land belongs to me. You are only foreigners and tenant farmers working for me.

²⁴"With every purchase of land you must grant the seller the right to buy it back. ²⁵If one of your fellow Israelites falls into poverty and is forced to sell some family land, then a close relative should buy it back for him. ²⁶If there is no close relative to buy the land, but the person who sold it gets enough money to buy it back, ²⁷he then has the right to redeem it from the one who bought it. The price of the land will be discounted according to the number of years until the next Year of Jubilee. In this way the original owner can then return to the land. ²⁸But if the original owner cannot afford to buy back the land, it will remain with the new owner until the next Year of Jubilee. In the jubilee year, the land must be returned to the original owners so they can return to their family land.

29"Anyone who sells a house inside a walled town has the right to buy it back for a full year after its sale. During that year, the seller retains the right to buy it back. 30But if it is not bought back within a year, the sale of the house within the walled town cannot be reversed. It will become the permanent property of the buyer. It will not be returned to the original owner in the Year of Jubilee. 31But a house in a village—a settlement without fortified walls—will be treated like property in the countryside. Such a house may be bought back at any time, and it must be returned to the original owner in the Year of Jubilee.

32"The Levites always have the right to buy back a house they have sold within the towns allotted to them. 33And any property that is sold by the Levites—all houses within the Levitical towns—must be returned in the Year of Jubilee. After all, the houses in the towns reserved for the Levites are the only property they own in all Israel. 34The open pastureland around the Levitical towns may never be sold. It is their permanent possession.

35"If one of your fellow Israelites falls into poverty and cannot support himself, support him as you would a foreigner or a temporary resident and allow him to live with you. 36Do not charge interest or make a profit at his expense. Instead, show your fear of God by letting him live with you as your relative. 37Remember, do not charge interest on money you lend him or make a profit on food you sell him. 38I am the Lord your God, who brought you out of the land of Egypt to give you the land of Canaan and to be your God.

39"If one of your fellow Israelites falls into poverty and is forced to sell himself to you, do not treat him as a slave. 40Treat him instead as a hired worker or as a temporary resident who lives with you, and he will serve you only until the Year of Jubilee. 41At that time he and his children will no longer be obligated to you, and they will return to their clans and go back to the land originally allotted to their ancestors. 42The people of Israel

are my servants, whom I brought out of the land of Egypt, so they must never be sold as slaves. 43Show your fear of God by not treating them harshly.

44"However, you may purchase male and female slaves from among the nations around you. 45You may also purchase the children of temporary residents who live among you, including those who have been born in your land. You may treat them as your property, 46passing them on to your children as a permanent inheritance. You may treat them as slaves, but you must never treat your fellow Israelites this way."

24:3 Hebrew *in the Tent of Meeting, outside the inner curtain of the Testimony;* see note on 16:13. 24:5 Hebrew ²⁄₁₀ *of an ephah* [4.4 liters]. 24:11 Hebrew *the Name;* also in 24:16b. 25:9 Hebrew *on the tenth day of the seventh month, on the Day of Atonement;* see 23:27a and the note there.

MARK 10:13-31

**O**ne day some parents brought their children to Jesus so he could touch and bless them. But the disciples scolded the parents for bothering him.

14When Jesus saw what was happening, he was angry with his disciples. He said to them, "Let the children come to me. Don't stop them! For the Kingdom of God belongs to those who are like these children. 15**I tell you the truth, anyone who doesn't receive the Kingdom of God like a child will never enter it."** 16Then he took the children in his arms and placed his hands on their heads and blessed them.

17As Jesus was starting out on his way to Jerusalem, a man came running up to him, knelt down, and asked, "Good Teacher, what must I do to inherit eternal life?"

18"Why do you call me good?" Jesus asked. "Only God is truly good. 19But to answer your question, you know the commandments: 'You must not murder. You must not commit adultery. You must not steal. You must not testify falsely. You must not cheat anyone. Honor your father and mother.'*"

20"Teacher," the man replied, "I've obeyed all these commandments since I was young."

21Looking at the man, Jesus felt genuine love for him. "There is still one thing you haven't done," he told him. "Go and sell all your possessions and give the money to the poor, and you will have treasure in heaven. Then come, follow me."

22At this the man's face fell, and he went away very sad, for he had many possessions.

23Jesus looked around and said to his disciples, "How hard it is for the rich to enter the Kingdom of God!" 24This amazed them. But Jesus said again, "Dear children, it is very hard* to enter the Kingdom of God. 25In fact, it is easier for a camel to go through the eye of a needle than for a rich person to enter the Kingdom of God!"

26The disciples were astounded. "Then who in the world can be saved?" they asked.

27Jesus looked at them intently and said, "Humanly speaking, it is impossible. But not with God. Everything is possible with God."

28Then Peter began to speak up. "We've given up everything to follow you," he said.

29"Yes," Jesus replied, "and I assure you that everyone who has given up house or brothers or sisters or mother or father or children or property, for my sake and for the Good News, 30will receive now in return a hundred times as many houses, brothers, sisters, mothers, children, and property—along with persecution. And in the world to come that person will have eternal life. 31But many who are the greatest now will be least important then, and those who seem least important now will be the greatest then.*"

10:19 Exod 20:12-16; Deut 5:16-20.   10:24 Some manuscripts read *very hard for those who trust in riches.* 10:31 Greek *But many who are first will be last; and the last, first.*

PSALM 44:9-26

But now you have tossed us aside
    in dishonor.
    You no longer lead our armies
        to battle.

10 You make us retreat from
        our enemies
    and allow those who hate us
        to plunder our land.
11 You have butchered us like sheep
    and scattered us among the
        nations.
12 You sold your precious people
        for a pittance,
    making nothing on the sale.
13 You let our neighbors mock us.
    We are an object of scorn and
        derision to those around us.
14 You have made us the butt of their
        jokes;
    they shake their heads at us
        in scorn.
15 We can't escape the constant
        humiliation;
    shame is written across our faces.
16 All we hear are the taunts of our
        mockers.
    All we see are our vengeful
        enemies.

17 All this has happened though we
        have not forgotten you.
    We have not violated your
        covenant.
18 Our hearts have not deserted you.
    We have not strayed from
        your path.
19 Yet you have crushed us in the
        jackal's desert home.
    You have covered us with
        darkness and death.
20 If we had forgotten the name
        of our God
    or spread our hands in prayer
        to foreign gods,
21 God would surely have known it,
    for he knows the secrets of every
        heart.
22 But for your sake we are killed
        every day;
    we are being slaughtered
        like sheep.

23 Wake up, O Lord! Why do you sleep?
    Get up! Do not reject us forever.
24 Why do you look the other way?
    Why do you ignore our suffering
        and oppression?

²⁵ We collapse in the dust,
   lying face down in the dirt.
²⁶ Rise up! Help us!
   Ransom us because of your
      unfailing love.

PROVERBS 10:20-21
The words of the godly are like sterling silver; the heart of a fool is worthless. □ The words of the godly encourage many, but fools are destroyed by their lack of common sense.

# MARCH 2

LEVITICUS 25:47–27:13
"Suppose a foreigner or temporary resident becomes rich while living among you. If any of your fellow Israelites fall into poverty and are forced to sell themselves to such a foreigner or to a member of his family, ⁴⁸they still retain the right to be bought back, even after they have been purchased. They may be bought back by a brother, ⁴⁹an uncle, or a cousin. In fact, anyone from the extended family may buy them back. They may also redeem themselves if they have prospered. ⁵⁰They will negotiate the price of their freedom with the person who bought them. The price will be based on the number of years from the time they were sold until the next Year of Jubilee—whatever it would cost to hire a worker for that period of time. ⁵¹If many years still remain until the jubilee, they will repay the proper proportion of what they received when they sold themselves. ⁵²If only a few years remain until the Year of Jubilee, they will repay a small amount for their redemption. ⁵³The foreigner must treat them as workers hired on a yearly basis. You must not allow a foreigner to treat any of your fellow Israelites harshly. ⁵⁴If any Israelites have not been bought back by the time the Year of Jubilee arrives, they and their children must be set free at that time. ⁵⁵For the people of Israel belong to me. They are my servants, whom I brought out of the land of Egypt. I am the LORD your God.

²⁶:¹"Do not make idols or set up carved images, or sacred pillars, or sculptured stones in your land so you may worship them. I am the LORD your God. ²You must keep my Sabbath days of rest and show reverence for my sanctuary. I am the LORD.

³"If you follow my decrees and are careful to obey my commands, ⁴I will send you the seasonal rains. The land will then yield its crops, and the trees of the field will produce their fruit. ⁵Your threshing season will overlap with the grape harvest, and your grape harvest will overlap with the season of planting grain. You will eat your fill and live securely in your own land.

⁶"I will give you peace in the land, and you will be able to sleep with no cause for fear. I will rid the land of wild animals and keep your enemies out of your land. ⁷In fact, you will chase down your enemies and slaughter them with your swords. ⁸Five of you will chase a hundred, and a hundred of you will chase ten thousand! All your enemies will fall beneath your sword.

⁹"I will look favorably upon you, making you fertile and multiplying your people. And I will fulfill my covenant with you. ¹⁰You will have such a surplus of crops that you will need to clear out the old grain to make room for the new harvest! ¹¹I will live among you, and I will not despise you. ¹²I will walk among you; I will be your God, and you will be my people. ¹³I am the LORD your God, who brought you out of the land of Egypt so you would no longer be their slaves. I broke the yoke of slavery from your neck so you can walk with your heads held high.

¹⁴"However, if you do not listen to me or obey all these commands, ¹⁵and if you break my covenant by rejecting my decrees, treating my regulations with

contempt, and refusing to obey my commands, [16]I will punish you. I will bring sudden terrors upon you—wasting diseases and burning fevers that will cause your eyes to fail and your life to ebb away. You will plant your crops in vain because your enemies will eat them. [17]I will turn against you, and you will be defeated by your enemies. Those who hate you will rule over you, and you will run even when no one is chasing you!

[18]"And if, in spite of all this, you still disobey me, I will punish you seven times over for your sins. [19]I will break your proud spirit by making the skies as unyielding as iron and the earth as hard as bronze. [20]All your work will be for nothing, for your land will yield no crops, and your trees will bear no fruit.

[21]"If even then you remain hostile toward me and refuse to obey me, I will inflict disaster on you seven times over for your sins. [22]I will send wild animals that will rob you of your children and destroy your livestock. Your numbers will dwindle, and your roads will be deserted.

[23]"And if you fail to learn the lesson and continue your hostility toward me, [24]then I myself will be hostile toward you. I will personally strike you with calamity seven times over for your sins. [25]I will send armies against you to carry out the curse of the covenant you have broken. When you run to your towns for safety, I will send a plague to destroy you there, and you will be handed over to your enemies. [26]I will destroy your food supply, so that ten women will need only one oven to bake bread for their families. They will ration your food by weight, and though you have food to eat, you will not be satisfied.

[27]"If in spite of all this you still refuse to listen and still remain hostile toward me, [28]then I will give full vent to my hostility. I myself will punish you seven times over for your sins. [29]Then you will eat the flesh of your own sons and daughters. [30]I will destroy your pagan shrines and knock down your places of worship. I will leave your lifeless corpses piled on top of your lifeless idols,* and I will despise you. [31]I will make your cities desolate and destroy your places of pagan worship. I will take no pleasure in your offerings that should be a pleasing aroma to me. [32]Yes, I myself will devastate your land, and your enemies who come to occupy it will be appalled at what they see. [33]I will scatter you among the nations and bring out my sword against you. Your land will become desolate, and your cities will lie in ruins. [34]Then at last the land will enjoy its neglected Sabbath years as it lies desolate while you are in exile in the land of your enemies. Then the land will finally rest and enjoy the Sabbaths it missed. [35]As long as the land lies in ruins, it will enjoy the rest you never allowed it to take every seventh year while you lived in it.

[36]"And for those of you who survive, I will demoralize you in the land of your enemies. You will live in such fear that the sound of a leaf driven by the wind will send you fleeing. You will run as though fleeing from a sword, and you will fall even when no one pursues you. [37]Though no one is chasing you, you will stumble over each other as though fleeing from a sword. You will have no power to stand up against your enemies. [38]You will die among the foreign nations and be devoured in the land of your enemies. [39]Those of you who survive will waste away in your enemies' lands because of their sins and the sins of their ancestors.

[40]"But at last my people will confess their sins and the sins of their ancestors for betraying me and being hostile toward me. [41]When I have turned their hostility back on them and brought them to the land of their enemies, then at last their stubborn hearts will be humbled, and they will pay for their sins. [42]Then I will remember my covenant with Jacob and my covenant with Isaac and my covenant with Abraham, and I will remember the land. [43]For the land must be abandoned to enjoy its

years of Sabbath rest as it lies deserted. At last the people will pay for their sins, for they have continually rejected my regulations and despised my decrees.

⁴⁴"But despite all this, I will not utterly reject or despise them while they are in exile in the land of their enemies. I will not cancel my covenant with them by wiping them out, for I am the LORD their God. ⁴⁵For their sakes I will remember my ancient covenant with their ancestors, whom I brought out of the land of Egypt in the sight of all the nations, that I might be their God. I am the LORD."

⁴⁶These are the decrees, regulations, and instructions that the LORD gave through Moses on Mount Sinai as evidence of the relationship between himself and the Israelites.

²⁷:¹THE LORD said to Moses, ²"Give the following instructions to the people of Israel. If anyone makes a special vow to dedicate someone to the LORD by paying the value of that person, ³here is the scale of values to be used. A man between the ages of twenty and sixty is valued at fifty shekels* of silver, as measured by the sanctuary shekel. ⁴A woman of that age is valued at thirty shekels* of silver. ⁵A boy between the ages of five and twenty is valued at twenty shekels of silver; a girl of that age is valued at ten shekels* of silver. ⁶A boy between the ages of one month and five years is valued at five shekels of silver; a girl of that age is valued at three shekels* of silver. ⁷A man older than sixty is valued at fifteen shekels of silver; a woman of that age is valued at ten shekels* of silver. ⁸If you desire to make such a vow but cannot afford to pay the required amount, take the person to the priest. He will determine the amount for you to pay based on what you can afford.

⁹"If your vow involves giving an animal that is acceptable as an offering to the LORD, any gift to the LORD will be considered holy. ¹⁰You may not exchange or substitute it for another animal—neither a good animal for a bad

one nor a bad animal for a good one. But if you do exchange one animal for another, then both the original animal and its substitute will be considered holy. ¹¹If your vow involves an unclean animal—one that is not acceptable as an offering to the LORD—then you must bring the animal to the priest. ¹²He will assess its value, and his assessment will be final, whether high or low. ¹³If you want to buy back the animal, you must pay the value set by the priest, plus 20 percent."

26:30 The Hebrew term (literally *round things*) probably alludes to dung.   27:3 Or *20 ounces* [570 grams].   27:4 Or *12 ounces* [342 grams].   27:5 Or *A boy . . . 8 ounces* [228 grams] *of silver; a girl . . . 4 ounces* [114 grams].   27:6 Or *A boy . . . 2 ounces* [57 grams] *of silver; a girl . . . 1.2 ounces* [34 grams].   27:7 Or *A man . . . 6 ounces* [171 grams] *of silver; a woman . . . 4 ounces* [114 grams].

## MARK 10:32-52

They [the disciples] were now on the way up to Jerusalem, and Jesus was walking ahead of them. The disciples were filled with awe, and the people following behind were overwhelmed with fear. Taking the twelve disciples aside, Jesus once more began to describe everything that was about to happen to him. ³³"Listen," he said, "we're going up to Jerusalem, where the Son of Man* will be betrayed to the leading priests and the teachers of religious law. They will sentence him to die and hand him over to the Romans.* ³⁴They will mock him, spit on him, flog him with a whip, and kill him, but after three days he will rise again."

³⁵Then James and John, the sons of Zebedee, came over and spoke to him. "Teacher," they said, "we want you to do us a favor."

³⁶"What is your request?" he asked.

³⁷They replied, "When you sit on your glorious throne, we want to sit in places of honor next to you, one on your right and the other on your left."

³⁸But Jesus said to them, "You don't know what you are asking! Are you able to drink from the bitter cup of suffering I am about to drink? Are you able to be baptized with the baptism of suffering I must be baptized with?"

<sup>39</sup>"Oh yes," they replied, "we are able!"

**Then Jesus told them, "You will indeed drink from my bitter cup and be baptized with my baptism of suffering.** <sup>40</sup>**But I have no right to say who will sit on my right or my left. God has prepared those places for the ones he has chosen."**

<sup>41</sup>When the ten other disciples heard what James and John had asked, they were indignant. <sup>42</sup>So Jesus called them together and said, "You know that the rulers in this world lord it over their people, and officials flaunt their authority over those under them. <sup>43</sup>But among you it will be different. Whoever wants to be a leader among you must be your servant, <sup>44</sup>and whoever wants to be first among you must be the slave of everyone else. <sup>45</sup>For even the Son of Man came not to be served but to serve others and to give his life as a ransom for many."

<sup>46</sup>Then they reached Jericho, and as Jesus and his disciples left town, a large crowd followed him. A blind beggar named Bartimaeus (son of Timaeus) was sitting beside the road. <sup>47</sup>When Bartimaeus heard that Jesus of Nazareth was nearby, he began to shout, "Jesus, Son of David, have mercy on me!"

<sup>48</sup>"Be quiet!" many of the people yelled at him.

But he only shouted louder, "Son of David, have mercy on me!"

<sup>49</sup>When Jesus heard him, he stopped and said, "Tell him to come here."

So they called the blind man. "Cheer up," they said. "Come on, he's calling you!" <sup>50</sup>Bartimaeus threw aside his coat, jumped up, and came to Jesus.

<sup>51</sup>"What do you want me to do for you?" Jesus asked.

"My rabbi,*" the blind man said, "I want to see!"

<sup>52</sup>And Jesus said to him, "Go, for your faith has healed you." Instantly the man could see, and he followed Jesus down the road.*

10:33a "Son of Man" is a title Jesus used for himself.
10:33b Greek *the Gentiles.*   10:51 Greek uses the Hebrew term *Rabboni.*   10:52 Or *on the way.*

## PSALM 45:1-17

*For the choir director: A love song to be sung to the tune "Lilies." A psalm\* of the descendants of Korah.*

<sup>1</sup> **B**eautiful words stir my heart.
 I will recite a lovely poem about
  the king,
 for my tongue is like the pen
  of a skillful poet.

<sup>2</sup> You are the most handsome of all.
 Gracious words stream from
  your lips.
 God himself has blessed
  you forever.

<sup>3</sup> Put on your sword, O mighty
  warrior!
 You are so glorious, so majestic!

<sup>4</sup> In your majesty, ride out to victory,
  defending truth, humility,
  and justice.
 Go forth to perform
  awe-inspiring deeds!

<sup>5</sup> Your arrows are sharp, piercing your
  enemies' hearts.
 The nations fall beneath
  your feet.

<sup>6</sup> Your throne, O God,* endures
  forever and ever.
 You rule with a scepter of justice.

<sup>7</sup> You love justice and hate evil.
 Therefore God, your God, has
  anointed you,
 pouring out the oil of joy on you
  more than on anyone else.

<sup>8</sup> Myrrh, aloes, and cassia perfume
  your robes.
 In ivory palaces the music
  of strings entertains you.

<sup>9</sup> Kings' daughters are among your
  noble women.
 At your right side stands the
  queen,
 wearing jewelry of finest gold
  from Ophir!

<sup>10</sup> Listen to me, O royal daughter;
  take to heart what I say.
 Forget your people and your
  family far away.

<sup>11</sup> For your royal husband delights
  in your beauty;

honor him, for he is your lord.
12 The princess of Tyre* will shower
    you with gifts.
    The wealthy will beg your favor.
13 The bride, a princess, looks glorious
    in her golden gown.
14 In her beautiful robes, she is led
    to the king,
    accompanied by her bridesmaids.
15 What a joyful and enthusiastic
    procession
    as they enter the king's palace!

16 Your sons will become kings like
    their father.
    You will make them rulers over
    many lands.
17 I will bring honor to your name
    in every generation.
    Therefore, the nations will praise
    you forever and ever.

**45:**TITLE Hebrew *maskil.* This may be a literary or musical
term.   **45:6** Or *Your divine throne.*   **45:12** Hebrew *The
daughter of Tyre.*

PROVERBS 10:22
The blessing of the LORD makes a person rich, and he adds no sorrow with it.

# MARCH
# 3

LEVITICUS 27:14—NUMBERS 1:54
"If someone dedicates a house to the
LORD, the priest will come to assess its
value. The priest's assessment will be final, whether high or low. 15 If the person
who dedicated the house wants to buy it
back, he must pay the value set by the
priest, plus 20 percent. Then the house
will again be his.

16"If someone dedicates to the LORD a
piece of his family property, its value will
be assessed according to the amount of
seed required to plant it—fifty shekels of
silver for a field planted with five bushels of barley seed.* 17 If the field is dedicated to the LORD in the Year of Jubilee,

then the entire assessment will apply.
18But if the field is dedicated after the
Year of Jubilee, the priest will assess the
land's value in proportion to the number
of years left until the next Year of Jubilee. Its assessed value is reduced each
year. 19 If the person who dedicated the
field wants to buy it back, he must pay
the value set by the priest, plus 20 percent. Then the field will again be legally
his. 20But if he does not want to buy it
back, and it is sold to someone else, the
field can no longer be bought back.
21When the field is released in the Year
of Jubilee, it will be holy, a field specially
set apart* for the LORD. It will become
the property of the priests.

22"If someone dedicates to the LORD
a field he has purchased but which is
not part of his family property, 23 the
priest will assess its value based on the
number of years left until the next Year
of Jubilee. On that day he must give the
assessed value of the land as a sacred
donation to the LORD. 24 In the Year of
Jubilee the field must be returned to the
person from whom he purchased it, the
one who inherited it as family property.
25(All the payments must be measured
by the weight of the sanctuary shekel,*
which equals twenty gerahs.)

26"You may not dedicate a firstborn
animal to the LORD, for the firstborn of
your cattle, sheep, and goats already belong to him. 27However, you may buy
back the firstborn of a ceremonially unclean animal by paying the priest's assessment of its worth, plus 20 percent.
If you do not buy it back, the priest will
sell it at its assessed value.

28"However, anything specially set
apart for the LORD—whether a person,
an animal, or family property—must
never be sold or bought back. Anything
devoted in this way has been set apart as
holy, and it belongs to the LORD. 29No
person specially set apart for destruction may be bought back. Such a person
must be put to death.

30"One tenth of the produce of the
land, whether grain from the fields or
fruit from the trees, belongs to the LORD

and must be set apart to him as holy. [31]If you want to buy back the LORD's tenth of the grain or fruit, you must pay its value, plus 20 percent. [32]Count off every tenth animal from your herds and flocks and set them apart for the LORD as holy. [33]You may not pick and choose between good and bad animals, and you may not substitute one for another. But if you do exchange one animal for another, then both the original animal and its substitute will be considered holy and cannot be bought back."

[34]These are the commands that the LORD gave through Moses on Mount Sinai for the Israelites.

[1:1]A YEAR after Israel's departure from Egypt, the LORD spoke to Moses in the Tabernacle* in the wilderness of Sinai. On the first day of the second month* of that year he said, [2]"From the whole community of Israel, record the names of all the warriors by their clans and families. List all the men [3]twenty years old or older who are able to go to war. You and Aaron must register the troops, [4]and you will be assisted by one family leader from each tribe.

[5]"These are the tribes and the names of the leaders who will assist you:

| Tribe | Leader |
|---|---|
| Reuben | Elizur son of Shedeur |
| [6] Simeon | Shelumiel son of Zurishaddai |
| [7] Judah | Nahshon son of Amminadab |
| [8] Issachar | Nethanel son of Zuar |
| [9] Zebulun | Eliab son of Helon |
| [10] Ephraim son of Joseph | Elishama son of Ammihud |
| Manasseh son of Joseph | Gamaliel son of Pedahzur |
| [11] Benjamin | Abidan son of Gideoni |
| [12] Dan | Ahiezer son of Ammishaddai |
| [13] Asher | Pagiel son of Ocran |
| [14] Gad | Eliasaph son of Deuel |
| [15] Naphtali | Ahira son of Enan |

[16]These are the chosen leaders of the community, the leaders of their ancestral tribes, the heads of the clans of Israel."

[17]So Moses and Aaron called together these chosen leaders, [18]and they assembled the whole community of Israel on that very day.* All the people were registered according to their ancestry by their clans and families. The men of Israel who were twenty years old or older were listed one by one, [19]just as the LORD had commanded Moses. So Moses recorded their names in the wilderness of Sinai.

[20-21]This is the number of men twenty years old or older who were able to go to war, as their names were listed in the records of their clans and families*:

| Tribe | Number |
|---|---|
| Reuben (Jacob's* oldest son) | 46,500 |
| [22-23] Simeon | 59,300 |
| [24-25] Gad | 45,650 |
| [26-27] Judah | 74,600 |
| [28-29] Issachar | 54,400 |
| [30-31] Zebulun | 57,400 |
| [32-33] Ephraim son of Joseph | 40,500 |
| [34-35] Manasseh son of Joseph | 32,200 |
| [36-37] Benjamin | 35,400 |
| [38-39] Dan | 62,700 |
| [40-41] Asher | 41,500 |
| [42-43] Naphtali | 53,400 |

[44]These were the men registered by Moses and Aaron and the twelve leaders of Israel, all listed according to their ancestral descent. [45]They were registered by families—all the men of Israel who were twenty years old or older and able to go to war. [46]The total number was 603,550.

[47]But this total did not include the Levites. [48]For the LORD had said to Moses, [49]"Do not include the tribe of Levi in the registration; do not count them with the rest of the Israelites. [50]Put the Levites in charge of the Tabernacle of the Covenant,* along with all its furnishings and equipment. They must carry the Tabernacle and all its furnishings as you travel, and they must take care of it and camp around it. [51]Whenever it is time for the Tabernacle to move, the Levites will take it down. And when it is time to stop, they will set it up again. But any unauthorized person who goes too near the Taberna-

cle must be put to death. ⁵²Each tribe of Israel will camp in a designated area with its own family banner. ⁵³But the Levites will camp around the Tabernacle of the Covenant to protect the community of Israel from the LORD's anger. The Levites are responsible to stand guard around the Tabernacle."

⁵⁴So the Israelites did everything just as the LORD had commanded Moses.

27:16 Hebrew *50 shekels* [20 ounces, or 570 grams] *of silver for a homer* [182 liters] *of barley seed.*   27:21 The Hebrew term used here refers to the complete consecration of things or people to the LORD, either by destroying them or by giving them as an offering; also in 27:28, 29. 27:25 Each shekel was about 0.4 ounces [11 grams] in weight.   1:1a Hebrew *the Tent of Meeting.*   1:1b This day in the ancient Hebrew lunar calendar occurred in April or May.   1:18 Hebrew *on the first day of the second month;* see 1:1.   1:20-21a In the Hebrew text, this phrase (*This is the number of men twenty years old or older who were able to go to war, as their names were listed in the records of their clans and families*) is repeated in 1:22, 24, 26, 28, 30, 32, 34, 36, 38, 40, 42.   1:20-21b Hebrew *Israel's.* The names "Jacob" and "Israel" are often interchanged throughout the Old Testament, referring sometimes to the individual patriarch and sometimes to the nation. 1:50 Or *Tabernacle of the Testimony;* also in 1:53.

## MARK 11:1-26

**A**s Jesus and his disciples approached Jerusalem, they came to the towns of Bethphage and Bethany on the Mount of Olives. Jesus sent two of them on ahead. ²"Go into that village over there," he told them. "As soon as you enter it, you will see a young donkey tied there that no one has ever ridden. Untie it and bring it here. ³If anyone asks, 'What are you doing?' just say, 'The Lord needs it and will return it soon.'"

⁴The two disciples left and found the colt standing in the street, tied outside the front door. ⁵As they were untying it, some bystanders demanded, "What are you doing, untying that colt?" ⁶They said what Jesus had told them to say, and they were permitted to take it. ⁷Then they brought the colt to Jesus and threw their garments over it, and he sat on it.

⁸Many in the crowd spread their garments on the road ahead of him, and others spread leafy branches they had cut in the fields. ⁹Jesus was in the center of the procession, and the people all around him were shouting,

"Praise God!*
    Blessings on the one who comes
        in the name of the LORD!
¹⁰ Blessings on the coming Kingdom of
        our ancestor David!
    Praise God in highest heaven!"*

¹¹So Jesus came to Jerusalem and went into the Temple. After looking around carefully at everything, he left because it was late in the afternoon. Then he returned to Bethany with the twelve disciples.

¹²The next morning as they were leaving Bethany, Jesus was hungry. ¹³He noticed a fig tree in full leaf a little way off, so he went over to see if he could find any figs. But there were only leaves because it was too early in the season for fruit. ¹⁴Then Jesus said to the tree, "May no one ever eat your fruit again!" And the disciples heard him say it.

¹⁵When they arrived back in Jerusalem, Jesus entered the Temple and began to drive out the people buying and selling animals for sacrifices. He knocked over the tables of the money changers and the chairs of those selling doves, ¹⁶and he stopped everyone from using the Temple as a marketplace.* ¹⁷He said to them, "The Scriptures declare, 'My Temple will be called a house of prayer for all nations,' but you have turned it into a den of thieves.'"*

¹⁸When the leading priests and teachers of religious law heard what Jesus had done, they began planning how to kill him. But they were afraid of him because the people were so amazed at his teaching.

¹⁹That evening Jesus and the disciples left* the city.

²⁰The next morning as they passed by the fig tree he had cursed, the disciples noticed it had withered from the roots up. ²¹Peter remembered what Jesus had said to the tree on the previous day and exclaimed, "Look, Rabbi! The fig tree you cursed has withered and died!"

²²Then Jesus said to the disciples, "Have faith in God. ²³I tell you the truth,

you can say to this mountain, 'May you be lifted up and thrown into the sea,' and it will happen. But you must really believe it will happen and have no doubt in your heart. [24]I tell you, you can pray for anything, and if you believe that you've received it, it will be yours. [25]But when you are praying, first forgive anyone you are holding a grudge against, so that your Father in heaven will forgive your sins, too.*"

11:9 Greek *Hosanna,* an exclamation of praise that literally means "save now"; also in 11:10.   11:9-10 Pss 118:25-26; 148:1.   11:16 Or *from carrying merchandise through the Temple.*   11:17 Isa 56:7; Jer 7:11.   11:19 Greek *they left;* other manuscripts read *he left.*   11:25 Some manuscripts add verse 26, *But if you refuse to forgive, your Father in heaven will not forgive your sins.* Compare Matt 6:15.

PSALM 46:1-11

*For the choir director: A song of the descendants of Korah, to be sung by soprano voices.**

[1] **God is our refuge and strength,
      always ready to help in times
      of trouble.**
[2] **So we will not fear when
      earthquakes come
      and the mountains crumble
      into the sea.**
[3] **Let the oceans roar and foam.
      Let the mountains tremble
      as the waters surge!**
                                    *Interlude*

[4] A river brings joy to the city
      of our God,
      the sacred home of the
      Most High.
[5] God dwells in that city; it cannot
      be destroyed.
      From the very break of day,
      God will protect it.
[6] The nations are in chaos,
      and their kingdoms crumble!
      God's voice thunders,
      and the earth melts!
[7] The LORD of Heaven's Armies is
      here among us;
      the God of Israel* is our fortress.
                                    *Interlude*

[8] Come, see the glorious works
      of the LORD:

      See how he brings destruction
      upon the world.
[9] He causes wars to end throughout
      the earth.
      He breaks the bow and snaps
      the spear;
      he burns the shields with fire.

[10] "Be still, and know that I am God!
      I will be honored by every nation.
      I will be honored throughout
      the world."

[11] The LORD of Heaven's Armies is
      here among us;
      the God of Israel is our fortress.
                                    *Interlude*

46:TITLE Hebrew *according to alamoth.*   46:7 Hebrew *of Jacob;* also in 46:11. See note on 44:4.

PROVERBS 10:23

**D**oing wrong is fun for a fool, but living wisely brings pleasure to the sensible.

# MARCH 4

NUMBERS 2:1–3:51

**T**hen the LORD gave these instructions to Moses and Aaron: [2]"When the Israelites set up camp, each tribe will be assigned its own area. The tribal divisions will camp beneath their family banners on all four sides of the Tabernacle,* but at some distance from it.

[3-4]"The divisions of Judah, Issachar, and Zebulun are to camp toward the sunrise on the east side of the Tabernacle, beneath their family banners. These are the names of the tribes, their leaders, and the numbers of their registered troops:

| | Tribe | Leader | Number |
|---|---|---|---|
| | Judah | Nahshon son of Amminadab | 74,600 |
| 5-6 | Issachar | Nethanel son of Zuar | 54,400 |
| 7-8 | Zebulun | Eliab son of Helon | 57,400 |

⁹So the total of all the troops on Judah's side of the camp is 186,400. These three tribes are to lead the way whenever the Israelites travel to a new campsite.

¹⁰⁻¹¹"The divisions of Reuben, Simeon, and Gad are to camp on the south side of the Tabernacle, beneath their family banners. These are the names of the tribes, their leaders, and the numbers of their registered troops:

| Tribe | Leader | Number |
|---|---|---|
| Reuben | Elizur son of Shedeur | 46,500 |
| ¹²⁻¹³ Simeon | Shelumiel son of Zurishaddai | 59,300 |
| ¹⁴⁻¹⁵ Gad | Eliasaph son of Deuel* | 45,650 |

¹⁶So the total of all the troops on Reuben's side of the camp is 151,450. These three tribes will be second in line whenever the Israelites travel.

¹⁷"Then the Tabernacle, carried by the Levites, will set out from the middle of the camp. All the tribes are to travel in the same order that they camp, each in position under the appropriate family banner.

¹⁸⁻¹⁹"The divisions of Ephraim, Manasseh, and Benjamin are to camp on the west side of the Tabernacle, beneath their family banners. These are the names of the tribes, their leaders, and the numbers of their registered troops:

| Tribe | Leader | Number |
|---|---|---|
| Ephraim | Elishama son of Ammihud | 40,500 |
| ²⁰⁻²¹ Manasseh | Gamaliel son of Pedahzur | 32,200 |
| ²²⁻²³ Benjamin | Abidan son of Gideoni | 35,400 |

²⁴So the total of all the troops on Ephraim's side of the camp is 108,100. These three tribes will be third in line whenever the Israelites travel.

²⁵⁻²⁶"The divisions of Dan, Asher, and Naphtali are to camp on the north side of the Tabernacle, beneath their family banners. These are the names of the tribes, their leaders, and the numbers of their registered troops:

| Tribe | Leader | Number |
|---|---|---|
| Dan | Ahiezer son of Ammishaddai | 62,700 |
| ²⁷⁻²⁸ Asher | Pagiel son of Ocran | 41,500 |
| ²⁹⁻³⁰ Naphtali | Ahira son of Enan | 53,400 |

³¹So the total of all the troops on Dan's side of the camp is 157,600. These three tribes will be last, marching under their banners whenever the Israelites travel."

³²In summary, the troops of Israel listed by their families totaled 603,550. ³³But as the LORD had commanded, the Levites were not included in this registration. ³⁴So the people of Israel did everything as the LORD had commanded Moses. Each clan and family set up camp and marched under their banners exactly as the LORD had instructed them.

³:¹THIS is the family line of Aaron and Moses as it was recorded when the LORD spoke to Moses on Mount Sinai: ²The names of Aaron's sons were Nadab (the oldest), Abihu, Eleazar, and Ithamar. ³These sons of Aaron were anointed and ordained to minister as priests. ⁴But Nadab and Abihu died in the LORD's presence in the wilderness of Sinai when they burned before the LORD the wrong kind of fire, different than he had commanded. Since they had no sons, this left only Eleazar and Ithamar to serve as priests with their father, Aaron.

⁵Then the LORD said to Moses, ⁶"Call forward the tribe of Levi, and present them to Aaron the priest to serve as his assistants. ⁷They will serve Aaron and the whole community, performing their sacred duties in and around the Tabernacle.* ⁸They will also maintain all the furnishings of the sacred tent,* serving in the Tabernacle on behalf of all the Israelites. ⁹Assign the Levites to Aaron and his sons. They have been given from among all the people of Israel to serve as their assistants. ¹⁰Appoint Aaron and his sons to carry out the duties of the

priesthood. But any unauthorized person who goes too near the sanctuary must be put to death."

[11]And the LORD said to Moses, [12]"Look, I have chosen the Levites from among the Israelites to serve as substitutes for all the firstborn sons of the people of Israel. The Levites belong to me, [13]for all the firstborn males are mine. On the day I struck down all the firstborn sons of the Egyptians, I set apart for myself all the firstborn in Israel, both of people and of animals. They are mine; I am the LORD."

[14]The LORD spoke again to Moses in the wilderness of Sinai. He said, [15]"Record the names of the members of the tribe of Levi by their families and clans. List every male who is one month old or older." [16]So Moses listed them, just as the LORD had commanded.

[17]Levi had three sons, whose names were Gershon, Kohath, and Merari.
[18]The clans descended from Gershon were named after two of his descendants, Libni and Shimei.
[19]The clans descended from Kohath were named after four of his descendants, Amram, Izhar, Hebron, and Uzziel.
[20]The clans descended from Merari were named after two of his descendants, Mahli and Mushi.
These were the Levite clans, listed according to their family groups.

[21]The descendants of Gershon were composed of the clans descended from Libni and Shimei. [22]There were 7,500 males one month old or older among these Gershonite clans. [23]They were assigned the area to the west of the Tabernacle for their camp. [24]The leader of the Gershonite clans was Eliasaph son of Lael. [25]These two clans were responsible to care for the Tabernacle, including the sacred tent with its layers of coverings, the curtain at its entrance, [26]the curtains of the courtyard that surrounded the Tabernacle and altar, the curtain at the courtyard entrance, the

ropes, and all the equipment related to their use.

[27]The descendants of Kohath were composed of the clans descended from Amram, Izhar, Hebron, and Uzziel. [28]There were 8,600* males one month old or older among these Kohathite clans. They were responsible for the care of the sanctuary, [29]and they were assigned the area south of the Tabernacle for their camp. [30]The leader of the Kohathite clans was Elizaphan son of Uzziel. [31]These four clans were responsible for the care of the Ark, the table, the lampstand, the altars, the various articles used in the sanctuary, the inner curtain, and all the equipment related to their use. [32]Eleazar, son of Aaron the priest, was the chief administrator over all the Levites, with special responsibility for the oversight of the sanctuary.

[33]The descendants of Merari were composed of the clans descended from Mahli and Mushi. [34]There were 6,200 males one month old or older among these Merarite clans. [35]They were assigned the area north of the Tabernacle for their camp. The leader of the Merarite clans was Zuriel son of Abihail. [36]These two clans were responsible for the care of the frames supporting the Tabernacle, the crossbars, the pillars, the bases, and all the equipment related to their use. [37]They were also responsible for the posts of the courtyard and all their bases, pegs, and ropes.

[38]The area in front of the Tabernacle, in the east toward the sunrise,* was reserved for the tents of Moses and of Aaron and his sons, who had the final responsibility for the sanctuary on behalf of the people of Israel. Anyone other than a priest or Levite who went too near the sanctuary was to be put to death.

[39]When Moses and Aaron counted the Levite clans at the LORD's command, the total number was 22,000 males one month old or older.

[40]Then the LORD said to Moses, "Now count all the firstborn sons in Israel who are one month old or older, and make a list of their names. [41]The Levites must be

reserved for me as substitutes for the firstborn sons of Israel; I am the LORD. And the Levites' livestock must be reserved for me as substitutes for the firstborn livestock of the whole nation of Israel."

42 So Moses counted the firstborn sons of the people of Israel, just as the LORD had commanded. 43 The number of firstborn sons who were one month old or older was 22,273.

44 Then the LORD said to Moses, 45 "Take the Levites as substitutes for the firstborn sons of the people of Israel. And take the livestock of the Levites as substitutes for the firstborn livestock of the people of Israel. The Levites belong to me; I am the LORD. 46 There are 273 more firstborn sons of Israel than there are Levites. To redeem these extra firstborn sons, 47 collect five pieces of silver* for each of them (each piece weighing the same as the sanctuary shekel, which equals twenty gerahs). 48 Give the silver to Aaron and his sons as the redemption price for the extra firstborn sons."

49 So Moses collected the silver for redeeming the firstborn sons of Israel who exceeded the number of Levites. 50 He collected 1,365 pieces of silver* on behalf of these firstborn sons of Israel (each piece weighing the same as the sanctuary shekel). 51 And Moses gave the silver for the redemption to Aaron and his sons, just as the LORD had commanded.

2:2 Hebrew *the Tent of Meeting;* also in 2:17.    2:14-15 As in many Hebrew manuscripts, Samaritan Pentateuch, and Latin Vulgate (see also 1:14); most Hebrew manuscripts read *son of Reuel.*    3:7 Hebrew *around the Tent of Meeting, doing service at the Tabernacle.*    3:8 Hebrew *the Tent of Meeting;* also in 3:25.    3:28 Some Greek manuscripts read *8,300;* see total in 3:39.    3:38 Hebrew *toward the sunrise, in front of the Tent of Meeting.*    3:47 Hebrew *5 shekels* [2 ounces or 57 grams].    3:50 Hebrew *1,365 shekels* [34 pounds or 15.5 kilograms].

## MARK 11:27–12:17

Again they entered Jerusalem. As Jesus was walking through the Temple area, the leading priests, the teachers of religious law, and the elders came up to him. 28 They demanded, "By what authority are you doing all these things? Who gave you the right to do them?"

29 "I'll tell you by what authority I do these things if you answer one question," Jesus replied. 30 "Did John's authority to baptize come from heaven, or was it merely human? Answer me!"

31 They talked it over among themselves. "If we say it was from heaven, he will ask why we didn't believe John. 32 But do we dare say it was merely human?" For they were afraid of what the people would do, because everyone believed that John was a prophet. 33 So they finally replied, "We don't know."

And Jesus responded, "Then I won't tell you by what authority I do these things."

12:1 THEN Jesus began teaching them with stories: "A man planted a vineyard. He built a wall around it, dug a pit for pressing out the grape juice, and built a lookout tower. Then he leased the vineyard to tenant farmers and moved to another country. 2 At the time of the grape harvest, he sent one of his servants to collect his share of the crop. 3 But the farmers grabbed the servant, beat him up, and sent him back empty-handed. 4 The owner then sent another servant, but they insulted him and beat him over the head. 5 The next servant he sent was killed. Others he sent were either beaten or killed, 6 until there was only one left— his son whom he loved dearly. The owner finally sent him, thinking, 'Surely they will respect my son.'

7 "But the tenant farmers said to one another, 'Here comes the heir to this estate. Let's kill him and get the estate for ourselves!' 8 So they grabbed him and murdered him and threw his body out of the vineyard.

9 "What do you suppose the owner of the vineyard will do?" Jesus asked. "I'll tell you—he will come and kill those farmers and lease the vineyard to others. 10 Didn't you ever read this in the Scriptures?

'The stone that the builders rejected
    has now become the cornerstone.
11 This is the LORD's doing,
    and it is wonderful to see.'*"

¹²The religious leaders* wanted to arrest Jesus because they realized he was telling the story against them—they were the wicked farmers. But they were afraid of the crowd, so they left him and went away.

¹³Later the leaders sent some Pharisees and supporters of Herod to trap Jesus into saying something for which he could be arrested. ¹⁴"Teacher," they said, "we know how honest you are. You are impartial and don't play favorites. You teach the way of God truthfully. Now tell us—is it right to pay taxes to Caesar or not? ¹⁵Should we pay them, or shouldn't we?"

Jesus saw through their hypocrisy and said, "Why are you trying to trap me? Show me a Roman coin,* and I'll tell you." ¹⁶When they handed it to him, he asked, "Whose picture and title are stamped on it?"

"Caesar's," they replied.

¹⁷**"Well, then," Jesus said, "give to Caesar what belongs to Caesar, and give to God what belongs to God."**

His reply completely amazed them.

**12:10-11** Ps 118:22-23.   **12:12** Greek *They*.
**12:15** Greek *a denarius*.

## PSALM 47:1-9

*For the choir director: A psalm of the descendants of Korah.*

¹ **C**ome, everyone! Clap your hands!
    Shout to God with joyful praise!
² For the LORD Most High is awesome.
    He is the great King of all
       the earth.
³ He subdues the nations before us,
    putting our enemies beneath
       our feet.
⁴ He chose the Promised Land
    as our inheritance,
       the proud possession of Jacob's
       descendants, whom he loves.
                                    *Interlude*

⁵ God has ascended with a mighty
    shout.
    The LORD has ascended with
       trumpets blaring.
⁶ Sing praises to God, sing praises;

sing praises to our King, sing
    praises!
⁷ For God is the King over all
    the earth.
    Praise him with a psalm!
⁸ God reigns above the nations,
    sitting on his holy throne.
⁹ The rulers of the world have
    gathered together
    with the people of the God
       of Abraham.
    For all the kings of the earth belong
       to God.
    He is highly honored everywhere.

## PROVERBS 10:24-25

**T**he fears of the wicked will be fulfilled; the hopes of the godly will be granted. □When the storms of life come, the wicked are whirled away, but the godly have a lasting foundation.

# MARCH 5

## NUMBERS 4:1-5:31

**T**hen the LORD said to Moses and Aaron, ²"Record the names of the members of the clans and families of the Kohathite division of the tribe of Levi. ³List all the men between the ages of thirty and fifty who are eligible to serve in the Tabernacle.*

⁴"The duties of the Kohathites at the Tabernacle will relate to the most sacred objects. ⁵When the camp moves, Aaron and his sons must enter the Tabernacle first to take down the inner curtain and cover the Ark of the Covenant* with it. ⁶Then they must cover the inner curtain with fine goatskin leather and spread over that a single piece of blue cloth. Finally, they must put the carrying poles of the Ark in place.

⁷"Next they must spread a blue cloth over the table where the Bread of the Presence is displayed, and on the cloth

they will place the bowls, pans, jars, pitchers, and the special bread. [8]They must spread a scarlet cloth over all of this, and finally a covering of fine goatskin leather on top of the scarlet cloth. Then they must insert the carrying poles into the table.

[9]"Next they must cover the lampstand with a blue cloth, along with its lamps, lamp snuffers, trays, and special jars of olive oil. [10]Then they must cover the lampstand and its accessories with fine goatskin leather and place the bundle on a carrying frame.

[11]"Next they must spread a blue cloth over the gold incense altar and cover this cloth with fine goatskin leather. Then they must attach the carrying poles to the altar. [12]They must take all the remaining furnishings of the sanctuary and wrap them in a blue cloth, cover them with fine goatskin leather, and place them on the carrying frame.

[13]"They must remove the ashes from the altar for sacrifices and cover the altar with a purple cloth. [14]All the altar utensils—the firepans, meat forks, shovels, basins, and all the containers—must be placed on the cloth, and a covering of fine goatskin leather must be spread over them. Finally, they must put the carrying poles in place. [15]The camp will be ready to move when Aaron and his sons have finished covering the sanctuary and all the sacred articles. The Kohathites will come and carry these things to the next destination. But they must not touch the sacred objects, or they will die. So these are the things from the Tabernacle that the Kohathites must carry.

[16]"Eleazar son of Aaron the priest will be responsible for the oil of the lampstand, the fragrant incense, the daily grain offering, and the anointing oil. In fact, Eleazar will be responsible for the entire Tabernacle and everything in it, including the sanctuary and its furnishings."

[17]Then the LORD said to Moses and Aaron, [18]"Do not let the Kohathite clans be destroyed from among the Levites! [19]This is what you must do so they will live and not die when they approach the most sacred objects. Aaron and his sons must always go in with them and assign a specific duty or load to each person. [20]The Kohathites must never enter the sanctuary to look at the sacred objects for even a moment, or they will die."

[21]And the LORD said to Moses, [22]"Record the names of the members of the clans and families of the Gershonite division of the tribe of Levi. [23]List all the men between the ages of thirty and fifty who are eligible to serve in the Tabernacle.

[24]"These Gershonite clans will be responsible for general service and carrying loads. [25]They must carry the curtains of the Tabernacle, the Tabernacle itself with its coverings, the outer covering of fine goatskin leather, and the curtain for the Tabernacle entrance. [26]They are also to carry the curtains for the courtyard walls that surround the Tabernacle and altar, the curtain across the courtyard entrance, the ropes, and all the equipment related to their use. The Gershonites are responsible for all these items. [27]Aaron and his sons will direct the Gershonites regarding all their duties, whether it involves moving the equipment or doing other work. They must assign the Gershonites responsibility for the loads they are to carry. [28]So these are the duties assigned to the Gershonite clans at the Tabernacle. They will be directly responsible to Ithamar son of Aaron the priest.

[29]"Now record the names of the members of the clans and families of the Merarite division of the tribe of Levi. [30]List all the men between the ages of thirty and fifty who are eligible to serve in the Tabernacle.

[31]"Their only duty at the Tabernacle will be to carry loads. They will carry the frames of the Tabernacle, the crossbars, the posts, and the bases; [32]also the posts for the courtyard walls with their bases, pegs, and ropes; and all the accessories and everything else related to their use. Assign the various loads to each man by name. [33]So these are the duties of the

Merarite clans at the Tabernacle. They are directly responsible to Ithamar son of Aaron the priest."

34So Moses, Aaron, and the other leaders of the community listed the members of the Kohathite division by their clans and families. 35The list included all the men between thirty and fifty years of age who were eligible for service in the Tabernacle, 36and the total number came to 2,750. 37So this was the total of all those from the Kohathite clans who were eligible to serve at the Tabernacle. Moses and Aaron listed them, just as the LORD had commanded through Moses.

38The Gershonite division was also listed by its clans and families. 39The list included all the men between thirty and fifty years of age who were eligible for service in the Tabernacle, 40and the total number came to 2,630. 41So this was the total of all those from the Gershonite clans who were eligible to serve at the Tabernacle. Moses and Aaron listed them, just as the LORD had commanded.

42The Merarite division was also listed by its clans and families. 43The list included all the men between thirty and fifty years of age who were eligible for service in the Tabernacle, 44and the total number came to 3,200. 45So this was the total of all those from the Merarite clans who were eligible for service. Moses and Aaron listed them, just as the LORD had commanded through Moses.

46So Moses, Aaron, and the leaders of Israel listed all the Levites by their clans and families. 47All the men between thirty and fifty years of age who were eligible for service in the Tabernacle and for its transportation 48numbered 8,580. 49When their names were recorded, as the LORD had commanded through Moses, each man was assigned his task and told what to carry.

And so the registration was completed, just as the LORD had commanded Moses.

5:1THE LORD gave these instructions to Moses: 2"Command the people of Israel to remove from the camp anyone who has a skin disease* or a discharge, or who has become ceremonially unclean by touching a dead person. 3This command applies to men and women alike. Remove them so they will not defile the camp in which I live among them." 4So the Israelites did as the LORD had commanded Moses and removed such people from the camp.

5Then the LORD said to Moses, 6"Give the following instructions to the people of Israel: If any of the people—men or women—betray the LORD by doing wrong to another person, they are guilty. 7They must confess their sin and make full restitution for what they have done, adding an additional 20 percent and returning it to the person who was wronged. 8But if the person who was wronged is dead, and there are no near relatives to whom restitution can be made, the payment belongs to the LORD and must be given to the priest. Those who are guilty must also bring a ram as a sacrifice, and they will be purified and made right with the LORD.* 9All the sacred offerings that the Israelites bring to a priest will belong to him. 10Each priest may keep all the sacred donations that he receives."

11And the LORD said to Moses, 12"Give the following instructions to the people of Israel.

"Suppose a man's wife goes astray, and she is unfaithful to her husband 13and has sex with another man, but neither her husband nor anyone else knows about it. She has defiled herself, even though there was no witness and she was not caught in the act. 14If her husband becomes jealous and is suspicious of his wife and needs to know whether or not she has defiled herself, 15the husband must bring his wife to the priest. He must also bring an offering of two quarts* of barley flour to be presented on her behalf. Do not mix it with olive oil or frankincense, for it is a jealousy offering—an offering to prove whether or not she is guilty.

16"The priest will then present her to

stand trial before the LORD. [17]He must take some holy water in a clay jar and pour into it dust he has taken from the Tabernacle floor. [18]When the priest has presented the woman before the LORD, he must unbind her hair and place in her hands the offering of proof—the jealousy offering to determine whether her husband's suspicions are justified. The priest will stand before her, holding the jar of bitter water that brings a curse to those who are guilty. [19]The priest will then put the woman under oath and say to her, 'If no other man has had sex with you, and you have not gone astray and defiled yourself while under your husband's authority, may you be immune from the effects of this bitter water that brings on the curse. [20]But if you have gone astray by being unfaithful to your husband, and have defiled yourself by having sex with another man—'

[21]"At this point the priest must put the woman under oath by saying, 'May the people know that the LORD's curse is upon you when he makes you infertile, causing your womb to shrivel* and your abdomen to swell. [22]Now may this water that brings the curse enter your body and cause your abdomen to swell and your womb to shrivel.*' And the woman will be required to say, 'Yes, let it be so.' [23]And the priest will write these curses on a piece of leather and wash them off into the bitter water. [24]He will make the woman drink the bitter water that brings on the curse. When the water enters her body, it will cause bitter suffering if she is guilty.

[25]"The priest will take the jealousy offering from the woman's hand, lift it up before the LORD, and carry it to the altar. [26]He will take a handful of the flour as a token portion and burn it on the altar, and he will require the woman to drink the water. [27]If she has defiled herself by being unfaithful to her husband, the water that brings on the curse will cause bitter suffering. Her abdomen will swell and her womb will shrink,* and her name will become a curse among her people. [28]But if she

has not defiled herself and is pure, then she will be unharmed and will still be able to have children.

[29]"This is the ritual law for dealing with suspicion. If a woman goes astray and defiles herself while under her husband's authority, [30]or if a man becomes jealous and is suspicious that his wife has been unfaithful, the husband must present his wife before the LORD, and the priest will apply this entire ritual law to her. [31]The husband will be innocent of any guilt in this matter, but his wife will be held accountable for her sin."

4:3 Hebrew *the Tent of Meeting;* also in 4:4, 15, 23, 25, 28, 30, 31, 33, 35, 37, 39, 41, 43, 47.   4:5 Or *Ark of the Testimony.*   5:2 Traditionally rendered *leprosy.* The Hebrew word used here describes various skin diseases. 5:8 Or *bring a ram for atonement, which will make atonement for them.*   5:15 Hebrew 1⁄10 *of an ephah* [2.2 liters].   5:21 Hebrew *when he causes your thigh to waste away.*   5:22 Hebrew *and your thigh to waste away.*   5:27 Hebrew *and her thigh will waste away.*

## MARK 12:18-37

Then Jesus was approached by some Sadducees—religious leaders who say there is no resurrection from the dead. They posed this question: [19]"Teacher, Moses gave us a law that if a man dies, leaving a wife without children, his brother should marry the widow and have a child who will carry on the brother's name.* [20]Well, suppose there were seven brothers. The oldest one married and then died without children. [21]So the second brother married the widow, but he also died without children. Then the third brother married her. [22]This continued with all seven of them, and still there were no children. Last of all, the woman also died. [23]So tell us, whose wife will she be in the resurrection? For all seven were married to her."

[24]Jesus replied, "Your mistake is that you don't know the Scriptures, and you don't know the power of God. [25]For when the dead rise, they will neither marry nor be given in marriage. In this respect they will be like the angels in heaven.

[26]"But now, as to whether the dead will be raised—haven't you ever read about this in the writings of Moses, in

the story of the burning bush? Long after Abraham, Isaac, and Jacob had died, God said to Moses,* 'I am the God of Abraham, the God of Isaac, and the God of Jacob.'* ²⁷So he is the God of the living, not the dead. You have made a serious error."

²⁸One of the teachers of religious law was standing there listening to the debate. He realized that Jesus had answered well, so he asked, "Of all the commandments, which is the most important?"

²⁹Jesus replied, "The most important commandment is this: 'Listen, O Israel! The LORD our God is the one and only LORD. ³⁰And you must love the LORD your God with all your heart, all your soul, all your mind, and all your strength.'* ³¹The second is equally important: 'Love your neighbor as yourself.'* No other commandment is greater than these."

³²The teacher of religious law replied, "Well said, Teacher. You have spoken the truth by saying that there is only one God and no other. ³³**And I know it is important to love him with all my heart and all my understanding and all my strength, and to love my neighbor as myself. This is more important than to offer all of the burnt offerings and sacrifices required in the law."**

³⁴Realizing how much the man understood, Jesus said to him, "You are not far from the Kingdom of God." And after that, no one dared to ask him any more questions.

³⁵Later, as Jesus was teaching the people in the Temple, he asked, "Why do the teachers of religious law claim that the Messiah is the son of David? ³⁶For David himself, speaking under the inspiration of the Holy Spirit, said,

'The LORD said to my Lord,
Sit in the place of honor at my
    right hand
    until I humble your enemies
    beneath your feet.'*

³⁷Since David himself called the Messiah 'my Lord,' how can the Messiah be his son?" The large crowd listened to him with great delight.

12:19 See Deut 25:5-6.   12:26a Greek *in the story of the bush? God said to him.*   12:26b Exod 3:6.   12:29-30 Deut 6:4-5.   12:31 Lev 19:18.   12:36 Ps 110:1.

## PSALM 48:1-14

*A song. A psalm of the descendants of Korah.*

¹ **H**ow great is the LORD,
    how deserving of praise,
in the city of our God,
    which sits on his holy mountain!
² It is high and magnificent;
    the whole earth rejoices to see it!
Mount Zion, the holy mountain,*
    is the city of the great King!
³ God himself is in Jerusalem's towers,
    revealing himself as its defender.

⁴ The kings of the earth joined forces
    and advanced against the city.
⁵ But when they saw it, they were
        stunned;
    they were terrified and ran away.
⁶ They were gripped with terror
    and writhed in pain like a woman
        in labor.
⁷ You destroyed them like the mighty
        ships of Tarshish
    shattered by a powerful east wind.

⁸ We had heard of the city's glory,
    but now we have seen it
        ourselves—
    the city of the LORD of Heaven's
        Armies.
It is the city of our God;
    he will make it safe forever.
                            *Interlude*

⁹ O God, we meditate on your
        unfailing love
    as we worship in your Temple.
¹⁰ As your name deserves, O God,
    you will be praised to the ends of
        the earth.
    Your strong right hand is filled
        with victory.
¹¹ Let the people on Mount Zion
        rejoice.
    Let all the towns of Judah be glad
    because of your justice.

¹² Go, inspect the city of Jerusalem.*
  Walk around and count the many
    towers.
¹³ Take note of the fortified walls,
    and tour all the citadels,
  that you may describe them
    to future generations.
¹⁴ For that is what God is like.
    He is our God forever and ever,
    and he will guide us until we die.

**48:2** Or *Mount Zion, in the far north;* Hebrew reads *Mount Zion, the heights of Zaphon.*   **48:12** Hebrew *Zion.*

PROVERBS 10:26

Lazy people irritate their employers,
like vinegar to the teeth or smoke in the
eyes.

# MARCH
# 6

NUMBERS 6:1–7:89

Then the Lord said to Moses, "Give the
following instructions to the people of
Israel.

²"If any of the people, either men or
women, take the special vow of a Nazirite, setting themselves apart to the Lord
in a special way, ³they must give up wine
and other alcoholic drinks. They must
not use vinegar made from wine or from
other alcoholic drinks, they must not
drink fresh grape juice, and they must
not eat grapes or raisins. ⁴As long as they
are bound by their Nazirite vow, they are
not allowed to eat or drink anything that
comes from a grapevine—not even the
grape seeds or skins.

⁵"They must never cut their hair
throughout the time of their vow, for
they are holy and set apart to the Lord.
Until the time of their vow has been fulfilled, they must let their hair grow long.
⁶And they must not go near a dead body
during the entire period of their vow to
the Lord. ⁷Even if the dead person is
their own father, mother, brother, or
sister, they must not defile themselves,
for the hair on their head is the symbol
of their separation to God. ⁸This requirement applies as long as they are set
apart to the Lord.

⁹"If someone falls dead beside them,
the hair they have dedicated will be defiled. They must wait for seven days and
then shave their heads. Then they will be
cleansed from their defilement. ¹⁰On
the eighth day they must bring two
turtledoves or two young pigeons to the
priest at the entrance of the Tabernacle.* ¹¹The priest will offer one of the
birds for a sin offering and the other for
a burnt offering. In this way, he will purify them* from the guilt they incurred
through contact with the dead body.
Then they must reaffirm their commitment and let their hair begin to grow
again. ¹²The days of their vow that were
completed before their defilement no
longer count. They must rededicate
themselves to the Lord as a Nazirite for
the full term of their vow, and each must
bring a one-year-old male lamb for a
guilt offering.

¹³"This is the ritual law for Nazirites.
At the conclusion of their time of separation as Nazirites, they must each go to the
entrance of the Tabernacle ¹⁴and offer
their sacrifices to the Lord: a one-year-
old male lamb without defect for a burnt
offering, a one-year-old female lamb
without defect for a sin offering, a ram
without defect for a peace offering, ¹⁵a
basket of bread made without yeast—
cakes of choice flour mixed with olive oil
and wafers spread with olive oil—along
with their prescribed grain offerings and
liquid offerings. ¹⁶The priest will present
these offerings before the Lord: first the
sin offering and the burnt offering;
¹⁷then the ram for a peace offering,
along with the basket of bread made
without yeast. The priest must also present the prescribed grain offering and
liquid offering to the Lord.

¹⁸"Then the Nazirites will shave their
heads at the entrance of the Tabernacle.
They will take the hair that had been dedicated and place it on the fire beneath the

peace-offering sacrifice. [19]After the Nazirite's head has been shaved, the priest will take for each of them the boiled shoulder of the ram, and he will take from the basket a cake and a wafer made without yeast. He will put them all into the Nazirite's hands. [20]Then the priest will lift them up as a special offering before the LORD. These are holy portions for the priest, along with the breast of the special offering and the thigh of the sacred offering that are lifted up before the LORD. After this ceremony the Nazirites may again drink wine.

[21]"This is the ritual law of the Nazirites, who vow to bring these offerings to the LORD. They may also bring additional offerings if they can afford it. And they must be careful to do whatever they vowed when they set themselves apart as Nazirites."

[22]Then the LORD said to Moses, [23]"Tell Aaron and his sons to bless the people of Israel with this special blessing:

[24] 'May the LORD bless you
    and protect you.
[25] May the LORD smile on you
    and be gracious to you.
[26] May the LORD show you his favor
    and give you his peace.'

[27]Whenever Aaron and his sons bless the people of Israel in my name, I myself will bless them."

[7:1]ON the day Moses set up the Tabernacle, he anointed it and set it apart as holy. He also anointed and set apart all its furnishings and the altar with its utensils. [2]Then the leaders of Israel—the tribal leaders who had registered the troops—came and brought their offerings. [3]Together they brought six large wagons and twelve oxen. There was a wagon for every two leaders and an ox for each leader. They presented these to the LORD in front of the Tabernacle.

[4]Then the LORD said to Moses, [5]"Receive their gifts, and use these oxen and wagons for transporting the Tabernacle.* Distribute them among the Levites according to the work they have to do." [6]So Moses took the wagons and oxen and presented them to the Levites. [7]He gave two wagons and four oxen to the Gershonite division for their work, [8]and he gave four wagons and eight oxen to the Merarite division for their work. All their work was done under the leadership of Ithamar son of Aaron the priest. [9]But he gave none of the wagons or oxen to the Kohathite division, since they were required to carry the sacred objects of the Tabernacle on their shoulders.

[10]The leaders also presented dedication gifts for the altar at the time it was anointed. They each placed their gifts before the altar. [11]The LORD said to Moses, "Let one leader bring his gift each day for the dedication of the altar."

[12]On the first day Nahshon son of Amminadab, leader of the tribe of Judah, presented his offering.

[13]His offering consisted of a silver platter weighing 3¼ pounds and a silver basin weighing 1¾ pounds* (as measured by the weight of the sanctuary shekel). These were both filled with grain offerings of choice flour moistened with olive oil. [14]He also brought a gold container weighing four ounces,* which was filled with incense. [15]He brought a young bull, a ram, and a one-year-old male lamb for a burnt offering, [16]and a male goat for a sin offering. [17]For a peace offering he brought two bulls, five rams, five male goats, and five one-year-old male lambs. This was the offering brought by Nahshon son of Amminadab.

[18]On the second day Nethanel son of Zuar, leader of the tribe of Issachar, presented his offering.

[19]His offering consisted of a silver platter weighing 3¼ pounds and a silver basin weighing 1¾ pounds (as measured by the weight of the sanctuary shekel). These were both filled with grain offerings of choice flour moistened with olive oil. [20]He

also brought a gold container weighing four ounces, which was filled with incense. [21]He brought a young bull, a ram, and a one-year-old male lamb for a burnt offering, [22]and a male goat for a sin offering. [23]For a peace offering he brought two bulls, five rams, five male goats, and five one-year-old male lambs. This was the offering brought by Nethanel son of Zuar.

[24]On the third day Eliab son of Helon, leader of the tribe of Zebulun, presented his offering.
[25]His offering consisted of a silver platter weighing 3¼ pounds and a silver basin weighing 1¾ pounds (as measured by the weight of the sanctuary shekel). These were both filled with grain offerings of choice flour moistened with olive oil. [26]He also brought a gold container weighing four ounces, which was filled with incense. [27]He brought a young bull, a ram, and a one-year-old male lamb for a burnt offering, [28]and a male goat for a sin offering. [29]For a peace offering he brought two bulls, five rams, five male goats, and five one-year-old male lambs. This was the offering brought by Eliab son of Helon.

[30]On the fourth day Elizur son of Shedeur, leader of the tribe of Reuben, presented his offering.
[31]His offering consisted of a silver platter weighing 3¼ pounds and a silver basin weighing 1¾ pounds (as measured by the weight of the sanctuary shekel). These were both filled with grain offerings of choice flour moistened with olive oil. [32]He also brought a gold container weighing four ounces, which was filled with incense. [33]He brought a young bull, a ram, and a one-year-old male lamb for a burnt offering, [34]and a male goat for a sin offering. [35]For a peace offering he brought two bulls, five rams, five male goats,

and five one-year-old male lambs. This was the offering brought by Elizur son of Shedeur.

[36]On the fifth day Shelumiel son of Zurishaddai, leader of the tribe of Simeon, presented his offering.
[37]His offering consisted of a silver platter weighing 3¼ pounds and a silver basin weighing 1¾ pounds (as measured by the weight of the sanctuary shekel). These were both filled with grain offerings of choice flour moistened with olive oil. [38]He also brought a gold container weighing four ounces, which was filled with incense. [39]He brought a young bull, a ram, and a one-year-old male lamb for a burnt offering, [40]and a male goat for a sin offering. [41]For a peace offering he brought two bulls, five rams, five male goats, and five one-year-old male lambs. This was the offering brought by Shelumiel son of Zurishaddai.

[42]On the sixth day Eliasaph son of Deuel, leader of the tribe of Gad, presented his offering.
[43]His offering consisted of a silver platter weighing 3¼ pounds and a silver basin weighing 1¾ pounds (as measured by the weight of the sanctuary shekel). These were both filled with grain offerings of choice flour moistened with olive oil. [44]He also brought a gold container weighing four ounces, which was filled with incense. [45]He brought a young bull, a ram, and a one-year-old male lamb for a burnt offering, [46]and a male goat for a sin offering. [47]For a peace offering he brought two bulls, five rams, five male goats, and five one-year-old male lambs. This was the offering brought by Eliasaph son of Deuel.

[48]On the seventh day Elishama son of Ammihud, leader of the tribe of Ephraim, presented his offering.
[49]His offering consisted of a silver platter weighing 3¼ pounds and a

silver basin weighing 1¾ pounds (as measured by the weight of the sanctuary shekel). These were both filled with grain offerings of choice flour moistened with olive oil. [50]He also brought a gold container weighing four ounces, which was filled with incense. [51]He brought a young bull, a ram, and a one-year-old male lamb for a burnt offering, [52]and a male goat for a sin offering. [53]For a peace offering he brought two bulls, five rams, five male goats, and five one-year-old male lambs. This was the offering brought by Elishama son of Ammihud.

[54]On the eighth day Gamaliel son of Pedahzur, leader of the tribe of Manasseh, presented his offering.

[55]His offering consisted of a silver platter weighing 3¼ pounds and a silver basin weighing 1¾ pounds (as measured by the weight of the sanctuary shekel). These were both filled with grain offerings of choice flour moistened with olive oil. [56]He also brought a gold container weighing four ounces, which was filled with incense. [57]He brought a young bull, a ram, and a one-year-old male lamb for a burnt offering, [58]and a male goat for a sin offering. [59]For a peace offering he brought two bulls, five rams, five male goats, and five one-year-old male lambs. This was the offering brought by Gamaliel son of Pedahzur.

[60]On the ninth day Abidan son of Gideoni, leader of the tribe of Benjamin, presented his offering.

[61]His offering consisted of a silver platter weighing 3¼ pounds and a silver basin weighing 1¾ pounds (as measured by the weight of the sanctuary shekel). These were both filled with grain offerings of choice flour moistened with olive oil. [62]He also brought a gold container weighing four ounces, which was filled with incense. [63]He brought a young bull, a ram, and a one-year-old male lamb for a burnt offering, [64]and a male goat for a sin offering. [65]For a peace offering he brought two bulls, five rams, five male goats, and five one-year-old male lambs. This was the offering brought by Abidan son of Gideoni.

[66]On the tenth day Ahiezer son of Ammishaddai, leader of the tribe of Dan, presented his offering.

[67]His offering consisted of a silver platter weighing 3¼ pounds and a silver basin weighing 1¾ pounds (as measured by the weight of the sanctuary shekel). These were both filled with grain offerings of choice flour moistened with olive oil. [68]He also brought a gold container weighing four ounces, which was filled with incense. [69]He brought a young bull, a ram, and a one-year-old male lamb for a burnt offering, [70]and a male goat for a sin offering. [71]For a peace offering he brought two bulls, five rams, five male goats, and five one-year-old male lambs. This was the offering brought by Ahiezer son of Ammishaddai.

[72]On the eleventh day Pagiel son of Ocran, leader of the tribe of Asher, presented his offering.

[73]His offering consisted of a silver platter weighing 3¼ pounds and a silver basin weighing 1¾ pounds (as measured by the weight of the sanctuary shekel). These were both filled with grain offerings of choice flour moistened with olive oil. [74]He also brought a gold container weighing four ounces, which was filled with incense. [75]He brought a young bull, a ram, and a one-year-old male lamb for a burnt offering, [76]and a male goat for a sin offering. [77]For a peace offering he brought two bulls, five rams, five male goats, and five one-year-old male lambs. This was the offering brought by Pagiel son of Ocran.

78On the twelfth day Ahira son of Enan, leader of the tribe of Naphtali, presented his offering.

79His offering consisted of a silver platter weighing 3¼ pounds and a silver basin weighing 1¾ pounds (as measured by the weight of the sanctuary shekel). These were both filled with grain offerings of choice flour moistened with olive oil. 80He also brought a gold container weighing four ounces, which was filled with incense. 81He brought a young bull, a ram, and a one-year-old male lamb for a burnt offering, 82and a male goat for a sin offering. 83For a peace offering he brought two bulls, five rams, five male goats, and five one-year-old male lambs. This was the offering brought by Ahira son of Enan.

84So this was the dedication offering brought by the leaders of Israel at the time the altar was anointed: twelve silver platters, twelve silver basins, and twelve gold incense containers. 85Each silver platter weighed 3¼ pounds, and each silver basin weighed 1¼ pounds. The total weight of the silver was 60 pounds* (as measured by the weight of the sanctuary shekel). 86Each of the twelve gold containers that was filled with incense weighed four ounces (as measured by the weight of the sanctuary shekel). The total weight of the gold was three pounds.* 87Twelve young bulls, twelve rams, and twelve one-year-old male lambs were donated for the burnt offerings, along with their prescribed grain offerings. Twelve male goats were brought for the sin offerings. 88Twenty-four bulls, sixty rams, sixty male goats, and sixty one-year-old male lambs were donated for the peace offerings. This was the dedication offering for the altar after it was anointed.

89Whenever Moses went into the Tabernacle to speak with the LORD, he heard the voice speaking to him from between the two cherubim above the Ark's cover—the place of atonement—that rests on the Ark of the Covenant.* The LORD spoke to him from there.

6:10 Hebrew the Tent of Meeting; also in 6:13, 18. 6:11 Or make atonement for them. 7:5 Hebrew the Tent of Meeting; also in 7:89. 7:13 Hebrew silver platter weighing 130 shekels [1.5 kilograms] and a silver basin weighing 70 shekels [800 grams]; also in 7:19, 25, 31, 37, 43, 49, 55, 61, 67, 73, 79, 85. 7:14 Hebrew 10 shekels [114 grams]; also in 7:20, 26, 32, 38, 44, 50, 56, 62, 68, 74, 80, 86. 7:85 Hebrew 2,400 shekels [27.6 kilograms]. 7:86 Hebrew 120 shekels [1.4 kilograms]. 7:89 Or Ark of the Testimony.

## MARK 12:38–13:13

Jesus also taught: "Beware of these teachers of religious law! For they like to parade around in flowing robes and receive respectful greetings as they walk in the marketplaces. 39And how they love the seats of honor in the synagogues and the head table at banquets. 40Yet they shamelessly cheat widows out of their property and then pretend to be pious by making long prayers in public. Because of this, they will be more severely punished."

41Jesus sat down near the collection box in the Temple and watched as the crowds dropped in their money. Many rich people put in large amounts. 42Then a poor widow came and dropped in two small coins.* 43Jesus called his disciples to him and said, "I tell you the truth, this poor widow has given more than all the others who are making contributions. 44For they gave a tiny part of their surplus, but she, poor as she is, has given everything she had to live on."

13:1As Jesus was leaving the Temple that day, one of his disciples said, "Teacher, look at these magnificent buildings! Look at the impressive stones in the walls."

2Jesus replied, "Yes, look at these great buildings. But they will be completely demolished. Not one stone will be left on top of another!"

3Later, Jesus sat on the Mount of Olives across the valley from the Temple. Peter, James, John, and Andrew came to him privately and asked him, 4"Tell us, when will all this happen? What sign will show us that these things are about to be fulfilled?"

⁵Jesus replied, "Don't let anyone mislead you, ⁶for many will come in my name, claiming, 'I am the Messiah.'* They will deceive many. ⁷And you will hear of wars and threats of wars, but don't panic. Yes, these things must take place, but the end won't follow immediately. ⁸Nation will go to war against nation, and kingdom against kingdom. There will be earthquakes in many parts of the world, as well as famines. But this is only the first of the birth pains, with more to come.

⁹"When these things begin to happen, watch out! You will be handed over to the local councils and beaten in the synagogues. You will stand trial before governors and kings because you are my followers. But this will be your opportunity to tell them about me.* ¹⁰For the Good News must first be preached to all nations.* ¹¹But when you are arrested and stand trial, don't worry in advance about what to say. Just say what God tells you at that time, for it is not you who will be speaking, but the Holy Spirit.

¹²"A brother will betray his brother to death, a father will betray his own child, and children will rebel against their parents and cause them to be killed. ¹³And everyone will hate you because you are my followers.* But the one who endures to the end will be saved."

12:42 Greek *two lepta, which is a kodrantes* [i.e., a quadrans]. 13:6 Greek *claiming, 'I am.'* 13:9 Or *But this will be your testimony against them.* 13:10 Or *all peoples.* 13:13 Greek *on account of my name.*

PSALM 49:1-20
*For the choir director: A psalm of the descendants of Korah.*

¹ Listen to this, all you people!
  Pay attention, everyone in the world!
² High and low,
  rich and poor—listen!
³ For my words are wise,
  and my thoughts are filled with insight.
⁴ I listen carefully to many proverbs
  and solve riddles with inspiration from a harp.

⁵ Why should I fear when trouble comes,
  when enemies surround me?
⁶ They trust in their wealth
  and boast of great riches.
⁷ Yet they cannot redeem themselves from death*
  by paying a ransom to God.
⁸ Redemption does not come so easily,
  for no one can ever pay enough
⁹ to live forever
  and never see the grave.

¹⁰ Those who are wise must finally die,
  just like the foolish and senseless,
  leaving all their wealth behind.
¹¹ The grave is their eternal home,
  where they will stay forever.
  They may name their estates after themselves,
¹² but their fame will not last.
  They will die, just like animals.
¹³ This is the fate of fools,
  though they are remembered as being wise.*      *Interlude*

¹⁴ Like sheep, they are led to the grave,*
  where death will be their shepherd.
  In the morning the godly will rule over them.
  Their bodies will rot in the grave,
  far from their grand estates.
¹⁵ But as for me, God will redeem my life.
  He will snatch me from the power of the grave.    *Interlude*

¹⁶ So don't be dismayed when the wicked grow rich
  and their homes become ever more splendid.
¹⁷ For when they die, they take nothing with them.
  Their wealth will not follow them into the grave.
¹⁸ In this life they consider themselves fortunate
  and are applauded for their success.
¹⁹ But they will die like all before them

and never again see the
light of day.
<sup>20</sup> People who boast of their wealth
don't understand;
they will die, just like animals.

**49:7** Or *no one can redeem the life of another.*    **49:13** The
meaning of the Hebrew is uncertain.    **49:14** Hebrew *Sheol;*
also in 49:14b, 15.

## PROVERBS 10:27-28
**F**ear of the Lord lengthens one's life,
but the years of the wicked are cut
short. □ The hopes of the godly result in
happiness, but the expectations of the
wicked come to nothing.

# MARCH
# 7

## NUMBERS 8:1–9:23
**T**he Lord said to Moses, <sup>2</sup>"Give Aaron
the following instructions: When you set
up the seven lamps in the lampstand,
place them so their light shines forward
in front of the lampstand." <sup>3</sup>So Aaron
did this. He set up the seven lamps so
they reflected their light forward, just as
the Lord had commanded Moses. <sup>4</sup>The
entire lampstand, from its base to its
decorative blossoms, was made of
beaten gold. It was built according to the
exact design the Lord had shown Moses.

<sup>5</sup>Then the Lord said to Moses, <sup>6</sup>"Now
set the Levites apart from the rest of the
people of Israel and make them ceremonially clean. <sup>7</sup>Do this by sprinkling
them with the water of purification, and
have them shave their entire body and
wash their clothing. Then they will be
ceremonially clean. <sup>8</sup>Have them bring a
young bull and a grain offering of
choice flour moistened with olive oil,
along with a second young bull for a sin
offering. <sup>9</sup>Then assemble the whole
community of Israel, and present the
Levites at the entrance of the Tabernacle.* <sup>10</sup>When you present the Levites

before the Lord, the people of Israel
must lay their hands on them. <sup>11</sup>Raising
his hands, Aaron must then present the
Levites to the Lord as a special offering
from the people of Israel, thus dedicat-
ing them to the Lord's service.

<sup>12</sup>"Next the Levites will lay their
hands on the heads of the young bulls.
Present one as a sin offering and the
other as a burnt offering to the Lord, to
purify the Levites and make them right
with the Lord.* <sup>13</sup>Then have the Levites
stand in front of Aaron and his sons,
and raise your hands and present them
as a special offering to the Lord. <sup>14</sup>In
this way, you will set the Levites apart
from the rest of the people of Israel, and
the Levites will belong to me. <sup>15</sup>After
this, they may go into the Tabernacle to
do their work, because you have purified them and presented them as a special offering.

<sup>16</sup>"Of all the people of Israel, the Le-
vites are reserved for me. I have claimed
them for myself in place of all the firstborn sons of the Israelites; I have taken
the Levites as their substitutes. <sup>17</sup>For all
the firstborn males among the people
of Israel are mine, both of people and of
animals. I set them apart for myself on
the day I struck down all the firstborn
sons of the Egyptians. <sup>18</sup>Yes, I have
claimed the Levites in place of all the
firstborn sons of Israel. <sup>19</sup>And of all the
Israelites, I have assigned the Levites to
Aaron and his sons. They will serve in
the Tabernacle on behalf of the Israelites and make sacrifices to purify* the
people so no plague will strike them
when they approach the sanctuary."

<sup>20</sup>So Moses, Aaron, and the whole
community of Israel dedicated the Levites, carefully following all the Lord's
instructions to Moses. <sup>21</sup>The Levites purified themselves from sin and washed
their clothes, and Aaron lifted them up
and presented them to the Lord as a
special offering. He then offered a sacrifice to purify them and make them
right with the Lord.* <sup>22</sup>After that the
Levites went into the Tabernacle to perform their duties, assisting Aaron and

his sons. So they carried out all the commands that the LORD gave Moses concerning the Levites.

²³The LORD also instructed Moses, ²⁴"This is the rule the Levites must follow: They must begin serving in the Tabernacle at the age of twenty-five, ²⁵and they must retire at the age of fifty. ²⁶After retirement they may assist their fellow Levites by serving as guards at the Tabernacle, but they may not officiate in the service. This is how you must assign duties to the Levites."

⁹:¹A YEAR after Israel's departure from Egypt, the LORD spoke to Moses in the wilderness of Sinai. In the first month* of that year he said, ²"Tell the Israelites to celebrate the Passover at the prescribed time, ³at twilight on the fourteenth day of the first month.* Be sure to follow all my decrees and regulations concerning this celebration."

⁴So Moses told the people to celebrate the Passover ⁵in the wilderness of Sinai as twilight fell on the fourteenth day of the month. And they celebrated the festival there, just as the LORD had commanded Moses. ⁶But some of the men had been ceremonially defiled by touching a dead body, so they could not celebrate the Passover that day. They came to Moses and Aaron that day ⁷and said, "We have become ceremonially unclean by touching a dead body. But why should we be prevented from presenting the LORD's offering at the proper time with the rest of the Israelites?"

⁸Moses answered, "Wait here until I have received instructions for you from the LORD."

⁹This was the LORD's reply to Moses. ¹⁰"Give the following instructions to the people of Israel: If any of the people now or in future generations are ceremonially unclean at Passover time because of touching a dead body, or if they are on a journey and cannot be present at the ceremony, they may still celebrate the LORD's Passover. ¹¹They must offer the Passover sacrifice one month later, at twilight on the fourteenth day

of the second month.* They must eat the Passover lamb at that time with bitter salad greens and bread made without yeast. ¹²They must not leave any of the lamb until the next morning, and they must not break any of its bones. They must follow all the normal regulations concerning the Passover.

¹³"But those who neglect to celebrate the Passover at the regular time, even though they are ceremonially clean and not away on a trip, will be cut off from the community of Israel. If they fail to present the LORD's offering at the proper time, they will suffer the consequences of their guilt. ¹⁴And if foreigners living among you want to celebrate the Passover to the LORD, they must follow these same decrees and regulations. The same laws apply both to native-born Israelites and to the foreigners living among you."

¹⁵On the day the Tabernacle was set up, the cloud covered it.* But from evening until morning the cloud over the Tabernacle looked like a pillar of fire. ¹⁶This was the regular pattern—at night the cloud that covered the Tabernacle had the appearance of fire. ¹⁷Whenever the cloud lifted from over the sacred tent, the people of Israel would break camp and follow it. And wherever the cloud settled, the people of Israel would set up camp. ¹⁸In this way, they traveled and camped at the LORD's command wherever he told them to go. Then they remained in their camp as long as the cloud stayed over the Tabernacle. ¹⁹If the cloud remained over the Tabernacle for a long time, the Israelites stayed and performed their duty to the LORD. ²⁰Sometimes the cloud would stay over the Tabernacle for only a few days, so the people would stay for only a few days, as the LORD commanded. Then at the LORD's command they would break camp and move on. ²¹Sometimes the cloud stayed only overnight and lifted the next morning. But day or night, when the cloud lifted, the people broke camp and moved on. ²²Whether the cloud stayed above the

Tabernacle for two days, a month, or a year, the people of Israel stayed in camp and did not move on. But as soon as it lifted, they broke camp and moved on. 23 So they camped or traveled at the LORD's command, and they did whatever the LORD told them through Moses.

8:9 Hebrew *the Tent of Meeting;* also in 8:15, 19, 22, 24, 26.    8:12 Or *to make atonement for the Levites.* 8:19 Or *make atonement for.*    8:21 Or *then made atonement for them to purify them.*    9:1 The first month of the ancient Hebrew lunar calendar usually occurs within the months of March and April.    9:3 This day in the ancient Hebrew lunar calendar occurred in late March, April, or early May.    9:11 This day in the ancient Hebrew lunar calendar occurred in late April, May, or early June. 9:15 Hebrew *covered the Tabernacle, the Tent of the Testimony.*

## MARK 13:14-37

"The day is coming when you will see the sacrilegious object that causes desecration* standing where he* should not be." (Reader, pay attention!) "Then those in Judea must flee to the hills. 15 A person out on the deck of a roof must not go down into the house to pack. 16 A person out in the field must not return even to get a coat. 17 How terrible it will be for pregnant women and for nursing mothers in those days. 18 And pray that your flight will not be in winter. 19 For there will be greater anguish in those days than at any time since God created the world. And it will never be so great again. 20 In fact, unless the Lord shortens that time of calamity, not a single person will survive. But for the sake of his chosen ones he has shortened those days.

21 "Then if anyone tells you, 'Look, here is the Messiah,' or 'There he is,' don't believe it. 22 For false messiahs and false prophets will rise up and perform signs and wonders so as to deceive, if possible, even God's chosen ones. 23 Watch out! I have warned you about this ahead of time!

24 "At that time, after the anguish of those days,

the sun will be darkened,
the moon will give no light,
25 the stars will fall from the sky,
and the powers in the heavens
will be shaken.*

26 Then everyone will see the Son of Man* coming on the clouds with great power and glory.* 27 And he will send out his angels to gather his chosen ones from all over the world*—from the farthest ends of the earth and heaven.

28 "Now learn a lesson from the fig tree. When its branches bud and its leaves begin to sprout, you know that summer is near. 29 In the same way, when you see all these things taking place, you can know that his return is very near, right at the door. 30 I tell you the truth, this generation* will not pass from the scene before all these things take place. 31 Heaven and earth will disappear, but my words will never disappear.

32 "However, no one knows the day or hour when these things will happen, not even the angels in heaven or the Son himself. Only the Father knows. 33 And since you don't know when that time will come, be on guard! Stay alert*!

34 "The coming of the Son of Man can be illustrated by the story of a man going on a long trip. When he left home, he gave each of his slaves instructions about the work they were to do, and he told the gatekeeper to watch for his return. 35 You, too, must keep watch! For you don't know when the master of the household will return—in the evening, at midnight, before dawn, or at daybreak. 36 Don't let him find you sleeping when he arrives without warning. 37 I say to you what I say to everyone: Watch for him!"

13:14a Greek *the abomination of desolation.* See Dan 9:27; 11:31; 12:11.    13:14b Or *it.*    13:24-25 See Isa 13:10; 34:4; Joel 2:10.    13:26a "Son of Man" is a title Jesus used for himself.    13:26b See Dan 7:13.    13:27 Greek *from the four winds.*    13:30 Or *this age,* or *this nation.* 13:33 Some manuscripts add *and pray.*

## PSALM 50:1-23
*A psalm of Asaph.*

1 The LORD, the Mighty One, is God,
and he has spoken;
he has summoned all humanity
from where the sun rises to
where it sets.

2 From Mount Zion, the perfection
of beauty,
God shines in glorious radiance.
3 Our God approaches,
and he is not silent.
Fire devours everything in his
way,
and a great storm rages around
him.
4 He calls on the heavens above and
earth below
to witness the judgment of his
people.
5 "Bring my faithful people to me—
those who made a covenant with
me by giving sacrifices."
6 Then let the heavens proclaim
his justice,
for God himself will be the judge.
*Interlude*

7 "O my people, listen as I speak.
Here are my charges against you,
O Israel:
I am God, your God!
8 I have no complaint about your
sacrifices
or the burnt offerings you
constantly offer.
9 But I do not need the bulls from
your barns
or the goats from your pens.
10 For all the animals of the forest
are mine,
and I own the cattle on a
thousand hills.
11 I know every bird on the mountains,
and all the animals of the field
are mine.
12 If I were hungry, I would not tell you,
for all the world is mine and
everything in it.
13 Do I eat the meat of bulls?
Do I drink the blood of goats?
14 Make thankfulness your sacrifice
to God,
and keep the vows you made
to the Most High.
15 Then call on me when you are
in trouble,
and I will rescue you,
and you will give me glory."

16 But God says to the wicked:
"Why bother reciting my decrees
and pretending to obey my
covenant?
17 For you refuse my discipline
and treat my words like trash.
18 When you see thieves, you approve
of them,
and you spend your time with
adulterers.
19 Your mouth is filled with
wickedness,
and your tongue is full of lies.
20 You sit around and slander your
brother—
your own mother's son.
21 While you did all this, I remained
silent,
and you thought I didn't care.
But now I will rebuke you,
listing all my charges against you.
22 Repent, all of you who forget me,
or I will tear you apart,
and no one will help you.
23 But giving thanks is a sacrifice that
truly honors me.
If you keep to my path,
I will reveal to you the salvation
of God."

PROVERBS 10:29-30
The way of the LORD is a stronghold to
those with integrity, but it destroys the
wicked. □ The godly will never be disturbed, but the wicked will be removed
from the land.

MARCH
8

NUMBERS 10:1–11:23
Now the LORD said to Moses, 2"Make
two trumpets of hammered silver for
calling the community to assemble and
for signaling the breaking of camp.
3 When both trumpets are blown, everyone must gather before you at the en-

trance of the Tabernacle.* [4]But if only one trumpet is blown, then only the leaders—the heads of the clans of Israel—must present themselves to you.

[5]"When you sound the signal to move on, the tribes camped on the east side of the Tabernacle must break camp and move forward. [6]When you sound the signal a second time, the tribes camped on the south will follow. You must sound short blasts as the signal for moving on. [7]But when you call the people to an assembly, blow the trumpets with a different signal. [8]Only the priests, Aaron's descendants, are allowed to blow the trumpets. This is a permanent law for you, to be observed from generation to generation.

[9]"When you arrive in your own land and go to war against your enemies who attack you, sound the alarm with the trumpets. Then the LORD your God will remember you and rescue you from your enemies. [10]Blow the trumpets in times of gladness, too, sounding them at your annual festivals and at the beginning of each month. And blow the trumpets over your burnt offerings and peace offerings. The trumpets will remind the LORD your God of his covenant with you. I am the LORD your God."

[11]In the second year after Israel's departure from Egypt—on the twentieth day of the second month*—the cloud lifted from the Tabernacle of the Covenant.* [12]So the Israelites set out from the wilderness of Sinai and traveled on from place to place until the cloud stopped in the wilderness of Paran.

[13]When the people set out for the first time, following the instructions the LORD had given through Moses, [14]Judah's troops led the way. They marched behind their banner, and their leader was Nahshon son of Amminadab. [15]They were joined by the troops of the tribe of Issachar, led by Nethanel son of Zuar, [16]and the troops of the tribe of Zebulun, led by Eliab son of Helon.

[17]Then the Tabernacle was taken down, and the Gershonite and Merarite divisions of the Levites were next in the line of march, carrying the Tabernacle with them. [18]Reuben's troops went next, marching behind their banner. Their leader was Elizur son of Shedeur. [19]They were joined by the troops of the tribe of Simeon, led by Shelumiel son of Zurishaddai, [20]and the troops of the tribe of Gad, led by Eliasaph son of Deuel.

[21]Next came the Kohathite division of the Levites, carrying the sacred objects from the Tabernacle. Before they arrived at the next camp, the Tabernacle would already be set up at its new location. [22]Ephraim's troops went next, marching behind their banner. Their leader was Elishama son of Ammihud. [23]They were joined by the troops of the tribe of Manasseh, led by Gamaliel son of Pedahzur, [24]and the troops of the tribe of Benjamin, led by Abidan son of Gideoni.

[25]Dan's troops went last, marching behind their banner and serving as the rear guard for all the tribal camps. Their leader was Ahiezer son of Ammishaddai. [26]They were joined by the troops of the tribe of Asher, led by Pagiel son of Ocran, [27]and the troops of the tribe of Naphtali, led by Ahira son of Enan.

[28]This was the order in which the Israelites marched, division by division.

[29]One day Moses said to his brother-in-law, Hobab son of Reuel the Midianite, "We are on our way to the place the LORD promised us, for he said, 'I will give it to you.' Come with us and we will treat you well, for the LORD has promised wonderful blessings for Israel!"

[30]But Hobab replied, "No, I will not go. I must return to my own land and family."

[31]"Please don't leave us," Moses pleaded. "You know the places in the wilderness where we should camp. Come, be our guide. [32]If you do, we'll share with you all the blessings the LORD gives us."

[33]They marched for three days after leaving the mountain of the LORD, with the Ark of the LORD's Covenant moving ahead of them to show them where to

stop and rest. [34]As they moved on each day, the cloud of the LORD hovered over them. [35]And whenever the Ark set out, Moses would shout, "Arise, O LORD, and let your enemies be scattered! Let them flee before you!" [36]And when the Ark was set down, he would say, "Return, O LORD, to the countless thousands of Israel!"

[11:1]SOON the people began to complain about their hardship, and the LORD heard everything they said. Then the LORD's anger blazed against them, and he sent a fire to rage among them, and he destroyed some of the people in the outskirts of the camp. [2]Then the people screamed to Moses for help, and when he prayed to the LORD, the fire stopped. [3]After that, the area was known as Taberah (which means "the place of burning"), because fire from the LORD had burned among them there.

[4]Then the foreign rabble who were traveling with the Israelites began to crave the good things of Egypt. And the people of Israel also began to complain. "Oh, for some meat!" they exclaimed. [5]"We remember the fish we used to eat for free in Egypt. And we had all the cucumbers, melons, leeks, onions, and garlic we wanted. [6]But now our appetites are gone. All we ever see is this manna!"

[7]The manna looked like small coriander seeds, and it was pale yellow like gum resin. [8]The people would go out and gather it from the ground. They made flour by grinding it with hand mills or pounding it in mortars. Then they boiled it in a pot and made it into flat cakes. These cakes tasted like pastries baked with olive oil. [9]The manna came down on the camp with the dew during the night.

[10]Moses heard all the families standing in the doorways of their tents whining, and the LORD became extremely angry. Moses was also very aggravated. [11]And Moses said to the LORD, "Why are you treating me, your servant, so harshly? Have mercy on me! What did I do to deserve the burden of all these people?

[12]Did I give birth to them? Did I bring them into the world? Why did you tell me to carry them in my arms like a mother carries a nursing baby? How can I carry them to the land you swore to give their ancestors? [13]Where am I supposed to get meat for all these people? They keep whining to me, saying, 'Give us meat to eat!' [14]I can't carry all these people by myself! The load is far too heavy! [15]If this is how you intend to treat me, just go ahead and kill me. Do me a favor and spare me this misery!"

[16]Then the LORD said to Moses, "Gather before me seventy men who are recognized as elders and leaders of Israel. Bring them to the Tabernacle* to stand there with you. [17]I will come down and talk to you there. I will take some of the Spirit that is upon you, and I will put the Spirit upon them also. They will bear the burden of the people along with you, so you will not have to carry it alone.

[18]"And say to the people, 'Purify yourselves, for tomorrow you will have meat to eat. You were whining, and the LORD heard you when you cried, "Oh, for some meat! We were better off in Egypt!" Now the LORD will give you meat, and you will have to eat it. [19]And it won't be for just a day or two, or for five or ten or even twenty. [20]You will eat it for a whole month until you gag and are sick of it. For you have rejected the LORD, who is here among you, and you have whined to him, saying, "Why did we ever leave Egypt?"'"

[21]But Moses responded to the LORD, "There are 600,000 foot soldiers here with me, and yet you say, 'I will give them meat for a whole month!' [22]Even if we butchered all our flocks and herds, would that satisfy them? Even if we caught all the fish in the sea, would that be enough?"

[23]Then the LORD said to Moses, "Has my arm lost its power? Now you will see whether or not my word comes true!"

10:3 Hebrew *Tent of Meeting.*   10:11a This day in the ancient Hebrew lunar calendar occurred in late April, May, or early June.   10:11b Or *Tabernacle of the Testimony.*
11:16 Hebrew *the Tent of Meeting.*

## MARK 14:1-21

It was now two days before Passover and the Festival of Unleavened Bread. The leading priests and the teachers of religious law were still looking for an opportunity to capture Jesus secretly and kill him. [2]"But not during the Passover celebration," they agreed, "or the people may riot."

[3]Meanwhile, Jesus was in Bethany at the home of Simon, a man who had previously had leprosy. While he was eating,* a woman came in with a beautiful alabaster jar of expensive perfume made from essence of nard. She broke open the jar and poured the perfume over his head.

[4]Some of those at the table were indignant. "Why waste such expensive perfume?" they asked. [5]"It could have been sold for a year's wages* and the money given to the poor!" So they scolded her harshly.

[6]But Jesus replied, "Leave her alone. Why criticize her for doing such a good thing to me? [7]You will always have the poor among you, and you can help them whenever you want to. But you will not always have me. [8]She has done what she could and has anointed my body for burial ahead of time. [9]I tell you the truth, wherever the Good News is preached throughout the world, this woman's deed will be remembered and discussed."

[10]Then Judas Iscariot, one of the twelve disciples, went to the leading priests to arrange to betray Jesus to them. [11]They were delighted when they heard why he had come, and they promised to give him money. So he began looking for an opportunity to betray Jesus.

[12]On the first day of the Festival of Unleavened Bread, when the Passover lamb is sacrificed, Jesus' disciples asked him, "Where do you want us to go to prepare the Passover meal for you?"

[13]So Jesus sent two of them into Jerusalem with these instructions: "As you go into the city, a man carrying a pitcher of water will meet you. Follow him. [14]At the house he enters, say to the owner, 'The Teacher asks: Where is the guest room where I can eat the Passover meal with my disciples?' [15]He will take you upstairs to a large room that is already set up. That is where you should prepare our meal." [16]So the two disciples went into the city and found everything just as Jesus had said, and they prepared the Passover meal there.

[17]In the evening Jesus arrived with the twelve disciples.* [18]As they were at the table* eating, Jesus said, "I tell you the truth, one of you eating with me here will betray me."

[19]Greatly distressed, each one asked in turn, "Am I the one?"

[20]He replied, "It is one of you twelve who is eating from this bowl with me. [21]For the Son of Man* must die, as the Scriptures declared long ago. But how terrible it will be for the one who betrays him. It would be far better for that man if he had never been born!"

14:3 Or *reclining.* 14:5 Greek *for 300 denarii.* A denarius was equivalent to a laborer's full day's wage. 14:17 Greek *the Twelve.* 14:18 Or *As they reclined.* 14:21 "Son of Man" is a title Jesus used for himself.

## PSALM 51:1-19

*For the choir director: A psalm of David, regarding the time Nathan the prophet came to him after David had committed adultery with Bathsheba.*

[1] Have mercy on me, O God,
        because of your unfailing
            love.
    Because of your great compassion,
        blot out the stain of my sins.
[2] Wash me clean from my guilt.
        Purify me from my sin.
[3] For I recognize my rebellion;
        it haunts me day and night.
[4] Against you, and you alone, have
            I sinned;
        I have done what is evil in your
            sight.
    You will be proved right in what
            you say,
        and your judgment against me
            is just.*
[5] For I was born a sinner—
        yes, from the moment my mother
            conceived me.

⁶ But you desire honesty from
　　the womb,*
　　teaching me wisdom even there.

⁷ Purify me from my sins,* and I will
　　be clean;
　　wash me, and I will be whiter than
　　snow.

⁸ Oh, give me back my joy again;
　　you have broken me—
　　now let me rejoice.

⁹ Don't keep looking at my sins.
　　Remove the stain of my guilt.

¹⁰ **Create in me a clean heart, O God.**
　　**Renew a loyal spirit within me.**

¹¹ **Do not banish me from your**
　　**presence,**
　　**and don't take your Holy Spirit***
　　**from me.**

¹² **Restore to me the joy of your**
　　**salvation,**
　　**and make me willing to**
　　**obey you.**

¹³ Then I will teach your ways to rebels,
　　and they will return to you.

¹⁴ Forgive me for shedding blood,
　　O God who saves;
　　then I will joyfully sing of your
　　forgiveness.

¹⁵ Unseal my lips, O Lord,
　　that my mouth may praise you.

¹⁶ You do not desire a sacrifice, or I
　　would offer one.
　　You do not want a burnt offering.

¹⁷ The sacrifice you desire is a broken
　　spirit.
　　You will not reject a broken and
　　repentant heart, O God.

¹⁸ Look with favor on Zion and
　　help her;
　　rebuild the walls of Jerusalem.

¹⁹ Then you will be pleased with
　　sacrifices offered in the right
　　spirit—
　　with burnt offerings and whole
　　burnt offerings.
　　Then bulls will again be sacrificed
　　on your altar.

**51:4** Greek version reads *and you will win your case in
court.* Compare Rom 3:4.　**51:6** Or *from the heart;* Hebrew
reads *in the inward parts.*　**51:7** Hebrew *Purify me with
the hyssop branch.*　**51:11** Or *your spirit of holiness.*

PROVERBS 10:31-32

The mouth of the godly person gives
wise advice, but the tongue that deceives
will be cut off. □ The lips of the godly
speak helpful words, but the mouth of
the wicked speaks perverse words.

# MARCH
# 9

NUMBERS 11:24–13:33

So Moses went out and reported the
LORD's words to the people. He gathered the seventy elders and stationed
them around the Tabernacle.* ²⁵And
the LORD came down in the cloud and
spoke to Moses. Then he gave the seventy elders the same Spirit that was
upon Moses. And when the Spirit rested
upon them, they prophesied. But this
never happened again.

²⁶Two men, Eldad and Medad, had
stayed behind in the camp. They were
listed among the elders, but they had
not gone out to the Tabernacle. Yet the
Spirit rested upon them as well, so they
prophesied there in the camp. ²⁷A
young man ran and reported to Moses,
"Eldad and Medad are prophesying in
the camp!"

²⁸Joshua son of Nun, who had been
Moses' assistant since his youth, protested, "Moses, my master, make them
stop!"

²⁹But Moses replied, "Are you jealous
for my sake? I wish that all the LORD's
people were prophets and that the LORD
would put his Spirit upon them all!"
³⁰Then Moses returned to the camp
with the elders of Israel.

³¹Now the LORD sent a wind that
brought quail from the sea and let them
fall all around the camp. For miles in
every direction there were quail flying
about three feet above the ground.* ³²So
the people went out and caught quail all

that day and throughout the night and all the next day, too. No one gathered less than fifty bushels*! They spread the quail all around the camp to dry. ³³But while they were gorging themselves on the meat—while it was still in their mouths— the anger of the LORD blazed against the people, and he struck them with a severe plague. ³⁴So that place was called Kibroth-hattaavah (which means "graves of gluttony") because there they buried the people who had craved meat from Egypt. ³⁵From Kibroth-hattaavah the Israelites traveled to Hazeroth, where they stayed for some time.

¹²:¹WHILE they were at Hazeroth, Miriam and Aaron criticized Moses because he had married a Cushite woman. ²They said, "Has the LORD spoken only through Moses? Hasn't he spoken through us, too?" But the LORD heard them. ³(Now Moses was very humble—more humble than any other person on earth.)

⁴So immediately the LORD called to Moses, Aaron, and Miriam and said, "Go out to the Tabernacle,* all three of you!" So the three of them went to the Tabernacle. ⁵Then the LORD descended in the pillar of cloud and stood at the entrance of the Tabernacle.* "Aaron and Miriam!" he called, and they stepped forward. ⁶And the LORD said to them, "Now listen to what I say:

"If there were prophets among you,
    I, the LORD, would reveal myself
        in visions.
    I would speak to them in dreams.
⁷ But not with my servant Moses.
    Of all my house, he is the one
        I trust.
⁸ I speak to him face to face,
    clearly, and not in riddles!
    He sees the LORD as he is.
So why were you not afraid
    to criticize my servant Moses?"

⁹The LORD was very angry with them, and he departed. ¹⁰As the cloud moved from above the Tabernacle, there stood Miriam, her skin as white as snow from leprosy.* When Aaron saw what had

happened to her, ¹¹he cried out to Moses, "Oh, my master! Please don't punish us for this sin we have so foolishly committed. ¹²Don't let her be like a stillborn baby, already decayed at birth."

¹³So Moses cried out to the LORD, "O God, I beg you, please heal her!"

¹⁴But the LORD said to Moses, "If her father had done nothing more than spit in her face, wouldn't she be defiled for seven days? So keep her outside the camp for seven days, and after that she may be accepted back."

¹⁵So Miriam was kept outside the camp for seven days, and the people waited until she was brought back before they traveled again. ¹⁶Then they left Hazeroth and camped in the wilderness of Paran.

¹³:¹THE LORD now said to Moses, ²"Send out men to explore the land of Canaan, the land I am giving to the Israelites. Send one leader from each of the twelve ancestral tribes." ³So Moses did as the LORD commanded him. He sent out twelve men, all tribal leaders of Israel, from their camp in the wilderness of Paran. ⁴These were the tribes and the names of their leaders:

| Tribe | Leader |
|---|---|
| Reuben | Shammua son of Zaccur |
| ⁵ Simeon | Shaphat son of Hori |
| ⁶ Judah | Caleb son of Jephunneh |
| ⁷ Issachar | Igal son of Joseph |
| ⁸ Ephraim | Hoshea son of Nun |
| ⁹ Benjamin | Palti son of Raphu |
| ¹⁰ Zebulun | Gaddiel son of Sodi |
| ¹¹ Manasseh son of Joseph | Gaddi son of Susi |
| ¹² Dan | Ammiel son of Gemalli |
| ¹³ Asher | Sethur son of Michael |
| ¹⁴ Naphtali | Nahbi son of Vophsi |
| ¹⁵ Gad | Geuel son of Maki |

¹⁶These are the names of the men Moses sent out to explore the land. (Moses called Hoshea son of Nun by the name Joshua.)

¹⁷Moses gave the men these instructions as he sent them out to explore the land: "Go north through the Negev into

the hill country. <sup>18</sup>See what the land is like, and find out whether the people living there are strong or weak, few or many. <sup>19</sup>See what kind of land they live in. Is it good or bad? Do their towns have walls, or are they unprotected like open camps? <sup>20</sup>Is the soil fertile or poor? Are there many trees? Do your best to bring back samples of the crops you see." (It happened to be the season for harvesting the first ripe grapes.)

<sup>21</sup>So they went up and explored the land from the wilderness of Zin as far as Rehob, near Lebo-hamath. <sup>22</sup>Going north, they passed through the Negev and arrived at Hebron, where Ahiman, Sheshai, and Talmai—all descendants of Anak—lived. (The ancient town of Hebron was founded seven years before the Egyptian city of Zoan.) <sup>23</sup>When they came to the valley of Eshcol, they cut down a branch with a single cluster of grapes so large that it took two of them to carry it on a pole between them! They also brought back samples of the pomegranates and figs. <sup>24</sup>That place was called the valley of Eshcol (which means "cluster"), because of the cluster of grapes the Israelite men cut there.

<sup>25</sup>After exploring the land for forty days, the men returned <sup>26</sup>to Moses, Aaron, and the whole community of Israel at Kadesh in the wilderness of Paran. They reported to the whole community what they had seen and showed them the fruit they had taken from the land. <sup>27</sup>This was their report to Moses: "We entered the land you sent us to explore, and it is indeed a bountiful country—a land flowing with milk and honey. Here is the kind of fruit it produces. <sup>28</sup>But the people living there are powerful, and their towns are large and fortified. We even saw giants there, the descendants of Anak! <sup>29</sup>The Amalekites live in the Negev, and the Hittites, Jebusites, and Amorites live in the hill country. The Canaanites live along the coast of the Mediterranean Sea* and along the Jordan Valley."

<sup>30</sup>But Caleb tried to quiet the people as they stood before Moses. "Let's go at once to take the land," he said. "We can certainly conquer it!"

<sup>31</sup>But the other men who had explored the land with him disagreed. "We can't go up against them! They are stronger than we are!" <sup>32</sup>So they spread this bad report about the land among the Israelites: "The land we traveled through and explored will devour anyone who goes to live there. All the people we saw were huge. <sup>33</sup>We even saw giants* there, the descendants of Anak. Next to them we felt like grasshoppers, and that's what they thought, too!"

11:24 Hebrew *the tent;* also in 11:26.   11:31 Or *there were quail 3 feet* [2 cubits or 92 centimeters] *deep on the ground.*   11:32 Hebrew *10 homers* [1.8 kiloliters].
12:4 Hebrew *the Tent of Meeting.*   12:5 Hebrew *the tent;* also in 12:10.   12:10 Or *with a skin disease.* The Hebrew word used here can describe various skin diseases.
13:29 Hebrew *the sea.*   13:33 Hebrew *nephilim.*

## MARK 14:22-52

**A**s they were eating, Jesus took some bread and blessed it. Then he broke it in pieces and gave it to the disciples, saying, "Take it, for this is my body."

<sup>23</sup>**And he took a cup of wine and gave thanks to God for it. He gave it to them, and they all drank from it.** <sup>24</sup>**And he said to them, "This is my blood, which confirms the covenant* between God and his people. It is poured out as a sacrifice for many.** <sup>25</sup>I tell you the truth, I will not drink wine again until the day I drink it new in the Kingdom of God."

<sup>26</sup>Then they sang a hymn and went out to the Mount of Olives.

<sup>27</sup>On the way, Jesus told them, "All of you will desert me. For the Scriptures say,

'God will strike* the Shepherd,
    and the sheep will be scattered.'

<sup>28</sup>But after I am raised from the dead, I will go ahead of you to Galilee and meet you there."

<sup>29</sup>Peter said to him, "Even if everyone else deserts you, I never will."

<sup>30</sup>Jesus replied, "I tell you the truth, Peter—this very night, before the rooster crows twice, you will deny three times that you even know me."

31"No!" Peter declared emphatically. "Even if I have to die with you, I will never deny you!" And all the others vowed the same.

32They went to the olive grove called Gethsemane, and Jesus said, "Sit here while I go and pray." 33He took Peter, James, and John with him, and he became deeply troubled and distressed. 34He told them, "My soul is crushed with grief to the point of death. Stay here and keep watch with me."

35He went on a little farther and fell to the ground. He prayed that, if it were possible, the awful hour awaiting him might pass him by. 36"Abba, Father,"* he cried out, "everything is possible for you. Please take this cup of suffering away from me. Yet I want your will to be done, not mine."

37Then he returned and found the disciples asleep. He said to Peter, "Simon, are you asleep? Couldn't you watch with me even one hour? 38Keep watch and pray, so that you will not give in to temptation. For the spirit is willing, but the body is weak."

39Then Jesus left them again and prayed the same prayer as before. 40When he returned to them again, he found them sleeping, for they couldn't keep their eyes open. And they didn't know what to say.

41When he returned to them the third time, he said, "Go ahead and sleep. Have your rest. But no—the time has come. The Son of Man is betrayed into the hands of sinners. 42Up, let's be going. Look, my betrayer is here!"

43And immediately, even as Jesus said this, Judas, one of the twelve disciples, arrived with a crowd of men armed with swords and clubs. They had been sent by the leading priests, the teachers of religious law, and the elders. 44The traitor, Judas, had given them a prearranged signal: "You will know which one to arrest when I greet him with a kiss. Then you can take him away under guard." 45As soon as they arrived, Judas walked up to Jesus. "Rabbi!" he exclaimed, and gave him the kiss.

46Then the others grabbed Jesus and arrested him. 47But one of the men with Jesus pulled out his sword and struck the high priest's slave, slashing off his ear.

48Jesus asked them, "Am I some dangerous revolutionary, that you come with swords and clubs to arrest me? 49Why didn't you arrest me in the Temple? I was there among you teaching every day. But these things are happening to fulfill what the Scriptures say about me."

50Then all his disciples deserted him and ran away. 51One young man following behind was clothed only in a long linen shirt. When the mob tried to grab him, 52he slipped out of his shirt and ran away naked.

14:24 Some manuscripts read *the new covenant.*
14:27 Greek *I will strike.* Zech 13:7.   14:36 *Abba* is an Aramaic term for "father."

## PSALM 52:1-9

*For the choir director: A psalm* of David, regarding the time Doeg the Edomite said to Saul, "David has gone to see Ahimelech."*

1 **W**hy do you boast about your
        crimes, great warrior?
    Don't you realize God's justice
        continues forever?
2 All day long you plot destruction.
    Your tongue cuts like a sharp razor;
    you're an expert at telling lies.
3 You love evil more than good
    and lies more than truth.
                            *Interlude*

4 You love to destroy others with
        your words,
    you liar!
5 But God will strike you down once
        and for all.
    He will pull you from your home
    and uproot you from the land
        of the living.        *Interlude*

6 The righteous will see it and
        be amazed.
    They will laugh and say,
7 "Look what happens to mighty
        warriors
    who do not trust in God.
    They trust their wealth instead

and grow more and more bold
in their wickedness."

⁸ But I am like an olive tree, thriving
in the house of God.
I will always trust in God's
unfailing love.
⁹ I will praise you forever, O God,
for what you have done.
I will trust in your good name
in the presence of your faithful
people.

52:TITLE Hebrew *maskil*. This may be a literary or musical
term.

## PROVERBS 11:1-3

The LORD detests the use of dishonest
scales, but he delights in accurate
weights. □ Pride leads to disgrace, but
with humility comes wisdom. □ Honesty
guides good people; dishonesty destroys
treacherous people.

# MARCH
# 10

## NUMBERS 14:1–15:16

Then the whole community began weeping aloud, and they cried all night. ²Their
voices rose in a great chorus of protest
against Moses and Aaron. "If only we had
died in Egypt, or even here in the wilderness!" they complained. ³"Why is the
LORD taking us to this country only to
have us die in battle? Our wives and our
little ones will be carried off as plunder!
Wouldn't it be better for us to return to
Egypt?" ⁴Then they plotted among themselves, "Let's choose a new leader and go
back to Egypt!"

⁵Then Moses and Aaron fell face
down on the ground before the whole
community of Israel. ⁶Two of the men
who had explored the land, Joshua son
of Nun and Caleb son of Jephunneh,
tore their clothing. ⁷They said to all the
people of Israel, "The land we traveled
through and explored is a wonderful

land! ⁸And if the LORD is pleased with
us, he will bring us safely into that land
and give it to us. It is a rich land flowing
with milk and honey. ⁹Do not rebel
against the LORD, and don't be afraid of
the people of the land. They are only
helpless prey to us! They have no protection, but the LORD is with us! Don't be
afraid of them!"

¹⁰But the whole community began to
talk about stoning Joshua and Caleb.
Then the glorious presence of the LORD
appeared to all the Israelites at the Tabernacle.* ¹¹And the LORD said to Moses,
"How long will these people treat me
with contempt? Will they never believe
me, even after all the miraculous signs I
have done among them? ¹²I will disown
them and destroy them with a plague.
Then I will make you into a nation
greater and mightier than they are!"

¹³But Moses objected. "What will the
Egyptians think when they hear about
it?" he asked the LORD. "They know full
well the power you displayed in rescuing your people from Egypt. ¹⁴Now if
you destroy them, the Egyptians will
send a report to the inhabitants of this
land, who have already heard that you
live among your people. They know,
LORD, that you have appeared to your
people face to face and that your pillar
of cloud hovers over them. They know
that you go before them in the pillar of
cloud by day and the pillar of fire by
night. ¹⁵Now if you slaughter all these
people with a single blow, the nations
that have heard of your fame will say,
¹⁶'The LORD was not able to bring them
into the land he swore to give them, so
he killed them in the wilderness.'

¹⁷"Please, Lord, prove that your power
is as great as you have claimed. For you
said, ¹⁸'The LORD is slow to anger and
filled with unfailing love, forgiving every
kind of sin and rebellion. But he does not
excuse the guilty. He lays the sins of the
parents upon their children; the entire
family is affected—even children in the
third and fourth generations.' ¹⁹In keeping with your magnificent, unfailing love,
please pardon the sins of this people, just

as you have forgiven them ever since they left Egypt."

²⁰Then the LORD said, "I will pardon them as you have requested. ²¹But as surely as I live, and as surely as the earth is filled with the LORD's glory, ²²not one of these people will ever enter that land. They have all seen my glorious presence and the miraculous signs I performed both in Egypt and in the wilderness, but again and again they have tested me by refusing to listen to my voice. ²³They will never even see the land I swore to give their ancestors. None of those who have treated me with contempt will ever see it. ²⁴But my servant Caleb has a different attitude than the others have. He has remained loyal to me, so I will bring him into the land he explored. His descendants will possess their full share of that land. ²⁵Now turn around, and don't go on toward the land where the Amalekites and Canaanites live. Tomorrow you must set out for the wilderness in the direction of the Red Sea.*"

²⁶Then the LORD said to Moses and Aaron, ²⁷"How long must I put up with this wicked community and its complaints about me? Yes, I have heard the complaints the Israelites are making against me. ²⁸Now tell them this: 'As surely as I live, declares the LORD, I will do to you the very things I heard you say. ²⁹You will all drop dead in this wilderness! Because you complained against me, every one of you who is twenty years old or older and was included in the registration will die. ³⁰You will not enter and occupy the land I swore to give you. The only exceptions will be Caleb son of Jephunneh and Joshua son of Nun.

³¹"'You said your children would be carried off as plunder. Well, I will bring them safely into the land, and they will enjoy what you have despised. ³²But as for you, you will drop dead in this wilderness. ³³And your children will be like shepherds, wandering in the wilderness for forty years. In this way, they will pay for your faithlessness, until the last of you lies dead in the wilderness.

³⁴"'Because your men explored the land for forty days, you must wander in the wilderness for forty years—a year for each day, suffering the consequences of your sins. Then you will discover what it is like to have me for an enemy.' ³⁵I, the LORD, have spoken! I will certainly do these things to every member of the community who has conspired against me. They will be destroyed here in this wilderness, and here they will die!"

³⁶The ten men Moses had sent to explore the land—the ones who incited rebellion against the LORD with their bad report—³⁷were struck dead with a plague before the LORD. ³⁸Of the twelve who had explored the land, only Joshua and Caleb remained alive.

³⁹When Moses reported the LORD's words to all the Israelites, the people were filled with grief. ⁴⁰Then they got up early the next morning and went to the top of the range of hills. "Let's go," they said. "We realize that we have sinned, but now we are ready to enter the land the LORD has promised us."

⁴¹But Moses said, "Why are you now disobeying the LORD's orders to return to the wilderness? It won't work. ⁴²Do not go up into the land now. You will only be crushed by your enemies because the LORD is not with you. ⁴³When you face the Amalekites and Canaanites in battle, you will be slaughtered. The LORD will abandon you because you have abandoned the LORD."

⁴⁴But the people defiantly pushed ahead toward the hill country, even though neither Moses nor the Ark of the LORD's Covenant left the camp. ⁴⁵Then the Amalekites and the Canaanites who lived in those hills came down and attacked them and chased them back as far as Hormah.

15:1THEN the LORD told Moses, ²"Give the following instructions to the people of Israel.

"When you finally settle in the land I am giving you, ³you will offer special gifts as a pleasing aroma to the LORD. These gifts may take the form of a burnt offering, a sacrifice to fulfill a vow, a voluntary offering, or an offering at any of your annual festivals, and they may be taken from your herds of cattle or your flocks of sheep and goats. 4When you present these offerings, you must also give the LORD a grain offering of two quarts* of choice flour mixed with one quart* of olive oil. 5For each lamb offered as a burnt offering or a special sacrifice, you must also present one quart of wine as a liquid offering.

6"If the sacrifice is a ram, give a grain offering of four quarts* of choice flour mixed with a third of a gallon* of olive oil, 7and give a third of a gallon of wine as a liquid offering. This will be a pleasing aroma to the LORD.

8"When you present a young bull as a burnt offering or as a sacrifice to fulfill a vow or as a peace offering to the LORD, 9you must also give a grain offering of six quarts* of choice flour mixed with two quarts* of olive oil, 10and give two quarts of wine as a liquid offering. This will be a special gift, a pleasing aroma to the LORD.

11"Each sacrifice of a bull, ram, lamb, or young goat should be prepared in this way. 12Follow these instructions with each offering you present. 13All of you native-born Israelites must follow these instructions when you offer a special gift as a pleasing aroma to the LORD. 14And if any foreigners visit you or live among you and want to present a special gift as a pleasing aroma to the LORD, they must follow these same procedures. 15Native-born Israelites and foreigners are equal before the LORD and are subject to the same decrees. This is a permanent law for you, to be observed from generation to generation. 16The same instructions and regulations will apply both to you and to the foreigners living among you."

14:10 Hebrew the Tent of Meeting.   14:25 Hebrew sea of reeds.   15:4a Hebrew 1⁄10 of an ephah [2.2 liters].
15:4b Hebrew 1⁄4 of a hin [1 liter]; also in 15:5.
15:6a Hebrew 2⁄10 of an ephah [4.4 liters].   15:6b Hebrew 1⁄3 of a hin [1.3 liters]; also in 15:7.   15:9a Hebrew 3⁄10 of an ephah [6.6 liters].   15:9b Hebrew 1⁄2 of a hin [2 liters]; also in 15:10.

## MARK 14:53-72

They took Jesus to the high priest's home where the leading priests, the elders, and the teachers of religious law had gathered. 54Meanwhile, Peter followed him at a distance and went right into the high priest's courtyard. There he sat with the guards, warming himself by the fire.

55Inside, the leading priests and the entire high council* were trying to find evidence against Jesus, so they could put him to death. But they couldn't find any. 56Many false witnesses spoke against him, but they contradicted each other. 57Finally, some men stood up and gave this false testimony: 58"We heard him say, 'I will destroy this Temple made with human hands, and in three days I will build another, made without human hands.' " 59But even then they didn't get their stories straight!

60Then the high priest stood up before the others and asked Jesus, "Well, aren't you going to answer these charges? What do you have to say for yourself?" 61But Jesus was silent and made no reply. Then the high priest asked him, "Are you the Messiah, the Son of the Blessed One?"

62Jesus said, "I AM.* And you will see the Son of Man seated in the place of power at God's right hand* and coming on the clouds of heaven.*"

63Then the high priest tore his clothing to show his horror and said, "Why do we need other witnesses? 64You have all heard his blasphemy. What is your verdict?"

"Guilty!" they all cried. "He deserves to die!"

65Then some of them began to spit at him, and they blindfolded him and beat him with their fists. "Prophesy to us," they jeered. And the guards slapped him as they took him away.

66Meanwhile, Peter was in the courtyard below. One of the servant girls who worked for the high priest came by 67and noticed Peter warming himself at the fire. She looked at him closely and said, "You were one of those with Jesus of Nazareth.*"

68But Peter denied it. "I don't know what you're talking about," he said, and he went out into the entryway. Just then, a rooster crowed.*

[69]When the servant girl saw him standing there, she began telling the others, "This man is definitely one of them!" [70]But Peter denied it again.

A little later some of the other bystanders confronted Peter and said, "You must be one of them, because you are a Galilean."

[71]Peter swore, "A curse on me if I'm lying—I don't know this man you're talking about!" [72]And immediately the rooster crowed the second time.

Suddenly, Jesus' words flashed through Peter's mind: "Before the rooster crows twice, you will deny three times that you even know me." And he broke down and wept.

14:55 Greek the Sanhedrin.   14:62a Or The 'I AM' is here; or I am the LORD. See Exod 3:14.   14:62b Greek at the right hand of the power. See Ps 110:1.   14:62c See Dan 7:13.   14:67 Or Jesus the Nazarene.   14:68 Some manuscripts do not include Just then, a rooster crowed.

## PSALM 53:1-6

*For the choir director: A meditation; a psalm\* of David.*

[1] Only fools say in their hearts,
    "There is no God."
  They are corrupt, and their actions
      are evil;
    not one of them does good!

[2] God looks down from heaven
      on the entire human race;
  he looks to see if anyone is truly wise,
    if anyone seeks God.
[3] But no, all have turned away;
    all have become corrupt.*
  No one does good,
    not a single one!

[4] Will those who do evil never learn?
    They eat up my people like bread
    and wouldn't think of praying
        to God.
[5] Terror will grip them,
      terror like they have never
        known before.
  God will scatter the bones
    of your enemies.

You will put them to shame, for
    God has rejected them.

[6] Who will come from Mount Zion to
    rescue Israel?
  When God restores his people,
    Jacob will shout with joy, and
      Israel will rejoice.

53:TITLE Hebrew *maskil*. This may be a literary or musical term.   53:3 Greek version reads *have become useless.* Compare Rom 3:12.

## PROVERBS 11:4

Riches won't help on the day of judgment, but right living can save you from death.

# MARCH 11

## NUMBERS 15:17–16:40

Then the LORD said to Moses, [18]"Give the following instructions to the people of Israel.

"When you arrive in the land where I am taking you, [19]and you eat the crops that grow there, you must set some aside as a sacred offering to the LORD. [20]Present a cake from the first of the flour you grind, and set it aside as a sacred offering, as you do with the first grain from the threshing floor. [21]Throughout the generations to come, you are to present a sacred offering to the LORD each year from the first of your ground flour.

[22]"But suppose you unintentionally fail to carry out all these commands that the LORD has given you through Moses. [23]And suppose your descendants in the future fail to do everything the LORD has commanded through Moses. [24]If the mistake was made unintentionally, and the community was unaware of it, the whole community must present a young bull for a burnt offering as a pleasing aroma to the LORD. It must be offered along with its prescribed grain offering

and liquid offering and with one male goat for a sin offering. ²⁵With it the priest will purify the whole community of Israel, making them right with the LORD,* and they will be forgiven. For it was an unintentional sin, and they have corrected it with their offerings to the LORD—the special gift and the sin offering. ²⁶The whole community of Israel will be forgiven, including the foreigners living among you, for all the people were involved in the sin.

²⁷"If one individual commits an unintentional sin, the guilty person must bring a one-year-old female goat for a sin offering. ²⁸The priest will sacrifice it to purify* the guilty person before the LORD, and that person will be forgiven. ²⁹These same instructions apply both to native-born Israelites and to the foreigners living among you.

³⁰"But those who brazenly violate the LORD's will, whether native-born Israelites or foreigners, have blasphemed the LORD, and they must be cut off from the community. ³¹Since they have treated the LORD's word with contempt and deliberately disobeyed his command, they must be completely cut off and suffer the punishment for their guilt."

³²One day while the people of Israel were in the wilderness, they discovered a man gathering wood on the Sabbath day. ³³The people who found him doing this took him before Moses, Aaron, and the rest of the community. ³⁴They held him in custody because they did not know what to do with him. ³⁵Then the LORD said to Moses, "The man must be put to death! The whole community must stone him outside the camp." ³⁶So the whole community took the man outside the camp and stoned him to death, just as the LORD had commanded Moses.

³⁷Then the LORD said to Moses, ³⁸"Give the following instructions to the people of Israel: Throughout the generations to come you must make tassels for the hems of your clothing and attach them with a blue cord. ³⁹When you see the tassels, you will remember and obey all the commands of the LORD instead of

following your own desires and defiling yourselves, as you are prone to do. ⁴⁰The tassels will help you remember that you must obey all my commands and be holy to your God. ⁴¹I am the LORD your God who brought you out of the land of Egypt that I might be your God. I am the LORD your God!"

16:1ONE day Korah son of Izhar, a descendant of Kohath son of Levi, conspired with Dathan and Abiram, the sons of Eliab, and On son of Peleth, from the tribe of Reuben. ²They incited a rebellion against Moses, along with 250 other leaders of the community, all prominent members of the assembly. ³They united against Moses and Aaron and said, "You have gone too far! The whole community of Israel has been set apart by the LORD, and he is with all of us. What right do you have to act as though you are greater than the rest of the LORD's people?"

⁴When Moses heard what they were saying, he fell face down on the ground. ⁵Then he said to Korah and his followers, "Tomorrow morning the LORD will show us who belongs to him* and who is holy. The LORD will allow only those whom he selects to enter his own presence. ⁶Korah, you and all your followers must prepare your incense burners. ⁷Light fires in them tomorrow, and burn incense before the LORD. Then we will see whom the LORD chooses as his holy one. You Levites are the ones who have gone too far!"

⁸Then Moses spoke again to Korah: "Now listen, you Levites! ⁹Does it seem insignificant to you that the God of Israel has chosen you from among all the community of Israel to be near him so you can serve in the LORD's Tabernacle and stand before the people to minister to them? ¹⁰Korah, he has already given this special ministry to you and your fellow Levites. Are you now demanding the priesthood as well? ¹¹The LORD is the one you and your followers are really revolting against! For who is Aaron that you are complaining about him?"

¹²Then Moses summoned Dathan

and Abiram, the sons of Eliab, but they replied, "We refuse to come before you! ¹³Isn't it enough that you brought us out of Egypt, a land flowing with milk and honey, to kill us here in this wilderness, and that you now treat us like your subjects? ¹⁴What's more, you haven't brought us into another land flowing with milk and honey. You haven't given us a new homeland with fields and vineyards. Are you trying to fool these men?* We will not come."

¹⁵Then Moses became very angry and said to the LORD, "Do not accept their grain offerings! I have not taken so much as a donkey from them, and I have never hurt a single one of them." ¹⁶And Moses said to Korah, "You and all your followers must come here tomorrow and present yourselves before the LORD. Aaron will also be here. ¹⁷You and each of your 250 followers must prepare an incense burner and put incense on it, so you can all present them before the LORD. Aaron will also bring his incense burner."

¹⁸So each of these men prepared an incense burner, lit the fire, and placed incense on it. Then they all stood at the entrance of the Tabernacle* with Moses and Aaron. ¹⁹Meanwhile, Korah had stirred up the entire community against Moses and Aaron, and they all gathered at the Tabernacle entrance. Then the glorious presence of the LORD appeared to the whole community, ²⁰and the LORD said to Moses and Aaron, ²¹"Get away from all these people so that I may instantly destroy them!"

²²But Moses and Aaron fell face down on the ground. "O God," they pleaded, "you are the God who gives breath to all creatures. Must you be angry with all the people when only one man sins?"

²³And the LORD said to Moses, ²⁴"Then tell all the people to get away from the tents of Korah, Dathan, and Abiram."

²⁵So Moses got up and rushed over to the tents of Dathan and Abiram, followed by the elders of Israel. ²⁶"Quick!" he told the people. "Get away from the tents of these wicked men, and don't touch anything that belongs to them. If

you do, you will be destroyed for their sins." ²⁷So all the people stood back from the tents of Korah, Dathan, and Abiram. Then Dathan and Abiram came out and stood at the entrances of their tents, together with their wives and children and little ones.

²⁸And Moses said, "This is how you will know that the LORD has sent me to do all these things that I have done—for I have not done them on my own. ²⁹If these men die a natural death, or if nothing unusual happens, then the LORD has not sent me. ³⁰But if the LORD does something entirely new and the ground opens its mouth and swallows them and all their belongings, and they go down alive into the grave,* then you will know that these men have shown contempt for the LORD."

³¹He had hardly finished speaking the words when the ground suddenly split open beneath them. ³²The earth opened its mouth and swallowed the men, along with their households and all their followers who were standing with them, and everything they owned. ³³So they went down alive into the grave, along with all their belongings. The earth closed over them, and they all vanished from among the people of Israel. ³⁴All the people around them fled when they heard their screams. "The earth will swallow us, too!" they cried. ³⁵Then fire blazed forth from the LORD and burned up the 250 men who were offering incense.

³⁶*And the LORD said to Moses, ³⁷"Tell Eleazar son of Aaron the priest to pull all the incense burners from the fire, for they are holy. Also tell him to scatter the burning coals. ³⁸Take the incense burners of these men who have sinned at the cost of their lives, and hammer the metal into a thin sheet to overlay the altar. Since these burners were used in the LORD's presence, they have become holy. Let them serve as a warning to the people of Israel."

³⁹So Eleazar the priest collected the 250 bronze incense burners that had been used by the men who died in the fire, and he hammered them into a thin

sheet to overlay the altar. [40]This would warn the Israelites that no unauthorized person—no one who was not a descendant of Aaron—should ever enter the LORD's presence to burn incense. If anyone did, the same thing would happen to him as happened to Korah and his followers. So the LORD's instructions to Moses were carried out.

15:25 Or *will make atonement for the whole community of Israel.* 15:28 Or *to make atonement for.* 16:5 Greek version reads *God has visited and knows those who are his.* Compare 2 Tim 2:19. 16:14 Hebrew *Are you trying to put out the eyes of these men?* 16:18 Hebrew *the Tent of Meeting;* also in 16:19, 42, 43, 50. 16:30 Hebrew *into Sheol;* also in 16:33. 16:36 Verses 16:36-50 are numbered 17:1-15 in Hebrew text.

## MARK 15:1-47

**V**ery early in the morning the leading priests, the elders, and the teachers of religious law—the entire high council*— met to discuss their next step. They bound Jesus, led him away, and took him to Pilate, the Roman governor.

[2]Pilate asked Jesus, "Are you the king of the Jews?"

Jesus replied, "You have said it."

[3]Then the leading priests kept accusing him of many crimes, [4]and Pilate asked him, "Aren't you going to answer them? What about all these charges they are bringing against you?" [5]But Jesus said nothing, much to Pilate's surprise.

[6]Now it was the governor's custom each year during the Passover celebration to release one prisoner—anyone the people requested. [7]One of the prisoners at that time was Barabbas, a revolutionary who had committed murder in an uprising. [8]The crowd went to Pilate and asked him to release a prisoner as usual.

[9]"Would you like me to release this 'King of the Jews'?" Pilate asked. [10](For he realized by now that the leading priests had arrested Jesus out of envy.) [11]But at this point the leading priests stirred up the crowd to demand the release of Barabbas instead of Jesus. [12]Pilate asked them, "Then what should I do with this man you call the king of the Jews?"

[13]They shouted back, "Crucify him!"

[14]"Why?" Pilate demanded. "What crime has he committed?"

But the mob roared even louder, "Crucify him!"

[15]So to pacify the crowd, Pilate released Barabbas to them. He ordered Jesus flogged with a lead-tipped whip, then turned him over to the Roman soldiers to be crucified.

[16]The soldiers took Jesus into the courtyard of the governor's headquarters (called the Praetorium) and called out the entire regiment. [17]They dressed him in a purple robe, and they wove thorn branches into a crown and put it on his head. [18]Then they saluted him and taunted, "Hail! King of the Jews!" [19]And they struck him on the head with a reed stick, spit on him, and dropped to their knees in mock worship. [20]When they were finally tired of mocking him, they took off the purple robe and put his own clothes on him again. Then they led him away to be crucified.

[21]A passerby named Simon, who was from Cyrene,* was coming in from the countryside just then, and the soldiers forced him to carry Jesus' cross. (Simon was the father of Alexander and Rufus.) [22]And they brought Jesus to a place called Golgotha (which means "Place of the Skull"). [23]They offered him wine drugged with myrrh, but he refused it.

[24]Then the soldiers nailed him to the cross. They divided his clothes and threw dice* to decide who would get each piece. **[25]It was nine o'clock in the morning when they crucified him. [26]A sign was fastened to the cross, announcing the charge against him. It read, "The King of the Jews." [27]Two revolutionaries* were crucified with him, one on his right and one on his left.***

[29]The people passing by shouted abuse, shaking their heads in mockery. "Ha! Look at you now!" they yelled at him. "You said you were going to destroy the Temple and rebuild it in three days. [30]Well then, save yourself and come down from the cross!"

[31]The leading priests and teachers of religious law also mocked Jesus. "He saved others," they scoffed, "but he can't

save himself! [32]Let this Messiah, this King of Israel, come down from the cross so we can see it and believe him!" Even the men who were crucified with Jesus ridiculed him.

[33]At noon, darkness fell across the whole land until three o'clock. [34]Then at three o'clock Jesus called out with a loud voice, *"Eloi, Eloi, lema sabachthani?"* which means "My God, my God, why have you abandoned me?"*

[35]Some of the bystanders misunderstood and thought he was calling for the prophet Elijah. [36]One of them ran and filled a sponge with sour wine, holding it up to him on a reed stick so he could drink. "Wait!" he said. "Let's see whether Elijah comes to take him down!"

[37]Then Jesus uttered another loud cry and breathed his last. [38]And the curtain in the sanctuary of the Temple was torn in two, from top to bottom.

[39]When the Roman officer* who stood facing him* saw how he had died, he exclaimed, "This man truly was the Son of God!"

[40]Some women were there, watching from a distance, including Mary Magdalene, Mary (the mother of James the younger and of Joseph*), and Salome. [41]They had been followers of Jesus and had cared for him while he was in Galilee. Many other women who had come with him to Jerusalem were also there.

[42]This all happened on Friday, the day of preparation,* the day before the Sabbath. As evening approached, [43]Joseph of Arimathea took a risk and went to Pilate and asked for Jesus' body. (Joseph was an honored member of the high council, and he was waiting for the Kingdom of God to come.) [44]Pilate couldn't believe that Jesus was already dead, so he called for the Roman officer and asked if he had died yet. [45]The officer confirmed that Jesus was dead, so Pilate told Joseph he could have the body. [46]Joseph bought a long sheet of linen cloth. Then he took Jesus' body down from the cross, wrapped it in the cloth, and laid it in a tomb that had been carved out of the rock. Then he rolled a stone in front of the entrance. [47]Mary Magdalene and Mary the mother of Joseph saw where Jesus' body was laid.

15:1 Greek *the Sanhedrin;* also in 15:43.   15:21 *Cyrene* was a city in northern Africa.   15:24 Greek *cast lots.* See Ps 22:18.   15:27a Or *Two criminals.*   15:27b Some manuscripts add verse 28, *And the Scripture was fulfilled that said, "He was counted among those who were rebels."* See Isa 53:12; also compare Luke 22:37.   15:34 Ps 22:1.   15:39a Greek *the centurion;* similarly in 15:44, 45.   15:39b Some manuscripts add *heard his cry and.*   15:40 Greek *Joses;* also in 15:47. See Matt 27:56.   15:42 Greek *It was the day of preparation.*

## PSALM 54:1-7

*For the choir director: A psalm* of David, regarding the time the Ziphites came and said to Saul, "We know where David is hiding." To be accompanied by stringed instruments.*

[1] Come with great power, O God, and
        rescue me!
    Defend me with your might.
[2] Listen to my prayer, O God.
    Pay attention to my plea.
[3] For strangers are attacking me;
        violent people are trying to
        kill me.
    They care nothing for God.
                                            *Interlude*

[4] But God is my helper.
    The Lord keeps me alive!
[5] May the evil plans of my enemies be
        turned against them.
    Do as you promised and put an
        end to them.

[6] I will sacrifice a voluntary offering
        to you;
    I will praise your name, O LORD,
        for it is good.
[7] For you have rescued me from
        my troubles
    and helped me to triumph over
        my enemies.

54:TITLE Hebrew *maskil.* This may be a literary or musical term.

## PROVERBS 11:5-6

The godly are directed by honesty; the wicked fall beneath their load of sin. □ The godliness of good people rescues them; the ambition of treacherous people traps them.

# MARCH
# 12

NUMBERS 16:41–18:32

**B**ut the very next morning the whole community of Israel began muttering again against Moses and Aaron, saying, "You have killed the LORD's people!" 42As the community gathered to protest against Moses and Aaron, they turned toward the Tabernacle and saw that the cloud had covered it, and the glorious presence of the LORD appeared.

43Moses and Aaron came and stood in front of the Tabernacle, 44and the LORD said to Moses, 45"Get away from all these people so that I can instantly destroy them!" But Moses and Aaron fell face down on the ground.

46And Moses said to Aaron, "Quick, take an incense burner and place burning coals on it from the altar. Lay incense on it, and carry it out among the people to purify them and make them right with the LORD.* The LORD's anger is blazing against them—the plague has already begun."

47Aaron did as Moses told him and ran out among the people. The plague had already begun to strike down the people, but Aaron burned the incense and purified* the people. 48He stood between the dead and the living, and the plague stopped. 49But 14,700 people died in that plague, in addition to those who had died in the affair involving Korah. 50Then because the plague had stopped, Aaron returned to Moses at the entrance of the Tabernacle.

17:1*THEN the LORD said to Moses, 2"Tell the people of Israel to bring you twelve wooden staffs, one from each leader of Israel's ancestral tribes, and inscribe each leader's name on his staff. 3Inscribe Aaron's name on the staff of the tribe of Levi, for there must be one staff for the leader of each ancestral tribe. 4Place these staffs in the Tabernacle in front of the Ark containing the tablets of the Covenant,* where I meet with you. 5Buds will sprout on the staff belonging to the man I choose. Then I will finally put an end to the people's murmuring and complaining against you."

6So Moses gave the instructions to the people of Israel, and each of the twelve tribal leaders, including Aaron, brought Moses a staff. 7Moses placed the staffs in the LORD's presence in the Tabernacle of the Covenant.* 8When he went into the Tabernacle of the Covenant the next day, he found that Aaron's staff, representing the tribe of Levi, had sprouted, budded, blossomed, and produced ripe almonds!

9When Moses brought all the staffs out from the LORD's presence, he showed them to the people. Each man claimed his own staff. 10And the LORD said to Moses: "Place Aaron's staff permanently before the Ark of the Covenant* to serve as a warning to rebels. This should put an end to their complaints against me and prevent any further deaths." 11So Moses did as the LORD commanded him.

12Then the people of Israel said to Moses, "Look, we are doomed! We are dead! We are ruined! 13Everyone who even comes close to the Tabernacle of the LORD dies. Are we all doomed to die?"

18:1THEN the LORD said to Aaron: "You, your sons, and your relatives from the tribe of Levi will be held responsible for any offenses related to the sanctuary. But you and your sons alone will be held responsible for violations connected with the priesthood.

2"Bring your relatives of the tribe of Levi—your ancestral tribe—to assist you and your sons as you perform the sacred duties in front of the Tabernacle of the Covenant.* 3But as the Levites go about all their assigned duties at the Tabernacle, they must be careful not to go near any of the sacred objects or the altar. If they do, both you and they will die. 4The Levites must join you in fulfilling their responsibilities for the care and maintenance of the Tabernacle,* but no unauthorized person may assist you.

⁵"You yourselves must perform the sacred duties inside the sanctuary and at the altar. If you follow these instructions, the LORD's anger will never again blaze against the people of Israel. ⁶I myself have chosen your fellow Levites from among the Israelites to be your special assistants. They are a gift to you, dedicated to the LORD for service in the Tabernacle. ⁷But you and your sons, the priests, must personally handle all the priestly rituals associated with the altar and with everything behind the inner curtain. I am giving you the priesthood as your special privilege of service. Any unauthorized person who comes too near the sanctuary will be put to death."

⁸The LORD gave these further instructions to Aaron: "I myself have put you in charge of all the holy offerings that are brought to me by the people of Israel. I have given all these consecrated offerings to you and your sons as your permanent share. ⁹You are allotted the portion of the most holy offerings that is not burned on the fire. This portion of all the most holy offerings—including the grain offerings, sin offerings, and guilt offerings—will be most holy, and it belongs to you and your sons. ¹⁰You must eat it as a most holy offering. All the males may eat of it, and you must treat it as most holy.

¹¹"All the sacred offerings and special offerings presented to me when the Israelites lift them up before the altar also belong to you. I have given them to you and to your sons and daughters as your permanent share. Any member of your family who is ceremonially clean may eat of these offerings.

¹²"I also give you the harvest gifts brought by the people as offerings to the LORD—the best of the olive oil, new wine, and grain. ¹³All the first crops of their land that the people present to the LORD belong to you. Any member of your family who is ceremonially clean may eat this food.

¹⁴"Everything in Israel that is specially set apart for the LORD* also belongs to you.

¹⁵"The firstborn of every mother, whether human or animal, that is offered to the LORD will be yours. But you must always redeem your firstborn sons and the firstborn of ceremonially unclean animals. ¹⁶Redeem them when they are one month old. The redemption price is five pieces of silver* (as measured by the weight of the sanctuary shekel, which equals twenty gerahs).

¹⁷"However, you may not redeem the firstborn of cattle, sheep, or goats. They are holy and have been set apart for the LORD. Sprinkle their blood on the altar, and burn their fat as a special gift, a pleasing aroma to the LORD. ¹⁸The meat of these animals will be yours, just like the breast and right thigh that are presented by lifting them up as a special offering before the altar. ¹⁹Yes, I am giving you all these holy offerings that the people of Israel bring to the LORD. They are for you and your sons and daughters, to be eaten as your permanent share. This is an eternal and unbreakable covenant* between the LORD and you, and it also applies to your descendants."

²⁰And the LORD said to Aaron, "You priests will receive no allotment of land or share of property among the people of Israel. I am your share and your allotment. ²¹As for the tribe of Levi, your relatives, I will compensate them for their service in the Tabernacle. Instead of an allotment of land, I will give them the tithes from the entire land of Israel.

²²"From now on, no Israelites except priests or Levites may approach the Tabernacle. If they come too near, they will be judged guilty and will die. ²³Only the Levites may serve at the Tabernacle, and they will be held responsible for any offenses against it. This is a permanent law for you, to be observed from generation to generation. The Levites will receive no allotment of land among the Israelites, ²⁴because I have given them the Israelites' tithes, which have

been presented as sacred offerings to the LORD. This will be the Levites' share. That is why I said they would receive no allotment of land among the Israelites."

25The LORD also told Moses, 26"Give these instructions to the Levites: When you receive from the people of Israel the tithes I have assigned as your allotment, give a tenth of the tithes you receive—a tithe of the tithe—to the LORD as a sacred offering. 27The LORD will consider this offering to be your harvest offering, as though it were the first grain from your own threshing floor or wine from your own winepress. 28You must present one-tenth of the tithe received from the Israelites as a sacred offering to the LORD. This is the LORD's sacred portion, and you must present it to Aaron the priest. 29Be sure to give to the LORD the best portions of the gifts given to you.

30"Also, give these instructions to the Levites: When you present the best part as your offering, it will be considered as though it came from your own threshing floor or winepress. 31You Levites and your families may eat this food anywhere you wish, for it is your compensation for serving in the Tabernacle. 32You will not be considered guilty for accepting the LORD's tithes if you give the best portion to the priests. But be careful not to treat the holy gifts of the people of Israel as though they were common. If you do, you will die."

16:46 Or *to make atonement for them.* 16:47 Or *and made atonement for.* 17:1 Verses 17:1-13 are numbered 17:16-28 in Hebrew text. 17:4 Hebrew *in the Tent of Meeting before the Testimony.* The Hebrew word for "testimony" refers to the terms of the LORD's covenant with Israel as written on stone tablets, which were kept in the Ark, and also to the covenant itself. 17:7 Or *Tabernacle of the Testimony;* also in 17:8. 17:10 Hebrew *before the Testimony;* see note on 17:4. 18:2 Or *Tabernacle of the Testimony.* 18:4 Hebrew *the Tent of Meeting;* also in 18:6, 21, 22, 23, 31. 18:14 The Hebrew term used here refers to the complete consecration of things or people to the LORD, either by destroying them or by giving them as an offering. 18:16 Hebrew *5 shekels* [2 ounces or 57 grams] *of silver.* 18:19 Hebrew *a covenant of salt.*

## MARK 16:1-20

Saturday evening, when the Sabbath ended, Mary Magdalene and Salome and Mary the mother of James went out and purchased burial spices so they could anoint Jesus' body. 2Very early on Sunday morning,* just at sunrise, they went to the tomb. 3On the way they were asking each other, "Who will roll away the stone for us from the entrance to the tomb?" 4But as they arrived, they looked up and saw that the stone, which was very large, had already been rolled aside.

5When they entered the tomb, they saw a young man clothed in a white robe sitting on the right side. The women were shocked, 6but the angel said, "Don't be alarmed. You are looking for Jesus of Nazareth,* who was crucified. He isn't here! He is risen from the dead! Look, this is where they laid his body. 7Now go and tell his disciples, including Peter, that Jesus is going ahead of you to Galilee. You will see him there, just as he told you before he died."

8The women fled from the tomb, trembling and bewildered, and they said nothing to anyone because they were too frightened.*

[*Shorter Ending of Mark*]

Then they briefly reported all this to Peter and his companions. Afterward Jesus himself sent them out from east to west with the sacred and unfailing message of salvation that gives eternal life. Amen.

[*Longer Ending of Mark*]

9After Jesus rose from the dead early on Sunday morning, the first person who saw him was Mary Magdalene, the woman from whom he had cast out seven demons. 10She went to the disciples, who were grieving and weeping, and told them what had happened. 11But when she told them that Jesus was alive and she had seen him, they didn't believe her.

12Afterward he appeared in a different form to two of his followers who were walking from Jerusalem into the country. 13They rushed back to tell the others, but no one believed them.

14Still later he appeared to the eleven disciples as they were eating together. He rebuked them for their stubborn unbelief because they refused to believe those who had seen him after he had been raised from the dead.*

15And then he told them, "Go into all the world and preach the Good News to everyone. 16Anyone who believes and is baptized will be saved. But anyone who refuses to believe will be condemned. 17These miraculous signs will accompany those who believe: They will cast out demons in my name, and they will speak in new languages.* 18They will be able to handle snakes with safety, and if they drink anything poisonous, it won't hurt them. They will be able to place their hands on the sick, and they will be healed."

19When the Lord Jesus had finished talking with them, he was taken up into heaven and sat down in the place of honor at God's right hand. 20And the disciples went everywhere and preached, and the Lord worked through them, confirming what they said by many miraculous signs.

16:2 Greek *on the first day of the week;* also in 16:9. 16:6 Or *Jesus the Nazarene.* 16:8 The most reliable early manuscripts of the Gospel of Mark end at verse 8. Other manuscripts include various endings to the Gospel. A few include both the "shorter ending" and the "longer ending." The majority of manuscripts include the "longer ending" immediately after verse 8. 16:14 Some early manuscripts add: *And they excused themselves, saying, "This age of lawlessness and unbelief is under Satan, who does not permit God's truth and power to conquer the evil (unclean) spirits. Therefore, reveal your justice now." This is what they said to Christ. And Christ replied to them, "The period of years of Satan's power has been fulfilled, but other dreadful things will happen soon. And I was handed over to death for those who have sinned, so that they may return to the truth and sin no more, and so they may inherit the spiritual, incorruptible, and righteous glory in heaven."* 16:17 Or *new tongues;* some manuscripts omit *new.*

## PSALM 55:1-23
*For the choir director: A psalm* of David, to be accompanied by stringed instruments.*

1 Listen to my prayer, O God.
    Do not ignore my cry for help!
2 Please listen and answer me,
    for I am overwhelmed by
    my troubles.
3 My enemies shout at me,
    making loud and wicked
    threats.
  They bring trouble on me
    and angrily hunt me down.

4 My heart pounds in my chest.
    The terror of death assaults me.
5 Fear and trembling overwhelm me,
    and I can't stop shaking.
6 Oh, that I had wings like a dove;
    then I would fly away and rest!
7 I would fly far away
    to the quiet of the wilderness.
                              *Interlude*
8 How quickly I would escape—
    far from this wild storm of
    hatred.

9 Confuse them, Lord, and frustrate
    their plans,
  for I see violence and conflict in
    the city.
10 Its walls are patrolled day and night
    against invaders,
  but the real danger is wickedness
    within the city.
11 Everything is falling apart;
    threats and cheating are rampant
    in the streets.

12 It is not an enemy who taunts me—
    I could bear that.
  It is not my foes who so arrogantly
    insult me—
  I could have hidden from them.
13 Instead, it is you—my equal,
    my companion and close friend.
14 What good fellowship we once
    enjoyed
  as we walked together to the
    house of God.

15 Let death stalk my enemies;
    let the grave* swallow them alive,
  for evil makes its home
    within them.

16 But I will call on God,
    and the LORD will rescue me.
17 Morning, noon, and night
    I cry out in my distress,
    and the LORD hears my voice.
18 He ransoms me and keeps me safe
    from the battle waged against me,
    though many still oppose me.
19 God, who has ruled forever,
    will hear me and humble them.
                              *Interlude*

For my enemies refuse to change
their ways;
they do not fear God.

20 As for my companion, he betrayed
his friends;
he broke his promises.
21 His words are as smooth as butter,
but in his heart is war.
His words are as soothing as lotion,
but underneath are daggers!

22 **Give your burdens to the Lord,**
**and he will take care of you.**
**He will not permit the godly to**
**slip and fall.**

23 But you, O God, will send the wicked
down to the pit of destruction.
Murderers and liars will die young,
but I am trusting you to save me.

55:TITLE Hebrew *maskil*. This may be a literary or musical
term.    55:15 Hebrew *let Sheol*.

PROVERBS 11:7
**W**hen the wicked die, their hopes die
with them, for they rely on their own
feeble strength.

# MARCH
# 13

NUMBERS 19:1–20:29
**T**he Lord said to Moses and Aaron,
2"Here is another legal requirement
commanded by the Lord: Tell the people of Israel to bring you a red heifer, a
perfect animal that has no defects and
has never been yoked to a plow. 3Give it
to Eleazar the priest, and it will be taken
outside the camp and slaughtered in his
presence. 4Eleazar will take some of its
blood on his finger and sprinkle it seven
times toward the front of the Tabernacle.* 5As Eleazar watches, the heifer
must be burned—its hide, meat, blood,
and dung. 6Eleazar the priest must then
take a stick of cedar,* a hyssop branch,

and some scarlet yarn and throw them
into the fire where the heifer is burning.
7"Then the priest must wash his
clothes and bathe himself in water.
Afterward he may return to the camp,
though he will remain ceremonially unclean until evening. 8The man who burns
the animal must also wash his clothes
and bathe himself in water, and he, too,
will remain unclean until evening. 9Then
someone who is ceremonially clean will
gather up the ashes of the heifer and deposit them in a purified place outside
the camp. They will be kept there for the
community of Israel to use in the water
for the purification ceremony. This ceremony is performed for the removal of
sin. 10The man who gathers up the ashes
of the heifer must also wash his clothes,
and he will remain ceremonially unclean
until evening. This is a permanent law
for the people of Israel and any foreigners who live among them.
11"All those who touch a dead human
body will be ceremonially unclean for
seven days. 12They must purify themselves on the third and seventh days
with the water of purification; then they
will be purified. But if they do not do
this on the third and seventh days, they
will continue to be unclean even after
the seventh day. 13All those who touch a
dead body and do not purify themselves
in the proper way defile the Lord's Tabernacle, and they will be cut off from
the community of Israel. Since the water of purification was not sprinkled on
them, their defilement continues.
14"This is the ritual law that applies
when someone dies inside a tent: All
those who enter that tent and those who
were inside when the death occurred
will be ceremonially unclean for seven
days. 15Any open container in the tent
that was not covered with a lid is also defiled. 16And if someone in an open field
touches the corpse of someone who was
killed with a sword or who died a natural
death, or if someone touches a human
bone or a grave, that person will be defiled for seven days.
17"To remove the defilement, put

some of the ashes from the burnt purification offering in a jar, and pour fresh water over them. 18Then someone who is ceremonially clean must take a hyssop branch and dip it into the water. That person must sprinkle the water on the tent, on all the furnishings in the tent, and on the people who were in the tent; also on the person who touched a human bone, or touched someone who was killed or who died naturally, or touched a grave. 19On the third and seventh days the person who is ceremonially clean must sprinkle the water on those who are defiled. Then on the seventh day the people being cleansed must wash their clothes and bathe themselves, and that evening they will be cleansed of their defilement.

20"But those who become defiled and do not purify themselves will be cut off from the community, for they have defiled the sanctuary of the LORD. Since the water of purification has not been sprinkled on them, they remain defiled. 21This is a permanent law for the people. Those who sprinkle the water of purification must afterward wash their clothes, and anyone who then touches the water used for purification will remain defiled until evening. 22Anything and anyone that a defiled person touches will be ceremonially unclean until evening."

20:1In the first month of the year,* the whole community of Israel arrived in the wilderness of Zin and camped at Kadesh. While they were there, Miriam died and was buried.

2There was no water for the people to drink at that place, so they rebelled against Moses and Aaron. 3The people blamed Moses and said, "If only we had died in the LORD's presence with our brothers! 4Why have you brought the congregation of the LORD's people into this wilderness to die, along with all our livestock? 5Why did you make us leave Egypt and bring us here to this terrible place? This land has no grain, no figs, no grapes, no pomegranates, and no water to drink!"

6Moses and Aaron turned away from the people and went to the entrance of the Tabernacle,* where they fell face down on the ground. Then the glorious presence of the LORD appeared to them, 7and the LORD said to Moses, 8"You and Aaron must take the staff and assemble the entire community. As the people watch, speak to the rock over there, and it will pour out its water. You will provide enough water from the rock to satisfy the whole community and their livestock."

9So Moses did as he was told. He took the staff from the place where it was kept before the LORD. 10Then he and Aaron summoned the people to come and gather at the rock. "Listen, you rebels!" he shouted. "Must we bring you water from this rock?" 11Then Moses raised his hand and struck the rock twice with the staff, and water gushed out. So the entire community and their livestock drank their fill.

12But the LORD said to Moses and Aaron, "Because you did not trust me enough to demonstrate my holiness to the people of Israel, you will not lead them into the land I am giving them!" 13This place was known as the waters of Meribah (which means "arguing") because there the people of Israel argued with the LORD, and there he demonstrated his holiness among them.

14While Moses was at Kadesh, he sent ambassadors to the king of Edom with this message:

"This is what your relatives, the people of Israel, say: You know all the hardships we have been through. 15Our ancestors went down to Egypt, and we lived there a long time, and we and our ancestors were brutally mistreated by the Egyptians. 16But when we cried out to the LORD, he heard us and sent an angel who brought us out of Egypt. Now we are camped at Kadesh, a town on the border of your land. 17Please let us travel through your land. We will be careful not to go through your fields and vineyards. We won't even drink water from your wells. We will stay on the king's road and never leave it until we have passed through your territory."

18But the king of Edom said, "Stay out of my land, or I will meet you with an army!"

19The Israelites answered, "We will stay on the main road. If our livestock drink your water, we will pay for it. Just let us pass through your country. That's all we ask."

20But the king of Edom replied, "Stay out! You may not pass through our land." With that he mobilized his army and marched out against them with an imposing force. 21Because Edom refused to allow Israel to pass through their country, Israel was forced to turn around.

22The whole community of Israel left Kadesh and arrived at Mount Hor. 23There, on the border of the land of Edom, the LORD said to Moses and Aaron, 24"The time has come for Aaron to join his ancestors in death. He will not enter the land I am giving the people of Israel, because the two of you rebelled against my instructions concerning the water at Meribah. 25Now take Aaron and his son Eleazar up Mount Hor. 26There you will remove Aaron's priestly garments and put them on Eleazar, his son. Aaron will die there and join his ancestors."

27So Moses did as the LORD commanded. The three of them went up Mount Hor together as the whole community watched. 28At the summit, Moses removed the priestly garments from Aaron and put them on Eleazar, Aaron's son. Then Aaron died there on top of the mountain, and Moses and Eleazar went back down. 29When the people realized that Aaron had died, all Israel mourned for him thirty days.

19:4 Hebrew *the Tent of Meeting.*   19:6 Or *juniper.*
20:1 The first month of the ancient Hebrew lunar calendar usually occurs within the months of March and April. The number of years since leaving Egypt is not specified.
20:6 Hebrew *the Tent of Meeting.*

## LUKE 1:1-25

**M**any people have set out to write accounts about the events that have been fulfilled among us. 2They used the eyewitness reports circulating among us from the early disciples.* 3**Having carefully investigated everything from the beginning, I also have decided to write a careful account for you, most honorable Theophilus, 4so you can be certain of the truth of everything you were taught.**

5When Herod was king of Judea, there was a Jewish priest named Zechariah. He was a member of the priestly order of Abijah, and his wife, Elizabeth, was also from the priestly line of Aaron. 6Zechariah and Elizabeth were righteous in God's eyes, careful to obey all of the Lord's commandments and regulations. 7They had no children because Elizabeth was unable to conceive, and they were both very old.

8One day Zechariah was serving God in the Temple, for his order was on duty that week. 9As was the custom of the priests, he was chosen by lot to enter the sanctuary of the Lord and burn incense. 10While the incense was being burned, a great crowd stood outside, praying.

11While Zechariah was in the sanctuary, an angel of the Lord appeared to him, standing to the right of the incense altar. 12Zechariah was shaken and overwhelmed with fear when he saw him. 13But the angel said, "Don't be afraid, Zechariah! God has heard your prayer. Your wife, Elizabeth, will give you a son, and you are to name him John. 14You will have great joy and gladness, and many will rejoice at his birth, 15for he will be great in the eyes of the Lord. He must never touch wine or other alcoholic drinks. He will be filled with the Holy Spirit, even before his birth.* 16And he will turn many Israelites to the Lord their God. 17He will be a man with the spirit and power of Elijah. He will prepare the people for the coming of the Lord. He will turn the hearts of the fathers to their children,* and he will cause those who are rebellious to accept the wisdom of the godly."

¹⁸Zechariah said to the angel, "How can I be sure this will happen? I'm an old man now, and my wife is also well along in years."

¹⁹Then the angel said, "I am Gabriel! I stand in the very presence of God. It was he who sent me to bring you this good news! ²⁰But now, since you didn't believe what I said, you will be silent and unable to speak until the child is born. For my words will certainly be fulfilled at the proper time."

²¹Meanwhile, the people were waiting for Zechariah to come out of the sanctuary, wondering why he was taking so long. ²²When he finally did come out, he couldn't speak to them. Then they realized from his gestures and his silence that he must have seen a vision in the sanctuary.

²³When Zechariah's week of service in the Temple was over, he returned home. ²⁴Soon afterward his wife, Elizabeth, became pregnant and went into seclusion for five months. ²⁵"How kind the Lord is!" she exclaimed. "He has taken away my disgrace of having no children."

1:2 Greek *from those who from the beginning were servants of the word.*   1:15 Or *even from birth.*   1:17 See Mal 4:5-6.

## PSALM 56:1-13

*For the choir director: A psalm of David, regarding the time the Philistines seized him in Gath. To be sung to the tune "Dove on Distant Oaks."*

¹ **O** God, have mercy on me,
    for people are hounding me.
    My foes attack me all day long.
² I am constantly hounded by those
        who slander me,
    and many are boldly attacking
        me.
³ But when I am afraid,
    I will put my trust in you.
⁴ I praise God for what he has
        promised.
    I trust in God, so why should
        I be afraid?
    What can mere mortals do to me?

⁵ They are always twisting what I say;
    they spend their days plotting to
        harm me.
⁶ They come together to spy on me—
    watching my every step, eager to
        kill me.
⁷ Don't let them get away with their
        wickedness;
    in your anger, O God, bring them
        down.

⁸ You keep track of all my sorrows.*
    You have collected all my tears in
        your bottle.
    You have recorded each one in
        your book.

⁹ My enemies will retreat when I call
        to you for help.
    This I know: God is on my side!
¹⁰ I praise God for what he has
        promised;
    Yes, I praise the LORD for what he
        has promised.
¹¹ I trust in God, so why should I be
        afraid?
    What can mere mortals do to me?

¹² I will fulfill my vows to you, O God,
    and will offer a sacrifice of thanks
        for your help.
¹³ For you have rescued me from
        death;
    you have kept my feet from
        slipping.
    So now I can walk in your presence,
        O God,
    in your life-giving light.

56:8 Or *my wanderings.*

## PROVERBS 11:8

**T**he godly are rescued from trouble, and it falls on the wicked instead.

# MARCH
# 14

## NUMBERS 21:1–22:20

The Canaanite king of Arad, who lived in the Negev, heard that the Israelites were approaching on the road through Atharim. So he attacked the Israelites and took some of them as prisoners. ²Then the people of Israel made this vow to the LORD: "If you will hand these people over to us, we will completely destroy* all their towns." ³The LORD heard the Israelites' request and gave them victory over the Canaanites. The Israelites completely destroyed them and their towns, and the place has been called Hormah* ever since.

⁴Then the people of Israel set out from Mount Hor, taking the road to the Red Sea* to go around the land of Edom. But the people grew impatient with the long journey, ⁵and they began to speak against God and Moses. "Why have you brought us out of Egypt to die here in the wilderness?" they complained. "There is nothing to eat here and nothing to drink. And we hate this horrible manna!"

⁶So the LORD sent poisonous snakes among the people, and many were bitten and died. ⁷Then the people came to Moses and cried out, "We have sinned by speaking against the LORD and against you. Pray that the LORD will take away the snakes." So Moses prayed for the people.

⁸Then the LORD told him, "Make a replica of a poisonous snake and attach it to a pole. All who are bitten will live if they simply look at it!" ⁹So Moses made a snake out of bronze and attached it to a pole. Then anyone who was bitten by a snake could look at the bronze snake and be healed!

¹⁰The Israelites traveled next to Oboth and camped there. ¹¹Then they went on to Iye-abarim, in the wilderness on the eastern border of Moab. ¹²From there they traveled to the valley of Zered Brook and set up camp. ¹³Then they moved out and camped on the far side of the Arnon River, in the wilderness adjacent to the territory of the Amorites. The Arnon is the boundary line between the Moabites and the Amorites. ¹⁴For this reason *The Book of the Wars of the LORD* speaks of "the town of Waheb in the area of Suphah, and the ravines of the Arnon River, ¹⁵and the ravines that extend as far as the settlement of Ar on the border of Moab."

¹⁶From there the Israelites traveled to Beer,* which is the well where the LORD said to Moses, "Assemble the people, and I will give them water." ¹⁷There the Israelites sang this song:

"Spring up, O well!
    Yes, sing its praises!
¹⁸ Sing of this well,
    which princes dug,
which great leaders hollowed out
    with their scepters and staffs."

Then the Israelites left the wilderness and proceeded on through Mattanah, ¹⁹Nahaliel, and Bamoth. ²⁰After that they went to the valley in Moab where Pisgah Peak overlooks the wasteland.*

²¹The Israelites then sent ambassadors to King Sihon of the Amorites with this message:

²²"Let us travel through your land. We will be careful not to go through your fields and vineyards. We won't even drink water from your wells. We will stay on the king's road until we have passed through your territory."

²³But King Sihon refused to let them cross his territory. Instead, he mobilized his entire army and attacked Israel in the wilderness, engaging them in battle at Jahaz. ²⁴But the Israelites slaughtered them with their swords and occupied their land from the Arnon River to the Jabbok River. They went only as far as the Ammonite border because the boundary of the Ammonites was fortified.* ²⁵So Israel captured all the towns of

the Amorites and settled in them, including the city of Heshbon and its surrounding villages. ²⁶Heshbon had been the capital of King Sihon of the Amorites. He had defeated a former Moabite king and seized all his land as far as the Arnon River. ²⁷Therefore, the ancient poets wrote this about him:

"Come to Heshbon and let it
be rebuilt!
Let the city of Sihon be restored.
²⁸ A fire flamed forth from Heshbon,
a blaze from the city of Sihon.
It burned the city of Ar in Moab;
it destroyed the rulers of the
Arnon heights.
²⁹ What sorrow awaits you, O people
of Moab!
You are finished, O worshipers
of Chemosh!
Chemosh has left his sons as
refugees,
his daughters as captives of Sihon,
the Amorite king.
³⁰ We have utterly destroyed them,
from Heshbon to Dibon.
We have completely wiped them out
as far away as Nophah and
Medeba.*"

³¹So the people of Israel occupied the territory of the Amorites. ³²After Moses sent men to explore the Jazer area, they captured all the towns in the region and drove out the Amorites who lived there. ³³Then they turned and marched up the road to Bashan, but King Og of Bashan and all his people attacked them at Edrei. ³⁴The LORD said to Moses, "Do not be afraid of him, for I have handed him over to you, along with all his people and his land. Do the same to him as you did to King Sihon of the Amorites, who ruled in Heshbon." ³⁵And Israel killed King Og, his sons, and all his subjects; not a single survivor remained. Then Israel occupied their land.

22:1THEN the people of Israel traveled to the plains of Moab and camped east of the Jordan River, across from Jericho. ²Balak son of Zippor, the Moabite king,

had seen everything the Israelites did to the Amorites. ³And when the people of Moab saw how many Israelites there were, they were terrified. ⁴The king of Moab said to the elders of Midian, "This mob will devour everything in sight, like an ox devours grass in the field!"

So Balak, king of Moab, ⁵sent messengers to call Balaam son of Beor, who was living in his native land of Pethor* near the Euphrates River.* His message said:

"Look, a vast horde of people has arrived from Egypt. They cover the face of the earth and are threatening me. ⁶Please come and curse these people for me because they are too powerful for me. Then perhaps I will be able to conquer them and drive them from the land. I know that blessings fall on any people you bless, and curses fall on people you curse."

⁷Balak's messengers, who were elders of Moab and Midian, set out with money to pay Balaam to place a curse upon Israel.* They went to Balaam and delivered Balak's message to him. ⁸"Stay here overnight," Balaam said. "In the morning I will tell you whatever the LORD directs me to say." So the officials from Moab stayed there with Balaam.

⁹That night God came to Balaam and asked him, "Who are these men visiting you?"

¹⁰Balaam said to God, "Balak son of Zippor, king of Moab, has sent me this message: ¹¹'Look, a vast horde of people has arrived from Egypt, and they cover the face of the earth. Come and curse these people for me. Then perhaps I will be able to stand up to them and drive them from the land.'"

¹²But God told Balaam, "Do not go with them. You are not to curse these people, for they have been blessed!"

¹³The next morning Balaam got up and told Balak's officials, "Go on home! The LORD will not let me go with you."

¹⁴So the Moabite officials returned to King Balak and reported, "Balaam

refused to come with us." ¹⁵Then Balak tried again. This time he sent a larger number of even more distinguished officials than those he had sent the first time. ¹⁶They went to Balaam and delivered this message to him:

"This is what Balak son of Zippor says: Please don't let anything stop you from coming to help me. ¹⁷I will pay you very well and do whatever you tell me. Just come and curse these people for me!"

¹⁸But Balaam responded to Balak's messengers, "Even if Balak were to give me his palace filled with silver and gold, I would be powerless to do anything against the will of the LORD my God. ¹⁹But stay here one more night, and I will see if the LORD has anything else to say to me."

²⁰That night God came to Balaam and told him, "Since these men have come for you, get up and go with them. But do only what I tell you to do."

21:2 The Hebrew term used here refers to the complete consecration of things or people to the LORD, either by destroying them or by giving them as an offering; also in 21:3. **21:3** *Hormah* means "destruction." **21:4** Hebrew *sea of reeds.* **21:16** *Beer* means "well." **21:20** Or *overlooks Jeshimon.* **21:24** Or *because the terrain of the Ammonite frontier was rugged;* Hebrew reads *because the boundary of the Ammonites was strong.* **21:30** Or *until fire spread to Medeba.* The meaning of the Hebrew is uncertain. **22:5a** Or *who was at Pethor in the land of the Amavites.* **22:5b** Hebrew *the river.* **22:7** Hebrew *set out with the money of divination in their hand.*

## LUKE 1:26-56

In the sixth month of Elizabeth's pregnancy, God sent the angel Gabriel to Nazareth, a village in Galilee, ²⁷to a virgin named Mary. She was engaged to be married to a man named Joseph, a descendant of King David. ²⁸Gabriel appeared to her and said, "Greetings, favored woman! The Lord is with you!*"

²⁹Confused and disturbed, Mary tried to think what the angel could mean. ³⁰"Don't be afraid, Mary," the angel told her, "for you have found favor with God! ³¹You will conceive and give birth to a son, and you will name him Jesus. ³²He will be very great and will be called the Son of the Most High. The Lord God will

give him the throne of his ancestor David. ³³And he will reign over Israel* forever; his Kingdom will never end!"

³⁴Mary asked the angel, "But how can this happen? I am a virgin."

³⁵The angel replied, "The Holy Spirit will come upon you, and the power of the Most High will overshadow you. So the baby to be born will be holy, and he will be called the Son of God. ³⁶What's more, your relative Elizabeth has become pregnant in her old age! People used to say she was barren, but she's now in her sixth month. ³⁷For nothing is impossible with God.*"

³⁸Mary responded, "I am the Lord's servant. May everything you have said about me come true." And then the angel left her.

³⁹A few days later Mary hurried to the hill country of Judea, to the town ⁴⁰where Zechariah lived. She entered the house and greeted Elizabeth. ⁴¹At the sound of Mary's greeting, Elizabeth's child leaped within her, and Elizabeth was filled with the Holy Spirit.

⁴²Elizabeth gave a glad cry and exclaimed to Mary, "God has blessed you above all women, and your child is blessed. ⁴³Why am I so honored, that the mother of my Lord should visit me? ⁴⁴When I heard your greeting, the baby in my womb jumped for joy. ⁴⁵You are blessed because you believed that the Lord would do what he said."

⁴⁶Mary responded,

"Oh, how my soul praises the Lord.
⁴⁷    How my spirit rejoices in God
        my Savior!
⁴⁸ For he took notice of his lowly
        servant girl,
        and from now on all generations
        will call me blessed.
⁴⁹ For the Mighty One is holy,
        and he has done great things
        for me.
⁵⁰ He shows mercy from generation
        to generation
        to all who fear him.
⁵¹ His mighty arm has done
        tremendous things!

He has scattered the proud and
     haughty ones.
52 He has brought down princes from
     their thrones
     and exalted the humble.
53 He has filled the hungry with good
     things
     and sent the rich away with
     empty hands.
54 He has helped his servant Israel
     and remembered to be merciful.
55 For he made this promise to our
     ancestors,
     to Abraham and his children
     forever."

56Mary stayed with Elizabeth about
three months and then went back to her
own home.

**1:28** Some manuscripts add *Blessed are you among
women.*   **1:33** Greek *over the house of Jacob.*   **1:37** Some
manuscripts read *For the word of God will never fail.*

## PSALM 57:1-11
*For the choir director: A psalm of David,
regarding the time he fled from Saul and
went into the cave. To be sung to the tune
"Do Not Destroy!"*

 1 **H**ave mercy on me, O God,
     have mercy!
     I look to you for protection.
     I will hide beneath the shadow
        of your wings
     until the danger passes by.
 2 I cry out to God Most High,*
     to God who will fulfill his purpose
        for me.
 3 He will send help from heaven to
        rescue me,
     disgracing those who hound me.
                              *Interlude*
     My God will send forth his unfailing
        love and faithfulness.

 4 I am surrounded by fierce lions
     who greedily devour human prey—
     whose teeth pierce like spears
        and arrows,
     and whose tongues cut
        like swords.

 5 Be exalted, O God, above the highest
        heavens!

     May your glory shine over all
        the earth.

 6 My enemies have set a trap for me.
     I am weary from distress.
     They have dug a deep pit in my path,
     but they themselves have fallen
        into it.            *Interlude*

 7 My heart is confident in you, O God;
     my heart is confident.
     No wonder I can sing your
        praises!
 8 Wake up, my heart!
     Wake up, O lyre and harp!
     I will wake the dawn with my song.
 9 **I will thank you, Lord, among all
        the people.
     I will sing your praises among
        the nations.
 10 For your unfailing love is as high
        as the heavens.
     Your faithfulness reaches to
        the clouds.**

 11 **Be exalted, O God, above the
        highest heavens.
     May your glory shine over all
        the earth.**

**57:2** Hebrew *El-Elyon.*

## PROVERBS 11:9-11
**W**ith their words, the godless destroy
their friends, but knowledge will rescue
the righteous. □ The whole city cele-
brates when the godly succeed; they
shout for joy when the wicked die.
□ Upright citizens are good for a city
and make it prosper, but the talk of the
wicked tears it apart.

# MARCH
# 15

## NUMBERS 22:21–23:30
**S**o the next morning Balaam got up, sad-
dled his donkey, and started off with the
Moabite officials. 22But God was angry

that Balaam was going, so he sent the angel of the LORD to stand in the road to block his way. As Balaam and two servants were riding along, 23Balaam's donkey saw the angel of the LORD standing in the road with a drawn sword in his hand. The donkey bolted off the road into a field, but Balaam beat it and turned it back onto the road. 24Then the angel of the LORD stood at a place where the road narrowed between two vineyard walls. 25When the donkey saw the angel of the LORD, it tried to squeeze by and crushed Balaam's foot against the wall. So Balaam beat the donkey again. 26Then the angel of the LORD moved farther down the road and stood in a place too narrow for the donkey to get by at all. 27This time when the donkey saw the angel, it lay down under Balaam. In a fit of rage Balaam beat the animal again with his staff.

28Then the LORD gave the donkey the ability to speak. "What have I done to you that deserves your beating me three times?" it asked Balaam.

29"You have made me look like a fool!" Balaam shouted. "If I had a sword with me, I would kill you!"

30"But I am the same donkey you have ridden all your life," the donkey answered. "Have I ever done anything like this before?"

"No," Balaam admitted.

31Then the LORD opened Balaam's eyes, and he saw the angel of the LORD standing in the roadway with a drawn sword in his hand. Balaam bowed his head and fell face down on the ground before him.

32"Why did you beat your donkey those three times?" the angel of the LORD demanded. "Look, I have come to block your way because you are stubbornly resisting me. 33Three times the donkey saw me and shied away; otherwise, I would certainly have killed you by now and spared the donkey."

34Then Balaam confessed to the angel of the LORD, "I have sinned. I didn't realize you were standing in the road to block my way. I will return home if you are against my going."

35But the angel of the LORD told Balaam, "Go with these men, but say only what I tell you to say." So Balaam went on with Balak's officials. 36When King Balak heard that Balaam was on the way, he went out to meet him at a Moabite town on the Arnon River at the farthest border of his land.

37"Didn't I send you an urgent invitation? Why didn't you come right away?" Balak asked Balaam. "Didn't you believe me when I said I would reward you richly?"

38Balaam replied, "Look, now I have come, but I have no power to say whatever I want. I will speak only the message that God puts in my mouth." 39Then Balaam accompanied Balak to Kiriath-huzoth, 40where the king sacrificed cattle and sheep. He sent portions of the meat to Balaam and the officials who were with him. 41The next morning Balak took Balaam up to Bamoth-baal. From there he could see some of the people of Israel spread out below him.

23:1THEN Balaam said to King Balak, "Build me seven altars here, and prepare seven young bulls and seven rams for me to sacrifice." 2Balak followed his instructions, and the two of them sacrificed a young bull and a ram on each altar.

3Then Balaam said to Balak, "Stand here by your burnt offerings, and I will go to see if the LORD will respond to me. Then I will tell you whatever he reveals to me." So Balaam went alone to the top of a bare hill, 4and God met him there. Balaam said to him, "I have prepared seven altars and have sacrificed a young bull and a ram on each altar."

5The LORD gave Balaam a message for King Balak. Then he said, "Go back to Balak and give him my message."

6So Balaam returned and found the king standing beside his burnt offerings with all the officials of Moab. 7This was the message Balaam delivered:

"Balak summoned me to come from Aram;

the king of Moab brought me
   from the eastern hills.
'Come,' he said, 'curse Jacob for me!
   Come and announce Israel's
      doom.'
⁸ But how can I curse those
   whom God has not cursed?
How can I condemn those
   whom the LORD has not
      condemned?
⁹ I see them from the cliff tops;
   I watch them from the hills.
I see a people who live by
   themselves,
   set apart from other nations.
¹⁰ Who can count Jacob's descendants,
   as numerous as dust?
Who can count even a fourth
   of Israel's people?
Let me die like the righteous;
   let my life end like theirs."

¹¹Then King Balak demanded of Balaam, "What have you done to me? I brought you to curse my enemies. Instead, you have blessed them!"

¹²But Balaam replied, "I will speak only the message that the LORD puts in my mouth."

¹³Then King Balak told him, "Come with me to another place. There you will see another part of the nation of Israel, but not all of them. Curse at least that many!" ¹⁴So Balak took Balaam to the plateau of Zophim on Pisgah Peak. He built seven altars there and offered a young bull and a ram on each altar.

¹⁵Then Balaam said to the king, "Stand here by your burnt offerings while I go over there to meet the LORD."

¹⁶And the LORD met Balaam and gave him a message. Then he said, "Go back to Balak and give him my message."

¹⁷So Balaam returned and found the king standing beside his burnt offerings with all the officials of Moab. "What did the LORD say?" Balak asked eagerly.

¹⁸This was the message Balaam delivered:

"Rise up, Balak, and listen!
   Hear me, son of Zippor.
¹⁹ God is not a man, so he does not lie.

He is not human, so he does not
   change his mind.
Has he ever spoken and failed
   to act?
Has he ever promised and not
   carried it through?
²⁰ Listen, I received a command
   to bless;
God has blessed, and I cannot
   reverse it!
²¹ No misfortune is in his plan
   for Jacob;
   no trouble is in store for Israel.
For the LORD their God is with them;
   he has been proclaimed
      their king.
²² God brought them out of Egypt;
   for them he is as strong as
      a wild ox.
²³ No curse can touch Jacob;
   no magic has any power against
      Israel.
For now it will be said of Jacob,
   'What wonders God has done
      for Israel!'
²⁴ These people rise up like a lioness,
   like a majestic lion rousing
      itself.
They refuse to rest
   until they have feasted on prey,
   drinking the blood of the
      slaughtered!"

²⁵Then Balak said to Balaam, "Fine, but if you won't curse them, at least don't bless them!"

²⁶But Balaam replied to Balak, "Didn't I tell you that I can do only what the LORD tells me?"

²⁷Then King Balak said to Balaam, "Come, I will take you to one more place. Perhaps it will please God to let you curse them from there."

²⁸So Balak took Balaam to the top of Mount Peor, overlooking the wasteland.* ²⁹Balaam again told Balak, "Build me seven altars, and prepare seven young bulls and seven rams for me to sacrifice." ³⁰So Balak did as Balaam ordered and offered a young bull and a ram on each altar.

23:28 Or *overlooking Jeshimon.*

## LUKE 1:57-80

When it was time for Elizabeth's baby to be born, she gave birth to a son. 58And when her neighbors and relatives heard that the Lord had been very merciful to her, everyone rejoiced with her.

59When the baby was eight days old, they all came for the circumcision ceremony. They wanted to name him Zechariah, after his father. 60But Elizabeth said, "No! His name is John!"

61"What?" they exclaimed. "There is no one in all your family by that name." 62So they used gestures to ask the baby's father what he wanted to name him. 63He motioned for a writing tablet, and to everyone's surprise he wrote, "His name is John." 64Instantly Zechariah could speak again, and he began praising God.

65Awe fell upon the whole neighborhood, and the news of what had happened spread throughout the Judean hills. 66Everyone who heard about it reflected on these events and asked, "What will this child turn out to be?" For the hand of the Lord was surely upon him in a special way.

67Then his father, Zechariah, was filled with the Holy Spirit and gave this prophecy:

68 **"Praise the Lord, the God of Israel,
because he has visited and
redeemed his people.**
69 He has sent us a mighty Savior*
from the royal line of his servant
David,
70 just as he promised
through his holy prophets
long ago.
71 Now we will be saved from our
enemies
and from all who hate us.
72 He has been merciful to our
ancestors
by remembering his sacred
covenant—
73 the covenant he swore with an oath
to our ancestor Abraham.
74 We have been rescued from our
enemies
so we can serve God without fear,
75 in holiness and righteousness
for as long as we live.

76 "And you, my little son,
will be called the prophet of the
Most High,
because you will prepare the way
for the Lord.
77 You will tell his people how to find
salvation
through forgiveness of their sins.
78 Because of God's tender mercy,
the morning light from heaven is
about to break upon us,*
79 to give light to those who sit in
darkness and in the shadow
of death,
and to guide us to the path
of peace."

80John grew up and became strong in spirit. And he lived in the wilderness until he began his public ministry to Israel.

1:69 Greek *has raised up a horn of salvation for us.*
1:78 Or *the Morning Light from heaven is about to visit us.*

## PSALM 58:1-11

*For the choir director: A psalm of David, to be sung to the tune "Do Not Destroy!"*

1 Justice—do you rulers* know the
meaning of the word?
Do you judge the people fairly?
2 No! You plot injustice in your hearts.
You spread violence throughout
the land.
3 These wicked people are born
sinners;
even from birth they have lied
and gone their own way.
4 They spit venom like deadly snakes;
they are like cobras that refuse
to listen,
5 ignoring the tunes of the snake
charmers,
no matter how skillfully they play.

6 Break off their fangs, O God!
Smash the jaws of these lions,
O LORD!
7 May they disappear like water into
thirsty ground.

Make their weapons useless in
their hands.*
8 May they be like snails that dissolve
into slime,
like a stillborn child who will
never see the sun.
9 God will sweep them away, both
young and old,
faster than a pot heats over
burning thorns.

10 The godly will rejoice when they
see injustice avenged.
They will wash their feet in the
blood of the wicked.
11 Then at last everyone will say,
"There truly is a reward for those
who live for God;
surely there is a God who judges
justly here on earth."

58:1 Or *you gods.*    58:7 Or *Let them be trodden down and
wither like grass.* The meaning of the Hebrew is uncertain.

## PROVERBS 11:12-13

It is foolish to belittle one's neighbor; a
sensible person keeps quiet. □ A gossip
goes around telling secrets, but those
who are trustworthy can keep a confidence.

## NUMBERS 24:1–25:18

By now Balaam realized that the Lord
was determined to bless Israel, so he did
not resort to divination as before. Instead, he turned and looked out toward
the wilderness, 2where he saw the people of Israel camped, tribe by tribe.
Then the Spirit of God came upon him,
3and this is the message he delivered:

"This is the message of Balaam son
of Beor,
the message of the man whose
eyes see clearly,

4 the message of one who hears the
words of God,
who sees a vision from the
Almighty,
who bows down with eyes
wide open:
5 How beautiful are your tents,
O Jacob;
how lovely are your homes,
O Israel!
6 They spread before me like palm
groves,*
like gardens by the riverside.
They are like tall trees planted by
the Lord,
like cedars beside the waters.
7 Water will flow from their buckets;
their offspring have all they need.
Their king will be greater than Agag;
their kingdom will be exalted.
8 God brought them out of Egypt;
for them he is as strong as
a wild ox.
He devours all the nations that
oppose him,
breaking their bones in pieces,
shooting them with arrows.
9 Like a lion, Israel crouches and
lies down;
like a lioness, who dares to
arouse her?
Blessed is everyone who blesses you,
O Israel,
and cursed is everyone who
curses you."

10King Balak flew into a rage against
Balaam. He angrily clapped his hands
and shouted, "I called you to curse my
enemies! Instead, you have blessed
them three times. 11Now get out of
here! Go back home! I promised to reward you richly, but the Lord has kept
you from your reward."

12Balaam told Balak, "Don't you remember what I told your messengers? I
said, 13'Even if Balak were to give me
his palace filled with silver and gold, I
would be powerless to do anything
against the will of the Lord.' I told you
that I could say only what the Lord says!
14Now I am returning to my own people.

But first let me tell you what the Israelites will do to your people in the future."

15 This is the message Balaam delivered:

"This is the message of Balaam son of Beor,
the message of the man whose eyes see clearly,
16 the message of one who hears the words of God,
who has knowledge from the Most High,
who sees a vision from the Almighty,
who bows down with eyes wide open:
17 I see him, but not here and now.
I perceive him, but far in the distant future.
A star will rise from Jacob;
a scepter will emerge from Israel.
It will crush the foreheads of Moab's people,
cracking the skulls of the people of Sheth.
18 Edom will be taken over,
and Seir, its enemy, will be conquered,
while Israel marches on in triumph.
19 A ruler will rise in Jacob
who will destroy the survivors of Ir."

20 Then Balaam looked over toward the people of Amalek and delivered this message:

"Amalek was the greatest of nations,
but its destiny is destruction!"

21 Then he looked over toward the Kenites and delivered this message:

"Your home is secure;
your nest is set in the rocks.
22 But the Kenites will be destroyed
when Assyria* takes you captive."

23 Balaam concluded his messages by saying:

"Alas, who can survive
unless God has willed it?
24 Ships will come from the coasts of Cyprus*;
they will oppress Assyria and afflict Eber,
but they, too, will be utterly destroyed."

25 Then Balaam and Balak returned to their homes.

25:1 WHILE the Israelites were camped at Acacia Grove,* some of the men defiled themselves by having* sexual relations with local Moabite women. 2 These women invited them to attend sacrifices to their gods, so the Israelites feasted with them and worshiped the gods of Moab. 3 In this way, Israel joined in the worship of Baal of Peor, causing the LORD's anger to blaze against his people.

4 The LORD issued the following command to Moses: "Seize all the ringleaders and execute them before the LORD in broad daylight, so his fierce anger will turn away from the people of Israel."

5 So Moses ordered Israel's judges, "Each of you must put to death the men under your authority who have joined in worshiping Baal of Peor."

6 Just then one of the Israelite men brought a Midianite woman into his tent, right before the eyes of Moses and all the people, as everyone was weeping at the entrance of the Tabernacle.* 7 When Phinehas son of Eleazar and grandson of Aaron the priest saw this, he jumped up and left the assembly. He took a spear 8 and rushed after the man into his tent. Phinehas thrust the spear all the way through the man's body and into the woman's stomach. So the plague against the Israelites was stopped, 9 but not before 24,000 people had died.

10 Then the LORD said to Moses, 11 "Phinehas son of Eleazar and grandson of Aaron the priest has turned my anger away from the Israelites by being as zealous among them as I was. So I stopped destroying all Israel as I had intended to do in my zealous anger. 12 Now tell him that I am making my special covenant of peace with him.

¹³In this covenant, I give him and his descendants a permanent right to the priesthood, for in his zeal for me, his God, he purified the people of Israel, making them right with me.*"

¹⁴The Israelite man killed with the Midianite woman was named Zimri son of Salu, the leader of a family from the tribe of Simeon. ¹⁵The woman's name was Cozbi; she was the daughter of Zur, the leader of a Midianite clan.

¹⁶Then the LORD said to Moses, ¹⁷"Attack the Midianites and destroy them, ¹⁸because they assaulted you with deceit and tricked you into worshiping Baal of Peor, and because of Cozbi, the daughter of a Midianite leader, who was killed at the time of the plague because of what happened at Peor."

24:6 Or like a majestic valley.   24:22 Hebrew Asshur; also in 24:24.   24:24 Hebrew Kittim.   25:1a Hebrew Shittim. 25:1b As in Greek version; Hebrew reads some of the men began having.   25:6 Hebrew the Tent of Meeting. 25:13 Or he made atonement for the people of Israel.

## LUKE 2:1-35

At that time the Roman emperor, Augustus, decreed that a census should be taken throughout the Roman Empire. ²(This was the first census taken when Quirinius was governor of Syria.) ³All returned to their own ancestral towns to register for this census. ⁴And because Joseph was a descendant of King David, he had to go to Bethlehem in Judea, David's ancient home. He traveled there from the village of Nazareth in Galilee. ⁵He took with him Mary, his fiancée, who was now obviously pregnant.

⁶And while they were there, the time came for her baby to be born. ⁷She gave birth to her first child, a son. She wrapped him snugly in strips of cloth and laid him in a manger, because there was no lodging available for them.

⁸That night there were shepherds staying in the fields nearby, guarding their flocks of sheep. ⁹Suddenly, an angel of the Lord appeared among them, and the radiance of the Lord's glory surrounded them. They were terrified, ¹⁰but the angel reassured them. "Don't

be afraid!" he said. "I bring you good news that will bring great joy to all people. ¹¹The Savior—yes, the Messiah, the Lord—has been born today in Bethlehem, the city of David! ¹²And you will recognize him by this sign: You will find a baby wrapped snugly in strips of cloth, lying in a manger."

¹³Suddenly, the angel was joined by a vast host of others—the armies of heaven—praising God and saying,

¹⁴ "Glory to God in highest heaven,
    and peace on earth to those with
      whom God is pleased."

¹⁵When the angels had returned to heaven, the shepherds said to each other, "Let's go to Bethlehem! Let's see this thing that has happened, which the Lord has told us about."

¹⁶They hurried to the village and found Mary and Joseph. And there was the baby, lying in the manger. ¹⁷After seeing him, the shepherds told everyone what had happened and what the angel had said to them about this child. ¹⁸All who heard the shepherds' story were astonished, ¹⁹but Mary kept all these things in her heart and thought about them often. ²⁰The shepherds went back to their flocks, glorifying and praising God for all they had heard and seen. It was just as the angel had told them.

²¹Eight days later, when the baby was circumcised, he was named Jesus, the name given him by the angel even before he was conceived.

²²Then it was time for their purification offering, as required by the law of Moses after the birth of a child; so his parents took him to Jerusalem to present him to the Lord. ²³The law of the Lord says, "If a woman's first child is a boy, he must be dedicated to the LORD."* ²⁴So they offered the sacrifice required in the law of the Lord—"either a pair of turtledoves or two young pigeons."*

²⁵At that time there was a man in Jerusalem named Simeon. He was righteous and devout and was eagerly waiting for the Messiah to come and

rescue Israel. The Holy Spirit was upon him [26] and had revealed to him that he would not die until he had seen the Lord's Messiah. [27] That day the Spirit led him to the Temple. So when Mary and Joseph came to present the baby Jesus to the Lord as the law required, [28] Simeon was there. He took the child in his arms and praised God, saying,

[29] "Sovereign Lord, now let your
      servant die in peace,
      as you have promised.
[30] I have seen your salvation,
[31]    which you have prepared
      for all people.
[32] He is a light to reveal God to the
      nations,
      and he is the glory of your people
      Israel!"

[33] Jesus' parents were amazed at what was being said about him. [34] **Then Simeon blessed them, and he said to Mary, the baby's mother, "This child is destined to cause many in Israel to fall, but he will be a joy to many others. He has been sent as a sign from God, but many will oppose him. [35] As a result, the deepest thoughts of many hearts will be revealed. And a sword will pierce your very soul."**

2:23 Exod 13:2.    2:24 Lev 12:8.

## PSALM 59:1-17

*For the choir director: A psalm of David, regarding the time Saul sent soldiers to watch David's house in order to kill him. To be sung to the tune "Do Not Destroy!"*

[1] Rescue me from my enemies,
      O God.
      Protect me from those who have
      come to destroy me.
[2] Rescue me from these criminals;
      save me from these murderers.
[3] They have set an ambush for me.
      Fierce enemies are out there
      waiting, LORD,
      though I have not sinned or
      offended them.
[4] I have done nothing wrong,
      yet they prepare to attack me.

      Wake up! See what is happening
      and help me!
[5] O LORD God of Heaven's Armies, the
      God of Israel,
      wake up and punish those hostile
      nations.
      Show no mercy to wicked traitors.
                      *Interlude*

[6] They come out at night,
      snarling like vicious dogs
      as they prowl the streets.
[7] Listen to the filth that comes from
      their mouths;
      their words cut like swords.
      "After all, who can hear us?"
      they sneer.
[8] But LORD, you laugh at them.
      You scoff at all the hostile
      nations.
[9] You are my strength; I wait for you
      to rescue me,
      for you, O God, are my fortress.
[10] In his unfailing love, my God will
      stand with me.
      He will let me look down in
      triumph on all my enemies.

[11] Don't kill them, for my people soon
      forget such lessons;
      stagger them with your power,
      and bring them to their knees,
      O Lord our shield.
[12] Because of the sinful things they say,
      because of the evil that is
      on their lips,
      let them be captured by their pride,
      their curses, and their lies.
[13] Destroy them in your anger!
      Wipe them out completely!
      Then the whole world will know
      that God reigns in Israel.*
                      *Interlude*

[14] My enemies come out at night,
      snarling like vicious dogs
      as they prowl the streets.
[15] They scavenge for food
      but go to sleep unsatisfied.*

[16] But as for me, I will sing about
      your power.
      Each morning I will sing with joy
      about your unfailing love.

For you have been my refuge,
a place of safety when I am
in distress.
[17] O my Strength, to you I sing
praises,
for you, O God, are my refuge,
the God who shows me unfailing
love.

**59:13** Hebrew *in Jacob*. See note on 44:4.   **59:15** Or *and growl if they don't get enough.*

## PROVERBS 11:14

**W**ithout wise leadership, a nation falls; there is safety in having many advisers.

# MARCH
# 17

## NUMBERS 26:1-51

**A**fter the plague had ended, the LORD said to Moses and to Eleazar son of Aaron the priest, [2]"From the whole community of Israel, record the names of all the warriors by their families. List all the men twenty years old or older who are able to go to war."

[3]So there on the plains of Moab beside the Jordan River, across from Jericho, Moses and Eleazar the priest issued these instructions to the leaders of Israel: [4]"List all the men of Israel twenty years old and older, just as the LORD commanded Moses."

This is the record of all the descendants of Israel who came out of Egypt.

[5]These were the clans descended from the sons of Reuben, Jacob's* oldest son:
The Hanochite clan, named after their ancestor Hanoch.
The Palluite clan, named after their ancestor Pallu.
[6] The Hezronite clan, named after their ancestor Hezron.
The Carmite clan, named after their ancestor Carmi.

[7]These were the clans of Reuben. Their registered troops numbered 43,730.

[8]Pallu was the ancestor of Eliab, [9]and Eliab was the father of Nemuel, Dathan, and Abiram. This Dathan and Abiram are the same community leaders who conspired with Korah against Moses and Aaron, rebelling against the LORD. [10]But the earth opened up its mouth and swallowed them with Korah, and fire devoured 250 of their followers. This served as a warning to the entire nation of Israel. [11]However, the sons of Korah did not die that day.

[12]These were the clans descended from the sons of Simeon:
The Jemuelite clan, named after their ancestor Jemuel.*
The Jaminite clan, named after their ancestor Jamin.
The Jakinite clan, named after their ancestor Jakin.
[13] The Zoharite clan, named after their ancestor Zohar.*
The Shaulite clan, named after their ancestor Shaul.

[14]These were the clans of Simeon. Their registered troops numbered 22,200.

[15]These were the clans descended from the sons of Gad:
The Zephonite clan, named after their ancestor Zephon.
The Haggite clan, named after their ancestor Haggi.
The Shunite clan, named after their ancestor Shuni.
[16] The Oznite clan, named after their ancestor Ozni.
The Erite clan, named after their ancestor Eri.
[17] The Arodite clan, named after their ancestor Arodi.*
The Arelite clan, named after their ancestor Areli.

[18]These were the clans of Gad. Their registered troops numbered 40,500.

[19]Judah had two sons, Er and Onan, who had died in the land of Canaan.

²⁰These were the clans descended from Judah's surviving sons:

The Shelanite clan, named after their ancestor Shelah.

The Perezite clan, named after their ancestor Perez.

The Zerahite clan, named after their ancestor Zerah.

²¹These were the subclans descended from the Perezites:

The Hezronites, named after their ancestor Hezron.

The Hamulites, named after their ancestor Hamul.

²²These were the clans of Judah. Their registered troops numbered 76,500.

²³These were the clans descended from the sons of Issachar:

The Tolaite clan, named after their ancestor Tola.

The Puite clan, named after their ancestor Puah.*

²⁴ The Jashubite clan, named after their ancestor Jashub.

The Shimronite clan, named after their ancestor Shimron.

²⁵These were the clans of Issachar. Their registered troops numbered 64,300.

²⁶These were the clans descended from the sons of Zebulun:

The Seredite clan, named after their ancestor Sered.

The Elonite clan, named after their ancestor Elon.

The Jahleelite clan, named after their ancestor Jahleel.

²⁷These were the clans of Zebulun. Their registered troops numbered 60,500.

²⁸Two clans were descended from Joseph through Manasseh and Ephraim.

²⁹These were the clans descended from Manasseh:

The Makirite clan, named after their ancestor Makir.

The Gileadite clan, named after their ancestor Gilead, Makir's son.

³⁰These were the subclans descended from the Gileadites:

The Iezerites, named after their ancestor Iezer.

The Helekites, named after their ancestor Helek.

³¹ The Asrielites, named after their ancestor Asriel.

The Shechemites, named after their ancestor Shechem.

³² The Shemidaites, named after their ancestor Shemida.

The Hepherites, named after their ancestor Hepher.

³³ (One of Hepher's descendants, Zelophehad, had no sons, but his daughters' names were Mahlah, Noah, Hoglah, Milcah, and Tirzah.)

³⁴These were the clans of Manasseh. Their registered troops numbered 52,700.

³⁵These were the clans descended from the sons of Ephraim:

The Shuthelahite clan, named after their ancestor Shuthelah.

The Bekerite clan, named after their ancestor Beker.

The Tahanite clan, named after their ancestor Tahan.

³⁶This was the subclan descended from the Shuthelahites:

The Eranites, named after their ancestor Eran.

³⁷These were the clans of Ephraim. Their registered troops numbered 32,500.

These clans of Manasseh and Ephraim were all descendants of Joseph.

³⁸These were the clans descended from the sons of Benjamin:

The Belaite clan, named after their ancestor Bela.

The Ashbelite clan, named after their ancestor Ashbel.

The Ahiramite clan, named after their ancestor Ahiram.

³⁹ The Shuphamite clan, named after their ancestor Shupham.*

The Huphamite clan, named after their ancestor Hupham.

40These were the subclans descended from the Belaites:

The Ardites, named after their ancestor Ard.*

The Naamites, named after their ancestor Naaman.

41These were the clans of Benjamin. Their registered troops numbered 45,600.

42These were the clans descended from the sons of Dan:

The Shuhamite clan, named after their ancestor Shuham.

43These were the Shuhamite clans of Dan. Their registered troops numbered 64,400.

44These were the clans descended from the sons of Asher:

The Imnite clan, named after their ancestor Imnah.

The Ishvite clan, named after their ancestor Ishvi.

The Beriite clan, named after their ancestor Beriah.

45These were the subclans descended from the Beriites:

The Heberites, named after their ancestor Heber.

The Malkielites, named after their ancestor Malkiel.

46Asher also had a daughter named Serah.

47These were the clans of Asher. Their registered troops numbered 53,400.

48These were the clans descended from the sons of Naphtali:

The Jahzeelite clan, named after their ancestor Jahzeel.

The Gunite clan, named after their ancestor Guni.

49The Jezerite clan, named after their ancestor Jezer.

The Shillemite clan, named after their ancestor Shillem.

50These were the clans of Naphtali. Their registered troops numbered 45,400.

51In summary, the registered troops of all Israel numbered 601,730.

26:5 Hebrew *Israel's;* see note on 1:20-21b.   26:12 As in Syriac version (see also Gen 46:10; Exod 6:15); Hebrew reads *Nemuelite . . . Nemuel.*   26:13 As in parallel texts at Gen 46:10 and Exod 6:15; Hebrew reads *Zerahite . . . Zerah.* 26:17 As in Samaritan Pentateuch and Greek and Syriac versions (see also Gen 46:16); Hebrew reads *Arod.* 26:23 As in Samaritan Pentateuch, Greek and Syriac versions, and Latin Vulgate (see also 1 Chr 7:1); Hebrew reads *The Punite clan, named after its ancestor Puvah.* 26:39 As in some Hebrew manuscripts, Samaritan Pentateuch, Greek and Syriac versions, and Latin Vulgate; most Hebrew manuscripts read *Shephupham.*   26:40 As in Samaritan Pentateuch, some Greek manuscripts, and Latin Vulgate; Hebrew lacks *named after their ancestor Ard.*

## LUKE 2:36-52

**A**nna, a prophet, was also there in the Temple. She was the daughter of Phanuel from the tribe of Asher, and she was very old. Her husband died when they had been married only seven years. 37Then she lived as a widow to the age of eighty-four.* She never left the Temple but stayed there day and night, worshiping God with fasting and prayer. 38She came along just as Simeon was talking with Mary and Joseph, and she began praising God. She talked about the child to everyone who had been waiting expectantly for God to rescue Jerusalem.

39When Jesus' parents had fulfilled all the requirements of the law of the Lord, they returned home to Nazareth in Galilee. 40There the child grew up healthy and strong. He was filled with wisdom, and God's favor was on him.

41Every year Jesus' parents went to Jerusalem for the Passover festival. 42When Jesus was twelve years old, they attended the festival as usual. 43After the celebration was over, they started home to Nazareth, but Jesus stayed behind in Jerusalem. His parents didn't miss him at first, 44because they assumed he was among the other travelers. But when he didn't show up that evening, they started looking for him among their relatives and friends.

45When they couldn't find him, they went back to Jerusalem to search for him there. ⁴⁶Three days later they finally discovered him in the Temple, sitting among the religious teachers, listening to them and asking questions. ⁴⁷All who heard him were amazed at his understanding and his answers.

⁴⁸His parents didn't know what to think. "Son," his mother said to him, "why have you done this to us? Your father and I have been frantic, searching for you everywhere."

⁴⁹**"But why did you need to search?" he asked. "Didn't you know that I must be in my Father's house?"*** ⁵⁰But they didn't understand what he meant.

⁵¹Then he returned to Nazareth with them and was obedient to them. And his mother stored all these things in her heart.

⁵²Jesus grew in wisdom and in stature and in favor with God and all the people.

2:37 Or *She had been a widow for eighty-four years.*
2:49 Or *"Didn't you realize that I should be involved with my Father's affairs?"*

PSALM 60:1-12
*For the choir director: A psalm of David useful for teaching, regarding the time David fought Aram-naharaim and Aram-zobah, and Joab returned and killed 12,000 Edomites in the Valley of Salt. To be sung to the tune "Lily of the Testimony."*

¹ **Y**ou have rejected us, O God, and broken our defenses.
    You have been angry with us; now restore us to your favor.
² You have shaken our land and split it open.
    Seal the cracks, for the land trembles.
³ You have been very hard on us, making us drink wine that sent us reeling.
⁴ But you have raised a banner for those who fear you—
    a rallying point in the face of attack.                    *Interlude*

⁵ Now rescue your beloved people. Answer and save us by your power.

⁶ God has promised this by his holiness*:
    "I will divide up Shechem with joy.
    I will measure out the valley of Succoth.
⁷ Gilead is mine, and Manasseh, too.
    Ephraim, my helmet, will produce my warriors,
    and Judah, my scepter, will produce my kings.
⁸ But Moab, my washbasin, will become my servant,
    and I will wipe my feet on Edom and shout in triumph over Philistia."

⁹ Who will bring me into the fortified city?
    Who will bring me victory over Edom?
¹⁰ Have you rejected us, O God?
    Will you no longer march with our armies?
¹¹ Oh, please help us against our enemies,
    for all human help is useless.
¹² With God's help we will do mighty things,
    for he will trample down our foes.

60:6 Or *in his sanctuary.*

PROVERBS 11:15
**T**here's danger in putting up security for a stranger's debt; it's safer not to guarantee another person's debt.

# MARCH 18

NUMBERS 26:52–28:15
**T**hen the LORD said to Moses, ⁵³"Divide the land among the tribes, and distribute the grants of land in proportion to the tribes' populations, as indicated by the number of names on the list. ⁵⁴Give the larger tribes more land and

the smaller tribes less land, each group receiving a grant in proportion to the size of its population. ⁵⁵But you must assign the land by lot, and give land to each ancestral tribe according to the number of names on the list. ⁵⁶Each grant of land must be assigned by lot among the larger and smaller tribal groups."

⁵⁷This is the record of the Levites who were counted according to their clans:

The Gershonite clan, named after their ancestor Gershon.

The Kohathite clan, named after their ancestor Kohath.

The Merarite clan, named after their ancestor Merari.

⁵⁸The Libnites, the Hebronites, the Mahlites, the Mushites, and the Korahites were all subclans of the Levites.

Now Kohath was the ancestor of Amram, ⁵⁹and Amram's wife was named Jochebed. She also was a descendant of Levi, born among the Levites in the land of Egypt. Amram and Jochebed became the parents of Aaron, Moses, and their sister, Miriam. ⁶⁰To Aaron were born Nadab, Abihu, Eleazar, and Ithamar. ⁶¹But Nadab and Abihu died when they burned before the LORD the wrong kind of fire, different than he had commanded.

⁶²The men from the Levite clans who were one month old or older numbered 23,000. But the Levites were not included in the registration of the rest of the people of Israel because they were not given an allotment of land when it was divided among the Israelites.

⁶³So these are the results of the registration of the people of Israel as conducted by Moses and Eleazar the priest on the plains of Moab beside the Jordan River, across from Jericho. ⁶⁴Not one person on this list had been among those listed in the previous registration taken by Moses and Aaron in the wilderness of Sinai. ⁶⁵For the LORD had said of them, "They will all die in the wilderness." Not one of them survived except Caleb son of Jephunneh and Joshua son of Nun.

²⁷:¹ONE day a petition was presented by the daughters of Zelophehad—Mahlah, Noah, Hoglah, Milcah, and Tirzah. Their father, Zelophehad, was a descendant of Hepher son of Gilead, son of Makir, son of Manasseh, son of Joseph. ²These women stood before Moses, Eleazar the priest, the tribal leaders, and the entire community at the entrance of the Tabernacle.* ³"Our father died in the wilderness," they said. "He was not among Korah's followers, who rebelled against the LORD; he died because of his own sin. But he had no sons. ⁴Why should the name of our father disappear from his clan just because he had no sons? Give us property along with the rest of our relatives."

⁵So Moses brought their case before the LORD. ⁶And the LORD replied to Moses, ⁷"The claim of the daughters of Zelophehad is legitimate. You must give them a grant of land along with their father's relatives. Assign them the property that would have been given to their father.

⁸"And give the following instructions to the people of Israel: If a man dies and has no son, then give his inheritance to his daughters. ⁹And if he has no daughter either, transfer his inheritance to his brothers. ¹⁰If he has no brothers, give his inheritance to his father's brothers. ¹¹But if his father has no brothers, give his inheritance to the nearest relative in his clan. This is a legal requirement for the people of Israel, just as the LORD commanded Moses."

¹²One day the LORD said to Moses, "Climb one of the mountains east of the river,* and look out over the land I have given the people of Israel. ¹³After you have seen it, you will die like your brother, Aaron, ¹⁴for you both rebelled against my instructions in the wilderness of Zin. When the people of Israel rebelled, you failed to demonstrate my holiness to them at the waters." (These are the waters of Meribah at Kadesh* in the wilderness of Zin.)

¹⁵Then Moses said to the LORD, ¹⁶"O LORD, you are the God who gives

breath to all creatures. Please appoint a new man as leader for the community. [17] Give them someone who will guide them wherever they go and will lead them into battle, so the community of the LORD will not be like sheep without a shepherd."

[18] The LORD replied, "Take Joshua son of Nun, who has the Spirit in him, and lay your hands on him. [19] Present him to Eleazar the priest before the whole community, and publicly commission him to lead the people. [20] Transfer some of your authority to him so the whole community of Israel will obey him. [21] When direction from the LORD is needed, Joshua will stand before Eleazar the priest, who will use the Urim—one of the sacred lots cast before the LORD—to determine his will. This is how Joshua and the rest of the community of Israel will determine everything they should do."

[22] So Moses did as the LORD commanded. He presented Joshua to Eleazar the priest and the whole community. [23] Moses laid his hands on him and commissioned him to lead the people, just as the LORD had commanded through Moses.

[28:1] THE LORD said to Moses, [2] "Give these instructions to the people of Israel: The offerings you present as special gifts are a pleasing aroma to me; they are my food. See to it that they are brought at the appointed times and offered according to my instructions.

[3] "Say to the people: This is the special gift you must present to the LORD as your daily burnt offering. You must offer two one-year-old male lambs with no defects. [4] Sacrifice one lamb in the morning and the other in the evening. [5] With each lamb you must offer a grain offering of two quarts* of choice flour mixed with one quart* of pure oil of pressed olives. [6] This is the regular burnt offering instituted at Mount Sinai as a special gift, a pleasing aroma to the LORD. [7] Along with it you must present the proper liquid offering of one quart of alcoholic drink with each lamb, poured out in the

Holy Place as an offering to the LORD. [8] Offer the second lamb in the evening with the same grain offering and liquid offering. It, too, is a special gift, a pleasing aroma to the LORD.

[9] "On the Sabbath day, sacrifice two one-year-old male lambs with no defects. They must be accompanied by a grain offering of four quarts* of choice flour moistened with olive oil, and a liquid offering. [10] This is the burnt offering to be presented each Sabbath day, in addition to the regular burnt offering and its accompanying liquid offering.

[11] "On the first day of each month, present an extra burnt offering to the LORD of two young bulls, one ram, and seven one-year-old male lambs, all with no defects. [12] These must be accompanied by grain offerings of choice flour moistened with olive oil—six quarts* with each bull, four quarts with the ram, [13] and two quarts with each lamb. This burnt offering will be a special gift, a pleasing aroma to the LORD. [14] You must also present a liquid offering with each sacrifice: two quarts* of wine for each bull, a third of a gallon* for the ram, and one quart* for each lamb. Present this monthly burnt offering on the first day of each month throughout the year.

[15] "On the first day of each month, you must also offer one male goat for a sin offering to the LORD. This is in addition to the regular burnt offering and its accompanying liquid offering."

28:2 Hebrew *the Tent of Meeting.*     27:12 Or *the mountains of Abarim.*     27:14 Hebrew *waters of Meribath-kadesh.*     28:5a Hebrew *⅒ of an ephah* [2.2 liters]; also in 28:13, 21, 29.     28:5b Hebrew *¼ of a hin* [1 liter]; also in 28:7.     28:9 Hebrew *²⁄₁₀ of an ephah* [4.4 liters]; also in 28:12, 20, 28.     28:12 Hebrew *⅒ of an ephah* [6.6 liters]; also in 28:20, 28.     28:14a Hebrew *½ of a hin* [2 liters].     28:14b Hebrew *⅓ of a hin* [1.3 liters].     28:14c Hebrew *¼ of a hin* [1 liter].

## LUKE 3:1-22

**I**t was now the fifteenth year of the reign of Tiberius, the Roman emperor. Pontius Pilate was governor over Judea; Herod Antipas was ruler* over Galilee; his brother Philip was ruler* over Iturea and Traconitis; Lysanias was ruler over Abilene. [2] Annas and Caiaphas were the high priests. At this time a message from God came to John son of Zechariah, who was living in the wilderness. ³Then John went from place to place on both sides of the Jordan River, preaching that people should be baptized to show that they had turned to God to receive forgiveness for their sins. ⁴Isaiah had spoken of John when he said,

"He is a voice shouting in the
    wilderness,
'Prepare the way for the LORD's
    coming!
Clear the road for him!
⁵ The valleys will be filled,
    and the mountains and hills
        made level.
The curves will be straightened,
    and the rough places made
        smooth.
⁶ And then all people will see
    the salvation sent from God.'"*

⁷When the crowds came to John for baptism, he said, "You brood of snakes! Who warned you to flee God's coming wrath? ⁸Prove by the way you live that you have repented of your sins and turned to God. Don't just say to each other, 'We're safe, for we are descendants of Abraham.' That means nothing, for I tell you, God can create children of Abraham from these very stones. ⁹Even now the ax of God's judgment is poised, ready to sever the roots of the trees. Yes, every tree that does not produce good fruit will be chopped down and thrown into the fire."

¹⁰The crowds asked, "What should we do?"

¹¹John replied, "If you have two shirts, give one to the poor. If you have food, share it with those who are hungry."

¹²Even corrupt tax collectors came to be baptized and asked, "Teacher, what should we do?"

¹³He replied, "Collect no more taxes than the government requires."

¹⁴"What should we do?" asked some soldiers.

John replied, "Don't extort money or make false accusations. And be content with your pay."

¹⁵Everyone was expecting the Messiah to come soon, and they were eager to know whether John might be the Messiah. ¹⁶John answered their questions by saying, "I baptize you with* water; but someone is coming soon who is greater than I am—so much greater that I'm not even worthy to be his slave and untie the straps of his sandals. He will baptize you with the Holy Spirit and with fire.* ¹⁷He is ready to separate the chaff from the wheat with his winnowing fork. Then he will clean up the threshing area, gathering the wheat into his barn but burning the chaff with never-ending fire." ¹⁸John used many such warnings as he announced the Good News to the people.

¹⁹John also publicly criticized Herod Antipas, the ruler of Galilee,* for marrying Herodias, his brother's wife, and for many other wrongs he had done. ²⁰So Herod put John in prison, adding this sin to his many others.

²¹One day when the crowds were being baptized, Jesus himself was baptized. As he was praying, the heavens opened, ²²and the Holy Spirit, in bodily form, descended on him like a dove. And a voice from heaven said, "You are my dearly loved Son, and you bring me great joy.*"

3:1a Greek *Herod was tetrarch.* Herod Antipas was a son of King Herod.    3:1b Greek *tetrarch;* also in 3:1c.    3:4-6 Isa 40:3-5 (Greek version).    3:16a Or *in.*    3:16b Or *in the Holy Spirit and in fire.*    3:19 Greek *Herod the tetrarch.* 3:22 Some manuscripts read *and today I have become your Father.*

PSALM 61:1-8
*For the choir director: A psalm of David, to be accompanied by stringed instruments.*

¹ **O God, listen to my cry!**
    **Hear my prayer!**
² **From the ends of the earth,**
    **I cry to you for help**
        **when my heart is overwhelmed.**
**Lead me to the towering rock**
        **of safety,**
³    for you are my safe refuge,
        a fortress where my enemies
            cannot reach me.

⁴ Let me live forever in your
sanctuary,
safe beneath the shelter
of your wings!            *Interlude*

⁵ For you have heard my vows, O God.
You have given me an inheritance
reserved for those who fear
your name.
⁶ Add many years to the life
of the king!
May his years span the
generations!
⁷ May he reign under God's protection
forever.
May your unfailing love and
faithfulness watch over him.
⁸ Then I will sing praises to your
name forever
as I fulfill my vows each day.

PROVERBS 11:16-17

**A** gracious woman gains respect, but
ruthless men gain only wealth. □ Your
kindness will reward you, but your cru-
elty will destroy you.

# MARCH
# 19

NUMBERS 28:16–29:40

"**O**n the fourteenth day of the first
month,* you must celebrate the LORD's
Passover. ¹⁷On the following day—the
fifteenth day of the month—a joyous,
seven-day festival will begin, but no
bread made with yeast may be eaten.
¹⁸The first day of the festival will be an
official day for holy assembly, and no ordinary work may be done on that day.
¹⁹As a special gift you must present a
burnt offering to the LORD—two young
bulls, one ram, and seven one-year-old
male lambs, all with no defects. ²⁰These
will be accompanied by grain offerings
of choice flour moistened with olive oil—
six quarts with each bull, four quarts with

the ram, ²¹and two quarts with each of
the seven lambs. ²²You must also offer a
male goat as a sin offering to purify yourselves and make yourselves right with the
LORD.* ²³Present these offerings in addition to your regular morning burnt offering. ²⁴On each of the seven days of the
festival, this is how you must prepare the
food offering that is presented as a special gift, a pleasing aroma to the LORD.
These will be offered in addition to the
regular burnt offerings and liquid offerings. ²⁵The seventh day of the festival
will be another official day for holy assembly, and no ordinary work may be
done on that day.

²⁶"At the Festival of Harvest,* when
you present the first of your new grain to
the LORD, you must call an official day
for holy assembly, and you may do no
ordinary work on that day. ²⁷Present a
special burnt offering on that day as a
pleasing aroma to the LORD. It will consist of two young bulls, one ram, and
seven one-year-old male lambs. ²⁸These
will be accompanied by grain offerings
of choice flour moistened with olive
oil—six quarts with each bull, four
quarts with the ram, ²⁹and two quarts
with each of the seven lambs. ³⁰Also, offer one male goat to purify yourselves
and make yourselves right with the
LORD. ³¹Prepare these special burnt offerings, along with their liquid offerings,
in addition to the regular burnt offering
and its accompanying grain offering. Be
sure that all the animals you sacrifice
have no defects.

²⁹:¹"CELEBRATE the Festival of Trumpets each year on the first day of the appointed month in early autumn.* You
must call an official day for holy assembly, and you may do no ordinary work.
²On that day you must present a burnt
offering as a pleasing aroma to the
LORD. It will consist of one young bull,
one ram, and seven one-year-old male
lambs, all with no defects. ³These must
be accompanied by grain offerings of
choice flour moistened with olive oil—
six quarts* with the bull, four quarts*

with the ram, ⁴and two quarts* with each of the seven lambs. ⁵In addition, you must sacrifice a male goat as a sin offering to purify yourselves and make yourselves right with the Lord.* ⁶These special sacrifices are in addition to your regular monthly and daily burnt offerings, and they must be given with their prescribed grain offerings and liquid offerings. These offerings are given as a special gift to the Lord, a pleasing aroma to him.

⁷"Ten days later, on the tenth day of the same month,* you must call another holy assembly. On that day, the Day of Atonement, the people must go without food and must do no ordinary work. ⁸You must present a burnt offering as a pleasing aroma to the Lord. It will consist of one young bull, one ram, and seven one-year-old male lambs, all with no defects. ⁹These offerings must be accompanied by the prescribed grain offerings of choice flour moistened with olive oil—six quarts of choice flour with the bull, four quarts of choice flour with the ram, ¹⁰and two quarts of choice flour with each of the seven lambs. ¹¹You must also sacrifice one male goat for a sin offering. This is in addition to the sin offering of atonement and the regular daily burnt offering with its grain offering, and their accompanying liquid offerings.

¹²"Five days later, on the fifteenth day of the same month,* you must call another holy assembly of all the people, and you may do no ordinary work on that day. It is the beginning of the Festival of Shelters,* a seven-day festival to the Lord. ¹³On the first day of the festival, you must present a burnt offering as a special gift, a pleasing aroma to the Lord. It will consist of thirteen young bulls, two rams, and fourteen one-year-old male lambs, all with no defects. ¹⁴Each of these offerings must be accompanied by a grain offering of choice flour moistened with olive oil—six quarts for each of the thirteen bulls, four quarts for each of the two rams, ¹⁵and two quarts for each of the four-

teen lambs. ¹⁶You must also sacrifice a male goat as a sin offering, in addition to the regular burnt offering with its accompanying grain offering and liquid offering.

¹⁷"On the second day of this seven-day festival, sacrifice twelve young bulls, two rams, and fourteen one-year-old male lambs, all with no defects. ¹⁸Each of these offerings of bulls, rams, and lambs must be accompanied by its prescribed grain offering and liquid offering. ¹⁹You must also sacrifice a male goat as a sin offering, in addition to the regular burnt offering with its accompanying grain offering and liquid offering.

²⁰"On the third day of the festival, sacrifice eleven young bulls, two rams, and fourteen one-year-old male lambs, all with no defects. ²¹Each of these offerings of bulls, rams, and lambs must be accompanied by its prescribed grain offering and liquid offering. ²²You must also sacrifice a male goat as a sin offering, in addition to the regular burnt offering with its accompanying grain offering and liquid offering.

²³"On the fourth day of the festival, sacrifice ten young bulls, two rams, and fourteen one-year-old male lambs, all with no defects. ²⁴Each of these offerings of bulls, rams, and lambs must be accompanied by its prescribed grain offering and liquid offering. ²⁵You must also sacrifice a male goat as a sin offering, in addition to the regular burnt offering with its accompanying grain offering and liquid offering.

²⁶"On the fifth day of the festival, sacrifice nine young bulls, two rams, and fourteen one-year-old male lambs, all with no defects. ²⁷Each of these offerings of bulls, rams, and lambs must be accompanied by its prescribed grain offering and liquid offering. ²⁸You must also sacrifice a male goat as a sin offering, in addition to the regular burnt offering with its accompanying grain offering and liquid offering.

²⁹"On the sixth day of the festival, sacrifice eight young bulls, two rams,

and fourteen one-year-old male lambs, all with no defects. [30]Each of these offerings of bulls, rams, and lambs must be accompanied by its prescribed grain offering and liquid offering. [31]You must also sacrifice a male goat as a sin offering, in addition to the regular burnt offering with its accompanying grain offering and liquid offering.

[32]"On the seventh day of the festival, sacrifice seven young bulls, two rams, and fourteen one-year-old male lambs, all with no defects. [33]Each of these offerings of bulls, rams, and lambs must be accompanied by its prescribed grain offering and liquid offering. [34]You must also sacrifice one male goat as a sin offering, in addition to the regular burnt offering with its accompanying grain offering and liquid offering.

[35]"On the eighth day of the festival, proclaim another holy day. You must do no ordinary work on that day. [36]You must present a burnt offering as a special gift, a pleasing aroma to the LORD. It will consist of one young bull, one ram, and seven one-year-old male lambs, all with no defects. [37]Each of these offerings must be accompanied by its prescribed grain offering and liquid offering. [38]You must also sacrifice one male goat as a sin offering, in addition to the regular burnt offering with its accompanying grain offering and liquid offering.

[39]"You must present these offerings to the LORD at your annual festivals. These are in addition to the sacrifices and offerings you present in connection with vows, or as voluntary offerings, burnt offerings, grain offerings, liquid offerings, or peace offerings."

[40]*So Moses gave all of these instructions to the people of Israel as the LORD had commanded him.

28:16 This day in the ancient Hebrew lunar calendar occurred in late March, April, or early May.    28:22 Or *to make atonement for yourselves;* also in 28:30. 28:26 Hebrew *Festival of Weeks.* This was later called the Festival of Pentecost (see Acts 2:1). It is celebrated today as Shavuat (or Shabuoth).    29:1 Hebrew *the first day of the seventh month.* This day in the ancient Hebrew lunar calendar occurred in September or October. This festival is celebrated today as Rosh Hashanah, the Jewish new year. 29:3a Hebrew *3/10 of an ephah* [6.6 liters]; also in 29:9, 14.

29:3b Hebrew *2/10 of an ephah* [4.4 liters]; also in 29:9, 14. 29:4 Hebrew *1/10 of an ephah* [2.2 liters]; also in 29:10, 15. 29:5 Or *to make atonement for yourselves.*    29:7 Hebrew *On the tenth day of the seventh month;* see 29:1 and the note there. This day in the ancient Hebrew lunar calendar occurred in September or October. It is celebrated today as Yom Kippur.    29:12a Hebrew *On the fifteenth day of the seventh month;* see 29:1, 7 and the notes there. This day in the ancient Hebrew lunar calendar occurred in late September, October, or early November.    29:12b Or *Festival of Booths,* or *Festival of Tabernacles.* This was earlier called the Festival of the Final Harvest or Festival of Ingathering (see Exod 23:16b). It is celebrated today as Sukkot (or Succoth).    29:40 Verse 29:40 is numbered 30:1 in Hebrew text.

## LUKE 3:23-38

Jesus was about thirty years old when he began his public ministry.

Jesus was known as the son of Joseph.
Joseph was the son of Heli.
[24] Heli was the son of Matthat.
Matthat was the son of Levi.
Levi was the son of Melki.
Melki was the son of Jannai.
Jannai was the son of Joseph.
[25] Joseph was the son of Mattathias.
Mattathias was the son of Amos.
Amos was the son of Nahum.
Nahum was the son of Esli.
Esli was the son of Naggai.
[26] Naggai was the son of Maath.
Maath was the son of Mattathias.
Mattathias was the son of Semein.
Semein was the son of Josech.
Josech was the son of Joda.
[27] Joda was the son of Joanan.
Joanan was the son of Rhesa.
Rhesa was the son of Zerubbabel.
Zerubbabel was the son of Shealtiel.
Shealtiel was the son of Neri.
[28] Neri was the son of Melki.
Melki was the son of Addi.
Addi was the son of Cosam.
Cosam was the son of Elmadam.
Elmadam was the son of Er.
[29] Er was the son of Joshua.
Joshua was the son of Eliezer.
Eliezer was the son of Jorim.
Jorim was the son of Matthat.
Matthat was the son of Levi.
[30] Levi was the son of Simeon.
Simeon was the son of Judah.
Judah was the son of Joseph.
Joseph was the son of Jonam.

Jonam was the son of Eliakim.
<sup>31</sup> Eliakim was the son of Melea.
Melea was the son of Menna.
Menna was the son of Mattatha.
Mattatha was the son of Nathan.
Nathan was the son of David.
<sup>32</sup> David was the son of Jesse.
Jesse was the son of Obed.
Obed was the son of Boaz.
Boaz was the son of Salmon.*
Salmon was the son of Nahshon.
<sup>33</sup> Nahshon was the son of
Amminadab.
Amminadab was the son of Admin.
Admin was the son of Arni.*
Arni was the son of Hezron.
Hezron was the son of Perez.
Perez was the son of Judah.
<sup>34</sup> Judah was the son of Jacob.
Jacob was the son of Isaac.
Isaac was the son of Abraham.
Abraham was the son of Terah.
Terah was the son of Nahor.
<sup>35</sup> Nahor was the son of Serug.
Serug was the son of Reu.
Reu was the son of Peleg.
Peleg was the son of Eber.
Eber was the son of Shelah.
<sup>36</sup> Shelah was the son of Cainan.
Cainan was the son of Arphaxad.
Arphaxad was the son of Shem.
Shem was the son of Noah.
Noah was the son of Lamech.
<sup>37</sup> Lamech was the son of Methuselah.
Methuselah was the son of Enoch.
Enoch was the son of Jared.
Jared was the son of Mahalalel.
Mahalalel was the son of Kenan.
<sup>38</sup> Kenan was the son of Enosh.*
Enosh was the son of Seth.
Seth was the son of Adam.
Adam was the son of God.

3:32 Greek *Sala,* a variant spelling of Salmon; also in 3:32b.
See Ruth 4:22.   3:33 Some manuscripts read *Amminadab
was the son of Aram. Arni* and *Aram* are alternate spellings
of Ram. See 1 Chr 2:9-10.   3:38 Greek *Enos,* a variant
spelling of Enosh; also in 3:38b. See Gen 5:6.

PSALM 62:1-12
*For Jeduthun, the choir director: A psalm
of David.*

<sup>1</sup> I wait quietly before God,
for my victory comes from him.

<sup>2</sup> He alone is my rock and my
salvation,
my fortress where I will never
be shaken.

<sup>3</sup> So many enemies against one man—
all of them trying to kill me.
To them I'm just a broken-down wall
or a tottering fence.
<sup>4</sup> They plan to topple me from my
high position.
They delight in telling lies
about me.
They praise me to my face
but curse me in their hearts.
*Interlude*

<sup>5</sup> Let all that I am wait quietly before
God,
for my hope is in him.
<sup>6</sup> He alone is my rock and my
salvation,
my fortress where I will not
be shaken.
<sup>7</sup> **My victory and honor come from
God alone.
He is my refuge, a rock where
no enemy can reach me.**
<sup>8</sup> **O my people, trust in him at
all times.
Pour out your heart to him,
for God is our refuge.**   *Interlude*

<sup>9</sup> Common people are as worthless as
a puff of wind,
and the powerful are not what
they appear to be.
If you weigh them on the scales,
together they are lighter than a
breath of air.

<sup>10</sup> Don't make your living by extortion
or put your hope in stealing.
And if your wealth increases,
don't make it the center
of your life.

<sup>11</sup> God has spoken plainly,
and I have heard it many times:
Power, O God, belongs to you;
<sup>12</sup> unfailing love, O Lord, is yours.
Surely you repay all people
according to what they have done.

PROVERBS 11:18-19

Evil people get rich for the moment, but the reward of the godly will last. □ Godly people find life; evil people find death.

## MARCH 20

NUMBERS 30:1–31:54

¹*Then Moses summoned the leaders of the tribes of Israel and told them, "This is what the LORD has commanded: ²A man who makes a vow to the LORD or makes a pledge under oath must never break it. He must do exactly what he said he would do.

³"If a young woman makes a vow to the LORD or a pledge under oath while she is still living at her father's home, ⁴and her father hears of the vow or pledge and does not object to it, then all her vows and pledges will stand. ⁵But if her father refuses to let her fulfill the vow or pledge on the day he hears of it, then all her vows and pledges will become invalid. The LORD will forgive her because her father would not let her fulfill them.

⁶"Now suppose a young woman makes a vow or binds herself with an impulsive pledge and later marries. ⁷If her husband learns of her vow or pledge and does not object on the day he hears of it, her vows and pledges will stand. ⁸But if her husband refuses to accept her vow or impulsive pledge on the day he hears of it, he nullifies her commitments, and the LORD will forgive her. ⁹If, however, a woman is a widow or is divorced, she must fulfill all her vows and pledges.

¹⁰"But suppose a woman is married and living in her husband's home when she makes a vow or binds herself with a pledge. ¹¹If her husband hears of it and does not object to it, her vow or pledge will stand. ¹²But if her husband refuses to accept it on the day he hears of it, her vow or pledge will be nullified, and the LORD will forgive her. ¹³So her husband may either confirm or nullify any vows or pledges she makes to deny herself. ¹⁴But if he does not object on the day he hears of it, then he is agreeing to all her vows and pledges. ¹⁵If he waits more than a day and then tries to nullify a vow or pledge, he will be punished for her guilt."

¹⁶These are the regulations the LORD gave Moses concerning relationships between a man and his wife, and between a father and a young daughter who still lives at home.

³¹:¹THEN the LORD said to Moses, ²"On behalf of the people of Israel, take revenge on the Midianites for leading them into idolatry. After that, you will die and join your ancestors."

³So Moses said to the people, "Choose some men, and arm them to fight the LORD's war of revenge against Midian. ⁴From each tribe of Israel, send 1,000 men into battle." ⁵So they chose 1,000 men from each tribe of Israel, a total of 12,000 men armed for battle. ⁶Then Moses sent them out, 1,000 men from each tribe, and Phinehas son of Eleazar the priest led them into battle. They carried along the holy objects of the sanctuary and the trumpets for sounding the charge. ⁷They attacked Midian as the LORD had commanded Moses, and they killed all the men. ⁸All five of the Midianite kings—Evi, Rekem, Zur, Hur, and Reba—died in the battle. They also killed Balaam son of Beor with the sword.

⁹Then the Israelite army captured the Midianite women and children and seized their cattle and flocks and all their wealth as plunder. ¹⁰They burned all the towns and villages where the Midianites had lived. ¹¹After they had gathered the plunder and captives, both people and animals, ¹²they brought them all to Moses and Eleazar the priest, and to the whole community of Israel, which was camped on the plains of Moab beside the Jordan River,

across from Jericho. ¹³Moses, Eleazar the priest, and all the leaders of the community went to meet them outside the camp. ¹⁴But Moses was furious with all the generals and captains* who had returned from the battle.

¹⁵"Why have you let all the women live?" he demanded. ¹⁶"These are the very ones who followed Balaam's advice and caused the people of Israel to rebel against the LORD at Mount Peor. They are the ones who caused the plague to strike the LORD's people. ¹⁷So kill all the boys and all the women who have had intercourse with a man. ¹⁸Only the young girls who are virgins may live; you may keep them for yourselves. ¹⁹And all of you who have killed anyone or touched a dead body must stay outside the camp for seven days. You must purify yourselves and your captives on the third and seventh days. ²⁰Purify all your clothing, too, and everything made of leather, goat hair, or wood."

²¹Then Eleazar the priest said to the men who were in the battle, "The LORD has given Moses this legal requirement: ²²Anything made of gold, silver, bronze, iron, tin, or lead—²³that is, all metals that do not burn—must be passed through fire in order to be made ceremonially pure. These metal objects must then be further purified with the water of purification. But everything that burns must be purified by the water alone. ²⁴On the seventh day you must wash your clothes and be purified. Then you may return to the camp."

²⁵And the LORD said to Moses, ²⁶"You and Eleazar the priest and the family leaders of each tribe are to make a list of all the plunder taken in the battle, including the people and animals. ²⁷Then divide the plunder into two parts, and give half to the men who fought the battle and half to the rest of the people. ²⁸From the army's portion, first give the LORD his share of the plunder—one of every 500 of the prisoners and of the cattle, donkeys, sheep, and goats. ²⁹Give this share of the army's half to Eleazar

the priest as an offering to the LORD. ³⁰From the half that belongs to the people of Israel, take one of every fifty of the prisoners and of the cattle, donkeys, sheep, goats, and other animals. Give this share to the Levites, who are in charge of maintaining the LORD's Tabernacle." ³¹So Moses and Eleazar the priest did as the LORD commanded Moses.

³²The plunder remaining from everything the fighting men had taken totaled 675,000 sheep and goats, ³³72,000 cattle, ³⁴61,000 donkeys, ³⁵and 32,000 virgin girls.

³⁶Half of the plunder was given to the fighting men. It totaled 337,500 sheep and goats, ³⁷of which 675 were the LORD's share; ³⁸36,000 cattle, of which 72 were the LORD's share; ³⁹30,500 donkeys, of which 61 were the LORD's share; ⁴⁰and 16,000 virgin girls, of whom 32 were the LORD's share. ⁴¹Moses gave all the LORD's share to Eleazar the priest, just as the LORD had directed him.

⁴²Half of the plunder belonged to the people of Israel, and Moses separated it from the half belonging to the fighting men. ⁴³It totaled 337,500 sheep and goats, ⁴⁴36,000 cattle, ⁴⁵30,500 donkeys, ⁴⁶and 16,000 virgin girls. ⁴⁷From the half-share given to the people, Moses took one of every fifty prisoners and animals and gave them to the Levites, who maintained the LORD's Tabernacle. All this was done as the LORD had commanded Moses.

⁴⁸Then all the generals and captains came to Moses ⁴⁹and said, "We, your servants, have accounted for all the men who went out to battle under our command; not one of us is missing! ⁵⁰So we are presenting the items of gold we captured as an offering to the LORD from our share of the plunder— armbands, bracelets, rings, earrings, and necklaces. This will purify our lives before the LORD and make us right with him.*"

⁵¹So Moses and Eleazar the priest received the gold from all the military commanders—all kinds of jewelry and crafted objects. ⁵²In all, the gold that the

generals and captains presented as a gift to the LORD weighed about 420 pounds.* 53All the fighting men had taken some of the plunder for themselves. 54So Moses and Eleazar the priest accepted the gifts from the generals and captains and brought the gold to the Tabernacle* as a reminder to the LORD that the people of Israel belong to him.

30:1 Verses 30:1-16 are numbered 30:2-17 in Hebrew text.    31:14 Hebrew *the commanders of thousands, and the commanders of hundreds;* also in 31:48, 52, 54.    31:50 Or *will make atonement for our lives before the LORD.*    31:52 Hebrew *16,750 shekels* [191 kilograms].    31:54 Hebrew *the Tent of Meeting.*

## LUKE 4:1-30

Then Jesus, full of the Holy Spirit, returned from the Jordan River. He was led by the Spirit in the wilderness,* 2where he was tempted by the devil for forty days. Jesus ate nothing all that time and became very hungry.

3Then the devil said to him, "If you are the Son of God, change this stone into a loaf of bread."

4But Jesus told him, "No! The Scriptures say, 'People do not live by bread alone.'*"

5Then the devil took him up and revealed to him all the kingdoms of the world in a moment of time. 6"I will give you the glory of these kingdoms and authority over them," the devil said, "because they are mine to give to anyone I please. 7I will give it all to you if you will worship me."

8Jesus replied, "The Scriptures say,

'You must worship the LORD
     your God
     and serve only him.'*"

9Then the devil took him to Jerusalem, to the highest point of the Temple, and said, "If you are the Son of God, jump off! 10For the Scriptures say,

'He will order his angels to protect
     and guard you.
11 And they will hold you up with
     their hands
     so you won't even hurt your foot
          on a stone.'*"

12Jesus responded, "The Scriptures also say, 'You must not test the LORD your God.'*"

13When the devil had finished tempting Jesus, he left him until the next opportunity came.

14Then Jesus returned to Galilee, filled with the Holy Spirit's power. Reports about him spread quickly through the whole region. 15He taught regularly in their synagogues and was praised by everyone.

16When he came to the village of Nazareth, his boyhood home, he went as usual to the synagogue on the Sabbath and stood up to read the Scriptures. 17The scroll of Isaiah the prophet was handed to him. He unrolled the scroll and found the place where this was written:

18 **"The Spirit of the LORD
     is upon me,
     for he has anointed me to bring
          Good News to the poor.
He has sent me to proclaim that
     captives will be released,
     that the blind will see,
that the oppressed will be set free,
19     and that the time of the LORD's
          favor has come.*"**

20He rolled up the scroll, handed it back to the attendant, and sat down. All eyes in the synagogue looked at him intently. 21Then he began to speak to them. "The Scripture you've just heard has been fulfilled this very day!"

22Everyone spoke well of him and was amazed by the gracious words that came from his lips. "How can this be?" they asked. "Isn't this Joseph's son?"

23Then he said, "You will undoubtedly quote me this proverb: 'Physician, heal yourself'—meaning, 'Do miracles here in your hometown like those you did in Capernaum.' 24But I tell you the truth, no prophet is accepted in his own hometown.

25"Certainly there were many needy widows in Israel in Elijah's time, when the heavens were closed for three and a half years, and a severe famine devastated the land. 26Yet Elijah was not sent to any of them. He was sent instead to a foreigner—a widow of Zarephath in the land of Sidon. 27And there were many lepers in Israel in the time of the prophet Elisha, but the only one healed was Naaman, a Syrian."

28When they heard this, the people in the synagogue were furious. 29Jumping up, they mobbed him and forced him to the edge of the hill on which the town was built. They intended to push him over the cliff, 30but he passed right through the crowd and went on his way.

4:1 Some manuscripts read *into the wilderness.* 4:4 Deut 8:3. 4:8 Deut 6:13. 4:10-11 Ps 91:11-12. 4:12 Deut 6:16. 4:18-19 Or *and to proclaim the acceptable year of the LORD.* Isa 61:1-2 (Greek version); 58:6.

## PSALM 63:1-11

*A psalm of David, regarding a time when David was in the wilderness of Judah.*

1 **O** God, you are my God;
   I earnestly search for you.
My soul thirsts for you;
   my whole body longs for you
in this parched and weary land
   where there is no water.
2 I have seen you in your sanctuary
   and gazed upon your power
      and glory.
3 Your unfailing love is better
   than life itself;
   how I praise you!
4 I will praise you as long as I live,
   lifting up my hands to you
      in prayer.
5 You satisfy me more than the
      richest feast.
   I will praise you with songs of joy.

6 I lie awake thinking of you,
   meditating on you through
      the night.
7 Because you are my helper,
   I sing for joy in the shadow
      of your wings.
8 I cling to you;
   your strong right hand holds
      me securely.

9 But those plotting to destroy me will
   come to ruin.

They will go down into the
   depths of the earth.
10 They will die by the sword
   and become the food of jackals.
11 But the king will rejoice in God.
   All who trust in him will
      praise him,
   while liars will be silenced.

## PROVERBS 11:20-21

**T**he LORD detests people with crooked hearts, but he delights in those with integrity. □ Evil people will surely be punished, but the children of the godly will go free.

# MARCH 21

## NUMBERS 32:1–33:39

**T**he tribes of Reuben and Gad owned vast numbers of livestock. So when they saw that the lands of Jazer and Gilead were ideally suited for their flocks and herds, 2they came to Moses, Eleazar the priest, and the other leaders of the community. They said, 3"Notice the towns of Ataroth, Dibon, Jazer, Nimrah, Heshbon, Elealeh, Sibmah,* Nebo, and Beon. 4The LORD has conquered this whole area for the community of Israel, and it is ideally suited for all our livestock. 5If we have found favor with you, please let us have this land as our property instead of giving us land across the Jordan River."

6"Do you intend to stay here while your brothers go across and do all the fighting?" Moses asked the men of Gad and Reuben. 7"Why do you want to discourage the rest of the people of Israel from going across to the land the LORD has given them? 8Your ancestors did the same thing when I sent them from Kadesh-barnea to explore the land. 9After they went up to the valley of Eshcol and explored the land, they discouraged the people of Israel from entering the land the LORD was giving them. ¹⁰Then the LORD was very angry with them, and he vowed, ¹¹'Of all those I rescued from Egypt, no one who is twenty years old or older will ever see the land I swore to give to Abraham, Isaac, and Jacob, for they have not obeyed me wholeheartedly. ¹²The only exceptions are Caleb son of Jephunneh the Kenizzite and Joshua son of Nun, for they have wholeheartedly followed the LORD.'

¹³"The LORD was angry with Israel and made them wander in the wilderness for forty years until the entire generation that sinned in the LORD's sight had died. ¹⁴But here you are, a brood of sinners, doing exactly the same thing! You are making the LORD even angrier with Israel. ¹⁵If you turn away from him like this and he abandons them again in the wilderness, you will be responsible for destroying this entire nation!"

¹⁶But they approached Moses and said, "We simply want to build pens for our livestock and fortified towns for our wives and children. ¹⁷Then we will arm ourselves and lead our fellow Israelites into battle until we have brought them safely to their land. Meanwhile, our families will stay in the fortified towns we build here, so they will be safe from any attacks by the local people. ¹⁸We will not return to our homes until all the people of Israel have received their portions of land. ¹⁹But we do not claim any of the land on the other side of the Jordan. We would rather live here on the east side and accept this as our grant of land."

²⁰Then Moses said, "If you keep your word and arm yourselves for the LORD's battles, ²¹and if your troops cross the Jordan and keep fighting until the LORD has driven out his enemies, ²²then you may return when the LORD has conquered the land. You will have fulfilled your duty to the LORD and to the rest of the people of Israel. And the land on the east side of the Jordan will be your property from the LORD. ²³But if you fail to keep your word, then you will have

sinned against the LORD, and you may be sure that your sin will find you out. ²⁴Go ahead and build towns for your families and pens for your flocks, but do everything you have promised."

²⁵Then the men of Gad and Reuben replied, "We, your servants, will follow your instructions exactly. ²⁶Our children, wives, flocks, and cattle will stay here in the towns of Gilead. ²⁷But all who are able to bear arms will cross over to fight for the LORD, just as you have said."

²⁸So Moses gave orders to Eleazar the priest, Joshua son of Nun, and the leaders of the clans of Israel. ²⁹He said, "The men of Gad and Reuben who are armed for battle must cross the Jordan with you to fight for the LORD. If they do, give them the land of Gilead as their property when the land is conquered. ³⁰But if they refuse to arm themselves and cross over with you, then they must accept land with the rest of you in the land of Canaan."

³¹The tribes of Gad and Reuben said again, "We are your servants, and we will do as the LORD has commanded! ³²We will cross the Jordan into Canaan fully armed to fight for the LORD, but our property will be here on this side of the Jordan."

³³So Moses assigned land to the tribes of Gad, Reuben, and half the tribe of Manasseh son of Joseph. He gave them the territory of King Sihon of the Amorites and the land of King Og of Bashan—the whole land with its cities and surrounding lands.

³⁴The descendants of Gad built the towns of Dibon, Ataroth, Aroer, ³⁵Atroth-shophan, Jazer, Jogbehah, ³⁶Beth-nimrah, and Beth-haran. These were all fortified towns with pens for their flocks.

³⁷The descendants of Reuben built the towns of Heshbon, Elealeh, Kiriathaim, ³⁸Nebo, Baal-meon, and Sibmah. They changed the names of some of the towns they conquered and rebuilt.

³⁹Then the descendants of Makir of the tribe of Manasseh went to Gilead and

conquered it, and they drove out the Amorites living there. 40So Moses gave Gilead to the Makirites, descendants of Manasseh, and they settled there. 41The people of Jair, another clan of the tribe of Manasseh, captured many of the towns in Gilead and changed the name of that region to the Towns of Jair.* 42Meanwhile, a man named Nobah captured the town of Kenath and its surrounding villages, and he renamed that area Nobah after himself.

33:1THIS is the route the Israelites followed as they marched out of Egypt under the leadership of Moses and Aaron. 2At the LORD's direction, Moses kept a written record of their progress. These are the stages of their march, identified by the different places where they stopped along the way.

3 They set out from the city of Rameses in early spring—on the fifteenth day of the first month*—on the morning after the first Passover celebration. The people of Israel left defiantly, in full view of all the Egyptians. 4Meanwhile, the Egyptians were burying all their firstborn sons, whom the LORD had killed the night before. The LORD had defeated the gods of Egypt that night with great acts of judgment!

5After leaving Rameses, the Israelites set up camp at Succoth.

6Then they left Succoth and camped at Etham on the edge of the wilderness.

7 They left Etham and turned back toward Pi-hahiroth, opposite Baal-zephon, and camped near Migdol.

8They left Pi-hahiroth and crossed the Red Sea* into the wilderness beyond. Then they traveled for three days into the Etham wilderness and camped at Marah.

9They left Marah and camped at Elim, where there were twelve springs of water and seventy palm trees.

10They left Elim and camped beside the Red Sea.*

11They left the Red Sea and camped in the wilderness of Sin.*

12 They left the wilderness of Sin and camped at Dophkah.

13 They left Dophkah and camped at Alush.

14They left Alush and camped at Rephidim, where there was no water for the people to drink.

15 They left Rephidim and camped in the wilderness of Sinai.

16They left the wilderness of Sinai and camped at Kibroth-hattaavah.

17 They left Kibroth-hattaavah and camped at Hazeroth.

18They left Hazeroth and camped at Rithmah.

19 They left Rithmah and camped at Rimmon-perez.

20They left Rimmon-perez and camped at Libnah.

21They left Libnah and camped at Rissah.

22 They left Rissah and camped at Kehelathah.

23 They left Kehelathah and camped at Mount Shepher.

24They left Mount Shepher and camped at Haradah.

25 They left Haradah and camped at Makheloth.

26They left Makheloth and camped at Tahath.

27 They left Tahath and camped at Terah.

28They left Terah and camped at Mithcah.

29 They left Mithcah and camped at Hashmonah.

30They left Hashmonah and camped at Moseroth.

31They left Moseroth and camped at Bene-jaakan.

32 They left Bene-jaakan and camped at Hor-haggidgad.

33 They left Hor-haggidgad and camped at Jotbathah.

34They left Jotbathah and camped at Abronah.

35 They left Abronah and camped at Ezion-geber.

³⁶They left Ezion-geber and camped at Kadesh in the wilderness of Zin. ³⁷They left Kadesh and camped at Mount Hor, at the border of Edom. ³⁸While they were at the foot of Mount Hor, Aaron the priest was directed by the LORD to go up the mountain, and there he died. This happened in midsummer, on the first day of the fifth month* of the fortieth year after Israel's departure from Egypt. ³⁹Aaron was 123 years old when he died there on Mount Hor.

32:3 As in Samaritan Pentateuch and Greek version (see also 32:38); Hebrew reads *Sebam*. 32:41 Hebrew *Havvoth-jair*. 33:3 This day in the ancient Hebrew lunar calendar occurred in late March, April, or early May. 33:8 Hebrew *the sea*. 33:10 Hebrew *sea of reeds;* also in 33:11. 33:11 The geographical name *Sin* is related to *Sinai* and should not be confused with the English word *sin*. 33:38 This day in the ancient Hebrew lunar calendar occurred in July or August.

## LUKE 4:31–5:11

Then Jesus went to Capernaum, a town in Galilee, and taught there in the synagogue every Sabbath day. ³²There, too, the people were amazed at his teaching, for he spoke with authority.

³³Once when he was in the synagogue, a man possessed by a demon—an evil* spirit—began shouting at Jesus, ³⁴"Go away! Why are you interfering with us, Jesus of Nazareth? Have you come to destroy us? I know who you are—the Holy One sent from God!"

³⁵Jesus cut him short. "Be quiet! Come out of the man," he ordered. At that, the demon threw the man to the floor as the crowd watched; then it came out of him without hurting him further.

³⁶Amazed, the people exclaimed, "What authority and power this man's words possess! Even evil spirits obey him, and they flee at his command!" ³⁷The news about Jesus spread through every village in the entire region.

³⁸After leaving the synagogue that day, Jesus went to Simon's home, where he found Simon's mother-in-law very sick with a high fever. "Please heal her," everyone begged. ³⁹Standing at her bedside, he rebuked the fever, and it left her. And she got up at once and prepared a meal for them.

⁴⁰As the sun went down that evening, people throughout the village brought sick family members to Jesus. No matter what their diseases were, the touch of his hand healed every one. ⁴¹Many were possessed by demons; and the demons came out at his command, shouting, "You are the Son of God!" But because they knew he was the Messiah, he rebuked them and refused to let them speak.

⁴²Early the next morning Jesus went out to an isolated place. The crowds searched everywhere for him, and when they finally found him, they begged him not to leave them. ⁴³But he replied, "I must preach the Good News of the Kingdom of God in other towns, too, because that is why I was sent." ⁴⁴So he continued to travel around, preaching in synagogues throughout Judea.*

⁵:¹ONE day as Jesus was preaching on the shore of the Sea of Galilee,* great crowds pressed in on him to listen to the word of God. ²He noticed two empty boats at the water's edge, for the fishermen had left them and were washing their nets. ³Stepping into one of the boats, Jesus asked Simon,* its owner, to push it out into the water. So he sat in the boat and taught the crowds from there.

⁴When he had finished speaking, he said to Simon, "Now go out where it is deeper, and let down your nets to catch some fish."

⁵"Master," Simon replied, "we worked hard all last night and didn't catch a thing. But if you say so, I'll let the nets down again." ⁶And this time their nets were so full of fish they began to tear! ⁷A shout for help brought their partners in the other boat, and soon both boats were filled with fish and on the verge of sinking.

⁸When Simon Peter realized what had happened, he fell to his knees before Jesus and said, "Oh, Lord, please leave me—I'm too much of a sinner to be around you." ⁹For he was awestruck

by the number of fish they had caught, as were the others with him. ¹⁰His partners, James and John, the sons of Zebedee, were also amazed.

Jesus replied to Simon, "Don't be afraid! From now on you'll be fishing for people!" ¹¹And as soon as they landed, they left everything and followed Jesus.

4:33 Greek *unclean*; also in 4:36.   4:44 Some manuscripts read *Galilee*.   5:1 Greek *Lake Gennesaret*, another name for the Sea of Galilee.   5:3 *Simon* is called "Peter" in 6:14 and thereafter.

## PSALM 64:1-10
*For the choir director: A psalm of David.*

¹ **O** God, listen to my complaint.
    Protect my life from my enemies'
    threats.
² Hide me from the plots of this
    evil mob,
    from this gang of wrongdoers.
³ They sharpen their tongues like
    swords
    and aim their bitter words
    like arrows.
⁴ They shoot from ambush at
    the innocent,
    attacking suddenly and fearlessly.
⁵ They encourage each other to do evil
    and plan how to set their traps in
    secret.
    "Who will ever notice?" they ask.
⁶ As they plot their crimes, they say,
    "We have devised the perfect
    plan!"
    Yes, the human heart and mind
    are cunning.

⁷ But God himself will shoot them
    with his arrows,
    suddenly striking them down.
⁸ Their own tongues will ruin them,
    and all who see them will shake
    their heads in scorn.
⁹ **Then everyone will be afraid;**
    **they will proclaim the mighty**
    **acts of God**
    **and realize all the amazing**
    **things he does.**
¹⁰ **The godly will rejoice in the Lord**
    **and find shelter in him.**
    **And those who do what is right**
    **will praise him.**

## PROVERBS 11:22
**A** beautiful woman who lacks discretion is like a gold ring in a pig's snout.

# MARCH 22

## NUMBERS 33:40–35:34
**A**t that time the Canaanite king of Arad, who lived in the Negev in the land of Canaan, heard that the people of Israel were approaching his land.

⁴¹Meanwhile, the Israelites left Mount Hor and camped at Zalmonah.
⁴²Then they left Zalmonah and camped at Punon.
⁴³They left Punon and camped at Oboth.
⁴⁴They left Oboth and camped at Iyeabarim on the border of Moab.
⁴⁵They left Iye-abarim* and camped at Dibon-gad.
⁴⁶They left Dibon-gad and camped at Almon-diblathaim.
⁴⁷They left Almon-diblathaim and camped in the mountains east of the river,* near Mount Nebo.
⁴⁸They left the mountains east of the river and camped on the plains of Moab beside the Jordan River, across from Jericho. ⁴⁹Along the Jordan River they camped from Beth-jeshimoth as far as the meadows of Acacia* on the plains of Moab.

⁵⁰While they were camped near the Jordan River on the plains of Moab opposite Jericho, the Lord said to Moses, ⁵¹"Give the following instructions to the people of Israel: When you cross the Jordan River into the land of Canaan, ⁵²you must drive out all the people living there. You must destroy all their carved and molten images and demolish all their pagan shrines. ⁵³Take

possession of the land and settle in it, because I have given it to you to occupy. ⁵⁴You must distribute the land among the clans by sacred lot and in proportion to their size. A larger portion of land will be allotted to each of the larger clans, and a smaller portion will be allotted to each of the smaller clans. The decision of the sacred lot is final. In this way, the portions of land will be divided among your ancestral tribes. ⁵⁵But if you fail to drive out the people who live in the land, those who remain will be like splinters in your eyes and thorns in your sides. They will harass you in the land where you live. ⁵⁶And I will do to you what I had planned to do to them."

³⁴:¹THEN the LORD said to Moses, ²"Give these instructions to the Israelites: When you come into the land of Canaan, which I am giving you as your special possession, these will be the boundaries. ³The southern portion of your country will extend from the wilderness of Zin, along the edge of Edom. The southern boundary will begin on the east at the Dead Sea.* ⁴It will then run south past Scorpion Pass* in the direction of Zin. Its southernmost point will be Kadesh-barnea, from which it will go to Hazar-addar, and on to Azmon. ⁵From Azmon the boundary will turn toward the Brook of Egypt and end at the Mediterranean Sea.*

⁶"Your western boundary will be the coastline of the Mediterranean Sea.

⁷"Your northern boundary will begin at the Mediterranean Sea and run east to Mount Hor, ⁸then to Lebo-hamath, and on through Zedad ⁹and Ziphron to Hazar-enan. This will be your northern boundary.

¹⁰"The eastern boundary will start at Hazar-enan and run south to Shepham, ¹¹then down to Riblah on the east side of Ain. From there the boundary will run down along the eastern edge of the Sea of Galilee,* ¹²and then along the Jordan River to the Dead Sea. These are the boundaries of your land."

¹³Then Moses told the Israelites, "This territory is the homeland you are to divide among yourselves by sacred lot. The LORD has commanded that the land be divided among the nine and a half remaining tribes. ¹⁴The families of the tribes of Reuben, Gad, and half the tribe of Manasseh have already received their grants of land ¹⁵on the east side of the Jordan River, across from Jericho toward the sunrise."

¹⁶And the LORD said to Moses, ¹⁷"Eleazar the priest and Joshua son of Nun are the men designated to divide the grants of land among the people. ¹⁸Enlist one leader from each tribe to help them with the task. ¹⁹These are the tribes and the names of the leaders:

| Tribe | Leader |
|---|---|
| Judah. . . . . . . . . . | Caleb son of Jephunneh |
| ²⁰ Simeon. . . . . . . | Shemuel son of Ammihud |
| ²¹ Benjamin. . . . . . . . . . | Elidad son of Kislon |
| ²² Dan . . . . . . . . . . . . . . . . . | Bukki son of Jogli |
| ²³ Manasseh son of Joseph . . . . . . . . | Hanniel son of Ephod |
| ²⁴ Ephraim son of Joseph . . . . . . . . . | Kemuel son of Shiphtan |
| ²⁵ Zebulun. . . . . . . | Elizaphan son of Parnach |
| ²⁶ Issachar . . . . . . . . . . . | Paltiel son of Azzan |
| ²⁷ Asher . . . . . . . . . . | Ahihud son of Shelomi |
| ²⁸ Naphtali. . . . . . | Pedahel son of Ammihud |

²⁹These are the men the LORD has appointed to divide the grants of land in Canaan among the Israelites."

³⁵:¹WHILE Israel was camped beside the Jordan on the plains of Moab across from Jericho, the LORD said to Moses, ²"Command the people of Israel to give to the Levites from their property certain towns to live in, along with the surrounding pasturelands. ³These towns will be for the Levites to live in, and the surrounding lands will provide pasture for their cattle, flocks, and other livestock. ⁴The pastureland assigned to the Levites around these towns will extend 1,500 feet* from the town walls in every direction. ⁵Measure off 3,000 feet* outside the town walls in every direction—east, south, west, north—with the town at the center. This area will

serve as the larger pastureland for the towns.

6"Six of the towns you give the Levites will be cities of refuge, where a person who has accidentally killed someone can flee for safety. In addition, give them forty-two other towns. 7In all, forty-eight towns with the surrounding pastureland will be given to the Levites. 8These towns will come from the property of the people of Israel. The larger tribes will give more towns to the Levites, while the smaller tribes will give fewer. Each tribe will give property in proportion to the size of its land."

9The LORD said to Moses, 10"Give the following instructions to the people of Israel.

"When you cross the Jordan into the land of Canaan, 11designate cities of refuge to which people can flee if they have killed someone accidentally. 12These cities will be places of protection from a dead person's relatives who want to avenge the death. The slayer must not be put to death before being tried by the community. 13Designate six cities of refuge for yourselves, 14three on the east side of the Jordan River and three on the west in the land of Canaan. 15These cities are for the protection of Israelites, foreigners living among you, and traveling merchants. Anyone who accidentally kills someone may flee there for safety.

16"But if someone strikes and kills another person with a piece of iron, it is murder, and the murderer must be executed. 17Or if someone with a stone in his hand strikes and kills another person, it is murder, and the murderer must be put to death. 18Or if someone strikes and kills another person with a wooden object, it is murder, and the murderer must be put to death. 19The victim's nearest relative is responsible for putting the murderer to death. When they meet, the avenger must put the murderer to death. 20So if someone hates another person and pushes him or throws a dangerous object at him and he dies, it is murder. 21Or if someone hates another person and hits him with a fist and he dies, it is murder. In such cases, the avenger must put the murderer to death when they meet.

22"But suppose someone pushes another person without having shown previous hostility, or throws something that unintentionally hits another person, 23or accidentally drops a huge stone on someone, though they were not enemies, and the person dies. 24If this should happen, the community must follow these regulations in making a judgment between the slayer and the avenger, the victim's nearest relative: 25The community must protect the slayer from the avenger and must escort the slayer back to live in the city of refuge to which he fled. There he must remain until the death of the high priest, who was anointed with the sacred oil.

26"But if the slayer ever leaves the limits of the city of refuge, 27and the avenger finds him outside the city and kills him, it will not be considered murder. 28The slayer should have stayed inside the city of refuge until the death of the high priest. But after the death of the high priest, the slayer may return to his own property. 29These are legal requirements for you to observe from generation to generation, wherever you may live.

30"All murderers must be put to death, but only if evidence is presented by more than one witness. No one may be put to death on the testimony of only one witness. 31Also, you must never accept a ransom payment for the life of someone judged guilty of murder and subject to execution; murderers must always be put to death. 32And never accept a ransom payment from someone who has fled to a city of refuge, allowing a slayer to return to his property before the death of the high priest. 33This will ensure that the land where you live will not be polluted, for murder pollutes the land. And no sacrifice except the execution of the murderer can purify the land from murder.* 34You must not defile the land where you live, for I live there myself. I am the LORD, who lives among the people of Israel."

33:45 As in 33:44; Hebrew reads *Iyim,* another name for Iye-abarim.   33:47 Or *the mountains of Abarim;* also in 33:48.   33:49 Hebrew *as far as Abel-shittim.* 34:3 Hebrew *Salt Sea;* also in 34:12.   34:4 Or *the ascent of Akrabbim.*   34:5 Hebrew *the sea;* also in 34:6, 7. 34:11 Hebrew *Sea of Kinnereth.*   35:4 Hebrew *1,000 cubits* [460 meters].   35:5 Hebrew *2,000 cubits* [920 meters].   35:33 Or *can make atonement for murder.*

## LUKE 5:12-28

In one of the villages, Jesus met a man with an advanced case of leprosy. When the man saw Jesus, he bowed with his face to the ground, begging to be healed. "Lord," he said, "if you are willing, you can heal me and make me clean."

13 Jesus reached out and touched him. "I am willing," he said. "Be healed!" And instantly the leprosy disappeared. 14 Then Jesus instructed him not to tell anyone what had happened. He said, "Go to the priest and let him examine you. Take along the offering required in the law of Moses for those who have been healed of leprosy.* This will be a public testimony that you have been cleansed."

15 But despite Jesus' instructions, the report of his power spread even faster, and vast crowds came to hear him preach and to be healed of their diseases. 16 But Jesus often withdrew to the wilderness for prayer.

17 One day while Jesus was teaching, some Pharisees and teachers of religious law were sitting nearby. (It seemed that these men showed up from every village in all Galilee and Judea, as well as from Jerusalem.) And the Lord's healing power was strongly with Jesus.

18 Some men came carrying a paralyzed man on a sleeping mat. They tried to take him inside to Jesus, 19 but they couldn't reach him because of the crowd. So they went up to the roof and took off some tiles. Then they lowered the sick man on his mat down into the crowd, right in front of Jesus. 20 Seeing their faith, Jesus said to the man, "Young man, your sins are forgiven."

21 But the Pharisees and teachers of religious law said to themselves, "Who does he think he is? That's blasphemy! Only God can forgive sins!"

22 Jesus knew what they were thinking, so he asked them, "Why do you question this in your hearts? 23 Is it easier to say 'Your sins are forgiven,' or 'Stand up and walk'? 24 So I will prove to you that the Son of Man* has the authority on earth to forgive sins." Then Jesus turned to the paralyzed man and said, "Stand up, pick up your mat, and go home!"

25 And immediately, as everyone watched, the man jumped up, picked up his mat, and went home praising God. 26 Everyone was gripped with great wonder and awe, and they praised God, exclaiming, "We have seen amazing things today!"

27 **Later, as Jesus left the town, he saw a tax collector named Levi sitting at his tax collector's booth. "Follow me and be my disciple," Jesus said to him. 28 So Levi got up, left everything, and followed him.**

5:14 See Lev 14:2-32.   5:24 "Son of Man" is a title Jesus used for himself.

## PSALM 65:1-13

*For the choir director: A song. A psalm of David.*

1 **W**hat mighty praise, O God,
    belongs to you in Zion.
  We will fulfill our vows to you,
2    for you answer our prayers.
  All of us must come to you.
3 Though we are overwhelmed
    by our sins,
  you forgive them all.
4 What joy for those you choose
    to bring near,
    those who live in your holy
      courts.
  What festivities await us
    inside your holy Temple.

5 You faithfully answer our prayers
    with awesome deeds,
    O God our savior.
  You are the hope of everyone
    on earth,
    even those who sail on
      distant seas.

⁶ You formed the mountains by
    your power
  and armed yourself with mighty
    strength.
⁷ You quieted the raging oceans
    with their pounding waves
  and silenced the shouting
    of the nations.
⁸ Those who live at the ends of the
    earth
    stand in awe of your wonders.
  From where the sun rises to where
    it sets,
    you inspire shouts of joy.

⁹ You take care of the earth and
    water it,
    making it rich and fertile.
  The river of God has plenty of water;
    it provides a bountiful harvest
    of grain,
    for you have ordered it so.
¹⁰ You drench the plowed ground
    with rain,
    melting the clods and leveling
    the ridges.
  You soften the earth with showers
    and bless its abundant crops.
¹¹ You crown the year with a bountiful
    harvest;
    even the hard pathways overflow
    with abundance.
¹² The grasslands of the wilderness
    become a lush pasture,
    and the hillsides blossom with joy.
¹³ The meadows are clothed with
    flocks of sheep,
    and the valleys are carpeted
    with grain.
    They all shout and sing for joy!

PROVERBS 11:23

The godly can look forward to a reward,
while the wicked can expect only judgment.

# MARCH 23

NUMBERS 36:1—
DEUTERONOMY 1:46

Then the heads of the clans of Gilead—descendants of Makir, son of Manasseh, son of Joseph—came to Moses and the family leaders of Israel with a petition. ²They said, "Sir, the LORD instructed you to divide the land by sacred lot among the people of Israel. You were told by the LORD to give the grant of land owned by our brother Zelophehad to his daughters. ³But if they marry men from another tribe, their grants of land will go with them to the tribe into which they marry. In this way, the total area of our tribal land will be reduced. ⁴Then when the Year of Jubilee comes, their portion of land will be added to that of the new tribe, causing it to be lost forever to our ancestral tribe."

⁵So Moses gave the Israelites this command from the LORD: "The claim of the men of the tribe of Joseph is legitimate. ⁶This is what the LORD commands concerning the daughters of Zelophehad: Let them marry anyone they like, as long as it is within their own ancestral tribe. ⁷None of the territorial land may pass from tribe to tribe, for all the land given to each tribe must remain within the tribe to which it was first allotted. ⁸The daughters throughout the tribes of Israel who are in line to inherit property must marry within their tribe, so that all the Israelites will keep their ancestral property. ⁹No grant of land may pass from one tribe to another; each tribe of Israel must keep its allotted portion of land."

¹⁰The daughters of Zelophehad did as the LORD commanded Moses. ¹¹Mahlah, Tirzah, Hoglah, Milcah, and Noah all married cousins on their father's side. ¹²They married into the clans of Manasseh son of Joseph. Thus, their

inheritance of land remained within their ancestral tribe.

13 These are the commands and regulations that the LORD gave to the people of Israel through Moses while they were camped on the plains of Moab beside the Jordan River across from Jericho.

1:1 THESE are the words that Moses spoke to all the people of Israel while they were in the wilderness east of the Jordan River. They were camped in the Jordan Valley* near Suph, between Paran on one side and Tophel, Laban, Hazeroth, and Di-zahab on the other.

2 Normally it takes only eleven days to travel from Mount Sinai* to Kadesh-barnea, going by way of Mount Seir. 3 But forty years after the Israelites left Egypt, on the first day of the eleventh month,* Moses addressed the people of Israel, telling them everything the LORD had commanded him to say. 4 This took place after he had defeated King Sihon of the Amorites, who had ruled in Heshbon, and King Og of Bashan, who had ruled in Ashtaroth and Edrei.

5 While the Israelites were in the land of Moab east of the Jordan River, Moses carefully explained the LORD's instructions as follows.

6 "When we were at Mount Sinai, the LORD our God said to us, 'You have stayed at this mountain long enough. 7 It is time to break camp and move on. Go to the hill country of the Amorites and to all the neighboring regions—the Jordan Valley, the hill country, the western foothills,* the Negev, and the coastal plain. Go to the land of the Canaanites and to Lebanon, and all the way to the great Euphrates River. 8 Look, I am giving all this land to you! Go in and occupy it, for it is the land the LORD swore to give to your ancestors Abraham, Isaac, and Jacob, and to all their descendants.'"

9 Moses continued, "At that time I told you, 'You are too great a burden for me to carry all by myself. 10 The LORD your God has increased your population, making you as numerous as the stars! 11 And may the LORD, the God of your ancestors, multiply you a thousand times more and bless you as he promised! 12 But you are such a heavy load to carry! How can I deal with all your problems and bickering? 13 Choose some well-respected men from each tribe who are known for their wisdom and understanding, and I will appoint them as your leaders.'

14 "Then you responded, 'Your plan is a good one.' 15 So I took the wise and respected men you had selected from your tribes and appointed them to serve as judges and officials over you. Some were responsible for a thousand people, some for a hundred, some for fifty, and some for ten.

16 "At that time I instructed the judges, 'You must hear the cases of your fellow Israelites and the foreigners living among you. Be perfectly fair in your decisions 17 and impartial in your judgments. Hear the cases of those who are poor as well as those who are rich. Don't be afraid of anyone's anger, for the decision you make is God's decision. Bring me any cases that are too difficult for you, and I will handle them.'

18 "At that time I gave you instructions about everything you were to do.

19 "Then, just as the LORD our God commanded us, we left Mount Sinai and traveled through the great and terrifying wilderness, as you yourselves remember, and headed toward the hill country of the Amorites. When we arrived at Kadesh-barnea, 20 I said to you, 'You have now reached the hill country of the Amorites that the LORD our God is giving us. 21 Look! He has placed the land in front of you. Go and occupy it as the LORD, the God of your ancestors, has promised you. Don't be afraid! Don't be discouraged!'

22 "But you all came to me and said, 'First, let's send out scouts to explore the land for us. They will advise us on the best route to take and which towns we should enter.'

23 "This seemed like a good idea to me, so I chose twelve scouts, one from each of your tribes. 24 They headed for

the hill country and came to the valley of Eshcol and explored it. 25They picked some of its fruit and brought it back to us. And they reported, 'The land the LORD our God has given us is indeed a good land.'

26"But you rebelled against the command of the LORD your God and refused to go in. 27You complained in your tents and said, 'The LORD must hate us. That's why he has brought us here from Egypt—to hand us over to the Amorites to be slaughtered. 28Where can we go? Our brothers have demoralized us with their report. They tell us, "The people of the land are taller and more powerful than we are, and their towns are large, with walls rising high into the sky! We even saw giants there—the descendants of Anak!"'

29"But I said to you, 'Don't be shocked or afraid of them! 30The LORD your God is going ahead of you. He will fight for you, just as you saw him do in Egypt. 31And you saw how the LORD your God cared for you all along the way as you traveled through the wilderness, just as a father cares for his child. Now he has brought you to this place.'

32"But even after all he did, you refused to trust the LORD your God, 33who goes before you looking for the best places to camp, guiding you with a pillar of fire by night and a pillar of cloud by day.

34"When the LORD heard your complaining, he became very angry. So he solemnly swore, 35'Not one of you from this wicked generation will live to see the good land I swore to give your ancestors, 36except Caleb son of Jephunneh. He will see this land because he has followed the LORD completely. I will give to him and his descendants some of the very land he explored during his scouting mission.'

37"And the LORD was also angry with me because of you. He said to me, 'Moses, not even you will enter the Promised Land! 38Instead, your assistant, Joshua son of Nun, will lead the people into the land. Encourage him, for he will lead Is-

rael as they take possession of it. 39I will give the land to your little ones—your innocent children. You were afraid they would be captured, but they will be the ones who occupy it. 40As for you, turn around now and go on back through the wilderness toward the Red Sea.*'

41"Then you confessed, 'We have sinned against the LORD! We will go into the land and fight for it, as the LORD our God has commanded us.' So your men strapped on their weapons, thinking it would be easy to attack the hill country.

42"But the LORD told me to tell you, 'Do not attack, for I am not with you. If you go ahead on your own, you will be crushed by your enemies.'

43"This is what I told you, but you would not listen. Instead, you again rebelled against the LORD's command and arrogantly went into the hill country to fight. 44But the Amorites who lived there came out against you like a swarm of bees. They chased and battered you all the way from Seir to Hormah. 45Then you returned and wept before the LORD, but he refused to listen. 46So you stayed there at Kadesh for a long time."

1:1 Hebrew *the Arabah;* also in 1:7.   1:2 Hebrew *Horeb,* another name for Sinai; also in 1:6, 19.   1:3 Hebrew *In the fortieth year, on the first day of the eleventh month.* This day in the ancient Hebrew lunar calendar occurred in January or February.   1:7 Hebrew *the Shephelah.* 1:40 Hebrew *sea of reeds.*

## LUKE 5:29–6:11

Later, Levi held a banquet in his home with Jesus as the guest of honor. Many of Levi's fellow tax collectors and other guests also ate with them. 30But the Pharisees and their teachers of religious law complained bitterly to Jesus' disciples, "Why do you eat and drink with such scum?*"

31Jesus answered them, "Healthy people don't need a doctor—sick people do. 32I have come to call not those who think they are righteous, but those who know they are sinners and need to repent."

33One day some people said to Jesus, "John the Baptist's disciples fast and pray regularly, and so do the disciples of the Pharisees. Why are your disciples always eating and drinking?"

34Jesus responded, "Do wedding guests fast while celebrating with the groom? Of course not. 35But someday the groom will be taken away from them, and then they will fast."

36Then Jesus gave them this illustration: "No one tears a piece of cloth from a new garment and uses it to patch an old garment. For then the new garment would be ruined, and the new patch wouldn't even match the old garment.

37"And no one puts new wine into old wineskins. For the new wine would burst the wineskins, spilling the wine and ruining the skins. 38New wine must be stored in new wineskins. 39But no one who drinks the old wine seems to want the new wine. 'The old is just fine,' they say."

6:1ONE Sabbath day as Jesus was walking through some grainfields, his disciples broke off heads of grain, rubbed off the husks in their hands, and ate the grain. 2But some Pharisees said, "Why are you breaking the law by harvesting grain on the Sabbath?"

3Jesus replied, "Haven't you read in the Scriptures what David did when he and his companions were hungry? 4He went into the house of God and broke the law by eating the sacred loaves of bread that only the priests can eat. He also gave some to his companions."

**5And Jesus added, "The Son of Man\* is Lord, even over the Sabbath."**

6On another Sabbath day, a man with a deformed right hand was in the synagogue while Jesus was teaching. 7The teachers of religious law and the Pharisees watched Jesus closely. If he healed the man's hand, they planned to accuse him of working on the Sabbath.

8But Jesus knew their thoughts. He said to the man with the deformed hand, "Come and stand in front of everyone." So the man came forward. 9Then Jesus said to his critics, "I have a question for you. Does the law permit good deeds on the Sabbath, or is it a day for doing evil? Is this a day to save life or to destroy it?"

10He looked around at them one by one and then said to the man, "Hold out your hand." So the man held out his hand, and it was restored! 11At this, the enemies of Jesus were wild with rage and began to discuss what to do with him.

5:30 Greek *with tax collectors and sinners?*   6:5 "Son of Man" is a title Jesus used for himself.

## PSALM 66:1-20
*For the choir director: A song. A psalm.*

1 **S**hout joyful praises to God, all
        the earth!
2    Sing about the glory of his name!
     Tell the world how glorious he is.
3 Say to God, "How awesome are
        your deeds!
     Your enemies cringe before
        your mighty power.
4 Everything on earth will worship
        you;
     they will sing your praises,
     shouting your name in glorious
        songs."                    *Interlude*

5 Come and see what our God
        has done,
     what awesome miracles he
        performs for people!
6 He made a dry path through
        the Red Sea,\*
     and his people went across
        on foot.
     There we rejoiced in him.
7 For by his great power he rules
        forever.
     He watches every movement
        of the nations;
     let no rebel rise in defiance.
                                *Interlude*

8 Let the whole world bless our God
        and loudly sing his praises.
9 Our lives are in his hands,
        and he keeps our feet from
        stumbling.
10 You have tested us, O God;
     you have purified us like silver.
11 You captured us in your net

and laid the burden of slavery
on our backs.
<sup></sup>¹² Then you put a leader over us.*
We went through fire and flood,
but you brought us to a place of
great abundance.

¹³ Now I come to your Temple with
burnt offerings
to fulfill the vows I made to you—
¹⁴ yes, the sacred vows that I made
when I was in deep trouble.
¹⁵ That is why I am sacrificing burnt
offerings to you—
the best of my rams as a pleasing
aroma,
and a sacrifice of bulls and male
goats.                              *Interlude*

¹⁶ Come and listen, all you who
fear God,
and I will tell you what he
did for me.
¹⁷ For I cried out to him for help,
praising him as I spoke.
¹⁸ If I had not confessed the sin
in my heart,
the Lord would not have listened.
¹⁹ But God did listen!
He paid attention to my prayer.
²⁰ Praise God, who did not ignore
my prayer
or withdraw his unfailing love
from me.

66:6 Hebrew *the sea.*  66:12 Or *You made people ride over
our heads.*

## PROVERBS 11:24-26

**G**ive freely and become more wealthy;
be stingy and lose everything. □The
generous will prosper; those who refresh others will themselves be refreshed. □People curse those who
hoard their grain, but they bless the one
who sells in time of need.

# MARCH 24

## DEUTERONOMY 2:1–3:29

"**T**hen we turned around and headed
back across the wilderness toward the
Red Sea,* just as the Lord had instructed me, and we wandered around
in the region of Mount Seir for a long
time.

²"Then at last the Lord said to me,
³'You have been wandering around in
this hill country long enough; turn to the
north. ⁴Give these orders to the people:
"You will pass through the country belonging to your relatives the Edomites,
the descendants of Esau, who live in
Seir. The Edomites will feel threatened,
so be careful. ⁵Do not bother them, for I
have given them all the hill country
around Mount Seir as their property,
and I will not give you even one square
foot of their land. ⁶If you need food to
eat or water to drink, pay them for it.
⁷For the Lord your God has blessed you
in everything you have done. He has
watched your every step through this
great wilderness. During these forty
years, the Lord your God has been with
you, and you have lacked nothing."'

⁸"So we bypassed the territory of our
relatives, the descendants of Esau, who
live in Seir. We avoided the road
through the Arabah Valley that comes
up from Elath and Ezion-geber.

"Then as we turned north along the
desert route through Moab, ⁹the Lord
warned us, 'Do not bother the Moabites,
the descendants of Lot, or start a war
with them. I have given them Ar as their
property, and I will not give you any of
their land.'"

¹⁰(A race of giants called the Emites
had once lived in the area of Ar. They
were as strong and numerous and tall as
the Anakites, another race of giants.
¹¹Both the Emites and the Anakites are
also known as the Rephaites, though the
Moabites call them Emites. ¹²In earlier

times the Horites had lived in Seir, but they were driven out and displaced by the descendants of Esau, just as Israel drove out the people of Canaan when the LORD gave Israel their land.)

¹³Moses continued, "Then the LORD said to us, 'Get moving. Cross the Zered Brook.' So we crossed the brook.

¹⁴"Thirty-eight years passed from the time we first left Kadesh-barnea until we finally crossed the Zered Brook! By then, all the men old enough to fight in battle had died in the wilderness, as the LORD had vowed would happen. ¹⁵The LORD struck them down until they had all been eliminated from the community.

¹⁶"When all the men of fighting age had died, ¹⁷the LORD said to me, ¹⁸'Today you will cross the border of Moab at Ar ¹⁹and enter the land of the Ammonites, the descendants of Lot. But do not bother them or start a war with them. I have given the land of Ammon to them as their property, and I will not give you any of their land.'"

²⁰(That area was once considered the land of the Rephaites, who had lived there, though the Ammonites call them Zamzummites. ²¹They were also as strong and numerous and tall as the Anakites. But the LORD destroyed them so the Ammonites could occupy their land. ²²He had done the same for the descendants of Esau who lived in Seir, for he destroyed the Horites so they could settle there in their place. The descendants of Esau live there to this day. ²³A similar thing happened when the Caphtorites from Crete* invaded and destroyed the Avvites, who had lived in villages in the area of Gaza.)

²⁴Moses continued, "Then the LORD said, 'Now get moving! Cross the Arnon Gorge. Look, I will hand over to you Sihon the Amorite, king of Heshbon, and I will give you his land. Attack him and begin to occupy the land. ²⁵Beginning today I will make people throughout the earth terrified because of you. When they hear reports about you, they will tremble with dread and fear.'"

²⁶Moses continued, "From the wil-derness of Kedemoth I sent ambassadors to King Sihon of Heshbon with this proposal of peace:

²⁷'Let us travel through your land. We will stay on the main road and won't turn off into the fields on either side. ²⁸Sell us food to eat and water to drink, and we will pay for it. All we want is permission to pass through your land. ²⁹The descendants of Esau who live in Seir allowed us to go through their country, and so did the Moabites, who live in Ar. Let us pass through until we cross the Jordan into the land the LORD our God is giving us.'

³⁰"But King Sihon of Heshbon refused to allow us to pass through, because the LORD your God made Sihon stubborn and defiant so he could help you defeat him, as he has now done.

³¹"Then the LORD said to me, 'Look, I have begun to hand King Sihon and his land over to you. Begin now to conquer and occupy his land.'

³²"Then King Sihon declared war on us and mobilized his forces at Jahaz. ³³But the LORD our God handed him over to us, and we crushed him, his sons, and all his people. ³⁴We conquered all his towns and completely destroyed* everyone—men, women, and children. Not a single person was spared. ³⁵We took all the livestock as plunder for ourselves, along with anything of value from the towns we ransacked.

³⁶"The LORD our God also helped us conquer Aroer on the edge of the Arnon Gorge, and the town in the gorge, and the whole area as far as Gilead. No town had walls too strong for us. ³⁷However, we avoided the land of the Ammonites all along the Jabbok River and the towns in the hill country—all the places the LORD our God had commanded us to leave alone.

³:¹"NEXT we turned and headed for the land of Bashan, where King Og and his entire army attacked us at Edrei. ²But the LORD told me, 'Do not be afraid of

him, for I have given you victory over Og and his entire army, and I will give you all his land. Treat him just as you treated King Sihon of the Amorites, who ruled in Heshbon.'

3"So the LORD our God handed King Og and all his people over to us, and we killed them all. Not a single person survived. 4We conquered all sixty of his towns—the entire Argob region in his kingdom of Bashan. Not a single town escaped our conquest. 5These towns were all fortified with high walls and barred gates. We also took many unwalled villages at the same time. 6We completely destroyed* the kingdom of Bashan, just as we had destroyed King Sihon of Heshbon. We destroyed all the people in every town we conquered— men, women, and children alike. 7But we kept all the livestock for ourselves and took plunder from all the towns.

8"So we took the land of the two Amorite kings east of the Jordan River—all the way from the Arnon Gorge to Mount Hermon. 9(Mount Hermon is called Sirion by the Sidonians, and the Amorites call it Senir.) 10We had now conquered all the cities on the plateau and all Gilead and Bashan, as far as the towns of Salecah and Edrei, which were part of Og's kingdom in Bashan. 11(King Og of Bashan was the last survivor of the giant Rephaites. His bed was made of iron and was more than thirteen feet long and six feet wide.* It can still be seen in the Ammonite city of Rabbah.)

12"When we took possession of this land, I gave to the tribes of Reuben and Gad the territory beyond Aroer along the Arnon Gorge, plus half of the hill country of Gilead with its towns. 13Then I gave the rest of Gilead and all of Bashan—Og's former kingdom—to the half-tribe of Manasseh. (This entire Argob region of Bashan used to be known as the land of the Rephaites. 14Jair, a leader from the tribe of Manasseh, conquered the whole Argob region in Bashan, all the way to the border of the Geshurites and Maacathites. Jair renamed this region after himself, calling it the Towns of Jair,* as it

is still known today.) 15I gave Gilead to the clan of Makir. 16But I also gave part of Gilead to the tribes of Reuben and Gad. The area I gave them extended from the middle of the Arnon Gorge in the south to the Jabbok River on the Ammonite frontier. 17They also received the Jordan Valley, all the way from the Sea of Galilee down to the Dead Sea,* with the Jordan River serving as the western boundary. To the east were the slopes of Pisgah.

18"At that time I gave this command to the tribes that would live east of the Jordan: 'Although the LORD your God has given you this land as your property, all your fighting men must cross the Jordan ahead of your Israelite relatives, armed and ready to assist them. 19Your wives, children, and numerous livestock, however, may stay behind in the towns I have given you. 20When the LORD has given security to the rest of the Israelites, as he has to you, and when they occupy the land the LORD your God is giving them across the Jordan River, then you may all return here to the land I have given you.'

21"At that time I gave Joshua this charge: 'You have seen for yourself everything the LORD your God has done to these two kings. He will do the same to all the kingdoms on the west side of the Jordan. 22Do not be afraid of the nations there, for the LORD your God will fight for you.'

23"At that time I pleaded with the LORD and said, 24'O Sovereign LORD, you have only begun to show your greatness and the strength of your hand to me, your servant. Is there any god in heaven or on earth who can perform such great and mighty deeds as you do? 25Please let me cross the Jordan to see the wonderful land on the other side, the beautiful hill country and the Lebanon mountains.'

26"But the LORD was angry with me because of you, and he would not listen to me. 'That's enough!' he declared. 'Speak of it no more. 27But go up to Pisgah Peak, and look over the land in every direction. Take a good look, but you may not cross the Jordan River. 28Instead, commission Joshua and encourage and strengthen him, for he will lead the people across the Jordan. He will give them all the land you now see before you as their possession.' 29So we stayed in the valley near Beth-peor."

2:1 Hebrew *sea of reeds.*    2:23 Hebrew *from Caphtor.*
2:34 The Hebrew term used here refers to the complete consecration of things or people to the LORD, either by destroying them or by giving them as an offering.    3:6 The Hebrew term used here refers to the complete consecration of things or people to the LORD, either by destroying them or by giving them as an offering. Also in 3:6b.    3:11 Hebrew *9 cubits* [4.1 meters] *long and 4 cubits* [1.8 meters] *wide.*
3:14 Hebrew *Havvoth-jair.*    3:17 Hebrew *from Kinnereth to the Sea of the Arabah, the Salt Sea.*

## LUKE 6:12-38

One day soon afterward Jesus went up on a mountain to pray, and he prayed to God all night. 13At daybreak he called together all of his disciples and chose twelve of them to be apostles. Here are their names:

14 Simon (whom he named Peter),
   Andrew (Peter's brother),
   James,
   John,
   Philip,
   Bartholomew,
15 Matthew,
   Thomas,
   James (son of Alphaeus),
   Simon (who was called the
      zealot),
16 Judas (son of James),
   Judas Iscariot (who later betrayed
      him).

17When they came down from the mountain, the disciples stood with Jesus on a large, level area, surrounded by many of his followers and by the crowds. There were people from all over Judea and from Jerusalem and from as far north as the seacoasts of Tyre and Sidon. 18They had come to hear him and to be healed of their diseases; and Jesus also cast out many evil* spirits. 19Everyone tried to touch him, because healing power went out from him, and he healed everyone.

20Then Jesus turned to his disciples and said,

"God blesses you who are poor,
   for the Kingdom of God is yours.
21 God blesses you who are hungry
      now,
   for you will be satisfied.
God blesses you who weep now,
   for in due time you will laugh.

22What blessings await you when people hate you and exclude you and mock you and curse you as evil because you follow the Son of Man. 23When that happens, be happy! Yes, leap for joy! For a great reward awaits you in heaven. And remember, their ancestors treated the ancient prophets that same way.

24 "What sorrow awaits you who
      are rich,
   for you have your only happiness
      now.
25 What sorrow awaits you who are
      fat and prosperous now,
   for a time of awful hunger
      awaits you.
What sorrow awaits you who
      laugh now,
   for your laughing will turn to
      mourning and sorrow.
26 What sorrow awaits you who are
      praised by the crowds,
   for their ancestors also praised
      false prophets.

27**"But to you who are willing to listen, I say, love your enemies! Do good to those who hate you. 28Bless those who curse you. Pray for those who hurt you.** 29If someone slaps you on one cheek, offer the other cheek also. If someone demands your coat, offer your shirt also. 30Give to anyone who asks; and when things are taken away from you, don't try to get them back. 31Do to others as you would like them to do to you.

32"If you love only those who love you, why should you get credit for that? Even sinners love those who love them! 33And if you do good only to those who do good to you, why should you get credit? Even sinners do that much! 34And if you lend money only to those who can repay you, why should you get credit? Even sinners will lend to other sinners for a full return.

³⁵"Love your enemies! Do good to them. Lend to them without expecting to be repaid. Then your reward from heaven will be very great, and you will truly be acting as children of the Most High, for he is kind to those who are unthankful and wicked. ³⁶You must be compassionate, just as your Father is compassionate.

³⁷"Do not judge others, and you will not be judged. Do not condemn others, or it will all come back against you. Forgive others, and you will be forgiven. ³⁸Give, and you will receive. Your gift will return to you in full—pressed down, shaken together to make room for more, running over, and poured into your lap. The amount you give will determine the amount you get back.*"

**6:18** Greek *unclean.*  **6:38** Or *The measure you give will be the measure you get back.*

## PSALM 67:1-7

*For the choir director: A song. A psalm, to be accompanied by stringed instruments.*

¹ **M**ay God be merciful and bless us.
    May his face smile with favor
        on us.                    *Interlude*

² May your ways be known
        throughout the earth,
    your saving power among people
        everywhere.
³ May the nations praise you, O God.
    Yes, may all the nations praise
        you.
⁴ Let the whole world sing for joy,
    because you govern the nations
        with justice
    and guide the people of the
        whole world.        *Interlude*

⁵ May the nations praise you, O God.
    Yes, may all the nations
        praise you.
⁶ Then the earth will yield its harvests,
    and God, our God, will richly
        bless us.
⁷ Yes, God will bless us,

and people all over the world
    will fear him.

## PROVERBS 11:27
**I**f you search for good, you will find favor; but if you search for evil, it will find you!

# MARCH 25

## DEUTERONOMY 4:1-49
"**A**nd now, Israel, listen carefully to these decrees and regulations that I am about to teach you. Obey them so that you may live, so you may enter and occupy the land that the LORD, the God of your ancestors, is giving you. ²Do not add to or subtract from these commands I am giving you. Just obey the commands of the LORD your God that I am giving you.

³"You saw for yourself what the LORD did to you at Baal-peor. There the LORD your God destroyed everyone who had worshiped Baal, the god of Peor. ⁴But all of you who were faithful to the LORD your God are still alive today—every one of you.

⁵"Look, I now teach you these decrees and regulations just as the LORD my God commanded me, so that you may obey them in the land you are about to enter and occupy. ⁶Obey them completely, and you will display your wisdom and intelligence among the surrounding nations. When they hear all these decrees, they will exclaim, 'How wise and prudent are the people of this great nation!' ⁷For what great nation has a god as near to them as the LORD our God is near to us whenever we call on him? ⁸And what great nation has decrees and regulations as righteous and fair as this body of instructions that I am giving you today?

⁹"But watch out! Be careful never to

forget what you yourself have seen. Do not let these memories escape from your mind as long as you live! And be sure to pass them on to your children and grandchildren. [10]Never forget the day when you stood before the LORD your God at Mount Sinai,* where he told me, 'Summon the people before me, and I will personally instruct them. Then they will learn to fear me as long as they live, and they will teach their children to fear me also.'

[11]"You came near and stood at the foot of the mountain, while flames from the mountain shot into the sky. The mountain was shrouded in black clouds and deep darkness. [12]And the LORD spoke to you from the heart of the fire. You heard the sound of his words but didn't see his form; there was only a voice. [13]He proclaimed his covenant—the Ten Commandments*—which he commanded you to keep, and which he wrote on two stone tablets. [14]It was at that time that the LORD commanded me to teach you his decrees and regulations so you would obey them in the land you are about to enter and occupy.

[15]"But be very careful! You did not see the LORD's form on the day he spoke to you from the heart of the fire at Mount Sinai. [16]So do not corrupt yourselves by making an idol in any form—whether of a man or a woman, [17]an animal on the ground, a bird in the sky, [18]a small animal that scurries along the ground, or a fish in the deepest sea. [19]And when you look up into the sky and see the sun, moon, and stars—all the forces of heaven—don't be seduced into worshiping them. The LORD your God gave them to all the peoples of the earth. [20]Remember that the LORD rescued you from the iron-smelting furnace of Egypt in order to make you his very own people and his special possession, which is what you are today.

[21]"But the LORD was angry with me because of you. He vowed that I would not cross the Jordan River into the good land the LORD your God is giving you as your special possession. [22]You will cross the Jordan to occupy the land, but I will not. Instead, I will die here on the east side of the river. [23]So be careful not to break the covenant the LORD your God has made with you. Do not make idols of any shape or form, for the LORD your God has forbidden this. [24]The LORD your God is a devouring fire; he is a jealous God.

[25]"In the future, when you have children and grandchildren and have lived in the land a long time, do not corrupt yourselves by making idols of any kind. This is evil in the sight of the LORD your God and will arouse his anger.

[26]"Today I call on heaven and earth as witnesses against you. If you break my covenant, you will quickly disappear from the land you are crossing the Jordan to occupy. You will live there only a short time; then you will be utterly destroyed. [27]For the LORD will scatter you among the nations, where only a few of you will survive. [28]There, in a foreign land, you will worship idols made from wood and stone—gods that neither see nor hear nor eat nor smell. [29]But from there you will search again for the LORD your God. And if you search for him with all your heart and soul, you will find him.

[30]"In the distant future, when you are suffering all these things, you will finally return to the LORD your God and listen to what he tells you. [31]For the LORD your God is a merciful God; he will not abandon you or destroy you or forget the solemn covenant he made with your ancestors.

[32]"Now search all of history, from the time God created people on the earth until now, and search from one end of the heavens to the other. Has anything as great as this ever been seen or heard before? [33]Has any nation ever heard the voice of God* speaking from fire—as you did—and survived? [34]Has any other god dared to take a nation for himself out of another nation by means of trials, miraculous signs, wonders, war, a strong hand, a powerful arm, and terrifying acts? Yet that is what the LORD

your God did for you in Egypt, right before your eyes.

[35]"He showed you these things so you would know that the LORD is God and there is no other. [36]He let you hear his voice from heaven so he could instruct you. He let you see his great fire here on earth so he could speak to you from it. [37]Because he loved your ancestors, he chose to bless their descendants, and he personally brought you out of Egypt with a great display of power. [38]He drove out nations far greater than you, so he could bring you in and give you their land as your special possession, as it is today.

[39]"So remember this and keep it firmly in mind: The LORD is God both in heaven and on earth, and there is no other. [40]If you obey all the decrees and commands I am giving you today, all will be well with you and your children. I am giving you these instructions so you will enjoy a long life in the land the LORD your God is giving you for all time."

[41]Then Moses set apart three cities of refuge east of the Jordan River. [42]Anyone who killed another person unintentionally, without previous hostility, could flee there to live in safety. [43]These were the cities: Bezer on the wilderness plateau for the tribe of Reuben; Ramoth in Gilead for the tribe of Gad; Golan in Bashan for the tribe of Manasseh.

[44]This is the body of instruction that Moses presented to the Israelites. [45]These are the laws, decrees, and regulations that Moses gave to the people of Israel when they left Egypt, [46]and as they camped in the valley near Beth-peor east of the Jordan River. (This land was formerly occupied by the Amorites under King Sihon, who ruled from Heshbon. But Moses and the Israelites destroyed him and his people when they came up from Egypt. [47]Israel took possession of his land and that of King Og of Bashan—the two Amorite kings east of the Jordan. [48]So Israel conquered the entire area from Aroer at the edge of the Arnon Gorge all the way to Mount Siri-

on,* also called Mount Hermon. [49]And they conquered the eastern bank of the Jordan River as far south as the Dead Sea,* below the slopes of Pisgah.)

**4:10** Hebrew *Horeb,* another name for Sinai; also in 4:15.
**4:13** Hebrew *the ten words.*    **4:33** Or *voice of a god.*
**4:48** As in Syriac version (see also 3:9); Hebrew reads *Mount Sion.*    **4:49** Hebrew *took the Arabah on the east side of the Jordan as far as the sea of the Arabah.*

## LUKE 6:39–7:10

Then Jesus gave the following illustration: "Can one blind person lead another? Won't they both fall into a ditch? [40]Students* are not greater than their teacher. But the student who is fully trained will become like the teacher.

[41]"And why worry about a speck in your friend's eye* when you have a log in your own? [42]How can you think of saying, 'Friend,* let me help you get rid of that speck in your eye,' when you can't see past the log in your own eye? Hypocrite! First get rid of the log in your own eye; then you will see well enough to deal with the speck in your friend's eye.

[43]"A good tree can't produce bad fruit, and a bad tree can't produce good fruit. [44]A tree is identified by its fruit. Figs never grow on thornbushes, nor grapes on bramble bushes. [45]**A good person produces good things from the treasury of a good heart, and an evil person produces evil things from the treasury of an evil heart. What you say flows from what is in your heart.**

[46]"So why do you keep calling me 'Lord, Lord!' when you don't do what I say? [47]I will show you what it's like when someone comes to me, listens to my teaching, and then follows it. [48]It is like a person building a house who digs deep and lays the foundation on solid rock. When the floodwaters rise and break against the house, it stands firm because it is well built. [49]But anyone who hears and doesn't obey is like a person who builds a house without a foundation. When the floods sweep down against that house, it will collapse into a heap of ruins."

7:1WHEN Jesus had finished saying all this to the people, he returned to Capernaum. 2At that time the highly valued slave of a Roman officer* was sick and near death. 3When the officer heard about Jesus, he sent some respected Jewish elders to ask him to come and heal his slave. 4So they earnestly begged Jesus to help the man. "If anyone deserves your help, he does," they said, 5"for he loves the Jewish people and even built a synagogue for us."

6So Jesus went with them. But just before they arrived at the house, the officer sent some friends to say, "Lord, don't trouble yourself by coming to my home, for I am not worthy of such an honor. 7I am not even worthy to come and meet you. Just say the word from where you are, and my servant will be healed. 8I know this because I am under the authority of my superior officers, and I have authority over my soldiers. I only need to say, 'Go,' and they go, or 'Come,' and they come. And if I say to my slaves, 'Do this,' they do it."

9When Jesus heard this, he was amazed. Turning to the crowd that was following him, he said, "I tell you, I haven't seen faith like this in all Israel!" 10And when the officer's friends returned to his house, they found the slave completely healed.

6:40 Or *Disciples.*   6:41 Greek *your brother's eye;* also in 6:42.   6:42 Greek *Brother.*   7:2 Greek *a centurion;* similarly in 7:6.

## PSALM 68:1-18

*For the choir director: A song. A psalm of David.*

1   Rise up, O God, and scatter your
        enemies.
     Let those who hate God run for
        their lives.
2   Blow them away like smoke.
     Melt them like wax in a fire.
     Let the wicked perish in the
        presence of God.
3   But let the godly rejoice.
     Let them be glad in God's
        presence.
     Let them be filled with joy.

4   Sing praises to God and to his name!
     Sing loud praises to him who
        rides the clouds.
     His name is the LORD—
        rejoice in his presence!

5   Father to the fatherless, defender
        of widows—
     this is God, whose dwelling
        is holy.
6   God places the lonely in families;
     he sets the prisoners free and
        gives them joy.
     But he makes the rebellious live in
        a sun-scorched land.

7   O God, when you led your people
        out from Egypt,
     when you marched through the
        dry wasteland,        *Interlude*
8   the earth trembled, and the heavens
        poured down rain
     before you, the God of Sinai,
     before God, the God of Israel.
9   You sent abundant rain, O God,
     to refresh the weary land.
10  There your people finally settled,
     and with a bountiful harvest,
        O God,
     you provided for your needy
        people.

11  The Lord gives the word,
     and a great army* brings the
        good news.
12  Enemy kings and their armies flee,
     while the women of Israel divide
        the plunder.
13  Even those who lived among the
        sheepfolds found treasures—
     doves with wings of silver
     and feathers of gold.
14  The Almighty scattered the enemy
        kings
     like a blowing snowstorm on
        Mount Zalmon.

15  The mountains of Bashan are
        majestic,
     with many peaks stretching high
        into the sky.
16  Why do you look with envy,
        O rugged mountains,

at Mount Zion, where God has
   chosen to live,
where the LORD himself will live
   forever?

<sup>17</sup> Surrounded by unnumbered
   thousands of chariots,
the Lord came from Mount Sinai
   into his sanctuary.
<sup>18</sup> When you ascended to the heights,
   you led a crowd of captives.
You received gifts from the people,
   even from those who rebelled
   against you.
Now the LORD God will live
   among us there.

**68:11** Or *a host of women.*

PROVERBS 11:28
Trust in your money and down you go!
But the godly flourish like leaves in
spring.

## MARCH
## 26

DEUTERONOMY 5:1–6:25
Moses called all the people of Israel together and said, "Listen carefully, Israel.
Hear the decrees and regulations I am
giving you today, so you may learn them
and obey them!

<sup>2</sup>"The LORD our God made a covenant
with us at Mount Sinai.* <sup>3</sup>The LORD did
not make this covenant with our ancestors, but with all of us who are alive today. <sup>4</sup>At the mountain the LORD spoke to
you face to face from the heart of the
fire. <sup>5</sup>I stood as an intermediary between
you and the LORD, for you were afraid of
the fire and did not want to approach the
mountain. He spoke to me, and I passed
his words on to you. This is what he said:

<sup>6</sup>"I am the LORD your God, who
   rescued you from the land of Egypt,
   the place of your slavery.

<sup>7</sup>"You must not have any other god
   but me.
<sup>8</sup>"You must not make for yourself an
idol of any kind, or an image of
anything in the heavens or on the
earth or in the sea. <sup>9</sup>You must not
bow down to them or worship
them, for I, the LORD your God, am
a jealous God who will not tolerate
your affection for any other gods.
I lay the sins of the parents upon
their children; the entire family is
affected—even children in the
third and fourth generations of
those who reject me. <sup>10</sup>But I lavish
unfailing love for a thousand
generations on those* who love
me and obey my commands.
<sup>11</sup>"You must not misuse the name of
the LORD your God. The LORD will
not let you go unpunished if you
misuse his name.
<sup>12</sup>"Observe the Sabbath day by
keeping it holy, as the LORD your
God has commanded you. <sup>13</sup>You
have six days each week for your
ordinary work, <sup>14</sup>but the seventh
day is a Sabbath day of rest
dedicated to the LORD your God. On
that day no one in your household
may do any work. This includes
you, your sons and daughters, your
male and female servants, your
oxen and donkeys and other
livestock, and any foreigners living
among you. All your male and
female servants must rest as you
do. <sup>15</sup>Remember that you were
once slaves in Egypt, but the LORD
your God brought you out with his
strong hand and powerful arm.
That is why the LORD your God has
commanded you to rest on the
Sabbath day.
<sup>16</sup>"Honor your father and mother, as
the LORD your God commanded
you. Then you will live a long, full
life in the land the LORD your God is
giving you.
<sup>17</sup>"You must not murder.

<sup>18</sup>"You must not commit adultery.

<sup>19</sup>"You must not steal.

<sup>20</sup>"You must not testify falsely against your neighbor.

<sup>21</sup>"You must not covet your neighbor's wife. You must not covet your neighbor's house or land, male or female servant, ox or donkey, or anything else that belongs to your neighbor.

<sup>22</sup>"The Lord spoke these words to all of you assembled there at the foot of the mountain. He spoke with a loud voice from the heart of the fire, surrounded by clouds and deep darkness. This was all he said at that time, and he wrote his words on two stone tablets and gave them to me.

<sup>23</sup>"But when you heard the voice from the heart of the darkness, while the mountain was blazing with fire, all your tribal leaders and elders came to me. <sup>24</sup>They said, 'Look, the Lord our God has shown us his glory and greatness, and we have heard his voice from the heart of the fire. Today we have seen that God can speak to us humans, and yet we live! <sup>25</sup>But now, why should we risk death again? If the Lord our God speaks to us again, we will certainly die and be consumed by this awesome fire. <sup>26</sup>Can any living thing hear the voice of the living God from the heart of the fire as we did and yet survive? <sup>27</sup>Go yourself and listen to what the Lord our God says. Then come and tell us everything he tells you, and we will listen and obey.'

<sup>28</sup>"The Lord heard the request you made to me. And he said, 'I have heard what the people said to you, and they are right. <sup>29</sup>Oh, that they would always have hearts like this, that they might fear me and obey all my commands! If they did, they and their descendants would prosper forever. <sup>30</sup>Go and tell them, "Return to your tents." <sup>31</sup>But you stand here with me so I can give you all my commands, decrees, and regulations. You must teach them to the people so they can obey them in the land I am giving them as their possession.'"

<sup>32</sup>So Moses told the people, "You must be careful to obey all the commands of the Lord your God, following his instructions in every detail. <sup>33</sup>Stay on the path that the Lord your God has commanded you to follow. Then you will live long and prosperous lives in the land you are about to enter and occupy.

<sup>6:1</sup>"These are the commands, decrees, and regulations that the Lord your God commanded me to teach you. You must obey them in the land you are about to enter and occupy, <sup>2</sup>and you and your children and grandchildren must fear the Lord your God as long as you live. If you obey all his decrees and commands, you will enjoy a long life. <sup>3</sup>Listen closely, Israel, and be careful to obey. Then all will go well with you, and you will have many children in the land flowing with milk and honey, just as the Lord, the God of your ancestors, promised you.

<sup>4</sup>"Listen, O Israel! The Lord is our God, the Lord alone.* <sup>5</sup>And you must love the Lord your God with all your heart, all your soul, and all your strength. <sup>6</sup>**And you must commit yourselves wholeheartedly to these commands that I am giving you today. <sup>7</sup>Repeat them again and again to your children. Talk about them when you are at home and when you are on the road, when you are going to bed and when you are getting up. <sup>8</sup>Tie them to your hands and wear them on your forehead as reminders. <sup>9</sup>Write them on the doorposts of your house and on your gates.**

<sup>10</sup>"The Lord your God will soon bring you into the land he swore to give you when he made a vow to your ancestors Abraham, Isaac, and Jacob. It is a land with large, prosperous cities that you did not build. <sup>11</sup>The houses will be richly stocked with goods you did not produce. You will draw water from cisterns you did not dig, and you will eat from vineyards and olive trees you did not plant. When you have eaten your fill in this land, <sup>12</sup>be careful not to forget the Lord, who rescued you from slavery

in the land of Egypt. [13] You must fear the LORD your God and serve him. When you take an oath, you must use only his name.

[14]"You must not worship any of the gods of neighboring nations, [15] for the LORD your God, who lives among you, is a jealous God. His anger will flare up against you, and he will wipe you from the face of the earth. [16] You must not test the LORD your God as you did when you complained at Massah. [17] You must diligently obey the commands of the LORD your God—all the laws and decrees he has given you. [18] Do what is right and good in the LORD's sight, so all will go well with you. Then you will enter and occupy the good land that the LORD swore to give your ancestors. [19] You will drive out all the enemies living in the land, just as the LORD said you would.

[20]"In the future your children will ask you, 'What is the meaning of these laws, decrees, and regulations that the LORD our God has commanded us to obey?'

[21]"Then you must tell them, 'We were Pharaoh's slaves in Egypt, but the LORD brought us out of Egypt with his strong hand. [22] The LORD did miraculous signs and wonders before our eyes, dealing terrifying blows against Egypt and Pharaoh and all his people. [23] He brought us out of Egypt so he could give us this land he had sworn to give our ancestors. [24] And the LORD our God commanded us to obey all these decrees and to fear him so he can continue to bless us and preserve our lives, as he has done to this day. [25] For we will be counted as righteous when we obey all the commands the LORD our God has given us.'"

5:2 Hebrew *Horeb*, another name for Sinai. 5:10 Hebrew *for thousands of those.* 6:4 Or *The LORD our God is one LORD;* or *The LORD our God, the LORD is one;* or *The LORD is our God, the LORD is one.*

## LUKE 7:11-35

Soon afterward Jesus went with his disciples to the village of Nain, and a large crowd followed him. [12] A funeral procession was coming out as he approached the village gate. The young man who had died was a widow's only son, and a large crowd from the village was with her. [13] When the Lord saw her, his heart overflowed with compassion. "Don't cry!" he said. [14] Then he walked over to the coffin and touched it, and the bearers stopped. "Young man," he said, "I tell you, get up." [15] Then the dead boy sat up and began to talk! And Jesus gave him back to his mother.

[16] Great fear swept the crowd, and they praised God, saying, "A mighty prophet has risen among us," and "God has visited his people today." [17] And the news about Jesus spread throughout Judea and the surrounding countryside.

[18] The disciples of John the Baptist told John about everything Jesus was doing. So John called for two of his disciples, [19] and he sent them to the Lord to ask him, "Are you the Messiah we've been expecting,* or should we keep looking for someone else?"

[20] John's two disciples found Jesus and said to him, "John the Baptist sent us to ask, 'Are you the Messiah we've been expecting, or should we keep looking for someone else?'"

[21] At that very time, Jesus cured many people of their diseases and illnesses, and he cast out evil spirits and restored sight to many who were blind. [22] Then he told John's disciples, "Go back to John and tell him what you have seen and heard—the blind see, the lame walk, the lepers are cured, the deaf hear, the dead are raised to life, and the Good News is being preached to the poor. [23] And tell him, 'God blesses those who do not turn away because of me.*'"

[24] After John's disciples left, Jesus began talking about him to the crowds. "What kind of man did you go into the wilderness to see? Was he a weak reed, swayed by every breath of wind? [25] Or were you expecting to see a man dressed in expensive clothes? No, people who wear beautiful clothes and live in luxury are found in palaces. [26] Were you looking for a prophet? Yes, and he is more than a prophet. [27] John is the man to whom the Scriptures refer when they say,

'Look, I am sending my messenger
    ahead of you,
and he will prepare your way
    before you.'*

28I tell you, of all who have ever lived,
none is greater than John. Yet even the
least person in the Kingdom of God is
greater than he is!"

29When they heard this, all the people—even the tax collectors—agreed
that God's way was right,* for they had
been baptized by John. 30But the Pharisees and experts in religious law rejected God's plan for them, for they had
refused John's baptism.

31"To what can I compare the people
of this generation?" Jesus asked. "How
can I describe them? 32They are like
children playing a game in the public
square. They complain to their friends,

'We played wedding songs,
    and you didn't dance,
so we played funeral songs,
    and you didn't weep.'

33For John the Baptist didn't spend his
time eating bread or drinking wine, and
you say, 'He's possessed by a demon.'
34The Son of Man,* on the other hand,
feasts and drinks, and you say, 'He's a
glutton and a drunkard, and a friend of
tax collectors and other sinners!' 35But
wisdom is shown to be right by the lives
of those who follow it.*"

7:19 Greek *Are you the one who is coming?* Also in 7:20.
7:23 Or *who are not offended by me.*   7:27 Mal 3:1.
7:29 Or *praised God for his justice.*   7:34 "Son of Man"
is a title Jesus used for himself.   7:35 Or *But wisdom is
justified by all her children.*

PSALM 68:19-35
**P**raise the Lord; praise God
    our savior!
    For each day he carries us in his
        arms.      *Interlude*
20 Our God is a God who saves!
    The Sovereign LORD rescues us
        from death.

21 But God will smash the heads of his
    enemies,
    crushing the skulls of those who
        love their guilty ways.

22 The Lord says, "I will bring my
    enemies down from Bashan;
    I will bring them up from the
        depths of the sea.
23 You, my people, will wash your feet
    in their blood,
    and even your dogs will get
        their share!"

24 Your procession has come into
    view, O God—
    the procession of my God and
        King as he goes into the
        sanctuary.
25 Singers are in front, musicians
    behind;
    between them are young women
        playing tambourines.
26 Praise God, all you people of Israel;
    praise the LORD, the source
        of Israel's life.
27 Look, the little tribe of Benjamin
    leads the way.
    Then comes a great throng of
        rulers from Judah
    and all the rulers of Zebulun
        and Naphtali.

28 Summon your might, O God.
    Display your power, O God, as you
        have in the past.
29 The kings of the earth are bringing
    tribute
    to your Temple in Jerusalem.
30 Rebuke these enemy nations—
    these wild animals lurking in
        the reeds,
    this herd of bulls among the
        weaker calves.
    Make them bring bars of silver
        in humble tribute.
    Scatter the nations that delight
        in war.
31 Let Egypt come with gifts of
    precious metals*;
    let Ethiopia* bow in submission
        to God.
32 Sing to God, you kingdoms of the
    earth.
    Sing praises to the Lord.
                *Interlude*
33 Sing to the one who rides across the
    ancient heavens,

his mighty voice thundering
from the sky.
³⁴ Tell everyone about God's power.
His majesty shines down on Israel;
his strength is mighty in the
heavens.
³⁵ God is awesome in his sanctuary.
The God of Israel gives power
and strength to his people.

Praise be to God!

68:31a Or *of rich cloth.*   68:31b Hebrew *Cush.*

PROVERBS 11:29-31
**T**hose who bring trouble on their families inherit the wind. The fool will be a
servant to the wise. □ The seeds of good
deeds become a tree of life; a wise person wins friends.* □ If the righteous are
rewarded here on earth, what will happen to wicked sinners?*

11:30 Or *and those who win souls are wise.*   11:31 Greek
version reads *If the righteous are barely saved, / what will
happen to godless sinners?* Compare 1 Pet 4:18.

# MARCH
# 27

DEUTERONOMY 7:1-8:20
"**W**hen the LORD your God brings you
into the land you are about to enter and
occupy, he will clear away many nations
ahead of you: the Hittites, Girgashites,
Amorites, Canaanites, Perizzites, Hivites, and Jebusites. These seven nations are greater and more numerous
than you. ²When the LORD your God
hands these nations over to you and you
conquer them, you must completely
destroy* them. Make no treaties with
them and show them no mercy. ³You
must not intermarry with them. Do not
let your daughters and sons marry their
sons and daughters, ⁴for they will lead
your children away from me to worship
other gods. Then the anger of the LORD
will burn against you, and he will

quickly destroy you. ⁵This is what you
must do. You must break down their pagan altars and shatter their sacred pillars. Cut down their Asherah poles and
burn their idols. ⁶For you are a holy
people, who belong to the LORD your
God. Of all the people on earth, the
LORD your God has chosen you to be his
own special treasure.

⁷"The LORD did not set his heart on
you and choose you because you were
more numerous than other nations, for
you were the smallest of all nations!
⁸Rather, it was simply that the LORD
loves you, and he was keeping the oath
he had sworn to your ancestors. That is
why the LORD rescued you with such a
strong hand from your slavery and from
the oppressive hand of Pharaoh, king of
Egypt. ⁹Understand, therefore, that the
LORD your God is indeed God. He is the
faithful God who keeps his covenant for
a thousand generations and lavishes his
unfailing love on those who love him
and obey his commands. ¹⁰But he does
not hesitate to punish and destroy those
who reject him. ¹¹Therefore, you must
obey all these commands, decrees, and
regulations I am giving you today.

¹²"If you listen to these regulations
and faithfully obey them, the LORD your
God will keep his covenant of unfailing
love with you, as he promised with an
oath to your ancestors. ¹³He will love
you and bless you, and he will give you
many children. He will give fertility to
your land and your animals. When you
arrive in the land he swore to give your
ancestors, you will have large harvests
of grain, new wine, and olive oil, and
great herds of cattle, sheep, and goats.
¹⁴You will be blessed above all the nations of the earth. None of your men or
women will be childless, and all your
livestock will bear young. ¹⁵And the
LORD will protect you from all sickness.
He will not let you suffer from the terrible diseases you knew in Egypt, but he
will inflict them on all your enemies!

¹⁶"You must destroy all the nations
the LORD your God hands over to
you. Show them no mercy, and do not

worship their gods, or they will trap you. [17]Perhaps you will think to yourselves, 'How can we ever conquer these nations that are so much more powerful than we are?' [18]But don't be afraid of them! Just remember what the LORD your God did to Pharaoh and to all the land of Egypt. [19]Remember the great terrors the LORD your God sent against them. You saw it all with your own eyes! And remember the miraculous signs and wonders, and the strong hand and powerful arm with which he brought you out of Egypt. The LORD your God will use this same power against all the people you fear. [20]And then the LORD your God will send terror* to drive out the few survivors still hiding from you!

[21]"No, do not be afraid of those nations, for the LORD your God is among you, and he is a great and awesome God. [22]The LORD your God will drive those nations out ahead of you little by little. You will not clear them away all at once, otherwise the wild animals would multiply too quickly for you. [23]But the LORD your God will hand them over to you. He will throw them into complete confusion until they are destroyed. [24]He will put their kings in your power, and you will erase their names from the face of the earth. No one will be able to stand against you, and you will destroy them all.

[25]"You must burn their idols in fire, and you must not covet the silver or gold that covers them. You must not take it or it will become a trap to you, for it is detestable to the LORD your God. [26]Do not bring any detestable objects into your home, for then you will be destroyed, just like them. You must utterly detest such things, for they are set apart for destruction.

[8:1]"BE careful to obey all the commands I am giving you today. Then you will live and multiply, and you will enter and occupy the land the LORD swore to give your ancestors. [2]Remember how the LORD your God led you through the wilderness for these forty years, humbling

you and testing you to prove your character, and to find out whether or not you would obey his commands. [3]Yes, he humbled you by letting you go hungry and then feeding you with manna, a food previously unknown to you and your ancestors. He did it to teach you that people do not live by bread alone; rather, we live by every word that comes from the mouth of the LORD. [4]For all these forty years your clothes didn't wear out, and your feet didn't blister or swell. [5]Think about it: Just as a parent disciplines a child, the LORD your God disciplines you for your own good.

[6]"So obey the commands of the LORD your God by walking in his ways and fearing him. [7]For the LORD your God is bringing you into a good land of flowing streams and pools of water, with fountains and springs that gush out in the valleys and hills. [8]It is a land of wheat and barley; of grapevines, fig trees, and pomegranates; of olive oil and honey. [9]It is a land where food is plentiful and nothing is lacking. It is a land where iron is as common as stone, and copper is abundant in the hills. [10]**When you have eaten your fill, be sure to praise the LORD your God for the good land he has given you.**

[11]**"But that is the time to be careful! Beware that in your plenty you do not forget the LORD your God and disobey his commands, regulations, and decrees that I am giving you today.** [12]For when you have become full and prosperous and have built fine homes to live in, [13]and when your flocks and herds have become very large and your silver and gold have multiplied along with everything else, be careful! [14]Do not become proud at that time and forget the LORD your God, who rescued you from slavery in the land of Egypt. [15]Do not forget that he led you through the great and terrifying wilderness with its poisonous snakes and scorpions, where it was so hot and dry. He gave you water from the rock! [16]He fed you with manna in the wilderness, a food unknown to your ancestors. He did this to humble

you and test you for your own good. ¹⁷He did all this so you would never say to yourself, 'I have achieved this wealth with my own strength and energy.' ¹⁸Remember the LORD your God. He is the one who gives you power to be successful, in order to fulfill the covenant he confirmed to your ancestors with an oath.

¹⁹"But I assure you of this: If you ever forget the LORD your God and follow other gods, worshiping and bowing down to them, you will certainly be destroyed. ²⁰Just as the LORD has destroyed other nations in your path, you also will be destroyed if you refuse to obey the LORD your God."

7:2 The Hebrew term used here refers to the complete consecration of things or people to the LORD, either by destroying them or by giving them as an offering; also in 7:26.   7:20 Often rendered *the hornet*. The meaning of the Hebrew is uncertain.

## LUKE 7:36–8:3

**O**ne of the Pharisees asked Jesus to have dinner with him, so Jesus went to his home and sat down to eat.* ³⁷When a certain immoral woman from that city heard he was eating there, she brought a beautiful alabaster jar filled with expensive perfume. ³⁸Then she knelt behind him at his feet, weeping. Her tears fell on his feet, and she wiped them off with her hair. Then she kept kissing his feet and putting perfume on them.

³⁹When the Pharisee who had invited him saw this, he said to himself, "If this man were a prophet, he would know what kind of woman is touching him. She's a sinner!"

⁴⁰Then Jesus answered his thoughts. "Simon," he said to the Pharisee, "I have something to say to you."

"Go ahead, Teacher," Simon replied.

⁴¹Then Jesus told him this story: "A man loaned money to two people— 500 pieces of silver* to one and 50 pieces to the other. ⁴²But neither of them could repay him, so he kindly forgave them both, canceling their debts. Who do you suppose loved him more after that?"

⁴³Simon answered, "I suppose the one for whom he canceled the larger debt."

"That's right," Jesus said. ⁴⁴Then he turned to the woman and said to Simon, "Look at this woman kneeling here. When I entered your home, you didn't offer me water to wash the dust from my feet, but she has washed them with her tears and wiped them with her hair. ⁴⁵You didn't greet me with a kiss, but from the time I first came in, she has not stopped kissing my feet. ⁴⁶You neglected the courtesy of olive oil to anoint my head, but she has anointed my feet with rare perfume.

⁴⁷"I tell you, her sins—and they are many—have been forgiven, so she has shown me much love. But a person who is forgiven little shows only little love." ⁴⁸Then Jesus said to the woman, "Your sins are forgiven."

⁴⁹The men at the table said among themselves, "Who is this man, that he goes around forgiving sins?"

⁵⁰And Jesus said to the woman, "Your faith has saved you; go in peace."

⁸:¹SOON afterward Jesus began a tour of the nearby towns and villages, preaching and announcing the Good News about the Kingdom of God. He took his twelve disciples with him, ²along with some women he had healed and from whom he had cast out evil spirits. Among them were Mary Magdalene, from whom he had cast out seven demons; ³Joanna, the wife of Chuza, Herod's business manager; Susanna; and many others who were contributing their own resources to support Jesus and his disciples.

7:36 Or *and reclined.*   7:41 Greek *500 denarii.* A denarius was equivalent to a laborer's full day's wage.

## PSALM 69:1-18

*For the choir director: A psalm of David, to be sung to the tune "Lilies."*

¹ **S**ave me, O God,
    for the floodwaters are up
        to my neck.
² Deeper and deeper I sink into
        the mire;

I can't find a foothold.
I am in deep water,
   and the floods overwhelm me.
3 I am exhausted from crying for help;
   my throat is parched.
My eyes are swollen with weeping,
   waiting for my God to help me.
4 Those who hate me without cause
   outnumber the hairs on my head.
Many enemies try to destroy me
   with lies,
   demanding that I give back what
   I didn't steal.

5 O God, you know how foolish I am;
   my sins cannot be hidden from
   you.
6 Don't let those who trust in you be
   ashamed because of me,
   O Sovereign LORD of Heaven's
   Armies.
Don't let me cause them to be
   humiliated,
   O God of Israel.
7 For I endure insults for your sake;
   humiliation is written all over
   my face.
8 Even my own brothers pretend they
   don't know me;
   they treat me like a stranger.

9 Passion for your house has
   consumed me,
   and the insults of those who
   insult you have fallen on me.
10 When I weep and fast,
   they scoff at me.
11 When I dress in burlap to show
   sorrow,
   they make fun of me.
12 I am the favorite topic of town
   gossip,
   and all the drunks sing about me.

13 But I keep praying to you, LORD,
   hoping this time you will show
   me favor.
In your unfailing love, O God,
   answer my prayer with your sure
   salvation.
14 Rescue me from the mud;
   don't let me sink any deeper!
Save me from those who hate me,

and pull me from these deep
   waters.
15 Don't let the floods overwhelm me,
   or the deep waters swallow me,
   or the pit of death devour me.

16 Answer my prayers, O LORD,
   for your unfailing love is
   wonderful.
Take care of me,
   for your mercy is so plentiful.
17 Don't hide from your servant;
   answer me quickly, for I am in
   deep trouble!
18 Come and redeem me;
   free me from my enemies.

**PROVERBS 12:1**
To learn, you must love discipline; it is stupid to hate correction.

# MARCH 28

**DEUTERONOMY 9:1–10:22**
"Listen, O Israel! Today you are about to cross the Jordan River to take over the land belonging to nations much greater and more powerful than you. They live in cities with walls that reach to the sky! 2 The people are strong and tall—descendants of the famous Anakite giants. You've heard the saying, 'Who can stand up to the Anakites?' 3 But recognize today that the LORD your God is the one who will cross over ahead of you like a devouring fire to destroy them. He will subdue them so that you will quickly conquer them and drive them out, just as the LORD has promised.

4 "After the LORD your God has done this for you, don't say in your hearts, 'The LORD has given us this land because we are such good people!' No, it is because of the wickedness of the other nations that he is pushing them out of your way. 5 It is not because you

are so good or have such integrity that you are about to occupy their land. The LORD your God will drive these nations out ahead of you only because of their wickedness, and to fulfill the oath he swore to your ancestors Abraham, Isaac, and Jacob. 6You must recognize that the LORD your God is not giving you this good land because you are good, for you are not—you are a stubborn people.

7"Remember and never forget how angry you made the LORD your God out in the wilderness. From the day you left Egypt until now, you have been constantly rebelling against him. 8Even at Mount Sinai* you made the LORD so angry he was ready to destroy you. 9This happened when I was on the mountain receiving the tablets of stone inscribed with the words of the covenant that the LORD had made with you. I was there for forty days and forty nights, and all that time I ate no food and drank no water. 10The LORD gave me the two tablets on which God had written with his own finger all the words he had spoken to you from the heart of the fire when you were assembled at the mountain.

11"At the end of the forty days and nights, the LORD handed me the two stone tablets inscribed with the words of the covenant. 12Then the LORD said to me, 'Get up! Go down immediately, for the people you brought out of Egypt have corrupted themselves. How quickly they have turned away from the way I commanded them to live! They have melted gold and made an idol for themselves!'

13"The LORD also said to me, 'I have seen how stubborn and rebellious these people are. 14Leave me alone so I may destroy them and erase their name from under heaven. Then I will make a mighty nation of your descendants, a nation larger and more powerful than they are.'

15"So while the mountain was blazing with fire I turned and came down, holding in my hands the two stone tablets inscribed with the terms of the covenant. 16There below me I could see that you

had sinned against the LORD your God. You had melted gold and made a calf idol for yourselves. How quickly you had turned away from the path the LORD had commanded you to follow! 17So I took the stone tablets and threw them to the ground, smashing them before your eyes.

18"Then, as before, I threw myself down before the LORD for forty days and nights. I ate no bread and drank no water because of the great sin you had committed by doing what the LORD hated, provoking him to anger. 19I feared that the furious anger of the LORD, which turned him against you, would drive him to destroy you. But again he listened to me. 20The LORD was so angry with Aaron that he wanted to destroy him, too. But I prayed for Aaron, and the LORD spared him. 21I took your sin—the calf you had made—and I melted it down in the fire and ground it into fine dust. Then I threw the dust into the stream that flows down the mountain.

22"You also made the LORD angry at Taberah,* Massah,* and Kibroth-hattaavah.* 23And at Kadesh-barnea the LORD sent you out with this command: 'Go up and take over the land I have given you.' But you rebelled against the command of the LORD your God and refused to put your trust in him or obey him. 24Yes, you have been rebelling against the LORD as long as I have known you.

25"That is why I threw myself down before the LORD for forty days and nights—for the LORD said he would destroy you. 26I prayed to the LORD and said, 'O Sovereign LORD, do not destroy them. They are your own people. They are your special possession, whom you redeemed from Egypt by your mighty power and your strong hand. 27Please overlook the stubbornness and the awful sin of these people, and remember instead your servants Abraham, Isaac, and Jacob. 28If you destroy these people, the Egyptians will say, "The Israelites died because the LORD wasn't able to bring them to the land he had promised to give them." Or they might say,

"He destroyed them because he hated them; he deliberately took them into the wilderness to slaughter them." <sup>29</sup>But they are your people and your special possession, whom you brought out of Egypt by your great strength and powerful arm.'

<sup>10:1</sup>"At that time the Lord said to me, 'Chisel out two stone tablets like the first ones. Also make a wooden Ark—a sacred chest to store them in. Come up to me on the mountain, <sup>2</sup>and I will write on the tablets the same words that were on the ones you smashed. Then place the tablets in the Ark.'

<sup>3</sup>"So I made an Ark of acacia wood and cut two stone tablets like the first two. Then I went up the mountain with the tablets in my hand. <sup>4</sup>Once again the Lord wrote the Ten Commandments* on the tablets and gave them to me. They were the same words the Lord had spoken to you from the heart of the fire on the day you were assembled at the foot of the mountain. <sup>5</sup>Then I turned and came down the mountain and placed the tablets in the Ark of the Covenant, which I had made, just as the Lord commanded me. And the tablets are still there in the Ark."

<sup>6</sup>(The people of Israel set out from the wells of the people of Jaakan* and traveled to Moserah, where Aaron died and was buried. His son Eleazar ministered as high priest in his place. <sup>7</sup>Then they journeyed to Gudgodah, and from there to Jotbathah, a land with many brooks and streams. <sup>8</sup>At that time the Lord set apart the tribe of Levi to carry the Ark of the Lord's Covenant, and to stand before the Lord as his ministers, and to pronounce blessings in his name. These are their duties to this day. <sup>9</sup>That is why the Levites have no share of property or possession of land among the other Israelite tribes. The Lord himself is their special possession, as the Lord your God told them.)

<sup>10</sup>"As for me, I stayed on the mountain in the Lord's presence for forty days and nights, as I had done the first

time. And once again the Lord listened to my pleas and agreed not to destroy you. <sup>11</sup>Then the Lord said to me, 'Get up and resume the journey, and lead the people to the land I swore to give to their ancestors, so they may take possession of it.'

<sup>12</sup>**"And now, Israel, what does the Lord your God require of you? He requires only that you fear the Lord your God, and live in a way that pleases him, and love him and serve him with all your heart and soul. <sup>13</sup>And you must always obey the Lord's commands and decrees that I am giving you today for your own good.**

<sup>14</sup>"Look, the highest heavens and the earth and everything in it all belong to the Lord your God. <sup>15</sup>Yet the Lord chose your ancestors as the objects of his love. And he chose you, their descendants, above all other nations, as is evident today. <sup>16</sup>Therefore, change your hearts* and stop being stubborn.

<sup>17</sup>"For the Lord your God is the God of gods and Lord of lords. He is the great God, the mighty and awesome God, who shows no partiality and cannot be bribed. <sup>18</sup>He ensures that orphans and widows receive justice. He shows love to the foreigners living among you and gives them food and clothing. <sup>19</sup>So you, too, must show love to foreigners, for you yourselves were once foreigners in the land of Egypt. <sup>20</sup>You must fear the Lord your God and worship him and cling to him. Your oaths must be in his name alone. <sup>21</sup>He alone is your God, the only one who is worthy of your praise, the one who has done these mighty miracles that you have seen with your own eyes. <sup>22</sup>When your ancestors went down into Egypt, there were only seventy of them. But now the Lord your God has made you as numerous as the stars in the sky!"

9:8 Hebrew *Horeb*, another name for Sinai.
9:22a *Taberah* means "place of burning." See Num 11:1-3.
9:22b *Massah* means "place of testing." See Exod 17:1-7.
9:22c *Kibroth-hattaavah* means "graves of craving." See Num 11:31-34.   10:4 Hebrew *the ten words.*   10:6 Or *set out from Beeroth of Bene-jaakan.*   10:16 Hebrew *circumcise the foreskin of your hearts.*

LUKE 8:4-21

One day Jesus told a story to a large crowd that had gathered from many towns to hear him: 5"A farmer went out to plant his seed. As he scattered it across his field, some seed fell on a footpath, where it was stepped on, and the birds ate it. 6Other seed fell among rocks. It began to grow, but the plant soon wilted and died for lack of moisture. 7Other seed fell among thorns that grew up with it and choked out the tender plants. 8Still other seed fell on fertile soil. This seed grew and produced a crop that was a hundred times as much as had been planted!" When he had said this, he called out, "Anyone with ears to hear should listen and understand."

9His disciples asked him what this parable meant. 10He replied, "You are permitted to understand the secrets* of the Kingdom of God. But I use parables to teach the others so that the Scriptures might be fulfilled:

'When they look, they won't
    really see.
When they hear, they won't
    understand.'*

11"This is the meaning of the parable: The seed is God's word. 12The seeds that fell on the footpath represent those who hear the message, only to have the devil come and take it away from their hearts and prevent them from believing and being saved. 13The seeds on the rocky soil represent those who hear the message and receive it with joy. But since they don't have deep roots, they believe for a while, then they fall away when they face temptation. 14The seeds that fell among the thorns represent those who hear the message, but all too quickly the message is crowded out by the cares and riches and pleasures of this life. And so they never grow into maturity. 15And the seeds that fell on the good soil represent honest, good-hearted people who hear God's word, cling to it, and patiently produce a huge harvest.

16"No one lights a lamp and then covers it with a bowl or hides it under a bed. A lamp is placed on a stand, where its light can be seen by all who enter the house. 17For all that is secret will eventually be brought into the open, and everything that is concealed will be brought to light and made known to all.

18"So pay attention to how you hear. To those who listen to my teaching, more understanding will be given. But for those who are not listening, even what they think they understand will be taken away from them."

19Then Jesus' mother and brothers came to see him, but they couldn't get to him because of the crowd. 20Someone told Jesus, "Your mother and your brothers are outside, and they want to see you."

21Jesus replied, "My mother and my brothers are all those who hear God's word and obey it."

8:10a Greek *mysteries*.    8:10b Isa 6:9 (Greek version).

PSALM 69:19-36

You know of my shame, scorn,
    and disgrace.
    You see all that my enemies
        are doing.
20 Their insults have broken my heart,
    and I am in despair.
    If only one person would show
        some pity;
    if only one would turn and
        comfort me.
21 But instead, they give me poison*
        for food;
    they offer me sour wine for
        my thirst.

22 Let the bountiful table set before
        them become a snare
    and their prosperity become
        a trap.*
23 Let their eyes go blind so they
        cannot see,
    and make their bodies shake
        continually.*
24 Pour out your fury on them;
    consume them with your
        burning anger.
25 Let their homes become desolate
    and their tents be deserted.

²⁶ To the one you have punished, they
        add insult to injury;
    they add to the pain of those you
        have hurt.
²⁷ Pile their sins up high,
    and don't let them go free.
²⁸ Erase their names from the
        Book of Life;
    don't let them be counted among
        the righteous.

²⁹ I am suffering and in pain.
    Rescue me, O God, by your saving
        power.

³⁰ Then I will praise God's name
        with singing,
    and I will honor him with
        thanksgiving.
³¹ For this will please the LORD more
        than sacrificing cattle,
    more than presenting a bull with
        its horns and hooves.
³² The humble will see their God at
        work and be glad.
    Let all who seek God's help be
        encouraged.
³³ For the LORD hears the cries
        of the needy;
    he does not despise his
        imprisoned people.

³⁴ Praise him, O heaven and earth,
    the seas and all that move in them.
³⁵ For God will save Jerusalem*
    and rebuild the towns of Judah.
    His people will live there
    and settle in their own land.
³⁶ The descendants of those who obey
        him will inherit the land,
    and those who love him will live
        there in safety.

**69:21** Or *gall.*   **69:22** Greek version reads *Let their
bountiful table set before them become a snare, / a trap that
makes them think all is well. / Let their blessings cause them
to stumble, / and let them get what they deserve.* Compare
Rom 11:9.   **69:23** Greek version reads *and let their backs
be bent forever.* Compare Rom 11:10.   **69:35** Hebrew
*Zion.*

## PROVERBS 12:2-3

**T**he LORD approves of those who are
good, but he condemns those who plan
wickedness. □ Wickedness never brings
stability, but the godly have deep roots.

# MARCH 29

DEUTERONOMY 11:1–12:32

"**Y**ou must love the LORD your God and
obey all his requirements, decrees, regulations, and commands. ²Keep in
mind that I am not talking now to your
children, who have never experienced
the discipline of the LORD your God or
seen his greatness and his strong hand
and powerful arm. ³They didn't see the
miraculous signs and wonders he performed in Egypt against Pharaoh and all
his land. ⁴They didn't see what the LORD
did to the armies of Egypt and to their
horses and chariots—how he drowned
them in the Red Sea* as they were chasing you. He destroyed them, and they
have not recovered to this very day!

⁵"Your children didn't see how the
LORD cared for you in the wilderness
until you arrived here. ⁶They didn't see
what he did to Dathan and Abiram (the
sons of Eliab, a descendant of Reuben)
when the earth opened its mouth in the
Israelite camp and swallowed them,
along with their households and tents
and every living thing that belonged to
them. ⁷But you have seen the LORD perform all these mighty deeds with your
own eyes!

⁸"Therefore, be careful to obey every
command I am giving you today, so you
may have strength to go in and take over
the land you are about to enter. ⁹If you
obey, you will enjoy a long life in the
land the LORD swore to give to your ancestors and to you, their descendants—
a land flowing with milk and honey!
¹⁰For the land you are about to enter
and take over is not like the land of
Egypt from which you came, where you
planted your seed and made irrigation
ditches with your foot as in a vegetable
garden. ¹¹Rather, the land you will soon
take over is a land of hills and valleys
with plenty of rain—¹²a land that the

LORD your God cares for. He watches over it through each season of the year!

¹³"If you carefully obey all the commands I am giving you today, and if you love the LORD your God and serve him with all your heart and soul, ¹⁴then he will send the rains in their proper seasons—the early and late rains—so you can bring in your harvests of grain, new wine, and olive oil. ¹⁵He will give you lush pastureland for your livestock, and you yourselves will have all you want to eat.

¹⁶"But be careful. Don't let your heart be deceived so that you turn away from the LORD and serve and worship other gods. ¹⁷If you do, the LORD's anger will burn against you. He will shut up the sky and hold back the rain, and the ground will fail to produce its harvests. Then you will quickly die in that good land the LORD is giving you.

¹⁸"So commit yourselves wholeheartedly to these words of mine. Tie them to your hands and wear them on your forehead as reminders. ¹⁹Teach them to your children. Talk about them when you are at home and when you are on the road, when you are going to bed and when you are getting up. ²⁰Write them on the doorposts of your house and on your gates, ²¹so that as long as the sky remains above the earth, you and your children may flourish in the land the LORD swore to give your ancestors.

²²"Be careful to obey all these commands I am giving you. Show love to the LORD your God by walking in his ways and holding tightly to him. ²³Then the LORD will drive out all the nations ahead of you, though they are much greater and stronger than you, and you will take over their land. ²⁴Wherever you set foot, that land will be yours. Your frontiers will stretch from the wilderness in the south to Lebanon in the north, and from the Euphrates River in the east to the Mediterranean Sea in the west.* ²⁵No one will be able to stand against you, for the LORD your God will cause the people to fear and dread you, as he promised, wherever you go in the whole land.

²⁶"Look, today I am giving you the choice between a blessing and a curse! ²⁷You will be blessed if you obey the commands of the LORD your God that I am giving you today. ²⁸But you will be cursed if you reject the commands of the LORD your God and turn away from him and worship gods you have not known before.

²⁹"When the LORD your God brings you into the land and helps you take possession of it, you must pronounce the blessing at Mount Gerizim and the curse at Mount Ebal. ³⁰(These two mountains are west of the Jordan River in the land of the Canaanites who live in the Jordan Valley,* near the town of Gilgal, not far from the oaks of Moreh.) ³¹For you are about to cross the Jordan River to take over the land the LORD your God is giving you. When you take that land and are living in it, ³²you must be careful to obey all the decrees and regulations I am giving you today.

¹²:¹"THESE are the decrees and regulations you must be careful to obey when you live in the land that the LORD, the God of your ancestors, is giving you. You must obey them as long as you live.

²"When you drive out the nations that live there, you must destroy all the places where they worship their gods—high on the mountains, up on the hills, and under every green tree. ³Break down their altars and smash their sacred pillars. Burn their Asherah poles and cut down their carved idols. Completely erase the names of their gods!

⁴"Do not worship the LORD your God in the way these pagan peoples worship their gods. ⁵Rather, you must seek the LORD your God at the place of worship he himself will choose from among all the tribes—the place where his name will be honored. ⁶There you will bring your burnt offerings, your sacrifices, your tithes, your sacred offerings, your offerings to fulfill a vow, your voluntary offerings, and your offerings of the

firstborn animals of your herds and flocks. ⁷There you and your families will feast in the presence of the LORD your God, and you will rejoice in all you have accomplished because the LORD your God has blessed you.

⁸"Your pattern of worship will change. Today all of you are doing as you please, ⁹because you have not yet arrived at the place of rest, the land the LORD your God is giving you as your special possession. ¹⁰But you will soon cross the Jordan River and live in the land the LORD your God is giving you. When he gives you rest from all your enemies and you're living safely in the land, ¹¹you must bring everything I command you—your burnt offerings, your sacrifices, your tithes, your sacred offerings, and your offerings to fulfill a vow—to the designated place of worship, the place the LORD your God chooses for his name to be honored.

¹²"You must celebrate there in the presence of the LORD your God with your sons and daughters and all your servants. And remember to include the Levites who live in your towns, for they will receive no allotment of land among you. ¹³Be careful not to sacrifice your burnt offerings just anywhere you like. ¹⁴You may do so only at the place the LORD will choose within one of your tribal territories. There you must offer your burnt offerings and do everything I command you.

¹⁵"But you may butcher your animals and eat their meat in any town whenever you want. You may freely eat the animals with which the LORD your God blesses you. All of you, whether ceremonially clean or unclean, may eat that meat, just as you now eat gazelle and deer. ¹⁶But you must not eat the blood. You must pour it out on the ground like water.

¹⁷"But you may not eat your offerings in your hometown—neither the tithe of your grain and new wine and olive oil, nor the firstborn of your flocks and herds, nor any offering to fulfill a vow, nor your voluntary offerings, nor your

sacred offerings. ¹⁸You must eat these in the presence of the LORD your God at the place he will choose. Eat them there with your children, your servants, and the Levites who live in your towns, celebrating in the presence of the LORD your God in all you do. ¹⁹And be very careful never to neglect the Levites as long as you live in your land.

²⁰"When the LORD your God expands your territory as he has promised, and you have the urge to eat meat, you may freely eat meat whenever you want. ²¹It might happen that the designated place of worship—the place the LORD your God chooses for his name to be honored—is a long way from your home. If so, you may butcher any of the cattle, sheep, or goats the LORD has given you, and you may freely eat the meat in your hometown, as I have commanded you. ²²Anyone, whether ceremonially clean or unclean, may eat that meat, just as you do now with gazelle and deer. ²³But never eat the blood, for the blood is the life, and you must not eat the lifeblood with the meat. ²⁴Instead, pour out the blood on the ground like water. ²⁵Do not eat the blood, so that all may go well with you and your children after you, because you will be doing what pleases the LORD.

²⁶"Take your sacred gifts and your offerings given to fulfill a vow to the place the LORD chooses. ²⁷You must offer the meat and blood of your burnt offerings on the altar of the LORD your God. The blood of your other sacrifices must be poured out on the altar of the LORD your God, but you may eat the meat. ²⁸Be careful to obey all my commands, so that all will go well with you and your children after you, because you will be doing what is good and pleasing to the LORD your God.

²⁹"When the LORD your God goes ahead of you and destroys the nations and you drive them out and live in their land, ³⁰do not fall into the trap of following their customs and worshiping their gods. Do not inquire about their gods, saying, 'How do these nations worship

their gods? I want to follow their example.' [31]You must not worship the LORD your God the way the other nations worship their gods, for they perform for their gods every detestable act that the LORD hates. They even burn their sons and daughters as sacrifices to their gods.

[32]*"So be careful to obey all the commands I give you. You must not add anything to them or subtract anything from them."

11:4 Hebrew *sea of reeds.*   11:24 Hebrew *to the western sea.*   11:30 Hebrew *the Arabah.*   12:32 Verse 12:32 is numbered 13:1 in Hebrew text.

## LUKE 8:22-39

One day Jesus said to his disciples, "Let's cross to the other side of the lake." So they got into a boat and started out. [23]As they sailed across, Jesus settled down for a nap. But soon a fierce storm came down on the lake. The boat was filling with water, and they were in real danger.

[24]The disciples went and woke him up, shouting, "Master, Master, we're going to drown!"

When Jesus woke up, he rebuked the wind and the raging waves. The storm stopped and all was calm! [25]Then he asked them, "Where is your faith?"

The disciples were terrified and amazed. "Who is this man?" they asked each other. "When he gives a command, even the wind and waves obey him!"

[26]So they arrived in the region of the Gerasenes,* across the lake from Galilee. [27]As Jesus was climbing out of the boat, a man who was possessed by demons came out to meet him. For a long time he had been homeless and naked, living in a cemetery outside the town.

[28]As soon as he saw Jesus, he shrieked and fell down in front of him. Then he screamed, "Why are you interfering with me, Jesus, Son of the Most High God? Please, I beg you, don't torture me!" [29]For Jesus had already commanded the evil* spirit to come out of him. This spirit had often taken control of the man. Even when he was placed under guard and put in chains and shackles, he simply broke them and rushed out into the wilderness, completely under the demon's power.

[30]Jesus demanded, "What is your name?"

"Legion," he replied, for he was filled with many demons. [31]The demons kept begging Jesus not to send them into the bottomless pit.*

[32]There happened to be a large herd of pigs feeding on the hillside nearby, and the demons begged him to let them enter into the pigs.

So Jesus gave them permission. [33]Then the demons came out of the man and entered the pigs, and the entire herd plunged down the steep hillside into the lake and drowned.

[34]When the herdsmen saw it, they fled to the nearby town and the surrounding countryside, spreading the news as they ran. [35]People rushed out to see what had happened. A crowd soon gathered around Jesus, and they saw the man who had been freed from the demons. He was sitting at Jesus' feet, fully clothed and perfectly sane, and they were all afraid. [36]Then those who had seen what happened told the others how the demon-possessed man had been healed. [37]And all the people in the region of the Gerasenes begged Jesus to go away and leave them alone, for a great wave of fear swept over them.

So Jesus returned to the boat and left, crossing back to the other side of the lake. [38]**The man who had been freed from the demons begged to go with him. But Jesus sent him home, saying,** [39]**"No, go back to your family, and tell them everything God has done for you."** So he went all through the town proclaiming the great things Jesus had done for him.

8:26 Other manuscripts read *Gadarenes;* still others read *Gergesenes;* also in 8:37. See Matt 8:28; Mark 5:1. 8:29 Greek *unclean.*   8:31 Or *the abyss,* or *the underworld.*

## PSALM 70:1-5

*For the choir director: A psalm of David, asking God to remember him.*

[1] **P**lease, God, rescue me!
   Come quickly, LORD, and help me.

² May those who try to kill me
  be humiliated and put to shame.
May those who take delight in my
    trouble
  be turned back in disgrace.
³ Let them be horrified by their
    shame,
  for they said, "Aha! We've got
    him now!"
⁴ But may all who search for you
  be filled with joy and gladness
    in you.
May those who love your salvation
  repeatedly shout, "God is great!"
⁵ But as for me, I am poor and needy;
  please hurry to my aid, O God.
You are my helper and my savior;
  O LORD, do not delay.

PROVERBS 12:4

**A** worthy wife is a crown for her husband, but a disgraceful woman is like cancer in his bones.

# MARCH
# 30

DEUTERONOMY 13:1–15:23

¹*"**S**uppose there are prophets among you or those who dream dreams about the future, and they promise you signs or miracles, ²and the predicted signs or miracles occur. If they then say, 'Come, let us worship other gods'—gods you have not known before—³do not listen to them. The LORD your God is testing you to see if you truly love him with all your heart and soul. ⁴Serve only the LORD your God and fear him alone. Obey his commands, listen to his voice, and cling to him. ⁵The false prophets or visionaries who try to lead you astray must be put to death, for they encourage rebellion against the LORD your God, who redeemed you from slavery and brought you out of the land of Egypt. Since they try to lead you astray from the way the LORD your God commanded you to live, you must put them to death. In this way you will purge the evil from among you.

⁶"Suppose someone secretly entices you—even your brother, your son or daughter, your beloved wife, or your closest friend—and says, 'Let us go worship other gods'—gods that neither you nor your ancestors have known. ⁷They might suggest that you worship the gods of peoples who live nearby or who come from the ends of the earth. ⁸But do not give in or listen. Have no pity, and do not spare or protect them. ⁹You must put them to death! Strike the first blow yourself, and then all the people must join in. ¹⁰Stone the guilty ones to death because they have tried to draw you away from the LORD your God, who rescued you from the land of Egypt, the place of slavery. ¹¹Then all Israel will hear about it and be afraid, and no one will act so wickedly again.

¹²"When you begin living in the towns the LORD your God is giving you, you may hear ¹³that scoundrels among you are leading their fellow citizens astray by saying, 'Let us go worship other gods'—gods you have not known before. ¹⁴In such cases, you must examine the facts carefully. If you find that the report is true and such a detestable act has been committed among you, ¹⁵you must attack that town and completely destroy* all its inhabitants, as well as all the livestock. ¹⁶Then you must pile all the plunder in the middle of the open square and burn it. Burn the entire town as a burnt offering to the LORD your God. That town must remain a ruin forever; it may never be rebuilt. ¹⁷Keep none of the plunder that has been set apart for destruction. Then the LORD will turn from his fierce anger and be merciful to you. He will have compassion on you and make you a large nation, just as he swore to your ancestors.

¹⁸"The LORD your God will be merciful only if you listen to his voice and keep all his commands that I am giving you today, doing what pleases him.

14:1"Since you are the people of the Lord your God, never cut yourselves or shave the hair above your foreheads in mourning for the dead. 2You have been set apart as holy to the Lord your God, and he has chosen you from all the nations of the earth to be his own special treasure.

3"You must not eat any detestable animals that are ceremonially unclean. 4These are the animals* you may eat: the ox, the sheep, the goat, 5the deer, the gazelle, the roe deer, the wild goat, the addax, the antelope, and the mountain sheep.

6"You may eat any animal that has completely split hooves and chews the cud, 7but if the animal doesn't have both, it may not be eaten. So you may not eat the camel, the hare, or the hyrax.* They chew the cud but do not have split hooves, so they are ceremonially unclean for you. 8And you may not eat the pig. It has split hooves but does not chew the cud, so it is ceremonially unclean for you. You may not eat the meat of these animals or even touch their carcasses.

9"Of all the marine animals, you may eat whatever has both fins and scales. 10You may not, however, eat marine animals that do not have both fins and scales. They are ceremonially unclean for you.

11"You may eat any bird that is ceremonially clean. 12These are the birds you may not eat: the griffon vulture, the bearded vulture, the black vulture, 13the kite, the falcon, buzzards of all kinds, 14ravens of all kinds, 15the eagle owl, the short-eared owl, the seagull, hawks of all kinds, 16the little owl, the great owl, the barn owl, 17the desert owl, the Egyptian vulture, the cormorant, 18the stork, herons of all kinds, the hoopoe, and the bat.

19"All winged insects that walk along the ground are ceremonially unclean for you and may not be eaten. 20But you may eat any winged bird or insect that is ceremonially clean.

21"You must not eat anything that has died a natural death. You may give it to a foreigner living in your town, or you may sell it to a stranger. But do not eat it yourselves, for you are set apart as holy to the Lord your God.

"You must not cook a young goat in its mother's milk.

22"You must set aside a tithe of your crops—one-tenth of all the crops you harvest each year. 23Bring this tithe to the designated place of worship—the place the Lord your God chooses for his name to be honored—and eat it there in his presence. This applies to your tithes of grain, new wine, olive oil, and the firstborn males of your flocks and herds. Doing this will teach you always to fear the Lord your God.

24"Now when the Lord your God blesses you with a good harvest, the place of worship he chooses for his name to be honored might be too far for you to bring the tithe. 25If so, you may sell the tithe portion of your crops and herds, put the money in a pouch, and go to the place the Lord your God has chosen. 26When you arrive, you may use the money to buy any kind of food you want—cattle, sheep, goats, wine, or other alcoholic drink. Then feast there in the presence of the Lord your God and celebrate with your household. 27And do not neglect the Levites in your town, for they will receive no allotment of land among you.

28"At the end of every third year, bring the entire tithe of that year's harvest and store it in the nearest town. 29Give it to the Levites, who will receive no allotment of land among you, as well as to the foreigners living among you, the orphans, and the widows in your towns, so they can eat and be satisfied. Then the Lord your God will bless you in all your work.

15:1"At the end of every seventh year you must cancel the debts of everyone who owes you money. 2This is how it must be done. Everyone must cancel the loans they have made to their fellow Israelites. They must not demand payment from their neighbors or relatives, for the LORD's time of release has arrived. ³This release from debt, however, applies only to your fellow Israelites—not to the foreigners living among you.

⁴"There should be no poor among you, for the LORD your God will greatly bless you in the land he is giving you as a special possession. ⁵You will receive this blessing if you are careful to obey all the commands of the LORD your God that I am giving you today. ⁶The LORD your God will bless you as he has promised. You will lend money to many nations but will never need to borrow. You will rule many nations, but they will not rule over you.

⁷"But if there are any poor Israelites in your towns when you arrive in the land the LORD your God is giving you, do not be hard-hearted or tightfisted toward them. ⁸Instead, be generous and lend them whatever they need. ⁹Do not be mean-spirited and refuse someone a loan because the year for canceling debts is close at hand. If you refuse to make the loan and the needy person cries out to the LORD, you will be considered guilty of sin. ¹⁰Give generously to the poor, not grudgingly, for the LORD your God will bless you in everything you do. ¹¹There will always be some in the land who are poor. That is why I am commanding you to share freely with the poor and with other Israelites in need.

¹²"If a fellow Hebrew sells himself or herself to be your servant* and serves you for six years, in the seventh year you must set that servant free.

¹³"When you release a male servant, do not send him away empty-handed. ¹⁴Give him a generous farewell gift from your flock, your threshing floor, and your winepress. Share with him some of the bounty with which the LORD your God has blessed you. ¹⁵Remember that you were once slaves in the land of Egypt and the LORD your God redeemed you! That is why I am giving you this command.

¹⁶"But suppose your servant says, 'I will not leave you,' because he loves you and your family, and he has done well with you. ¹⁷In that case, take an awl and push it through his earlobe into the door. After that, he will be your servant for life. And do the same for your female servants.

¹⁸"You must not consider it a hardship when you release your servants. Remember that for six years they have given you services worth double the wages of hired workers, and the LORD your God will bless you in all you do.

¹⁹"You must set aside for the LORD your God all the firstborn males from your flocks and herds. Do not use the firstborn of your herds to work your fields, and do not shear the firstborn of your flocks. ²⁰Instead, you and your family must eat these animals in the presence of the LORD your God each year at the place he chooses. ²¹But if this firstborn animal has any defect, such as lameness or blindness, or if anything else is wrong with it, you must not sacrifice it to the LORD your God. ²²Instead, use it for food for your family in your hometown. Anyone, whether ceremonially clean or unclean, may eat it, just as anyone may eat a gazelle or deer. ²³But you must not eat the blood. You must pour it out on the ground like water."

13:1 Verses 13:1-18 are numbered 13:2-19 in Hebrew text. 13:15 The Hebrew term used here refers to the complete consecration of things or people to the LORD, either by destroying them or by giving them as an offering; similarly in 13:17. 14:4 The identification of some of the animals and birds listed in this chapter is uncertain. 14:7 Or *coney,* or *rock badger.* 15:12 Or *If a Hebrew man or woman is sold to you.*

LUKE 8:40–9:6

On the other side of the lake the crowds welcomed Jesus, because they had been waiting for him. ⁴¹Then a man named Jairus, a leader of the local synagogue, came and fell at Jesus' feet, pleading with him to come home with him. ⁴²His only daughter,* who was twelve years old, was dying.

As Jesus went with him, he was surrounded by the crowds. ⁴³A woman in the crowd had suffered for twelve years with constant bleeding,* and she could find no cure. ⁴⁴Coming up behind Jesus, she touched the fringe of his robe. Immediately, the bleeding stopped.

⁴⁵"Who touched me?" Jesus asked.

Everyone denied it, and Peter said, "Master, this whole crowd is pressing up against you."

⁴⁶But Jesus said, "Someone deliberately touched me, for I felt healing power go out from me." ⁴⁷When the woman realized that she could not stay hidden, she began to tremble and fell to her knees before him. The whole crowd heard her explain why she had touched him and that she had been immediately healed. ⁴⁸"Daughter," he said to her, "your faith has made you well. Go in peace."

⁴⁹While he was still speaking to her, a messenger arrived from the home of Jairus, the leader of the synagogue. He told him, "Your daughter is dead. There's no use troubling the Teacher now."

⁵⁰But when Jesus heard what had happened, he said to Jairus, "Don't be afraid. Just have faith, and she will be healed."

⁵¹When they arrived at the house, Jesus wouldn't let anyone go in with him except Peter, John, James, and the little girl's father and mother. ⁵²The house was filled with people weeping and wailing, but he said, "Stop the weeping! She isn't dead; she's only asleep."

⁵³But the crowd laughed at him because they all knew she had died. ⁵⁴Then Jesus took her by the hand and said in a loud voice, "My child, get up!" ⁵⁵And at that moment her life* returned, and she immediately stood up! Then Jesus told them to give her something to eat. ⁵⁶Her parents were overwhelmed, but Jesus insisted that they not tell anyone what had happened.

⁹:¹One day Jesus called together his twelve disciples* and gave them power and authority to cast out demons and to heal all diseases. ²Then he sent them out to tell everyone about the Kingdom of God and to heal the sick. ³"Take nothing for your journey," he instructed

them. "Don't take a walking stick, a traveler's bag, food, money,* or even a change of clothes. ⁴Wherever you go, stay in the same house until you leave town. ⁵And if a town refuses to welcome you, shake its dust from your feet as you leave to show that you have abandoned those people to their fate."

⁶So they began their circuit of the villages, preaching the Good News and healing the sick.

8:42 Or *His only child, a daughter.* 8:43 Some manuscripts add *having spent everything she had on doctors.* 8:55 Or *her spirit.* 9:1 Greek *the Twelve;* other manuscripts read *the twelve apostles.* 9:3 Or *silver coins.*

PSALM 71:1-24

❶ Lord, I have come to you
for protection;
don't let me be disgraced.
² Save me and rescue me,
for you do what is right.
Turn your ear to listen to me,
and set me free.
³ Be my rock of safety
where I can always hide.
Give the order to save me,
for you are my rock and
my fortress.
⁴ My God, rescue me from the power
of the wicked,
from the clutches of cruel
oppressors.
⁵ O Lord, you alone are my hope.
I've trusted you, O Lord, from
childhood.
⁶ Yes, you have been with me
from birth;
from my mother's womb you
have cared for me.
No wonder I am always
praising you!
⁷ My life is an example to many,
because you have been my
strength and protection.
⁸ That is why I can never stop
praising you;
I declare your glory all day long.
⁹ And now, in my old age, don't set
me aside.
Don't abandon me when my
strength is failing.

¹⁰ For my enemies are whispering
against me.
They are plotting together
to kill me.
¹¹ They say, "God has abandoned him.
Let's go and get him,
for no one will help him now."

¹² O God, don't stay away.
My God, please hurry to help me.
¹³ Bring disgrace and destruction on
my accusers.
Humiliate and shame those
who want to harm me.
¹⁴ But I will keep on hoping for
your help;
I will praise you more and more.
¹⁵ I will tell everyone about your
righteousness.
All day long I will proclaim your
saving power,
though I am not skilled with
words.*
¹⁶ I will praise your mighty deeds,
O Sovereign LORD.
I will tell everyone that you alone
are just.

¹⁷ O God, you have taught me from my
earliest childhood,
and I constantly tell others about
the wonderful things you do.
¹⁸ Now that I am old and gray,
do not abandon me, O God.
Let me proclaim your power to this
new generation,
your mighty miracles to all who
come after me.

¹⁹ Your righteousness, O God, reaches
to the highest heavens.
You have done such wonderful
things.
Who can compare with you,
O God?
²⁰ You have allowed me to suffer
much hardship,
but you will restore me to life again
and lift me up from the depths
of the earth.
²¹ You will restore me to even greater
honor
and comfort me once again.

²² Then I will praise you with music
on the harp,
because you are faithful to your
promises, O my God.
I will sing praises to you with
a lyre,
O Holy One of Israel.
²³ I will shout for joy and sing your
praises,
for you have ransomed me.
²⁴ I will tell about your righteous deeds
all day long,
for everyone who tried to hurt me
has been shamed and humiliated.

71:15 Or *though I cannot count it.*

## PROVERBS 12:5-7

The plans of the godly are just; the advice of the wicked is treacherous. □ The words of the wicked are like a murderous ambush, but the words of the godly save lives. □ The wicked die and disappear, but the family of the godly stands firm.

# MARCH 31

## DEUTERONOMY 16:1-17:20

"In honor of the LORD your God, celebrate the Passover each year in the early spring, in the month of Abib,* for that was the month in which the LORD your God brought you out of Egypt by night. ²Your Passover sacrifice may be from either the flock or the herd, and it must be sacrificed to the LORD your God at the designated place of worship—the place he chooses for his name to be honored. ³Eat it with bread made without yeast. For seven days the bread you eat must be made without yeast, as when you escaped from Egypt in such a hurry. Eat this bread—the bread of suffering—so that as long as you live you will remember the day you departed from Egypt. ⁴Let no yeast be found in any house throughout your land for those seven days. And when you sacrifice the Passover lamb on the evening of the first day, do not let any of the meat remain until the next morning.

⁵"You may not sacrifice the Passover in just any of the towns that the LORD your God is giving you. ⁶You must offer it only at the designated place of worship—the place the LORD your God chooses for his name to be honored. Sacrifice it there in the evening as the sun goes down on the anniversary of your exodus from Egypt. ⁷Roast the lamb and eat it in the place the LORD your God chooses. Then you may go back to your tents the next morning. ⁸For the next six days you may not eat any bread made with yeast. On the seventh day proclaim another holy day in honor of the LORD your God, and no work may be done on that day.

⁹"Count off seven weeks from when you first begin to cut the grain at the time of harvest. ¹⁰Then celebrate the Festival of Harvest* to honor the LORD your God. Bring him a voluntary offering in proportion to the blessings you have received from him. ¹¹This is a time to celebrate before the LORD your God at the designated place of worship he will choose for his name to be honored. Celebrate with your sons and daughters, your male and female servants, the Levites from your towns, and the foreigners, orphans, and widows who live among you. ¹²Remember that you were once slaves in Egypt, so be careful to obey all these decrees.

¹³"You must observe the Festival of Shelters* for seven days at the end of the harvest season, after the grain has been threshed and the grapes have been pressed. ¹⁴This festival will be a happy time of celebrating with your sons and daughters, your male and female servants, and the Levites, foreigners, orphans, and widows from your towns. ¹⁵For seven days you must celebrate this festival to honor the LORD your God at the place he chooses, for it

is he who blesses you with bountiful harvests and gives you success in all your work. This festival will be a time of great joy for all.

¹⁶"Each year every man in Israel must celebrate these three festivals: the Festival of Unleavened Bread, the Festival of Harvest, and the Festival of Shelters. On each of these occasions, all men must appear before the LORD your God at the place he chooses, but they must not appear before the LORD without a gift for him. ¹⁷All must give as they are able, according to the blessings given to them by the LORD your God.

¹⁸"Appoint judges and officials for yourselves from each of your tribes in all the towns the LORD your God is giving you. They must judge the people fairly. ¹⁹You must never twist justice or show partiality. Never accept a bribe, for bribes blind the eyes of the wise and corrupt the decisions of the godly. ²⁰Let true justice prevail, so you may live and occupy the land that the LORD your God is giving you.

²¹"You must never set up a wooden Asherah pole beside the altar you build for the LORD your God. ²²And never set up sacred pillars for worship, for the LORD your God hates them.

¹⁷:¹"NEVER sacrifice sick or defective cattle, sheep, or goats to the LORD your God, for he detests such gifts.

²"When you begin living in the towns the LORD your God is giving you, a man or woman among you might do evil in the sight of the LORD your God and violate the covenant. ³For instance, they might serve other gods or worship the sun, the moon, or any of the stars—the forces of heaven—which I have strictly forbidden. ⁴When you hear about it, investigate the matter thoroughly. If it is true that this detestable thing has been done in Israel, ⁵then the man or woman who has committed such an evil act must be taken to the gates of the town and stoned to death. ⁶But never put a person to death on the testimony of only one witness. There must always be

two or three witnesses. [7] The witnesses must throw the first stones, and then all the people may join in. In this way, you will purge the evil from among you.

[8]"Suppose a case arises in a local court that is too hard for you to decide—for instance, whether someone is guilty of murder or only of manslaughter, or a difficult lawsuit, or a case involving different kinds of assault. Take such legal cases to the place the LORD your God will choose, [9] and present them to the Levitical priests or the judge on duty at that time. They will hear the case and declare the verdict. [10]You must carry out the verdict they announce and the sentence they prescribe at the place the LORD chooses. You must do exactly what they say. [11]After they have interpreted the law and declared their verdict, the sentence they impose must be fully executed; do not modify it in any way. [12]Anyone arrogant enough to reject the verdict of the judge or of the priest who represents the LORD your God must die. In this way you will purge the evil from Israel. [13]Then everyone else will hear about it and be afraid to act so arrogantly.

[14]"You are about to enter the land the LORD your God is giving you. When you take it over and settle there, you may think, 'We should select a king to rule over us like the other nations around us.' [15]If this happens, be sure to select as king the man the LORD your God chooses. You must appoint a fellow Israelite; he may not be a foreigner.

[16]"The king must not build up a large stable of horses for himself or send his people to Egypt to buy horses, for the LORD has told you, 'You must never return to Egypt.' [17]The king must not take many wives for himself, because they will turn his heart away from the LORD. And he must not accumulate large amounts of wealth in silver and gold for himself.

[18]**"When he sits on the throne as king, he must copy for himself this body of instruction on a scroll in the presence of the Levitical priests.** [19]**He must always keep that copy with**

**him and read it daily as long as he lives. That way he will learn to fear the LORD his God by obeying all the terms of these instructions and decrees.** [20]This regular reading will prevent him from becoming proud and acting as if he is above his fellow citizens. It will also prevent him from turning away from these commands in the smallest way. And it will ensure that he and his descendants will reign for many generations in Israel."

16:1 Hebrew *Observe the month of Abib, and keep the Passover unto the LORD your God.* Abib, the first month of the ancient Hebrew lunar calendar, usually occurs within the months of March and April.   16:10 Hebrew *Festival of Weeks;* also in 16:16. This was later called the Festival of Pentecost (see Acts 2:1). It is celebrated today as Shavuat (or Shabuoth).   16:13 Or *Festival of Booths,* or *Festival of Tabernacles;* also in 16:16. This was earlier called the Festival of the Final Harvest or Festival of Ingathering (see Exod 23:16b). It is celebrated today as Sukkot (or Succoth).

## LUKE 9:7-27

**W**hen Herod Antipas, the ruler of Galilee,* heard about everything Jesus was doing, he was puzzled. Some were saying that John the Baptist had been raised from the dead. [8]Others thought Jesus was Elijah or one of the other prophets risen from the dead.

[9]"I beheaded John," Herod said, "so who is this man about whom I hear such stories?" And he kept trying to see him.

[10]When the apostles returned, they told Jesus everything they had done. Then he slipped quietly away with them toward the town of Bethsaida. [11]But the crowds found out where he was going, and they followed him. He welcomed them and taught them about the Kingdom of God, and he healed those who were sick.

[12]Late in the afternoon the twelve disciples came to him and said, "Send the crowds away to the nearby villages and farms, so they can find food and lodging for the night. There is nothing to eat here in this remote place."

[13]But Jesus said, "You feed them."

"But we have only five loaves of bread and two fish," they answered. "Or are you expecting us to go and buy enough food for this whole crowd?" [14]For there were about 5,000 men there.

Jesus replied, "Tell them to sit down in groups of about fifty each." [15]So the people all sat down. [16]Jesus took the five loaves and two fish, looked up toward heaven, and blessed them. Then, breaking the loaves into pieces, he kept giving the bread and fish to the disciples so they could distribute it to the people. [17]They all ate as much as they wanted, and afterward, the disciples picked up twelve baskets of leftovers!

[18]One day Jesus left the crowds to pray alone. Only his disciples were with him, and he asked them, "Who do people say I am?"

[19]"Well," they replied, "some say John the Baptist, some say Elijah, and others say you are one of the other ancient prophets risen from the dead."

[20]Then he asked them, "But who do you say I am?"

Peter replied, "You are the Messiah* sent from God!"

[21]Jesus warned his disciples not to tell anyone who he was. [22]"The Son of Man* must suffer many terrible things," he said. "He will be rejected by the elders, the leading priests, and the teachers of religious law. He will be killed, but on the third day he will be raised from the dead."

[23]Then he said to the crowd, "If any of you wants to be my follower, you must turn from your selfish ways, take up your cross daily, and follow me. [24]If you try to hang on to your life, you will lose it. But if you give up your life for my sake, you will save it. [25]And what do you benefit if you gain the whole world but are yourself lost or destroyed? [26]If anyone is ashamed of me and my message, the Son of Man will be ashamed of that person when he returns in his glory and in the glory of the Father and the holy angels. [27]I tell you the truth, some standing here right now will not die before they see the Kingdom of God."

**9:7** Greek *Herod the tetrarch.* Herod Antipas was a son of King Herod and was ruler over Galilee.   **9:20** Or *the Christ. Messiah* (a Hebrew term) and *Christ* (a Greek term) both mean "the anointed one."   **9:22** "Son of Man" is a title Jesus used for himself.

## PSALM 72:1-20
*A psalm of Solomon.*

[1] **G**ive your love of justice to the
    king, O God,
       and righteousness to the
          king's son.
[2] Help him judge your people in the
       right way;
    let the poor always be treated
       fairly.
[3] May the mountains yield prosperity
       for all,
    and may the hills be fruitful.
[4] Help him to defend the poor,
    to rescue the children of the
       needy,
    and to crush their oppressors.
[5] May they fear you as long as the
       sun shines,
    as long as the moon remains
       in the sky.
    Yes, forever!

[6] May the king's rule be refreshing
       like spring rain on freshly
          cut grass,
    like the showers that water
       the earth.
[7] May all the godly flourish during
       his reign.
    May there be abundant prosperity
       until the moon is no more.
[8] May he reign from sea to sea,
    and from the Euphrates River*
       to the ends of the earth.
[9] Desert nomads will bow before him;
    his enemies will fall before him
       in the dust.
[10] The western kings of Tarshish
       and other distant lands
    will bring him tribute.
    The eastern kings of Sheba and Seba
    will bring him gifts.
[11] All kings will bow before him,
    and all nations will serve him.

[12] He will rescue the poor when they
       cry to him;
    he will help the oppressed, who
       have no one to defend them.
[13] He feels pity for the weak and
       the needy,

and he will rescue them.
14 He will redeem them from
      oppression and violence,
   for their lives are precious to him.

15 Long live the king!
   May the gold of Sheba be given
      to him.
   May the people always pray
      for him
   and bless him all day long.
16 May there be abundant grain
      throughout the land,
   flourishing even on the hilltops.
   May the fruit trees flourish like the
      trees of Lebanon,
   and may the people thrive like
      grass in a field.
17 May the king's name endure
      forever;
   may it continue as long as the
      sun shines.

May all nations be blessed
      through him
   and bring him praise.

18 Praise the LORD God, the God
      of Israel,
   who alone does such wonderful
      things.
19 Praise his glorious name forever!
   Let the whole earth be filled with
      his glory.
   Amen and amen!

20 (This ends the prayers of David
      son of Jesse.)

72:8 Hebrew *the river*.

## PROVERBS 12:8-9

**A** sensible person wins admiration, but a warped mind is despised. □ Better to be an ordinary person with a servant than to be self-important but have no food.